Inside Social Life

Readings in Sociological Psychology and Microsociology

Third Edition

Spencer E. Cahill

University of South Florida

Roxbury Publishing Company

Los Angeles, California

Library of Congress Cataloging-in-Publication Data

Inside social life: readings in sociological psychology and microsociology/[compiled] by
Spencer E. Cahill. — 3rd ed.
p. cm.
Includes bibliographical references.
ISBN 1-891487-42-6
1. Social psychology. 2. Microsociology. I. Cahill, Spencer.
HM1033.I57 2001
302–dc21

00-020821
CIP

Publisher: Claude Teweles
Managing Editor: Dawn VanDercreek
Production Editor: Carla Max-Ryan
Typography: Synergistic Data Systems
Cover Design: Marnie Kenney

Printed on acid-free paper in the United States of America. This paper meets the standards for recy-
cling of the Environmental Protection Agency.

ISBN 1-891487-42-6

Roxbury Publishing Company
P.O. Box 491044
Los Angeles, California 90049-9044
Tel.: (310) 473-3312 • Fax: (310) 473-4490
E-mail: roxbury@roxbury.net
Website: www.roxbury.net

Contents

Part I: Human Being and Social Reality

1. Neurology and the Soul 2

Oliver Sacks
With descriptions of some of his patients, neurologist Sacks illustrates that human experience and neurology mutually influence each other.

2. Culture and Human Nature 6

Clifford Geertz
Geertz argues that human nature is incomplete without culture and the guidance of systems of significant symbols.

3. Islands of Meaning 10

Eviatar Zerubavel
An examination of how individuals socially divide reality into discrete categories of experience or islands of meaning.

Part II: The Social Construction of Self

4. The Self as Sentiment and Reflection 16

Charles Horton Cooley
This is the classic statement of Cooley's theory of the "looking-glass self."

5. The Self as Social Structure 21

George Herbert Mead
Mead's analysis of the social origins and character of the self inspired the development of a distinctively sociological psychology.

Part III: The Social Construction of Subjective Experience

Part IV: The Self and Social Interaction

---

* Denotes chapters new to the Third Edition

Part V: Social Interaction and Order

Part VI: Social Interaction and Relationships

---

* Denotes chapters new to the Third Edition

Part VII: Structures of Social Life

Part VIII: The Construction of Social Structures

---

* Denotes chapters new to the Third Edition

Part IX: The Politics of Social Reality

* Denotes chapters new to the Third Edition

Part X: Postmodern Social Reality

Kenneth J. Gergen
Gergen argues that the widely varied and constantly changing experiences of contemporary social life encourage a fragmented and fluctuating sense of self.

Introduction

The concerns of sociology are popularly viewed as far removed from the concerns of daily social life and those who live it. Sociologists seem more interested in countless responses to questionnaires, official statistics, organizational charts, disembodied institutions like *the* family and social systems of national and international scope themselves, rather than with what actual people say, do, and feel in the course of their daily social lives. That is one side of sociology and an important one. But there is another side that looks *inside* social life and people who live it.

The term *microsociology* is commonly used to distinguish this side of sociology from macrosociology, with which the discipline is popularly associated. Microsociology concerns the daily details of how actual people create and sustain the social relationships, organizations, and systems that macrosociology studies in the abstract. Its topics, for example, include how speakers take turns in conversation; how passing strangers exchange glances, then quickly look away from one another; or how talk, costume, and conduct serve to produce and maintain the very social worlds that people inhabit in their daily lives. They include the social worlds of playgrounds, basketball courts, sidewalks, hospitals, restaurants, and offices. These are only a few of the places sociologists have gone to study and understand social life from the inside.

Many sociologists do not stop there but also look inside the hearts and minds of individuals who inhabit different social worlds. They examine relationships between people's social and subjective experience—their thoughts, feelings, and private views of themselves. Sociologists share this field of study with psychologists, and it is commonly referred to as *social psychology*. However, sociologists and psychologists generally approach the study of interrelations between social life and individuals' inner lives from different directions. Psychologists tend to look for the operation of universal principles of human psychology in social life, while sociologists consider the social variability of subjective experience to be more significant and informative. This has led to the cumbersome expressions "sociological social psychology" and "psychological social psychology." But there is a more economical way of drawing this distinction: Psychologists can retain the title "social psychology" if sociologists claim the title *sociological psychology* as their own. This latter expression clearly refers to a psychology based on a distinctively sociological understanding of the human condition in all its varied forms.

The concerns of microsociology and sociological psychology are not unrelated to those of macrosociology. Although individuals daily produce and reproduce the social worlds that they inhabit, they do not do so under circumstances of their choosing. Recurring patterns of interaction result in relatively stable features or structures of social life. For example, people routinely place one another into different gender, ethnic, and other social categories, treating one another differently based on such identifications. Organized patterns of social life result in unequal distributions of resources and power among people. Such social divisions and hierarchies or social structures influence interaction in ways that tend to lead to their perpetuation. As previously suggested, microsociology examines how individuals interactionally produce and reproduce the social divisions, organizations, institutions, and systems that macrosociology studies in the abstract. Microsociology and sociological psychology also address how social structures influence different individuals' social lives and subjective experience. They thereby complement macrosociology and bring alive the study of human social life.

***

The readings collected in this volume provide an introduction to sociological psychology and microsociology. College students are often introduced to these fields of study in courses with titles like "Social Psychology" or "The Individual in Society." This volume is intended for them and for other readers who are interested in the inner workings of social life and how each of us influences and is influenced by it. The volume includes both statements of theoretical positions and empirical studies that draw and elaborate upon those positions.

Some of the selections included herein are considered classics of sociological psychology and microsociology. Others are more recent and have yet to weather the test of time. This combination of classic and more current readings offer a sense of the intellectual roots of sociological psychology and microsociology, as well as proof of their continuing vitality. The selections can be read in any order, although I have tried to arrange them so that each one builds on preceding ideas and empirical findings. Regardless of which articles you read first, my hope is that they convey an appreciation of the intricate artfulness of daily social action and the fascinating variety of human social experience.

Appreciating that today's instructors and students are sensitive to the issue of sexism in writing, I would like to add a note about gender usage in this anthology. Because many of the selections were originally published some years ago, a few use the masculine generic and contain other references to gender that may seem insensitive to the contemporary reader.

Nine of the selections included in this Third Edition of *Inside Social Life* are new, and one is from the First Edition. These new articles address such topics as:

- The social history of grief
- Experiencing critical illness
- Interacting in public bathrooms
- Everyday social life in nursing homes
- Constructing stories of a codependent self
- Mass media's construction of social problems
- Dynamics of popularity among adolescent girls
- The interactional and definitional work of waitresses
- Social and psychological sources of organized mass murder

Introductions to each section *and* article both identify and explain central issues, key concepts, and relationships among topics.

I was greatly aided in this revision by the comments and evaluations that instructors forwarded to the publisher and by informal conversations with colleagues. I especially thank Jennifer Dunn for convincing me of the importance of placing contemporary social life in historical perspective. I am most grateful to Kathy Charmaz, Marianne Cutler, Tom Kando, Nick Larsen, Kent Sandstrom, Michael Schwalbe, and Anne Statham for their thoughtful comments on the second edition and helpful suggestions for revision. As I did in the introduction to the first two editions, I also thank Gerald Handel for first suggesting that I undertake this project, Claude Teweles for his continuing encouragement and patience, and, as always, Donileen Loseke for everything. Finally, I thank my former students and colleagues at Skidmore College and my students and colleagues at the University of South Florida for their stimulation, inspiration, guidance, and support. ✦

Uses of the Selections

Inside Social Life can be used effectively as a single assigned text. However, for instructors who wish to use this anthology to supplement another text, the following chart may be helpful. It groups selections by topics that are conventionally used to organize courses in social psychology and microsociology. Primary and secondary emphases are listed separately. (Parentheses indicate an alternative primary use for a selection.) ✦

Topic	Primary Emphasis	Secondary Emphasis
Cognition and Perception	1, 3, 8, 9	5, 24
Emotions	10, 11, 18, 22, (31)	4, 27
Self and Identity	4, 5, 7, 13, 14	12, 20, 32, 35, (6), (15), (36)
Socialization	6, (11)	4, 5, 8, 22, 29, 35
Social Interaction	12, 16, 17, 19	28
Social Relationships	20, 21, 22, (23)	18, 25
Culture	2, 25	9, 10, 34
Social Organization and Institutions	24, 26, 28, 31	27, 35
Gender	29, (6), (15)	22, 27
Class and Ethnicity	27, 30	
Deviance and Social Control	32, 33	9, 23, 30
Social Problems	15, 23, 34, 35	30, 33
Social Change	36	10

About the Contributors

Patricia Adler is a professor of sociology at the University of Colorado. She is the author of *Wheeling and Dealing* (1985) and coauthor of *Peer Power* (1997).

Peter Adler is a professor of sociology at the University of Denver. He is a coauthor, with Patricia Adler, of *Backboards and Blackboards* (1991) and *Peer Power* (1997).

Elijah Anderson is a professor of sociology at the University of Pennsylvania. He is the author of *A Place on the Corner* (1976), *Streetwise* (1990), and *The Code of the Streets* (1999).

Leon Anderson is a professor of sociology at Ohio University. He is a coauthor of the multiple award-winning *Down on Their Luck* (1993).

Arnold Arluke is a professor of sociology at Northeastern University. He is the coauthor of award-winning *Regarding Animals* (1996) and other books.

Howard Becker is a professor of sociology at the University of Washington–Seattle. His books include *Outsiders* (1963) and *Art Worlds* (1982).

Joel Best is a professor of sociology at the University of Delaware. He is the author of *Threatened Children* (1990), *Controlling Vice* (1998), and *Random Violence* (1999).

Herbert Blumer (1900–1987) was a prominant advocate for the sociological perspective of symbolic interactionism and professor of sociology at the University of California at Berkeley before his death. Among his many articles and books, the most widely read is *Symbolic Interactionism: Perspective and Method* (1969).

Spencer E. Cahill is a professor of interdisciplinary social sciences and sociology at the University of South Florida. He is the editor of this volume.

Candace Clark is a professor of sociology at Montclair State University. She is the author of *Misery and Company* (1997).

Charles Horton Cooley (1864–1929), an economist turned sociologist, had a long teaching career at the University of Michigan. His major works are *Human Nature and Social Order* (1902), *Social Organization* (1909), and *Social Process* (1918).

Timothy Diamond is a professor of sociology at Western Michigan University and the author of *Making Grey Gold* (1992).

Donna Eder is a professor of sociology at Indiana University and the author of *School Talk* (1995) and several influential articles on adolescent peer culture.

Robin Eggleston is a practicing social worker in upstate New York.

Gary Alan Fine is a professor of sociology at Northwestern University. His books include *With the Boys* (1987), *Kitchens* (1996), and the award-winning *Morel Tales* (1998).

Arthur W. Frank is a professor of sociology at the University of Calgary and the author of *At the Will of the Body* (1991) and *The Wounded Storyteller* (1995).

Clifford Geertz is a professor of social sciences in the Institute for Advanced Study at Princton University. He is the author of several influential articles, essays, and books including *The Interpretation of Cultures* (1973) and *After the Fact* (1995).

Kenneth J. Gergen is a professor of psychology at Swarthmore College. He is the author of several books including *The Saturated Self* (1991), *Realities and Relationships* (1997), and *An Invitation to Social Construction* (1999).

Erving Goffman (1922–1982) was Benjamin Franklin Professor of Anthropology and Sociology at the University of Pennsylvania and President of the American Sociological Association at the time of his death. His many influential books include *The Presentation of Self in Everyday Life* (1959), *Asylums* (1961), *Relations in Public* (1971), and *Frame Analysis* (1974).

Leslie Irvine is a professor of sociology at the University of Colorado and the author of *Codependent Forevermore* (1999).

David A. Karp is a professor of sociology at Boston College. He is a coauthor of *Being Urban* (1991) and the author of the award-winning *Speaking of Sadness* (1996).

Sherryl Kleinman is a professor of sociology at the University of North Carolina at Chapel Hill. She is the author of *Equals Before God* (1984) and *Opposing Ambitions* (1996).

Robert Jay Lifton is Distinguished Professor of Psychiatry and Psychology at the John Jay College of the City University of New York. He is the author of several books including *Death in Life* (1968), *The Nazi Doctors* (1986), and *The Protean Self* (1993).

Lyn H. Lofland is a professor of sociology at the University of California at Davis. Her books include *A World of Strangers* (1972) and *The Public Realm* (1998).

Douglas Mason-Schrock is completing his Ph.D. in sociology at North Carolina State University.

George Herbert Mead (1863–1931) profoundly influenced early generations of American sociologists while a professor of philosophy at the University of Chicago. His published lectures and other work provided the basis for a distinctively sociological psychology and include *Mind, Self, and Society* (1934), *The Philosophy of the Act* (1938), and numerous articles.

Greta Foff Paules is a cultural anthropologist and the author of *Dishing It Out* (1991).

Oliver Sacks is a professor of neurology at the Albert Einstein College of Medicine. He is the author of many popular books including *The Man Who Mistook His Wife for a Hat* (1987) and *Awakenings* (1990).

Allen C. Smith III is a professor in the office of educational development at the University of North Carolina School of Medicine.

David Snow is a professor of sociology at the University of Arizona. He is the author of several important works and a coauthor of the multiple award-winning *Down on Their Luck* (1993).

Sheldon Stryker is a professor of sociology at Indiana University at Bloomington. He is the author of *Symbolic Interactionism: A Social Structural Version* (1980).

Barrie Thorne is a professor of sociology and women's studies at the University of California at Berkeley. She is a coauthor of *She Said/He Said* (1976) and the author of *Gender Play* (1993).

Diane Vaughan is a professor of sociology at Boston College. She is the author of *Uncoupling* (1990) and the award-winning *The Challenger Launch Decision* (1996).

Lev Vygotsky (1896–1934) was an influential Russian psychologist who died of tuberculosis only ten years after beginning his study of psychology. Among his extensive writings during that decade, *Language and Thought* (1934) is the most widely read today.

Ronald Wardhaugh is a professor of linguistics at the University of Toronto. His books include *How Conversation Works* (1985) and *Introduction to Sociolinguistics* (1988 and 1992).

Eviatar Zerubavel is a professor of sociology at Rutgers University. He is the author of several books including *Hidden Rhythms* (1981) and *The Fine Line* (1991). ✦

Part I

Human Being and Social Reality

The study and understanding of any subject must start with something—with some general ideas about that subject. The subject of sociological psychology and microsociology is human experience, both shared and private. Thus, sociological psychology and microsociology must start with some general ideas about human nature, human experience, and social existence. The three selections in this section advance some ideas about these fundamental questions. They provide conceptual foundations on which a study and understanding of human social life and experience can be built. Although only one article is written by a sociologist, all three provide conceptual pillars that securely support sociological psychology and microsociology. They also remind us that more popular ways of thinking about human beings and social life may not do justice to their fascinating complexity. ✦

1

Neurology and the Soul

Oliver Sacks

The history of Western thought is full of dualistic conceptions of human nature. Human "being" is variously separated into body and soul, sensation and reason, and physicality and mentality. These separations of human being into distinct and opposing parts have led to a number of debates over which side predominates. Does nature or nurture primarily determine individuals' thoughts, feelings, and behavior? Is the principal source of human knowledge perception or reflection? Is "mind" just another word for the biochemical operations of the nervous system, or is mind irreducible to biological processes? Although these and related debates continue, the view that emphasizes the bodily and physical side of human being seems to have the advantage today. At least medical treatment of the bodily being is generally accepted as the solution to a growing variety of human ills and troubles. There is presumably a drug, diet, or exercise program that can cure almost any condition.

This is the approach to curing human ills and troubles that Oliver Sacks, the neurologist and noted author of such books as Awakenings and The Man Who Mistook His Wife for a Hat, had learned in medical school. However, as he reports in this selection, his experiences with patients have led him to doubt the wisdom of that approach. He could not predict nor explain how particular patients would respond to certain medical treatment, based solely on his knowledge of their physical condition and the physiological effects of the administered treatment. Their symptoms and responses to treatment could not be understood apart from their past lives and current circumstances. As a result, Sacks concluded that it was not enough merely to treat a disease or lesion. He had to consider and treat the whole person.

Sacks' conclusion not only challenges contemporary medical practice, but also the dualistic and mechanistic conceptions of the human being that have characterized Western thought for centuries. Body and mind are inextricably locked together in what Sacks terms "the economy of the person." The nervous system is not a machine or biochemical computer that produces thoughts, feelings, and behavior according to some innate program. Rather, it continually evolves as it adapts to the individual's ever-changing experiences. It is influenced as much by perception, thought, and feeling as it influences them. Thus, understanding human being requires an understanding of more than human biology—it also requires an understanding of human experience. And human experience is the subject matter of sociological psychology and microsociology.

There is a tendency in neurology and pathology to talk about "the lesion," to see the process and end of medicine as delineating and "treating" the lesion. But the effects of a lesion, of any dysfunction, cannot help ramifying throughout the economy of the organism, forcing one to consider the organism as a whole.

The first patients I saw when I finished my [medical] training were patients with migraine. My first thoughts were that migraine was a simple pathology, or pathophysiology, which would require a pill, a medication, and that the beginning and end of medicine was to make the diagnosis and to give the pill. But there were many patients who shook me. One in particular was a young mathematician who described to me how every week he had a sort of cycle. He would start to get nervous and irritable on Wednesday, and this would become worse by Thursday; by Friday, he could not work. On Saturday he was greatly agitated, and on Sunday he would have a terrible migraine. But then, toward afternoon, the migraine would die away. Sometimes, as a migraine disappears, the person may break out in a gentle sweat; he may pass pints of urine. It is almost as if there is a catharsis at both physiological and emotional levels. As the migraine and the tension drained out of this man, he would feel himself refreshed, renewed; he would feel calm and creative; and on Sunday evening, Monday, and Tuesday, he did original work in mathematics. Then he would start getting irritable again.

When I "cured" this man of his migraines, I also "cured" him of his mathematics. Along with the pathology, the creativity also disappeared, and this made it clear that one had to inspect the economy of the person, the economy of this strange cycle of illness and misery each week, culminating in a migraine and then followed by a wonderful transcendent sort of health and creativity. It is not sufficient just to make a diagnosis of migraine and give a pill. One has to inquire into the entire human drama that surrounds the attacks, to explore what they might mean in a particular person. One has to take not just a "medical" history, but must try to construct a complete human narrative.

The second group of patients I encountered were those I describe in my book *Awakenings*. As a student I had vaguely heard of the great sleeping sickness, the *encephalitis lethargica*, which had become a worldwide pandemic in the 1920s; but it was only in 1966, when I arrived at a hospital in New York, that I saw for the first time the full, and almost unimaginable, depth and strangeness of the states that this might bring about. When I came to the hospital, I found some eighty patients who were, for the most part, completely "frozen," frozen in strange statuesque attitudes—and some of them had been in this state for forty years. Many of them had curious "crises" at times, in which their frozenness would be replaced by sudden spasmodic activity, "forced" movements, "forced" behaviors, compulsions of every kind.

In the summer of 1969, it became possible to give these patients a new "awakening" drug, L-DOPA, and with it, in that summer, they were released from their decades-long symptoms and syndromes, and became startlingly, wonderfully, alive. Then, in the fall, all sorts of problems appeared—recurrences of old symptoms, new symptoms of all sorts, sudden oscillations between states of immobility and excitement. Some of these setbacks, it was evident, had simple physiological causes: 90 percent or more of the motor-regulatory systems of the brain had been devastated, and the relatively few regulatory cells left were being overstimulated, and exhausted, by the drug. But this, it was equally evident, was not the whole of the matter: some patients with the grossest physiological damage did relatively well, and other patients, with less organic damage, did very badly.

One such patient (Rose R.), for example, was deeply nostalgic, and when she was "awakened" to 1969 she found it intolerable: "I can't bear it," she said, "everything is gone. Everything which meant anything has vanished and gone." And her "awakening" had a deeply anachronistic quality: she spoke of figures from the 1920s as if they were still alive; she had mannerisms, turns of phrase that had been obsolete for forty years but that still seemed entirely current and contemporary to her. She said, "I *know* it's 1969, but I *feel* I'm twenty-one." And she added, "I can't bear the present time—all this television, trash, nonsense. None of it means anything to me." And, perhaps in accordance with this state of mind, she suddenly ceased to respond to L-DOPA, and reverted again to the catatonic state she had been in for forty years; we were never able again, by chemical means, to make any change in her condition.

Another patient (Miron V.), who at first did very badly on L-DOPA, swinging unpredictably between stupor and frenzy, did far better and ceased to swing, when he found his family, who had been cut off from him for years; and when, additionally, we were able to set up a cobbler's bench at last in the hospital, so that he could resume the work he had once loved and which had been essential in giving him a sense of purpose and identity. Bringing these back—work and love, meaning—"centered" him, gave him back a firm base of identity and health, and alleviated the violent physiological oscillations he had been having.

Whatever went wrong on the ward or in their inner lives would instantly throw these patients into physiological problems of all sorts. Thus, there was a sudden access of tics, crises, recurrent Parkinsonism, etc., in September 1969, when a new hospital director abruptly dissolved the patient community, forbade visiting, and instituted a new, repressive regime; and whatever went right, humanly and morally, would as promptly serve to alleviate these problems (as with Miron V.). I had, as I had had with my migraine patients, a sense of complete psychophysical transparency, or continuity, of the physical and the mental dissolving into each other—never a sense of two elements or realms. "Awakening," it became clear, was not just a matter of a chemical, but of everything that constituted, in moral and human experience, "a life."

We had at first thought in narrow, chemical terms, believing that it would be sufficient to animate the patients chemically with L-DOPA, and then let them go. But L-DOPA, it was soon clear, was only the beginning. What was then necessary, after the first excitement had come and gone, was "reality," the sense of a real life, an identity; it was necessary for them to find or make a life with purpose and meaning and individuality and dignity.

This, it might be said, is true of us all, but it was especially clear in these neurologically damaged patients, who had so little of the normal resilience the rest of us have, and so great a tendency to disintegrate physiologically. These patients had an exaggerated need to find ways of centering and organizing their so greatly disturbed physiology. Thus, studying them, in their extremity, made clearer what is needed and sought by us all.

One such way of "centering," of recalling a self, the active powers of a self, from the abyss of pathology, can be given by music, by art of all kinds. In Parkinsonism, in postencephalitic syndromes, patients become deeply inert. *Inert*, etymologically, is the privative of *art*: indeed, the word was originally *inart*. And one of the cures for inertia is art: thus, one would see patients completely frozen, unable to take a single step, without inner impulse or activity, but almost miraculously able, in the presence of music, to walk, to dance, to move and to talk normally.

One such postencephalitic patient, a former music teacher, said she had been "de-musicked" by her disease; but, even before L-DOPA, she would suddenly recover herself, albeit briefly, if she was "re-musicked." Other patients would suddenly "come to"—that is, recover their lost mobility and initiative and will and identity—if one engaged them in play: playing ball, playing cards, any sort of play.

Art and play, drama and rite, had a therapeutic power as strong as any drug; but, it was clear, these worked in a different way. They worked, one felt, *to evoke a self*, and not in some partial and mechanical way.

When I first started seeing patients, my thinking was mechanical, physiological. But it soon became clear that I needed always to address myself to the individual person and to his needs, and that I could not understand what was going on without this. More and more I started to think of medicine as not just treating the lesion or the disease. One has to treat the lesion, but one has, equally, to pay attention to the entire individual.

Implied in all this is the necessity for an adequate concept of the individual and of mind, a concept of how individual persons grow and become, and how their growing and becoming are correlated with their physical bodies. Dualistic approaches prevent us from developing such a con-

cept. The body remains, resolutely, a "machine," with the mind divorced from it, as a sort of "ghost."

There have always been mechanical views of the nervous system: in the seventeenth century, Leibniz compared it to a mill; in the nineteenth century, it was often compared to a telephone exchange. In this century, it is usually compared to a computer. This model sees the brain as a glorified machine, as an immensely intricate but relatively fixed set of nervous connections, programmed to carry out different sets of nervous operations. But the world is not labeled, it does not feed us instructions and information, and there is much to indicate that, in higher nervous systems at least, there is not all that much "programming" built in. The world does not have a predetermined structure: our structuring of the world is our own—our brains create structures in the light of our experiences.

Faced with the necessity of survival, for making order in a teeming and chaotic world—"a booming, buzzing chaos," as William James called it—the brain is highly plastic and adapts itself at each moment. The infant, the human infant at least, is born into chaos, at least so far as complex perceptions and cognitions go. The infant immediately starts exploring the world, looking, feeling, touching, smelling, as all higher animals do, from the moment of birth. Sensation alone is not enough; it must be combined with movement, with emotion, with action. Movement and sensation together become integrated to form a "category," a coherent brain response, a category which is the antecedent of a "meaning." Subsequent explorations—feeling the same object at different times, in different contexts—are never quite the same, so that the initial category is revised, recategorized, and re-recategorized, again and again. Given this incessant recategorization, no perception, no image, no memory, one would expect, would ever be precisely repeated or the same. Yet through this structuring and restructuring the infant, the growing individual, constructs a self and a world.

It is characteristic of a creature, in contrast to a computer, that nothing is ever precisely repeated or reproduced; that there is, rather, a continual revision and reorganization of perception and memory, so that no two experiences (or their neural bases) are ever precisely the same. Experience is ever-changing, like Heraclitus' stream. This stream-like quality of mind and perception, of consciousness and life, cannot be caught in any mechanical model. One is not an immaterial soul, floating around in a machine. I do not feel alive, psychologically alive, except insofar as a stream of feeling—perceiving, imagining, remembering, reflecting, revising, recategorizing—runs through me. I am that stream—that stream is me.

This is totally different from Hume's denial of identity and his reduction of mental life to nothing but "a bundle or collection of different sensations, which succeed each other with an inconceivable rapidity, and are in a perpetual flux and movement." We are not incoherent, a bundle of sensations, but a "self," rising from experience, continually growing and revised. The brain is not a bundle of impersonal processes, an "It," with the "mind," the "self," hovering mysteriously above it. It is a confederation, an organic unity, of innumerable categorizations of its own activities, and from these, its self-reflection, there arises consciousness, the Mind, a metastructure built upon the real worlds in the brain.

In his last letter Goethe wrote, "The Ancients said that the animals are taught through their organs; let me add to this, so are men, but they have the advantage of teaching their organs in return." Through experience, education, art, and life, we teach our brains. This is a neurological learning, so that finally neurology and the soul do come together completely in a way which dignifies neurology, and which is no indignity to the soul.

Reprinted from: Oliver Sacks, "Neurology and the Soul" in *New York Review of Books*, Volume 37 (November 22, 1990), pp. 44–50. Copyright © 1990 by Oliver Sacks. Reprinted by permission of International Creative Management, Inc. ✦

2

Culture and Human Nature

Clifford Geertz

Many thinkers who are influenced by evolutionary theory emphasize similarities between humans and other species. Yet anyone who seriously compares humans to other species cannot help but conclude that we are unique within the animal kingdom. For good or ill, we have brought heat to frigid climates, illuminated the darkness, erected magnificent buildings, and invented terrifying devices with which to destroy them. The accomplishments of other animals do not even compare. In adapting to the environments that we inhabit, we humans have adapted those environments to our needs, desires, and dreams to an extent unparalleled by any other species. There is clearly something different about us.

In this selection, the anthropologist Clifford Geertz argues that what sets us apart from other species is our use and dependence upon culture or systems of significant symbols. According to Geertz, once culture emerged in the course of human evolution, it shaped our subsequent biological evolution. Our evolutionary ancestors had to adapt not only to their natural environment but also to the cultural environments that they created. That gave a selective advantage to those who were most skilled in the use of significant symbols, resulting in the gradual evolution of Homo sapiens with our complex central nervous system. This gives us a highly flexible but biologically unfinished nature.

Compared to other animals, we are instinctionally "underdetermined." Our genes may provide the basic ground plans for how we live but few specifics. We require another source of guidance in order to survive, and culture provides that guidance. According to Geertz, culture is a set of control mechanisms over behavior that compensates for the relative lack of genetic control over human behavior. Thus, our culture is an essential aspect of our nature; not culture in general but the specific culture or system of significant symbols that we learn and use. Universal human nature consists of little more than the capacity to acquire the specific human nature of a particular culture.

Geertz's arguments imply that the search for human universals can only lead to empty abstractions. For example, universal human psychology does not determine a particular individual's thoughts, feelings, and actions. It only provides a broad outline that the individual's culture and experience must fill in. We are cultural by nature, and, therefore, human nature and psychology is as diverse as human cultures. In an important sense, there is no meaningful human psychology but many human psychologies. We can only understand those varied psychologies if we understand the specific human cultures or systems of significant symbols that govern them. That is one of the central tasks of sociological psychology.

Geertz wrote this essay in the 1950s and followed the convention at that time of using the expression "Man" in the generic sense to refer to all humans, including women and children. This generic use of "Man" confuses one sex and all of humanity and is fortunately rare today. It might be useful mentally to translate "Man" to "Human" as you read this selection.

. . . I want to propose two ideas. The first is that culture is best seen not as complexes of concrete behavior patterns—customs, usages, traditions, habit clusters—but as a set of control mechanisms—plans, recipes, rules, instructions—for governing behavior. The second idea is that man is precisely the animal most desperately dependent upon such extragenetic, outside-the-skin control mechanisms, such cultural programs, for ordering his behavior.

. . . The "control mechanism" view of culture begins with the assumption that human thought is basically both social and public—that its natural habitat is the house yard, the marketplace, and the town square. Thinking consists not of "happenings in the head" (though happenings there and elsewhere are necessary for it to occur) but of a traffic in what have been called, by G. H. Mead and others, significant symbols—words for the most part but also gestures, drawings, musical sounds, mechanical devices like clocks, or natural objects like jewels—anything, in fact, that is disengaged from its mere actuality and used to impose meaning upon experience. From the point of view of any particular individual, such symbols are largely given. He finds them already current in the community when he is born, and they remain, with some additions, subtractions, and partial alterations he may or may not have had a hand in, in circulation there until after he dies. While he lives he uses them, or some of them, sometimes deliberately and with care, most often spontaneously and with ease, but always with the same end in view: to put a construction upon events through which he lives, to orient himself within "the ongoing course of experienced things," to adopt a vivid phrase of John Dewey's.

Man is so in need of such symbolic sources of illumination to find his bearings in the world because the nonsymbolic sort that are constitutionally ingrained in his body cast so diffused a light. The behavior patterns of lower animals are, at least to a much greater extent, given to them with their physical structure; genetic sources of information order their actions within much narrower ranges of variation, the narrower and more thoroughgoing the lower the animal. For man, what are innately given are extremely general response capacities, which although they make possible far greater plasticity, complexity, and, on the scattered occasions when everything works as it should, effectiveness of behavior, leave it much less precisely regulated. This, then, is the second face of our argument: Undirected by culture patterns—organized systems of significant symbols—man's behavior would be virtually ungovernable, a mere chaos of pointless acts and exploding emotions, his experience virtually shapeless. Culture, the accumulated totality of such patterns, is not just an ornament of human existence but . . . an essential condition for it.

. . . Some of the most telling evidence in support of such a position comes from recent advances in our understanding of what used to be called the descent of man: the emergence of *Homo sapiens* out of his general primate background. . . . In the current view, the evolution of *Homo sapiens*—modern man—out of his immediate pre-*sapiens* background got definitely under way nearly four million years ago with the appearance of the now famous Australopithecines—the so-called ape men of southern and eastern Africa—and culminated with the emergence of *sapiens* himself only some one to two hundred thousand years ago. Thus, as at least elemental forms of cultural, or if you wish protocultural, activity (simple toolmaking, hunting, and so on) seem to have been present among some of the Australopithecines, there was an overlap of, as I say, well

over a million years between the beginning of culture and the appearance of man as we know him today. The precise dates . . . are not critical; what is critical is that there was an overlap and that it was a very extended one. The final phases of the phylogenetic history of man took place in the same grand geological era—the so-called Ice Age—as the initial phases of his cultural history. Men have birthdays, but man does not.

What this means is that culture, rather than being added on, so to speak, to a finished or virtually finished animal, was ingredient, and centrally ingredient, in the production of that animal itself. The slow, steady, almost glacial growth of culture through the Ice Age altered the balance of selection pressures for the evolving *Homo* in such a way as to play a major directive role in his evolution. The perfection of tools, the adoption of organized hunting and gathering practices, the beginnings of true family organization, the discovery of fire, and, most critically, though it is as yet extremely difficult to trace it out in any detail, the increasing reliance upon systems of significant symbols (language, art, myth, ritual) for orientation, communication, and self-control all created for man a new environment to which he was then obliged to adapt. As culture, step by infinitesimal step, accumulated and developed, a selective advantage was given to those individuals in the population most able to take advantage of it—the effective hunter, the persistent gatherer, the adept toolmaker, the resourceful leader—until what had been a small-brained, protohuman *Homo australopithecus* became the large-brained fully human *Homo sapiens*. Between the cultural pattern, the body, and the brain, a positive feedback system was created in which each shaped the progress of the other, a system in which the interaction among increasing tool use, the changing anatomy of the hand, and the expanding representation of the thumb on the cortex is only one of the more graphic examples. By submitting himself to governance by symbolically mediated programs for producing artifacts, organizing social life, or expressing emotions, man determined, if unwittingly, the culminating stages of his own biological destiny. Quite literally, though quite inadvertently, he created himself.

Though, as I mentioned, there were a number of important changes in the gross anatomy of genus *Homo* during this period of his crystallization—in skull shape, dentition, thumb size, and so on—by far the most important and dramatic were those that evidently took place in the central nervous system; for this was the period when the human brain, and most particularly the forebrain, ballooned into its present top-heavy proportions. . . . [T]hough the Australopithecines had a torso and arm configuration not drastically different from our own, and a pelvis and leg formation at least well-launched toward our own, they had cranial capacities hardly larger than those of the living apes—that is to say, about a third to a half of our own. What sets true man off most distinctly from protomen is apparently not overall bodily form but complexity of nervous organization. The overlap period of cultural and biological change seems to have consisted in an intense concentration on neural development and perhaps associated refinements of various behaviors—of the hands, bipedal locomotion, and so on—for which the basic anatomical foundations—mobile shoulders and wrists, a broadened ilium, and so on—had already been securely laid. In itself, this is perhaps not altogether startling; but, combined with what I have already said, it suggests some conclusions about what sort of animal man is. . . .

Most bluntly, it suggests that there is no such thing as a human nature independent of culture. Men without culture would not be the clever savages of Golding's *Lord of the Flies* thrown back upon the cruel wisdom of their animal instincts. . . . They would be unworkable monstrosities with very few useful instincts, fewer recognizable sentiments, and no intellect: mental basket cases. As our central nervous system—and most particularly its crowning curse and glory, the neocortex—grew up in great part in interaction with culture, it is incapable of directing our behavior or organizing our experience without the guidance provided by systems of significant symbols. What happened to us in the Ice Age is that we were obliged to abandon the regularity and precision of detailed genetic control over our conduct for the flexibility and adaptability of a more generalized, though of course no less real, genetic control over it. To supply the additional information necessary to be able to act, we were forced, in turn, to rely more and more heavily on cultural sources—the accumulated fund of significant symbols. Such symbols are thus not mere expressions, instrumentalities, or correlates of our biological, psychological, and social existence; they

are prerequisites of it. Without men, no culture, certainly; but equally, and more significantly, without culture, no men.

We are, in sum, incomplete or unfinished animals who complete or finish ourselves through culture—and not through culture in general but through highly particular forms of it: Dobuan and Javanese, Hopi and Italian, upper-class and lower-class, academic and commercial. Man's great capacity for learning, his plasticity, has often been remarked, but what is even more critical is his extreme dependence upon a certain sort of learning: the attainment of concepts, the apprehension and application of specific systems of symbolic meaning. Beavers build dams, birds build nests, bees locate food, baboons organize social groups, and mice mate on the basis of forms of learning that rest predominantly on the instructions encoded in their genes and evoked by appropriate patterns of external stimuli: physical keys inserted into organic locks. But men build dams or shelters, locate food, organize their social groups, or find sexual partners under the guidance of instructions encoded in flow charts and blueprints, hunting lore, moral systems and aesthetic judgments: conceptual structures molding formless talents.

We live, as one writer has neatly put it, in an "information gap." Between what our body tells us and what we have to know in order to function, there is a vacuum we must fill ourselves, and we fill it with information (or misinformation) provided by our culture. The boundary between what is innately controlled and what is culturally controlled in human behavior is an ill-defined and wavering one. Some things are, for all intents and purposes, entirely controlled intrinsically: we need no more cultural guidance to learn how to breathe than a fish needs to learn how to swim. Others are almost certainly largely cultural; we do not attempt to explain on a genetic basis why some men put their trust in centralized planning and others in the free market, though it might be an amusing exercise. Almost all complex human behavior is, of course, the interactive, nonadditive outcome of the two. Our capacity to speak is surely innate; our capacity to speak English is surely cultural. Smiling at pleasing stimuli and frowning at unpleasing ones are surely in degree genetically determined (even apes screw up their faces at noxious odors); but sardonic smiling and burlesque frowning are equally surely predominantly cultural, as is perhaps demonstrated by the Balinese definition of a madman as someone who, like an American, smiles when there is nothing to laugh at. Between the basic ground plans for our life that our genes lay down—the capacity to speak or to smile—and the precise behavior we in fact execute—speaking English in a certain tone of voice, smiling enigmatically in a delicate social situation—lies a complex set of significant symbols under whose direction we transform the first into the second, the ground plans into activity. . . . One of the most significant facts about us may finally be that we all begin with the natural equipment to live a thousand kinds of life but end in the end having lived only one.

. . . When seen as a set of symbolic devices for controlling behavior, extrasomatic sources of information, culture provides the link between what men are intrinsically capable of becoming and what they actually, one by one, in fact become. Becoming human is becoming individual, and we become individual under the guidance of cultural patterns, historically created systems of meaning in terms of which we give form, order, point and direction to our lives. And the cultural patterns involved are not general but specific—not just "marriage" but a particular set of notions about what men and women are like, how spouses should treat one another, or who should properly marry whom; not just "religion" but belief in the wheel of karma, the observance of a month of fasting, or the practice of cattle sacrifice. Man is to be defined neither by his innate capacities alone . . . nor by his actual behaviors alone . . . but rather by the link between them, by the way in which the first is transformed into the second, his generic potentialities focused into his specific performances. It is in man's career, in its characteristic course, that we can discern, however dimly, his nature, and though culture is but one element in determining that course, it is hardly the least important. As culture shaped us as a single species—and is no doubt still shaping us—so too it shapes us as separate individuals. . . .

Reprinted from: Clifford Geertz, "The Impact of the Concept of Culture on the Concept of Man" in Platt (ed.), *New Views of the Nature of Man*, pp. 106–108, 110–114, 115–116. Copyright © 1965 by The University of Chicago Press. Reprinted by permission. ✦

3

Islands of Meaning

Eviatar Zerubavel

We commonly assume that our experience is of a world "out there," and that the external world exists independently of our experience of it. We seldom appreciate how much interpretation guides and shapes our experience. We look out the window and see a toddler who is running down the sidewalk fall and start to cry. We then watch his mother run to his aid and pick him up in order to comfort him. But what we actually saw was a small animate object quickly go from a vertical to a horizontal position, followed by loud, piercing sounds, and then the appearance of a larger animate object that elevated the smaller one off the ground. Toddler, cry, mother, and comfort are significant symbols through which we filtered those perceptions. These symbols and their meanings constitute our experience as much as, if not more than, our perceptions. And we did not invent those symbols and their meanings; we learned them from others. In this important respect, then, the reality we experience day by day and moment by moment is a socially constructed reality.

As Eviatar Zerubavel notes in this selection, we divide what we experience into distinct categories or "islands of meaning." We lump together things we consider similar, ignoring their differences, and separate them from other things, ignoring similarities and exaggerating differences. The world we experience does not come prepackaged in such categories. We pack it into them and, as Zerubavel observes, our packaging of experience into discrete categories of meaning is an "inevitably arbitrary act." There are an indefinite variety of ways to break up reality into such discrete islands of meaning, as the cultural and historical variety of human classification systems attests.

Zerubavel notes that language largely guides our classification of our experiences. We learn a logic of classification when we learn a language and other significant symbols, and we learn language and other systems of significant symbols from others. In this way, society teaches us how to perceive our world, shape it into discrete islands of meaning, and construct reality. This is one of the ways in which culture completes our unfinished human nature. It provides the social lenses through which we can see meaningful shapes in our shapeless experience. And individuals who acquire the social lenses of different cultures see, and therefore live, in different realities. We must understand what others are seeing in order to understand how they think, feel, and act, and that requires an inspection of the social lenses—the systems of significant symbols—through which they are looking.

We transform the natural world into a social one by carving out of it mental chunks we then treat as if they were discrete, totally detached from their surroundings. The way we mark off islands of property is but one example of the general process by which we create meaningful social entities.

In order to endow the things we perceive with meaning, we normally ignore their uniqueness and regard them as typical members of a particular class of objects (a relative, a present), acts (an apology, a crime), or events (a game, a conference). After all, "If each of the many things in the world were taken as distinct, unique, a thing in itself unrelated to any other thing, perception of the world would disintegrate into complete meaninglessness."[1] Indeed, things become meaningful only when placed in some category. A clinical symptom, for instance, is quite meaningless until we find some diagnostic niche (a cold, an allergic reaction) within which to situate and thus make sense of it. Our need to arrange the world around us in categories is so great that, even when we encounter mental odds and ends that do not seem to belong in any conventional category, we nonetheless "bend" them so as to fit them into one anyway, as we usually do with the sexually ambiguous or the truly novel work of art. When such adjustment does not suffice, we even create special categories (avant-garde, others, miscellaneous) for these mental pariahs. . . .

Creating islands of meaning entails two rather different mental processes—lumping and splitting. On the one hand, it involves grouping "similar" items together in a single mental cluster—sculptors and filmmakers ("artists"), murder and arson ("felonies"), foxes and camels ("animals"). At the same time, it also involves separating in our mind "different" mental clusters from one another—artists from scientists, felonies from misdemeanors, animals from humans. In order to carve out of the flux surrounding us meaningful entities with distinctive identities, we must experience them as separate from one another.

Separating one island of meaning from another entails the introduction of some mental void between them. As we carve discrete mental chunks out of continuous streams of experience, we normally visualize substantial gaps separating them from one another. Such mental versions of the great divides that split continuous stretches of land following geological upheavals underlie our basic experience of mental entities as situated amid blank stretches of emptiness. It is our perception of the void among these islands of meaning that makes them separate in our mind, and its magnitude reflects the degree of separateness we perceive among them.

Gaps are critical to our ability to experience insular entities. The experiential separateness of the self, for example, is clearly enhanced by the actual gap of "personal space" that normally envelops it. By literally insulating the self from contact with others, such a gap certainly promotes its experience as an insular entity. A similar experience of an island situated in a vacuum often leads us to confine our horizons to, and never venture beyond, our neighborhood, hometown, or country. The great divides we visualize between women and men, children and adults, and blacks and whites likewise promote our perception of such entities as discrete. . . .

I have thus far drawn a deliberately one-sided picture of reality as an array of insular entities neatly separated from one another by great divides. Such discontinuity, however, is not as inevitable as we normally take it to be. It is a pronouncedly mental scalpel that helps us carve discrete mental slices out of reality. . . . The scalpel, of course, is a *social* scalpel. It is society that underlies the way we generate meaningful mental entities.

Reality is not made up of insular chunks unambiguously separated from one another by sharp divides, but rather, of vague, blurred-edge essences that often "spill over" into one another. It normally presents itself not in black and white, but, rather, in subtle shades of gray, with mental twilight zones as well as intermediate essences connecting entities. Segmenting it into discrete islands of meaning usually rests on some social convention, and most boundaries are, therefore, mere social artifacts. As such, they often vary

from one society to another as well as across historical periods within each society. Moreover, the precise location—not to mention the very existence—of such mental partitions is often disputed even within any given society. . . .

Breaking up reality into discrete islands of meaning is, thus, an inevitably arbitrary act. The very existence of dividing lines (not to mention their location) is a matter of convention. It is by pure convention, for example, that we regard Danish and Norwegian as two separate languages yet Galician as a mere dialect of Portuguese. It is likewise by sheer convention that we draw a line between heroin and other lethal substances such as alcohol and tobacco (not to mention its own chemical cousins, which we use as pain-killers or as controlled substitutes for heroin itself). It is mere convention that similarly leads us to regard cooking or laundering as "service" occupations and fishermen or raftsmen as less skilled than assembly-line workers or parking-lot attendants. Just as arbitrary is the way in which we carve supposedly discrete species out of the continuum of living forms, separate the masculine from the feminine, cut up continuous stretches of land into separate continents (Europe and Asia, North and Central America), or divide the world into time zones. Nor are there any natural divides separating childhood from adulthood, winter from spring, or one day from the next (both my children, indeed, used to refer to the morning before their last afternoon nap as "yesterday"), and if we attribute distinctive qualities to decades ("the Roaring Twenties") or centuries ("nineteenth-century architecture"), it is only because we happen to count by tens. Had we used nine, instead, as the basis of our counting system, we would have undoubtedly discovered the historical significance of 9-, 81-, and 729-year cycles and generated fin-de-siecle and millenary frenzy around the years 1944 and 2187. We probably would also have experienced our midlife crisis at the age of thirty-six!

It is we ourselves who create categories and force reality into supposedly insular compartments. Mental divides as well as the "things" they delineate are pure artifacts that have no basis whatsoever in reality. A category, after all, is "a group of things [yet] things do not present themselves . . . grouped in such a way . . . [Nor is their resemblance] enough to explain how we are led to group . . . them together in a sort of ideal sphere, enclosed by definite limits."[2] Classification is an artificial process of concept formation rather than of discovering clusters that already exist. Entities such as "vitamins," "politicians," "art," and "crime" certainly do not exist "out there." The way we construct them resembles the way painters and photographers create pictures by mentally isolating supposedly discrete slices of reality from their immediate surroundings. In the real world, there are no divides separating one insular "thing" from another. . . .

And yet, while boundaries and mental fields may not exist "out there," neither are they generated solely by our own mind. The discontinuities we experience are neither natural nor universal, yet they are not entirely personal either. We may not all classify reality in a precisely identical manner, yet we certainly do cut it up into rather similar mental chunks with pretty similar outlines. It is indeed a mind that organizes reality in accordance with a specific logic, yet it is usually a group mind using an unmistakably social logic (and therefore also producing an unmistakably social order). When we cut up the world, we usually do it not as humans or as individuals but rather as members of societies.

The logic of classification is something we must learn. Socialization involves learning not only society's norms but also its distinctive classificatory schemes. Being socialized or acculturated entails knowing not only how to behave, but also how to perceive reality in a socially appropriate way. An anthropologist who studies another culture, for example, must learn "to see the world as it is constituted for the people themselves, to assimilate their distinctive categories. . . . [H]e may have to abandon the distinction between the natural and the supernatural, relocate the line between life and death, accept a common nature in mankind and animals."[3] Along similar lines, by the time she is three, a child has already internalized the conventional outlines of the category "birthday present" enough to know that, if someone suggests that she bring lima beans as a present, he must be kidding.

Whenever we classify things, we always attend some of their distinctive features in order to note similarities and contrasts among them while ignoring all the rest as irrelevant. The length of a film, for example, or whether it is in color or black and white is quite irrelevant to the way it is rated, whereas the color of a dress is totally irrelevant to

where it is displayed in a department store. What to stress among what is typically a "plethora of viable alternatives" is largely a social decision,[4] and being socialized entails knowing which features are salient for differentiating items from one another and which ones ought to be ignored as irrelevant. It involves learning, for example, that, whereas adding cheese makes a hamburger a "cheeseburger," adding lettuce does not make it a "lettuceburger," and that it is the kind of meat and not the condiment that goes with it that gives a sandwich it distinctive identity. It likewise involves learning that the sex of the person for whom they are designed is probably the most distinctive feature of clothes (in department stores men's shirts are more likely to be displayed alongside men's pajamas than alongside women's blouses), and that the way it is spelled may help us locate an eggplant in a dictionary but not in a supermarket. Similarly, we learn that in order to find a book in a bookstore we must attend its substantive focus and the first letters of its author's last name (and ignore, for example, the color of its cover), yet that in order to find it in a book exhibit we must first know who published it. (We also learn that bookstores regard readers' ages as a critical feature of books, thus displaying children's books on dogs alongside children's books on boats rather than alongside general books on dogs). We likewise learn that, in supermarkets, low-sodium soup is located near the low-sugar pineapple slices ("diet food"), marzipan near the anchovy paste ("gourmet food"), and canned corn near the canned pears (rather than by the fresh or frozen corn). And so we learn that, for the purpose of applying the incest taboo, brotherhood "counts" as a measure of proximity to oneself, whereas having the same blood type is irrelevant.

Separating the relevant (figure) from the irrelevant (ground) is not a spontaneous act. Classifying is a normative process, and it is society that leads us to perceive things as similar to or different from one another through unmistakably social "*rules* of irrelevance"[5] that specify which differences are salient for differentiating entities from one another and which ones are only negligible differences among variants of a single entity. Ignoring differences which "make no difference" involves some social pressure to disregard them. Though we often notice them, we learn to ignore them as irrelevant, just as we inhibit our perception of its ground in order to perceive the figure. Along the same lines, ignoring the stutter or deformity of another is not a spontaneous act but rather a social display of tact. It is rules of irrelevance that likewise lead judges, professors, and doctors to display "affective neutrality"[6] and acquit innocent defendants, reward good students, and do their best to save patients' lives even when they personally despise them. They also lead bureaucrats who screen applications to exclude applicants' sex or race from their official considerations even if they are personally attentive to it.

The social construction of discontinuity is accomplished largely through language:

> We dissect nature along lines laid down by our native languages. The categories . . . we isolate from the world of phenomena we do not find there because they stare every observer in the face. . . . [T]he world is presented in a kaleidoscopic flux of impressions which has to be organized by our minds. We cut nature up . . . as we do, largely because we are parties to an agreement to organize it in this way—an agreement that . . . is codified in the patterns of our language. . . . [W]e cannot talk at all except by subscribing to the organization and classification of data which the agreement decrees.[7]

Not only does language allow us to detach mental entities from their surroundings and assign them fixed, decontextualized meanings, it also enables us to transform experiential continuums into discontinuous categories ("long" and "short," "hot" and "cold"). As we assign them separate labels, we come to perceive mental essences such as "professionals," "criminals," or "the poor" as if they were indeed discrete. It is language that allows us to carve out of a continuous voice range the discrete categories "alto" and "soprano," distinguish "herbs" (basil, dill) from leaves we would never allow on our table, define vague discomfort in seemingly sharp categories such as "headache" or "nausea," and perceive after shave lotion as actually different from eau de toilette or cologne. At the same time, it is our ability to assign them a common label that also allows us to lump things together in our mind. Only the concept "classical," for example, makes Ravel's music similar to Vivaldi's, and only the concept "alcoholic" makes wine seem "closer" to vodka than to grape juice.

Since it is the very basis of social reality, we often forget that language rests on mere convention and regard such mental entities, which are our own creation, as if they were real. . . .

By the same token, as we divide a single continuous process into several conceptual parts ("cause" and "effect," "life" and "death") we often commit the fallacy of misplaced concreteness and regard such purely mental constructs as if they were actually separate. We likewise reify the mental divide separating "white-collar" from "manual" labor as well as the purely mental outlines of such entities as races, classes, families, and nations. Like the dwellers of Plato's proverbial cave, we are prisoners of our own minds, mistaking mere social conceptions for actual experiential perceptions.

It is society that helps us carve discrete islands of meaning out of our experience. Only English speakers, for example, can "hear" the gaps between the separate words in "perhapstheyshouldhavetrieditearlier," which everyone else hears as a single chain of sound. Along similar lines, while people who hear jazz for the first time can never understand why a seemingly continuous stretch of music is occasionally interrupted by bursts of applause, jazz connoisseurs can actually "hear" the purely mental divides separating piano, bass, or drum "solos" from mere "accompaniment." Being a member of society entails "seeing" the world through special mental lenses. It is these lenses, which we acquire only through socialization, that allow us to "perceive things." The proverbial Martian cannot see the mental partitions separating Catholics from Protestants, classical from popular music, or the funny from the crude. Like the contours of constellations, we "see" such fine lines only when we learn that we should expect them there. As real as they may feel to us, boundaries are mere figments of our minds. Only the socialized can "see" them. To all cultural outsiders they are totally invisible.

Only through such "glasses" can entities be "seen." As soon as we remove them, boundaries practically disappear and the "things" they delineate fade away. What we then experience is as continuous as is Europe or the Middle East when seen from space or in ancient maps, or our own neighborhood when fog or heavy snow covers curbs and property lines, practically transforming familiar milieux into a visually undifferentiated flux. This is the way reality must appear to the unsocialized—a boundless, unbroken world with no lines. That is the world we would have inhabited were it not for society.

Notes

1. George G. Simpson, *Principles of Animal Taxonomy* (New York: Columbia University Press, 1961), p. 2.
2. Emile Durkheim and Marcel Mauss, *Primitive Classification* (Chicago: University of Chicago Press, 1973), pp. 7–8.
3. Rodney Needham, "Introduction" to Durkheim and Mauss, *Primitive Classification*, p. viii.
4. Steven J. Gould, "Taxonomy as Politics: The Harm of False Classification," *Dissent*, Winter 1990, p. 73.
5. Erving Goffman, *Encounters* (Indianapolis: Bobbs-Merrill, 1961), pp. 19–26.
6. Talcott Parsons, *The Social System* (New York: Free Press, 1964), pp. 60, 435, 458–62.
7. Benjamin Whorf, "Science and Linguistics," in *Language, Thought, and Reality* (Cambridge: MIT Press, 1956), pp. 213–214.

Part II

The Social Construction of Self

The experience of self is central to being human. Humans could not experience a meaningful reality unless they could symbolically convey meanings to themselves as well as to others. In order to do so, they must think of and act toward themselves as if they were someone else. We get angry at, talk to, encourage, and congratulate ourselves much as we do one another. From the perspective of sociological psychology, this is the essence of the human self: to be both the subject and object of one's own thoughts and actions. And the self that is the object of our thoughts and actions is as much socially constructed as any other object of our experience. Our self becomes real to us as we act toward ourselves as others do. We interpret and define our thoughts, feelings, and actions in terms of shared symbols. The selections in this section examine the social character of the self, the process of its acquisition and its reconstruction. ✦

4

The Self as Sentiment and Reflection

Charles Horton Cooley

Charles Horton Cooley was an economist by training who made important contributions to the development of sociological psychology. The influence of Adam Smith's theory of human sentiments is obvious in this selection, which was written around the turn of the twentieth century. In Theory of Moral Sentiments *(1759), Smith maintains that individuals' sympathetic identification with one another's situation provides the moral foundation of human social life. For Cooley, the human self also rests on individuals' emotional responsiveness to one another. He argues that sentiment is the core of the human self and is central to its development. Accordingly, a sense of appropriation is the source of this self-feeling. The individual not only appropriates people and material objects by claiming them as "mine," but he or she also appropriates images of himself or herself reflected in others' treatment of him or her.*

This is what is commonly known as Cooley's theory of "the looking-glass self." Cooley suggests that the individual can only reflect upon and form images of himself or herself through the imaginary adoption of someone else's perspective. The individual imagines how he or she must appear to someone, imagines how that person must be judging his or her appearance and behavior, and consequently feels either pride or shame. Such socially reflected images inform the individual of who and what she or he is, and the consequent feelings of pride and shame provide the grounds for her or his sense of self-worth or esteem.

Cooley's young daughter M. was an important source of inspiration for his theory of the looking-glass self. He closely observed and took meticulous notes on her behavior. Cooley was particularly taken by her use of first-person pronouns like "mine" and "my." As Cooley notes, unlike most other expressions, these pronouns mean something or someone quite different, depending on who is speaking. M. could only have learned to use pronouns correctly by reflecting how oth-ers use them—by the imaginary adoption of other people's perspectives. Cooley was also amazed at how early in life M. was aware of her influence over others. She recognized the reflections of her own actions in how others responded to her. For us, as for M., others' responses are the looking glass in which we see reflected images of ourselves. It is from these socially reflected images that we construct a self and our feelings about it.

It is well to say at the outset that by the word "self" in this discussion is meant simply that which is designated in common speech by the pronouns of the first person singular, "I," "me," "my," "mine," and "myself." "Self" and "ego" are used by metaphysicians and moralists in many other senses, more or less remote from the "I" of daily speech and thought, and with these I wish to have as little to do as possible. What is here discussed is what psychologists call the empirical self, the self that can be apprehended or verified by ordinary observation. I qualify it by the word social not as implying the existence of a self that is not social—for I think that the "I" of common language always has more or less distinct reference to other people as well as the speaker—but because I wish to emphasize and dwell upon the social aspect of it.

The distinctive thing in the idea, for which the pronouns of the first person are names, is apparently a characteristic kind of feeling which may be called the my-feeling or sense of appropriation. Almost any sort of ideas may be associated with this feeling, and that alone, it would seem, is the determining factor in the matter. As Professor James says in his admirable discussion of the self, the words "me" and "self" designate "all the things which have the power to produce in a stream of consciousness excitement of a certain peculiar sort. . . ." The social self is simply any idea, or system of ideas, drawn from the communicative life, that the mind cherishes as its own. Self-feeling has its chief scope within the general life, not outside of it. . . .

That the "I" of common speech has a meaning which includes some sort of reference to other persons is involved in the very fact that the word and the ideas it stands for are phenomena of language and the communicative life. It is doubtful whether it is possible to use language at all without thinking more or less distinctly of someone else, and certainly the things to which we give names, and which have a large place in reflective thought, are almost always those which are impressed upon us by our contact with other people. Where there is no communication there can be no nomenclature and no developed thought. What we call "me," "mine," or "myself" is, then, not something separate from the general life, but the most interesting part of it, a part whose interest arises from the very fact that it is both general and individual. That is, we care for it just because it is that phase of the mind that is living and striving in the common life, trying to impress itself upon the minds of others. "I" is a militant social tendency, working to hold and enlarge its place in the general current of tendencies. So far as it can, it waxes, as all life does. To think of it as apart from society is a palpable absurdity of which no one could be guilty who really *saw* it as a fact of life. . . .

If a thing has no relation to others of which one is conscious, he is unlikely to think of it at all, and if he does think of it, he cannot, it seems to me, regard it as emphatically *his*. The appropriative sense is always the shadow, as it were, of the common life, and when we have it, we have a sense of the latter in connection with it. Thus, if we think of a secluded part of the woods as "ours," it is because we think, also, that others do not go there. . . .

The reference to other persons involved in the sense of self may be distinct and particular, as when a boy is ashamed to have his mother catch him at something she has forbidden; or it may be vague and general, as when one is ashamed to do something which only his conscience, expressing his sense of social responsibility, detects and disapproves; but it is always there. There is no sense of "I," as in pride or shame, without its correlative sense of you, or he, or they. Even the miser gloating over his hidden gold can feel the "mine" only as he is aware of the world of men over whom he has secret power; and the case is very similar with all kinds of hidden treasure. Many painters, sculptors, and writers have loved to withhold their work from the world, fondling it in seclusion until they were quite done with it; but the delight in this, as in all secrets, depends upon a sense of the value of what is concealed.

In a very large and interesting class of cases, the social reference takes the form of a somewhat definite imagination of how one's self—that is, any idea he appropriates—appears in a particular

mind; and the kind of self-feeling one has is determined by the attitude toward this attributed to that other mind. A social self of this sort might be called the reflected or looking-glass self:

> "Each to each a looking-glass
> Reflects the other that doth pass."

As we see our face, figure, and dress in the glass, and are interested in them because they are ours, and pleased or otherwise with them according as they do or do not answer to what we should like them to be; so in imagination we perceive in another's mind some thought of our appearance, manners, aims, deeds, character, friends, and so on, and are variously affected by it.

A self-idea of this sort seems to have three principal elements: the imagination of our appearance to the other person; the imagination of his judgment of that appearance; and some sort of self-feeling, such as pride or mortification. The comparison with a looking glass hardly suggests the second element, the imagined judgment, which is quite essential. The thing that moves us to pride or shame is not the mere mechanical reflection of ourselves, but an imputed sentiment, the imagined effect of this reflection upon another's mind. This is evident from the fact that the character and weight of that other, in whose mind we see ourselves, makes all the difference with our feeling. We are ashamed to seem evasive in the presence of a straightforward man, cowardly in the presence of a brave one, gross in the eyes of a refined one, and so on. We always imagine, and in imagining share, the judgments of the other mind. A man will boast to one person of an action—say some sharp transaction in trade—which he would be ashamed to own to another. . . .

[This] view [of] "self" and the pronouns of the first person . . . was impressed on me by observing my child M. at the time when she was learning to use these pronouns. When she was two years and two weeks old, I was surprised to discover that she had a clear notion of the first and second persons when used possessively. When asked, "Where is your nose?" she would put her hand upon it and say "my." She also understood that when someone else said "my" and touched an object, it meant something opposite to what was meant when she touched the same object and used the same word. Now, anyone who will exercise his imagination upon the question of how this matter must appear to a mind having no means of knowing anything about "I" and "my," except what it learns by hearing them used, will see that it should be very puzzling. Unlike other words, the personal pronouns have apparently no uniform meaning, but convey different and even opposite ideas when employed by different persons. It seems remarkable that children should master the problem before they arrive at the considerable power of abstract reasoning. How should a little girl of two, not particularly reflective, have discovered that "my" was not the sign of a definite object like other words, but meant something different with each person who used it? And, still more surprising, how should she have achieved the correct use of it with reference to herself which, it would seem, *could not be copied from anyone else*, simply because no one else used it to describe what belonged to her? The meaning of words is learned by associating them with other phenomena. But how is it possible to learn the meaning of one which, as used by others, is never associated with the same phenomenon as when properly used by one's self? Watching her use of the first person, I was at once struck with the fact that she employed it almost wholly in a possessive sense, and that, too, when in an aggressive, self-assertive mood. It was extremely common to see R. tugging at one end of a plaything and M. at the other, screaming, "My, my." "Me" was sometimes nearly equivalent to "my" and was also employed to call attention to herself when she wanted something done for her. Another common use of "my" was to demand something she did not have at all. Thus, if R. had something the like of which she wanted, say a cart, she would exclaim, "Where's *my* cart?"

It seemed to me that she might have learned the use of these pronouns as follows. The self-feeling had always been there. From the first week she had wanted things and cried and fought for them. She had also become familiar by observation and opposition with similar appropriative activities on the part of R. Thus, she not only had the feeling herself, but by associating it with its visible expression had probably defined it, sympathized with it, resented it, in others. Grasping, tugging, and screaming would be associated with the feeling in her own case and would recall the feeling when observed in others. They would constitute a language, precedent to the use of first-person pronouns, to express the self-idea. All was ready, then, for the word to name this experi-

ence. She now observed that R., when contentiously appropriating something, frequently exclaimed, "my," "mine," "give it to *me*," "I want it," and the like. Nothing more natural, then, than that she should adopt these words as names for a frequent and vivid experience with which she was already familiar in her own case and had learned to attribute to others. Accordingly, it appeared to me, as I recorded in my notes at the time, that "'my' and 'mine' are simply names for concrete images of appropriativeness," embracing both the appropriative feeling and its manifestation. If this is true, the child does not at first work out the I-and-you idea in an abstract form. The first-person pronoun is a sign of a concrete thing, after all, but that thing is not primarily the child's body, or his muscular sensations as such, but the phenomenon of aggressive appropriation, practiced by himself, witnessed in others, and incited and interpreted by a hereditary instinct. This seems to get over the difficulty mentioned above, namely, the seeming lack of a common content between the meaning of "my" when used by another and when used by one's self. This common content is found in the appropriative feeling and the visible and audible signs of that feeling. An element of difference and strife comes in, of course, in the opposite actions or purposes which the "my" of another and one's own "my" are likely to stand for. When another person says "mine" regarding something which I claim, I sympathize with him enough to understand what he means, but it is a hostile sympathy, overpowered by another and more vivid "mine" connected with the idea of drawing the object my way.

In other words, the meaning of "I" and "mine" is learned in the same way that the meanings of hope, regret, chagrin, disgust, and thousands of other words of emotion and sentiment are learned: that is, by having the feeling, imputing it to others in connection with some kind of expression, and hearing the word along with it. As to its communication and growth, the self-idea is in no way peculiar that I see, but essentially like other ideas. In its more complex forms, such as are expressed by "I" in conversation and literature, it is a social sentiment, or type of sentiments, defined and developed by intercourse. . . .

I imagine, then, that as a rule the child associates "I" and "me" at first only with those ideas regarding which his appropriative feeling is aroused and defined by opposition. He appropriates his nose, eye, or foot in very much the same way as a plaything—by antithesis to other noses, eyes, and feet, which he cannot control. It is not uncommon to tease little children by proposing to take away one of these organs, and they behave precisely as if the "mine" threatened were a separable object—which it might be for all they know. And, as I have suggested, even in adult life, "I," "me," and "mine" are applied with a strong sense of their meaning only to things distinguished as peculiar to us by some sort of opposition or contrast. They always imply social life and relation to other persons. That which is most distinctively mine is very private, it is true, but it is that part of the private which I am cherishing in antithesis to the rest of the world, not the separate but the special. The aggressive self is essentially a militant phase of the mind, having for its apparent function the energizing of peculiar activities, and, although the militancy may not go on in an obvious, external manner, it always exists as a mental attitude. . . .

The process by which self-feeling of the looking-glass sort develops in children may be followed without much difficulty. Studying the movements of others as closely as they do, they soon see a connection between their own acts and changes in those movements; that is, they perceive their own influence or power over persons. The child appropriates the visible actions of his parent or nurse, over which he finds he has some control, in quite the same way as he appropriates one of his own members or a plaything; and he will try to do things with this new possession, just as he will with his hand or his rattle. A girl six months old will attempt in the most evident and deliberate manner to attract attention to herself, to set going by her actions some of those movements of other persons that she has appropriated. She has tasted the joy of being a cause, of exerting social power, and wishes more of it. She will tug at her mother's skirts, wriggle, gurgle, stretch out her arms, etc., all the time watching for the hoped-for effect. . . .

The young performer soon learns to be different things to different people, showing that he begins to apprehend personality and to foresee its operation. If the mother or nurse is more tender than just, she will almost certainly be "worked" by systematic weeping. It is a matter of common observation that children often behave worse with their mother than with other and less sympathetic

people. Of the new persons that a child sees, it is evident that some make a strong impression and awaken a desire to interest and please them, while others are indifferent or repugnant. Sometimes the reason can be perceived or guessed, sometimes not; but the fact of selective interest, admiration, and prestige is obvious before the end of the second year. By that time a child already cares much for the reflection of himself upon one personality and little for that upon another. Moreover, he soon claims intimate and tractable persons as *mine*, classes them among his other possessions, and maintains his ownership against all comers. M., at three years of age, vigorously resented R.'s claim upon their mother. The latter was "*my* mamma," whenever the point was raised.

Strong joy and grief depend upon the treatment this rudimentary social self receives. . . . At about fifteen months old [M.] had become "a perfect little actress," seeming to live largely in imaginations of her effect upon other people. She constantly and obviously laid traps for attention, and looked abashed or wept at any signs of disapproval or indifference. At times it would seem as if she could not get over these repulses, but would cry long in a grieved way, refusing to be comforted. If she hit upon any little trick that made people laugh, she would be sure to repeat it, laughing loudly and affectedly in imitation. She had quite a repertory of these small performances, which she would display to a sympathetic audience, or even try upon strangers. I have seen her at sixteen months, when R. refused to give her the scissors, sit down and make-believe cry, putting up her underlip and sniffling, meanwhile looking up now and then to see what effect she was producing. . . .

Progress from this point is chiefly in the way of a greater definiteness, fullness, and inwardness in the imagination of the other's state of mind. A little child thinks of and tries to elicit certain visible or audible phenomena, and does not go beyond them; but what a grown-up person desires to produce in others is an internal, invisible condition which his own richer experience enables him to imagine, and of which expression is only the sign. Even adults, however, make no separation between what other people think and the visible expression of that thought. They imagine the whole thing at once, and their idea differs from that of a child chiefly in the comparative richness and complexity of the elements that accompany and interpret the visible or audible sign. There is also a progress from the naive to the subtle in socially self-assertive action. A child obviously and simply, at first, does things for effect. Later there is an endeavor to suppress the appearance of doing so; affection, indifference, contempt, etc., are simulated to hide the real wish to affect the self-image. . . .

Reprinted from: Charles Horton Cooley, "The Self as Sentiment and Reflection" in *Human Nature and the Social Order*, pp. 168–170, 179–184, 189–194, 196–199. Copyright © 1983 by Transaction Publishers. Reprinted by permission. ✦

5

The Self as Social Structure

George Herbert Mead

George Herbert Mead is probably the most important figure in the development of sociological psychology. His characterizations of the self and its development are central to distinctively sociological understandings of the human condition. This selection is taken from Mind, Self, and Society, which is Mead's best-known work, even though he did not actually write it. It was reconstructed from the class notes of students who took a course of that same title from Mead at the University of Chicago in the 1920s. Mead makes a number of important points about the human self in this selection: the self is separate from the body; it arises in social experience; but it is more than a mere product of socially reflected self-images.

According to Mead, language is crucial to the development of the self. When we speak, we hear ourselves and respond to what we are saying in similar ways, as do those whom we are addressing. In speaking, we are both the subject and an object of our own action. Moreover, because what we say means more or less the same to us as to those being addressed, we can assume their role and anticipate their likely reaction to what we are saying. Mead observes that, once children start to acquire language, they literally begin to take on the roles of others in play. They play at being a mother, father, or superhero. In so doing, the child addresses himself or herself in the role of those whom Mead calls significant others and responds accordingly. At this stage, the child develops separate selves that answer to each role he or she plays. That is why, Mead argues, a multiple personality is, in a certain sense, normal. It is when the child starts playing games that he or she begins to tie these multiple selves together into a unified whole.

Games involve the rule-governed coordination of a variety of distinct roles. In order to successfully play a game, the child must simultaneously assume the roles of all the other players. For example, in Mead's favorite example of baseball, a first baseman cannot successfully complete a double play unless she or he takes the role and anticipates the reactions of both the shortstop and the second baseman to a ground ball hit in their direction. By simultaneously assuming such interrelated roles, the individual adopts the perspective of an organized community or generalized other toward himself or herself. Such a generalized perspective provides the individual with a unified view of self. As Mead notes, this implies that the structure of the self will reflect the structure of the various groups of which the individual is a member.

However, in Mead's view, the self consists of more than the "me" that is the object of others' actions. The self is both subject and object. The subject or "I" responds to the object or "me," sometimes questioning and challenging it. The self is not a thing but a process—a continuous interchange between subject and object, "I" and "me." Mead provides a profoundly social, although not socially deterministic, view of the self. The self is profoundly social not only in the sense that it arises in social experience, but also in the sense that it is a social process—a continuous inner conversation between an "I" and a "me." Social experience may make that conversation possible, but it does not determine what will emerge from it. It can be as lively, creative, and unpredictable as the most entertaining conversation among individuals.

The self has the characteristic that it is an object to itself, and that characteristic distinguishes it from other objects and from the body. It is perfectly true that the eye can see the foot, but it does not see the body as a whole. We cannot see our backs; we can feel certain portions of them, if we are agile, but we cannot get an experience of our whole body. There are, of course, experiences which are somewhat vague and difficult of location, but the bodily experiences are for us organized about a self. The foot and hand belong to the self. We can see our feet, especially if we look at them from the wrong end of an opera glass, as strange things which we have difficulty in recognizing as our own. The parts of the body are quite distinguishable from the self. We can lose parts of the body without any serious invasion of the self. The mere ability to experience different parts of the body is not different from the experience of a table. The table presents a different feel from what the hand does when one hand feels another, but it is an experience of something with which we come definitely into contact. The body

21

does not experience itself as a whole, in the sense in which the self in some way enters into the experience of the self.

It is the characteristic of the self as an object to itself that I want to bring out. This characteristic is represented in the word "self," which is a reflexive, and indicates that which can be both subject and object. This type of object is essentially different from other objects. . . .

The self, as that which can be an object to itself, is essentially a social structure, and it arises in social experience. . . . The individual experiences himself as such, not directly, but only indirectly, from the particular standpoint of other individual members of the same social group, or from the generalized standpoint of the social group as a whole to which he belongs. For he enters his own experience as a self or individual, not directly or immediately, not by becoming a subject to himself, but only insofar as he first becomes an object to himself, just as other individuals are objects to him or in his experience; and he becomes an object to himself only by taking the attitudes of other individuals toward himself within a social environment or context of experience and behavior in which both he and they are involved.

After a self has arisen, it in a certain sense provides for itself its social experiences, and so we can conceive of an absolutely solitary self. But it is impossible to conceive of a self arising outside of social experience. When it has arisen, we can think of a person in solitary confinement for the rest of his life, but who still has himself as a companion, and is able to think and to converse with himself as he had communicated with others. . . . We are continually following up our own address to other persons by an understanding of what we are saying, and using that understanding in the direction of our continued speech. We are finding out what we are going to say, what we are going to do, by trolling the process itself. In the conversation of gestures, what we say calls out a certain response in another and that in turn changes our own action, so that we shift from what we started to do because of the reply the other makes. The conversation of gestures is the beginning of communication. The individual comes to carry on a conversation of gestures with himself. He says something, and that calls out a certain reply in himself which makes him change what he was going to say. One starts to say something, we will presume an unpleasant something, but when he

starts to say it, he realizes it is cruel. The effect on himself of what he is saying checks him; there is here a conversation of gestures between the individual and himself. We mean by significant speech that the action is one that affects the individual himself, and that the effect upon the individual himself is part of the intelligent carrying out of the conversation with others. Now we, so to speak, amputate that social phase and dispense with it for the time being, so that one is talking to one's self as one would talk to another person. . . .

We have discussed the social foundations of the self. . . . We may now explicitly raise the question as to the nature of the "I" which is aware of the social "me." . . . The "I" reacts to the self which arises through taking the attitudes of others. Through taking those attitudes, we have introduced the "me" and we react to it as an "I."

The "I" is the response of the individual to the attitude of the community as this appears in his own experience. His response to that organized attitude in turn changes it. . . . [T]his is a change which is not present in his own experience until after it takes place. The "I" appears in our experience in memory. It is only after we have acted that we know what we have done; it is only after we have spoken that we know what we have said. The adjustment to that organized world which is present in our own nature is one that represents the "me" and is constantly there. But if the response to it is a response which is of the nature of the conversation of gestures, if it creates a situation which is in some sense novel, if one puts up his side of the case, asserts himself over against others and insists that they take a different attitude toward himself, then there is something important occurring that is not previously present in experience. . . . Such a novel reply to the social situation . . . constitutes the "I" as over against the "me."

The problem now presents itself as to how, in detail, a self arises. We have to note something of the background of its genesis. . . . We have seen . . . that there are certain gestures that affect the organism as they affect other organisms and may, therefore, arouse in the organism responses of the same character as aroused in the other. Here, then, we have a situation in which the individual may at least arouse responses in himself and reply to these responses, the condition being that the social stimuli have an effect on the individual which is like that which they have on the other.

That, for example, is what is implied in language; otherwise, language as significant symbol would disappear, since the individual would not get the meaning of that which he says. . . . It is out of that sort of language that the mind of Helen Keller was built up. As she has recognized, it was not until she could get into communication with other persons through symbols which could arouse in herself the responses they arouse in other people that she could get what we term a mental content, or a self.

Another set of background factors in the genesis of the self is represented in the activities of play and the game.

We find [among] children . . . invisible, imaginary companions. . . . [Children] organize in this way the responses which they call out in other persons and call out also in themselves. Of course, this playing with an imaginary companion is only a peculiarly interesting phase of ordinary play. Play in this sense, especially the stage which precedes the organized games, is a play at something. A child plays at being a mother, at being a teacher, at being a policeman, that is, he is taking different roles, as we say. We have something that suggests this in what we call the play of animals: a cat will play with her kittens, and dogs play with each other. Two dogs playing with each other will attack and defend, in a process which if carried through would amount to an actual fight. There is a combination of responses which checks the depth of the bite. But we do not have in such a situation the dogs taking a definite role in the sense that a child deliberately takes the role of another. This tendency on the part of the children is what we are working with in the kindergarten where the roles which the children assume are made the basis for training. When a child does assume a role he has in himself the stimuli which call out that particular response or group of responses. He may, of course, run away when he is chased, as the dog does, or he may turn around and strike back just as the dog does in his play. But that is not the same as playing at something. Children get together to "play Indian." This means that the child has a certain set of stimuli which call out in itself the responses that they would call out in others, and which answer to an Indian. In the play period the child utilizes his own responses to these stimuli which he makes use of in building a self. The response which he has a tendency to make to these stimuli organizes them. He plays

that he is, for instance, offering himself something, and he buys it; he gives a letter to himself and takes it away; he addresses himself as a parent, as a teacher; he arrests himself as a policeman. He has a set of stimuli which call out in himself the sort of responses they call out in others. He takes this group of responses and organizes them into a certain whole. Such is the simplest form of being another to one's self. It involves a temporal situation. The child says something in one character and responds in another character, and then his responding in another character is a stimulus to himself in the first character, and so the conversation goes on. A certain organized structure arises in him and in his other which replies to it, and these carry on the conversation of gestures between themselves.

If we contrast play with the situation in an organized game, we note the essential difference that the child who plays in a game must be ready to take the attitude of everyone else involved in that game, and that these different roles must have a definite relationship to each other. Taking a very simple game such as hide-and-seek, everyone, with the exception of the one who is hiding, is a person who is hunting. A child does not require more than the person who is hunted and the one who is hunting. If a child is playing in the first sense he just goes on playing, but there is no basic organization gained. In that early stage he passes from one role to another just as a whim takes him. But in a game where a number of individuals are involved, then the child taking one role must be ready to take the role of everyone else. If he gets in a "ball nine," he must have the responses of each position involved in his own position. He must know what everyone else is going to do in order to carry out his own play. He has to take all of these roles. They do not all have to be present in consciousness at the same time, but at some moments he has to have three or four individuals present in his own attitude, such as the one who is going to throw the ball, the one who is going to catch it, and so on. These responses must be, in some degree, present in his own make-up. In the game, then, there is a set of responses of such others so organized that the attitude of one calls out the appropriate attitudes of the other.

This organization is put in the form of the rules of the game. Children take a great interest in rules. They make rules on the spot in order to help themselves out of difficulties. Part of the enjoyment of the game is to get these rules. Now, the rules are the set of responses which a particular attitude calls out. You can demand a certain response in others if you take a certain attitude. These responses are all in yourself as well. There you get an organized set of such responses as that to which I have referred, which is something more elaborate than the roles found in play. Here there is just a set of responses that follow on each other indefinitely. At such a stage we speak of a child as not yet having a fully developed self. The child responds in a fairly intelligent fashion to the immediate stimuli that come to him, but they are not organized. He does not organize his life as we would like to have him do, namely, as a whole. There is just a set of responses of the type of play. The child reacts to a certain stimulus, and the reaction is in himself that is called out in others, but he is not a whole self. In his game he has to have an organization of these roles; otherwise, he cannot play the game. The game represents the passage in the life of the child from taking the role of others in play to the organized part that is essential to self-consciousness in the full sense of the term.

The fundamental difference between the game and play is that in the latter the child must have the attitude of all the others involved in that game. The attitudes of the other players which the participant assumes organize into a sort of unit, and it is that organization which controls the response of the individual. The illustration used was of a person playing baseball. Each one of his own acts is determined by his assumption of the action of the others who are playing the game. What he does is controlled by his being everyone else on that team, at least insofar as those attitudes affect his own particular response. We get then an "other" which is an organization of the attitudes of those involved in the same process.

A multiple personality is in a certain sense normal. . . . There is usually an organization of the whole self with reference to the community to which we belong, and the situation in which we find ourselves. What the society is, whether we are living with people of the present, people of our own imaginations, people of the past, varies, of course, with different individuals. Normally, within the sort of community as a whole to which we belong, there is a unified self, but that may be broken up. To a person who is somewhat unstable and in whom there is a line of cleavage, certain activities become impossible, and that set of activities may separate and evolve into another self. Two separate "me's" and "I's," two different selves result, and that is the condition under which there is a tendency to break up the personality. There is an account of a professor of education who disappeared, was lost to the community, and later turned up in a logging camp in the West. He freed himself of his occupation and turned to the woods where he felt, if you like, more at home. The pathological side of it was the forgetting, the leaving out of the rest of the self. This result involved getting rid of certain bodily memories which would identify the individual to himself. We often recognize the lines of cleavage that run through us. We would be glad to forget certain things, get rid of things the self is bound up with in past experiences. What we have here is a situation in which there can be different selves, and it is dependent upon the set of social reactions that is involved as to which self we are going to be.

The unity and structure of the complete self reflects the unity and structure of the social process as a whole; and each of the elementary selves of which it is composed reflects the unity and structure of one of the various aspects of that process in which the individual is implicated. In other words, the various elementary selves which constitute, or are organized into, a complete self are the various aspects of the structure of that complete self answering to the various aspects of the structure of the social process as a whole; the structure of the complete self is thus a reflection of the complete social process. The organization and unification of a social group is identical with the organization and unification of any one of the selves arising within the social process in which that group is engaged, or which it is carrying on.

The organized community or social group which gives to the individual his unity of self may be called "the generalized other." The attitude of the generalized other is the attitude of the whole community.

I have emphasized what I have called the structures upon which the self is constructed, the framework of the self, as it were. . . . We cannot be ourselves unless we are also members in whom there is a community of attitudes which control the attitudes of all. We cannot have rights unless we have common attitudes. That which we have acquired as self-conscious persons makes us such members of society and gives us selves. Selves can exist only in definite relationships to other selves. No hard-and-fast line can be drawn between our own selves and the selves of others, because our own selves exist and enter as such into our experience only insofar as the selves of others exist and enter as such into our experience also. The individual possesses a self only in relation to the selves of the other members of his social group; and the structure of his self expresses or reflects the general behavior pattern of this social group to which he belongs; just as does the structure of the self of every other individual belonging to this social group.

6

Fashioning Gender Identity

Spencer E. Cahill

Gender identity is one of the earliest components of children's self-definitions. Most five-year-olds routinely refer to themselves as a boy or a girl and insist that others do so as well. There are many explanations for this early acquisition of gender identity. Some assume that hormones biologically determine gender identification, while more Freudian explanations attribute it to children's psychological identification with same-sex parents or other adults. Others maintain that gender identification is a by-product of children's cognitive development, while still others contend that it is just another learned behavior resulting from patterns of reward and punishment. Cooley's and Mead's accounts of the social development of the self suggest an alternative explanation. This selection illustrates that alternative explanation and the importance of socially constructed personal appearances to the process of gender identity acquisition.

Both Cooley and Mead propose that the individual acquires a self by taking the attitude of others toward herself or himself, and we have different attitudes about males and females. At birth, infants are immediately identified as male or female. From that time forward, caretakers commonly groom, dress, and decorate infants so that their appearance clearly announces their sex to others. This is of no small importance because there is considerable evidence that we have different attitudes about male and female infants and treat them differently.

Once children begin to acquire their native language, they begin to learn about this sexual classification of people. They learn that people belong to discrete categories like "mommies" and "daddies," "boys" and "girls," "women" and "men." They also learn to place people into the socially appropriate categories based on perceptible differences in appearance—differences that are mostly created through grooming and dress. When children enter what Mead called the play stage of self-development, they begin to play at being these different kinds of people, commonly donning a socially appropriate costume when doing so. Others' responses to this role playing and corresponding appearance management informs children that no matter how they dress they cannot escape their socially ascribed sex. They consequently take these attitudes of others toward themselves and embrace their socially bestowed gender identity as their own.

That is, children do not recognize or define themselves as a boy or a girl until they see and understand the reflections of themselves in the looking glass of others' responses to them.

This selection describes the process of the social development of gender identity in more detail. It also illustrates many of the ideas discussed in earlier selections about social classification and the social origins of the self. It empirically illustrates that sex and gender, like all systems of classification, are socially constructed and how gender identity, like other dimensions of the self, arises in social experience.

The transsexual . . . Agnes changed her identity nearly three years before undergoing sex reassignment surgery. After five years of covertly consuming synthetic estrogens (Garfinkel 1967, pp. 285–288), two months of dieting, and much rehearsal, Agnes transformed herself into a female on a late August day in 1956.

> Taking a room in a downtown hotel, she changed into female clothes and went to a local beauty shop where her hair, which was short, was cropped and rearranged in the Italian cut Sophia Loren had made popular. (Garfinkel 1967, p. 145)

On her return home by bus that evening, Agnes was the proud recipient of several soldiers' attentions. Although still haunted by her past life as a male and the secret of her masculine genitalia, Agnes was a female for many if not most intents and purposes from that day forward.

Like the rest of Agnes's story, the manner of her identity transformation is of more than passing interest to students of social life. Agnes's masculine genitalia did not prevent her from being seen as a female nor did her pharmaceutically produced feminine form automatically make her a female in other's eyes. Rather, she secured her claim to a female identity by changing her clothing and hairstyle. The more general sociological lesson is obvious. In everyday social life, the identification of people as male or female has less to do with anatomical characteristics than with what Goffman (1963, p. 25) termed "personal front"— "the complex of clothing, make-up, hairdo and other surface decorations" the individual carries on his or her person. That is the complex of materials out of which male and female identities are commonly fashioned in our society. By implication, they may also be among the materials out of which self-identified males and females are biographically fashioned.

This article concerns the biographical fashioning of self-identified males and females in early childhood. During my 18 months as a volunteer staff member of both a university-affiliated and a parent cooperative preschool in Southern California, I observed the children who attended those schools under a variety of circumstances and interviewed a number of them and their parents. In addition, I subsequently recorded informal discussions with the parents of other children in fieldnotes. The following empirical exploration of the contributions of appearance management to young children's gender socialization is based upon these fieldnotes and others' observations and findings. . . .

Establishing Gender Identities

In our society and probably most others, an infant's external genitalia are visually inspected moments after birth, and, in most cases, he or she is immediately identified as a boy or a girl. . . . [Although] parents are subsequently reassured of their infant's ascribed sex-class identity every time they change the infant's diapers or bathe him or her . . . others who have contact with the infant seldom have the benefit of that anatomical reassurance. Moreover, as the often reported "Baby X" studies suggest, we are not very adept at ascertaining the ascribed sex-class identity of a clothed infant in the absence of other identifying information. The adult participants in those two studies played with one of three infants who were dressed in either "a yellow jumpsuit" (Seavey, Katz and Zalk 1975, p. 105) or an undershirt and diapers (Sidorowicz and Lunney 1980, p. 70), and some were given no hint as to the sex-class identity of the infant with whom they played. When subsequently asked, the overwhelming majority of these uninformed participants mis-

identified the infant's ascribed sex-class placement. Such presumed indications of masculinity and femininity as body shape, physical strength (Seavey, Katz and Zalk 1975, p. 107) and frequency of smiling (Sidorowicz and Lunney 1980, p. 71) proved unreliable.

Yet . . . we implicitly consider an infant's ascribed sex-class identity as prescribing how we should view and treat him or her. When, for example, college students were shown a videotape of an infant crying in response to the opening and closing of a jack-in-the-box, those who had been told that the infant was a boy attributed the crying to anger while those who had been told the infant was a girl reported that "she" was frightened (Condry and Condry 1976). It would seem that we respond not so much to infants but to sex-class identified infants. That is apparently why, despite the obvious risk of clever retorts at our expense, we sometimes ask an infant's accompanying caregiver the literally ambiguous question: "What is it?" We are not simply asking whether the infant is a boy or a girl but thereby also requesting guidance in how we should respond to and talk about him or her. It is seldom necessary to request such guidance, however.

For the most part, parents and other caregivers in our society silently announce their infants' sex-class identities "to whom it may concern" by draping and decorating infants in what might best be termed "sartorial symbols" of sex-class identities. They often color code infants in terms of the traditional masculine blue and feminine pink, commonly dress them in miniaturized versions of adults' sex-class associated costumes, and sometimes even tape bows to female infants' hairless heads. Such conventional, sartorial symbols of sex-class identities enable anyone who comes into contact with an infant to immediately identify the infant as a boy or a girl. In Gregory Stone's (1962, p. 106) phrase, they "invest" the infant with a sex-class identity.

Moreover, the sartorial investiture of infants with sex-class identities also serves indirectly to invest them with presumed male or female human natures. To borrow from Stone (1962, p. 106), "the responses of the world toward the child are differently mobilized" depending on whether there is a bow taped to or a baseball cap resting upon the child's head. For example, as the findings of [a] previously mentioned stud[y] suggest, we tend to view an infant who has a bow taped on her head as . . . frightened rather than angry when she cries. In contrast, we tend to view an infant who is wearing a baseball cap as . . . angry rather than frightened when he cries. Because of these divergent views of differently dressed infants, we tend to treat them differently and thereby encourage them to behaviorally express their presumed male or female human natures. The psychiatrist Robert Stoller (1968, pp. 62–63) once observed that "one can see evidence" of children's "unquestioned femininity or masculinity" by the time they begin to walk. That may be so, but much effort goes into producing this evidence not the least of which is the effort devoted to the sex-class management of infant's personal fronts. It is because of such efforts that we look for evidence of infants' masculinity or femininity and act so as to insure that they will provide behavioral evidence of such presumed male or female human natures.

Recognizing Gendered Identities

Although young children may be behaviorally expressing their presumed masculinity or femininity by the time they begin to walk, they are undoubtedly unaware that they are doing so until somewhat later in their biographies. Before they can appreciate the gender expressive significance of their behavior to others, they must first learn that their social environment is populated by two distinct categories of persons. It is not until they begin to acquire their native language that they start to learn this fundamentally important lesson about the world into which they were born.

Young children's exposure to the everyday usage of such identifying verbal labels as "mommy" and "daddy," "girl" and "boy," and "lady" and "man" encourages them to sort people into sex-class related categories (Cahill 1986, pp. 299–302). Although it may be some time before they understand that such two-term collections of identifying verbal labels all point to a single, underlying system of dichotomous classification, children as young as two years of age identify clothed individuals in photographs as "mommies," "daddies," "boys," and "girls" with a high degree of accuracy. . . . (Thompson 1975). However, it is doubtful whether young children would do so unless there were obvious perceptible similarities among and differences between these categories of persons. As a number of students of

language acquisition have concluded . . . perceptible similarities are the most important determinates of young children's categorical applications of their rudimentary vocabularies.

It seems that as children begin to acquire their native language they develop tentative hypotheses about the criteria on which others' application of sex-class related identifying terms is based. They then empirically test those hypotheses, heed others' responses to their own applications of sex-class related identifying terms, and thereby acquire a practical understanding of common associations between various aspects of personal appearance and sex-class identification. For example, the following occurred on a preschool playground. I (C) was sitting on the side of a sandbox, and a 35-month-old boy (S) was standing in between my legs. He reached up and tugged my beard.

S: That daddy! That daddy!

C: My beard?

S: Yeah. That daddy.

I later learned that this boy's father had not been clean-shaven since before the boy's birth. Thus, rather than indicating that his "daddy" and I shared this perceptible characteristic, the boy was apparently testing his hypothesis that a beard was a sign of "daddiness," of membership in that class of persons called "daddy."

As might be expected, some individuals' personal fronts are confusing to young children in this regard. For example, I (C) was holding a 39-month-old girl (K) when a male preschool teacher (J) with a full beard and mid-back length hair which was gathered together into a "pony tail" approached. The young girl looked at me and then at the teacher.

K: You a boy. He a girl 'cause got a pony tail.

C: Oh yeah?

K: (looking at J) You got a pony tail.

J: Yes.

The young girl then looked back at me and grinned. While this girl seemed to recognize that the teacher was not "really" a girl, she obviously considered a "pony tail" a sign of "girlness." Indeed, she may well have been attempting to elicit a response from either the teacher or me which would clarify the confusing sex-class identifying implications of the teacher's personal front.

For the most part, however, our sex-class related management of both our own and our children's personal fronts does heighten the perceptual similarity of males and of females and the perceptual dissimilarity between males and females. It is primarily these perceptual similarities and differences that direct young children's application of sex-class related identifying terms in our society. . . . Although adults sometimes do instruct young children about the defining anatomical characteristics of males and females, those instructions are often more confusing than enlightening in a society in which bodies are typically clothed. For example, I was once approached by a 37-month-old girl on a preschool playground who informed me "you a girl." When I asked why I was a girl, she replied: "Cause no got penis." This girl was apparently applying a recently learned but misleading lesson when no one has a visible penis as is commonly the case in our society.

Like this girl, children apparently do take adults' instructions regarding the sex-class identifying implications of anatomical characteristics to heart, but those instructions are simply of little practical utility or significance to them. When, for example, four- to six-year-olds were asked what was the most important consideration in deciding whether someone was a boy or a girl, many referred to the genitals, yet hair length had the greatest influence on their sex-class related identifications of "anatomically correct" dolls with different body shapes and wigs (Thompson and Bentler 1971). We adults may implicitly assume that anatomical characteristics are the most obvious grounds for sex-class identification, but that is not obvious to young children as the following anecdote dramatically illustrates.

A colleague's four-year-old son and his father enrolled in a father-son swimming class at the local YMCA. The participants swam in the nude, but some of the fathers wore bathing caps. On the way home from the first session, the boy asked his father why so many "women" had attended the class. When his father inquired "what women," the boy replied: "You know, in the hats."

Regardless of what adults may tell young children, they know that it is bathing caps, hairstyle, clothing and other surface decorations which make someone either a mommy or a daddy, a woman or a man, or a boy or a girl in everyday social life. That is the lesson they learn through observation and practical experimentation with the identity transforming power of appearance management.

Exploring Gendered Identities

Soon after children acquire their native language, as George Herbert Mead first suggested, they start behaviorally to explore the social identities or "roles" which are implicitly encoded in the everyday usage of that language. In Mead's (1934, pp. 150–151, emphasis added) words, the play of young children

> . . . is play *at* something. A child plays at being a mother, at being a policeman: that is, it is taking different roles.

Moreover, as Stone (1962, p. 109) noted some years later, this role playing commonly involves "dressing out" of the roles or social identities which others consider the child's own and "dressing into" those which he or she is temporarily assuming. For example, the younger children in the preschools at which I observed often assumed the identities of so-called "superheroes" such as "Superman," "Batman," and "Wonderwoman." Appearance management was an integral part of this role playing. The children would fashion a "superhero" cape out of paper and tape or by tying the sleeves of their jackets around their necks. When the materials necessary to fashion such a cape were not available, the children would protest that they could not play "superhero" despite reassurances from teachers and other adults to the contrary. Moreover, children typically would not answer to their given names when wearing one of these makeshift capes but only to one of the identifying terms associated with a "superhero" cape. To adult eyes, these children may have only been playing, but it seems in their own eyes they were magically transforming themselves into different kinds of persons by altering their personal fronts.

It is particularly notable in the context of this analysis that the younger children at these preschools paid little attention to inconsistencies between the gendered identities which they sartorially assumed and their ascribed sex-class identities. For example, it was not uncommon for young boys to assume the identity of "Wonderwoman" nor for girls to assume the identity of "Superman." It was also not uncommon for these children to engage in what adults call "cross-dressing." Most did so occasionally, and some did so routinely as illustrated by the following excerpt from an interview of a mother (M) of a 35-month-old girl.

> M: You know my daughter S— has this short hair cut and people are always saying what a nice boy she is.
>
> C: Does she get upset?
>
> M: No. In fact, some days she comes down and says that she wants to be a boy today. It's amazing how she already knows about clothes and all. When she wants to be a boy she puts on jeans and finds dirty socks. Not dirty, but older white socks that are . . .
>
> C: Dingy?
>
> M: Yeah, dingy.

Like Agnes, this young girl was already a sophisticated, practical sociologist. She knew that by altering her personal front she could transform her sex-class identity in others' eyes, and as Cooley (1922) reminds us, our identities are little more than reflections in others' eyes.

However, those with whom a child has regular contact are typically informed of his or her ascribed sex-class identity. Although they may temporarily indulge the child's sartorial assumption of gendered identities which are inconsistent with his or her ascribed sex-class identity, in most cases they will eventually discourage him or her from doing so. For example, the following occurred in a preschool classroom. Two 40-month-old boys (S, T) were playing doctor when a 38-month-old boy (E) who was wearing a "dress-up" dress and high heeled shoes approached.

> E: Fix me (pointing to the unfastened zipper in the dress).
>
> S: You're not a girl.
>
> T: You're a boy.
>
> S: Those are girl things.
>
> *E hurriedly slips out of the dress and kicks off the shoes.*

Through experiences such as this, most children quickly learn that the alchemy of appearance management is limited. Ultimately, it does not enable them to escape the sex-class identity with which others have [invested] and continue to invest them.

In addition to discouraging "cross-dressing," others also encourage young children to "dress into" their ascribed sex-class identity. For example, a preschool aide (A) encountered a 39-month-old girl (S) who was dressed in a bright yellow sunsuit bordered with lace and matching sun bonnet. The girl snapped the straps of the sunsuit with her thumbs and looked at the aide.

> S: I got lace.
>
> A: You're all girl aren't you S—? You're so sweet.

At other times this encouragement of children's sartorial expression of ascribed sex-class identities takes the form of invidious comparisons as the following illustrates.

> A 43-month-old and 37-month-old girl who are both wearing summer dresses are sitting on a preschool playground. Another 37-month-old girl who is dressed in jeans and a smock is standing nearby. A preschool aide walks by and addresses the two girls in summer dresses. "There's a couple of pretty girls." The other girl pulls her smock away from her body, looks at the aide, and remarks: "My dress." In response, the aide asks: "K—, why doesn't your mom ever put you in a real dress?"

In a variety of ways, therefore, both adults and older peers implicitly instruct young children that they are obliged to manage their personal front so that it clearly announces their ascribed sex-class identity. Others thereby implicitly inform young children that they have little choice but to embrace that identity as their own. . . .

Embracing Gendered Identities

Some years ago, Nelson Foote (1951, p. 17) noted that self-identification involves both appropriation of and commitment to an identity. He then observed that

> . . . the compulsive effect of identification upon behavior must arise from absence of alternatives, from unquestioned acceptance of the identities cast upon one by circumstances beyond his control (or thought to be). (Foote 1951, p. 19)

In most cases, others' responses to a child's experimentation with the identity transforming power of appearance management prevents the child from escaping his or her ascribed sex-class identity. From the child's perspective, that identity is cast upon him or her by circumstances that are beyond his or her sartorial control. Thus . . . ascribed sex-class identities do begin to have a "compulsive" effect on most children's behavior by the end of the preschool-age period of their biographies. Having been fashioned into self-identified males and females by others, they begin to fashion themselves into gendered persons.

One of the most obvious indications of older preschool-age children's commitment to their ascribed sex-class identity is their unswerving dedication to its sartorial expression. For example, a 60-month-old boy who had unusually long hair which was often gathered together into a pony tail attended one of the preschools at which I observed. One morning the boy's mother visited his preschool teacher to protest the school's dress code. When the boy's mother started to gather his hair into a pony tail that morning, he told her that his teacher had said that he could not wear a pony tail at school anymore. The teacher informed the mother that she had never said anything of the kind. The boy later admitted that he simply did not want "girl's hair" anymore. On another occasion at the same preschool, I observed a 55-month-old boy refuse a woman's offer to help him put on a necklace because, in his words, it was "for girls." When the woman told him that he could wear the necklace and pretend that he was a king, he again refused. He emphatically reminded her that he was not a "king" but a "boy." Perhaps kings could wear necklaces as the woman suggested, but this boy was well aware that doing so was no way to confirm his identity as a boy.

Many mothers have also told me of their frustration with their preschool age daughters' sudden refusal to wear slacks and insistence upon wearing dresses regardless of the weather or impracticality of engaging in certain activities when doing so. However, girls of this age do not seem as concerned as boys about avoiding sartorial symbols of the other sex-class identity. For example, I often saw the older girls at the preschools at which I observed wearing one of the boys' caps or jackets but never saw an older boy wearing a girl's hat or jacket. . . .

For whatever reason, it seems that we consider a greater diversity of personal fronts compatible with a female identity than with a male identity in this society. A girl with short hair who is wearing jeans and a flannel shirt will commonly be recognized by others as a girl if she also wears earrings or a necklace. That is exactly why boys must not wear earrings or a necklace if they hope socially to confirm their identity as a boy. Men may wear an earring or a necklace or a pony tail and still socially confirm their male identity, but boys do not have that luxury. Excluding the genitalia which are typically concealed, young boys and young girls are commonly indistinguishable from one another except for some small, sartorial badge of female identity. Thus, young boys must vigilantly avoid any and all sartorial symbols of female identity in order socially to confirm their identities as boys. . . .

Aligning Appearance With Gendered Identities

Although most children are clearly committed to their ascribed sex-class identities by the end of the preschool-age period of their biographies, they do not simply conform to conventional standards of sex-class related appearance management as a result. Rather, they continue to experiment with the management of their personal fronts while simultaneously attempting to "align" (Stokes and Hewitt 1976) the resulting sartorial expressions with their presumed masculinity or femininity. For example, I observed a 55-month-old boy (S) slip into a red "dress-up" dress in a preschool classroom and then walk over to a 51-month-old girl (M).

S: TA-DA-DA (in an affected high pitched voice).

M: Silly.

S: TA-DA-DA.

M: You're silly.

S: DA-TA-TA (in an affected low pitched voice while slipping out of the dress) SUUUPerman!

As M's comments indicate, S's behavior while wearing the dress was accountably "silly" or playful and, consequently, the sex-class identifying implications of the dress were not taken seriously. As if that were not enough to establish the expressive unseriousness of the dress, S then emerged from that feminine cocoon in an unmistakably masculine form. He thereby maintained his social claim to the identity of boy despite having worn the dress.

Children's experimentation with their personal fronts also takes unexpected expressive turns requiring improvisation in order to confirm their presumed masculinity or femininity. For example, I overheard the following playground conversation between two five-year-old girls (F, R) and a five-year-old boy (N), all of whom were painting their faces with watercolors.

R: I have to put on make-up 'cause I'm on a date.

F: I'm wearing make-up 'cause I'm going to the doctor.

N: I got mine on 'cause it's Halloween.

Once the girls defined the watercolors as "make-up," the boy apparently needed an explanation or account to neutralize the sex-class identifying implication of its use. His solution was ingenious. He declared that it was the one day of the year on which males can wear make-up with impunity. It is apparently through experiences such as these that children gain an increasingly sophisticated, practical understanding of the elasticity of and points at which conventional standards of sex-class related appearance management snap back with an identity undermining force. . . .

Conclusion

Although primarily suggestive, the preceding examination of young children's gender socialization . . . indicate[s] that appearance management is a principal mechanism of [gender identity acquisition]. Sex-class related appearance management socially invests infants with sex-class identities and, thereby, with male and female human natures. It also promotes young children's sex-class identification of both others and themselves. In addition, others' responses to children's experimentation with the identity transforming power of appearance management encourages them to embrace behaviorally their ascribed sex-class identities. They consequently begin to align their sartorial expression with . . . conventional . . . standards of sex-class related appearance management and to manage their personal fronts so as to announce clearly their ascribed sex-class identities to others. [They thereby become gendered persons to themselves as well as to others.]

References

Cahill, S. 1986. "Language Practices and Self-Definition: The Case of Gender Identity Acquisition." *The Sociological Quarterly* 27: 295–311.

Condry, J. and S. Condry. 1976. "Sex Differences: A Study of the Eye of the Beholder." *Child Development* 47: 812–819.

Cooley, C. H. 1922. *Human Nature and Social Order.* New York: Scribner's.

Foote, N. 1951. "Identification as the Basis for a Theory of Motivation." *American Sociological Review* 16: 14–21.

Garfinkel, H. 1967. *Studies in Ethnomethodology.* Englewood Cliffs, NJ: Prentice Hall.

Goffman, E. 1963. *Behavior in Public Places.* New York: Basic Books.

Mead, G. H. (1934) 1962. *Mind, Self, and Society.* Edited by C. Morris. Chicago, IL: University of Chicago Press.

Seavey, C., P. Katz, and S. R. Zalk. 1975. "Baby X: The Effect of Gender Labels on Adult Responses to Infants." *Sex Roles* 1: 103–109.

Sidorowicz, L. and G. S. Lunney. 1980. "Baby X Revisited." *Sex Roles* 6: 67–73.

Stokes, R. and J. Hewitt. 1976. "Aligning Actions." *American Sociological Review* 41: 838–849.

Stoller, R. 1968. *Sex and Gender.* New York: Science House.

Stone, G. 1962. "Appearance and the Self." Pp. 86–118 in *Human Behavior and Social Processes,* edited by A. Rose. Boston: Houghton Mifflin.

Thompson, S. 1975. "Gender Labels and Early Sex Role Development." *Child Development* 46: 339–347.

Thompson, S. and P. M. Bentler. 1971. "The Priority of Cues in Sex Discrimination by Children and Adults." *Developmental Psychology* 5: 181–185.

7

Narratives of the Codependent Self

Leslie Irvine

Social experience not only gives rise to the self, as Mead argues and the previous selection empirically demonstrates. It also sustains, often gradually changes, and sometimes radically transforms individuals' selves. Individuals sustain their selves through the stories or narratives that they tell others and themselves. Those stories are anchored in social relationships and associations. When important relationships and associations end, individuals' selves are often the casualties of what Leslie Irvine calls the "narrative wreckage" of shattered stories. In such cases, the individual needs new stories of the self and new relationships and associations in which to anchor it. Today, many people find those new stories and social anchorage in Twelve Step, self-help groups like Alcoholics or Codependents Anonymous. These groups provide individuals with what Irvine calls "narrative formulas" that guide them in constructing new stories of the self and receptive audiences for those stories. Those narrative formulas also provide individuals with accounts that excuse them of responsibility for past problems. Those accounts encourage individuals to stop condemning their old selves and get on with constructing new ones.

In this selection, Leslie Irvine describes how members of Codependents Anonymous (CoDA) construct stories of self and, thereby, transform their "selves." She notes that individuals commonly come to CoDA when an important relationship ends. They have lost the social anchor for stories that sustain their prior self and must repair their damaged selves. CoDA provides them with accounts for their failed relationships, a narrative formula for new stories of self, and a social anchor for those stories. However, as Irvine argues, it is not enough for members of CoDA merely to tell a new story of codependence and convince others of that story in order to repair their damaged selves. They must also convince themselves of this new story of the self. This new story must become part of their internal conversations. Although Irvine learned how to tell a story of

codependency and convince others of it, unlike many members of CoDA, she never defined her self as "codependent" because she did not believe the story she was telling. Yet, Irvine had another story of her self—she was a sociologist doing research—and the social anchors of her University and colleagues for that story. The explicit stories of self of CoDA members help us recognize what we all do although often more implicitly. Whatever our definition of self, we must sustain it through the stories we tell one another and ourselves that are firmly anchored in social relationships and what Irvine calls "institutions."

This is a study of how disrupted lives can be made livable again. It draws on ethnographic research in Codependents Anonymous, a Twelve Step group known simply as CoDA. CoDA is a psychospiritual self-help program that attracts people who have experienced a divorce or the breakup of a committed relationship—or a series of such events. CoDA offers people a way to account for their experience, and consequently, a way of making sense of their lives. What dedicated members claim to gain from the group is a sense of self. I took their claims seriously, and tried to understand what makes that sense possible. This, then, is primarily a study of the experience of selfhood. . . .

Although I refer to the "members" of CoDA—and that is how they refer to themselves—the criteria for membership are ephemeral and subjective. The CoDA Preamble, recited at every meeting, explains the "only requirement for membership is a desire for healthy and fulfilling relationships with others and ourselves" (CoDA 1988). Thus, you may consider yourself a member of CoDA simply by attending a single meeting. . . .

During the seventeen months that I studied CoDA, I attended over two hundred meetings on Long Island and in New York City. This represents over four hundred hours of observation. Much of the time, I participated in the meetings, which is to say that I talked about myself. I did not have to make up a story about codependency, as I would have if I had tried to "pass" in AA. . . . The meaning of codependency is sufficiently open that it can accommodate the events of any life. Each individual has the freedom, indeed the right, to decide what his or her codependency means. Thus,

I was able to share without lying. Moreover, I am convinced that, in this setting, participation was the sociologically ethical thing to do. . . . CoDA's norms make continuous detached observation impossible, and I wanted to spend sufficient time in at least one group to learn about its culture. Therefore, in most meetings, I participated as well as observed. In groups that I visited only once or a few times, I was able to observe without participating. . . .

People are . . . pushed [into CoDA] by the disruption that comes with "uncoupling," or ending a relationship. If codependency is "about" anything, it is about resolving the disruption that uncoupling does to the self. With very few exceptions, people seek out CoDA after the breakup of a serious, committed relationship or in a relationship's terminal stages. Every one of the thirty-six people I interviewed had done so. Breaking up was a constant theme in the meetings I attended. In some cases, the breakups had to do with children. A divorce separates a father from his children and he must adjust to seeing them only on weekends. Or, a sporadically employed, alcoholic, thirty-something son wants to move back home for the third time, and his mother, tired of having money stolen from her purse, wants to bring herself to say "no." This kind of uncoupling certainly differs from separation and divorce. Nevertheless, it can bring similar social and emotional disruption. Consequently, some people in this situation also seek support in CoDA. More often, however, the breakups involved divorce. . . .

Just as becoming a couple involves more than sharing a phone number and checking account, uncoupling, too, involves more than establishing physical separation. Some of the members of CoDA described the experience to me in these words:

> It was completely draining. I lost my whole life. (*woman, thirty-six*)

> What does it feel like? It feels empty. That you can't figure a freaking thing out. That you feel so . . . so helpless. (*man, forty-two*)

> I was devastated. My life stopped for about four months. (*woman, forty-five*)

The language is telling: "I lost my whole life." "It feels empty." "My life stopped . . . " What they are describing, although no one put it in these particular words, is the loss of selfhood. They had lost the ability to tell stories of themselves that made sense. Marriage and committed relations provide formulas and contexts for your stories. . . . People do not simply make up stories about themselves on a whim. Rather, they draw plots, scripts, casts, and audiences from institutions. . . . I mean "institution" to refer to patterns of activities organized around a similar goal. Marriage and relationships, as institutions, provide opportunities for people to "be" or "become" themselves because they anchor the stories told by those within them. When a relationship ends, that institutional anchor is dislodged. This is at the heart of the "narrative wreckage" that the members of CoDA described. Uncoupling disrupted the continuity in their existing stock of stories. It derailed the plots. It removed key characters. It made future chapters or episodes unimaginable. It meant that two people whose language had evolved from "I" to "we" must now think of themselves as "I" again. . . .

Implicit in becoming an "I" again is the question of "Who will I be now, without this other person?" In this sense, uncoupling does have a positive side to it, in that it offers opportunities to pursue avenues not possible within the relationship. But there are often obstacles to taking hold of those opportunities and answering the question of "Who will I be?" For with the loss comes the specter of self-doubt: "Can I trust my judgment, in light of having failed?"

The implication of failure may seem implausible in times when divorce and separation have become commonplace. Yet, even today, "relationships are almost universally viewed in success/failure terms," writes McCall (1982). . . . Even if you do not take your own divorce as a sign of failure, others often see it in that light. . . . [Divorce] is still widely held as indicative of some personal flaw. For example, socializing with couples becomes difficult after uncoupling, and not only because of the inevitable "splitting of friends." . . . Divorced people report feeling that married friends exclude them from social interaction because they seem to find them threatening in some way. . . .

The stories people tell after uncoupling must redeem this experience of failure. On the way to answering the question of "Who will I be now," they must also answer the question of "What happened?" Lurking beneath this are questions such as "Why me?" "What's wrong with me?" And,

"What am I really like?" To provide satisfying answers, uncoupling stories must take the form of "accounts" (Scott and Lyman 1968). Accounts are "linguistic devices [that] explain unanticipated or untoward behavior" (46). They either mitigate responsibility for your conduct or accept responsibility but neutralize the consequences of doing so. Accounts that accomplish the former are known as "excuses"; those that accomplish the latter are called "justifications." By either relieving or neutralizing personal responsibility, accounts help to diminish blame and, therefore, reduce the effects of stigma. Moreover, accounts not only convey information to *others*; they explain your own conduct to *yourself.* In so doing, they restore your own sense of self-approval.

For accounts to be honored, they have to use vocabulary that is "anchored in the background expectations of the situation" (Scott and Lyman 1968, 53). Self-consciously or not, audiences have standards for what they will find credible. Anyone who has been late for an important engagement or stopped for speeding knows this well. Accounts must be consistent with what "everybody knows" about what they purport to explain, or at least with what "everybody" in a particular setting "knows." In the case of uncoupling, accounts have to convey legitimate reasons for breaking up. In middle-class American culture, it is generally legitimate to emphasize the importance of the individual over the relationship. Although few people would give fulfillment as the sole reason for breaking up, the sense of obligation to oneself constitutes an appropriate explanation for doing so. . . . People repair the "narrative wreckage" of uncoupling and, consequently, redeem damaged selves, using accounts that follow standards set by their audiences—including themselves. These standards—and new audiences—then become important in the revision of the story of who they are.

There are, then, crucial ways that selfhood, as a narrative accomplishment, depends on institutions. Marriages and relationships, as institutions, provide anchors for the stories of the self. When these anchors are lost, others must replace them. Until then, life "feels empty," and "everything falls apart." . . .

At CoDA meetings, one concern dominates all others. This is the idea of a "real" self that is solely and completely your own possession. . . . At the meetings, [members] learn to piece together events of their lives using an institutionalized formula. Each meeting brings a new installment to the story. The narrator and the listeners situate the new information within the context of existing themes. With each telling, the narrators integrate new experiences and insights into an evolving "socio-biography" (Plummer 1983; Wuthnow 1994), which is a story about one's life and one's formative experiences that is created in a public setting. At each CoDA meeting, the narrators pick up the story where it left off, taking it in a new direction, and taking the story of the self in a new direction as well. Over the long term, the narrator and the group remember these themes and, consequently, legitimate them as the narrator's identity. . . .

The audience at CoDA meetings holds specific expectations about what constitutes a "good" story of codependency and recovery. By listening to hundreds of people share, I began to understand their expectations. I began to see the characteristic sequence through which believers in codependency order the events of their lives. This sequence, or "narrative formula," as I call it, follows a five part chronology that produces a special type of life history. . . .

'Abusive' Childhoods

Codependency, as the text read at each meeting explains, "is born out of our sometimes moderately, sometimes extremely dysfunctional family systems." Since all families are dysfunctional—either "moderately" or "extremely"—all manner of experiences become reframed to this end. In this view, families, by definition, "abuse" their children. As a result, any and everyone's family history becomes reconceptualized as "abusive." Those who do not come from families of addicts or alcoholics—and this includes most CoDA members—find other sorts of problems. I was struck by the ways that seemingly unexceptional childhoods became "dysfunctional." Even in the absence of any obvious family troubles, members went to great lengths to find or invent them. For example, I found that childhood "abuse" included general inadequacy, overwork, and Catholicism.

> There's no drug addiction or alcoholism in my immediate family . . . Just a super codependent, shame-based family. I just never felt good enough. (*woman, age thirty-six*)

There was so much abuse in my family. Abuse and neglect. There was always food on the table, always a roof over our heads. But my parents were both working all the time and never there for us. It was so abusive emotionally. Really dysfunctional. (*man, age forty-one*)

Nobody in my family was alcoholic or into drugs. We were just guilt-ridden Catholics. (*woman, age thirty-eight*)

Granted, some members of CoDA did give accounts of authentic-seeming physical and emotional mistreatment they endured as children. For the most part, however, I found that the term "abuse" was used indiscriminately. When a person cannot recall an instance of "abuse," it does not imply its absence, but its severity. The inability to recall "abuse" allegedly means that the "victim" has "denied" the experience in order to survive it. The "abuse" must have been so intense that the mind blocked it out as a survival mechanism. For example:

My upbringing was so dysfunctional that it's hard to remember. I shut down so much. (*woman, age forty-two*)

I can't remember anything before the age of 21, so I know it must have been pretty bad. My parents must have abused me so bad that I just shut down in order to survive it. (*man, age forty-five*)

Thus, [in these ways,] every childhood becomes an "abusive" childhood. . . . Narratives of codependency—and narratives in general—do not correspond with any objective reality. That is not their point. Their point is to show how a particular "past came to be, and how, ultimately, it gave birth to the present" (McAdams 1993, 102). Audiences have standards for what constitutes a "good" story, and the person who shares in CoDA must adhere to them. The question is not whether any given item is true, but whether it makes for a "good" story. What is interesting about forgotten instances of childhood "abuse" is not their veracity. It is how they make particular kinds of stories possible, and so remake the lives of those who tell them. . . . The person who begins a commitment to CoDA and its discourse enters a world in which all families are considered "abusive." Within the group, you can only legitimately tell stories that begin with "abuse." Were it not for the "abuse," your life would have turned out differently. Since you have ended up in CoDA, the "abuse" *must* have happened. Consequently, members develop stories about "abusive" childhoods, and those stories become their experience. . . .

Excusing Dysfunction

The narrative continues with a description of how the "abusive" childhood set you up for "dysfunction." The chronology makes the present seem like the logical and even inevitable, outcome of the past. . . . It attributes your recent past or present situation to undiagnosed codependency, which originated in childhood circumstances. By blaming relationship troubles on your unrecognized codependency in this way, the account reduces individual blame and its accompanying stigma.

As was the case with "abuse," what constitutes "dysfunction" varies widely. Within the discourse, any relationship or situation that has a less-than-satisfactory outcome qualifies as "dysfunctional." To be sure, someone occasionally described an appalling emotional or physical situation. But, often as not, the term described far less dramatic elements of dissatisfaction. Consider these examples from one small group:

A man described a vague but troubling need to be "in control" of his relationship to his girlfriend. I say "vague" because he never got around to explaining what he actually did to be controlling, but kept repeating phrases such as, "I've got to surrender my need to be in control. It's so 'dysfunctional'," and "Having to be in control leads to a lot of 'dysfunction' in my life." . . .

A woman voiced concern about feeling resentment over her daughter-in-law's absence from a family gathering. She saw this as an attempt by the younger woman to ruin her day. "She shouldn't be able to control my feelings," the woman said. "This has taught me that I've got to detach. I won't be part of that 'dysfunction.'"

A woman expressed pride in her new ability to "take care of" herself by refusing to baby-sit for a family member who had asked her to do so on the spur of the moment. To do otherwise would have encouraged "dysfunction."

A man talked about a recent meal at a restaurant. The waitress had made an error in his order, and he did not bring it to her attention.

He wondered what makes him "relate to people in such 'dysfunctional' ways."

A man described his general feelings of resentment and anger stemming from his "dysfunctional" relationship with this mother. She had recently recommended that he go to see the movie *Nell*, and he struggled to figure out why.

I offer these illustrations not to question their putative "dysfunction," but to highlight its role in the narrative. These were clearly instances that had not gone the way the speakers had hoped. By calling them "dysfunctional," the speakers could excuse their own role in the outcome. They could blame it on an intrinsic flaw, or "dysfunction," in the relationship, thereby, relieving themselves of their share of the interactional responsibility. They could acknowledge that they acted badly, but disavow responsibility by claiming that, in light of such "dysfunction," things could not have gone otherwise. Things may have gone wrong, but through no fault of their own. In this way, "dysfunction" can excuse entire relationships, as well as discrete interactional instances:

I married my father. I grew up thinking that he was what a husband should be like. So I went out and married a man just like him. What else did I know? My relationship with my husband brought out all the issues I had with my father. All I knew was dysfunction. (*woman, age thirty-six*)

I realize now that I picked her because she repeated all that chaos from when I was growing up. It was hell—both the marriage and my childhood. I did some really rotten things, I know, but it's because of the total dysfunction I saw as a kid. What I thought was love was really something else, some toxic stuff that went on at home. I acted the same way I saw my parents act. (*man, age thirty-nine*)

'Hitting Bottom'

The term is self-explanatory. Although the "bottom" differs among speakers, it is always an emotional low point.

I hit my bottom around Christmas. I couldn't stop crying, and being a man, you know, I wondered what was wrong with me! [he chuckles] But I just couldn't do anything else. It was miserable. Miserable. (*man, forty-nine*)

When I was at my bottom, I went and brought a piece of hose, you know, to use in my exhaust pipe. I just wanted to have it around, to keep that option open. I was walking around feeling this dread, this constant feeling of dread. And in my more lucid moments I would say, "Geez, I've really got to do something or I'm going to end up dead." (*woman, age thirty-seven*)

The account of the "bottom" is an important aspect of the narrative. It foregrounds a self that has not only endured hardship and conflict, but one that has found an intriguing solution. The "bottom" brings richness and complexity to the self that will emerge from the story. As the narrative progresses, having survived the "bottom" will suggest a competence and maturity that help redeem the self from failure. More immediately, it introduces an optimistic tone to the narrative. . . . Sociologically speaking, optimism reveals the narrator's underlying faith in the belief that life can be good and that one is, to some extent, able to direct oneself toward that good life.

You really do, you hit bottom and you say, "Look, I'm happy for the air that I'm breathing," and you start from there and everything else is a plus. (*man, age forty-five*)

[The relationship] didn't serve me anymore. It was really devastating to realize that it didn't serve my growth. It brought me to a big dead end. And then I found CoDA, and it opened up a whole new avenue for me. (*woman, age thirty-six*)

Working a Program

This refers to how each speaker describes what he or she is doing to encourage recovery from codependency. . . .

This is where, to use a Twelve Step phrase, you show that you can not only "talk the talk," but also "walk the walk." You demonstrate to yourself and to the group that you are serious about recovery. It is not simply something that you talk about once a week, but it is something that you "work on" the remaining six days, as well. Typically, speakers describe working through particular Steps or what they are doing to "get in touch with" themselves. The Steps, incidentally, involve a continuous process of self-assessment. You never "complete" the Twelve Steps. The "personal inventory" of Steps Four and Ten must be taken regularly. Consequently, the amends of Step Eight must be periodically made to those you have wronged. For example, in one depiction of working through Step Six, a striking platinum blonde woman in her early forties described how she had become "entirely ready to have God remove all [her] defects of character." This Sixth Step assumes that you have already worked through the Fifth, which requires admitting "to God, to ourselves, and to another human being the exact nature of our wrongs." On this particular evening, the woman spoke of defensively clinging to one of her "defects of character," which was a hatred for her mother. She had finally become ready to give up that hatred, with the help of her Higher Power. She believed that she had been born to a mother who "abused" her, she said, in order to learn how to "take care" of herself emotionally. She had hated her mother for not loving her, but now saw that she had learned from the "abuse." For a long time, she had not known how to "take care" of herself, and although the details remained cloudy in her account, she said she had learned enough to begin to do so, and so, was ready to have her Higher Power eliminate her hatred for her mother.

What constitutes "working a Program" can vary widely, since each person alone knows best what he or she should do to foster recovery. It is difficult to fake—or at least it would have been for me. For this reason, I never spoke in front of the entire group. Because I was not "working a Program," I could not have given the group what they were expecting to hear, and if I had, I would have felt deceptive for doing so. In small group sharing, I could talk about other things. When I had to talk about "working a Program," I said things like "trying to figure out what's best for me."

My experience illustrates an important point: it is not enough to simply tell a story about yourself; you must also believe in your own story. Although I understood the formula for a narrative of codependency, I did not "become" codependent because I did not believe in that story as who I "am." I seem to have managed impressions successfully enough to have others attribute a codependent identity to me; no one ever called it into question, and , on several occasions, "my" codependency was even the subject of friendly teasing. But the impressions others had

of me did not translate into my identifying myself in that way. . . .

Although I could tell a story that convinced others that I belonged in the group, I never convinced myself or even tried to. . . .

Redeeming the Past

Here, the speaker talks about life in recovery. He or she recounts how codependency, though painful, was ultimately beneficial for personal "growth." The hardship it brought is portrayed as all for the best, thereby showing that he or she has indeed learned something through the misfortune. Consider the woman who said:

> I finally have come to the other side of the anger, the blaming, the bitterness, and finally have been truly able to see the benefits of it, that the characteristics that developed out of the abuse and dysfunction—I'm realizing that maybe if these things hadn't happened, I might not have the characteristics that I have today. (*age forty-five*)

Another had this to say:

> I think the pain was all worth it when I see what's happened for my growth.
> (*age forty-six*)

Good stories need satisfying endings. Since the lives of those telling the stories are still in progress, the endings must tolerate ambiguity. They must keep a number of alternatives open for the future, and they must have the flexibility to change as the tellers change. Yet, they must not have so much openness that they suggest immaturity and a lack of resolve. In sharing, ambiguity is accomplished through recovery cliches such as "Taking care of" or "Believing in myself" and "Getting in touch with my feelings." These and similarly vague phrases indicate a positive course of action for the future without pinning you down to specifics. For example:

> The biggest help to me has been being honest with myself. CoDA has given me the courage to believe in myself and not believe all the lies from the past, from the way I was raised. (*woman, forty-five*)

Even if life had not yet taken a turn for the better, narrators seemed certain that things would improve in due time. They played up a sense of mastery over their lives—if tentative—as in "I'm not sure how this will end up, but I'll be fine as long as I keep doing what I've learned to do." For example:

> I've been in a real crummy spot, and it's been hard to try to do recovery and keep it all together. CoDA has made me realize that I have no control over what my wife decides to do. I can just take care of myself and know that, whatever happens, I'll get through it. (*man, thirty-seven*)

With such endings—"Whatever happens, I'll get through it"—narrators affirm the "growth" of the self. They suggest the ability to reconcile the tough issues of adult life with their own capabilities and goals. This new skill at reconciliation is recognized as what was lacking in their lives before recovery.

The idea of a life in recovery raises a question. If people go to CoDA when a relationship ends, but continue to attend long after the sting of uncoupling has subsided, what, then, do they see themselves "recovering" *from*? I met people who had spent three, four, and even five years in the group. They came to CoDA on the heels of disruption and stayed. What were they *doing* there? Quite simply, they were "recovering" from codependency, but they never got a clean bill of health.

The discourse builds in large part on a medical metaphor: it portrays codependency as a *condition*. It causes varying degrees of discomfort and inconvenience. It requires varying levels of intervention. But it forever affects the way you go about your life, and it never completely heals. Once people identify themselves as codependents, they can never fully "recover." Even though the pain of a particular relationship may pass, the underlying condition that fostered the troublesome "dysfunction" does not. Your codependency may go into a remission of sorts as you begin to make "healthier" choices, but it will never go away. As a condition, it requires continuous monitoring, hence continued participation in CoDA. This subtly but effectively transforms your purpose for attending. People come to the group for support during uncoupling. In the course of repairing the damage, they discover (or create) so many fundamental problems that they end up with a lifelong project. The loss starts the introspection, but it often continues long afterwards.

Meanwhile, however, a more social phenomenon has also taken place, through the development of a socio-biography. By the time the crisis period ends, people feel little need to move on. They have "become" codependent—or at least they have in the sense that they see *themselves* that way. It is true that, as Wuthnow puts it, "people in groups do not simply tell stories—they become their stories" (1994, 301). But they must also find their own stories convincing. The existence of an established narrative formula of codependency does not reduce the experience of having a self to mastering a story. . . .

Because the narrative of the self is, as Gagnon (1992) put it, an "internal conversation," the experience of selfhood hinges as much or more on believing in your *own* stories than on getting *others* to believe them. The narrative accomplishment of selfhood is decidedly not analogous to [managing others' impressions]. . . . What I am describing is much more internal; it is impression management *directed at yourself*. . . .

If CoDA members are indicative of anything, they are indicative of the strength and ubiquity of the belief in the essential self, experienced as continuous and coherent. This continuity and coherence takes the form of a running story that people tell to themselves, as well as to other people. While the story has integrity, it also leaves room for a great deal of ambiguity, for it is not yet finished.

This does not mean that stories of the self are capriciously cobbled together; rather, they are grounded in institutions, which give life to the internal conversations. Neither does it mean that institutions simply provide a set and setting for your narrative performances, only to fade away after the show. Rather, they remain long after the curtain falls. We cannot "do" selfhood alone, but it must work when we are alone if it is to work in front of others.

References

Codependents Anonymous (CoDA). 1988. *Preamble and Welcome*. Phoenix: CoDA Service Office.

Gagnon, John. 1992. "The Self, Its Voices, and Their Discord." Pp. 221–243 in *Investigating Subjectivity*, edited by Carolyn Ellis and Michael Flaherty. Newbury Park, CA: Sage.

McAdams, Dan P. 1993. *The Stories We Live By: Personal Myths and the Making of the Self*. New York: Guilford Press.

McCall, George. 1982. "Becoming Unrelated: The Management of Bond Dissolution." Pp. 211–232 in *Personal Relationships, vol. 4, Dissolving Personal Rela-*

tionships, edited by Steven Duck. London: Academic Press.

Plummer, Ken. 1983. *Documents of Life: An Introduction to the Problems and Literature of Humanistic Method.* London, UK: George Allen and Unwin.

Scott, Marvin and Standford Lyman. 1968. "Accounts." *American Sociological Review* 33:46–62.

Wuthnow, Robert. 1994. *Sharing the Journey: Support Groups and America's New Quest for Community.* New York: Free Press.

Part III

The Social Construction of Subjective Experience

In the earlier selection, "The Self as Social Structure," Mead observes that, once the self has arisen, individuals have themselves as companions. They are able to think and converse with themselves as they have communicated with others. They are able to define and interpret their own experience through inner conversations. Yet, individuals can do so only because they have communicated with others. The language, symbols, and understandings that individuals draw upon in conversing with themselves are not of their own invention. They are used by and learned from others with whom the individual has communicated. Thus, the individual's inner reality is as much socially constructed as the outer reality that she or he shares with others.

The selections in this section address the social construction of subjective experience. They examine the social shaping of individuals' thoughts, experience of bodily states, and emotions. Each illustrates that sociological study and understanding, rather than being skin deep, reach deep inside individuals' minds and hearts. They can do so because the social life among individuals gets under their skin, creating social lives within each person. ✦

8

The Development of Language and Thought

Lev Vygotsky

Lev Vygotsky was a research fellow at the Moscow Institute of Psychology from 1924 up to his untimely
death in 1934 at 38 years of age. Although a prolific
writer during that decade, few outside the former Soviet
Union knew of Vygotsky's writing until the early
1960s, when his book Thought and Language was
first published in English. This selection is from a later
edition of that volume and demonstrates what many
Western readers now know: Vygotsky, like Mead and
Cooley, provided a basis for the development of a distinctively sociological psychology.

Throughout his writing, Vygotsky stressed the social
origins of human thought. He proposed that the initial
direction of human psychological development runs
from the "interpsychological" to the "intrapsychological," or from the social to the individual. This pro-
posal directly challenged what was then, and still remains, the prevailing view of psychological
development as a gradual accommodation of subjective
desires and thoughts to social existence and objective
reasoning. The cognitive developmental theory of Jean
Piaget, a popular example of this general view, was the
principal target of Vygotsky's criticism in this selection.

As Vygotsky notes, Piaget's general view of human
psychological development was not unique but rather
was borrowed from psychoanalysis. Like Freud, Piaget
assumed that the individual is born with unrealistic desires and thoughts. According to Freud, the individual is
initially governed by the pleasure principle, but the
gratification of his or her innate desires is frustrated by
the necessity of adapting to the environment in order to
survive. The ego develops out of this clash between the
pleasure and reality principles, resulting in the repression of the individual's unrealistic desires and thoughts
within the unconscious realm of the id. The individual
then confronts the additional demands of the social environment, giving rise to a superego or social conscience.

Piaget's proposed stages of cognitive development
mirrored Freud's sequence of psychosexual development. According to Piaget, the individual's thought is
initially idiosyncratic and fantastic or "autistic." It then
becomes egocentric, as the individual attempts to
change the environment to her or his needs and desires.
This self-centeredness gradually disappears, as the individual interacts with others and learns that there are
other perspectives besides his or her own. His or her
thought gradually becomes socialized, directed, and objective rather than subjective. The intrapsychological is
gradually replaced by the interpsychological.

Piaget based this proposed sequence of cognitive development on his observation of children's play. He observed that preschool-age children talk to themselves or
engage in what he termed egocentric speech far more
than school-age children who engage in more socialized speech.

Vygotsky was unconvinced by this evidence. He
proposed an alternative explanation of young children's so-called egocentric speech, based on the results
of his own experiments. Those experiments indicated
that children's egocentric speech increases when they
confront a problem. Vygotsky therefore concluded that
this egocentric speech is not self-centered, but self-di-
recting. Children are apparently attempting to talk
themselves through the problem, much as others have
verbally directed them through problems in the past.
Egocentric speech is not, then, a preliminary to socialized or communicative speech, but rather its product.
According to Vygotsky, it is a transitional stage in the
development from communicative to inner speech.
Inner speech or thought is merely egocentric speech become silent. The development of human speech and
thought moves from the intersubjective to the subjective, rather than the reverse, as Piaget and Freud would
have it. As Vygotsky suggested, thought—even autistic
thought—is impossible without a language and symbols
with which to think. And language and symbols are acquired through communication with others. That is the
source of even our most private, idiosyncratic, and fantastic thoughts.

Psychology owes a great deal to Jean Piaget. It is
not an exaggeration to say that he revolutionized
the study of the child's speech and thought. He
developed the clinical method for exploring children's ideas that has since been widely used. He
was the first to investigate the child's perception
and logic systematically; moreover, he brought to

his subject a fresh approach of unusual amplitude and boldness.

Piaget, however, did not escape the duality characteristic of [modern] psychology. He tried to hide behind the wall of facts, but facts "betrayed" him, for they led to problems. Problems gave birth to theories, in spite of Piaget's determination to avoid them by closely following the experimental facts and disregarding, for the time being, that the very choice of experiments is determined by hypotheses. But facts are always examined in the light of some theory and, therefore, cannot be disentangled from philosophy.

According to Piaget, the bond uniting all the specific characteristics of the child's logic is the egocentrism of occupying an intermediate position, genetically, structurally, and functionally, between autistic and directed thought.

The idea of the polarity of directed and undirected . . . thought is borrowed from psychoanalysis. . . . We find the same idea in Freud, who claims that the pleasure principle precedes the reality principle. . . . Piaget says:

> Directed thought is conscious, i.e., it pursues an aim which is present to the mind of the thinker; it is intelligent, which means that it is adapted to reality and tries to influence it; it admits of being true or false (empirically or logically true), and it can be communicated by language. Autistic thought is subconscious, which means that the aims it pursues and the problems it tries to solve are not present in consciousness; it is not adapted to reality, but creates for itself a dream world of imagination; it tends not to establish truths, but to satisfy desires, and it remains strictly individual and incommunicable as such by means of language. On the contrary, it works chiefly by images, and in order to express itself, has recourse to indirect methods, evoking by means of symbols and myths the feeling by which it is led. (Piaget 1959:43)

Directed thought is social. As it develops, it is increasingly influenced by the laws of experience and of logic proper. Autistic thought, on the contrary, is individualistic and obeys a set of special laws of its own:

> Now between autism and intelligence there are many degrees, varying with their capacity for being communicated. These intermediate varieties must, therefore, be subject to a special logic, intermediate too between the logic of autism and that of intelligence. The chief of

those intermediate forms, i.e., the type of thought, which like that exhibited by our children seeks to adapt itself to reality but does not communicate itself as such, we propose to call *egocentric* thought. (Piaget 1959:45)

While its main function is still the satisfaction of personal needs, it already includes some mental adaptation, some of the reality orientation typical of the thought of adults. The egocentric thought of the child "stands midway between autism in the strict sense of the word and socialized thought" (Piaget 1969:208). This is Piaget's basic hypothesis.

Piaget emphasizes that egocentric speech does not provide communication. . . . [It] is, therefore, useless. It plays no essential role in child behavior. It is speech for the child's sake, which is incomprehensible for others and which is closer to a verbal dream than to a conscious activity.

But if such speech plays no positive role in child behavior, if it is a mere accompaniment, it is but a symptom of weakness and immaturity in the child's thinking, a symptom that must disappear in the course of child development. Useless and unconnected with the structure of activity, this accompaniment should become weaker and weaker until it completely disappears from the routine of the child's speech.

Data collected by Piaget seemingly supports this point of view. The coefficient of egocentric speech decreases with age and reaches zero at the age of seven or eight—which means that egocentric speech is not typical for school children. Piaget, however, assumes that the loss of egocentric speech does not preclude children from remaining cognitively egocentric. Egocentric thought simply changes the form of its manifestation, appearing now in abstract reasoning and in the new symptoms that have no semblance to egocentric talk. In conformity with his idea of the uselessness of egocentric speech, Piaget claims that this speech "folds" and dies out at the threshold of school age.

We in our turn conducted our own experiments aimed at understanding the function and fate of egocentric speech. The data obtained led us to a new comprehension of this phenomenon that differs greatly from that of Piaget. Our investigation suggests that egocentric speech does play a specific role in the child's activity.

In order to determine what causes egocentric talk, what circumstances provoke it, we organized the children's activities in much the same way Piaget did, but we added a series of frustrations and difficulties. For instance, when a child was getting ready to draw, he would suddenly find that there was no paper, or no pencil of the color he needed. In other words, by obstructing his free activity, we made him face problems.

We found that in these difficult situations the coefficient of egocentric speech almost doubled, in comparison with Piaget's normal figure for the same age and also in comparison with our figure for children not facing these problems. The child would try to grasp and to remedy the situation in talking to himself: "Where's the pencil? I need a blue pencil. Never mind, I'll draw with the red one and wet it with water; it will become dark and look like blue."

In the same activities without impediments, our coefficient of egocentric talk was even slightly lower than Piaget's. It is legitimate to assume, then, that a disruption in the smooth flow of activity is an important stimulus for egocentric speech. This discovery fits in with two premises to which Piaget himself refers several times in his book. One of them is the so-called law of awareness, which was formulated by Claparede and which states that an impediment or disturbance in an automatic activity makes the author aware of this activity. The other premise is that speech is an expression of that process of becoming aware.

Indeed, the above-mentioned phenomena were observed in our experiments: egocentric speech appeared when a child tried to comprehend the situation, to find a solution, or to plan a nascent activity. The older children behaved differently: they scrutinized the problem, thought (which was indicated by long pauses), and then found a solution. When asked what he was thinking about, such a child answered more in a line with the "thinking aloud" of a preschooler. We thus assumed that the same mental operations that the preschooler carries out through voiced egocentric speech are already relegated to soundless inner speech in school children.

Our findings indicate that egocentric speech does not long remain a mere accompaniment to the child's activity. Besides being a means of expression and of release of tension, it soon becomes an instrument of thought in the proper sense—in seeking and planning the solution of a problem. An accident that occurred during one of our experiments provides a good illustration of one way in which egocentric speech may alter the course of an activity: a child of five and a half was drawing a streetcar when the point of his pencil broke. He tried, nevertheless, to finish the circle of [the] wheel, pressing down on the pencil very hard, but nothing showed on the paper except a deep colorless line. The child muttered to himself, "It's broken," put aside the pencil, took watercolors instead, and began drawing a *broken* streetcar after an accident, continuing to talk to himself from time to time about the change in his picture. The child's accidentally provoked egocentric utterance so manifestly affected his activity that it is impossible to mistake it for a mere byproduct, an accompaniment not interfering with the melody. Our experiments showed highly complex changes in the interrelation of activity and egocentric talk. We observed how egocentric speech at first marked the end result or a turning point in an activity, then was gradually shifted toward the middle and finally to the beginning of the activity, taking on a directing, planning function and raising the child's acts to the level of purposeful behavior. What happens here is similar to the well-known developmental sequence in the naming of drawings. A small child draws first, then decides what it is that he has drawn; at a slightly older age, he names his drawing when it is half-done; and finally, he decides beforehand what he will draw.

The revised conception of the function of egocentric speech must also influence our conception of its later fate and must be brought to bear on the issue of its disappearance at school age. Experiments can yield indirect evidence but no conclusive answer about the causes of this disappearance.

There is, of course, nothing to this effect in Piaget, who believes that egocentric speech simply dies off. The development of inner speech in the child receives little specific elucidation in his studies. But since inner speech and voiced egocentric speech fulfill the same function, the implication would be that if, as Piaget maintains, egocentric speech precedes socialized speech, then inner speech also must precede socialized speech—an assumption untenable from the genetic point of view.

However, Piaget's theoretical position apart, his own findings and some of our data suggest that egocentric speech is actually an intermediate stage leading to inner speech. Of course, this is only a hypothesis, but, taking into account the present state of our knowledge about the child's speech, it is the most plausible one. If we compare the amount of what might be called egocentric speech in children and adults, we would have to admit that the "egocentric" speech of adults is much richer. From the point of view of functional psychology, all silent thinking is nothing but "egocentric" speech. John B. Watson would have said that such speech serves individual rather than social adaptation. The first feature uniting the inner speech of adults with the egocentric speech of children is its function as speech-for-oneself. If one turns to Watson's experiment and asks a subject to solve some problem thinking aloud, one would find that such thinking aloud of an adult has a striking similarity to the egocentric speech of children. Second, these two forms also have the same structural characteristics: out of context they would be incomprehensible to others because they omit to mention what is obvious to the speaker. These similarities lead us to assume that when egocentric speech disappears, it does not simply atrophy but "goes underground," i.e., turns into inner speech.

Our observation that at the age when this change is taking place children facing difficult situations resort now to egocentric speech, now to silent reflection, indicates that the two can be functionally equivalent. It is our hypothesis that the processes of inner speech develop and become stabilized approximately at the beginning of school age and that this causes the quick drop in the egocentric speech observed at this stage.

The above-mentioned experiments and considerations hardly support Piaget's hypothesis concerning the egocentrism of six-year-olds. At least the phenomenon of egocentric speech, viewed from our perspective, fails to confirm his assumptions.

The cognitive function of egocentric speech, which is most probably connected with the development of inner speech, by no means is a reflection of the child's egocentric thinking, but rather shows that under certain circumstances egocentric speech is becoming an agent of realistic thinking. Piaget assumed that if 40–47 percent of the speech of a child of six and a half is egocentric, then his thinking must be egocentric within the same range. Our investigation showed, however, that there can be no connection between egocentric talk and egocentric thinking whatso-

ever—which means that the major implication drawn from Piaget's data might be wrong.

We thus have an experimental fact that has nothing to do with the correctness or falsity of our own hypothesis concerning the fate of egocentric speech. This is the factual evidence that the child's egocentric speech does not reflect egocentric thinking, but rather carries out an opposite function, that of realistic thinking.

Limited in scope as our findings are, we believe that they help one to see in a new and broader perspective the general direction of the development of speech and thought. In Piaget's view, the two functions follow a common path, from autistic to socialized speech, from subjective fantasy to the logic of relations. In the course of this change, the influence of adults is deformed by the psychic processes of the child, but it wins out in the end. The development of thought is, to Piaget, a story of the gradual socialization of deeply intimate, personal, autistic mental states. Even social speech is represented as following, not preceding, egocentric speech.

The hypothesis we propose reverses this course. Let us look at the direction of thought development during one short interval, from the appearance of egocentric speech to its disappearance, in the framework of language development as a whole.

We consider that the total development runs as follows: the primary function of speech, in both children and adults, is communication, social contact. The earliest speech of the child is, therefore, essentially social. At first it is global and multifunctional; later, its functions become differentiated. At a certain age the social speech of the child is quite sharply divided into egocentric speech and communicative speech. (We prefer to use the term *communicative* for the form of speech that Piaget calls *socialized*, as though it had been something else before becoming social. From our point of view, the two forms, communicative and egocentric, are both social, though their functions differ.) Egocentric speech emerges when the child transfers social, collaborative forms of behavior to the sphere of inner-personal psychic functions. The child's tendency to transfer to his inner processes the behavior patterns that formerly were social is well known to Piaget. He describes in another context how arguments between children give rise to the beginnings of logical reflection. Something similar happens, we

OR DO WE CONSIDER CHILDREN READY FOR SCHOOL WHEN THEY HAVE DEVELOPED THE CAPACITY FOR INNER SPEECH?

believe, when the child starts conversing with himself as he has been doing with others. When circumstances force him to stop and think, he is likely to think aloud. Egocentric speech, splintered off from general social speech, in time leads to inner speech, which serves both autistic and logical thinking.

Egocentric speech as a separate linguistic form is the highly important genetic link in the transition from vocal to inner speech, an intermediate stage between the differentiation of the functions of vocal speech and the final transformation of one part of vocal speech into inner speech. It is this transitional role of egocentric speech that lends it such great theoretical interest. The whole conception of speech development differs profoundly in accordance with the interpretation given to the role of egocentric speech. Thus, our schema of development—first social, then egocentric, then inner speech—contrasts . . . with Piaget's . . . sequence—from non-verbal autistic thought through egocentric thought and speech to socialized speech and logical thinking.

The . . . most serious conclusion that can be drawn from our critical analysis concerns the alleged opposition of two forms of thinking: autistic and realistic. This opposition served as a basis for Piaget's theory, as well as for the psychoanalytical approach to child development. We think that it is incorrect to oppose the principle of satisfaction of needs to the principle of adaptation to reality. The very concept of need, if taken from the perspective of development, necessarily contains the notion of satisfaction of need through a certain adjustment to reality.

Need and adaptation must be considered in their unity. What we have in well-developed autistic thinking, i.e., an attempt to attain an imaginary satisfaction of desires that failed to be satisfied in real life, is a product of a long development. Autistic thinking, therefore, is a late product of the development of realistic, conceptual thinking. Piaget, however, chose to borrow from Freud the idea that the pleasure principle precedes the reality principle.

We see how different is the picture of the development of the child's speech and thought, depending on what is considered to be a starting point of such development. In our conception, the true direction of the development of thinking is not from the individual to the social, but from the social to the individual.

References

Piaget, Jean. 1959. *The Language and Thought of the Child*. London: Routledge and Kegan Paul.

——. 1969. *Judgement and Reasoning in the Child*. London: Routledge and Kegan Paul.

9

The Social Basis of Drug-Induced Experience

Howard Becker

Howard Becker studied marijuana users in the late 1940s when few Americans, mostly jazz musicians, used the drug. His was a landmark study. Becker discovered that socialization was required in order for an individual to experience a marijuana high. The user had to learn to perceive the drug's effects, to associate those effects with the drug, and to define those effects as pleasurable. As marijuana use became more common, most people learned these lessons from friends, movies, and what they read before ever using the drug. Yet, the high that they experienced was as much a product of socialization as that of earlier marijuana users. Although it may be harder not to perceive the effects of many other drugs, the example of the marijuana high suggests a more general conclusion about drug-induced experiences. Such experiences are not automatic consequences of the drug's physiological effects, but rather are products of users' interpretations of those effects.

Becker draws upon that general lesson in this selection written in the 1960s in response to the then widespread concern about LSD-induced psychosis. Although there were numerous reports at the time of psychotic reactions to LSD use, Becker notes that many people were apparently using the drug without experiencing any adverse psychological effects. The obvious question is, what might distinguish LSD users who experience psychotic reactions from those who do not? Becker's answer is that they interpret the effects of the drug differently, depending on their experience with the drug and with other LSD users. Inexperienced users, without the benefit of experienced users' interpretations of the drug's effects, are the most likely candidates for LSD-induced psychosis. The effects of the drug may resemble the psychotic symptoms that they have seen in movies or read or learned about in abnormal-psychology classes. Consequently, users conclude that they are

going crazy. Experienced users probably have a much different interpretation of LSD's effects, which they share with inexperienced users whom they know. The result is a much different experience for the inexperienced.

Becker's analysis of drug-induced experiences has broad implications. If drug-induced experiences are, at least in part, products of interpretation, then so too are other experiences of bodily states. As with perceptions of the external environment, individuals do not automatically react to physical sensations but define and interpret them. They cannot do anything they please with either the external environment or their bodies, but they can interpret their perceptions of them in an indefinite variety of ways. Social experience is the source of those possible interpretations. It shapes drug-induced experiences, sexual experiences, and experiences of illness, fatigue, and pain, to name but a few. Physiological sensations are only the raw material out of which bodily experiences are socially constructed.

In 1938, Albert Hoffman discovered the peculiar effects of lysergic acid diethylamide (LSD-25) on the mind. He synthesized the drug in 1943 and, following the end of World War II, it came into use in psychiatry, both as a method of simulating psychosis for clinical study and as a means of therapy. In the early 1960s, Timothy Leary, Richard Alpert, and others began using it with normal subjects as a means of "consciousness expansion." Their work received a great deal of publicity, particularly after a dispute with Harvard authorities over its potential danger. Simultaneously, LSD-25 became available on the underground market and, although no one has accurate figures, the number of people who have used or continue to use it is clearly very large.

In spite of [those who] allege that LSD is extremely dangerous, that it produces psychosis, I think it is fair to say that the evidence of its danger is by no means decisive. If the drug does . . . cause . . . a bona fide psychosis, it will be the only case in which anyone can state with authority that they found *the* unique cause of any such phenomenon. . . . Whatever the ultimate findings of pharmacologists and others . . . studying the drug, sociologists are unlikely to accept such an asocial and unicausal explanation of any form of complex social behavior. But if we refuse to accept the explanations of others, we are obligated to provide one of our own. In what follows, I consider the reports of LSD-induced psychoses and try to relate them to what is known of the social psychology and sociology of drug use. . . .

I must add a cautionary disclaimer. I have not examined thoroughly the literature on LSD. . . . What I have to say about it is necessarily speculative with respect to its effects; what I have to say about the conditions under which it is used is also speculative, but is based in part on interviews with a few users. . . .

The Subjective Effects of Drugs

The physiological effects of drugs can be ascertained by standard techniques of physiological and pharmacological research. Scientists measure and have explanations for the actions of many drugs on such observable indices as the heart and respiratory rates, the level of various chemicals in the blood, and the secretion of enzymes and hormones. In contrast, the subjective changes produced by a drug can be ascertained only by asking the subject, in one way or another, how he feels. (To be sure, one can measure the drug's effect on certain measures of psychological functioning—the ability to perform some standardized task, such as placing pegs in a board or remembering nonsense syllables—but this does not tell us what the drug experience is like.)

We take medically prescribed drugs because we believe they will cure or control a disease from which we are suffering; the subjective effects they produce are either ignored or defined as noxious side effects. But some people take some drugs precisely because they want to experience these subjective effects; they take them, to put it colloquially, because they want to get "high." These recreationally used drugs have become the focus of sociological research, because the goal of an artificially induced change in consciousness seems to many immoral, and those who so believe have been able to transform their belief into law. Drug users thus come to sociological attention as lawbreakers, and the problems typically investigated have to do with explaining their lawbreaking.

Nevertheless, some sociologists, anthropologists, and social psychologists have investigated the problem of drug-induced subjective experience in its own right. Taking their findings together, the following conclusions seem justified.

First, many drugs, including those used to produce changes in subjective experience, have a great variety of effects and the user may single out many of them, one of them, or none of them as definite experiences he is undergoing. He may be totally unaware of some of the drug's effects, even when they are physiologically gross, although in general the grosser the effects the harder they are to ignore. When he does perceive the effects, he may not attribute them to drug use but dismiss them as due to some other cause, such as fatigue or a cold. Marijuana users, for example, may not even be aware of the drug's effects when they first use it, even though it is obvious to others that they are experiencing them (Becker 1963:41–58).

Second, and in consequence, the effects of the same drug may be experienced quite differently by different people or by the same people at different times. Even if physiologically observable effects are substantially the same in all members of the species, individuals can vary widely in those to which they choose to pay attention. Thus, Aberle (1966) remarks on the quite different experiences [American] Indians and experimental subjects have with peyote; and Blum (1964) reports a wide variety of experiences with LSD, depending on the circumstances under which it was taken.

Third, since recreational users take drugs in order to achieve some subjective state not ordinarily available to them, it follows that they will expect and be most likely to experience those effects which produce a deviation from conventional perceptions and interpretations of internal and external experience. Thus, distortions in perception of time and space and shifts in judgments of the importance and meaning of ordinary events constitute the most commonly reported effects.

Fourth, any of a great variety of effects may be singled out by the user as desirable or pleasurable, as the effects for which he has taken the drug. Even effects which seem to the uninitiated to be uncomfortable, unpleasant, or frightening—perceptual distortions or visual and auditory hallucinations—can be defined by users as a goal to be sought.

Fifth, how a person experiences the effects of a drug depends greatly on the way others define those effects for him. The total effect of a drug is likely to be a melange of differing physical and psychological sensations. If others whom the user believes to be knowledgeable single out certain effects as characteristic and dismiss others, he is likely to notice those they single out as characteristic of his own experience. If they define certain effects as transitory, he is likely to believe that those effects will go away. All this supposes, of course, that the definition offered the user can be validated in his own experience, that something contained in the drug-induced melange of sensations corresponds to it.

Such a conception of the character of the drug experience has its roots, obviously, in Mead's theory of the self and the relation of objects to the self. In that theory, objects (including the self) have meaning for the person only as he imputes meaning to them in the course of his interaction with them. The meaning is not given in the object, but is lodged there as the person acquires a conception of the kind of action that can be taken with, toward, by, and for it. Meanings arise in the course of social interaction, deriving their character from the consensus participants develop about the object in question. The findings of such research on the character of drug-induced experience are therefore predictable from Mead's theory.

Drug Psychoses

The scientific literature and, even more, the popular press frequently state that recreational drug use produces a psychosis. The nature of "psychosis" is seldom defined, as though it were intuitively clear. Writers usually seem to mean a mental disturbance of some unspecified kind, involving auditory and visual hallucinations, an inability to control one's stream of thought, and a tendency to engage in socially inappropriate behavior, either because one has lost the sense that it is inappropriate or because one cannot stop oneself. In addition, and perhaps most important, psychosis is thought to be a state that will last long beyond the specific event that provoked it. However it occurred, it is thought to mark a more or less permanent change in the psyche and this, after all, is why we usually think of it as such a bad thing. Over-indulgence in alcohol produces many of the symptoms cited, but this frightens no one, because we understand that they will soon go away.

Verified reports of drug-induced psychoses are scarcer than one might think. Nevertheless, let us assume that these reports have not been fabricated, but represent an interpretation by the reporter of something that really happened. In the light of the findings just cited, what kind of event can we imagine to have occurred that might have been interpreted as a "psychotic episode?" (I use the word "imagine" advisedly, for the available case reports usually do not furnish sufficient material to allow us to do more than imagine what might have happened.)

The most likely sequence of events is this. The inexperienced user has certain unusual subjective experiences, which he may or may not attribute to having taken the drug. He may find his perception of space distorted, so that he has difficulty climbing a flight of stairs. He may find his train of thought so confused that he is unable to carry on a normal conversation and hears himself making totally inappropriate remarks. He may see or hear things in a way that he suspects is quite different from the way others see and hear them.

Whether or not he attributes what is happening to the drug, the experiences are likely to be upsetting. One of the ways we know that we are normal human beings is that our perceptual world, on the evidence available to us, seems to be pretty much the same as other people's. We see and hear the same things, make the same kind of sense out of them and, where perceptions differ, can explain the difference by a difference in situation or perspective. We may take for granted that the inexperienced drug user, though he wanted to get "high," did not expect an experience so radical as to call into question that common-sense set of assumptions.

In any society whose culture contains notions of sanity and insanity, the person who finds his subjective state altered in the way described may think he has become insane. We learn at a young age that a person who "acts funny," "sees things," "hears things," or has other bizarre and unusual experiences may have become "crazy," "nuts," "loony," or a host of other synonyms. When a drug user identifies some of these untoward events occurring in his own experience, he may decide that he merits one of those titles—that he has lost his grip on reality, his control of himself, and has in fact "gone crazy." The interpretation implies the corollary that the change is irreversible or, at least, that things are not going to be changed back very easily. The drug experience, perhaps originally intended as a momentary entertainment, now looms as a momentous event which will disrupt one's life, possibly permanently. Faced with this conclusion, the person develops a full-blown anxiety attack, but it is an anxiety caused by his reaction to the drug experience rather than a direct consequence of the drug use itself. (In this connection, it is interesting that, in the published reports of LSD psychoses, acute anxiety attacks appear as the category of untoward reactions.)

It is perhaps easier to grasp what this must feel like if we imagine that, having taken several social drinks at a party, we were suddenly to see varicolored snakes peering out at us from behind the furniture. We would instantly recognize this as a sign of delirium tremens, and would no doubt become severely anxious at the prospect of having developed such a serious mental illness. Some such panic is likely to grip the recreational user of drugs who interprets his experience as a sign of insanity.

Though I have put the argument with respect to the inexperienced user, long-time users of recreational drugs sometimes have similar experiences. They may experiment with a higher dosage than they are used to and experience effects unlike anything they have known before. This can easily occur when using drugs purchased in the illicit market, where quality may vary greatly, so that the user inadvertently gets more than he can handle.

The scientific literature does not report any verified cases of people acting on their distorted perceptions so as to harm themselves and others, but such cases have been reported in the press. Press reports of drug-related events are very unreliable, but it may be that users have, for instance, stepped out of a second story window, deluded by the drug into thinking it only a few feet to the ground. If such cases have occurred, they too may be interpreted as examples of psychosis, but a different mechanism than the one just discussed would be involved. The person, presumably, would have failed to make the necessary correction for the drug-induced distortion, a correction, however, that experienced users assert can be made. Thus, a novice marijuana user will find it difficult to drive while "high," but experienced users can control their thinking and actions so as to behave appropriately. Although it is commonly assumed that a person under the influence of LSD must avoid ordinary social situations for 12

or more hours, I have been told of at least one user who takes the drug and then goes to work; she explained that, once you learn "how to handle it" (i.e., make the necessary corrections for distortions caused by the drug), there is no problem.

In short, the most likely interpretation we can make of the drug-induced psychoses reported is that they are either severe anxiety reactions to an event interpreted and experienced as insanity, or failures by the user to correct, in carrying out some ordinary action, for the perceptual distortions caused by the drug. If the interpretation is correct, then untoward mental effects produced by drugs depend in some part on its physiological action, but to a much larger degree find their origin in the definitions and conceptions the user applies to that action. These can vary with the individual's personal makeup, a possibility psychiatrists are most alive to, or with the groups he participates in, the trail I shall pursue here.

The Influence of Drug-Using Cultures

While there are no reliable figures, it is obvious that a very large number of people use recreational drugs, primarily marijuana and LSD. From the previous analysis one might suppose that, therefore, a great many people would have disquieting symptoms and, given the ubiquity in our society of the concept of insanity, that many would decide they had gone crazy and thus have a drug-induced anxiety attack. But very few such reactions occur. Although there must be more than are reported in the professional literature, it is unlikely that drugs have this effect in any large number of cases. If they did, there would necessarily be many more verified accounts than are presently available. Since the psychotic reaction stems from a definition of the drug-induced experience, the explanation of this paradox must lie in the availability of competing definitions of the subjective states produced by drugs.

Competing definitions come to the user from other users who, to his knowledge, have had sufficient experience with the drug to speak with authority. He knows that the drug does not produce permanent disabling damage in all cases, for he can see that these other users do not suffer from it. The question, of course, remains whether it may not produce damage in some cases and whether his is one of them, no matter how rare.

When someone experiences disturbing effects, other users typically assure him that the change in his subjective experience is neither rare nor dangerous. They have seen similar reactions before and may even have experienced them themselves with no lasting harm. In any event, they have some folk knowledge about how to handle the problem.

They may, for instance, know of an antidote for the frightening effects; thus, marijuana users, confronted with someone who had gotten "too high," encourage him to eat, an apparently effective counter-measure. They talk reassuringly about their own experiences, "normalizing" the frightening symptom by treating it, matter-of-factly, as temporary. They maintain surveillance over the affected person, preventing any physically or socially dangerous activity. They may, for instance, keep him from driving or from making a public display that will bring him to the attention of the police or others who would disapprove of his drug use. They show him how to allow for the perceptual distortion the drug causes and teach him how to manage interaction with nonusers.

They redefine the experience he is having as desirable rather than frightening, as the end for which the drug is taken. What they tell him carries conviction, because he can see that it is not some idiosyncratic belief but is instead culturally shared. It is what "everyone" who uses the drug knows. In all these ways, experienced users prevent the episode from having lasting effects and reassure the novice that whatever he feels will come to a timely and harmless end.

The anxious novice thus has an alternative to defining his experience as "going crazy." He may redefine the event immediately or, having been watched over by others throughout the anxiety attack, decide that it was not so bad after all and not fear its reoccurrence. He "learns" that his original definition was "incorrect" and that the alternative offered by other users more nearly describes what he has experienced.

Available knowledge does not tell us how often this mechanism comes into play or how effective it is in preventing untoward psychological reactions; no research has been addressed to this point. In the case of marijuana, at least, the paucity of reported cases of permanent damage, coupled with the undoubted increase in use, suggests that it may be an effective mechanism.

For such a mechanism to operate, a number of conditions must be met. First, the drug must not produce, quite apart from the user's interpretations, permanent damage to the mind. No amount of social redefinition can undo the damage done by toxic alcohols, or the effects of a lethal dose of an opiate or barbiturate. This analysis, therefore, does not apply to drugs known to have such effects.

Second, users of the drug must share a set of understandings—a culture—which includes, in addition to material on how to obtain and ingest the drug, definitions of the typical effects, the typical course of the experience, the permanence of the effects, and a description of methods for dealing with someone who suffers an anxiety attack because of drug use or attempts to act on the basis of distorted perceptions. Users should have available to them, largely through face-to-face participation with other users but possibly in such other ways as reading as well, the definitions contained in that culture, which they can apply in place of the common-sense definitions available to the inexperienced man in the street.

Third, the drug should ordinarily be used in group settings, where other users can present the definitions of the drug-using culture to the person whose inner experience is so unusual as to provoke use of the common-sense category of insanity. Drugs for which technology and custom promote group use should produce a lower incidence of "psychotic episodes."

The last two conditions suggest, as is the case, that marijuana, surrounded by an elaborate culture and ordinarily used in group settings, should produce few "psychotic" episodes. At the same time, they suggest the prediction that drugs which have not spawned a culture and are ordinarily used in private, such as barbiturates, will produce more such episodes.

Non-User Interpretations

A user suffering from drug-induced anxiety may also come into contact with non-users who will offer him definitions, depending on their own perspectives and experiences, that may validate the diagnosis of "going crazy" and thus prolong the episode, possibly producing relatively permanent disability. These non-users include family members and police, but most important among them are psychiatrists and psychiatrically oriented physicians. (Remember that when we speak of reported cases of psychosis, the report is ordinarily made by a physician, though police may also use the term in reporting a case to the press.)

Medical knowledge about the recreational use of drugs is spotty. Little research has been done, and its results are not at the fingertips of physicians who do not specialize in the area. (In the case of LSD, of course, there has been a good deal of research, but its conclusions are not clear and, in any case, have not yet been spread throughout the profession.) Psychiatrists are not anxious to treat drug users, so few of them have accumulated any clinical experience with the phenomenon. Nevertheless, a user who develops severe and uncontrollable anxiety will probably be brought, if he is brought anywhere, to a physician for treatment. Most probably, he will be brought to a psychiatric hospital, if one is available; if not, to a hospital emergency room, where a psychiatric resident will be called once the connection with drugs is established, or to a private psychiatrist.

Physicians, confronted with a case of drug-induced anxiety and lacking specific knowledge of its character or proper treatment, rely on a kind of generalized diagnosis. They reason that people probably do not use drugs unless they are suffering from a severe underlying personality disturbance; that use of the drug may allow repressed conflicts to come into the open where they will prove unmanageable; that the drug in this way provokes a true psychosis; and, therefore, that the patient confronting them is psychotic. Furthermore, even though the effects of the drug wear off, the psychosis may not, for the repressed psychological problems it has brought to the surface may not recede as it is metabolized and excreted from the body.

Given such a diagnosis, the physician knows what to do. He hospitalizes the patient for observation and prepares, where possible, for long-term therapy designed to repair the damage done to the psychic defenses or to deal with the conflict unmasked by the drug. Both hospitalization and therapy are likely to reinforce the definition of the drug experience as insanity, for in both the patient will be required to "understand" that he is mentally ill as a precondition for return to the world.

The physician, then, does *not* treat the anxiety attack as a localized phenomenon, to be treated in a symptomatic way, but as an outbreak of a serious disease heretofore hidden. He may thus prolong the serious effects beyond the time they might have lasted had the user instead come into contact with other users. This analysis, of course, is frankly speculative; what is required is a study of the way physicians treat cases of the kind described and, especially, comparative study of the effects of treatment of drug-induced anxiety attacks by physicians and by drug users.

Another category of non-users deserves mention. Literary men and journalists publicize definitions of drug experiences, either of their own invention or those borrowed from users, psychiatrists, or police. (Some members of this category use drugs themselves, so it may be a little confusing to classify them as non-users; in any case, the definitions are provided outside the ordinary channels of communication in the drug-using world.) The definitions of literary men—novelists, essayists, and poets—grow out of a long professional tradition, beginning with De Quincey's *Confessions*, and are likely to be colored by that tradition. Literary descriptions dwell on the fantasy component of the experience, on its cosmic and ineffable character, and on the threat of madness. Such widely available definitions furnish some of the substance out of which a user may develop his own definition, in the absence of definitions from the drug-using culture.

Journalists use any of a number of approaches conventional in their craft; what they write is greatly influenced by their own professional needs. They must write about "news," about events which have occurred recently and require reporting and interpretation. Furthermore, they need "sources," persons to whom authoritative statements can be attributed. Both needs dispose them to reproduce the line taken by law-enforcement officials and physicians, for news is often made by the passage of a law or by a public statement in the wake of an alarming event, such as a bizarre murder or suicide. So journalistic reports frequently dwell on the theme of madness or suicide, a tendency intensified by the newsman's desire to tell a dramatic story. Some journalists, of course, will take the other side in the argument, but even then, because they argue against the theme of madness, the emphasis on that theme is maintained. Public discussion of drug use tends to strengthen those stereotypes that would lead users who suffer disturbing effects to interpret their experience as "going crazy."

Conclusion

The preceding analysis, to repeat, is supported at only a few points by available research; most of what has been said is speculative. The theory, however, gains credibility in several ways. Many of its features follow directly from a Meadian social psychology and the general plausibility of that scheme lends it weight. Furthermore, it is consistent with much of what social scientists have discovered about the nature of drug-induced experiences. In addition, the theory makes sense of some commonly reported and otherwise inexplicable phenomena, such as variations in the number of "psychotic" episodes attributable to recre-

ational drug use. Finally, and much the least important, it is in accord with my haphazard and informal observations of LSD use.

References

Aberle, David. 1966. *The Peyote Religion Among the Navaho*. Chicago: Aldine.

Becker, Howard. 1963. *The Outsiders*. New York: The Free Press.

Blum, Richard. 1964. *Utopiates*. New York: Atherton Press.

10

The Social Shaping of Grief

Lyn H. Lofland

If, and if so how much, social experience shapes human emotions is a matter of continuing controversy. There are reasons to suspect that people everywhere express anger, fear, happiness, and sadness similarly and may even experience these emotions for similar, although not identical reasons. Likewise, different groups have widely different mourning customs, but everyone everywhere apparently grieves over the death of a loved one. The question remains: Just how universal and how socially variable are human emotions?

Lyn Lofland addresses that question with respect to grief in this selection, using a historical perspective. As she notes, many contemporary writers argue that grief is a natural human reaction to the loss of a loved one. They maintain that its symptoms and course are determined by human nature and not by social experience. Unconvinced of that, Lofland describes how the character of relationships, the definition and prevalence of death, understandings of the self, and opportunities for private emotional reflection have historically changed in Western societies. She proposes that these changes have intensified the sense of loss and experience of grief when a loved one dies. We apparently experience grief less often but more deeply than our ancestors.

Lofland does not resolve the question of how universal or diverse human emotions are. What she does demonstrate is that the expression, course, intensity, and duration of even apparently universal emotions like grief may be historically and culturally quite diverse. We cannot merely assume that people throughout history and everywhere experience similar emotions similarly. No matter how universal emotion may be, social experience, interpretations, and circumstances may shape how individuals experience that emotion. Understanding human emotion requires an understanding of how individuals' subjective experience reflects their social experience.

One of the recurring tensions in the study of human beings arises over the question of how similar, historically and cross-culturally, the species may be. This issue of the universality, or more accurately, the *extent* of the universality of human nature seems to be an extraordinarily complex one. Consider how believable we find points of view on the issue which are diametrically opposed. Humanists have tended to argue with Terence that "nothing human is alien to me." And out of our capacity to understand, to find meaning, to take delight in music and poetry and drama and art and letters that have traveled great distances in time and space, we judge the arguments of the humanists to be fully plausible. Conversely, historians and anthropologists, especially, have emphasized the incredible diversity of humankind, the extraordinary capacity of the species to generate different ways of being in the world. And when we read well-developed portraits of other cultural groups or of our own group in other times, we know that the anthropologists and the historians are correct. Surely it must be that we find both kinds of answers satisfying because, as many scholars have concluded, both kinds of answers are true. It is not a question of *whether* all humans are like or unlike all other humans. Rather, it is—and this is far more complex—a question of how humans are alike and how they differ.

In what follows, I will address the question of human similarity/difference relative only to emotional experience and, even more narrowly, relative only to a single emotional experience, that of grief. I want to look at the issue of just how deeply social arrangements penetrate into private emotion; just how molded by culture and history even intimate internal experience may be. Grief—defined here as a response to the involuntary loss through death of a human being who is viewed as significant by the actor of reference—offers an especially strategic case for considering such matters. It is, at least in what we know of its modern form, intensely felt and of long duration. It is emotion "writ large" in its overwhelming rather than subtle effects. Of equal strategic import, grief seems linked to some very basic processes of human attachment, to concerns with the social bond. To begin to understand something of the variation or universality of the emotional experience of grief, then, is to probe deeply into the variation and the universality of the human condition.

Over the past forty years a serious and considerable literature on grief has emerged. From clinical evidence, interview studies, and first-person accounts, we know a great deal about the internal experiences and private actions of persons who have suffered the death of someone close. The population on which this knowledge is based is quite diverse in terms of class but admittedly limited relative to nationality and in terms of the relation between deceased and the survivor. Most descriptions come from British and American widows, bereaved parents, and widowers. For those persons, however, the picture that emerges from the literature is a consistent and convincing one: grief is an emotional experience that is both searing and long-lasting. Its "symptomatology" (varying somewhat from individual to individual and within individuals from time to time) includes such diverse physical and mental feelings and activities as: sleeplessness, restlessness, loss of appetite, frustration, hallucinations, "irrational" behavior, shortness of breath, heaviness in the chest, nausea, headaches, uncontrolled weeping, sadness, despair, hopelessness, apathy, and irritability . . . [It is generally agreed] that over time the symptoms gradually subside and, while they may never completely disappear, they usually become sufficiently mild for the individual to experience herself or himself as "normal" once again. Current assessments of how long this takes range from one to three years and, during this period, the bereaved seem to be especially vulnerable to physiological and psychological disorders. In sum, the literature tells us that the normal grief experience—normal at least for a significant number of modern Americans and British—is painful, debilitating, and relatively long-lasting.

The question at issue, then, is whether and to what degree this experience partakes of the universal or the particular in the human condition.

Grief and Available [Evidence]

As I noted above, the empirical materials out of which our knowledge of the modern grief experience emerge are considerable and convincing. But they apply, let me emphasize again, to a quite limited population. Once our attention shifts from contemporary Europeans (mostly British) and Americans (mostly white), we find a paucity of [evidence]. The fact of the matter is that the clinical experiences and the interview studies, as well as extensive first person accounts which allow us direct access to others' internal feelings and private actions, are themselves modern and primarily Western creations and they have been utilized primarily by modern Westerners relative to modern Westerners. There simply is no comparable historical data and data on modern non-Western populations are extremely limited.

What we do know a great deal about is mourning, both cross-culturally and historically. The human record is filled with rich descriptions of what people do at the time of death of one of their number—both in terms of social arrangements (for example, body disposal rituals) and of individual activities (for example, self-mutilation). While the terms grief and mourning are frequently used as synonyms, scholars have found it essential to differentiate between them. Grief refers to what is *felt*, mourning to what is *done*. . . .

It is, of course, tempting to try to *infer* grief from mourning, and many have made such an attempt. But . . . as Rosenblatt, Walsh, and Jackson conclude in their 1976 volume, *Grief and Mourning in Cross-Cultural Perspective*, ...

> Unfortunately, the gap between what we would like to investigate in the area of emotional expression and what the ethnographic literature allows us to investigate is enormous. It is impossible to study cross-culturally the fine grain of emotional behavior, to probe for similarities and the differences in most of the behaviors that have been described in the literature on grief in the United States. . . . Even if the behaviors were described, it would still be necessary to have data on how these behaviors are defined and understood by the people in each society. But these data are lacking. (p. 14)

In sum, while there is little in the available record to tell us that the modern grief experience is not a universal, there is also little there to tell us that it is. Despite this, most contemporary discussions of the experience appear to assume—often implicitly—that in important respects, grief transcends space and time. I want now, briefly, to examine this point of view.

Grief in Contemporary Thought

I think it is fair to say that a good deal of the serious scholarly work on grief as well, as the popular discourses on the topic, tend to view it as if it were a non-fatal disease, not unlike the common cold. Whether one is a thirteenth-century Chinese peasant or a twentieth-century Welsh mineworker, the "syndrome" is essentially the same. Sometimes this conception is quite explicit. . . . More frequently, it is implicit, contained within the assumption that grief has a "normal course"— a set of expected symptoms which will progress in a generally predictable manner and which, unless environmental conditions intervene to prolong them or to escalate them to a more serious level, will eventually disappear. It is in the assumption of the normal course that grief is revealed as a universal of the human condition, for the "course"—like the course of a disease—is biologically grounded. What will "trigger" the onset of symptoms (i.e., who is defined as significant) is assumed to be variable, but once triggered, the "normal" internal experience is everywhere and always the same.

The most sophisticated rendering of this point of view is to be found in the works of scholars concerned with the relationship between grief and mourning and critical of the de-ritualized character of much modern public mourning. Ariès (1974) and Gorer (1965), for example, argue that among modern Westerners, the decline of well-developed death rituals has pathologically extended grief's "normal course." Humans in other times and other places know the same grief feelings that modern humans know. But because of effective public ceremonies, these feelings persist for a much shorter period of time. . . .

Scholars like . . . Ariès and Gorer would certainly agree that the grief experience is affected by social conditions. Their arguments about the relation between grief and mourning, however, imply that the effect [is] limited to grief's onset and duration. I propose, in contrast, that social shaping is of a profound character, potentially rendering all aspects of the experience—its symptoms or texture, its shapes or phasing, as well as its onset and duration—highly variable across space and time.

Shaping the Grief Experience

While we do not have the requisite [evidence] on grief to document its vulnerability to social shaping, we do have [evidence], especially from social history, on crucial experiential compo-

nents. These components are: (1) the level of significance of the other who dies; (2) the definition of the situation surrounding death; (3) the character of the self experiencing a loss through death; and (4) the interactional setting/situation in which the three prior components occur. From an interactionist perspective, it would be commonplace to assert that as these components of a death situation varied, so would human action. I want here simply to assert that as these components vary, so will human feeling. In this section, I will present data which suggest variation in these components and which thus support the hypothesis of profound social shaping of the grief experience. The discussion here will also provide a framework for understanding why, among Americans and British, grief is so painful, debilitating, and long-lasting.

The Level of Significance of the Other

The historical record would seem to indicate quite clearly that societal patterns of relational investment are variable; that is, *which* others become significant and *how* significant they are change as time and space change. The first part of this assertion regarding the variability of who is routinely significant to whom is relatively unproblematic. To say in group A, cousins have strong attachments to one another while in Group B, the cousin relationship is not recognized is merely to state a social scientific commonplace. However, the second part of the assertion regarding variability in level of significance is perhaps less obvious. I have elsewhere (Lofland, 1982) argued that it is fruitful to conceive of human attachment as being formed by multiple building blocks or "threads of connectedness." I suggested that there are seven of these. We are linked to others by *roles* we play, by the *help* we receive, by the wider *network* of others made available to us, by the *selves* others create and sustain, by the *comforting myths* they allow us, by the *reality* they validate for us, and by the *futures* they make possible. I do not claim that this listing is exhaustive. But it is useful in thinking about, among other matters, the possible patterned variation in levels of significance that others may have for us.

Having broken down human attachment into separate pieces, it becomes possible to ask whether there might not be cultural and historical differences in the way these individual pieces get put together, as well as in preferences for their construction. One can imagine, for example, a human group in which the "threads" or linkages are quite widely distributed such that any single relationship is relatively *low in significance*. This would seem to be exactly what Edmund Volkart ([1957] 1976) was suggesting [some years ago] in his classic "Bereavement and Mental Health."

> In his study of the Ifaluk people, [M.E.] Spiro was puzzled by some features of bereavement behavior there. When a family member died, the immediate survivors displayed considerable pain and distress, which behavior was in accordance with local custom. However, as soon as the funeral was over, the bereaved were able to laugh, smile, and behave in general as if they had suffered no loss or injury at all. . . . In terms of the thesis being developed here . . . [we can argue that] in self-other relations among the Ifaluk, the other is not valued by the self as a unique and necessary personality. . . . Multiple and interchangeable personnel performing the same functions for the individual provide the individual with many psychological anchors in his social environment; the death of any one person leaves the others and thus diminishes the loss. (pp. 247–249)

Conversely, one can also imagine a human group in which a typical actor is connected to an individual other by *multiple* threads, but with the total number of relationships maintained by the actor being quite small. In such a situation, any single relationship is relatively *high in significance*. The work of a number of social scientists would suggest that this is the dominant contemporary pattern of connectedness in the West—a pattern that is of relatively recent vintage, at least among Europeans. Intimacy (that is, the sharing of many facets of self, the multiple-threaded connection, with only a few others) would appear to be a product of Western individualization, urbanization and industrialization. . . . Certainly the intense bonding and heavy relational investment characteristic of the modern parent-child relationship seems not to be universal. Mitterauer and Sieder (1982), writing of the eighteenth- and nineteenth-century European peasant family argue that

> . . . little importance was attached to actual parentage. Foster children might be taken in, orphans of relations or neighbors; young relations often came into the household as men- or maidservants and were then treated as children of the family. On the other hand, people often sent their children into service at an early age and without a great sense of loss. (p. 61)

The point here is not to argue that modern multi-threaded, intense relationships are unique nor to suggest that parental love is a recent phenomenon. . . . The point is simply that (1) there is some evidence to suggest historical and cultural variation in the typical patterning of relationships; that (2) differing patterns imply differing levels of relational significance; and that (3) differing levels of significance suggest differences in the grief experience.

The Definition of the Situation

Death itself is certainly one universal of the human condition. But the *experience of death* is a variable—both among individuals within a particular social grouping and, more importantly and of exclusive concern here, among social groupings. That is, the definition of the situation of death is not always and everywhere the same. There are many senses in which this is true; I wish here to point only to two of these.

First, what death looks like *philosophically* or ideologically is enormously variable. . . . [E]ven a cursory perusal of the anthropological, historical, and/or philosophical literature will remind us that the beliefs, symbols, and values associated with death share in that incredible cultural diversity which seems to be a signal characteristic of our species.

There is a second sense in which the experience of death—the definition of the situation of death—varies. What death looks like *demographically*—its frequency, size, and shape—is not always and everywhere the same. For the contemporary Westener, for example, death is a relative rarity. The current American mortality rate of less than 9 in 1,000, with the associated life expectancy of approximately 73 years, means that for many of us, the first personally meaningful death we will encounter will be those of our parents and these will occur when we are middle aged. When we marry, we have every reason to believe that while the union may very well be prematurely severed by divorce, it is unlikely to be prematurely severed by death. The current infant mortality rate in the United States is about 1 percent (lower in much of Western Europe). That rate, combined with quite low age specific rates among children means few parents will suffer the deaths of their babies and even fewer will suffer the deaths of their older offspring. Contemporary parents, then, have every reason to expect that their children will bury them, not the reverse. What is of interest here is that this situation appears to be *historically deviant*. The modern death pattern (characteristic of the developed nations) is a very recent phenomenon—the consequence of an unprecedented mortality revolution (Goldscheider, 1976). Throughout most of human history (and in many parts of the world yet today), the demographic picture is a very different one. In the premodern world, death was not a rarity but an experiential constant. Goldscheider suggests an "ideal typical" mortality rate of 50 per 1,000, but with frequent fluctuations in that rate up to 200, 300, or even 400 per 1,000. Similarly, infant mortality rates ran about 35 percent of births and, for example, in Brittany in France, in the seventeenth and eighteenth centuries (which is considered relatively typical), half of the children did not survive beyond their tenth year. Given such figures, it is hardly surprising that evidence from historians suggests that, at least in some times and places in Europe, deaths of children and spouses were sufficiently routine to engender practices expressing that routine. Mitterauer and Sieder (1982), for example, note that

> Changes in membership took place so frequently in a European peasant household of the eighteenth or nineteenth century that there could be no comparable sense of loss throughout the group. If a young wife died after a few years of marriage—and this happened quite often because of the great danger at and after childbirth—a second marriage was contracted after only a short period of mourning. A new housewife was needed to help in the management of the farm. Parents had to assume that several of their children would die young. . . . Soon after one child had died, the next might come into the world, and so on until the end of the woman's period of fertility. (p. 61)

Similarly, the "feeling rules" (Hochschild, 1979) of colonial Puritans (Keyssar, 1980) . . . as well as Elizabethans also support the interpretation that much historic death was defined as routine. Lu Emily Pearson (1980) reports, for example, that Eliazbethan widows were " . . . given little time to mourn. . . . As soon as a widow laid the body of her husband in the tomb, she was expected to bury her independence and her grief

. . . [and to put herself] into the hands of [her] nearest kin who might proceed . . . to launch [her] into matrimony again" (pp. 407–408).

In sum, there is strong historical evidence to suggest that the definition of the situation of death varies across time and space—varies both in terms of the philosophical lens though which death is viewed and defined and in terms of frequency, shape, and size of death which calls for definition. As such, surely, the emotional response to death—the grief—must vary as well.

The Character of the Self

Some of the most challenging work in social history and in social psychology in recent decades has dealt with the difficult but intriguing question of space-time variation in the character of the self. In the main, scholars have argued that such variation does exist and does so along a number of different dimensions. For example, the degree of *separateness* of the self has been explored. . . . Morris's (1972) *The Discovery of the Individual, 1050–1200* is perhaps the most convincing treatment of the topic. As he argues:

> Western culture has developed [a] sense of individuality to an extent exceptional among civilizations of the world. In primitive societies, the training of the child is usually directed to his learning the traditions of the tribe so that he may find his identity, not in anything peculiar to himself, but in the common mind of his people. . . . Our difficulty in understanding [the Ancient Greeks] is largely due to the fact that they have no equivalent to our concept of "person" while their vocabulary was rich in words which express community of being. . . . Belief in reincarnation [in the Asiatic and Eastern Tradition] virtually excludes individuality in the Western sense, for each person is but a manifestation of the life within him, which will be reborn, after his apparent death, in another form. Taking a world view, one might almost regard [Western individualism] as an eccentricity among cultures. (p. 2)

Similarly, . . . Turner (1976) . . . [has] provided evidence for a recent shift in the *location* of the "true self" from an anchorage in "institution" to an anchorage in "impulse." . . .

Specifying exactly how such changes in the character of the self link to the character of emotional experience is far beyond the capabilities of current research and analysis. But it is surely not outside the realm of social scientific common-sense to expect that as selves are differentially separated . . . [and] located . . . they will also be differentially sentienced. And, there is research which points to such a difference.

Writing about the contrasts between modern (nineteenth- and twentieth-century) and early modern (sixteenth- through eighteenth-century) Europeans and Americans, Fox and Quitt [1980] describe one significant point of contrast: the honeymoon. . . .The absence of the honeymoon in pre-1800 Europe and America and its subsequent appearance reflects, they argue, a change in feelings about feelings.

> A honeymoon, with its exclusive preoccupation with pleasure and feelings, would not be compatible with the temperament of those early modern people who denied or distrusted their inner selves, who tried to eradicate or control their appetites, who renounced or moderated the promptings of the flesh. *A modern honeymoon requires a different temperament, one that seeks to give free play to inner feelings.* (p. 32, emphasis added)

The contemporary grief experience, with its intensity, with the exquisite range of its symptoms and with its considerable duration, would seem to be remarkably well-matched to the modern penchant for "exploring and expressing one's deepest strivings" and to the modern temperament which "seeks to give free play to inner feelings." To the degree that this penchant and temperament is culturally and historically variable, that is, to the degree that there is cultural and historical variability in the self which grieves, then, surely, the grief itself must vary.

The Interactional Setting/Situation

The modern literature on grief is replete with descriptions of private activities in which bereaved persons engage which keep their attention riveted to their loss. Quite typically and literally, they seek the lost person. Taking long solitary walks, scanning faces for a glimpse of the dead other is not unusual behavior. . . . They may fully hallucinate the other's presence or merely fantasize it or more simply, remember it. But through such hallucination or fantasy or memory, a strong sense of the loss is maintained. . . . They visit places and look at objects rich in associations with the lost other; going over photographs again and again, for example, or returning repeatedly to a particular cafe. . . . They take for themselves the

dead other's possessions, keeping clothes in the closet, for example, or appropriating jewelry or books. . . . For our purposes here, what is particularly striking about these descriptions of behavior patterns among the bereaved is that they could only occur among persons who have access to considerable periods of solitude and privacy and who are embedded in an interactional setting/situation that is neither populated by large numbers of demanding others nor characterized by serious restrictions of space or time. And the kind of interactional situation is, without question, historically variable.

The activities of the modern bereaved are the activities of persons who live in households—in interactional settings—which are relatively spacious and which contain only a few others. As David Popenoe (1985) notes, in the United States and Sweden, as examples, "daily domestic life . . . takes place in a very tiny group. In [many] households . . . there is, [in fact] *no* other person in the same domicile" (p. 26). Contrast this situation with Galdin's (1977) description of a typical Colonial American household—a description which seems equally applicable to most living arrangements throughout history and to many yet today.

> People were almost always within monitoring range of one another. Families were large and houses small; of the few rooms there were, most were multipurpose. Even if a person were alone in a room, almost all of his activities could be overheard, since plaster walls were virtually nonexistent. Furthermore, within a room, private space was minimized, since beds were typically shared and benches were more common than single chairs. (pp. 35–36)

When these living situations coincided with pressures toward speedy "replacement" of spouse or infant or parent, for example, it is difficult to see how the bereaved had the time, the space, or the privacy necessary for the incessant focusing on loss that now seems typical. Thus, to the degree that the emotional experience of grief is associated with the interactional context in which the grieving person is embedded, that experience must be variable.

Concluding Remarks

In the preceding, I have suggested that the modern emotional experience of grief, as documented by a considerable literature, may not be universal of the human condition. It seems likely that since everywhere and always humans form attachments, everywhere and always they know grief. But it seems equally likely that the character of that grief—its shape and texture and length—is quite variable. Whether the modern experience is a unique one cannot be determined at this time. Certainly the particular concatenation of circumstances which produce it may be unique: (1) a relational pattern which links individuals to a small number of highly significant others; (2) a definition of death as personal annihilation and as unusual and tragic except among the aged; (3) selves which take very seriously their emotional states; and (4) interactional settings which provide rich opportunities to contemplate loss. But that is not to say that other combinations of components might not generate the same result. Thus, it would be a mistake to conceive of changes in the grief experience in any unilinear way. Neither the history of humankind nor the history of Western social orders should be read as a history of a progressive intensification of that experience. "Evolutionary" thinking of this sort has led us astray in our attempts to understand other phenomena (for example, the family, the city) and there is no reason to believe it will serve us better in this context. What is needed is an openness to the possibility of finding some rather messy patterns of similarities and differences in the grief experience across time and space. What is needed, also, is the willingness to replace sweeping generalizations about grief with its careful and delimited depiction.

References

Ariès, Philippe. 1974. *Western Attitudes Toward Death From the Middle Ages to the Present.* Baltimore, MD: Johns Hopkins University Press.

Fox, Vivian C., and Martin H. Quitt. 1980. *Loving, Parenting, and Dying: The Family Cycle in England and America, Past and Present.* New York: Psychohistory Press.

Galdin, Howard. 1977. "Private Lives and Public Order: A Critical View of the History of Intimate Relations in the United States." Pp. 33–72 in George Levinger and Harold L. Raush (eds.), *Close Relationships: Perspectives on the Meaning of Intimacy.* Amherst: University of Massachusetts Press.

Goldscheider, Calvin. 1976. "The Mortality Revolution." Pp. 163–189 in Edwin Schneidman (ed.), *Death: Current Perspectives.* Palo Alto, CA: Mayfield.

Gorer, Geoffrey. 1965. *Death, Grief, and Mourning in Contemporary Britain.* London: Cresset Press.

Hochschild, Arlie. 1979. "Emotion Work, Feeling Rules, and Social Structure." *American Journal of Sociology,* 85 (November): 551–575.

Keyssar, Alexander. 1980. "Widowhood in Eighteenth-Century Massachusetts." Pp. 425–455 in Vivian C. Fox and Martin H. Quitt (eds.), *Loving, Parenting, and Dying: The Family Cycle in England and America, Past and Present.* New York: Psychohistory Press.

Lofland, Lyn H. 1982. "Loss and Human Connection: An Exploration Into the Nature of the Social Bond." Pp. 219–242 in William Ickes and Eric S. Knowles (eds.), *Personality, Roles, and Social Behavior.* New York: Springer-Verlag.

Mitterauer, Michael, and Reinhard Sieder. 1982. *The European Family: Patriarchy to Partnership From the Middle Ages to the Present.* Trans. Karla Oosterveen and Manfred Hörzinger. Oxford: Basil Blackwell.

Morris, John. 1972. *The Discovery of the Individual, 1050–1200.* New York: Harper & Row.

Pearson, Lu Emily. 1980. "Changes Wrought by Death." Pp. 407–421 in Vivian C. Fox and Martin H. Quitt (eds.), *Loving, Parenting, and Dying: The Family Cycle in England and America, Past and Present.* New York: Psychohistory Press.

Popenoe, David. 1985. *Private Pleasure, Public Plight: American Metropolitan Community Life in Comparative Perspective.* New Brunswick, NJ: Transaction Books.

Rosenblatt, Paul C., R. P. Walsh, and D. A. Jackson. 1976. *Grief and Mourning in Cross-Cultural Perspective.* New Haven, CT: Human Relations Area Files Press.

Turner, Ralph. 1976. "The Real Self: From Institution to Impulse." *American Journal of Sociology,* 81 (March): 989–1016.

Volkart, Edmund H. (with the collaboration of Stanley T. Michael). [1957] 1976. "Bereavement and Mental Health." Pp. 239–257 in Robert Fulton (ed.), *Death and Identity.* Rev. ed. Bowie, MD: The Charles Press.

11

Managing Emotions in Medical School

Allen C. Smith III
and
Sherryl Kleinman

For many years, students of social life ignored emotions. That changed in the late 1970s when a number of sociologists began to study and write about the social shaping and consequences of human emotions. Among them, Arlie Russell Hochschild proposed that human emotions are shaped by learned but implicit "feeling rules." According to her, individuals manage not only their outward expression of emotions but also their very feelings in order to conform to such rules. They not only express but also attempt to feel what they think they should be feeling. Further, Hochschild suggested that feeling rules vary not just historically and cross-culturally but also within societies. For example, she illustrated that feeling rules vary among occupations within our own society.

If that is the case, then occupational training necessarily involves some emotional socialization. Initiates into an occupation need to learn new feeling rules and develop new emotion management skills. Such emotional socialization may be most apparent in professional schools. As Zerubavel noted in an earlier selection, professionals such as judges, professors, and doctors are expected to put personal feelings aside and display "affective neutrality" in their work. That expectation may be most difficult for doctors who must touch and treat the human body in ways that would evoke repulsion or arousal in most of us.

This selection examines the emotional socialization of medical students. As Smith and Kleinman document, medical students' education includes subtle instruction in the feeling rules of their chosen occupation and practice in emotion management. Students learn, if they do not already know, that doctors do not let their emotions interfere with their work. Yet, the students' contact and treatment of the human body during their training often provokes professionally inappropriate and un-

comfortable emotions. Although these feelings are seldom explicitly discussed, medical school encourages students to adopt emotion management strategies through which emotions are shaped to conform to professional feeling rules. Over time, most students come not only to display affective neutrality toward the human body, but also to feel affectively neutral about it. However, as Smith and Kleinman note, that too can cause problems if they carry this affective neutrality into their personal lives.

This example provides a particularly clear picture of how emotions are socially shaped. For the most part, we learn feeling rules and how to manage emotions gradually over many years. It is only when we must suddenly conform to new feeling rules, as medical students must, that our management of emotions becomes self-conscious and obvious to us. Yet, medical students' management of emotions merely helps us see what we are all doing less self-consciously most of the time—managing emotions.

[handwritten: → DOES THIS RELATE TO AFFECTIVE RESPONSES TO ART / AESTHETICS?]

All professionals develop a perspective different from, and sometimes at odds with, that of the public. "Professionals" are supposed to know more than their clients and to have personable, but not personal, relationships with them. Social distance between professional and client is expected. Except for scattered social movements within the professions in the late 1960s and 1970s . . . professionals expect to have an "affective neutrality" (Parsons 1951) or a "detached concern" for clients (Lief and Fox 1963). Because we associate authority in this society with an unemotional persona, affective neutrality reinforces professionals' power and keeps clients from challenging them. One element of professional socialization, then, is the development of appropriately controlled affect.

Medicine is the archetypal profession, and norms guiding the physician's feelings are strong. Physicians ideally are encouraged to feel moderate sympathy toward patients, but excessive concern and all feelings based on the patient's or the physician's individuality are proscribed. Presumably, caring too much for the patient can interfere with delivering good service. Other feelings such as disgust or sexual attraction, considered natural in the personal sphere, violate fundamental medical ideals. Doctors are supposed to treat all patients alike (that is, well) regardless of personal attributes, and without emotions that might disrupt the clinical process or the doctor-patient relationship. . . . [D]etachment presumably helps doctors to deal with death and dying, with the pressure of making mistakes, and with the uncertainty of medical knowledge.

In this paper we examine another provocative issue—the physical intimacy inherent in medicine—and ask how medical students manage their inappropriate feelings as they make contact with the human body with all of their senses. We look closely at the situations that make them most uncomfortable: disassembling the dead human body (i.e., autopsy and dissection) and making "intimate" contact with living bodies (i.e., pelvic, rectal, and breast examinations). From the beginning of medical training, well before students take on clinical responsibility, dealing with the human body poses a problem for them. Clothed in multiple meanings and connected to important rituals and norms, the body demands a culturally defined respect and provokes deep feelings. Even a seemingly routine physical calls for a physical intimacy that would evoke strong feelings in a personal context, feelings which are unacceptable in medicine.

The ideology of affective neutrality is strong in medicine; yet no courses in the medical curriculum deal directly with emotion management, specifically learning to change or eliminate inappropriate feelings (Hochschild 1983). Rather, two years of participant observation in a medical school revealed that discussion of the students' feelings is taboo; their development toward emotional neutrality remains part of the hidden curriculum. Under great pressure to prove themselves worthy of entering the profession, students are afraid to admit that they have uncomfortable feelings about patients or procedures, and hide those feelings behind a "cloak of competence" (Haas and Shaffir 1977). Beneath their surface presentations, how do students deal with the "unprofessional" feelings they bring over from the personal realm? Because faculty members do not address the problem, students are left with an individualistic outlook: they expect to get control of themselves through sheer will-power.

Despite the silence surrounding this topic, the faculty, the curriculum, and the organization of medical school do provide students with resources for dealing with their problem. The culture of medicine that informs teaching and provides the feeling rules also offers unspoken supports for dealing with unwanted emotions. Students draw on aspects of their experience in medical school to manage their emotions. . . . In this case study of the professionalization of emotions, we examine how students learn to handle unsettling reactions to patients and procedures in a context in which faculty members expect students to socialize themselves.

Methods and Setting

We studied students as they encountered the human body in clinical situations during the first three years of their training at a major medical school in the southeast. The first author conducted participant observation for two and one-half years. . . . Over the same period we conducted open-ended, in-depth interviews with 16 first-year, 13 second-year, and 15 third-year students, and with 18 others, including residents, attending physicians, nurses, spouses, and a counselor in the student health service. . . .

The school is a well-established university-based program with a traditional four-year curriculum. . . . Students have direct contact with the human body in a variety of situations. They begin dissection in gross anatomy on the third day of the first year. For 70 hours they progressively disassemble a preserved human body (cadaver), removing, examining, and discarding tissue while searching for specific "structures." Beginning in the first year, students spend 20 hours practicing a limited set of physical examination skills on each other. Although they do not examine the breasts, genitals, or rectum in these sessions, the practice still becomes uncomfortable at certain points, such as listening to the heart and examining the abdomen.

In the second year, students also practice examination skills for about 10 hours with patients in the hospital. Again, the breasts, genitals, and rectum are excluded unless a specific instructor requires them for his or her group of students. In a special session in the second year, students learn to conduct the gynecological examination. . . . Each student practices the basic examination once. Another special session, the autopsy, also is required in the second year. The autopsy is more upsetting to students than dissection, largely because the body is freshly dead and is accompanied by personal information in the patient's medical record. As one student put it, the body is "much closer to life than the smoked herring (cadaver) in gross anatomy."

In the third-year clerkships, the students conduct physical examinations and assist with a wide variety of tests and procedures. Depending on the relationships they establish with residents and faculty, clerks are included in much of the clinical service offered in the hospital. . . .

The Student's Problem

As they encounter the human body, students experience a variety of uncomfortable feelings including embarrassment, disgust, and arousal. Medical school, however, offers a barrier against these feelings by providing the anesthetic effect of long hours and academic pressure.

> You know the story. On call every third night, and stay in the hospital late most other evenings. I don't know how you're supposed to think when you're that tired, but you do, plod through the day insensitive to everything. (Third-year male)

Well before entering medical school, students learn that their training will involve constant pressure and continuing fatigue. Popular stories prepare them for social isolation, the impossibility of learning everything, long hours, test anxiety, and the fact that medical school will permeate their lives. These difficulties and the sacrifices that they entail legitimate the special status of the profession the students are entering. They also blunt the students' emotional responses.

Yet uncomfortable feelings break through. Throughout the program, students face provocative situations—some predictable, others surprising. They find parts of their training, particularly dissection and the autopsy, bizarre or immoral when seen from the perspective they had "for 25 years" before entering medical school.

> Doing the pelvis, we cut it across the waist. . . . Big saws! The mad scientist! People wouldn't believe what we did in there. The cracking sound! That day was more than anxiety. We were really violating that person. . . . Drawn and quartered. (First-year male)

> I did my autopsy 10 days ago. That shook me off my feet. Nothing could have prepared me for it. The person was my age. . . . She just looked (pause) asleep. Not like the cadaver.

> Fluid, blood, smell. It smelled like a butcher shop. And they handled it like a butcher shop. The technicians. Slice, move, pull, cut . . . all the organs inside, pulled out in 10 minutes. I know it's absurd, but what if she's not really dead? She doesn't look like it. (Second-year female)

The "mad scientist" and the "butcher" violate the students' images of medicine. Even in more routine kinds of contact, the students sometimes feel that they are ignoring the sanctity of the body and breaking social taboos.

Much of the students' discomfort is based on the fact that the bodies they have contact with are or were *people*. Suddenly students feel uncertain about the relationship of the person to the body, a relationship they had previously taken for granted.

> It felt tough when we had to turn the whole body over from time to time (during dissection). It felt like real people. (First-year female)

> OK. Maybe he was a father, but the father part is gone. This is just the body. That sounds religious. Maybe it is. How else can I think about it? (First-year male)

When the person is somehow reconnected to the body, such as when data about the living patient who died are brought into the autopsy room, students feel less confident and more uneasy.

Students find contact with the sexual body particularly stressful. In the anatomy lab, in practice sessions with other students, and in examining patients, students find it difficult to feel neutral as contact approaches the sexual parts of the body.

> When you listen to the heart you have to work around the breast, and move it to listen to one spot. I tried to do it with minimum contact, without staring at her tit . . . breast. . . . The different words (pause) shows I was feeling both things at once. (Second-year male)

Though they are rarely aroused, students worry that they will be. They feel guilty, knowing that sexuality is proscribed in medicine, and they feel embarrassed. Most contact involves some feelings, but contact with the sexual body presents a bigger problem.

On occasion students feel unsure about differences between the personal and the professional perspectives. Recalling the first day of "surface anatomy," when they are expected to remove their shirts in order to examine each other's backs before beginning dissection of the back, students remember an unspoken tension. The lab manual suggests that women wear bathing suit tops, but few students read it in advance. Some of the few women who comply wear bras.

> I remember surface anatomy. That first day when they asked us to take our shirts off, including the girls. That was real uncomfortable. You know (pause) seeing some of the girls in bras. Some of them were wearing swimsuit tops. But (pause) and drawing on their chests. So I got a guy for a partner. (First-year male)

> What's the difference between a bra and a bathing suit top? Don't know. But there is one! (First-year female)

When students are standing in the anatomy lab beside the cadavers, the difference between a bra and a bathing suit is surprisingly hard to describe. The differences are clear from a personal perspective, but in the technical objectivity of the laboratory, the details and meanings of the personal perspective seem elusive and irrational.

Students also feel disgust. They see feces, smell vomit, touch wounds, and hear bone saws, encountering many repulsive details with all of their senses.

> One patient was really gross! He had something that kept him standing, and coughing all the time. Coughing phlegm, and that really bothers me. Gross! Just something I don't like. Some smelled real bad. I didn't want to examine their axillae. Stinking armpits! It was just not something I wanted to do. (Second-year female)

When the ugliness is tied to living patients, the aesthetic problem is especially difficult. On opening the bowels of the cadaver, for example, students permit themselves some silent expressions of discomfort, but even a wince is unacceptable with repugnant living patients.

To make matters worse, students learn early on that they are not supposed to talk about their feelings with faculty members or other students. Feelings remain private. The silence encourages students to think about their problem as an individual matter, extraneous to the "real work" of medical school. They speak of "screwing up your courage," "getting control of yourself," "being tough enough," and "putting feelings aside." They worry that the faculty would consider them incompetent and unprofessional if they admitted their problem.

> I would be embarrassed to talk about it. You're supposed to be professional here. Like there's an unwritten rule about how to talk. (First-year female)

> It wouldn't be a problem if I weren't in medicine. But doctors just aren't supposed to feel that way. (Interviewer) How do you know? (Student) I don't know how, just sense it. It's macho, the control thing. Like, "Med student, get a grip on yourself." It's just part of medicine. It's a norm, expected. (First-year male)

The "unwritten rule" is relaxed enough sometimes to permit discussion, but the privacy that surrounds these rare occasions suggests the degree to which the taboo exists. At times, students signal their uncomfortable feelings—rolling their eyes, turning away, and sweating—but such confirmation is limited. Exemplifying pluralistic ignorance, each student feels unrealistically inadequate in comparison with peers (yet another uncomfortable feeling). Believing that other students are handling the problem better than they are, each student manages his or her feelings privately, only vaguely aware that all students face the same problem.

The silence continues in the curriculum; discomfort with medical intimacy is not mentioned officially. The issue is broached once or twice in class with comments such as "You can expect to be aroused sometimes, examining an attractive woman." Yet there is no discussion, and such rare exceptions occur only according to individual faculty members' initiative. . . .

Emotion Management Strategies

How do students manage their uncomfortable and "inappropriate" feelings? The deafening silence surrounding the issue keeps them from defining the problem as shared, or from working out common solutions. They cannot develop strategies collectively, but their solutions are not individual. Rather, students use the same basic emotion management strategies because social norms, faculty models, curricular priorities, and official and unofficial expectations provide them with uniform guidelines and resources for managing their feelings.

Transforming the Contact

Students feel uncomfortable because they are making physical contact with people in ways they would usually define as appropriate only in a personal context, or as inappropriate only in a personal context, or as inappropriate in any context. Their most common solution to this problem is cognitive. Mentally they transform the body and their contact with it into something entirely different from the contacts they have in their personal lives. Students transform the person into a set of esoteric body parts and change their intimate contact with the body into a mechanical or analytic problem.

> I just told myself, "OK, doc, you're here to find out what's wrong, and that includes the axillae (armpits)." And I detach a little, reduce the person for a moment. . . . Focus real hard on the detail at hand, the fact, or the procedure or question. Like with the cadaver. Focus on a vessel. Isolate down to whatever you're doing. (Second year female)

> Well, with the pelvic training (pause) I concentrated on the procedure, the sequence, and the motions. . . . With the 22-year-old, I concentrated on the order, sequence (pause), and on the details to check. (Second-year male)

Feeling guilty about "mangling" a cadaver, one student begins to ask difficult questions about nerves in the neck. Feeling "uneasy" about a pelvic exam, another student concentrates on the Bartholin gland, which is hidden under more disturbing flesh. Distinct from the body as a whole, these anatomical and procedural details become personally insignificant but academically important. Students learn to recognize them, even if they do not always understand how the specifics will be important in medicine. In the process, the body loses its provocative, personal significance.

Students also transform the moment of contact into a complex intellectual puzzle, the kind of challenge they faced successfully during previous years of schooling. They interpret details according to logical patterns and algorithms, and find answers as they master the rules.

> It helped to know that we were there for a training experience. My anxiety became the anxiety of learning enough. We saw a movie on traumas, like gunshots, burns, explosions. If I had just come off the street, I would have felt sick. But I focused on learning. Occupying my

> mind with learning and science. (Second-year male)

> The patient is really like a math word problem. You break it down into little pieces and put them together. The facts you get from a history and physical, from the labs and chart. They fit together, once you begin to see how to do it. . . . It's an intellectual challenge. (Third-year female)

Defining contact as a part of scientific medicine makes the students feel safe. They are familiar with and confident about science, they feel supported by its cultural and curricular legitimacy, and they enjoy rewards for demonstrating their scientific know-how. In effect, science itself is an emotion management strategy. By competing for years for the highest grades, these students have learned to separate their feelings from the substance of their classes and to concentrate on the impersonal facts of the subject matter. In medical school they use these "educational skills" not only for academic success but also for emotion management.

The curriculum supports the students' efforts to focus on subpersonal facts and details. In 20 courses over the first two years, texts and teachers disassemble the body into systems and subsystems. Students are presented with an impossibly large number of anatomical and pathophysiological details which define the body as a collection of innumerable smaller objects in a complex system. Furthermore, faculty members reward students for recognizing and reciting the relevant facts and details and for reporting them in a succinct and unemotional fashion. Intellectualization is not merely acceptable; it is celebrated as evidence of superior performance in modern medicine. The curriculum equips the students with the substantive basis for their intellectual transformations of the body, and rewards them for using it.

The scientific, clinical language that the students learn also supports intellectualization. It is complex, esoteric, and devoid of personal meanings. "Palpating the abdomen" is less personal than "feeling the belly."

> When we were dissecting the pelvis, the wrong words kept coming to mind, and it was uncomfortable. I tried to be sure to use the right words, penis and testicles (pause) not cock and balls. Even just thinking. Would have been embarrassing to make that mistake that

day. School language, it made it into a science project. (First-year female)

Further, the structure of the language, as in the standard format for the presentation of a case, helps the students to think and speak impersonally. Second-year students learn that there is a routine, acceptable way to summarize a patient: chief complaint, history of present illness, past medical history, family history, social history, review of systems, physical findings, list of problems, medical plan. In many situations they must reduce the sequence to a two- or three-minute summary. Faculty members praise the students for their ability to present the details quickly. Medical language labels and conveys clinical information, and it leads the students away from their emotions.

Transformation sometimes involves changing the body into a nonhuman object. Students think of the body as a machine or as an animal specimen, and recall earlier, comfortable experiences in working on that kind of object. The body is no longer provocative because it is no longer a body.

> After we had the skin off (the cadaver), it was pretty much like a cat or something. It wasn't pleasant, but it wasn't human either. (First-year female)

> (The pelvic exam) is pretty much like checking a broken toaster. It isn't a problem. I'm good at that kind of thing. (Second-year male)

> You can't tell what's wrong without looking under the hood. It's different when I'm talking with a patient. But when I'm examining them it's like an automobile engine.... There's a bad connotation with that, but it's literally what I mean. (Third-year male)

Working on a cat, a toaster, or an engine, the student effaces the person and proceeds "as if" contact were something entirely different (Hochschild 1983). The secularized body is sometimes disturbing to students ("It's just like any meat"). At other times it is reassuringly neutral; contact becomes truly impersonal.

The curriculum supports these dehumanizing transformations by eliminating the person in most of the students' contact with the body. Contact is usually indirect, based on photographs, X-rays (and several newer technologies), clinical records, diagrams, and written words. Students would have to make an effort to reconnect these images to the people they remotely represent. It is harder to disregard the person in direct contact, but such

contact constitutes a very small part of the students' school time in the first three years. In addition, a large part of the students' direct contact occurs with a cadaver in the anatomy lab. Contact with living persons represents less than three percent of their school time over the first three years. Students must take the final step in transforming the body into a specific nonhuman thing, but the curriculum provides the first step by separating the body from the person.

Accentuating the Positive

As we hinted in the previous section, transforming body contact into an analytic event does not merely rid students of their uncomfortable feelings, producing neutrality. It often gives them opportunities to have good feelings about what they are doing. Their comfortable feelings include the excitement of practicing "real medicine," the satisfaction of learning, and the pride of living up to medical ideals. Students identify much of their contact with the body as "real medicine," asserting that such contact separates medicine from other professions. As contact begins in dissection and continues through the third-year clinical clerkships, students feel excited about their progress.

> I can't remember what it was like before coming. It's enveloping. When I wake up I start thinking about being in med school. It's like a honeymoon, knowing I'll be a MD some day. It's just a real good feeling. I don't know how long it will last. And the work is demanding, almost all my time. But it is real, and it does make gross (lab) easier. Lab makes it real, even if it is gross. (First-year male)

> This (dissection) is the part that is really medical school. Not like any other school. It feels like an initiation rite, something like when I joined a fraternity. We were really going to work on people. (First-year male)

After years of anticipation, they are actually entering the profession; occasions of body contact mark their arrival and their progress. The students also feel a sense of privilege and power.

> This is another part that is unique to med school. The professor told us we are the only ones who can do this legally. It is special (pause) and uneasy. (First-year female)

> I remember my second patient. An older guy. . . . There I was, a second-year student

who didn't know much of anything, and I could have done anything I wanted. He would have done whatever I told him. (Second-year male)

Eventually students see contact as their responsibility and their right, and forget the sense of privilege they felt at the beginning. Still, some excitement returns as they take on clinical responsibility in the third year. All of these feelings can displace the discomfort which also attends most contact.

Contact also provides a compelling basis for several kinds of learning, all of which the students value. They sense that they learn something important in contact, something richer than the "dry facts" of textbooks and lectures. Physicians, they believe, rely on touch, not on text.

> I guess I learned the intuitive part in the practice sessions (on physical examination skills). After all that training in science, this was different . . . Like feeling someone's side. Feeling (pause) it begins to mean something. . . . All the courses don't mean anything 'til I have them in my fingertips, my ears. (First-year male)

> The bimanual (in the pelvic exam) was different. Like I knew that I was supposed to feel (with my hands), but I didn't feel anything. Like when you palpate the spleen. Most people never feel it. So this is just another of those. I had read the book on the exam, and it seemed like an ancient rite. It felt good to have a sense of it after that evening. . . . (Second-year male)

Students also develop clinical intuition and a fascination for the body and the "personality" of its parts. They find the learning that occurs with contact gratifying, sometimes satisfying a long-standing curiosity, and frequently symbolizing the power of medicine.

Similarly, students can intensify the good feelings that come with practicing medical ideals. By attending to those ideals, students can feel a pride which overrides any spontaneous discomfort.

> If it's something uneasy, like moving her (breast) to listen to her heart, I also know that I'm doing the right thing. It's both, and it feels good to know I'm doing it right. (Second-year male)

> The personal stuff just doesn't apply to the real exam of a patient. This is a completely differ-

ent relationship than any other in my life. It's my job. It would be inappropriate if I didn't examine them, touch them. It's expected. (Second-year female)

In proceeding with contact despite their discomfort, the students are "doing it right," and that feels good. Some feel pleased about passing important landmarks in their training. Some feel proud of "practicing good medicine." Pride and self-respect diminish awkwardness and embarrassment.

There are two ways in which students accentuate their pride and excitement. First, they can "go with" the good feelings that arise spontaneously. Second, they can create good feelings when they do not arise naturally. By transforming an uncomfortable contact into an analytic event, students can produce the feelings of excitement and satisfaction that they have learned to associate with problem solving. Transformation and accentuating the positive are mutually reinforcing strategies.

Using the Patient

Students sometimes take patients' feelings into account as a means of managing their own discomfort. They do this in two different ways: empathizing with the patient and blaming the patient. When they are uncomfortable, students can control their feelings by shifting their awareness away from their own feelings and to the patient's. Empathizing with the patient, they distract themselves from their own feelings. At the same time, they can feel good about "putting the patient first."

> Sure, my feelings matter. But theirs do too, even more. I'm here for them, and it's only right to give theirs priority. It feels good to listen to them, to try to understand (pause) to care. And I don't feel so weird. (Second-year male)

Empathy, then, can be an effective emotion management strategy as well as an appropriate professional quality.

Students sometimes use the patient as an external locus for their own uncomfortable feelings. They make the patient responsible for their feelings, blaming the patient or simply projecting their own feelings onto the patient. A student can manage feelings of sexual awkwardness, for example, by defining the patient as inappropriately sexual.

I know he is embarrassed. I would be. (Interviewer) Are you embarrassed too? (Student) Yeah. Maybe part of it's mine. No just his. Embarrassed isn't quite the right word. Uneasy. But he might be embarrassed too! (Second-year female)

My very first patient was a young girl, 14 years old. I had been told she was a pediatrics patient, but I sure didn't expect a 14-year-old (pause) and well-developed. I think she was promiscuous. I forgot to do the heart at first. Went all the way to the end and then said, "I'll have to listen to your heart." It was extremely uncomfortable. (Third-year male)

Labeling the patient as "promiscuous," the student can forgive himself his awkwardness and perhaps replace it with feelings of superiority or anger. Patients can be difficult in many ways. . . . Yet in order to manage their own feelings, students sometimes manufacture or exaggerate negative conclusions about the patient or project their own feelings onto the patient, where they are less threatening.

Laughing About It

Students can find or create humor in the situations that provoke their discomfort. Humor is an acceptable way for people to acknowledge a problem and to relieve tension without having to confess weaknesses. In this case, joking also lets other students know that they are not alone with the problem.

When the others are talking it's usually about unusual stuff, like jokes about huge breasts. . . . Talking in small groups would help. The sexual aspect is there. Are they normal or abnormal? What's going on? (Second-year male)

The way we talk. Before we wouldn't talk about the penis or vagina. Now we do casually, with folks in medicine. And we say more about what's happening with us sexually. Lots of comments about ejaculation, orgasms, getting it back in less than 20 minutes, that kind of thing. Some of it is serious learning conversation. Sometimes it's just joking banter. (Second-year female)

By redefining the situation as at least partially humorous, students reassure themselves that they can handle the challenge. They believe that the problem can't be so serious if there is a funny side to it. Joking also allows them to relax a little and to set ideals aside for a time.

Where do students learn to joke in this way? The faculty, including the residents (who are the real teachers on the clinical teams), participate freely, teaching the students that humor is an acceptable way to talk about uncomfortable encounters in medicine.

We get all our grandmotherly types around the first day of (gross anatomy) lab, in case some of (the students) wimp out. Wonder why it's such a problem. (Faculty member)

If I had to examine her I'd toss my cookies. I mean she is enormous. That's it! Put it in the chart! Breasts too large for examination! (Resident) (The team had just commented on a variety of disturbing behaviors that they observed with the patient.)

None of these comments is particularly funny out of context and without the gestures and tone of voice that faculty members use to embellish their words. Yet the humor is evident in person. . . . Eager to please the faculty and to manage their emotions, students quickly adopt the faculty's humor. Joking about patients and procedures means sharing something special with the faculty, becoming a colleague. The idea implicit in the humor, that feelings are real despite the rule against discussing them, is combined with an important sense of "we-ness" that the students value.

Unlike the students' other strategies, joking occurs primarily when they are alone with other medical professionals. Jokes are acceptable in the hallways, over coffee, or in physicians' workrooms, but usually are unacceptable when outsiders might overhear. Joking is backstage behavior. Early in their training, students sometimes make jokes in public, perhaps to strengthen their identity as "medical student," but most humor is in-house, reserved for those who share the problem and have a sense of humor about it.

Avoiding the Contact

Students sometimes avoid the kinds of contact that give rise to unwanted emotions. They control the visual field during contact, and eliminate or abbreviate particular kinds of contact.

We did make sure that it was covered. The parts we weren't working on. The head, the genitals. All of it really. It is important to keep them wrapped and moist, so they wouldn't get moldy. That made sense. But when the cloth slipped, someone made sure to cover it back up, even if just a little (pubic) hair showed. (First-year female)

Keeping personal body parts covered in the lab and in examinations prevents mold, maintains a sterile field, and protects the patient's modesty. Covers also eliminate disturbing sites and protect students from their feelings. Such nonprofessional purposes are sometimes most important. Some students, for example, examine the breasts by reaching under the patient's gown, bypassing the visual examination emphasized in training.

Students also avoid contact by abbreviating or eliminating certain parts of the physical examination, moving or looking away, or being absent. Absence is usually not an option, but many students use the less obvious variations.

I had most trouble with the genitalia. . . . Quite an ordeal. Taking the skin off. The girls did the actual dissection. I went into the corner and read. Turned my back. Didn't want to be involved. (First-year male)

At the genitals, I was embarrassed. I had never touched a guy's genitals before. Even though this was medical, it was a pretty quick exam. I mimicked the preceptor, but I didn't really have any knowledge of it. It was not comfortable. (Second-year female)

The students explain their limited and "deferred" examinations by claiming inexperience or appealing to the patient's needs: "Four or five others will be doing it. Why should I make the patient uncomfortable?" Some students admit they use these arguments to avoid or postpone disturbing contact.

Conveniently, the faculty do not supervise students' contact with patients in the second and third years. When the faculty members are present they do the work themselves, leaving the students to observe. This lack of supervision gives students the freedom to learn without the pressure of criticism. It also gives them opportunities to avoid the kinds of contact that make them uncomfortable.

Also, faculty members protect students from contact with the parts of the body that make them most uneasy. There is no pressure to continue with "surface anatomy," where students examine each other in the region of the body to be dissected. In fact, students stop after the first three or four sessions; some students do not participate at all. There are limits on the range of physical examination skills that the students practice with

each other and in the gynecological training session: the student does not examine the breasts and does not conduct the rectal component of the examination in this session. There is a policy excluding the genitals and the rectum in practice sessions with patients in the second year. The faculty rarely challenge students who "defer" the breast, rectal, and genital examinations in the clerkships, and they abbreviate such contact in their own work.

Mostly, (the residents) don't do the breasts, pelvic, or rectal. We had a woman with a vaginal discharge (noted in the chart), but I didn't do a pelvic on the workup. Almost never. Sometimes a quick external check. That is the extent of their concern. For most docs and residents those are outside their area of expertise. If they think an exam should be done, they call in a consult, like GYN. . . . On medicine, the rectal is often important. I did a couple. Hopefully, the resident or attending did it. We thought we should do screening on the breasts, but I only did one or two. (Third-year male).

If you skip the genitals or rectal, and you note "exam deferred" in the chart, there's no problem. Sometimes they tell you to go ahead and do it, but there's no problem. So long as they don't think you just forgot. Just say "pelvic deferred." (Third-year female)

Silent acceptance of the boundary around the sexual parts of the body suggests that the faculty *do* regard and treat the sexual body as "different," despite the official line (neutrality) that conceals the difference. As neutrality fails and feelings arise, the faculty give the students, and themselves, permission to reduce or eliminate the kinds of contact they find most upsetting.

Taking Medicine Home

In their studies, students gradually come to see the human body as an interesting object, separate from the person. This new, intellectualized body is stripped of the meanings the students knew before coming to medical school. The impersonal body is relatively neutral and easy to contact clinically, but students have a vague and unsettling sense of loss.

The heart. I know it's just a blood pump. Mostly muscle. Valves. But it's something more, too. Interesting to touch it, see it. But it felt funny. Like (pause) I went up in my head when we lifted out his heart. Funny feeling (pause) partly physical. Won't be any place to go when we open his head. (First-year female)

I had to confront the fact that we are just flesh, made of flesh, like the animals we eat. It took a week to work it out, partly. (Second-year male)

According to the official perspective of the school, the body is "just" a complex object. The heart may be an awesome, marvelous pump, but something which has been valuable is lost during professionalization. Mysterious and romantic meanings are publicly discarded, and students are not sure what their world will be like without them. They try to shift culturally sacred meanings from the body to the abstract person, and their efforts do diminish the uncomfortable feelings that spill over into medicine from their personal lives. Yet the new perspective is sometimes awkward at school, and it creates other issues for students as medical neutrality spills over into their personal lives.

For some students, medical training creates a problem as new meanings for the body and for body contact go home with them at night. The clinical perspective enters into moments of contact with spouses and friends, an arena where personal meanings are important.

I have learned enough to find gross problems. And they taught us that breast cancer is one of the biggest threats to a woman's health. OK. So I can offer my expertise. But I found myself examining her, right in the middle of making love. Not cool! (Second year male)

I'm learning, but it's still a little uncomfortable. I'm sure glad I could talk about it with my wife. It felt like something about my masculinity. In GYN you don't think so much in sexual terms. Not with that big piece of metal (the speculum) in her. But there's no metal at home, and I still don't feel the same about it. They say you get over this pretty quick. I wonder how. What will it be like later? (Third-year male)

Particularly in the sexual domain, the progressive neutralization of the body threatens personal meanings that the students have long attached to physical intimacy. Without alternative meanings that could promise a comparable sense of attachment and gratification, some students fear that the special power of intimacy may be lost as they neu-

tralize the body for medicine. Acknowledging the threatening quality of intimacy in personal life, some students are also concerned that they may bring their emotion management strategies home and use them in unhealthy ways to minimize personal pains.

For other students, neutralizing the body at school helps them to achieve greater intimacy at home. If intimacy has been over romanticized in their personal relationships, for example, it can become less awesome and more manageable as they redefine it for medicine.

Well, it's been fun, trying things on him. I'd practice things like the ear exam, or (pause) we didn't do the (male) genitals at school. I tried it at home. He was real good about it, and I think I learned something. I was glad to have a chance before trying it on a real patient. And we talked afterward, more than we usually do. (Second-year female)

I had fallen way behind in touching (in my personal life). It had gotten so touching wasn't an option for me. But I'm catching up. It's an option. It's allowed. Almost like I'm practicing on my patients. . . . I don't know if that makes sense. Like I have been blocking on touching every time. But with patients I get beyond the blocks, and I can sense a little of what it's like. Look! I'm out here beyond the blocks, and it's OK! Then I can try it a little more in my personal life. (Third-year female)

As some special meanings are stripped away, these students can proceed more comfortably with personal intimacy. Their training demystifies physical intimacy, making it easier to discuss it with personal partners. In some cases they find it easier to initiate contact. Whether the effect is comfortable or threatening, the fact that students bring home their professional perspective on the body indicates the strength of the training process, particularly as it affects the personal body. Maintaining a personal perspective at home becomes yet another challenge that many students face.

Conclusion

Medical students sometimes feel attracted to or disgusted by the human body. They want to do something about these feelings, but they find that the topic is taboo. Even among themselves, students generally refrain from talking about their problem. Yet despite the silence, the culture and organization of medical school provide students with supports and guidelines for managing their emotions. Affective socialization proceeds with no deliberate control, but with profound effect. . . .

Analytic transformation is the students' primary [emotion management] strategy, and it does tend to produce affective neutrality. As we stated, however, the medical culture provides other strategies that involve strong feelings instead of the neutrality of medical ideals. The particular feelings allowed by faculty members and by the culture fit with the basis of all occupations that have achieved the honorific title of "profession": acquiring hierarchical distance from clients (if not always emotional indifference). Much of the humor that students learn puts down patients who are aesthetically, psychologically, or socially undesirable. . . . Blaming patients and avoiding uncomfortable contact lend power to the physician's role. Even the effort to accentuate the comfortable feelings which come with learning contributes to the distance. In concentrating on the medical problem, students distance themselves from their patients. . . . All of these strategies maintain the kind of professional distance that characterizes modern medical culture, a distance which provides for comfortable objectivity as well as scientific medical care.

One of the students' strategies, however, operates differently. Empathizing with patients diminishes the students' discomfort and directs attention to the patient's feelings and circumstances. Students are taught that excessive concern for patients can cloud their clinical judgment, but moderate concern allows them to manage their own feelings *and* to pay close attention to the patient. . . .

We suspect that the patterns we found in medical education occur as well in other professional schools and situations. Most health professionals face similar challenges and maintain a similar silence about them (Pope, Keith-Spiegel, and Tabachnik 1986). Comparably provocative challenges exist elsewhere, requiring potentially similar strategies of change and control. . . .

Our study suggests that the emotional socialization of professional training will influence the character of performance in the workplace and will have consequences for life outside the workplace. Medical students accept that they must change their perspective on the body in order to practice medicine, but they worry about the consequences. Often using the word "desensitization," they are concerned that medical training will dull their emotional responses too generally.

> Those feelings just get in the way. They don't fit, and I'm going to learn to get rid of them. Don't know how yet, and some of the possibilities are scary. What's left when you succeed? But what choice is there? (Second-year female)

> It's kind of dehumanizing. We just block off the feelings, and I don't know what happens to them. This is pretty important to me. I'm working to keep a sense of myself through all this. (Third-year male)

Quietly, because their concern is private and therefore uncertain, students ask questions we might all ask. Will we lose our sensitivity to those we serve? To others in our lives? To ourselves? Will we even know it is happening?

References

Haas, J. and W. Shaffir. 1977. "The Professionalization of Medical Students: Developing Competence and a Cloak of Competence." *Symbolic Interaction* 1: 71–88.

Hochschild, A. 1983. *The Managed Heart.* Berkeley: University of California Press.

Lief, H. and R. Fox. 1963. "Training for Detached Concern in Medical Students." Pp. 12–35 in *The Psychological Basis of Medical Practice*, edited by H. Lief. New York: Harper and Row.

Parsons, T. 1951. *The Social System.* New York: Free Press.

Pope, K., P. Keith-Spiegel, and B. Tabachnik. 1986. "Sexual Attraction to Clients: The Human Therapist and the (Sometimes) Inhuman Training System." *American Psychologist* 42(2): 147–158.

Part IV

The Self and Social Interaction

The self not only arises in social experience, as discussed in Part II, but is also sustained and changed through social interaction. The individual continually interacts with others. Each of those interactions provides the individual with reflected images of himself or herself. The way that others respond to the individual conveys their attitude toward him or her; and, as Cooley and Mead explained, the individual takes each attitude in kind. The self-images reflected in others' responses to the individual sometimes confirm, occasionally undermine, and gradually alter the individual's view of himself or herself.

However, the individual is not a passive participant in these interactions with others. Social interaction is a process of mutual influence. The individual influences as much how others view and respond to her or him as they influence the individual. Through influence over others, the individual can shape the very self-images that others reflect back. Moreover, the individual converses with herself or himself, whether interacting with others or alone.

The individual can inwardly challenge and counter the self-images that external life reflects, at least for a while. One's inner conversations may temporarily drown out others' external voices, especially if they are not in unison. If they are, however, the individual will have difficulty preventing those voices from echoing throughout these inward conversations.

The selections in this section address various aspects of the interrelationship between the self and social interaction. They examine how individuals influence others' views of them, how reflected self-images influence and sometimes transform individuals' views of themselves, how individuals resist the influence of social experience, and how they collectively construct stories about themselves and, thereby, their identities. These selections collectively demonstrate the old adage that no man or woman is an island or, more accurately, that no self is. Rather, the human self rests on the shifting sands of social experience. ✦

12

The Presentation of Self

Erving Goffman

The name Erving Goffman is virtually synonymous with microsociology. Throughout his life, Goffman argued that social interaction should be studied as a topic in its own right. He maintained that social interaction has its own logic and structure, regardless of the participants' personality characteristics or the social organizational and institutional context in which it occurs. That position is the basis for Goffman's very novel and influential analysis of the self. He was not interested in the individual's subjective self or inner conversations but rather in the social definition and construction of the public self during social interaction.

Goffman's approach to this topic is commonly described as dramaturgical. That is, Goffman views the self, social interaction, and life as dramatic or theatrical productions. Individuals are social actors who play different parts in the varied scenes of social life. Every time individuals interact with one another, they enact a self, influencing others' definition of them and of the situation. They usually arrive at a working consensus concerning the definition of each other's self and of the situation that consequently guides their interaction. Although social actors' performances are sometimes clumsy and unconvincing, they generally cooperate to save each other's individual shows and their collective show as a whole.

Goffman's dramaturgical analysis is more than a creative use of metaphor. We humans cannot peer into one another's hearts and minds, nor can we ever know another's "real" or "true" self. Our knowledge of each other is limited to what we can observe. Our definition of one another's self is necessarily based on appearance, conduct, and the settings in which we interact. In turn, we present a self to one another through how we look and act, and where we go. Regardless of whether these self-presentations are intentional or unintentional, honest or dishonest, they are nonetheless performances. The self is not a material thing that the individual carries around and can show others. It must be dramatically realized on each and every occasion of social interaction.

Goffman wrote this selection in the 1950s and a few of his illustrative examples trade upon prevailing stereotypes of women at that time. Although contemporary readers may find those dated examples to be sexist, they do not detract from Goffman's insight into the drama of everyday social life.

When an individual enters the presence of others, they commonly seek to acquire information about him or to bring into play information about him already possessed. They will be interested in his general socio-economic status, his conception of self, his attitude toward them, his competence, his trustworthiness, etc. Although some of this information seems to be sought almost as an end in itself, there are usually quite practical reasons for acquiring it. Information about the individual helps to define the situation, enabling others to know in advance what he will expect of them and what they may expect of him. Informed in these ways, the others will know how best to act in order to call forth a desired response from him.

For those present, many sources of information become accessible and many carriers (or "sign-vehicles") become available for conveying this information. If unacquainted with the individual, observers can glean clues from his conduct and appearance which allow them to apply their previous experience with individuals roughly similar to the one before them or, more important, to apply untested stereotypes to him. They can also assume from past experience that only individuals of a particular kind are likely to be found in a given social setting. They can rely on what the individual says about himself or on documentary evidence he provides as to who and what he is. If they know, or know of, the individual by virtue of experience prior to the interaction, they can rely on assumptions as to the persistence and generality of psychological traits as a means of predicting his present and future behavior.

However, during the period in which the individual is in the immediate presence of the others, few events may occur which directly provide the others with the conclusive information they will need, if they are to direct wisely their own activity. Many crucial facts lie beyond the time and place of interaction or lie concealed within it. For example, the "true" or "real" attitudes, beliefs, and emotions of the individual can be ascertained only indirectly, through his avowals or through what appears to be involuntary expressive behavior. Similarly, if the individual offers the others a product or service, they will often find that during the interaction there will be no time and place immediately available for eating the pudding that the proof can be found in. They will be forced to accept some events as conventional or natural signs of something not directly available to the senses. In Ichheiser's terms,[1] the individual will have to act so that he intentionally or unintentionally expresses himself, and the others will in turn have to be *impressed* in some way by him.

Taking communication in both its narrow and broad sense, one finds that when the individual is in the immediate presence of others, his activity will have a promissory character. The others are likely to find that they must accept the individual on faith, offering him a just return, while he is present before them, in exchange for something whose true value will not be established until after he has left their presence. (Of course, the others also live by inference in their dealings with the physical world, but it is only in the world of social interaction that the objects about which they make inferences will purposely facilitate and hinder this inferential process.) The security that they justifiably feel in making inferences about the individual will vary, of course, depending on such factors as the amount of information they already possess about him; but no amount of such past evidence can entirely obviate the necessity of acting on the basis of inferences.

Let us now turn from the others to the point of view of the individual who presents himself before them. He may wish them to think highly of him, or to think that he thinks highly of them, or to perceive how in fact he feels toward them, or to obtain no clear-cut impression; he may wish to ensure sufficient harmony, so that the interaction can be sustained, or to defraud, get rid of, confuse, mislead, antagonize, or insult them. Regardless of the particular objective which the individual has in mind and of his motive for having this objective, it will be in his interests to control the conduct of the others, especially their responsive treatment of him. This control is achieved largely by influencing the definition of the situation which the others come to formulate, and he can influence this definition by expressing himself in

such a way as to give them the kind of impression that will lead them to act voluntarily in accordance with his own plan. Thus, when an individual appears in the presence of others, there will usually be some reason for him to mobilize his activity, so that it will convey an impression to others, which it is in his interests to convey. Since a girl's dormitory mates will glean evidence of her popularity from the calls she receives on the phone, we can suspect that some girls will arrange for calls to be made, and Willard Waller's finding can be anticipated:

> It has been reported by many observers that a girl who is called to the telephone in the dormitories will often allow herself to be called several times, in order to give all the other girls ample opportunity to hear her paged.[2]

I have said that when an individual appears before others, his actions will influence the definition of the situation which they come to have. Sometimes the individual will act in a thoroughly calculating manner, expressing himself in a given way solely in order to give the kind of impression to others that is likely to evoke from them a specific response he is concerned to obtain. Sometimes the individual will be calculating in his activity but be relatively unaware that this is the case. Sometimes he will intentionally and consciously express himself in a particular way, but chiefly because the tradition of his group or social status require this kind of expression and not because of any particular response (other than vague acceptance or approval) that is likely to be evoked from those impressed by the expression. Sometimes the traditions of an individual's role will lead him to give a well-designed impression of a particular kind, and yet he may be neither consciously nor unconsciously disposed to create such an impression. The others, in their turn, may be suitably impressed by the individual's efforts to convey something, or may misunderstand the situation and come to conclusions that are warranted neither by the individual's intent nor by the facts. In any case, in so far as the others act *as if* the individual had conveyed a particular impression, we may take a functional or pragmatic view and say that the individual has "effectively" projected a given definition of the situation and "effectively" fostered the understanding that a given state of affairs obtains.

There is one aspect of the others' response that bears special comment here. Knowing that the individual is likely to present himself in a light that is favorable to him, the others may divide what they witness into two parts: a part that is relatively easy for the individual to manipulate at will, being chiefly his verbal assertions, and a part in regard to which he seems to have little concern or control, being chiefly derived from the expressions he gives off. The others may then use what are considered to be the ungovernable aspects of his expressive behavior as a check upon the validity of what is conveyed by the governable aspects. In this a fundamental asymmetry is demonstrated in the communication process, the individual presumably being aware of only one stream of his communication, the witnesses of this stream and of one other. For example, in Shetland Isle one crofter's wife, in serving native dishes to a visitor from the mainland of Britain, would listen with a polite smile to his polite claims of liking what he was eating; at the same time, she would take note of the rapidity with which the visitor lifted his fork or spoon to his mouth, the eagerness with which he passed food into his mouth, and the gusto expressed in chewing the food, using these signs as a check on the stated feelings of the eater. The same woman, in order to discover what one acquaintance (A) "actually" thought of another acquaintance (B), would wait until B was in the presence of A but engaged in conversation with still another person (C). She would then covertly examine the facial expressions of A as he regarded B in conversation with C. Not being in conversation with B, and not being directly observed by him, A would sometimes relax usual constraints and tactful deceptions, and freely express what he was "actually" feeling about B. This Shetlander, in short, would observe the unobserved observer.

Now given the fact that others are likely to check up on the more controllable aspects of behavior by means of the less controllable, one can expect that sometimes the individual will try to exploit this very possibility, guiding the impression he makes through behavior felt to be reliably informing. For example, in gaining admission to a tight social circle, the participant observer may not only wear an accepting look while listening to an informant, but may also be careful to wear the same look when observing the informant talking to others; observers of the observer will then not as easily discover where he actually stands. A specific illustration may be cited from Shetland Isle. When a neighbor dropped in to have a cup of tea, he would ordinarily wear at least a hint of an expectant warm smile as he passed through the door into the cottage. Since lack of physical obstructions outside the cottage and lack of light within it usually made it possible to observe the visitor unobserved as he approached the house, islanders sometimes took pleasure in watching the visitor drop whatever expression he was manifesting and replace it with a sociable one just before reaching the door. However, some visitors, in appreciating that this examination was occurring, would blindly adopt a social face a long distance from the house, thus ensuring the projection of a constant image.

This kind of control upon the part of the individual reinstates the symmetry of the communication process, and sets the stage for a kind of information game—a potentially infinite cycle of concealment, discovery, false revelation, and rediscovery. It should be added that since the others are likely to be relatively unsuspicious of the presumably unguided aspect of the individual's conduct, he can gain much by controlling it. The others, of course, may sense that the individual is manipulating the presumably spontaneous aspects of his behavior, and seek in this very act of manipulation some shading of conduct that the individual has not managed to control. This again provides a check upon the individual's behavior, this time his presumably uncalculated behavior, thus re-establishing the asymmetry of the communication process. Here, I would like only to add the suggestion that the arts of piercing an individual's effort at calculated unintentionality seem better developed than our capacity to manipulate our own behavior; so that, regardless of how many steps have occurred in the information game, the witness is likely to have the advantage over the actor, and the initial asymmetry of the communication process is likely to be retained.

When we allow that the individual projects a definition of the situation when he appears before others, we must also see that the others, however passive their role may seem to be, will themselves effectively project a definition of the situation by virtue of their response to the individual and by virtue of any lines of action they initiate to him. Ordinarily, the definitions of the situation projected by the several different participants are sufficiently attuned to one another so that open contradiction will not occur. I do not mean that there will be the kind of consensus that arises when each individual present candidly expresses what he really feels and honestly agrees with the expressed feelings of the others present. This kind of harmony is an optimistic ideal and in any case not necessary for the smooth working of society. Rather, each participant is expected to suppress his immediate heartfelt feelings, conveying a view of the situation which he feels the others will be able to find at least temporarily acceptable. The maintenance of this surface of agreement, this veneer of consensus, is facilitated by each participant concealing his own wants behind statements which assert values to which everyone present feels obliged to give lip service. Further, there is usually a kind of division of definitional labor. Each participant is allowed to establish the tentative official ruling regarding matters which are vital to him but not immediately important to others, e.g., the rationalizations and justifications by which he accounts for his past activity. In exchange for this courtesy, he remains silent or non-committal on matters important to others but not immediately important to him. We have then a kind of interactional *modus vivendi*. Together, the participants contribute to a single over-all definition of the situation, which involves not so much a real agreement as to what exists, but rather a real agreement as to whose claims concerning what issues will be temporarily honored. Real agreement will also exist concerning the desirability of avoiding an open conflict of definitions of the situation. I will refer to this level of agreement as a "working consensus." It is to be understood that the working consensus established in one interaction setting will be quite different in content from the working consensus established in a different type of setting. Thus, between two friends at lunch, a reciprocal show of affection, respect, and concern for the other is maintained. In service occupations, on the other hand, the specialist often maintains an image of disinterested involvement in the problem of the client; while the client responds with a show of respect for the competence and integrity of the specialist. Regardless of such differences in content, however, the general form of these working arrangements is the same.

In noting the tendency for a participant to accept the definitional claims made by the others present, we can appreciate the crucial importance of the information that the individual *initially* possesses or acquires concerning his fellow participants; for it is on the basis of this initial information that the individual starts to define the situation and starts to build up lines of responsive action. The individual's initial projection commits him to what he is proposing to be and requires him to drop all pretenses of being other things. As the interaction among the participants progresses, additions and modifications in this initial informational state will of course occur, but it is essential that these later developments be related without contradiction to, and even built up from, the initial positions taken by the several participants. It would seem that an individual can more easily make a choice as to what line of treatment to demand from and extend to the others present at the beginning of an encounter than he can alter the line of treatment that is being pursued, once the interaction is under way.

In everyday life, of course, there is a clear understanding that first impressions are important. Thus, the work adjustment of those in service occupations will often hinge upon a capacity to seize and hold the initiative in the service relation, a capacity that will require subtle aggressiveness on the part of the server when he is of lower socio-economic status than his client. W. F. Whyte suggests the waitress as an example:

> The first point that stands out is that the waitress who bears up under pressure does not simply respond to her customers. She acts with some skill to control their behavior. The first question to ask when we look at the customer relationship is, 'Does the waitress get the jump on the customer, or does the customer get the jump on the waitress?' The skilled waitress realizes the crucial nature of this question. . . .
>
> The skilled waitress tackles the customer with confidence and without hesitation. For example, she may find that a new customer has seated himself before she could clear off the dirty dishes and change the cloth. He is now leaning on the table studying the menu. She greets him, says, "May I change the cover, please?" and, without waiting for an answer, takes his menu away from him so that he moves back from the table, and she goes about her work. The relationship is handled politely

but firmly, and there is never any question as to who is in charge.[3]

When the interaction that is initiated by "first impressions" is itself merely the initial interaction in an extended series of interactions involving the same participants, we speak of "getting off on the right foot" and feel that it is crucial that we do so. Thus, one learns that some teachers take the following view:

> You can't ever let them get the upper hand on you or you're through. So I start out tough. The first day I get a new class in, I let them know who's boss. . . . You've got to start off tough, then you can ease up as you go along. If you start out easy-going, when you try to get tough, they'll just look at you and laugh.[4]

Similarly, attendants in mental institutions may feel that, if the new patient is sharply put in his place the first day on the ward and made to see who is boss, much future difficulty will be prevented.

Given the fact that the individual effectively projects a definition of the situation when he enters the presence of others, we can assume that events may occur within the interaction which contradict, discredit, or otherwise throw doubt upon this projection. When these disruptive events occur, the interaction itself may come to a confused and embarrassed halt. Some of the assumptions upon which the responses of the participants had been predicated become untenable, and the participants find themselves lodged in an interaction for which the situation has been wrongly defined and is now no longer defined. At such moments the individual whose presentation has been discredited may feel ashamed, while the others present may feel hostile; and all the participants may come to feel ill at ease, nonplussed, out of countenance, embarrassed, experiencing the kind of anomy that is generated when the minute social system of face-to-face interaction breaks down.

In stressing the fact that the initial definition of the situation projected by an individual tends to provide a plan for the co-operative activity that follows—in stressing this action point of view—we must not overlook the crucial fact that any projected definition of the situation also has a distinctive moral character. It is this moral character of projections that will chiefly concern us in this report. Society is organized on the principle that any individual who possesses certain social characteristics has a moral right to expect that others will value and treat him in an appropriate way. Connected with this principle is a second, namely that an individual who implicitly or explicitly signifies that he has certain social characteristics ought in fact to be what he claims he is. In consequence, when an individual projects a definition of the situation and thereby makes an implicit or explicit claim to be a person of a particular kind, he automatically exerts a moral demand upon the others, obliging them to value and treat him in the manner that persons of his kind have a right to expect. He also implicitly foregoes all claims to be things he does not appear to be and, hence, foregoes the treatment that would be appropriate for such individuals. The others find, then, that the individual has informed them as to what is and as to what they *ought* to see as the "is."

One cannot judge the importance of definitional disruptions by the frequency with which they occur, for apparently they would occur more frequently, were not constant precautions taken. We find that preventive practices are constantly employed to avoid these embarrassments and that corrective practices are constantly employed to compensate for discrediting occurrences that have not been successfully avoided. When the individual employs these strategies and tactics to protect his own projections, we may refer to them as "defensive practices"; when a participant employs them to save the definition of the situation projected by another, we speak of "protective practices" or "tact." Together, defensive and protective practices comprise the techniques employed to safeguard the impression fostered by an individual during his presence before others. It should be added that, while we may be ready to see that no fostered impression would survive if defensive practices were not employed, we are less ready perhaps to see that few impressions could survive, if those who received the impression did not exert tact in their reception of it.

In addition to the fact that precautions are taken to prevent disruption of projected definitions, we may also note that an intense interest in these disruptions comes to play a significant role in the social life of the group. Practical jokes and social games are played, in which embarrassments which are to be taken unseriously are purposely engineered. Fantasies are created, in which devastating exposures occur. Anecdotes from the past—real, embroidered, or fictitious—are told and retold, detailing disruptions which occurred, almost occurred, or occurred and were admirably resolved. There seems to be no grouping which does not have a ready supply of these games, reveries, and cautionary tales, to be used as a source of humor, a catharsis for anxieties, and a sanction for inducing individuals to be modest in their claims and reasonable in their projected expectations. The individual may tell himself through dreams of getting into impossible positions. Families tell of the time a guest got his dates mixed and arrived when neither the house nor anyone in it was ready for him. Journalists tell of times when an all too meaningful misprint occurred, and the paper's assumption of objectivity or decorum was humorously discredited. Public servants tell of times a client ridiculously misunderstood form instructions, giving answers which implied an unanticipated and bizarre definition of the situation.[5] Seamen, whose home away from home is rigorously he-man, tell stories of coming back home and inadvertently asking mother to "pass the fucking butter."[6] Diplomats tell of the time a near-sighted queen asked a republican ambassador about the health of his king. . . .[7]

For the purpose of this report, interaction (that is, face-to-face interaction) may be roughly defined as the reciprocal influence of individuals upon one another's actions when in one another's immediate physical presence. An interaction may be defined as all the interaction which occurs throughout any one occasion when a given set of individuals are in one another's continuous presence; the term "an encounter" would do as well. A "performance" may be defined as all the activity of a given participant on a given occasion which serves to influence in any way any of the other participants. Taking a particular participant and his performance as a basic point of reference, we may refer to those who contribute the other performances as the audience, observers, or co-participants. The pre-established pattern of action, which is unfolded during a performance and which may be presented or played through on other occasions, may be called a "part" or "routine." . . .

When an individual plays a part, he implicitly requests his observers to take seriously the impression that is fostered before them. They are asked to believe that the character they see actually possesses the attributes he appears to possess,

that the task he performs will have the consequences that are implicitly claimed for it, and that, in general, matters are what they appear to be. In line with this, there is the popular view that the individual offers his performance and puts on his show "for the benefit of other people." It will be convenient to begin a consideration of performances by turning the question around and looking at the individual's own belief in the impression of reality that he attempts to engender in those among whom he finds himself.

At one extreme, one finds that the performer can be fully taken in by his own act; he can be sincerely convinced that the impression of reality which he stages is the real reality. When his audience is also convinced in this way about the show he puts on—and this seems to be the typical case—then, for the moment at least, only the sociologist or the socially disgruntled will have any doubts about the "realness" of what is presented.

At the other extreme, we find that the performer may not be taken in at all by his own routine. This possibility is understandable, since no one is in quite as good an observational position to see through the act as the person who puts it on. Coupled with this, the performer may be moved to guide the conviction of his audience only as a means to other ends, having no ultimate concern in the conception that they have of him or of the situation. When the individual has no belief in his own act and no ultimate concern with the beliefs of his audience, we may call him cynical, reserving the term "sincere" for individuals who believe in the impression fostered by their own performance. It should be understood that the cynic, with all his professional disinvolvement, may obtain unprofessional pleasures from his masquerade, experiencing a kind of gleeful spiritual aggression from the fact that he can toy at will with something his audience must take seriously.

It is not assumed, of course, that all cynical performers are interested in deluding their audiences for purposes of what is called "self-interest" or private gain. A cynical individual may delude his audience for what he considers to be their own good, or for the good of the community, etc. For illustrations of this we need not appeal to sadly enlightened showmen, such as Marcus Aurelius or Hsun Tzu. We know that in service occupations practitioners who may otherwise be sincere are sometimes forced to delude their customers, because their customers show such a heartfelt demand for it. Doctors who are led into giving placebos, filling-station attendants who resignedly check and recheck tire pressures for anxious women motorists, shoe clerks who sell a shoe that fits but tell the customer it is the size she wants to hear—these are cynical performers whose audiences will not allow them to be sincere. . . .

[W]hile the performance offered by impostors and liars is quite flagrantly false and differs in this respect from ordinary performances, both are similar in the care their performers must exert in order to maintain the impression that is fostered. Whether an honest performer wishes to convey the truth or whether a dishonest performer wishes to convey a falsehood, both must take care to enliven their performances with appropriate expressions, exclude from their performances expressions that might discredit the impression being fostered, and take care lest the audience impute unintended meanings. Because of these shared dramatic contingencies, we can profitably study performances that are quite false in order to learn about ones that are quite honest.

In our society, the character one performs and one's self are somewhat equated, and this self-as-character is usually seen as something housed within the body of its possessor, especially the upper parts thereof, being a nodule, somehow, in the psychobiology of personality. I suggest that this view is an implied part of what we are all trying to present, but provides, just because of this, a bad analysis of the presentation. In this report, the performed self was seen as some kind of image, usually creditable, which the individual on stage and in character effectively attempts to induce others to hold in regard to him. While this image is entertained *concerning* the individual, so that a self is imputed to him, this self itself does not derive from its possessor, but from the whole scene of his action, being generated by that attribute of local events which renders them interpretable by witnesses. A correctly staged and performed scene leads the audience to impute a self to a performed character, but this imputation—this self—is a *product* of a scene that comes off, and is not a *cause* of it. The self, then, as a performed character, is not an organic thing that has a specific location, whose fundamental fate is to be born, to mature, and to die; it is a dramatic effect arising diffusely from a scene that is presented, and the characteristic issue, the crucial concern, is whether it will be credited or discredited.

In analyzing the self, then, we are drawn from its possessor, from the person who will profit or lose most by it; for he and his body merely provide the peg on which something of collaborative manufacture will be hung for a time. And the means for producing and maintaining selves do not reside inside the peg; in fact, these means are often bolted down in social establishments. . . .

The whole machinery of self-production is cumbersome, of course, and sometimes breaks down, exposing its separate components. . . . But well oiled, impressions will flow from it fast enough to put us in the grips of one of our types of reality—the performance will come off, and the firm self accorded each performed character will appear to emanate intrinsically from its performer. . . .

In developing the conceptual framework employed in this report, some language of the stage was used. . . . [However], this report is not concerned with aspects of theater that creep into everyday life. It is concerned with the structure of social encounters—the structure of those entities in social life that come into being whenever persons enter one another's immediate physical presence. The key factor in this structure is the maintenance of a single definition of the situation, this definition having to be expressed, and this expression sustained in the face of a multitude of potential disruptions.

A character staged in a theater is not in some ways real, nor does it have the same kind of real consequences as does the thoroughly contrived character performed by a confidence man; but the *successful* staging of either of these types of false figures involves use of *real* techniques—the same techniques by which everyday persons sustain their real social situations. Those who conduct face-to-face interaction on a theater's stage must meet the key requirement of real situations, they must expressively sustain a definition of the situation, but this they do in circumstances that have facilitated their developing an apt terminology for the interactional tasks that all of us share.

Notes

1. Gustav Ichheiser, "Misunderstandings in Human Relations," Supplement to *The American Journal of Sociology,* LV (September 1949), pp. 6–7.

2. Willard Waller, "The Rating and Dating Complex," *American Sociological Review*, II, p. 730.

3. W. F. Whyte, "When Workers and Customers Meet," Chap. VII, *Industry and Society*, ed. W. F. Whyte (New York: McGraw-Hill, 1946), pp. 132–33.

4. Teacher interview quoted by Howard S. Becker, "Social Class Variations in the Teacher-Pupil Relationship," *Journal of Educational Sociology*, XXV, p. 459.

5. Peter Blau, "Dynamics of Bureaucracy" (Ph.D. dissertation, Department of Sociology, Columbia University, forthcoming, University of Chicago Press), pp. 127–29.

6. Walter M. Beattie, Jr., "The Merchant Seamen" (unpublished M.A. Report, Department of Sociology, University of Chicago, 1950), p. 35.

7. Sir Frederick Ponsonby, *Recollections of Three Reigns* (New York: Dutton, 1952), p. 46.

13

The Gloried Self

*Patricia Adler
and
Peter Adler*

This selection dramatically illustrates the interrelation between public self-images and individuals' self-concepts or sense of their "true" selves. Patricia and Peter Adler describe how sudden celebrity transformed the self-conceptions of players for a highly successful college basketball program. These players not only saw themselves reflected in others' treatment of them, but also on the television screen and in the pages of newspapers and magazines. The Adlers remind us that others' reactions to an individual are not the only source of self-images today. For celebrities at least, the mass media are also a source of stylized and often exaggerated self-images.

The Adlers also remind us that individuals are not passively molded by socially reflected or media images of themselves. With the encouragement of their coaches, the players attempted to resist the influence of both the hero worship by fans and media hype. Ultimately, however, the glory was too intoxicating and the media portrayals too seductive. What started out as a mere act to give reporters and fans what they expected became a trap. The more effectively the players presented themselves as the media portrayed them, the more the players thought of themselves in those terms.

As the Adlers observe, such celebrity and glory are not without cost. An individual's self-concept is usually multi-dimensional. It consists of an organized complex of social identities and corresponding self-evaluations. We each may think of ourselves as serious students, good friends, insensitive sons or daughters, relatively unattractive romantic partners, mediocre athletes, and so on. We may consider some of these identities more important than others, but we consider all dimensions of who and what we "really" are. It was just such multi-dimensionality that the basketball players sacrificed for glory. Their identity as basketball players engulfed other dimensions of their self-concepts. The Adlers describe how the brilliant glory of socially reflected and media self-images can blind an individual to other prior

or possible identities. They leave us to ponder the question, what might happen to such an individual's self-concept when his or her glory fades?

In this paper we describe and analyze a previously unarticulated form of self-identity: the "gloried" self, which arises when individuals become the focus of intense interpersonal and media attention, leading to their achieving celebrity. The articulation of the gloried self not only adds a new concept to our self-repertoire but also furthers our insight into self-concept formation in two ways: it illustrates one process whereby dynamic contradictions between internal and external pressures become resolved, and it highlights the ascendance of an unintended self-identity in the face of considerable resistance.

The development of the gloried self is an outgrowth of individuals becoming imbued with celebrity. . . . Development of a gloried self is caused in part by the treatment of individuals' selves as objects by others. A "public person" is created, usually by the media, which differs from individuals' private personas. These public images are rarely as intricate or as complex as individuals' [personal] selves; often, they draw on stereotypes or portray individuals in extreme fashion to accentuate their point. Yet the power of these media portrayals, reinforced by face-to-face encounters with people who hold these images, often causes individuals to objectify their selves to themselves. Individuals thus become initially alienated from themselves through the separation of their self-concept from the conception of their selves held by others. Ultimately, they resolve this disparity and reduce their alienation by changing their self-images to bridge the gap created by others' perceptions of them, even though they may fight this development as it occurs.

Characteristically, the gloried self is a greedy self, seeking to ascend in importance and to cast aside other self-dimensions as it grows. It is an intoxicating and riveting self, which overpowers other aspects of the individual and seeks increasing reinforcement to fuel its growth. Yet at the same time, its surge and display violate societal mores of modesty in both self-conception and self-presentation. Individuals thus become embroiled in inner conflict between their desire for recognition, flattery, and importance and the inclination to keep feeding this self-affirming element, and the socialization that urges them to fight such feelings and behavioral impulses. That the gloried self succeeds in flourishing, in spite of [the] individuals' struggle against it, testifies to its inherent power and its drive to eclipse other self-dimensions.

Drawing on ethnographic data gathered in a college athletics setting, we discuss the creation and the character of the gloried self, showing its effects on the individuals in whom it develops. . . . Over a five-year period (1980–1985), we conducted a participant-observation study of a major college basketball program. . . . The research was conducted at a medium-sized (6,000 students) private university (hereafter referred to as "the University") in the mid south central portion of the United States, with a predominantly white, suburban, middle-class student body. The basketball program was ranked in the top 40 of Division I NCAA schools throughout our research, and in the top 20 for most of two seasons. The team played in post-season tournaments every year, and in four complete seasons won approximately four times as many games as it lost. Players generally were recruited from the surrounding area; they were predominantly black (70 percent) and ranged from lower to middle class. . . . We analyze [these] athletes' experiences and discuss the aggrandizing effects of celebrity in fostering the gloried self's ascent to prominence. Then we look at the consequent changes and diminishments in the self that occur as the price of this self-aggrandizement. . . .

The Experience of Glory

Experiencing glory was exciting, intoxicating, and riveting. Two self-dimensions were either created or expanded in the athletes we studied: the reflected self and the media self. . . .

The Reflected Self

As a result of the face-to-face interactions between team members and people they encountered through their role as college athletes, the athletes' impressions of themselves were modified and changed. As Cooley (1902) and Mead (1934) were the first to propose, individuals engage in role-taking; their self-conceptions are products of social interaction, affected by the reflected impressions of others. According to

Cooley (1902), these "looking-glass" selves are formed through a combination of cognitive and affective forces; although individuals react intellectually to the impressions they perceive others are forming about them, they also develop emotional reactions about these judgments. Together, these reactions are instrumental in shaping their self-images. . . .

The forging and modification of reflected selves began as team members perceived how people *treated* them; subsequently, they formed *reactions* to that treatment. One of the first things they all noticed was that they were sought intensely by strangers. Large numbers of people, individually and in groups, wanted to be near them, to get their autographs, to touch them, and to talk to them. People treated them with awe and respect. One day, for example, the head coach walked out of his office and found a woman waiting for him. As he turned towards her, she threw herself in front of him and began to kiss his feet, all the while telling him what a great man he was. More commonly, fans who were curious about team matters approached players, trying to engage them in conversation. These conversations sometimes made the players feel awkward, because, although they wanted to be polite to their fans, they had little to say to them. Carrying on an interaction was often difficult. As one player said:

> People come walking up to you, and whether they're timid or pushy, they still want to talk. It's like, here's their hero talking face-to-face with them, and they want to say anything just so they can have a conversation with them. It's *hero-worshipping*. But what do you actually say to your hero when you see him?

These interactions, then, often took the form of ritualized pseudo-conversations, in which players and their fans offered each other stylized but empty words.

Many fans [identified the players] socially and expect[ed] them to respond in kind. Players found themselves thrust into a "psuedo-intimacy" (Bensman and Lilienfeld 1979) with these fans, who had seen them so often at games and on television. Yet their relationship with the players was one-sided; fans often expected players to reciprocate their feelings of intimacy. As a result of their celebrity, team members . . . were open to engagement in personal interaction with individuals whom they did not know at all.

Players also found themselves highly prized in interacting with boosters (financial supporters of the team). Boosters showered all players with invitations to their houses for team meetings or dinner. They fought jealously to have players seen with them or gossiped about as having been in their houses. It soon became apparent to players that boosters derived social status from associating with them. . . . This situation caused players to recognize that they were "glory bearers," so filled with glory that they could confer it on anyone by their mere presence. They experienced a sense of the "Midas touch": They had an attribute (fame) that everybody wanted and which could be transmitted. Their ability to cast glory onto others and their desirability to others because of this ability became an important dimension of their new, reflected self-identity.

The Media Self

A second dimension of the self created from the glory experience was influenced largely by media portrayals. . . . Most of the athletes who came to the University had received some media publicity in high school (68 percent); but the national level of the print and video coverage they received after arriving, coupled with the intensity of the constant focus, caused them to develop more compelling and more salient media selves than they had possessed previously.

Radio, television, and newspaper reporters covering the team often sought out athletes for "human interest" stories. These features presented media-framed angles that cast athletes into particular roles and tended to create new dimensions of their selves. Images were created from a combination of individuals' actual behavior and reporters' ideas of what made good copy. Thus, through media coverage, athletes were cast into molds that frequently were distorted or exaggerated reflections of their behavior and self-conceptions.

Team members, for whom the media had created roles, felt as if they had to live up to these portrayals. For instance, two players were depicted as "good students"—shy, quiet, religious, and diligent. Special news features emphasized their outstanding traits, illustrating how they went regularly to class, were humanitarian, and cared about graduating. Yet one of them lamented:

> Other kids our age, they go to the fair and they walk around with a beer in their hand, or a cigarette; but if me and Dan were to do that, then people would talk about that. We can't go over to the clubs, or hang around, without it relaying back to Coach. We can't even do things around our teammates, because they expect us to be a certain way. The media has created this image of us as the "good boys," and now we have to live up to it.

Other players (about 20 percent) were embraced for their charismatic qualities; they had naturally outgoing personalities and the ability to excite a crowd. These players capitalized on the media coverage, exaggerating their antics to gain attention and fame. Yet the more they followed the media portrayal, the more likely it was to turn into a caricature of their selves. One player described how he felt when trapped by his braggart media self:

> I used to like getting in the paper. When reporters came around, I would make those Mohammed Ali type outbursts—I'm gonna do this, I'm gonna do that. And they come around again, stick a microphone in your face, 'cause they figure somewhere Washington will have another outburst. But playing that role died out in me. I think sometimes the paper pulled out a little too much from me that wasn't me. But people seen me as what the paper said, and I had to play that role.

Particular roles notwithstanding, all the players shared the media-conferred sense of self as celebrity. Raised to the status of stars, larger than life, they regularly read their names and statements in the newspaper, saw their faces on television, or heard themselves whispered about on campus. One team member described the consequences of this celebrity:

> We didn't always necessarily agree with the way they wrote about us in the paper, but people who saw us expected us to be like what they read there. A lot of times it made us feel uncomfortable, acting like that, but we had to act like they expected us to, for the team's sake. We had to act like this was what we was really like.

Ironically, however, the more they interacted with people through their dramaturgically induced media selves, the more many of the team members felt familiar and comfortable with those selves ("We know what to do, we don't have to think about it no more"). The media presented the selves and the public believed in them, so the athletes continued to portray them. Even though they attempted to moderate these selves, part of them pressed for their legitimacy and acceptance. Over time, the athletes believed these portrayals increasingly and transformed their behavior into more than mere "impression management" (Goffman 1959). . . . [They] went through a gradual process of . . . becoming more engrossed or more deeply involved in their media selves. The recurrent social situations of their everyday lives served as the foils against which both their public and their private selves developed. The net effect of having these selves placed upon them and of interacting through them with others was that athletes eventually integrated them into their core self.

Self-Aggrandizement

Athletes were affected profoundly by encounters with the self-images reflected onto them by others, both in person and through the media. It was exciting and gratifying to be cast as heroes. Being presented with these images and feeling obligated to interact with people through them, athletes added a new self to their repertoire: a glorified self. This self had a greater degree of aggrandizement than their previous identities. The athletes may have dreamed of glory, but until now they had never formed a structured set of relationships with people who accorded it to them. Yet although they wanted to accept and enjoy this glory, to allow themselves to incorporate it into a full-blown self-identity, they felt hesitant and guilty. They wrestled with the competing forces of their desires for extravagant pleasure and pride and the normative guidelines of society, which inhibited these desires. The athletes' struggle with factors inhibiting and enhancing their self-aggrandizement shows how and why they ultimately developed gloried selves.

Inhibiting Factors

Players knew they had to be careful both about feeling important and about showing these feelings. The norms of our society dictate a more modest, more self-effacing stance. Consequently, the players worked hard to suppress their growing feelings of self-aggrandizement in several ways. First, they drew on their own feelings of *fear* and *insecurity*. Although it violated the norms of their peer culture to reveal these feelings, most of the athletes we interviewed (92 percent) had doubts or worries about their playing abilities or futures.

Second, they tried to *discount* the flattery of others as exaggerated or false. . . . Athletes . . . tended to evaluate their behavior less globally than did their audience and to interpret their successes as based less on their own outstanding characteristics than on some complex interaction of circumstances.

Third, the athletes' feelings of importance and superiority were constrained by the actions of the coach and by the norms of their peer subculture. For his part, the coach tried to keep players' self-aggrandizement in check by *puncturing* them whenever he thought they were becoming too "puffed" (conceited). He "dragged" (criticized, mocked) them both in team meetings and in individual sessions, trying to achieve the right balance of confidence and humility.

In addition, players punctured their teammates by ridiculing each other publicly in their informal sessions in the dorms. Each one claimed to be the best player on the team, and had little praise for others. The athletes did not actually think their teammates had no talent; rather, the peer subculture allowed little room for "glory passing." As a result, except for the braggarts (about 20 percent of the group), none of the players expressed in public how good they felt and how much they enjoyed being treated as stars. Instead, they tried largely to suppress the feelings of excitement, intoxication, and aggrandizement, not to let themselves be influenced by the reflected sense of glory. As one player remarked:

> You feel it coming up on you and you know you got to fight it. You can't be letting your head get all out of control.

Fourth, the coach helped to *normalize* the athletes' experiences and reactions by placing them in the occupational perspective. Being adulated was part of the job, he believed, and this job was no more special than any other. . . . He conveyed this sense of occupational duty to his players and assistants. Like him, they had to "get with the program," to play to the public and help support people's sense of involvement with the team. In public, then, players feigned intimacy with total strangers and allowed themselves to be worshiped, meanwhile being told that this was merely a job.

Enhancing Factors

Yet as tired as they were, as repetitive as this behavior became, the athletes knew that this job was unlike any other. The excitement, the centrality, and the secrecy, which did not exist in the everyday world made this arena different. As one assistant coach explained:

> The times were exciting. There was always something going on, something happening, some new event occurring each day. We felt like we were newsmakers, we were important. We touched so many more lives, were responsible for so many more people, and so many more people cared, wanted to know something from us. It was very intoxicating. Everyone even close felt the excitement, just from elbow-rubbing.

Athletes also were influenced in their developing feelings of self-importance by the concrete results of their behavior. . . . [T]hey were able to observe the outcomes of their behavior and to use them to form and modify assessments of their selves. Thus, when the team was winning, their feelings of importance, grandeur, talent, and invincibility soared; when they lost, they felt comparatively incompetent, powerless, and small. Because the team's record throughout our research period was overwhelmingly successful, team members reviewed the outcomes of their contests and the season records, and concluded that they were fine athletes and local heroes. . . .

One result of receiving such intense personal interest and media attention was that players developed "big heads." They were admired openly by so many people and their exploits were regarded as so important that they began to feel more notable. Although they tried to remain modest, all of the players found that their celebrity caused them to lose control over their sense of self-importance. As one player observed:

> You try not to let it get away from you. You feel it coming all around you. People building you up. You say to yourself that you're the same guy you always were and that nothing has changed. But what's happening to you is so unbelievable. Even when you were sitting at home in high school imagining what college ball would be like, you could not imagine this. All the media, all the fans, all the pressure. And all so suddenly, with no time to prepare or ease into it. Doc, it got to go to your head. You try to fight it, and you think you do, but

you got to be affected by it, you got to get a big head.

Although the players fought to normalize and diminish their feelings of self-aggrandizement, they were swept away in spite of themselves by the allure of glory, to varying degrees. Their sense of glory fed their egos, exciting them beyond their ability to manage or control it. They had never before been such glory-generating figures, had never felt the power that was now invested in them by the crowds or worshipful fans. They developed deep, powerful feelings affirming how important they had become and how good it felt.

All the members of the University's basketball program developed gloried selves, although the degree varied according to several factors. To some extent, their aggrandizement and glorification were affected by the level of attention they received. Individuals with more talent, who held central roles as team stars, were the focus of much media and fan attention. Others, who possessed the social and interpersonal attributes that made them good subjects for reporters, fruitful topics of conversation for boosters, and charismatic crowd pleasers, also received considerable notice. In addition, those who were more deeply invested in the athletic role were more likely to develop stronger gloried selves. They looked to this arena for their greatest rewards and were the most susceptible to its aggrandizing influence. Finally, individuals resisted or yielded to the gloried self depending on personal attributes. Those who were . . . more modest and more self-effacing tried harder to neutralize the effects and had more difficulty in forging grandiose self-conceptions than those who were boastful or pretentious.

The Price of Glory

Athletes' self-aggrandizement, as we have seen, was a clear consequence of the glory experience. Self-diminishment was a corresponding and concomitant effect. Athletes paid a price for becoming gloried in the form of self-narrowing or self-erosion. They sacrificed both the multidimensionality of their current selves and the potential breadth of their future selves; various dimensions of their identities were either diminished, detached, or somehow changed as a result of their increasing investment in their gloried selves.

Self-Immediacy

One of the first consequences of the ascent of the gloried self was a loss of future orientation. In all their lives, from the most celebrated player to the least, these individuals had never experienced such a level of excitement, adulation, intensity, and importance. These sensations were immediate and real, flooding all team members' daily lives and overwhelming them. As a result, their focus turned toward their present situation and became fixed on it.

This reaction was caused largely by the absorbing quality of the moment. During the intensity of the season (and to a lesser extent during the off-season), their basketball obligations and involvements were prominent. When they were lying exhausted in their hotel rooms, hundreds of miles from campus, or on their beds after a grueling practice, the responsibilities of school seemed remote and distant. One player described his state of preoccupation:

> I've got two finals tomorrow and one the next day. I should be up in the room studying right now. But how can I get my mind on that when I know I've got to guard Michael Jordan tomorrow night?

Their basketball affairs were so much more pressing, not only in the abstract but also because other people made specific demands on them, that it was easy to relegate all other activities to a position of lesser importance.

Many players who had entered college expecting to prepare themselves for professional or business careers were distracted from those plans and relinquished them (71 percent). The demands of the basketball schedule became the central focus of their lives; the associated physical, social, and professional dimensions took precedence over all other concerns. Despite their knowledge that only two percent of major-college players eventually play in the NBA (Coakley 1986; Leonard and Reyman 1988), they all clung to the hope that they would be the ones to succeed. One of the less outstanding athletes on the team expressed the players' commonly held attitude toward their present and their future:

> You have to have two goals, a realistic and an unrealistic. Not really an unrealistic, but a dream. We all have that dream. I know the odds are against it, but I feel realistically that I can make the NBA. I have to be in the gym every day, lift weights, more or less sacrifice my life to basketball. A lot.

To varying degrees, all players ceased to think about their futures other than as a direct continuation of the present. They were distracted from long-term planning and deferment of gratification in favor of the enormous immediate gratification they received from their fans and from celebrity. What emerged was a self that primarily thought about only one source of gratification—athletic fame—and that imagined and planned for little else.

The players imagined vaguely that if they did not succeed as professional athletes, a rich booster would provide them with a job. Although they could observe older players leaving the program without any clear job opportunities, they were too deeply absorbed in the present to recognize the situation. Ironically, they came to college believing that it would expand their range of opportunities . . . yet they sacrificed the potential breadth of their future selves by narrowing their range of vision to encompass only that which fed their immediate hunger for glory.

Diminished Awareness

Locked into a focus on the present and stuck with a vision of themselves that grew from their celebrity status, all team members, to varying degrees, became desensitized to the concerns of their old selves. They experienced a heightened sensitivity and reflectivity toward the gloried self and a loss of awareness of the self-dimensions unrelated to glory. Nearly everyone they encountered interacted with them, at least in part, through their gloried selves. As this self-identity was fed and expanded, their other selves tended to atrophy. At times the athletes seemed to be so blinded by their glory that they would not look beyond it. . . .

This diminished awareness had several consequences. First, in becoming so deeply absorbed in their gloried selves, athletes relegated non-athletic concerns to secondary, tertiary, or even lesser status. These concerns included commitments to friends, relatives, and school. For example, many athletes (54 percent) began each semester vowing that it would be different this time, but each semester they "forgot" to go to class. Reflecting on this occurrence, one player mused:

You don't think, it's not like you goin' to be a bad boy today, or you goin' to pull the wool over someone's eyes. You just plain ol' forget. You sleep through it.

For a while the athletes could ignore the facts and the consequences of their behavior, but this denial wore thin as the semester progressed, and they fell behind more noticeably. Then they moved into a stage of neutralization, blaming boring professors, stupid courses, exhaustion, coaches' demands, or injury.

Second, their new personas were expanded, even in their interactions with friends. Players referred to this situation as being "puffed," and each accused the others of it:

Sometimes I can't even talk to Rich no more. He's so puffed in the head you can't get him to talk sense, he's lost touch with reality. It's like it's full of jello in there and he's talking a bunch of hot air.

What the athletes sensed as filling the heads of these puffed players was the self-image created by the glory experience.

Third, some athletes plunged into various acts because these acts fed their gloried selves (60 percent). They distanced themselves from their old values and took potentially career-ending risks. For example, when a player who filled a substitute role was "red-shirted" (excused from play without losing his scholarship or expending a year of eligibility) for the year because of injury, he was willing to give up this desirable and protective status when asked to do so by the coach. He was convinced easily, despite his secondary position, that the team could not function without him; like others, he blocked off the warnings and the caution that stemmed from an awareness of other needs and interests. The same lack of reflectiveness and self-awareness prevented players with chronic injuries, those who were hobbling and could no longer jump, from admitting to themselves that their playing days were over, that their gloried selves had to retire.

Self-Detachment

For some team members and at times for all, the distinction between their gloried selves and their other selves became more than a separation; the distance and the lack of reflectiveness grew into detachment. In the most extreme cases (18 percent), some athletes developed a barrier between this new, exciting, glamorous self and their old, formerly core selves. They found it increasingly difficult to break through that barrier. They experienced a dualism between these selves, as if occasionally they represented discrete individuals and not multiple facets of the same person; at times, they shifted back and forth between them. Ultimately, the different images became so disparate that they could not be fused, or else individuals became so deeply involved in their gloried selves that they lost control over their efforts to constrain and integrate them. The more these individuals interacted with others through this self, the more it developed a life and a destiny of its own.

For instance, one of the most popular players on the team developed a gloried self that was tied to his self-proclaimed nickname "Apollo." Charismatic and enthusiastic whenever he was in public, he generated enormous amounts of attention and adulation through his outgoing personality. On the court he would work the crowd, raising their emotions, exhorting them to cheer, and talking brashly to opposing players. Reporters thronged to him, because he was colorful, lively, and quotable. In public settings, he was always referred to by his nickname.

Yet, although this player deliberately had created the Apollo identity, eventually it began to control him. It led him to associate at times with people who valued him only for that self; it surfaced in interactions with friends when he had not called it forth. It led him to detach himself from responsibility for things he did while in that persona. As he reported:

I had a summer job working for some booster at a gas station. I figured he wanted to show off that he had Apollo pumping his gas. I'd go into my act for the customers and the other employees, how fine I was, lotta times show up late or not at all. I figured he wouldn't fire me. But he did. Looking back, I can't see how I just up and blew that job. That ain't like me. That was Apollo done that, not me.

Other team members, who did not go so far as to create separate identities for their gloried selves, still experienced feelings of bifurcation. Their former selves were mundane and commonplace compared to their new, vibrant selves. These contrasting selves called forth different kinds of character and behavior. At times, the team members found it difficult to think of themselves as integrated persons, incorporating these divergent identities into one overall self. Feelings of fragmentation haunted them.

Discussion

As we have shown, high school graduates entered the world of college athletics and underwent a fundamental transformation. Thrust into a whirlwind of adulation and celebrity, they reacted to the situation through a process of simultaneous self-aggrandizement and self-diminishment. The gloried self expanded, overpowering all . . . other . . . self-dimensions; it became the aspect of self in which they lived and invested. They immersed themselves single-mindedly in this portion of their selves, and the feedback and gratification they derived from this identity dwarfed their other identities. They had not anticipated this situation, but gradually, as they were drawn into the arena of glory, they were swept away by stardom and fame. Their commitment to the athletic self grew beyond anything they had ever imagined or intended. Once they had experienced the associated power and centrality, they were reluctant to give them up. They discarded their other aspirations, lost touch with other dimensions of their selves (even to the point of detachment), and plunged themselves into the gloried self.

Athletes' gloried selves arose originally as dramaturgical constructions. Other people, through the media or face to face, conferred these identities on athletes through their expectations of them. Athletes responded by playing the corresponding roles because of organizational loyalty, interactional obligations, and enjoyment.

Yet in contrast to other roles, which can be played casually and without consequence, athletes' actions in these roles increased their commitment and their self-involvement in them and made the athletes "more or less unavailable for alternative lines of action" (Kornhauser 1962:321). The gloried self not only influenced athletes' future behavior but also transformed their self-conceptions and identities. . . . [This] entire process . . . illustrates the relationship between dramaturgical roles and real selves, showing how the former comes to impinge upon and influence the latter.

References

Bensman, Joseph and Robert Lilienfeld. 1979. *Between Public and Private*. New York: Free Press.

Coakley, Jay J. 1986. *Sport in Society*. 3d ed. St. Louis: Mosby.

Cooley, Charles H. 1902. *Human Nature and Social Order*. New York: Scribners.

Goffman, Erving. 1959. *The Presentation of Self in Everyday Life*. New York: Doubleday.

Kornhauser, William. 1962. "Social Bases of Political Commitment: A Study of Liberals and Radicals." Pp. 321–339 in *Human Behavior and Social Processes*, ed. A.M. Rose. Boston: Houghton Mifflin.

Leonard, Wilbert and Jonathon Reyman. 1988. "The Odds of Attaining Professional Athlete Status: Refining the Computations." *Sociology of Sports Journal* 5 162–169.

Mead, George Herbert. 1934. *Mind, Self, and Society*. Chicago: University of Chicago Press.

14

Salvaging the Self From Homelessness

*David Snow
and
Leon Anderson*

The Adlers' study of college basketball players illustrates how socially reflected self-images can profoundly
alter individuals' self-conceptions. In this selection,
Snow and Anderson illustrate how individuals defend
their self-conceptions from socially reflected self-images
with the example of the homeless. The contrast between the social and psychological fates of the Adlers'
basketball players and the homeless is a stark one. As
Snow and Anderson report, the domiciled who are fortunate enough not to live on the streets commonly ignore, often insult, and sometimes harass the homeless.
Such demeaning treatment continually reminds the
homeless of their "stigmatized status" or spoiled social
identity. However, the homeless whom Snow and Anderson studied do not meekly succumb to the influence
of such unflattering self-images. Rather, they actively
attempt to salvage some sense of self-worth from the
wreckage of their daily encounters with the domiciled.

The homeless primarily rely on what Snow and Anderson call "identity talk" for this purpose. They attempt
verbally to convince themselves, one another, and occasionally even the domiciled that they are not who and
what their current circumstances, appearance, and
conduct would seem to suggest. The homeless sometimes verbally distance themselves from their apparently spoiled social identity by claiming a more valued
personal identity. Other times, they verbally embrace
such seemingly spoiled social identities as "bum" or
"tramp," while definitionally imbuing these titles with
nobility. And they often engage in fictive storytelling
about their past, their likely future, and even their present.

Although the homeless sometimes psychologically
succumb to the unflattering self-images that they constantly face, they more often succeed in countering
them. Their success in this regard is a tribute to the
human spirit and to the ability of individuals to defend
their self-conceptions from socially reflected self-images. However, what Snow and Anderson suggest but
never explicitly address is that the homeless seem to
support or at least not directly challenge one another's
identity talk. It is an open question just how long the
homeless or anyone else could resist the influence of socially reflected self-images, especially demeaning ones,
without a little help from their friends. Many of the selections in this volume suggest the answer: not very
long.

To be homeless in America is to have fallen to the
bottom of the status system; it is also to be confronted with gnawing doubts about self-worth. . . .
Such [a] vexing concern [is] not just the psychic fall-
out of having descended onto the streets, but [is]
also stoked by encounters with the domiciled that
constantly remind the homeless of where they
stand in relation to others.

One such encounter occurred early in the
course of our fieldwork [among the homeless in
Austin, Texas]. It was late afternoon, and the
homeless were congregating in front of the [Sal-
vation Army or] Sally [as the homeless called it]
for dinner. A school bus approached that was
packed with Anglo junior high school students
being bused from an eastside barrio school to
their upper-middle- and upper-class homes in the
city's northwest neighborhoods. As the bus rolled
by, a fusillade of coins came flying out the windows, as the students made obscene gestures and
shouted, "Get a job." Some of the homeless ges-
tured back, some scrambled for the scattered
coins—mostly pennies—others angrily threw the
coins at the bus, and a few seemed oblivious to
the encounter. For the passing junior high
schoolers, the exchange was harmless fun, a way
to work off the restless energy built up in school;
but for the homeless, it was a stark reminder of
their stigmatized status and of the extent to which
they are the objects of negative attention.

Initially, we did not give much thought to this
encounter. We were more interested in other issues and were neither fully aware of the frequency of such occurrences nor appreciative of
their psychological consequences. We quickly
came to learn, however, that this was hardly an
isolated incident. The buses passed by the Sally
every weekday afternoon during the school year;

other domiciled citizens occasionally found pleasure in driving by and similarly hurling insults at
the homeless and pennies at their feet; and . . . the
hippie tramps and other homeless in the university area were derisively called "Drag worms," the
police often harassed the homeless, and a number of neighborhoods took turns vilifying and derogating them.

Not all encounters with the domiciled are so
stridently and intentionally demeaning, of course,
but they are no less piercingly stigmatizing. One
Saturday morning, for instance, as we walked
with Willie Hastings and Ron Whitaker along a
downtown street, a woman with a station wagon
full of children drove by. As they passed, several
of the children pointed at us and shouted, "Hey,
Mama, look at the street people!" Ron responded
angrily:

> "Mama, look at the street people!" You know,
> it pisses me off the way fucking thieves steal
> shit and they can still hold their heads high
> 'cause they got money. Sure, they have to go
> to prison sometimes, but when they're out,
> nobody looks down on them. But I wouldn't
> steal from nobody, and look how those kids
> stare at us!

The pain of being objects of curiosity and negative attention is experienced fairly regularly by the
homeless, but they suffer just as frequently from
what has been called "attention deprivation." In
The Pursuit of Attention, Charles Derber (1979:42)
commented that "members of the subordinate
classes are regarded as less worthy of attention in
relations with members of dominant classes and
so are subjected to subtle yet systematic face-to-
face deprivation." For no one is Derber's observation more true than for the homeless, who are
routinely ignored or avoided by the domiciled. . . .
[P]edestrians frequently avert their eyes when
passing the homeless on the sidewalk, and they
often hasten their pace and increase the distance
between themselves and the homeless when they
sense they may be targeted by a panhandler.
Pedestrians sometimes go as far as to cross the
street in order to avoid anticipated interaction
with the homeless. Because of the fear and anxiety presumably engendered in the domiciled by
actual or threatened contact with the homeless,
efforts are often made at the community level . . .
to regulate and segregate the homeless both spatially and institutionally. Although these avoidance rituals and segregative measures are not as

overtly demeaning as the more active and immediate kinds of negative attention the homeless
receive, they can be equally stigmatizing, for they
also cast the homeless as objects of contamination. This, too, constitutes an assault upon the self,
albeit a more subtle and perhaps more insidious
one.

Occurring alongside the negative attention
and attention deprivation, the homeless experience . . . an array of gestures and acts that are frequently altruistic and clearly indicative of goodwill. People do, on occasion, give to panhandlers
and beggars out of sincere concern rather than
merely to get them off their backs. Domiciled citizens sometimes even provide assistance without
being asked. One evening, for instance, we found
Pat Manchester sitting on a bench near the university, eating pizza. "Man, I was just sitting here,"
he told us, "and this dude walked by and gave me
half a pizza and two dollar bills." Several of the
students who worked at restaurants in the
unviersity area occasionally brought leftovers to
Rhyming Mike and other hippie tramps. Other
community members occasionally took street
people to their home for a shower, dinner, and a
good night's sleep. Even Jorge Herrera, who was
nearly incoherent, appeared never to wash or
bathe, and was covered with rashes and open
sores, was the recipient of such assistance. Twice,
during our field research, he appeared on the
streets after a brief absence in clean clothes,
shaved, and with a new haircut. When we asked
about the changes in his appearance, he told us
that someone had taken him home, cleaned him
up, and let him spend the night. These kinds of
unorganized, sporadic gestures of goodwill
clearly facilitate the survival of some of the homeless, but the numbers they touch in comparison
to those in need are minuscule. Nor do they
occur in sufficient quantity or consistently
enough to neutralize the stigmatizing and demeaning consequences of not only being on the
streets but being objects of negative attention or
little attention at all.

In addition to those who make sporadic gestures of goodwill, thousands of domiciled citizens
devote occasional time and energy to serving the
homeless in an organized fashion in churches,
soup kitchens, and shelters. Angels House kitchen
was staffed in part by such volunteers, and their
support was essential to the operation of the
kitchen. Yet the relationship between these well-

meaning volunteers and the homeless is highly structured and sanitized. The volunteers typically prepare sandwiches and other foods in a separate area from the homeless or encounter them only across the divide of a serving counter that underscores the distance between the servers and the served. Thus, however sincere and helpful the efforts of domiciled volunteers, the structure of their encounters with the homeless often underscores the immense status differences and thereby reminds the homeless again of where they stand in relation to others. . . .

The task the homeless face of salvaging the self is not easy, especially since wherever they turn they are reminded that they are at the very bottom of the status system. As Sonny McCallister lamented shortly after he became homeless, "The hardest thing's been getting used to the way people look down on street people. It's real hard to feel good about yourself when almost everyone you see is looking down on you." Tom Fisk, who had been on the streets longer, agreed. But he said that he had become more calloused over time:

> I used to let it bother me when people stared at me while I was trying to sleep on the roof of my car or change clothes out of my trunk, but I don't let it get to me anymore. I mean, they don't know who I am, what gives them the right to judge me? I know I'm okay.

But there was equivocation and uncertainty in his voice. Moreover, even if he no longer felt the stares and comments of others, he still had to make sense of the distance between himself and them.

How, then, do the homeless deal with the negative attention they receive or the indifference they encounter as they struggle to survive materially? How do they salvage their selves? . . . We address these questions in the remainder of [this] chapter.

Constructing Identity-Oriented Meaning

[I]nteraction between two or more individuals minimally requires that they be situated or placed as social objects. In other words, situationally specific identities must be established. Such identities can be established in two ways: they can be attributed or imputed by others, or they can be claimed or asserted by the actor. The former can

be thought of as social or role identities in that they are imputations based primarily on information gleaned from the appearance or behavior of others and from the time and location of their action, as when children in a passing car look out the window and yell, "Hey, Mama, look at the street people!" or when junior high school students yell out the windows of their school bus to the homeless lining up for dinner in front of the Sally, "Get a job, you bums!" In each case, the homeless in question have been situated as social objects and thus assigned social identities.

When individuals claim or assert an identity, by contrast, they attribute meaning to themselves. Such self-attributions can be thought of as personal identities rather than social identities, in that they are self-designations brought into play or avowed during the course of actual or anticipated interaction with others. Personal identities may be consistent with imputed social identities, as when Shotgun claims to be "a tramp," or inconsistent, as when Tony Jones yells back to the passing junior high schoolers, "Fuck you, I ain't no lazy bum!" The presented personal identities of individuals who are frequent objects of negative attention or attention deprivation, as are the homeless, can be especially revealing, because they offer a glimpse of how those people deal interactionally with their pariah-like status and the demeaning social identities into which they are frequently cast. Personal identities thus provide . . . insight into the ways the homeless attempt to salvage the self.

What, then, are the personal identities that the homeless construct and negotiate when in interaction with others? Are they merely a reflection of the highly stereotypic and stigmatized identities attributed to them, or do they reflect a more positive sense of self or at least an attempt to carve out and sustain a less demeaning self-conception?

The construction of personal identity typically involves a number of complementary activities: (a) procurement and arrangement of physical setting and props; (b) cosmetic face work or the arrangement of personal appearance; (c) selective association with other individuals and groups; and (d) verbal construction and assertion of personal identity. Although some of the homeless engage in conscious manipulation of props and appearance—for example, Pushcart, with his fully loaded shopping cart, and Shotgun, who fancies himself a con artist—most do not resort to such measures. Instead, the primary means by which the homeless announce their personal identities is verbal. They engage, in other words, in a good bit of identity talk. This is understandable, since the homeless seldom have the financial or social resources to pursue the other identity construction activities. Additionally, since the structure of their daily routines ensures that they spend a great deal of time waiting here and there, they have ample opportunity to converse with each other.

Sprinkled throughout these conversations with each other, as well as those with agency personnel and, occasionally, with the domiciled, are numerous examples of identity talk. Inspection of the instances of the identity talk to which we were privy yielded three generic patterns: (1) distancing; (2) embracement; and (3) fictive storytelling. . . . We elaborate in turn each of [these] generic patterns [and] their varieties. . . .

Distancing

When individuals have to enact roles, associate with others, or utilize institutions that imply social identities inconsistent with their actual or desired self-conceptions, they often attempt to distance themselves from those roles, associations, or institutions. A substantial proportion of the identity talk we recorded was consciously focused on distancing from other homeless individuals, from street and occupational roles, and from the caretaker agencies servicing the homeless. Nearly a third of the identity statements were of this variety.

Associational Distancing

Since a claim to a particular self is partly contingent on the imputed social identities of the person's associates, one way people can substantiate that claim when their associates are negatively evaluated is to distance themselves from those associates. This distancing technique manifested itself in two ways among the homeless: disassociation from the homeless as a general social category, and disassociation from specific groupings of homeless individuals.

Categoric associational distancing was particularly evident among the recently dislocated. Illustrative is Tony Jones's comment in response to our initial query about life on the streets:

I'm not like the other guys who hang out down at the Sally. If you want to know about street people, I can tell you about them; but you can't really learn about street people from studying me, because I'm different.

Such categorical distancing also occurred among those individuals who saw themselves as on the verge of getting off the street. After securing two jobs in the hope of raising enough money to rent an apartment, Ron Whitaker indicated, for example, that he was different from other street people. "They've gotten used to living on the streets and they're satisfied with it, but not me!" he told us. "Next to my salvation, getting off the streets is the most important thing in my life." This variety of categorical distancing was particularly pronounced among homeless individuals who had taken jobs at the Sally and thus had one foot off the streets. These individuals were frequently criticized by other homeless for their condescending attitude. As Marilyn put it, "As soon as these guys get inside, they're better than the rest of us. They've been out on the streets for years, and as soon as they're inside, they forget it."

Among the outsiders who had been on the streets for some time and who appeared firmly rooted in that life-style there were few examples of categorical distancing. Instead, these individuals frequently distinguished themselves from other groups of homeless. This form of associational distancing was most conspicuous among those, such as the hippie tramps and redneck bums, who were not regular social-service or shelter users and who saw themselves as especially independent and resourceful. These individuals not only wasted little time in pointing out that they were "not like those Sally users," but were also given to derogating the more institutionally dependent. Indeed, although they are among the furthest removed from a middle-class lifestyle, they sound at times much like middle-class citizens berating welfare recipients. As Marilyn explained, "A lot of these people staying at the Sally, they're reruns. Every day they're wanting something. People get tired of giving. All you hear is gimme, gimme. And we transients are getting sick of it."

Role Distancing

Role distancing, the second form of distancing employed by the homeless, involves a self-conscious attempt to foster the impression of a lack of commitment or attachment to a particular role in order to deny the self implied. Thus, when individuals find themselves cast into roles in which the social identities implied are inconsistent with desired or actual self-conceptions, role distancing is likely to occur. Since the homeless routinely find themselves being cast into or enacting low-status, negatively evaluated roles, it should not be surprising that many of them attempt to disassociate themselves from those roles.

As did associational distancing, role distancing manifested itself in two ways: distancing from the general role of street person, and distancing from specific occupational roles. The former, which is also a type of categorical distancing, was particularly evident among the recently dislocated. It was not uncommon for these individuals to state explicitly that they should "not be mistaken as a typical street person." Role distancing of the less categoric and more situationally specific type was most evident among those who performed day labor, such as painters' helpers, hod carriers, warehouse and van unloaders, and those in unskilled service occupations, such as dishwashing and janitorial work. As we saw earlier, the majority of the homeless we encountered would avail themselves of such job opportunities, but they seldom did so enthusiastically, since the jobs offered low status and low wages. This was especially true of the straddlers and some of the outsiders, who frequently reminded others of their disdain for such jobs and of the belief that they deserved better, as exemplified by the remarks of a drunk young man who had worked the previous day as a painter's helper: "I made $36 off the Labor Corner, but it was just nigger work. I'm twenty-four years old, man. I deserve better than that."

Similar distancing laments were frequently voiced over the disparity between job demands and wages. We were conversing with a small gathering of homeless men on a Sunday afternoon, for example, when one of them revealed that earlier in the day he had turned down a job to carry shingles up a ladder for $4 an hour because he found it demeaning to "do that hard a work for that low a pay." Since day-labor jobs seldom last for more than six hours, perhaps not much is lost monetarily in foregoing such jobs, in comparison to what can be gained in pride. But even when the ratio of dollars to pride appears to make rejection costly, as in the case of permanent jobs, dissatisfaction with the low status of menial jobs may prod some homeless individuals to engage in the

ultimate form of role distancing by quitting currently held jobs. As Ron Whitaker recounted the day after he quit in the middle of his shift as a dishwasher at a local restaurant:

> My boss told me, "You can't walk out on me." And I told her, "Fuck you, just watch me. I'm gonna walk out of here right now." And I did. "You can't walk out on me," she said. I said, "Fuck you, I'm gone."

The foregoing illustrations suggest that the social identities lodged in available work roles are frequently inconsistent with the desired or idealized self-conceptions of some of the homeless. Consequently, "bitching about," "turning down," and even "blowing off" such work may function as a means of social-identity disavowal, on the one hand, and personal-identity assertion on the other. Such techniques provide a way of saying, "Hey, I have some pride. I'm in control. I'm my own person." This is especially the case among those individuals for whom such work is no longer just a stopgap measure but an apparently permanent feature of their lives.

Institutional Distancing

An equally prevalent distancing technique involved the derogation of the caretaker agencies that attended to the needs of the homeless. The agency that was the most frequent object of these harangues was the Sally. Many of the homeless who used it described it as a greedy corporation run by inhumane personnel more interested in lining their own pockets than in serving the needy. Willie Hastings claimed, for example, that "the major is money-hungry and feeds people the cheapest way he can. He never talks to people except to gripe at them." He then added that the "Sally is supposed to be a Christian organization, but it doesn't have a Christian spirit. It looks down on people. . . . The Salvation Army is a national business that is more worried about making money than helping people." Ron Whitaker concurred, noting on another occasion that the "Sally here doesn't nearly do as much as it could for people. The people who work there take bags of groceries and put them in their cars. People donate to the Sally, and then the workers there cream off the best." Another straddler told us after he had spent several nights at the winter shelter, "If you spend a week here, you'll see how come people lose hope. You're treated just like an animal."

Because the Salvation Army is the only local facility that provides free shelter, breakfast, and dinner, attention is understandably focused on it. But that the Sally would be frequently derogated by the people whose survival it facilitates may appear puzzling at first glance, especially given its highly accommodative orientation. The answer lies in part in the organization and dissemination of its services. Clients are processed in an impersonal, highly structured assembly line-like fashion. The result is a leveling of individual differences and a decline in personal autonomy. Bitching and complaining about such settings create psychic distance from the self-implied and secure a modicum of personal autonomy. This variety of distancing, though observable among all of the homeless, was most prevalent among . . . individuals [who] have used street agencies over a long period of time. [T]heir self concepts are . . . deeply implicated in them, thus necessitating distancing from those institutions and the self-implied. Criticizing the Sally, then, provides some users with a means of dealing with the implications of their dependency on it. It is, in short, a way of presenting and sustaining a somewhat contrary personal identity. . . .

Embracement

Embracement connotes a person's verbal and expressive confirmation of acceptance of and attachment to the social identity associated with a general or specific role, a set of social relationships, or a particular ideology. So defined, embracement implies that social identity is congruent with personal identity. Thus, embracement involves the avowal of implied social identities, rather than their disavowal, as in the case of distancing. Thirty-four percent of the identity statements were of this variety.

Role Embracement

The most conspicuous kind of embracement encountered was categoric role embracement, which typically manifested itself by the avowal and acceptance of street-role identities, such as tramp and bum. Occasionally we would encounter an individual who would immediately announce that he or she was a tramp or a bum. A case in point is provided by our initial encounter with Shotgun, when he proudly told us that he was "the tramp who was on the front page of yesterday's newspaper." In that and subsequent conversations, his talk was peppered with references to himself as a tramp. He said, for example, that he had appeared on a television show in St. Louis as a tramp and that he "tramped" his way across the country, and he revealed several "cons" that "tramps use to survive on the road."

Shotgun and others like him identified themselves as traditional "brethren of the road" tramps. A number of other individuals identified themselves as "hippie tramps." When confronted by a passing group of young punk-rockers, for instance, Gimpy Dan and several other hippie tramps voiced agreement with the remark one made that "these kids will change but we'll stay the same." As if to buttress this claim, they went on to talk about "Rainbow," . . . [an] annual gathering of old hippies which functions in part as a kind of identity-reaffirmation ritual. For these street people, there was little doubt about who they were; they not only saw themselves as hippie tramps, but they embraced that identity both verbally and expressively.

This sort of embracement also surfaced on occasion with skid row-like bums, as was evidenced by Gypsy Bill's repeated references to himself as a bum. As a corollary of such categoric role embracement, most individuals who identified themselves as tramps or bums adopted nicknames congruent with these roles, such as Shotgun, Boxcar Billie, Gypsy Bill, and Pushcart. Such street names thus symbolize a break with their domiciled past and suggest, as well, a fairly thoroughgoing embracement of life on the streets.

Role-specific embracement was also encountered occasionally, as when Gypsy would refer to himself as an "expert dumpster diver." Many street people occasionally engage in this survival activity, but relatively few pridefully identify with it. Other role-specific survival activities embraced included panhandling, small-time drug-dealing, and performing, such as playing a musical instrument or singing on a street corner for money. "Rhyming Mike" . . . made his money by composing short poems for spare change from passers-by, and routinely referred to himself as a street poet. For some homeless individuals, then, the street roles and routines they enact function as sources of positive identity and self-worth.

Associational Embracement

A second variety of embracement entails reference to oneself as a friend or as an individual who takes his or her social relationships seriously. Gypsy provides a case in point. On one occasion, he told us that he had several friends who either refused or quit jobs at the Sally because they "weren't allowed to associate with other guys on the streets who were their friends." Such a policy struck him as immoral. "They expect you to forget who your friends are and where you came from when you go to work there," he told us angrily. "They asked me to work there once and I told them, 'No way.' I'm a bum and I know who my friends are." Self-identification as a person who willingly shared limited resources, such as cigarettes and alcohol, also occurred frequently, particularly among self-avowed tramps and bums.

Associational embracement was also sometimes expressed in claims of protecting buddies. . . . [For example,] JJ and Indio repeatedly said they "looked out for each other." When Indio was telling about having been assaulted and robbed while walking through an alley, JJ said, almost apologetically, "It wouldn't have happened if I was with you. I wouldn't have let them get away with that." Similar claims were made to one of us, as when two [individuals] said one evening after an ambiguous encounter with a clique of half a dozen other street people, "If it wasn't for us, they'd have had your ass."

Although protective behaviors that entailed risk were seldom observed, protective claims, and particularly promises, were heard frequently. Whatever the relationship between such claims and action, they not only illustrate adherence to the moral code of "what goes around, comes around," but they also express the claimant's desire to be identified as a trustworthy friend.

Ideological Embracement

The third variety of embracement entails adherence to an ideology or an alternative reality and the avowal of a personal identity that is cognitively congruent with that ideology. Banjo, for example, routinely identifies himself as a Christian. He painted on his banjo case "Wealth Means Nothing Without God," and his talk is sprinkled with references to his Christian beliefs. He can often be found giving testimony about "the power and grace of Jesus" to other homeless

around the Sally, and he witnesses regularly at the Central Assembly of God Church. Moreover, he frequently points out that his religious beliefs transcend his situation on the streets. As he told us once, "It would have to be a bigger purpose than just money to get me off the streets, like a religious mission."

A source of identity as powerful as religion, but less common, is the occult and related alternative realities. Since traditional occupational roles are not readily available to the homeless as a basis for identity, and since few street people have the material resources that can be used for construction of positive personal identities, it is little wonder that some of them find in alternative realities a locus for a positive identity. [For example,] Tanner Sutton identifies himself as a "spirit guide" who can see into the future, prophesying, for instance, that "humans will be transformed into another life form."

Like mainstream religious traditions and occult realities, conversionist, restorative ideologies, such as that associated with Alcoholics Anonymous, provide an identity for some homeless people who are willing to accept AA's doctrines and adhere to its program. Interestingly, AA's successes seldom remain on the streets. Consequently, those street people who have previously associated with AA seldom use it as a basis for identity assertion. Nonetheless, it does constitute a potentially salient identity peg. . . .

Fictive Storytelling

A third form of identity talk engaged in by the homeless is fictive storytelling about past, present, or future experiences and accomplishments. We characterize as fictive stories those that range from minor exaggerations of experience to full-fledged fabrications. We observed two types of fictive storytelling: embellishment of the past and present, and fantasizing about the future. Slightly more than a third of the identity statements we recorded fell into one of these two categories.

Embellishment

By *embellishment*, we refer to the exaggeration of past *or* present experiences with fanciful and fictitious particulars so as to assert a positive personal identity. Embellishment involves enlargement of the truth, an overstatement of what transpired or is unfolding. Embellished stories, then, are only partly fictional.

Examples of embellishment for identity construction abound among the homeless. Although a wide array of events and experiences, ranging from the accomplishments of offspring to sexual and drinking exploits and predatory activities, were embellished, such storytelling was most commonly associated with past and current occupational and financial themes. The typical story of financial embellishment entailed an exaggerated claim regarding past or current wages. A case in point is provided by a forty-year-old homeless man who spent much of his time hanging around a bar boasting about having been offered a job as a Harley-Davidson mechanic for $18.50 per hour, although at the same time he constantly begged for cigarettes and spare change for beer.

Equally illustrative of such embellishment was an encounter we overheard between Marilyn, who was passing out discarded burritos, and a homeless man in his early twenties. After this fellow had taken several burritos, he chided Marilyn for being "drunk." She yelled back angrily, "I'm a sheetrock taper and I make 14 bucks an hour. What the fuck do you make?" In addition to putting the young man in his place, Marilyn thus announced to him and to others overhearing the encounter her desired identity as a person who earns a good wage and must, therefore, be treated respectfully. Subsequent interaction with her revealed that she worked only sporadically, and then most often for not much more than minimum wage. There was, then, a considerable gap between claims and reality.

Disjunctures between identity assertions and reality appear to be quite common and were readily discernible on occasion, as in the case of a forty-five-year-old [man] from Pittsburgh who had been on the streets for a year and who was given to substantial embellishment of his former military experiences. On several occasions, he was overheard telling about "patrolling the Alaskan/Russian border in Alaskan Siberia" and his encounters with Russian guards who traded him vodka for coffee. Since there is no border between Alaska and Siberia, it is obvious that this tale is outlandish. Nonetheless, such tales, however embellished, can be construed as attempts to communicate specifics about the person and the person's sense of self. Additionally, they focus a ray of positive attention on the storyteller and

thereby enable him or her to garner momentarily a valued resource that is typically in short supply on the streets.

Fantasizing

The second type of fictive storytelling among the homeless is verbal fantasizing, which involves the articulation of fabrications about the speaker's future. Such fabrications place the narrator in positively framed situations that seem far removed from, if at all connected to, his or her past and present. These fabrications are almost always benign, usually have a Walter Mitty/pipe dream quality to them, and vary from fanciful reveries involving little self-deception to fantastic stories in which the narrator appears to be taken in by his or her constructions.

Regardless of the degree of self-deception, the verbal fantasies we heard were generally organized around one or more of four themes: self-employment, money, material possessions, and women. Fanciful constructions concerning self-employment usually involved business schemes. On several occasions, for example, Tony Jones told us and others about his plans to set up a little shop near the university to sell leather hats and silver work imported from New York. In an even more expansive vein, two [men] who had befriended each other seemed to be scheming constantly about how they were going to start one lucrative business after another. Once, we overheard them talking about "going into business" for themselves, "either roofing houses or rebuilding classic cars and selling them." A few days later, they were observed trying to find a third party to bankroll one of these business ventures, and they even asked us if we "could come up with some cash."

An equally prominent source of fanciful identity construction is the fantasy of becoming rich. Some of the homeless just daydreamed about what they would do if they had a million dollars. Pat Manchester, for instance, assured us that, if he "won a million dollars in a lottery," he was mature enough that he "wouldn't blow it." Others made bold claims about future riches without offering any details. And still others confidently spun fairly detailed stories about being extravagant familial providers in the future, as Tom Fisk did when he returned to town after a futile effort to establish himself in a city closer to his girlfriend. Despite his continuing financial setbacks, he assured us, "I'm going to get my fiancé a new pet monkey, even if it costs a thousand dollars. And I'm going to get her two parrots too, just to show her how much I love her."

Fanciful identity assertions were also constructed around material possessions and sexual encounters with women. These two identity pegs were clearly illustrated one evening among several homeless men along the city's major nightlife strip. During the course of making numerous overtures to passing women, two of the fellows jointly fantasized about how they would attract these women in the future. "Man, these chicks are going to be all over us when we come back into town with our new suits and Corvettes," one exclaimed. The other added, "We'll have to get some cocaine, too. Cocaine will get you women every time." This episode and fantasy occurred early in the second month of our fieldwork, and we quickly came to learn that such fantasizing was fairly commonplace and that it was typically occasioned by "women-watching," which exemplifies one of the ways in which homeless men are both deprived of attention and respond to that deprivation.

One place homeless men would often watch women was along a jogging trail in one of the city's parks adjacent to the river. Here, on warm afternoons, they would drink beer and call out to women who jogged or walked along the trail or came to the park to sun themselves. Most of the women moved nervously by, ignoring the overtures of the men. But some responded with a smile, a wave, or even a quick "Hi!" Starved for female attention, the homeless men are quick to fantasize, attributing great significance to the slightest response. One Saturday afternoon, for example, as we were sitting by the jogging trail drinking beer with Pat Manchester and Ron Whitaker, we noticed several groups of young women who had laid out blankets on the grassy strip that borders the trail. Pat and Ron were especially interested in the women who were wearing shorts and halter tops. Pat called out for them to take their tops off. It was not clear that they heard him, but he insisted, "They really want it. I can tell they do." He suggested we go over with him to "see what we can get," but he was unwilling to go by himself. Instead, he constructed a fantasy in which the young women were very interested in him. Occasionally, the women glanced toward us with apprehension, and Pat always acted as

though it was a sign of interest. "If I go over there and they want to wrap me up in that blanket and fuck me," he said, "man, I'm going for it." Nonetheless, he continued to sit and fantasize, unwilling to acknowledge openly the obdurate reality staring him in the face.

Although respectable work, financial wealth, material possessions, and women are intimately interconnected in actuality, only one or two of the themes were typically highlighted in the stories we heard. Occasionally, however, we encountered a particularly accomplished storyteller who wove together all four themes in a grand scenario. Such was the case with the [man] from Pittsburgh who told the following tale over a meal of bean stew and stale bread at the Sally, and repeated it after lights-out as he lay on the concrete floor of the winter warehouse: "Tomorrow morning I'm going to get my money and say, 'Fuck this shit.' I'm going to catch a plane to Pittsburgh and tomorrow night I'll take a hot bath, have a dinner of linguine and red wine in my own restaurant, and have a woman hanging on my arm." When encountered on the street the next evening, he attempted to explain his continued presence on the streets by saying, "I've been informed that all my money is tied up in a legal battle back in Pittsburgh," an apparently fanciful amplification of the original fabrication. . . .

Conclusion

Many of the homeless are, [then], active agents in the construction and negotiation of identities as they interact with others. They do not, in other words, passively accept the social identities their appearance sometimes exudes or into which they are cast. This is not to suggest that the homeless do not sometimes view themselves in terms of the more negative, stereotypical identities frequently imputed to them. One afternoon, for example, we encountered Gypsy stretched out on a mattress in the back of his old car. Drunk and downhearted, he muttered glumly:

I've just about given up on life. I can't get any work and all my friends do is keep me drunk. Crazy, just crazy—that's all I am. Don't have any desire to do anything for myself. This car is all I've got, and even it won't work. It's not even worth trying. I'm nothing but an asshole and a bum anymore.

But on other occasions, as we have seen, Gypsy was not only more cheerful but even managed to cull shreds of self-respect and dignity from his pariah-like existence. Moreover, we found that self-deprecating lamentations like Gypsy's were relatively rare compared to the avowal of positive personal identities. This should not be particularly surprising, since every human needs to be an object of value and since the homeless have little to supply that sense of value other than their own identity-construction efforts. . . .

In this chapter we have explored the ways the homeless deal with their plight . . . by attempting to construct and maintain a sense of . . . self-worth that helps them stay afloat. Not all of the homeless succeed, of course. The selves of some have been so brutalized that they are abandoned in favor of alcohol, drugs, or out-of-this-world fantasies. And many would probably not score high on a questionnaire evaluating self-esteem. But the issue for us has not been how well the homeless fare in comparison to others on measures of self esteem, but that they do, in fact, attempt to salvage the self, and that this struggle is an ongoing feature of the experience of living on the streets.

The homeless we studied are not the only individuals who have fallen or been pushed through the cracks of society who nevertheless try to carve a modicum of . . . personal significance out of what must seem to those perched higher in the social order as a [meaningless] void. Other examples of such salvaging work have been found in mental hospitals, concentration camps, and among black street corner men. In these and presumably in other such cases of marginality, the attempt to carve out and maintain a sense of . . . self-worth seems especially critical for survival because it is the one thread that enables those situated at the bottom to salvage their humanity. It follows, then, that it is not out of disinterest that some people find it difficult to salvage their respective selves, but that it results instead from the scarcity of material and social resources at their disposal. That many of the homeless are indeed able to . . . secure a measure of self-worth testifies to their psychological resourcefulness and resolve, and to the resilience of the human spirit.

Reference

Derber, Charles. 1979. *The Pursuit of Attention.* New York: Oxford University Press.

15

Constructing Transsexual Selves

Douglas Mason-Schrock

In an earlier selection, Leslie Irvine explained how, after failed relationships, individuals reconstruct their selves by telling stories. This selection examines a similar process among transsexuals. However, unlike members of Codependents Anonymous (CoDA), transsexuals must construct selves that their bodies contradict. Rather than reconstruct a new self, as members of CoDA do, transsexuals must tell stories that connect a current self to a past self that was always present but long suppressed.

In this selection, Mason-Schrock examines these stories or self-narratives and how they create a transsexual self. He shows that male-to-female transsexuals tell of early cross-dressing, being caught doing so, and of failure at athletics. They attribute earlier, conventionally masculine pursuits to denial of their true selves because of social pressures. They similarly dismiss earlier self-identification as homosexual, transvestite, or cross-dresser. Through these stories of early femininity and subsequent denial, the male-to-female transsexual convinces others and herself that her true, feminine self is trapped inside the wrong body.

However, as Mason-Schrock also demonstrates, the transsexual does not invent such narratives in isolation. Like the individual who learns from CoDA how to tell stories that support his or her new "codependent" self, the transsexual learns how to tell her story from the transgender community. She learns from transgender magazines, web sites, television shows, and in support groups what counts as evidence of transsexuality, denial, and a variety of "identity slogans." When she tells her story or self-narrative in support groups, other transsexuals provide guidance, affirm her transsexual identity, and ignore information that might contradict it. Like the stories of members of CoDA, the transsexual's self-narrative is not so much her own but given to her by the transgender community.

The transsexual's narrative creation and maintenance of self is rather obvious because it involves such a radical change in identity. Yet, like transsexuals, we all create and maintain selves through the stories we tell. We emphasize parts of our past, ignore others, and dismiss still others when telling these stories, much like transsexuals do. And, like transsexuals, we learn how to tell the stories that we do from others and depend on them to accept or at least not challenge our stories. This is yet another way that the self is created, maintained, and sometimes changed through social interaction.

Stories are like containers that hold us together; they give us a sense of coherence and continuity. By telling what happened to us once upon a time, we make sense of who we are today. To fashion a biographical story imposes a comforting order on our experience, but how do we arrive at stories that feel right, that point to authentic selfhood? One way to find out is to examine how people create new self-narratives to support a radical change in identity. We might find . . . that stories are not simply told about a preexisting self but that stories, and their collective creation, bring [experientially] real "true selves" into being.

Transsexuals provide an intriguing opportunity to study this process of self-construction. The desired identity change is indeed radical: from one gender to another. Typically transsexuals, like those described here, believe they were born in wrong-sexed bodies and want to remedy the mistake, eventually through surgery. The process entails relearning how to do gender, down to the smallest details of self-presentation. The process is also anguishing, in that transsexuals often face rejection from family and friends. In addition, there are problems of finding ways to pay for therapy, electrolysis, hormone treatments, and surgery. To be willing to endure this process, one must believe firmly that the "true self" demands it. . . .

Transsexuals face a peculiar difficulty [fashioning a new sense of self] because their bodies, as signifiers, belie the new gender identities they want to claim. Moreover, in Western cultures, the body is taken to be an unequivocal sign of gender; thus it is not easy for those born with penises to define themselves as "female inside." The implication is that transsexuals must look elsewhere, beyond their natural bodies, for signs of the gendered character of their "true selves."

One place where they learn to look is the past. Through participating in the so-called "transgender community," they learn how to scan their biographies for evidence of a differently gendered "true self." In this paper, I focus on how transsexuals learn to do this—that is, how they learn, from others in the transgender community, to find biographical evidence of a differently gendered "true self" and to fashion this information into a story that leads inexorably to the identity "transsexual." By studying this process among transsexuals—whose identity dilemmas are severe and thus call for a highly visible response—we can gain insight into the generic process of self-construction through narrative. . . .

The Transgender Community

My involvement in the transgender community began after I found an advertisement for a therapist who specialized in "transgender issues." When I called her and explained my research interests, she said that she co-led a transgender support group and invited me to the next meeting.

I attended eight . . . of these meetings over a 15 month period. Each meeting lasted about three hours. Between 10 and 26 cross-dressers, transsexuals, and sometimes their significant others were present at each meeting. . . . Beside the regular meetings, I also attended the group's annual Christmas party and went to a hockey game with a born male dressed as a woman. . . .

I also read magazines, pamphlets, and short articles written and distributed by various transgender organizations. In addition, I found an Internet community of trangendcrists and consistently read two "semi-private" e-mail lists, and lurked on a weekly real-time support group for transgenderists on America Online. . . . Other data derived from interviews with 10 transsexuals whom I met at support group meetings. . . .

Making the Differently Gendered 'True Self'

"A girl brain in a boy body," said one interviewee when I asked her what it meant to be transsexual. Transsexuals believed they were *born* into the wrong-sexed bodies. Through biological miswiring, they felt they had been given a body signifying a gender different from that of their "true self." This biological view of gender implied that transsexuals' differently gendered "true

selves" had existed from birth. Consequently, to be secure in their new self-definitions, they had to find evidence that they had always been different. Together they found such evidence in their biographies. That is, they collectively reinterpreted certain past events as evidence of transsexuality. This reinterpretation took place while presenting their self-narratives to each other. Transsexuals most often told stories of childhood events. This was where the remaking of the self began.

Childhood Stories

During an interview, one male-to-female transsexual had difficulty defining transsexualism. She said that nobody had ever asked her to do that before, and added:

> I guess that it would be whatever the medical term or psychological term is. I'm not exactly sure. But it always has been there since I can remember; probably at four years old I felt more female than . . . male.

During support group meetings and interviews, and on computer networks, transgenderists often said, "I've felt different *as long as I can remember.*" Early memories of feeling ambivalent about gender, or memories of doing gender unconventionally, were regarded as key pieces of evidence for transsexuality. Transsexuals viewed childhood as a time when their authentic impulses had not yet been stifled by restrictive gender boundaries. At that time, the "true self" reigned. To construct their new identity, transsexuals most often told childhood stories about (1) actual or fantasized cross-dressing experiences, (2) getting caught cross-dressing, and (3) sport participation. What mattered was how these stories were interpreted.

Early cross-dressing stories. Children learn early to attribute their own and others' gender on the basis of clothing (Cahill 1989), and as adults, they take this cultural sign of gender for granted. Male-to-female transsexuals viewed early cross-dressing experiences as evidence of always having possessed a differently gendered "true self." The cross-dressing activities described in these stories varied considerably in duration and frequency. Some transsexuals recounted elaborate stories of cross-dressing throughout childhood. For example, one male-to-female transsexual in her mid-forties offered the following story in an interview:

I was five years old and I had a female cousin that was the same age as me. . . . Our grandmother kept us during the day while my mom and her mom worked. . . . I think I initiated it, I believe, I can't exactly remember, but it was like, "Let's just change clothes." It was a two-story house; we always played upstairs. We kind of had the run of the house 'cause Granny couldn't negotiate well. We just changed [clothes] for one afternoon: I was basically Jane and she was John. . . . I always thought that it seemed like little girls were so much different, and that's the way I really wanted to be. I saw myself more as her than I did as the little boy. And that's when it all started. And we did it quite often over the course of probably two years. . . .

Most stories of early cross-dressing suggested that at first it was undertaken almost on a whim. This account by a 40-year-old was typical:

I was five years old. We lived in town, but there was an old family homeplace that nobody was living in at the time. . . . I was just exploring in the attic one day and found a black dress hanging from a nail in the rafters. I just tried it on and it felt good. I started going through all the drawers, finding other things to try on. And over the years following that—the house had no closets; they used wardrobes—I emptied out one of the wardrobes and turned that into my wardrobe. As I found bits and pieces of clothing that appealed to me, I just added them to my wardrobe.

This person remembered cross-dressing at the homeplace until she went to college. When she told a similar version of this story at a support group meeting, several members smiled and nodded. These responses not only affirmed the individual narrator's transsexual identity, but also conveyed the message that telling stories of early cross-dressing was an acceptable way to show that the identity fit. . . .

Other transsexuals did not cross-dress for long periods during childhood, but they remembered a brief time when they tried it or told of fantasizing about it. In an interview, a male-to-female transsexual told the following story:

I know a lot of people start [cross-dressing] when they are five years old. At that age I really didn't have that much of an opportunity. That was about the age when my sister moved out of the house. My mother was a fairly intimidating person. . . . I do remember

that when I was growing up there were mostly girls in the neighborhood; there were very few boys. I was over at a house . . . and saw a [woman's] bathing suit and started to try it on. Somebody came in and saw that and said "I'm going to tell," so I stopped and nothing ever came out of that. Then for a long time it was just fantasizing about dressing as or being a girl.

Transsexuals' stories about early cross-dressing varied considerably. Some said they did it consistently for a number of years; others said they only fantasized about it. Three group members only recalled their earliest memories of cross-dressing while under hypnosis. . . . The main point . . . is not the accuracy of the accounts but the fact that during support group meetings, all variations of the narratives were affirmed as evidence of transsexuality.

The most commonly accepted evidence of transsexualism in the transgender community was cross-dressing or fantasizing about cross-dressing as a *child*. The age at which one began such activities was significant, because transsexuals believed that the "true self" was most likely to express itself at an early age. One person I interviewed said she remembered beginning to cross-dress at age three. Transsexuals believed that the "true self" was more likely to govern one's actions in childhood because its impulses had not yet been constrained by parents, teachers, and peers.

The age at which a person began cross-dressing was also viewed as a way to distinguish transsexuals from both erotic transvestites and cross-dressers. By emphasizing the early age of actual or fantasized cross-dressing, transsexuals dissociated themselves from transvestites, who usually told of beginning to cross-dress during adolescence for erotic purposes. By stressing that their early feelings and activities reflected an *exclusively* gendered "true self," rather [than] merely an *aspect* of self, transsexuals distanced themselves from cross-dressers, who often talked about cross-dressing as if it were a hobby. By emphasizing differences, support group members policed the boundaries . . . between the three closely related identities: transvestite, cross-dresser, and transsexual.

It was especially important to make such distinctions because most transsexuals had defined themselves as cross-dressers. Policing also took place when support group members told stories about dressing in women's clothing as adults. At one meeting, several cross-dressers exchanged accounts of dressing up as women for Halloween, with emphasis on humorous aspects of fooling friends or restroom episodes. No transsexuals joined in with similar stories. A construction worker—a newcomer who hadn't yet publicly labeled herself a cross-dresser or a transsexual—was asked by a cross-dresser if she had ever "dressed up" for Halloween. She replied:

Halloween is for dressing in costumes, and this is not a costume. It is part of who I am, part of me. If I dressed at Halloween it would be like saying that this is false, but it isn't, it's real. Femininity is an art form. I practice the art of femininity.

Transsexuals affirmed her story with comments such as "I know what you mean." One male transsexual, who lived full-time as a woman, added that she now dresses in women's clothes daily, and it's just "the natural thing to do." Transsexuals' reactions indicated that, as a group, they were indeed different from the cross-dressers—and thus also showed the newcomer whom she resembled most closely.

Getting caught cross-dressing. One meeting, which was called "Family Issues Night," started with an exchange of stories about coming out to family members. During a lull in the conversation, the group leader asked a longtime member to talk about her family situation. She told the group about cross-dressing as a child and gave a detailed account of getting caught cross-dressed. Her parents sent her regularly to a psychiatrist for several months, until she learned to tell the man "what he wanted to hear." This experience, she said, led her to question for many years the normality of cross-dressing. Other transsexuals responded by telling their own stories about getting caught; often they emphasized that it made them ashamed.

Overall, these stories helped to create the notion that the "true self" was constrained by forces *outside* the individual. Because the transsexuals felt that their differently gendered "true self" had always existed, the stories helped to explain why they had denied its existence for 30 to 40 years. By stressing the negative social consequences in telling each other these stories, getting caught became a "turning point" in transsexuals' self-narratives. . . . The turning point, however, did not bring

them closer to self-actualization; rather, it estranged them from the "true self." Any periodic cessation of cross-dressing thus could be attributed to pressure from others. A previously quoted transsexual exemplified this point in telling how she and her cross-dressing cousin were caught by an older cousin:

A cousin of mine that was probably ten years older caught us one day and she just about came unglued. She thought it was about the worst thing that any kids could ever do. . . . It was a big long lecture. I will never forget it . . . threatening to tell my parents, and her parents, and our grandmother, and all this stuff. Sort of put the fear of God into us for a while. I think after that it sort of started winding down with the two of us because we realized . . . that "hey, maybe this is not right, this is not the way." Before, it was kind of fun and games; there was nothing real serious about it.

One born male in her mid-thirties (who started to live full-time as a woman about five months after the interview) felt that being prohibited from cross-dressing squelched the natural development of her differently gendered "true self." In an interview, she said:

I knew it was antisocial behavior [but] . . . looking back on it, I wish it had been different. I wish I would have been like the kid in school that was beat up because he was a sissy, just because maybe now I'd be much farther along. . . . I have about two or three years before I can get surgery. I feel that had I been more honest with my feelings at an earlier age, or allowed myself to express myself the way I wanted to at an earlier age, that I'd be different—more of a complete person now. About that age I started to internalize my feelings and my tendencies, and bury it.

Negative social reactions to cross-dressing or other "cross-gendered" activities, such as little boys acting feminine, were seen as building up barriers to the expression of the differently gendered "true self." Transsexuals regarded such negative responses as the foundation for full-blown denial (which I will discuss in detail below). Stories about getting caught thus linked childhood cross-dressing stories with denial narratives. Weaving these stories together made them appear, at least on the surface, to be seamless constructions of self-meaning.

Participation in sports. Evidence of a differently gendered "true self" was also common in the transsexuals' stories about participating in sports as youths. Because participation in sports is one of the most common and potent signifiers of masculinity . . . these stories were powerful resources for constructing a differently gendered "true self." Most of the born males emphasized that they were naturally inept at sports, while the born female stressed her athletic prowess as a child.

During support group meetings, the born males often casually mentioned their lack of athletic ability. At one meeting, for example, a male-to-female transsexual gave a detailed account of an early cross-dressing experience and added, "I was also the last one picked for team sports." This abrupt change of topic threw me off guard; yet the group members took it in stride, and many nodded in agreement. These short utterances, often made without warning or elaboration, seemed like misplaced fragments, but in fact they created further evidence for the existence of a differently gendered "true self." They were like transsexual identity slogans.

When the transsexuals offered self-narratives, these identity slogans blossomed into elaborate stories rich in color, with the distinct air of the differently gendered "true self." One born male, whose father and older brother had been successful in multiple high school sports, told the following story in an interview:

> When I was in elementary school still, something that was real significant for me was that I'm not very good in sports. One of my vivid memories was in gym class. They'd choose two captains for the teams, and then the two captains would go back and forth . . . picking other team members and picking the best people first and the worst last, and—which I think is a terrible thing to do, I can't believe they do that to kids—and I would always be down near the bottom. And it was just such an agonizing thing, just sitting there waiting and waiting, three people left, two people left. So that was something that was really traumatic for me all throughout my childhood. . . . Playing little league baseball, basketball, and football—spectacularly unsuccessful. And finally by the time I was sixteen, baseball was the last thing that I dropped out of, and I felt like a real failure.

Another male-to-female transsexual, who was in her mid-forties, described her experiences as a boy in elementary school.

> People other than your parents start putting the binary notion of gender identity onto you, and that's when I started feeling bad. (Q: How do you mean, bad?) Out of place. Even in grade school I didn't want to play with the boys. I didn't want to play football, or basketball, or baseball, or any of those things. I wanted to play jump rope with the girls. By the time I got to third grade, the teachers didn't want me to do that anymore. . . . Of course, I'm sure you've heard this before, I was always the last person picked for the teams when the boys chose up sides, just because I had no interest whatsoever in those kinds of things. So I was ostracized continuously for my lack of athletic prowess, which didn't bother me at all because I had no interest whatsoever in having athletic prowess.

Telling stories about their lack of accomplishments in sports helped male-to-female transsexuals create evidence of their differently gendered "true self." Because they believe they were born in the wrong body, they felt they had always had a female "true self." Consequently, if they had not excelled at sports, as they believed "real" boys do, they saw this as further proof of transsexuality.

In contrast to male-to-female transsexuals, the born female I interviewed stressed his physical ability. Although he didn't participate in organized sport as a youth, he raised the issue of physical toughness, which is often part of athletics. He thus stressed characteristics and activities that are conventionally associated with maleness and masculinity in our culture. When I asked him what he meant by calling himself a tomboy who "liked to climb trees," he said:

> Well, I have younger brothers and sisters, and growing up I was the one who would have to protect them when they got into situations with older children. I had the tendency of somehow getting under the skin of some people and I was always having to defend myself. Girls in particular . . . would not have a one-to-one confrontation; it was usually three-to-one against me. . . . If you really want to cause pain, pulling hair really doesn't do it; you twist. All you have to do is pull their hair and twist it, and they would let go and it was over in a short period of time.

The female-to-male transsexual reinterpreted these biographical episodes as evidence of transsexuality. Support group members agreed, believing that the aggressive behavior exhibited by this born female as a young girl was evidence that he had always had a differently gendered "true self."

Stories of Denial

Interpreting early cross-dressing and sports experiences as signs of a differently gendered "true self" helped the transsexuals define themselves as having been born in the wrong-sexed body. Yet they also had to explain away prior involvement in activities that signified their unwanted gender identity. If a male-to-female transsexual had been successful at sports or had signified conventional masculinity most of her life, this history had to be reinterpreted to support her new gender identity. If it was not reinterpreted, she might doubt that she was really a transsexual. If the transsexual had been trying to present a virtual identity to others, they simply could have avoided giving discrediting information (Goffman 1963, 95). But because they were doing identity work to create a[n] [experientially] real "true self," they had to find a way to reconcile discrepant biographical data.

To resolve this identity dilemma, transsexuals gave accounts of being "in denial" before they came to terms with transsexuality. Denial narratives were perhaps the most powerful identity-making resource shared in the transgender community. These narratives were fashioned from psychological rhetoric and thus had scientific legitimacy. To transsexuals, denial meant repressing their "true selves" and thus denying who they really were. This allowed male-to-female transsexuals to interpret the past expression of masculinity as the presentation of a false self (and vice versa for born females). Thus denial narratives helped them explain away things that might have undermined their claims to possessing differently gendered "true selves."

Presenting a denial narrative could facilitate a complete change in identity over a short period, as in the following example. A born male who had been attending meetings for several months consistently introduced herself as a cross-dresser until one meeting, when she introduced herself as "just myself." She explained that she wasn't sure anymore what it meant to be a cross-dresser. As I wrote in my field notes, she talked about a story that happened earlier in the week. She got a catalog in the mail and said:

> I was flipping through the catalog and got to the lingerie section. They have live models who model the bras and panties and I was looking at a bra and you could see a significant portion of her breast and I sort of wondered if that was for sale also.

This story expressed the narrator's desire to change her *body*, not only her clothing, and primed the group for her identity transition. At the following meeting, she introduced herself, with some hesitation, by saying, "I'm coming to realize that I'm a transsexual." She went on to explain that it was difficult to say this in front of the others because she had been "struggling to get through denial." Group members offered her support; some said she was brave and courageous for taking such a big step. By invoking the denial narrative, she completed her identity change in the eyes of the group. No one dared ask whether she really had been in denial because so many others relied on denial narratives to sustain their own claims to transsexuality.

Like other stories considered acceptable for transsexual identity-making, allusions to denial were constantly worked into group discussions. Denial was often mentioned in brief but significant ways during support group meetings. Transsexuals got the most mileage from denial narratives, however, when telling their complete life histories. These accounts of denial referred to three principal kinds of experiences: (1) self-distractions, (2) masculinity/femininity pursuits, and (3) self-mislabeling.

Self-Distractions. Tales of denial emphasizing self-distractions were accounts of life events that diverted transsexuals' attention from seeing their "true selves." Interviewees said they turned to drugs or sources of bliss to hide their transsexuality. Many said that awareness of the social consequences of stigmatization caused them to find ways to suppress their unconventional "true feelings." One transsexual in her mid-thirties explained in an interview how she was able to repress her "true self" through substance use.

> In high school I smoked a lot of pot and drank a lot, which covered up the emotions really well. At that age, about sixteen or seventeen, I found out that I could escape through drugs and alcohol. I got to college and pretty much

did the same thing. Somehow, miraculously, I was able to graduate with a very decent GPA—and I drank like crazy the whole time and did drugs. I guess I was able to control it enough to manage my life and appear to the rest of the world to be a sane, normal person. But at the same time, I was drinking almost constantly, burying these feelings. . . . I could feel like dressing up like a girl but open a beer instead—and maybe belch and feel all better.

As this person went on to say, even the euphoria of love was a drug that could mask the "true self."

While we were in the euphoria of love, I didn't drink, which was okay. I just wanted to be on the same plane she was. Then all of a sudden about three months later, the euphoria of love started to wear a little thin and those feelings just came flying in for the first time in about 10 or 15 years. It all came back. (Q: The dressing?) The dressing and the transsexuality. Before, I could keep it at bay.

Transsexuals felt that denial, although often strong enough to shut out the "true self" for many years, was always at risk of collapsing. When transsexuals presented denial narratives, they split the self in two: (1) the protagonist of "true self," who worked relentlessly to tear down the barriers of denial, and (2) the antagonist or socially aware "self," who struggled to make repairs. Eventually, they felt, the "true self" proved to have more stamina and the barriers could not withstand the pressure; the "true self" thus won out in this "romance narrative." . . .

Although stories of substance abuse were most common, self-distraction narratives included a variety of preoccupations. For example, the born female said he had so many other problems in his life, including health difficulties and family problems, that he wasn't able to focus on gender-related issues until very recently. Transsexuals could search their biographies for virtually any event in their lives that demanded a great deal of time or emotional energy, and could reinterpret it as a period of denial.

Masculinity/femininity pursuits. Whereas self-distracton narratives focused on doing things or being in situations that inhibited self-reflection, masculinity/femininity pursuits were stories about trying to conform to conventional notions of gender. By defining as *denial* the behavior stereotypically associated with the gender category they were leaving behind, transsexuals were able to gloss over these biographical contradictions. For instance, one born male had been a successful football player in high school. Later, as an adult man, this person had won a community award for organizing and coaching Little League sports. At the time of the interview, she viewed what others called "successes" as efforts to sustain denial.

When I asked one transsexual when she first wanted to cross-dress in public, she responded with the following story of a masculinity pursuit.

Wishing to do so? I didn't let myself wish to do so. Like I said, I was wearing a mustache so I wouldn't even attempt to do so. I'd shave it off every once in a while. I would pretend that I was shaving it off so I could get it to grow back thicker, but what I was shaving it off for was because that way I could cross over. I wouldn't have to stick my fingers above my upper lip to try to see what I looked like.

She saw her previous cultivation of a mustache, a physical sign of masculinity, as a way to deny her differently gendered "true self." Similarly, another born male I interviewed told of previously lifting weights in an attempt to make her body more muscular and more masculine. The transsexuals viewed as denial their past attempt to sculpt their bodies to "give off" (Goffman 1959: 2) signs of masculinity because these attempts contradicted what they currently felt existed deep inside themselves.

Besides the display of physical signs of masculinity, sometimes the main theme of masculinity pursuits was overconformity to traditional gender norms. During one interview a transsexual—who, as a man, had had three unsuccessful marriages to women—explained that she had signified a particular abusive aspect of masculinity in sustaining denial:

When it came to women, I was a son-of-a-bitch. . . . I really was. I treated women like dirt. [I'd tell them,] "You don't know what you're talking about. Let me just do everything, you just sit back and go with the flow. You're not smart enough. You don't know what's going on in the world" . . . to quote it on your tape, it may not seem right, but "Finger them, fuck them, and forget them" . . . was my attitude: Let's see how many women I could lay in the course of a week, or in the course of a month. It was like a game, but even when all of this was going on, inside I was hating what I was doing. [I'd think,] "I don't know this person; the real person is in here." And when I am seeing the woman that I am with, I am thinking, "I would love to *be* you." I would love to be them . . . it was like I was a different person. It was almost like standing back and watching somebody else do these things. Even now, especially now, when I look back it's like I don't believe all that. (Q: And you were doing those things to—) To compensate for—I thought that if I'm real macho, if I'm a real *"man man"* or *"boy boy"* or teenager, or whatever it is, then people aren't going to notice this little feminine side in me that's wanting to come out and just touch somebody or be real gentle.

Ironically, this person wanted to be the kind of person he treated so badly. She said she didn't like the things she had done, but did them because she was trying to be a man. This guilt (about treating women badly) helped solidify the interpretation of denial because it was interpreted as signaling that *something* was wrong with how she had acted as a man.

Masculinity/femininity pursuits also took the form of hobbies. When I walked into the living room of one interviewee's townhouse, the first thing I noticed, with some unease, was a collection of large hunting knives, a few pieces of which were on display on a coffee table. This born male said she had collected these knives in an attempt to conform to traditional masculinity. In addition, this 44-year-old newly defined transsexual told the following story of denial:

Then I started, over a period of a couple years, going through these cycles of really getting into [cross-dressing] and saying "I'm going to go forward," and then stopping and saying, "No, this is out of hand" and engage[ing] in some hobby or activity that would serve as a vehicle for repression. I went through a bit of collecting guns, going to gun shows, and doing a lot of shooting, 'cause that was a really *manly* thing to do. I went through a bit of wearing Redman hats and driving around in pickup trucks and going to mud bog races and those kinds of things 'cause that's the *manly* thing to do. I bought a Harley and went down to Daytona for bike week with half a million Harley riders. Did that for several years because that's the manly thing to do. Of course, the last time I did it I wore a pink lace camisole and stockings and garter belt underneath my leather jacket and my jeans.

Masculinity/femininity pursuits sometimes involved attempts to become involved in single-gendered groups. The born female I interviewed described his attempts to get involved with a group of women whom he had worked with as a "she." As he explained:

I had tried to get involved with the females in the departments. A few of us would . . . go out to eat one night [a month] and kid around— and I just felt isolated in talking about what dresses they were wearing, or makeup. Just those kinds of things; they don't seem to interest me. I don't wear much makeup. I don't like wearing heels, stockings, and jewelry, and to talk about the patterns for material for curtains and the latest recipe. Every once [in a while I'll] talk about a recipe. But spend the whole evening involved with those kinds of things? It wasn't me. I'd rather talk philosophy, gardening. There was a limit in how much I could fit in women's groups.

In attempting to do gender in a traditionally feminine manner, this transsexual remembered feeling uncomfortable. Only after joining the transgender support group and hearing dozens of stories about feeling inauthentic while doing gender conventionally did he interpret his feelings as signs of a differently gendered "true self."

Self-mislabeling. Besides attempting to align the narrator with gender-appropriate activities, some transsexuals' stories of denial emphasized "self-mislabeling." These accounts most often involved defining oneself as a transvestite or cross-dresser, although labeling oneself homosexual, androgynous, or even a sensitive male was not infrequent. After becoming active in the transgender subculture, transsexuals learned to interpret their experiments with these identities as denial. One born male, who recently had begun living full-time as a women, said in an interview:

At one point I thought, . . . "I like dressing like a girl but the only thing I know is there are gay people and straight people, [so] I must be a gay person," and that pushed me into that life for awhile and I stayed there before I realized that I didn't quite identify [with them].

In this person's account of self-mislabeling, she implied that a limited knowledge about alternative identities, specifically *transsexual*, led her to falsely identify as homosexual, thus denying her "true self."

Eight of the nine male-to-female transsexuals I interviewed had previously labeled themselves transvestites or cross-dressers. Unlike other stories of denial, these accounts were often brief and vague. Interviewees often tried to gloss this prior identity confusion by making statements such as, "When I was in denial I thought I might be a transvestite." At the support group meetings, no one was ever asked to clarify such statements. One possible reason why they avoided moving beyond surface details was that doing so could raise a potentially embarrassing question: How could they be sure that the label *transsexual* was correct and not just another mistake? Honoring vague accounts at strategic moments thus helped maintain the power of denial narratives and sanctioned the identity *transsexual*.

When I asked one transsexual how she realized she wasn't a transvestite, she first brought up other narrative evidence—talking about cross-dressing at an early age. Then she raised the following dilemma:

> The problem is if you asked me that question in 1985, I would've told you that I dressed for erotic stimulation and that I was a transvestite, and it was not a means of denying transsexualism.

Another born male—who had started defining herself as transsexual only a few months before our interview—framed the dilemma more sharply:

> I know up here (point to head) something is not male. And yet there is absolutely no direct sensory input that confirms it. None. And this builds up an undercurrent of skepticism that can just undercut everything. If I don't dress [as a woman], I'm denying part of me that I know exists. If I do dress [as a woman], I'm denying part of me that I do see. So, which is denial?

As these quotes imply, it is often hard to grasp what constitutes denial, especially if one attempts to distinguish between truly being in denial and falsely thinking that one is in denial. What criteria does a behavior or attitude have to meet in order to qualify as denial? In the transgender community, an account was viewed as an instance of denial if it fit with other acceptable self-narratives. That is, as long as a story pointed to the existence of a differently gendered "true self," it was legitimate and unquestioned in the group.

Self-Narratives as Collective Creations

Although an isolated individual who felt inauthentic doing gender conventionally could have invented stories similar to those discussed above (because they relied heavily on stereotypical views of gender), they would have been much less powerful without group affirmation. It was the transgender community that cemented the interpretation of gender nonconformity as evidence of transsexuality rather than homosexuality. In this community in the United States, with its over 200 local support groups and national and regional conferences, the templates for self-narratives were made and used. These narrative forms also were maintained and transmitted through community publications, computer networks, and television talk shows. The community functioned in four key ways to help individuals fashion their own self-narratives: (1) modeling, (2) guiding, (3) affirming, and (4) tactful blindness.

Modeling

At support group meetings, the narratives were maintained and transferred to new members largely through *modeling*. In this process, first of all, those transsexuals who were adept at telling self-narratives did so voluntarily. In telling their stories, they gave the new members clues about the types of significant events to look for in their own biographies. If the newcomers listened closely, they could find the rhetorical tools that could be used, with some slight alterations, to signify their own differently gendered "true selves."

One way in which established members did this was by tagging on relevant identity slogans while ostensibly talking about something else. At several of the meetings, transsexuals introduced themselves as "transsexual" and added something like "and I've been cross-dressing since I was five years old." This was somewhat of a ritual; if one person started it, most of the other transsexuals followed with similar introductions. Referencing acceptable self-narratives in this way alerted new members that talking about childhood cross-dressing was linked somehow to transsexualism. In addition, the modeling, or ritualistic repeating of the introduction by those already "in the know," helped to legitimate and sustain childhood cross-dressing stories as an acceptable way to claim a differently gendered "true self."

To make modeling work, it was particularly important for transsexuals well versed in their self-narratives to publicly declare themselves as *transsexuals*, because both cross-dressers and transsexuals attended the meetings. This allowed newcomers who weren't sure what identity to choose to distinguish between the self-narratives of transsexuals and those of cross-dressers. Then they could examine their own biographies to see which kind of story fit them better. For instance, when one transsexual went to her first support group meeting, told her story, and then heard other stories, she said she was "amazed" and felt as though she had "come home." Despite her uncertainty about her identity before the meeting, hearing transsexuals tell stories similar to hers helped convince her that she was a transsexual.

Transsexuals also could learn to model the narratives by reading transgender community publications. On the semi-private e-mail computer list to which I belonged (which had more than 300 subscribers), new subscribers were required to submit an "intro" to the group after about a month. Most of these intros were autobiographical and pointed to certain life events that could be interpreted as clues to a differently gendered "true self." In these biographical statements, new subscribers mimicked the postings of regular members; thus they often wrote about feeling different as long as they could remember, the time when they first cross-dressed, and failure in sports.

In many stories in *Tapestry*, the most popular magazine of the transgender community, the authors referred to these community narratives. In one such article (Montgomery 1993), a female-to-male transsexual wrote about his life before he came to terms with his differently gendered "true self."

> I kept running as fast as I could, burning the candle at both ends. . . . I couldn't remember what someone had said a second after they had said it. Alcohol and drugs had eaten my mind, my feelings, and my heart away.

He went on:

> Something was missing. I didn't know what and I was too scared to find out. . . . The something that was missing was me; the part that I kept running from all these years. I didn't begin to feel whole again until I started to validate me, the one I had stuffed so far down he

> was killing me for not letting him out. My soul was dying.

In the first passage, the author used a self-distraction denial narrative, implying that alcohol and drugs had numbed him. A prospective transsexual who read this article might reflect on his or her own use of drugs or alcohol and might redefine this behavior as denial. In the second passage, without using the word *denial*, the author clarified what denial means. He interpreted feelings of emptiness in his life as signifying that he was repressing his "true self."

Overall, this passage might lead a reader to interpret a lack of personal meaning or sense of belonging, or anything related to feeling that "something was missing," as signs of repressing his or her differently gendered "true self." Some members of the support group apparently had picked up this message from the transgender community. Four said they were so depressed before they "came to terms" with transsexualism that they sought professional help. At the time of their interviews, they all interpreted these periods of despair as evidence that they were repressing their differently gendered "true selves."

The identity "transsexual," although stigmatized, is becoming culturally viable (Garber 1992). . . . As a result, transsexuals' self-narratives can be heard on television talk shows and, recently, in feature films. One interviewee said she first heard transsexuals' stories on the *Sally Jessy Raphael Show*. She saw parts of her life in their stories, called the "expert doctor" who had appeared on the show, and then drove across four states to see him. The doctor "diagnosed" her as transsexual (or affirmed her narrative) and helped her find a support group.

Guiding

Whereas modeling concerned studying others' stories and figuring out how to apply them to one's self, guiding was more interactive. Established members often asked newcomers questions about their pasts, which drew out stories that fit the subculture's acceptable narrative forms. This process was like the collective opening up of a person's biography to highlight life events that the group perceived as evidence of transsexuality. The new member then could tell stories about these highlighted biographical passages at this and future gatherings, and his or her differently gendered "true self" thus could be affirmed by others.

For example, when a new member voluntarily revealed a little about himself or herself (showing willingness to self-disclose) but didn't use an acceptable self-narrative, a regular member sometimes asked, "So when did you *first* cross-dress?" After introducing myself at the first meeting I attended, I was asked if I had ever dressed or been dressed in "female clothes." After I said that my older sister once might have dressed me as a girl, one member uttered a conspicuously satisfied "Hmmm." If my agenda had been to look for my "true self" rather than to conduct research, I might have seen this early life event as a sign of "who I really am."

Guiding was sometimes more overt. At two of the eight meetings I attended—each of which included several first-timers—the coleader/therapist asked if anyone had ever "purged their feminine clothing." Almost everyone raised a hand. On both occasions, a longtime member explained that she had conducted more than 10 purges in the past 20 years, and added that she had only recently realized that her feelings were not going to fade. Similarly, on one of these occasions, a member in her sixties told the group:

> I went through phases of purging for close to fifty years. I've burned enough clothes to fill this entire room. I'm really serious, this entire room. I just don't do it anymore because I know I'll regret it later.

These exchanges helped newcomers to define past purges as futile attempts to deny "who they really are." In addition, they helped preserve purging stories as identity-making tools for everyone. Because these occasions were initiated and guided by the therapist who "specialized in transgender issues," the self-narratives seemed all the more legitimate means of claiming a differently gendered "true self."

Guiding and modeling pointed to pieces of biography that were crucial parts of the transsexual narrative. Newcomers who learned what these were could then use them in assembling the puzzling pieces of their differently gendered "true selves." The passing down of the narratives to newcomers not only aided in the newcomers' own quest for personal meaning, but also preserved the rhetorical tools as they became old-timers themselves. Eventually they would become the givers, rather than the receivers, of identity-making clues.

Affirming

Modeling and guiding worked, especially in interactions, because of the audience members' reactions to the stories. Identities, like all things, become meaningful through the response of others (Stone 1981). At support group meetings, when someone talked about recent events in his or her life, he or she might touch on one of the acceptable self-narratives. After mentioning a significant piece of biographical evidence, others reacted in subtle ways—usually with "um-hums," nods, smiles, or sometimes sighs or "ahs." These "murmurings" (Goffman 1974: 541) validated the story as well as the narrator's identity.

At one meeting, for example, a participant described being tormented by the question of whether she wanted to tell a friend, who knew her as a man, about her desire to become a woman. When asked why she wanted to tell, she explained that it was becoming difficult to continue presenting an inauthentic self to someone who was close to her. She added that she had been in denial for a long time and did not want to deny her "true self" to a good friend. When denial of the "true self" was brought up, some members nodded or smiled. The speaker had touched on an acceptable community narrative for self-construction. The listeners' responses delicately but unmistakably reinforced the speaker's differently gendered "true self," and also marked denial narratives as a resource on which transsexuals could draw to fashion a new identity.

Tactful Blindness

Besides making overt responses, transsexuals sometimes affirmed self-narratives by not questioning their validity or logical coherence. Self-narratives always have loose ends and can be unraveled by anyone who wishes to do so. Transsexuals thus practiced "tact" (Goffman 1967:29) when they ignored discrepancies and implausibilities in each other's stories. By doing so, the support group members nurtured the fragile new identities they were trying to acquire. This collective "looking the other way" also shielded the practice of using self-narratives to create evidence of a "true self" that did not yet exist.

Thus a certain tactful blindness allowed people with diverse biographies to see themselves as possessing similar "true selves." At one meeting, for example, a born male who had been a competitive cyclist and remembered (under hypnosis) cross-dressing just once as a child was sitting next to a born male who had never participated in sports and had cross-dressed throughout childhood. Both identified as transsexual; this identity was affirmed and supported by group members when they told their contrasting stories. No one ever questioned how such different experiences could be unequivocal evidence of the same kind of "true self."

Overall, the creation and maintenance of acceptable narratives was a community effort. The transgender community created the culture, which in turn provided resources for identity work. The resources available to transgenderists often fed on each other. For example, transgender support groups, including the one I attended, often had libraries of publications to help newcomers understand what they were experiencing. National publications listed local support groups, Internet groups, and places offering therapeutic and medical help. People I interviewed passed all sorts of information about transgender issues between themselves and (on a few occasions) to me. The narrative construction of "true selves" required a great deal of cooperation.

Conclusion

Transsexuals used self-narratives to convincingly invent a differently gendered "true self," but they didn't invent or use self-narratives in isolation. Subcultural involvement, at some level, was essential. My analysis shows that not only frameworks for interpreting identities . . . but also symbolic resources for making those identities are created subculturally. Through modeling, guiding, affirming, and tactful blindness, transsexuals created and learned the narrative forms that sustained an identity which their physical bodies could not. . . .

Transsexuals are not the only ones who construct their identities through storytelling. . . . [A] sense of continuity and coherence is difficult to sustain in our present society. Indeed, we may face complex situations and diverse self-presenta-

tional demands that can make us feel fragmented. Living in such a world increases opportunities to contradict ourselves. Adding to this problem is the fact that all of us have conflicting impulses to act. Over the life course, the self-contradictions multiply; thus it becomes more difficult to maintain a coherent self. Under these conditions, self-narratives may become even more important for self-making because of their power to create order out of chaos.

To maintain a sense of wholeness and continuity, we must revise, edit, and sometimes completely rewrite our "true selves." Sometimes we can do this alone. At other times, when the stakes are high or when the confusion is great, we may need to turn to others for help. Doing this work with similar others guarantees the existence of an audience willing to affirm a new "true self," regardless of what outsiders may think of it. As the case of transsexuals shows, interacting with others gives us what we need to make the self as real and true as it can be.

References

Cahill, Spencer E. 1989. "Fashioning Males and Females: Appearance Management and the Social Reproduction of Gender." *Symbolic Interaction* 2:281–298.

Garber, Marjorie. 1992. *Vested Interests: Cross-Dressing and Cultural Anxiety*. New York: Routledge.

Goffman, Erving. 1959. *The Presentation of Self in Everyday Life*. New York: Anchor.

———. 1963. *Stigma: Notes on the Management of Spoiled Identity*. Englewood Cliffs, NJ: Prentice Hall.

———. 1967. *Interaction Ritual*. New York: Pantheon.

———. 1974. *Frame Analysis*. New York: Harper.

Montgomery, Taylor. 1993. "Take It as You Find It or Do With It As You Will." *Tapestry* 65:30–32.

Stone, Gregory. 1981. "Appearance and the Self: A Slightly Revised Version." Pp. 87–102 in *Social Psychology Through Symbolic Interaction*, edited by Gregory Stone and Harvey Farberman. Waltham, MA: Ginn.

Part V

Social Interaction and Order

Social interaction has an organization all its own, apart from the participants' particular characteristics and the larger social environments in which it occurs. Indeed, social interaction is meaningful because it is patterned, organized, and orderly. Participants commonly share an implicit understanding of its organization and, therefore, similar expectations of what each is likely to do under different circumstances. This shared but implicit understanding turns both action and inaction, the expected and unexpected, into meaningful events. For example, individuals who are acquainted expect to exchange greetings when they meet. If we walk past those whom we know without greeting them, they will probably consider it a snub. Our failure to greet them is meaningful, because they expect a greeting. Although we may blatantly ignore expected patterns of interaction, we do so at the risk of sending unintended messages to others and often unflattering ones about ourselves.

One of the principal tasks of microsociology is to investigate and describe recurrent patterns of interaction and the principles of their organization. The goal is to understand how individuals achieve mutual understanding and collectively construct meaningful social lives. That is the focus of the selections in this section. They describe the organization of different aspects of social interaction, explain individuals' commitment to sustaining orderly patterns of interaction, and illustrate how such patterns of interaction provide the glue of social life. ✦

16

Face-Work and Interaction Rituals

Erving Goffman

An earlier selection by Erving Goffman examined some of the dramatic or theatrical characteristics of social interaction. It described how individuals enact selves and reach a working consensus concerning the respective parts each will play in the course of their interaction. In this selection, Goffman observes that individuals effectively claim positive social value or "face" through the lines they take or parts they perform during interaction. He also argues, as Snow and Anderson's selection about the homeless suggests, that individuals are emotionally invested in claiming and maintaining face. The embarrassment we experience when we stumble, forget our lines, or otherwise bungle a social performance clearly demonstrates his argument.

According to Goffman, the maintenance of face requires that individuals uphold an expressive order. That is, an individual must meet others' expectations of how the type of person that she or he claims to be should act. In turn, others must treat her or him as that type of person. Thus, the maintenance of face depends on an implicit agreement: I will protect your face, if you protect mine. We usually honor this agreement because of our common emotional investment in face, resulting in our self-regulated participation in orderly patterns of social interaction.

Goffman describes two basic kinds of face-work that characterize such orderly interaction. The first is self-explanatory: we attempt to avoid places, people, situations, and topics that might threaten our own or others' face and attempt to ignore events that do. However, we do not always succeed, which necessitates the second kind of face-work, or what Goffman calls the corrective process.

Goffman describes the corrective process as a "ritual" for two reasons. First, it consists of a routine interchange of "moves." When a threat to face occurs, we expect the involved parties to engage in a sequence of familiar acts and interpret the absence of any such moves in terms of that expected pattern. If, for example, an individual who has offended someone fails to offer an apology, we are likely to conclude that he or she is cold and uncaring. This example illustrates how socially expected patterns of interaction turn both action and inaction into meaningful events.

Second, the corrective process is like a religious ritual, expressing individuals' mutual reverence for face. The countless times a day that we say "excuse me," "I'm sorry," and "thank you" indicate just how highly we regard both our own and others' face. Thus, Goffman's characterization of face as "sacred" is at most only a slight exaggeration.

Every person lives in a world of social encounters, involving him either in face-to-face or mediated contact with other participants. In each of these contacts, he tends to act out what is sometimes called a line—that is, a pattern of verbal and nonverbal acts by which he expresses his view of the situation and through this his evaluation of the participants, especially himself. Regardless of whether a person intends to take a line, he will find that he has done so in effect. The other participants will assume that he has more or less willfully taken a stand, so that if he is to deal with their response to him he must take into consideration the impression they have possibly formed of him.

The term *face* may be defined as the positive social value a person effectively claims for himself by the line others assume he has taken during a particular contact. Face is an image of self-delineated in terms of approved social attributes—albeit an image that others may share, as when a person makes a good showing for his profession or religion by making a good showing for himself.

A person tends to experience an immediate emotional response to the face which a contact with others allows him; he cathects his face; his "feelings" become attached to it. If the encounter sustains an image of him that he has long taken for granted, he probably will have few feelings about the matter. If events establish a face for him that is better than he might have expected, he is likely to "feel good"; if his ordinary expectations are not fulfilled, one expects that he will "feel bad" or "feel hurt." In general, a person's attachment to a particular face, coupled with the ease with which disconfirming information can be conveyed by himself and others, provides one reason why he finds that participation in any contact with others is a commitment. A person will also have feelings about the face sustained for the other participants; and, while these feelings may differ in quantity and direction from those he has for his own face, they constitute an involvement in the face of others that is as immediate and spontaneous as the involvement he has in his own face. One's own face and the face of others are constructs of the same order; it is the rules of the group and the definition of the situation which determine how much feeling one is to have for face and how this feeling is to be distributed among the faces involved.

A person may be said to *have*, or *be in*, or *maintain* face when the line he effectively takes presents an image of him that is internally consistent, that is supported by judgments and evidence conveyed by other participants, and that is confirmed by evidence conveyed through impersonal agencies in the situation. At such times the person's face clearly is something that is not lodged in or on his body, but rather something that is diffusely located in the flow of events in the encounter and becomes manifest only when these events are read and interpreted for the appraisals expressed in them.

The line maintained by and for a person during contact with others tends to be of a legitimate institutionalized kind. During a contact of a particular type, an interactant of known or visible attributes can expect to be sustained in a particular face and can feel that it is morally proper that this should be so. Given his attributes and the conventionalized nature of the encounter, he will find a small choice of lines will be open to him and a small choice of faces will be waiting for him. Further, on the basis of a few known attributes, he is given the responsibility of possessing a vast number of others. His co-participants are not likely to be conscious of the character of many of these attributes until he acts perceptibly in such a way as to discredit his possession of them; then everyone becomes conscious of these attributes and assumes that he willfully gave a false impression of possessing them.

Thus, while concern for face focuses the attention of the person on the current activity, he must, to maintain face in this activity, take into consideration his place in the social world beyond it. A person who can maintain face in the current situation is someone who has abstained from certain actions in the past that would have been difficult to face up to later. In addition, he fears loss of face now partly because the others may take this as a sign that consideration for his feelings need not be shown in the future. There is nevertheless a limitation to this interdependence between the current situation and the wider social world: an encounter with people whom he will not have dealings with again leaves him free to take a high line that the future will discredit, or free to suffer humiliations that would make future dealing with them an embarrassing thing to have to face.

A person may be said to *be in wrong face* when information is brought forth in some way about his social worth which cannot be integrated, even with effort, into the line that is being sustained for him. A person may be said to *be out of face* when he participates in a contact with others without having ready a line of the kind participants in such situations are expected to take. The intent of many pranks is to lead a person into showing a wrong face or no face, but there will also be serious occasions, of course, when he will find himself expressively out of touch with the situation.

When a person senses that he is in face, he typically responds with feelings of confidence and assurance. Firm in the line he is taking, he feels that he can hold his head up and openly present himself to others. He feels some security and some relief—as he also can when the others feel he is in wrong face but successfully hide these feelings from him.

When a person is in wrong face or out of face, expressive events are being contributed to the encounter which cannot be readily woven into the expressive fabric of the occasion. Should he sense that he is in wrong face or out of face, he is likely to feel ashamed and inferior because of what has happened to the activity on his account and because of what may happen to his reputation as a participant. Further, he may feel bad because he had relied upon the encounter to support an image of self to which he has become emotionally attached and which he now finds threatened. Felt lack of judgmental support from the encounter may take him aback, confuse him, and momentarily incapacitate him as an interactant. His manner and bearing may falter, collapse, and crumble. He may become embarrassed and chagrined; he may become shamefaced. The feeling, whether warranted or not, that he is perceived in a flustered state by others, and that he is presenting no usable line, may add further injuries to his feelings, just as his change from being in wrong face or out of face to being shamefaced can add further disorder to the expressive organization of the situation. Following common usage, I shall employ the term *poise* to refer to the capacity to suppress and conceal any tendency to become shamefaced during encounters with others.

In our Anglo-American society, as in some others, the phrase "to lose face" seems to mean to be in wrong face, to be out of face, or to be shamefaced. The phrase "to save one's face" appears to refer to the process by which the person sustains an impression for others that he has not lost face. . . .

As an aspect of the social code of any social circle, one may expect to find an understanding as to how far a person should go to save his face. Once he takes on a self-image expressed through face, he will be expected to live up to it. In different ways in different societies, he will be required to show self-respect, abjuring certain actions because they are above or beneath him, while forcing himself to perform others, even though they cost him dearly. By entering a situation in which he is given a face to maintain, a person takes on the responsibility of standing guard over the flow of events as they pass before him. He must ensure that a particular *expressive order* is sustained—an order that regulates the flow of events, large or small, so that anything that appears to be expressed by them will be consistent with his face. When a person manifests these compunctions primarily from duty to himself, one speaks in our society of pride; when he does so because of duty to wider social units, and receives support from these units in doing so, one speaks of honor. When these compunctions have to do with postural things, with expressive events derived from the way in which the person handles his body, his emotions, and the things with which he has physical contact, one speaks of dignity, this being an aspect of expressive control that is always praised and never studied. In any case, while his social face can be his most personal possession and the center of his security and pleasure, it is only on loan to him from society; it will be withdrawn, unless he conducts himself in a way that is worthy of it. Approved attributes and their relation to face make of every man his own jailer; this is a fundamental social constraint, even though each man may like his cell.

Just as the member of any group is expected to have self-respect, so also he is expected to sustain a standard of considerateness; he is expected to go to certain lengths to save the feelings and the face of others present, and he is expected to do this willingly and spontaneously because of emotional identification with the others and with their feelings. In consequence, he is disinclined to witness the defacement of others. The person who can witness another's humiliation and unfeelingly retain a cool countenance himself is said in our society to be "heartless," just as he who can unfeelingly participate in his own defacement is thought to be "shameless."

The combined effect of the rule of self-respect and the rule of considerateness is that the person tends to conduct himself during an encounter so as to maintain both his own face and the face of the other participants. This means that the line taken by each participant is usually allowed to prevail, and each participant is allowed to carry off the role he appears to have chosen for himself. A state where everyone temporarily accepts everyone else's line is established. This kind of mutual acceptance seems to be a basic structural feature of interaction, especially the interaction of face-to-face talk. It is typically a "working" acceptance, not a "real" one, since it tends to be based not on agreement of candidly expressed heartfelt evaluations, but upon a willingness to give temporary lip service to judgments with which the participants do not really agree.

The mutual acceptance of lines has an important conservative effect upon encounters. Once the person initially presents a line, he and the others tend to build their later responses upon it, and in a sense, become stuck with it. Should the person radically alter his line, or should it become discredited, then confusion results, for the participants will have prepared and committed themselves for actions that are now unsuitable. . . .

By *face-work* I mean to designate the actions taken by a person to make whatever he is doing consistent with face. Face-work serves to counteract "incidents"—that is, events whose effective symbolic implications threaten face. Thus, poise is one important type of face-work, for through poise the person controls his embarrassment and hence the embarrassment that he and others might have over his embarrassment. Whether or not the full consequences of face-saving actions are known to the person who employs them, they often become habitual and standardized practices; they are like traditional plays in a game or traditional steps in a dance. Each person, sub-culture, and society seems to have its own characteristic repertoire of face-saving practices. It is to this repertoire that people partly refer when they ask what a person or culture is "really" like. And yet the particular set of practices stressed by particular persons or groups seems to be drawn from a single logically coherent framework of possible practices. It is as if face, by its very nature, can be saved only in a certain number of ways, and as if each social grouping must make its selections from this single matrix of possibilities.

The members of every social circle may be expected to have some knowledge of face-work and some experience in its use. In our society, this kind of capacity is sometimes called tact, *savoir-faire*, diplomacy, or social skill. Variation in social skill pertains more to the efficacy of face-work than to the frequency of its application, for almost all acts involving others are modified, prescriptively or proscriptively, by considerations of face. If a person is to employ his repertoire of face-saving practices, obviously he must first become aware of the interpretation that others may have placed upon his acts and the interpretation that he ought perhaps to place upon theirs. In other words, he must exercise perceptiveness. But even if he is properly alive to symbolically conveyed judgements and is socially skilled, he must yet be willing to exercise his perceptiveness and his skill; he must, in short, be prideful and considerate. Admittedly, of course, the possession of perceptiveness and social skill so often leads to their application in our society that terms such as politeness or tact fail to distinguish between the inclination to exercise such capacities and the capacities themselves.

I have already said that the person will have two points of view—a defensive orientation toward saving his own face and a protective orientation toward saving the others' face. Some practices will be primarily defensive and others primarily protective, although in general, one may expect these two perspectives to be taken at the same time. In trying to save the face of others, the person must choose a tack that will not lead to loss of his own; in trying to save his own face, he must consider the loss of face that his action may entail for others.

In many societies, there is a tendency to distinguish three levels of responsibility that a person may have for a threat to face that his actions have created. First, he may appear to have acted innocently; his offense seems to be unintended and unwitting, and those who perceive his act can feel that he would have attempted to avoid it had he foreseen its offensive consequences. In our society, one calls such threats to face *faux pas, gaffes, boners,* or *bricks.* Secondly, the offending person may appear to have acted maliciously and spitefully, with the intention of causing open insult. Thirdly, there are incidental offenses; these arise as an unplanned but sometimes anticipated by-product of action—action the offender performs in spite of its offensive consequences, although not out of spite. From the point of view of a particular participant, these three types of threat can be introduced by the participant himself against his own face, by himself against the face of the others, by the others against their own face, or by the others against himself. Thus, the person may find himself in many different relations to a threat to face. If he is to handle himself and others well in all contingencies, he will have to have a repertoire of face-saving practices for each of these possible relations to threat.

The Basic Kinds of Face-Work

The Avoidance Process

The surest way for a person to prevent threats to his face is to avoid contacts in which these threats are likely to occur. In all societies, one can observe this in the avoidance relationship and in the tendency for certain delicate transactions to be conducted by go-betweens. Similarly, in many societies, members know the value of voluntarily making a gracious withdrawal before an anticipated threat to face has had a chance to occur.

Once the person does chance an encounter, other kinds of avoidance practices come into play. As defensive measures, he keeps off topics and away from activities that would lead to the expression of information that is inconsistent with the line he is maintaining. At opportune moments he will change the topic of conversation or the direction of activity. He will often present initially a front of diffidence and composure, suppressing any show of feeling, until he has found out what kind of line the others will be ready to support for him. Any claims regarding self may be made with belittling modesty, with strong qualifications, or with a note of unseriousness; by hedging in these ways, he will have prepared a self for himself that will not be discredited by exposure, personal failure, or the unanticipated acts of others. And if he does not hedge his claims about self, he will at least attempt to be realistic about them, knowing that otherwise events may discredit him and make him lose face.

Certain protective maneuvers are as common as these defensive ones. The person shows respect and politeness, making sure to extend to others any ceremonial treatment that might be their due. He employs discretion; he leaves unstated facts that might implicitly or explicitly contradict and embarrass the positive claims made by others. He employs circumlocutions and deceptions, phrasing his replies with careful ambiguity, so that the others' face is preserved even if their welfare is not. He employs courtesies, making slight modifications of his demands on or appraisals of the others, so that they will be able to define the situation as one in which their self-respect is not threatened. In making a belittling demand upon the others, or in imputing uncomplimentary attributes to them, he may employ a joking manner, allowing them to take the lie that they are good sports, able to relax from their ordinary standards of pride and honor. And before engaging in a potentially offensive act, he may provide explanations as to why the others ought not to be affronted by it. For example, if he knows that it will be necessary to withdraw from the encounter before it has terminated, he may tell the others in advance that it is necessary for him to leave, so that they will have faces that are prepared for it. But neutralizing the potentially offensive act need not be done verbally; he may wait for a propitious moment or natural break—for example, in conversation, a momentary lull when no one speaker can be affronted—and then leave, in this way using the context instead of his words as a guarantee of inoffensiveness.

When a person fails to prevent an incident, he can still attempt to maintain the fiction that no threat to face has occurred. The most blatant example of this is found where the person acts as if an event that contains a threatening expression has not occurred at all. He may apply this studied non-observance to his own acts—as when he does not by any outward sign admit that his stomach is rumbling—or to the acts of others, as when he does not "see" that another has stumbled. Social life in mental hospitals owes much to this process; patients employ it in regard to their own peculiarities, and visitors employ it, often with tenuous desperation, in regard to patients. In general, tactful blindness of this kind is applied only to events that, if perceived at all, could be perceived and interpreted only as threats to face.

A more important, less spectacular kind of tactful overlooking is practiced when a person openly acknowledges an incident as an event that has occurred, but not as an event that contains a threatening expression. If he is not the one who is responsible for the incident, then his blindness will have to be supported by his forbearance; if he is the doer of the threatening deed, then his blindness will have to be supported by his willingness to seek a way of dealing with the matter, which leaves him dangerously dependent upon the cooperative forbearance of the others.

Another kind of avoidance occurs when a person loses control of his expressions during an encounter. At such times he may try not so much to overlook the incident as to hide or conceal his activity in some way, thus making it possible for the others to avoid some of the difficulties created by a participant who has not maintained face. Correspondingly, when a person is caught out of face because he had not expected to be thrust into interaction, or because strong feelings have disrupted his expressive mask, the others may protectively turn away from him or his activity for a moment, to give him time to assemble himself.

The Corrective Process

When the participants in an undertaking or encounter fail to prevent the occurrence of an event that is expressively incompatible with the judgments of social worth that are being maintained, and when the event is of the kind that is difficult to overlook, then the participants are likely to give it accredited status as an incident—to ratify it as a threat that deserves direct official attention—and to proceed to try to correct for its effects. At this point, one or more participants find themselves in an established state of ritual disequilibrium or disgrace, and an attempt must be made to re-establish a satisfactory ritual state for them. I use the term *ritual* because I am dealing with acts through whose symbolic component the actor shows how worthy he is of respect or how worthy he feels others are of it. The imagery of equilibrium is apt here, because the length and intensity of the corrective effort is nicely adapted to the persistence and intensity of the threat. One's face, then, is a sacred thing, and the expressive order required to sustain it is, therefore, a ritual one.

The sequence of acts set in motion by an acknowledged threat to face, and terminating in the re-establishment of ritual equilibrium, I shall call an *interchange*. Defining a message or move as everything conveyed by an actor during a turn at taking action, one can say that an interchange will involve two or more moves and two or more participants. Obvious examples in our society may be found in the sequence of "Excuse me" and "Certainly" and in the exchange of presents or visits. The interchange seems to be a basic concrete unit of social activity and provides one natural empirical way to study interaction of all kinds. Face-saving practices can be usefully classified according to their position in the natural sequence of moves that comprise this unit. Aside from the event which introduces the need for a corrective interchange, four classic moves seem to be involved.

There is, first, the challenge, by which participants take on the responsibility of calling attention to the misconduct; by implication, they suggest that the threatened claims are to stand firm and that the threatening event itself will have to be brought back into line.

The second move consists of the offering, whereby a participant, typically the offender, is given a chance to correct for the offense and re-establish the expressive order. Some classic ways of making this move are available. On the one hand, an attempt can be made to show that what admittedly appeared to be a threatening expression is really a meaningless event, or an unintentional act, or a joke not meant to be taken seriously, or an unavoidable, "understandable" product of extenuating circumstances. On the other hand, the meaning of the event may be granted and effort concentrated on the creator of it. Information may be provided to show that the creator was under the influence of something and not himself, or that he was under the command of somebody else and not acting for himself. When a person claims that an act was meant in jest, he may go on and claim that the self that seemed to lie behind the act was also projected as a joke. When a person suddenly finds that he has

demonstrably failed in capacities that the others assumed him to have and to claim for himself—such as the capacity to spell, to perform minor tasks, to talk without malapropisms, and so on—he may quickly add, in a serious or unserious way, that he claims these incapacities as part of his self. The meaning of the threatening incident thus stands, but it can now be incorporated smoothly into the flow of expressive events.

As a supplement to or substitute for the strategy of redefining the offensive act or himself, the offender can follow two other procedures: he can provide compensations to the injured—when it is not his own face that he has threatened; or he can provide punishment, penance, and expiation for himself. These are important moves or phases in the ritual interchange. Even though the offender may fail to prove his innocence, he can suggest through these means that he is now a renewed person, a person who has paid for his sin against the expressive order and is once more to be trusted in the judgmental scene. Further, he can show that he does not treat the feelings of the others lightly, and that, if their feelings have been injured by him, however innocently, he is prepared to pay a price for his action. Thus, he assures the others that they can accept his explanations without this acceptance constituting a sign of weakness and a lack of pride on their part. Also, by his treatment of himself, by his self-castigation, he shows that he is clearly aware of the kind of crime he would have committed had the incident been what it first appeared to be, and that he knows the kind of punishment that ought to be accorded to one who would commit such a crime. The suspected person thus shows that he is thoroughly capable of taking the role of the others toward his own activity, that he can still be used as a responsible participant in the ritual process, and that the rules of conduct which he appears to have broken are still sacred, real, and unweakened. An offensive act may arouse anxiety about the ritual code; the offender allays this anxiety by showing that both the code and he as an upholder of it are still in working order.

After the challenge and the offering have been made, the third move can occur; the persons to whom the offering is made can accept it as a satisfactory means of re-establishing the expressive order and the faces supported by this order. Only then can the offender cease the major part of his ritual offering.

In the terminal move of the interchange, the forgiven person conveys a sign of gratitude to those who have given him the indulgence of forgiveness.

The phases of the corrective process—challenge, offering, acceptance, and thanks—provide a model for interpersonal ritual behavior, but a model that may be departed from in significant ways. For example, the offended parties may give the offender a chance to initiate the offering on his own before a challenge is made and before they ratify the offense as an incident. This is a common courtesy, extended on the assumption that the recipient will introduce a self-challenge. Further, when the offended persons accept the corrective offering, the offender may suspect that this has been grudgingly done from tact, and so he may volunteer additional corrective offerings, not allowing the matter to rest until he has received a second or third acceptance of his repeated apology. Or the offended persons may tactfully take over the role of the offender and volunteer excuses for him that will, perforce, be acceptable to the offended persons.

An important departure from the standard corrective cycle occurs when a challenged· offender patently refuses to heed the warning and continues with his offending behavior, instead of setting the activity to rights. This move shifts the play back to the challengers. If they countenance the refusal to meet their demands, then it will be plain that their challenge was a bluff and that the bluff has been called. This is an untenable position; a face for themselves cannot be derived from it, and they are left to bluster. To avoid this fate, some classic moves are open to them. For instance, they can resort to tactless, violent retaliation, destroying either themselves or the person who had refused to heed their warning. Or they can withdraw from the undertaking in a visible huff—righteously indignant, outraged, but confident of ultimate vindication. Both tacks provide a way of denying the offender his status as an interactant, and hence denying the reality of the offensive judgment he has made. Both strategies are ways of salvaging face, but for all concerned the costs are usually high. It is partly to forestall such scenes that an offender is usually quick to offer apologies; he does not want the affronted persons to trap themselves into the obligation to resort to desperate measures.

It is plain that emotions play a part in these cycles of response, as when anguish is expressed because of what one has done to another's face, or anger because of what has been done to one's own. I want to stress that these emotions function as moves, and fit so precisely into the logic of the ritual game that it would seem difficult to understand them without it. In fact, spontaneously expressed feelings are likely to fit into the formal pattern of the ritual interchange more elegantly than consciously designed ones.

Making Points— The Aggressive Use of Face-Work

Every face-saving practice which is allowed to neutralize a particular threat opens up the possibility that the threat will be willfully introduced for what can be safely gained by it. If a person knows that this modesty will be answered by others' praise of him, he can fish for compliments. If his own appraisal of self will be checked against incidental events, then he can arrange for favorable incidental events to appear. If others are prepared to overlook an affront to them and act forbearingly, or to accept apologies, then he can rely on this as a basis for safely offending them. He can attempt by sudden withdrawal to force the others into a ritually unsatisfactory state, leaving them to flounder in an interchange that cannot readily be completed. Finally, at some expense to himself, he can arrange for the others to hurt his feelings, thus forcing them to feel guilt, remorse, and sustained ritual disequilibrium.

When a person treats face-work not as something he need be prepared to perform, but rather as something that others can be counted on to perform or to accept, then an encounter or an undertaking becomes less a scene of mutual considerateness than an arena in which a contest or match is held. The purpose of the game is to preserve everyone's line from an inexcusable contradiction, while scoring as many points as possible against one's adversaries and making as many gains as possible for oneself. An audience to the struggle is almost a necessity. The general method is for the person to introduce favorable facts about himself and unfavorable facts about the others in such a way that the only reply the others will be able to think up will be one that terminates the interchange in a grumble, a meager excuse, a face-saving I-can-take-a-joke laugh, or an empty stereotyped comeback of the "Oh yeah?" or "That's what you think" variety. The losers in such cases will have to cut their losses, tacitly grant the loss of a point, and attempt to do better in the next interchange. . . .

In aggressive interchanges, the winner not only succeeds in introducing information favorable to himself and unfavorable to the others, but also demonstrates that as interactant he can handle himself better than his adversaries. Evidence of this capacity is often more important than all the other information the person conveys in the interchange, so that the introduction of a "crack" in verbal interaction tends to imply that the initiator is better at footwork than those who must suffer his remarks. However, if they succeed in making a successful parry of the thrust and then a successful riposte, the instigator of the play must not only face the disparagement with which the others have answered him but also accept the fact that his assumption of superiority in footwork has proven false. He is made to look foolish; he loses face. Hence, it is always a gamble to "make a remark." The tables can be turned and the aggressor can lose more than he could have gained had his move won the point. . . .

Cooperation in Face-Work

Since each participant in an undertaking is concerned, albeit for differing reasons, with saving his own face and the face of the others, then tacit cooperation will naturally arise so that the participants together can attain their shared but differently motivated objectives.

One common type of tacit cooperation in face-saving is the tact exerted in regard to face-work itself. The person not only defends his own face and protects the face of the others, but also acts so as to make it possible and even easy for the others to employ face-work for themselves and him. He helps them to help themselves and him. Social etiquette, for example, warns men against asking for New Year's Eve dates too early in the season, lest the girl find it difficult to provide a gentle excuse for refusing. This second-order tact can be further illustrated by the widespread practice of negative-attribute etiquette. The person who has an unapparent negatively valued attribute often finds it expedient to begin

an encounter with an unobtrusive admission of his failing, especially with persons who are uninformed about him. The others are thus warned in advance against making disparaging remarks about his kind of person and are saved from the contradiction of acting in a friendly fashion to a person toward whom they are unwittingly being hostile. This strategy also prevents the others from automatically making assumptions about him which place him in a false position and saves him from painful forbearance or embarrassing remonstrances.

Tact, in regard to face-work, often relies for its operation on a tacit agreement to do business through the language of hint—the language of innuendo, ambiguities, well-placed pauses, carefully worded jokes, and so on. The rule regarding this unofficial kind of communication is that the sender ought not to act as if he had officially conveyed the message he has hinted at, while the recipients have the right and the obligation to act as if they have not officially received the message contained in the hint. Hinted communication, then, is deniable communication; it need not be faced up to. It provides a means by which the person can be warned that his current line or the current situation is leading to loss of face, without this warning itself becoming an incident.

Another form of tacit cooperation, and one that seems to be much used in many societies, is reciprocal self-denial. Often the person does not have a clear idea of what would be a just or acceptable apportionment of judgments during the occasion, and so he voluntarily deprives or depreciates himself while indulging and complimenting the others, in both cases carrying the judgments safely past what is likely to be just. The favorable judgments about himself he allows to come from others; the unfavorable judgments of himself are his own contributions. This "after you, Alphonse" technique works, of course, because in depriving himself, he can reliably anticipate that the others will compliment or indulge him. Whatever allocation of favors is eventually established, all participants are first given a chance to show that they are not bound or constrained by their own desires and expectations, that they have a properly modest view of themselves, and that they can be counted upon to support the ritual code. . . .

A person's performance of face-work, extended by his tacit agreement to help others perform theirs, represents his willingness to abide by the ground rules of social interaction. Here is the hallmark of his socialization as an interactant. If he and the others were not socialized in this way, interaction in most societies and most situations would be a much more hazardous thing for feelings and faces. The person would find it impractical to be oriented to symbolically conveyed appraisals of social worth, or to be possessed of feelings—that is, it would be impractical for him to be a ritually delicate object. . . . It is no wonder that trouble is caused by a person who cannot be relied upon to play the face-saving game. . . .

Conclusion

Throughout this paper it has been implied that underneath their differences in culture, people everywhere are the same. If persons have a universal human nature, they themselves are not to be looked to for an explanation of it. One must look rather to the fact that societies everywhere, if they are to be societies, must mobilize their members as self-regulating participants in social encounters. One way of mobilizing the individual for this purpose is through ritual: he is taught to be perceptive; to have feelings attached to self and a self expressed through face; to have pride, honor, and dignity; to have considerateness; to

have tact and a certain amount of poise. These are some of the elements of behavior which must be built into the person, if practical use is to be made of him as an interactant, and it is these elements that are referred to in part when one speaks of universal human nature.

Universal human nature is not a very human thing. By acquiring it, the person becomes a kind of construct, built up not from inner psychic propensities but from moral rules that are impressed upon him from without. These rules, when followed, determine the evaluation he will make of himself and of his fellow-participants in the encounter, the distribution of his feelings, and the kinds of practices he will employ to maintain a specified and obligatory kind of ritual equilibrium. The general capacity to be bound by moral rules may well belong to the individual, but the particular set of rules which transforms him into a human being derives from requirements established in the ritual organization of social encounters. . . .

17

The Interaction Order of Public Bathrooms

Spencer E. Cahill

This selection illustrates the dramatic and ritual character of everyday social life that Goffman identified with the example of routine behavior in public bathrooms. From Goffman's dramaturgical perspective, bathrooms are backstage regions where individuals can temporarily retire from their frontstage performances. However, public bathrooms do not insulate individuals from potential audiences. When not concealed in toilet stalls, they must be ready to perform and to uphold what Goffman called "the interaction order." Yet, individuals in public bathrooms routinely engage in acts that are inconsistent with their frontstage performances and undermine the "sacred" face they claim through those performances. Thus, public bathrooms are scenes of many socially delicate situations that reveal just how loyal we are to the commonly understood but unspoken rules that govern everyday social interaction.

First, this selection illustrates that much behavior in public bathrooms consists of what Goffman called "interpersonal rituals." Individuals show respect for one another by honoring one another's right to be let alone and the turn order of queues. They show respect for their relationships with others by acknowledging those with whom they are previously acquainted. Other ritual conduct in public bathrooms addresses the socially delicate situations that occur within them. For example, men using adjacent urinals do not glance at one another and then look away as they might under other circumstances but keep their eyes glued to the wall directly in front of them. Other ritual conduct counteracts the profaning implications of the acts for which public bathrooms are explicitly designed.

Second, this selection illustrates the variety of backstage behaviors that routinely occur in public bathrooms. In addition to the acts for which they are explicitly designed, individuals retreat to bathrooms to inspect and repair their frontstage appearance and costumes or "personal fronts." They retreat to bathrooms when overcome by emotion. And, groups who are acting as an ensemble or "performance team" retreat to bathrooms to boost team morale, rehearse lines, and give one another direction.

Both forms of routine behavior in public bathrooms, ritual and backstage, reveal many of the usually unrecognized standards that govern everyday social interaction and our usually unrecognized commitment to them. Backstage behavior reveals, by way of contrast, the behavioral standards that govern our frontstage performances. And, our ritual conduct in public bathrooms demonstrates just how committed we are to upholding the expressive order that sustains the "sacredness" of our own and others' "face." The usually unnoticed but exquisite orderliness of everyday social interaction clearly does not stop at the bathroom door.

[Some] years ago the anthropologist Horace Miner (1955) suggested, with tongue planted firmly in cheek, that many of the rituals that behaviorally express and sustain the central values of our culture occur in bathrooms. Whether Miner realized it or not . . . there was more to this thesis than his humorous interpretation of bathroom rituals suggests. As Erving Goffman (1959: 112–113) once observed, the vital secrets of our public shows are often visible in those settings that serve as backstage regions relative to our public performances:

> it is here that illusions and impressions are openly constructed. . . . Here the performer can relax; he can drop his front, forgo speaking his lines, and step out of character.

Clearly, bathrooms or, as they are often revealingly called, restrooms, are such backstage regions. By implication, therefore, systematic study of bathroom behavior may yield valuable insights into the character and requirements of our routine public performances. . . .

This study is . . . concerned with routine bathroom behavior. Over a nine-month period, five student research assistants and I spent over one hundred hours observing behavior in the bathrooms of such public establishments as shopping malls, student centers on college campuses, and restaurants and bars at various locations in the Northeastern United States. These observations were recorded in fieldnotes and provide the empirical basis for the following analysis.

The Performance Regions of Public Bathrooms

Needless to say, one of the behaviors for which bathrooms are explicitly designed is defecation. In our society, as Goffman (1959: 121) observed, "defecation involves an individual in activity which is defined as inconsistent with the cleanliness and purity standards" that govern our public performances.

> Such activity also causes the individual to disarrange his clothing and to "go out of play," that is, to drop from his face the expressive mask that he employs in face-to-face interaction. At the same time it becomes difficult for him to reassemble his personal front should the need to enter into interaction occur.

When engaged in the act of defecation, therefore, individuals seek to insulate themselves from potential audiences in order to avoid discrediting the expressive masks that they publicly employ. . . .

In an apparent attempt to provide such privacy, toilets in many public bathrooms are surrounded by partially walled cubicles with doors that can be secured against potential intrusions. Public bathrooms that do not provide individuals this protection from potential audiences are seldom used for the purpose of defecation. In the course of our research, for example, we never observed an individual using an unenclosed toilet for this purpose. If a bathroom contained both enclosed and unenclosed toilets . . . individuals ignored the unenclosed toilets even when queues had formed outside of the enclosed toilets. In a sense, therefore, the cubicles that typically surround toilets in public bathrooms, commonly called stalls, physically divide such bathrooms into two distinct performance regions.

Indeed, Goffman (1971: 32) has used the term "stall" to refer to any "well-bounded space to which individuals lay temporary claim, possession being on an all-or-nothing basis." . . . [A] toilet stall is clearly a member of this sociological family of ecological arrangements. Sociologically speaking, however, it is not physical boundaries, per se, that define a space as a stall but the behavioral regard given such boundaries. For example, individuals who open or attempt to open the door of an occupied toilet stall typically provide a remedy for this act, in most cases a brief apology such as "Whoops" or "Sorry." By offering such a remedy, the offending individual implicitly defines the attempted intrusion as a [violation] and, thereby, af-

firms his or her belief in a rule that prohibits such intrusions (Goffman 1971: 113). In this sense, toilet stalls provide occupying individuals not only physical protection against potential audiences but normative protection as well.

In order to receive this protection, however, occupying individuals must clearly inform others of their claim to such a stall. Although individuals sometimes lean down and look under doors of toilet stalls for feet, they typically expect occupying individuals to mark their claim to a toilet stall by securely closing the door. On one occasion, a middle-aged woman began to push open the unlocked door of a toilet stall. Upon discovering that the stall was occupied, she immediately said, "I'm sorry," and closed the door. When a young woman emerged from the stall a couple minutes later, the older woman apologized once again but pointed out that "the door was open." The young woman responded, "it's okay," thereby minimizing the offense and perhaps acknowledging a degree of culpability on her part.

As is the case with many physical barriers to perception (Goffman 1963: 152), the walls and doors of toilet stalls are also treated as if they cut off more communication than they actually do. Under most circumstances, the walls and doors of toilet stalls are treated as if they were barriers to conversation. Although acquainted individuals may sometimes carry on a conversation through the walls of a toilet stall if they believe the bathroom is not otherwise occupied, they seldom do so if they are aware that others are present. Moreover, individuals often attempt to ignore offensive sounds and smells that emanate from occupied toilet stalls, even though the exercise of such "tactful blindness" (Goffman 1955: 219) is sometimes a demanding task. In any case, the walls and doors of toilet stalls provide public actors with both physical and normative shields behind which they can perform potentially discrediting acts.

Toilet stalls in public bathrooms are, therefore, publicly accessible yet private backstage regions. Although same-sexed clients of a public establishment may lay claim to any unoccupied toilet stall in the bathroom designated for use by persons of their sex, once such a claim is laid, once the door to the stall is closed, it is transformed into the occupying individual's private, albeit temporary, retreat from the demands of public life. While occupying the stall, that individual can engage in a variety of potentially discrediting acts with impunity.

When not concealed behind the protective cover of a toilet stall, however, occupants of public bathrooms may be observed by others. . . . Same-sexed clients of a public establishment can enter and exit at will the bathroom designated for their use, and it may be simultaneously occupied by as many individuals as its physical dimensions allow. By implication, occupants of public bathrooms must either perform or be ready to perform for an audience. As a result, the behavior that routinely occurs in the "open region" of a public bathroom, that area that is not enclosed by toilet stalls, resembles, in many important respects, the behavior that routinely occurs in other public settings.

The Ritual of Public Bathrooms

As Goffman (1971) convincingly argued, much of this behavior can best be described as "interpersonal rituals." Emile Durkheim (1965), in his [classic] analysis of religion, defined a ritual as a perfunctory, conventionalized act which expresses respect and regard for some object of "ultimate value." . . . Drawing inspiration from Durkheim, Goffman (1971: 63) pointed out that despite the increasing secularizaiton of our society there remain

> brief rituals one individual performs for and to another, attesting to civility and good will on the performer's part and to the recipient's possession of a small patrimony of sacredness.

Still borrowing from Durkheim . . . Goffman (1971: 62) divided these interpersonal rituals into two classes: positive and negative.

According to Durkheim, negative rituals express respect and regard for objects of ultimate value by protecting them from profanation. According to Goffman (1971: 62), negative interpersonal rituals involve the behavioral honoring of the scared individual's right to private "preserves" and "to be let alone." As previously noted, for example, individuals typically refrain from physically, conversationally, or visually intruding on an occupied toilet stall. In doing so, they implicitly honor the occupying individual's right to be let alone and in this respect perform a negative interpersonal ritual.

Similarly, the queues that typically form in public bathrooms when the demand for sinks, urinals, and toilet stalls exceeds the available supply are also products of individuals' mutual performance of negative interpersonal rituals. Individuals typically honor one another's right to the turn claimed by taking up a position in such a queue, even when "creature releases" (Goffman 1963: 69) threaten to break through their self-control. Young children provide an occasional exception, sometimes ignoring the turn-order of such queues. Yet even then the child's caretaker typically requests, on the child's behalf, the permission of those waiting in the queue. Between performances at a music festival, for example, a preschool-age girl and her mother were observed rapidly walking toward the entrance to a women's bathroom out of which a queue extended for several yards down a nearby sidewalk. As they walked past those waiting in the queue, the mother repeatedly asked "Do you mind? She really has to go."

However, the interpersonal rituals that routinely occur in the open region of public bathrooms are not limited to negative ones. If individuals possess a small patrimony of sacredness, then, as Durkheim (1974: 37) noted, "the greatest good is in communion" with such sacred objects. When previously acquainted individuals come into contact with one another, therefore, they typically perform conventionalized acts, positive interpersonal rituals, that express respect and regard for their previous communion with one another. In a sense, negative and positive interpersonal rituals are two sides of the same expressive coin. Whereas negative interpersonal rituals symbolically protect individuals from profanation by others, positive interpersonal rituals symbolically cleanse communion between individuals of its potentially defiling implications. Although a positive interpersonal ritual may consist of no more than a brief exchange of greetings, failure to at least acknowledge one's previous communion with another is, in effect, to express disregard for the relationship and, by implication, the other individual's small patrimony of sacredness (Goffman 1971: 62–94).

Even when previously acquainted individuals come into contact with one another in a public bathroom, therefore, they typically acknowledge their prior relationship. In fact, the performance of such positive interpersonal rituals sometimes interfered with the conduct of our research. On one occasion, for example, a member of the research team was in the open region of an otherwise unoccupied men's bathroom. While he was writing some notes about an incident that had just occurred, an acquaintance entered.

A: Hey _____! (walks to the urinal and unzips his pants) Nothing like pissin.

O: Yup.

A: Wh'da hell ya doin? (walks over to a sink and washes hands)

O: Writing.

A: Heh, heh, yea. About people pissin. . . . That's for you.

O: Yup.

A: Take care.

O: Mmm. Huh.

As this incident illustrates, individuals must be prepared to perform positive interpersonal rituals when in the open region of public bathrooms, especially those in public establishments with a relatively stable clientele. Whereas some of these may consist of no more than a brief exchange of smiles, others may involve lengthy conversations that reaffirm the participants' shared biography.

In contrast, when unacquainted individuals come into contact with one another in the open regions of public bathrooms, they typically perform a brief, negative interpersonal ritual that Goffman (1963: 84) termed "civil inattention." In its canonical form,

> one gives to another enough visual notice to demonstrate that one appreciates that the other is present . . . while at the next moment withdrawing one's attention from him so as to express that he does not constitute a target of special curiosity or design.

Through this brief pattern of visual interaction, individuals both acknowledge one another's presence and, immediately thereafter, one another's right to be let alone.

A variation on the canonical form of civil attention is also commonly performed in the open region of public bathrooms, most often by men using adjacent urinals. Although masculine clothing permits males to urinate without noticeably disturbing their clothed appearance, they must still partially expose their external genitalia in order to do so. Clearly, the standards of modesty that govern public behavior prohibit even such limited exposure of the external genitalia. Although the sides of some urinals and the urinating individual's back provide partial barriers to perception, they do not provide protection against the glances of someone occupying an adjacent urinal. In our society, however, "when bodies are naked, glances are clothed" (Goffman 1971: 46). What men typically give one another when using adjacent urinals is not, therefore, civil inattention but "nonperson treatment" (Goffman 1963: 83–84): that is, they treat one another as if they were part of the setting's physical equipment, as "objects not worthy of a glance." When circumstances allow, of course, unacquainted males typically avoid occupying adjacent urinals and, thereby, this ritually delicate situation.

It is not uncommon, however, for previously acquainted males to engage in conversation while using adjacent urinals. For example, the following interaction was observed in the bathroom of a restaurant.

> A middle-aged man is standing at one of two urinals. Another middle-aged man enters the bathroom and, as he approaches the available urinal, greets the first man by name. The first man quickly casts a side-long glance at the second and returns the greeting. He then asks the second man about his "new granddaughter," and they continue to talk about grandchildren until one of them zips up his pants and walks over to a sink. Throughout the conversation, neither man turned his head so as to look at the other.

As this example illustrates, urinal conversations are often characterized by a lack of visual interaction between the participants. Instead of looking at one another while listening . . . participants in such conversations typically fix their gaze on the wall immediately in front of them, an intriguing combination of the constituent elements of positive and negative interpersonal rituals. Although ritually celebrating their prior communion with one another, they also visually honor one another's right to privacy.

Due to the particular profanations and threats of profanations that characterize public bathrooms, moreover, a number of variations on these general patterns also commonly occur. In our society, as Goffman (1971: 41) observed, bodily excreta are considered "agencies of defilement." Although supported by germ theory, this view involves somewhat more than a concern for hygiene. Once such substances as urine, fecal matter, menstrual discharge and flatus leave individuals' bodies, they acquire the power to profane even though they may not have the power to infect. In any case, many of the activities in which individuals engage when in bathrooms are considered both self-profaning and potentially profaning to others. As a result, a variety of ritually delicate situations often arise in public bathrooms.

For example, after using urinals and toilets, individuals' hands are considered contaminated and, consequently, a source of contamination to others. In order to demonstrate both self-respect and respect for those with whom they might come into contact, individuals are expected to and often do wash their hands after using urinals and toilets. Sinks for this purpose are typically located in the open region of public bathrooms, allowing others to witness the performance of this restorative ritual. Sometimes, however, public bathrooms are not adequately equipped for this purpose. Most commonly, towel dispensers are empty or broken. Although individuals sometimes do not discover this situation until after they have already washed their hands, they often glance at towel dispensers as they walk from urinals and toilet stalls to sinks. If they discover that the towel dispensers are empty or broken, there is typically a moment of indecision. Although they sometimes proceed to wash their hands and then dry them on their clothes, many times they hesitate, facially display disgust, and audibly sigh. By performing these gestures-in-the-round, they express a desire to wash their hands; their hands remain contaminated, but their regard for their own and others' sacredness is established.

Because the profaning power of odor operates over a distance and in all directions, moreover, individuals who defecate in public bathrooms not only temporarily profane themselves but also risk profaning the entire setting. If an individual is clearly responsible for the odor of feces or flatus that fills a bathroom, therefore, he or she must rely on others to identify sympathetically with his or her plight and, consequently, exercise tactful blindness. However, this is seldom left to chance. When other occupants of the bathroom are acquaintances, the offending individual may offer a

subtle, self-derogatory display as a defensive, face-saving measure (Goffman 1955). Upon emerging from toilet stalls, for example, such persons sometimes look at acquaintances and facially display disgust. Self-effacing humor is also occasionally used in this way. On one occasion, for example, an acquaintance of a member of the research team emerged from a toilet stall after having filled the bathroom with a strong fecal odor. He walked over to a sink, smiled at the observer, and remarked: "Something died in there." Through such subtle self-derogation, offending individuals metaphorically split themselves into two parts: a sacred self that assigns blame and a blame-worthy animal self. Because the offending individual assigns blame, moreover, there is no need for others to do so (Goffman 1971: 113).

If other occupants of the bathroom are unfamiliar to the offending individual, however, a somewhat different defensive strategy is commonly employed. Upon emerging from a toilet stall, individuals who are clearly responsible for an offensive odor seldom engage in visual interaction with unacquainted others. In so doing, they avoid visually acknowledging not only the presence of others but others' acknowledgement of their own presence as well. In a sense, therefore, the offending individual temporarily suspends his or her claim to the status of sacred object, an object worthy of such visual regard. The assumption seems to be that by suspending one's claim to this status, others need not challenge it and are, consequently, more likely to exercise tactful blindness in regard to the offense.

Thus, despite Miner's humorous misidentification and interpretation of bathroom rituals, there is something to recommend the view that many of the rituals that behaviorally express and sustain the central values of our culture occur in bathrooms. Although those "central values do but itch a little," as Goffman (1971: 185) noted, "everyone scratches." And, it must be added, they often scratch in public bathrooms. However, routine bathroom behavior consists of more than the interpersonal rituals that are found in other public settings or variations on their general theme.

Backstage Behavior in Public Bathrooms

Clearly, public establishments differ in the degree to which their clients observe generally accepted standards of behavioral propriety. Moreover, the behavior that routinely occurs within an establishment's bathrooms typically reflects the degree of behavioral "tightness or looseness" (Goffman 1963: 200) that characterizes that establishment. For example, bathrooms in neighborhood bars are characterized by considerably more behavioral looseness than are bathrooms in expensive restaurants. Regardless of the degree of tightness or looseness that characterizes the frontstage region of a public establishment, however, somewhat greater behavioral looseness will be found in the establishment's bathrooms. After all, even the open region of a public bathroom is backstage relative to the setting beyond its doors. As such, public bathrooms offer individuals at least some relief from the behavioral harness that the frontstage audience's eyes impose upon them. . . .

Managing Personal Fronts

When in a public setting, as Goffman (1963: 24) pointed out, individuals are expected to have their "faculties in readiness for any face-to-face interaction that might come" their way. One of the most evident means by which individuals express such readiness is "through the disciplined management of personal appearance or 'personal front,' that is, the complex of clothing, make-up, hairdo, and other surface decorations" that they carry about on their person (Goffman 1963: 25). Of course, keeping one's personal front in a state of good repair requires care and effort. . . . However, individuals who are inspecting or repairing their personal fronts in public encounter difficulties in maintaining the degree of interactional readiness often expected of them; their attention tends to be diverted from the social situations that surround them (Goffman 1963: 66). For the most part, therefore, close [inspection] and major adjustments of personal fronts are confined to backstage regions such as public bathrooms.

Most public bathrooms are equipped for this purpose. Many offer coin-operated dispensers of a variety of "personal care products" . . . and almost all have at least one mirror. The most obvious reason for the presence of mirrors in public bathrooms is that the act of defecation and, for females, urination, requires individuals to literally "drop" their personal fronts. In order to ensure that they have adequately reconstructed their personal front after engaging in such an act, individuals must and typically do perform what

Lofland (1972) has termed a "readiness check." For example, the following was observed in the men's bathroom of a neighborhood bar:

> A young man emerges from a toilet stall and, as he passes the mirror, hesitates. He glances side-long at his reflection, gives a nod of approval and then walks out the door.

When such a readiness check reveals flaws in the individual's personal front, he or she typically makes the appropriate repairs: Shirts are often retucked into pants and skirts, skirts are rotated around the waist, and pants are tugged up and down.

Because bodily movement and exposure to the elements can also disturb a disciplined personal front, the post-defecation or urination readiness check sometimes reveals flaws in individuals' personal fronts that are the result of normal wear and tear. Upon emerging from toilet stalls and leaving urinals, therefore, individuals sometimes repair aspects of their personal fronts that are not normally disturbed in the course of defecating or urinating. For example, the following was observed in the women's bathroom of a student center on a college campus.

> A young woman emerges from a toilet stall, approaches a mirror, and inspects her reflection. She then removes a barrette from her hair, places the barrette in her mouth, takes a comb out of her coat pocket, and combs her hair while smoothing it down with her other hand. With the barrette still in her mouth, she stops combing her hair, gazes intently at the mirror and emits an audible "ick." She then places the barrette back in her hair, pinches her cheeks, takes a last look at her reflection and exits.

Interestingly, as both this example and the immediately preceding one illustrate, individuals sometimes offer visible or audible evaluations of their reflections when inspecting and repairing their personal front, a finding that should delight proponents of Meadian sociological psychology. Public bathrooms may protect individuals from the critical reviews of external audiences, but they do not protect them from those of their internal audience.

In any case, public bathrooms are as much "self-service" repair shops for personal fronts as they are socially approved shelters for physiological acts that are inconsistent with the cleanliness and purity standards that govern our public performances. In fact, individuals often enter public bathrooms with no apparent purpose other than the management of their personal front. For example, it is not uncommon for males to enter public bathrooms, walk directly to the nearest available mirror, comb their hair, rearrange their clothing, and then immediately exit. In our society, of course, females are often expected to present publicly a more extensively managed personal front than are males. Consequently, females often undertake extensive repairs in public bathrooms. For example, the following was observed in the women's bathroom of a student center on a college campus:

> Two young women enter, one goes to a toilet stall and the other immediately approaches a mirror. The second woman takes a brush out of her bookbag, throws her hair forward, brushes it, throws her hair back, and brushes it into place. She returns the brush to her bookbag, smooths down her eyebrows, and wipes underneath her eyes with her fingers. She then removes a tube of lipstick from her bookbag, applies it to her lips, and uses her finger to remove the lipstick that extends beyond the natural outline of her lips. As her friend emerges from the toilet stall, she puts the lipstick tube back into her bookbag, straightens her collar so that it stands up under her sweater and then exits with her friend.

Even though individuals routinely inspect and repair their personal fronts in the open regions of public bathrooms, they often do so furtively. When others enter the bathroom, individuals sometimes suspend inspecting or repairing their personal fronts until the new arrivals enter toilet stalls or approach urinals. In other cases, they hurriedly complete these activities before they can be witnessed. . . . Despite the furtiveness that sometimes characterizes individuals' inspection and repair of their personal fronts, however, the open region of a public bathroom is often the only available setting in which they can engage in these activities without clearly undermining their frontstage performances. As Lofland (1972: 101) observed in a somewhat different context, "it is apparently preferable to be witnessed by a few . . . in a brief episode of backstage behavior than to be caught . . . with one's presentation down" on the frontstage.

Going Out of Play

While a disciplined personal front may serve to express interactional readiness, public actors must also "exert a kind of discipline or tension" in regard to their bodies in order to actually maintain the degree of interactional readiness that is expected of them (Goffman 1963: 24). After all, a variety of bodily processes can drain individuals' attention away from the social world around them, causing them to turn inward and, interactionally speaking, to go out of play. Of course, the ostensive purpose of public bathrooms and their toilet stalls is to provide public actors with socially approved shelters in which to indulge such bodily processes. . . .

In addition to creature releases that threaten to slip through an individual's self-control, emotional reactions may also cause individuals to go out of play. In such cases, individuals may conclude that precipitant leave-taking is preferable to going out of play in full view of their frontstage audience. Under these circumstances, therefore, they may quickly retreat to the protective cover of a toilet stall. Although it is difficult for an observer to ascertain if this has taken place, it was the research team's impression that incidents, such as those described by Margaret Atwood (1969: 71) in her novel, *The Edible Woman*, are not uncommon. The narrator, Marian, was sitting with some friends in a bar when she noticed "a large drop of something wet" on the table near her hand.

> I poked it with my finger and smudged it around a little before I realized with horror that it was a tear. I must be crying then . . . I was going to break down and make a scene, and I couldn't. I slid out of my chair, trying to be as inconspicuous as possible, walked across the room avoiding the other tables with great care, and went to the Ladies Powder Room. Checking first to make sure no one else was in there—I couldn't have witnesses—I locked myself into one of the plushy-pink cubicles and wept for several minutes.

Depending on how precipitant such leave-taking is, of course, same-sexed members of the individual's frontstage audience may feel justified in conversationally intruding on this private preserve in order to inquire about his or her well-being. It is probably easier, however, to deflect such questions from behind the protective cover of a toilet stall than it would be if the frontstage audience witnessed such a display of emotion.

Parallel to individuals who retire to toilet stalls when they are overcome with emotion, entire "performance teams" (Goffman 1959: 77–105) sometimes retreat into public bathrooms in order to conceal the paralyzing embarrassment that results when a collective performance [collapses]. . . . For example, the following conversation between three young women was recorded in the bathroom of a student center on a college campus. Although the incident that led to this conversation was not observed, it obviously resulted in such paralyzing embarrassment.

A: That was sooo embarrassing! I can't believe that just happened. (general laughter)

B: He must think we are the biggest bunch of losers.

A: I can't believe I just screamed loud enough for everyone to hear.

C: It really wasn't all that loud. I'm sure he didn't hear you.

A: How can you say that? He turned around just as I said it. Why didn't you guys tell me he was standing right there?

B: _____, we didn't see him right away, and I did try to tell you but you were so busy talking that I . . .

A: I can't believe that just happened. I feel like such an asshole.

B: Don't worry 'bout it. At least he knows who you are now. Are you ready?

A: I'm so embarrassed. What if he's still out there?

B: You're gonna have to see him at some point.

In addition to concealing a temporary loss of control, these defensive strategies also buy individuals and performance teams time, as this example illustrates, in which to gather themselves together before once again facing the frontstage audience.

However, occupants of public bathrooms and their toilet stalls who use them for purposes other than those for which they were explicitly designed must exercise some caution. Unusual or unusually loud noises and unusually long occupancy, if someone is aware of the duration of the occupancy, may lead others to intrude upon these private preserves. By implication, individu-

als who use public bathrooms and their toilet stalls in order to conceal autoerotic activities, the usage of illicit drugs, emotional reactions, or other potentially discrediting acts must still exercise a degree of self-control.

Staging Talk

As Goffman (1959: 175) observed, performance teams routinely use backstage regions to gather themselves together [and] discuss . . . problems involved in the staging of their collective performance:

> Here the team can run through its performance, checking for offending expressions when no audience is present to be affronted by them; here poor members of the team . . . can be schooled or dropped from the performance.

In the conversation reproduced above, for example, B and C not only attempt to belittle the discrediting implications of A's earlier actions, but B also schools A in the art of staging collective performances. If, according to B, A had paid more attention to the other team members' directional cues, she could have avoided this embarrassing incident.

In addition to retreating into public bathrooms after the failure of a collective performance, performance teams also retire to public bathrooms in order to take preventive measures against such an occurrence. Here the team may agree upon collusive signals, rehearse their planned performance, and exchange strategic information. In bathrooms in bars, for example, performance teams were sometimes overheard discussing the planned targets of members' erotic overtures, the overtures they had received, the source of such overtures, and their likely responses. By providing other members of a performance team with such strategic information, of course, an individual may prevent them from interfering with his or her personal project and may even enlist their aid in accomplishing it.

Sometimes, moreover, the backstage discussions that occur in public bathrooms are at least partially concerned with a team member's morale or that of the entire team. In the previously discussed conversation between the three young women, for example, B and C attempt to boost A's morale by both belittling the discrediting implications of her earlier actions and encouraging her to "go on with the show." As Goffman (1959:

175) pointed out, backstage derogation of the audience is another strategy that performance teams commonly employ in order to maintain their morale. For example, a young woman was overheard making the following remark to two other young women in the bathroom of a popular nightclub.

> You guys think I'm obnoxious! WELL just take a look at _____, my God!

In any case, both performance teams and individual performers . . . routinely use public bathrooms as staging areas for their public performances. . . .

Conclusion

The behavior that routinely occurs within [public bathrooms] reveals, by way of contrast, some of the requirements that we must meet in order to maintain an unblemished public face. As the preceding analysis indicates, typical bathroom behaviors include the open staging of public performances, the concealment of emotional reactions, the indulgence of creature releases, and the inspection and repair of personal fronts. If, moreover, public bathrooms are backstage regions relative to the public settings beyond their doors, then the behaviors that tend to be confined to public bathrooms are inconsistent with the behavioral standards that govern our public performances. By implication, therefore, these standards would seem to require the presentation of a disciplined personal front, the avoidance of visible concern with its maintenance, the suppression of animal natures, some minimal degree of interactional readiness, and performances that appear "only natural." Without such readily accessible backstage regions as public bathrooms, it becomes increasingly difficult to fulfill these requirements; much of what we do in public bathrooms, then, is what we must not do elsewhere but what we must do somewhere.

In addition to noting such backstage behavior, the preceding analysis indicates that a number of interpersonal rituals found in other public settings are also routinely performed in public bathrooms. Although, at first glance, this finding may seem to contradict the characterization of public bathrooms as backstage regions, even "loosely defined" social situations are, in Goffman's (1963: 241) words, "tight little rooms." In fact, it may be within such loosely defined situations that the central values of our culture itch the most and are, by implication, most in need of scratching. Within public bathrooms, the animal natures behind our expressive masks and the blemishes underneath our disciplined personal fronts are often exposed. When we find ourselves in such ritually delicate situations, we need assurances that we retain our small patrimony of sacredness despite evidence to the contrary. In a sense, interpersonal rituals are routinely performed in public bathrooms because of, rather than in spite of, their backstage character.

In short, systematic study of routine bathroom behavior reveals just how loyal members of this society are to the central values and behavioral standards that hold our collective lives together. Whatever else they may do, users of public bathrooms continue to bear the "cross of personal character" (Goffman 1971: 185), and, as long as they continue to carry this burden, remain self-regulating participants in the "interaction order" (Goffman 1983).

References

Atwood, M. (1969) *The Edible Woman*. Boston: Little, Brown.

Durkheim, E. (1974) *Sociology and Philosophy*. (D. F. Pocock, trans.). New York: Free Press (originally published in 1924).

———. (1965) *The Elementary Forms of the Religious Life*. (J. W. Swain, trans.). New York: Free Press (originally published in 1915).

Goffman, E. (1983) "The interaction order." *Amer. Soc. Rev.* 48 (February): 1–17.

———. (1971) *Relations in Public: Microstudies in Public Order*. New York: Basic Books.

———. (1963) *Behavior in Public Places: Notes on the Social Organization of Gatherings*. New York: Free Press.

———. (1959) *The Presentation of Self in Everyday Life*. Garden City, NY: Doubleday.

———. (1955) "On face-work: An analysis of ritual elements of social interaction." *Psychiatry* 18 (August): 213–231.

Lofland, L. (1972) "Self-management in public settings: Part I." *Urban Life* 1 (April): 93–108.

Miner, H. (1955) "Body ritual among the Nacirema." *Amer. Anthropologist* 58 (June): 503–507.

18

Wheelchair Users' Interpersonal Management of Emotions

*Spencer E. Cahill
and
Robin Eggleston*

Everyday interaction is characterized by not only an expressive order, but an emotional order as well. This is nowhere more apparent than in public places where strangers and casual acquaintances routinely meet and sometimes interact. There, calm composure usually prevails and open expressions of intense emotions are rare. Yet, underneath this calm veneer, emotions such as fear, embarrassment, anger, and resentment often boil. This selection illustrates the considerable emotion work required to keep those emotions from boiling over into public interactions with the example of wheelchair users' public experience.

Wheelchair users' public experience is especially emotional. They often find themselves in embarrassing situations. They are treated both rudely and with kindness. They routinely receive needed and unneeded, wanted and unwanted, helpful and harmful assistance from others. All of these circumstances stir their emotions. Yet, as this selection illustrates, wheelchair users usually avoid publicly expressing their embarrassment, anger, and resentment so as to avoid evoking emotions in others. This is only one of the ways that wheelchair users manage both their own and others' emotions in public.

Although unusually demanding, wheelchair users' emotion work in public places illustrates the effort required to sustain the emotional tranquility of everyday public life. Like wheelchair users, we often make humorous remarks to relieve the tension of problematic situations. We suppress our anger so as not to provoke

others'. We act graciously toward those who treat us both ungraciously and overgraciously so as not to anger or embarrass them. We manage our own emotions so as to manage others' and thereby sustain the emotional orderliness of everyday social interaction.

Since the 1970s, students of social life have learned many lessons about the social sources and consequences of emotions. Many of us now appreciate that social life is as much an affair of the heart as of the head, but perhaps we do not appreciate this fact deeply enough. We still tend to concentrate on individuals' socially guided management of their own emotions to the neglect of their management of one another's. . . .

Yet, as Goffman (1963a, 1971) demonstrates convincingly, individuals in public places attempt to assure one another of their civility and goodwill so as not to evoke embarrassment, fear, or anger in others or in themselves. Although they often appear emotionally reserved and indifferent, that appearance is a consequence of emotion work rather than its absence. . . . The study of public life has much to teach us about the emotional dynamics of social interaction and life, if only we are willing to learn from those who notice what we usually miss. [And, when it comes to the interpersonal management of emotions], those whose principal mode of mobility is a wheelchair cannot help noticing what the rest of us can overlook more easily. . . .

Our specific focus is the emotional dilemmas faced by wheelchair users when in public places. We begin by briefly describing the inspiration and empirical basis of our analysis. Then we examine three general types of emotional challenges that wheelchair users confront in public places. Our purpose is not only to provide some insight into wheelchair users' public lives but also to draw from their example more general lessons about the emotional dynamics of contemporary public life and the interpersonal dynamics of emotion management. . . .

The Instruction of Wheelchair Use and Users

Our collective interest in wheelchair users' public experiences grew out of conversations between the first author and second author, who has used an electrically powered wheelchair as her principal mode of public mobility [for some time]. At the urging of the first author, she started to make fieldnotes of her daily participant observation of the social life of a wheelchair user. . . . [T]he first author supplemented these with fieldnotes that he made when using a wheelchair in public places for the specific purpose of participant observation. . . . We also collected and read wheelchair users' autobiographical accounts. . . . In addition, we collectively conducted and recorded interviews with seven women and five men who regularly use a wheelchair in public places. . . .

Although initially we did not intend to focus on the emotional challenges of public wheelchair use, emotional dilemmas loomed large in our own and our informants' accounts and in the published accounts of other wheelchair users' public experiences. Gradually we became convinced that those dilemmas contained a revealing story about the place of wheelchair users in public life, about contemporary public life more generally, and about interpersonal processes of emotion management. The following analysis tells that story.

The Emotional Demands of Public Wheelchair Use

For many wheelchair users, the very decision to venture into public places is emotionally turbulent. The desire for autonomy and for the many pleasures that only public places offer collides with fears—among others, fear of moving past and among much larger vehicles. There is the fear of upsetting others that has kept one of our informants, who recently started using a wheelchair, from using it in restaurants.

> I think it's hard for people to eat food close to people who are ill. There's something about the process of eating that makes people even more uptight about disease. . . . My rolling in probably wouldn't affect people in that way, but in the back of my mind I'm afraid it would. I'll have to get over that.

Wheelchair users also fear, with justification, being an embarrassing and embarrassed public spectacle.

Humoring Embarrassment

Like those whom one of our informants calls "stand-up people," wheelchair users face a variety of embarrassing possibilities whenever they venture into public places. For any number of reasons, they may lose control over self or situation (Gross and Stone 1964), falling short of what is generally expected of public actors. Wheelchair users, however, face a number of uniquely embarrassing contingencies because the physical environment, both natural and constructed, is unfriendly to their mode of mobility. Rain and snow can leave them immobile and embarrassingly in need of rescue. Doorway thresholds, uneven sidewalks, and unanticipated depressions at the bottom of curb cuts may cause a wheelchair to tip over, leaving its occupant embarrassingly sprawled on the ground. Crowded and narrow passageways may make it nearly impossible for wheelchair users to avoid knocking merchandise off shelves, rolling into standing strangers, or struggling to maneuver around tight corners in front of anxiously paralyzed bystanders. Although wheelchair users do not welcome such discomfort, many become quite adept at easing the "dis-ease" (Gross and Stone 1964:2) of potentially embarrassing situations because they face them so often.

Humor is the most common and perhaps most effective strategy that wheelchair users employ for this purpose. . . . [L]aughing at or joking about embarrassing events reduces their seriousness and thereby lessens potentially embarrassing concern about them. Laughter and humor are also means of allaying anxiety (Coser 1959:174), which can serve a dual definitional purpose. A wheelchair user's potentially embarrassing situation often provokes anxiety in witnesses to her or his plight. Defining the situation as laughable can ease everyone's particular "dis-ease," as the second author learned when shopping at a clothing store.

> I wheeled up to the entrance to a dressing room while my friend held a number of garments. I forgot to set the brakes on my chair, so when I started to raise myself up with my crutches the chair went rolling backwards while I went falling forward onto the floor. My friend stood there with this look of alarm until I started laughing. The two of us started laughing, and then a saleswoman came rushing over: "My goodness, are you all right?" I

answered "Yes, I'm fine" while still laughing. Her facial expression went from alarm to unconcern in a flash, once she realized we were laughing.

Through incidents like this, wheelchair users acquire the experiential wisdom that a sense of humor is "a tremendous asset."

> . . . if you can laugh at yourself, no matter what. . . . And if it's funny to me first, then my feelings aren't hurt. And you don't feel self-conscious because you can laugh with me.

As this 60-year-old woman had learned from countless falls in public places, laughter can both prevent and relieve hurt feelings, anxious self-consciousness, and the contagious "dis-ease" of embarrassment.

On the other hand, humor sometimes has the opposite effect. A woman who had been using a wheelchair in public for only six months told us of her recent experience in a shopping mall bathroom.

> There was a whole line of people waiting to get into these two stalls. It was packed. And I'm trying to back up and not doing a very good job of it and having to start over again, bumping into the washbasin. I finally get myself around, with all these people obviously watching me. There was dead silence. So I finally got myself out, and I looked up at all these people and I went "Now, I would like a big round of applause, please." Nobody did anything. It was like you can't make a joke about this stuff. I thought "Give me a break."

Like hospital patients who joke with the medical staff about death (Emerson 1969), this woman apparently exceeded the topical limits of her audience's sense of humor. At least they blatantly refused her invitation to laugh at her plight and reduce its definitional seriousness (Coser 1959:172). This incident illustrates one of the emotional dilemmas that wheelchair users face when in public places: they must attempt to remain poised and good-humored in frustrating and potentially embarrassing circumstances without thereby increasing others' already considerable discomfort at those circumstances. In public places they often have the double duty of managing their own and others' emotions (Hochschild 1979). . . .

This is clearly the case when wheelchair users are interrogated by curious children, as often happens, about their unusual mode of mobility and physical condition. All but one of our informants report that they gladly answer such young interrogators' questions. One informant, whose left leg had been amputated, had an uncommon sense of humor, but his openness with young children was not unusual.

> Kids go "Where's your leg?" "It's gone. If you find it, I'll give you fifty cents. I've been looking for that damn thing all week." "Can I see it?" "Sure." I take my pants up, show the stump. "Wow, it's gone. You're not sitting on it." "Yep, it's gone." They're frank. They're very candid.

Inquisitive children's accompanying adult caretakers, however, seldom appreciate their young charges' candor. As the man quoted above reported, "The parents turn blue. They turn shades of pink and red. I have to protect the kids from the parents. They want to jerk them away." Other informants reported similar experiences.

> And children, you find that they come up and ask "How come you're in a chair? You mean you can't walk? Really?" But if there's an adult with them, they tend to pull the child back. "Oh now, don't disturb her." And I say "They're not disturbing me."

If our informants are at all representative, most wheelchair users not only graciously endure and satisfy young children's uncivil curiosity when in public places. They also attempt to manage the embarrassment (and sometimes the wrath) of those curious children's adult caretakers in the interest of child protection. Whatever emotion work (Hochschild 1979:561–563) is done is usually done by them.

Fred Davis (1961:127) once observed that "in our society the visibly handicapped are customarily accorded, save by children, the surface acceptance of democratic manners guaranteed to nearly all." He may have been right about children, but many wheelchair users probably would find his attribution of democratic manners to children's elders a bit too generous. In both our own and our informants' experience, most adults indeed accord wheelchair users the surface acceptance of civil inattention in public places (Goffman 1963a:84). Yet there are more than a few exceptions. These include walkers, as they are sometimes called by wheelchair users, who proclaim their admiration of a wheelchair user at the expense of his or her right to be let alone in public (Goffman 1971:62). The older the walker and the younger the wheelchair user, the more common this treatment seems. The second author, for example, who is in her early twenties, is routinely approached by considerably older strangers, who cheerfully inform her that they think she "is wonderful." Although clearly complimentary, such unexpected and seemingly groundless public praise is an embarrassment. Simultaneously flattered, embarrassed, and resentful of the intrusion, the wheelchair user faces the dilemma of formulating an appropriate response, and usually settles for a half-hearted "thank you."

Wheelchair users commonly resolve the emotional dilemmas of their public lives in this way. They expressively mask their own emotions so as to manage others'. They cover their embarrassment with good humor, relieving witnesses' emotional discomfort. They hide resentment behind calm graciousness, saving forward strangers the embarrassment that would be caused by expressing such resentment. Even when wheelchair users feel fully justified in their emotional reactions, their public expression often contrasts sharply with their private feelings. The example of righteous anger suggests some reasons why.

Embarrassing Anger

Like children (Cahill 1990), wheelchair users are alternately treated like "open persons" (Goffman 1963a:126) and subjected to "nonperson" treatment in public places (Goffman 1963a:84). Although both forms of treatment betray others' surface acceptance of wheelchair users, the latter is usually the more maddening. Occupants of various service roles are the culprits mentioned most often. Apparently uncomfortable salesclerks may busy themselves folding merchandise as if a potential customer in a wheelchair were invisible. Restaurant personnel may huddle behind a wheelchair user, close enough to let her overhear their discussion of "where to put her." All kinds of service workers may treat a wheelchair user's walking companions as his or her spokespersons and caretakers. Sometimes they return change to such companions after receiving payment from the wheelchair user, or ask her companions "And what would she like?"

Such nonperson treatment often provokes wheelchair users' anger but seldom the expression of that anger. As one of our informants told us, "I just want to reach out and grab a hold of them and shake them for all they're worth. But I just sit back, and I grit my teeth." Our informants report that they usually try to respond to nonperson treatment not with anger but with calm reminders of their presence and ability to speak for themselves. They also report that this strategy is usually effective in eliciting an embarrassed apology and more civil treatment.

Yet no matter how common and how effective such gentle reminders are, wheelchair users sometimes reveal their anger at nonperson treatment through hostile comments and tone. When a waiter asked the wife of one of our informants whether "he will be getting out of the chair," our informant sarcastically replied, "Yes, he will." Such hostile expressions can be even more effective than calm reminders in eliciting embarrassed apologies, but at the expense of leaving the wheelchair user feeling embarrassed and guilty about his or her lack of emotional poise. In this respect and most others, wheelchair users are as much children of their emotional culture . . . as are most contemporary Americans. To borrow a distinction from Hochschild (1990:122–24), our "feeling rules" sometimes prescribe anger but our "expression rules" proscribe its expression. These contradictions lead to conflicting feelings of justifiable anger and guilt at expressing the anger. Wheelchair users are not alone in experiencing such contradictory feelings in public or elsewhere.

Private guilt and embarrassment are not the only potentially unwelcome consequences of wheelchair users' public expressions of anger. Rather than eliciting embarrassed apologies, their anger may be returned, as one of our informants learned when she protested a robustly walking man's choice of parking places.

> I've had a guy park in a handicapped parking spot and I've gone up and said: "Look, do you realize you're parked in a handicapped parking spot?" And he said "I know it, and I'm sick of you people getting all the good spots. It's reverse discrimination. I'm sick of being discriminated against." "Well," I said, "I'm going to call the police and you can tell your story to them." And he says, "Go ahead. I've had it. It's about time."

Although this man moved his car when our informant wheeled to the nearest public telephone, it was a harder-won moral victory than she had anticipated. . . . [Thus,] wheelchair users who publicly express moral outrage must be prepared to receive what they give. Their angry protest may be met with angry resistance, creating an embarrassing and sometimes alarming public scene that they must then manage or escape.

The angry protests of self-appointed defenders of wheelchair users' public privileges are no less instructive in this regard. One of our informants, who drove a car with hand controls that was otherwise unremarkable, told us of the following public encounter:

> I pull the car into a handicapped place, and this car pulls up alongside me with two young women in it. One of them leans over and says, "You know you're in a handicapped place." And I said, "Yes, I'm disabled." And then she says, "You don't look disabled." And I don't usually do this kind of thing, but I just said, "What does disabled look like?" And they just drove off. Maybe I shouldn't have done that, but it was one of those days.

The informant's hostile retort and the tinge of guilt he apparently felt as a result illustrate both the possible subjective costs and the interpersonal risks of publicly expressing anger. This is one horn of an emotional dilemma that wheelchair users often face in public. Should they suppress their righteous anger and forgo the satisfaction that its expression often brings, or should they assume the costs and risks of expression? As suggested previously, our informants, like the second author, commonly resolve this dilemma in favor of suppression—if not of their anger, then at least of expression.

That decision, however, does not always save wheelchair users from the embarrassing public scenes that angry protests can create. Their walking companions see to that, as a 34-year-old paraplegic woman explains.

> After thirteen and a half years you've heard just about everything, so it's like "Oh, you know." But it's my friends who [say] "Can you imagine the nerve? Let's get out of here." They've actually made me leave. My ex-boyfriend, we got up from the table and walked out . . . it started when they didn't know where to put me, and then the waitress ignored me. And he had just had it. He said "We're out of here." I said "Don't make an issue out of it." "The issue's made." Got my purse, got my coat, and we started to leave. We had the man-

ager on our coattails. I think that's more embarrassing.

As Goffman (1963b:31) observes, "[T]he person with a courtesy stigma can in fact make both the stigmatized and normal uncomfortable" by confronting everyone "with too much morality." Walkers who befriend and accompany wheelchair users in public are apparently no exception. Their easy susceptibility to moral outrage may lead to public scenes that their wheelchair-using companions would just as soon avoid. As if their occasional nonperson treatment were not painful enough, wheelchair users also must sometimes bear the embarrassment of their defenders' self-righteous zeal.

Wheelchair users' experiences with public anger are not unique. Regardless of our mode of mobility, public expressions of anger are risky: they can provoke angry retaliation and create embarrassing scenes. For most of us, much of the time, those potential costs seem to outweigh whatever personal satisfaction we might gain by expressing our righteous rage. Consequently we "surface act" (Hochschild 1979:558) so as to prevent our anger from reaching the surface. Thus, public appearances of emotional indifference are sometimes just that—appearances. Wheelchair users' experiences in public places remind us of how much emotion work may be invested in maintaining those appearances.

Ingratiating Sympathy

Prevailing expression rules, possible retaliation, and potential embarrassment are not the only deterrents to wheelchair users' public expression of righteous anger. They also know that they cannot afford to alienate the walkers who populate the public places they frequent. Experience has taught them that their uncooperative bodies and, more commonly, the unfriendliness of the physical environment to their mode of mobility sometimes leave them hopelessly dependent on others' sympathetic assistance. They may need waiters to move chairs away from a table so that they can wheel their own under it, or to store their wheelchair after transferring to a chair with legs. Often they must rely on strangers to fetch items from shelves that are either too high or too low for them to reach. They may wheel down a curb cut on one side of a street only to find a curb on the other side, over which anonymous passersby must help them if they are to continue along their intended path. Like one of our informants, they may find themselves in a restaurant or bar without "handicap accessible" toilet facilities and themselves without same-sexed companionship, and thus may require the assistance of total strangers to use those much-needed facilities. Or, like another of our informants, they may need to flag down a passing motorist on a city street to help them replace a foot on the footrest of their wheelchair after it has been dislodged by an involuntary spasm. These are only a few of the circumstances in which wheelchair users find themselves requiring the sympathetic assistance of walkers with whom they are unacquainted. . . .

Whatever its form, that assistance qualifies as sympathetic. According to Clark (1987:296), sympathy consists of "empathy plus sentiment, empathy plus display or all three." The assistance that walkers sometimes provide wheelchair users in public places has at least two of those components. It involves empathetic role-taking and is a culturally recognized expression of sympathy, even if not motivated by sincere "fellow-feeling" or sentiment. Regardless of the motivation, its provision stirs emotions.

Although many wheelchair users do not hesitate to ask for assistance when they need it, they are as aware of, and as strongly committed to, prevailing sympathy etiquette (Clark 1987) as other rules of feeling and expression. Therefore they often find themselves torn between concern about making excessive claims on others' sympathy and their immediate need for sympathetic assistance. Guilt is the typical result.

> If I'm in the grocery store, and I need something, and I ask somebody to get it [I say] "Oh, I'm sorry." And I find myself making excuses, saying things like "Oh, it's just not been my day" or "it seems everything I want today is up too high." I feel like I'm putting people out of their way. I feel like I'm imposing on someone to ask for help.

This informant told us that she did not have to apologize or explain herself because "people would bend over backwards to help you," but she seemed implicitly to know better. Even while she laid claim to others' sympathy, her apologies and accounts demonstrated her awareness of sympathy etiquette and its proscription against excessive claims (Clark 1987:305–307). Her guilty penance of remedial work (Goffman 1971:108–18) may have assured her benefactors that she would claim no more sympathy, time, and attention than necessary.

This wheelchair user's sensitivity to the sacrifices of sympathetically helpful strangers is not unusual. Wheelchair users often are forced to request sympathetic assistance from strangers in order to continue on their daily rounds, but still feel a pang of guilt when doing so. Those who have some choice may feel somewhat more than a guilty pang. . . . For example, one of our informants, who could walk short distances with the aid of a cane, often [felt like a fraud who was exploiting strangers' kindness].

> I've had people do double and triple takes when I get up out of my wheelchair. . . . Sometimes when I'm using my chair in the grocery store and I can't reach something, I get up; sometimes I ask people to get it for me. I mean, that's where I feel like a fraud, because I can get up. But if I get up, then I feel like a fraud because people can tell that I'm using a wheelchair but I don't need to—I mean I don't *have* to.

Like this woman, many wheelchair users are aware that they must appear strong, independent, and brave so as to avoid "being perceived as self-pitying" and overdemanding of others' sympathy (Clark 1987:307). To avoid such a perception and the resulting guilt, they may take needless risks and expend needless energy rather than requesting even minor aid from strangers. The micropolitical benefits of such dogged self-reliance may also help to compensate for inefficient expenditures of time, energy, and personal safety.

Even if wheelchair users defiantly refuse to pay the subjective price of guilt when requesting and accepting sympathetic assistance, they pay an interpersonal price. Whatever the benefits, as Clark (1987:299–300) observes, receiving sympathy obligates the recipient to repay the granter with "emotional commodities such as gratitude, deference and future sympathy." And deferential gratitude is the only emotional currency with which wheelchair users can repay strangers whom they are unlikely to encounter in the future. Using such currency to compensate helpful and sympathetic strangers for their sacrifices is not without micropolitical implications: Wheelchair users thereby elevate their benefactors' interactional standing or "place" at the expense of their own (Clark 1990).

Wheelchair users often pay that price cheerfully when they require and request sympathetic assistance, but those are not the only occasions on which they are expected to pay it. Walkers who are unknown to wheelchair users provide sympathetic assistance not only when it is requested, but also when it is not. The first author learned this in the opening moments of his first public appearance in a wheelchair.

> I got the chair unfolded and assembled and started wheeling down the hallway. As I was approaching the door, a woman walked alongside my chair and asked: "Are you going that way?" Assuming that she meant toward the door, I answered "Yes." She gracefully moved in front of me and opened the first of the double doors. I thanked her. She then just as gracefully opened the outer door once I was through the first, and again I thanked her.

From all reports, this is not an unusual experience for wheelchair users. Walkers often quicken or slow their pace so as to be in a position to open and hold doors for wheelchair users whom they do not know. They offer to push occupied wheelchairs up steep inclines, and sometimes begin to do so without warning. Also, they volunteer to fold and load wheelchairs into users' cars and vans. These are only a few examples of the unsolicited assistance that wheelchair users report receiving from strangers. . . .

[Yet], unsolicited acts of sympathetic assistance place wheelchair users under no less of an obligation than acts that are requested. It is still generally expected that the recipient will repay the granter with "deferential gratitude," and the micropolitical cost of that repayment may be even greater than for requested acts of sympathetic assistance. Simmel offers a theoretical explanation:

> Once we have received something good from another person . . . we no longer can make up for it completely. The reason is that his gift, because it was first, has a voluntary character which no return gift can have (1950:392).

This voluntary character is absent from the provision of sympathetic assistance in response to a request from an apparently "sympathy worthy" (Clark 1987:297–298) wheelchair user. If the provision of the requested assistance is of little moment to the person asked, as is commonly the case, then provision is no less obligatory than repayment. To refuse such a request is to risk being judged hatefully heartless. In contrast, an unsolicited act of sympathetic assistance contains what Simmel (1950:393) calls "the decisive element of . . . freedom," which is absent from the deferential gratitude offered in return. Moreover, as Clark (1990:315) observes, the donor of an emotional gift such as sympathetic assistance "gets to impose his or her definition of what the other wants or needs." To accept such an emotional gift is not only to "contract an irredeemable obligation" (Simmel 1950:393) but also to concede definitional authority over one's own wants and needs to another, thereby doubly diminishing the recipient's interactional standing. Thus the micropolitical implications of the kindness often displayed toward wheelchair users in public places can be quite unkind.

This is not to say that wheelchair users never appreciate unsolicited offers and acts of sympathetic assistance. One of our informants reports that he adjusts the speed of his wheelchair in relation to the reflections of approaching walkers in glass doors so as to ensure that they will reach the door slightly before him and will open and hold it for him voluntarily. At times he is more than willing to absorb the micropolitical losses caused by accepting such a minor expression of sympathetic kindness, and he is not alone.

Yet neither he nor other wheelchair users appreciate all the unsolicited assistance that sympathetic walkers shower on them. Sometimes they resent the costs in definitional authority or in mere time and energy that such acts of kindness impose. In the 1970s, for example, one of our informants was mistaken for a wounded veteran of the Vietnam war by a bouncer at a popular country and western bar. Before our informant could correct the misidentification, the bouncer carried him and his chair past the long queue of people awaiting admittance to the bar, forcibly removed some patrons from a table, and then offered the table to our informant and his companions. When the bouncer left to order "drinks on the house," our informant's wife wisely advised him, "Don't you dare tell him you're not a vet." For the rest of the evening, our informant and his companions were held hostage to the bouncer's definition of the situation, and had to feign knowledge of Vietnamese geography. Another informant reports that bartenders routinely refuse to accept payment for his drinks, insisting that his "money's no good here." A relatively well-paid civil servant, our informant resented the definitional implication that he was unable to pay his own way, but sometimes "let it go because they just wouldn't take my money." At times, too, unsolicited assistance merely makes wheelchair users' lives more difficult, as when walkers insist on helping a wheelchair user disassemble, fold, and load the wheelchair into a car or van, taking twice as long to do so as the user commonly takes and sometimes damaging the wheelchair in the process.

Even more maddening are those occasions on which self-appointed benefactors bear some responsibility for the wheelchair user's plight. One of our informants reported that she called a restaurant to inquire if it was accessible to wheelchair users. After being assured that it was, she made reservations for the following evening.

> [W]e got there to find that they had four or five steps, and there was no way I was going to get up there. So the owner of the restaurant and several of the male kitchen help came out and just picked my chair right up. They made every effort, once I got there, to help, which was really nice, but at the same time I was not happy after what they'd told me. . . . I get embarrassed when people make too much fuss over me.

This embarrassed and unhappy, if not angry, woman never returned to the restaurant in question. Yet on the evening of her first and only visit, she graciously thanked its owner and his employees for helping her over, through, and out of a predicament into which he had lured her. Her apparently insincere expression of seemingly undeserved gratitude is not aberrant among wheelchair users who receive unsolicited and unwelcome acts of sympathetic assistance. Here again, wheelchair users' public expression and their private feelings often contrast sharply.

At least our informants often express gratitude for unsolicited offers and acts of assistance even when they are unneeded, unwelcome, inconvenient, embarrassing, and demeaning. They know all too well the consequences of not doing so: their self-appointed benefactors, as well as those who witness his or her charity, are likely to judge them harshly for any hint of ingratitude. One of our informants learned this on his first trip to a highly recommended barbershop.

> I drove over there and got out of my car and wheeled up to the door. I opened the door and prepared to go in, and one of the two barbers came out and grabbed my handles. Now, as I've said, I like to do and insist on doing things for myself, but this fellow would not let go of the handles. I had my brakes on, preventing him from pushing me, but he insisted that he was going to push me over the threshold. . . . And finally . . . I forget what he said, but I asked for an apology. And he said "Okay, I apologize, but you have a chip on your shoulder, don't you?"

Like recipients of other forms of charity, wheelchair users who refuse or resist unsolicited acts of sympathetic assistance risk being viewed as having . . . "a chip on their shoulders." For many wheelchair users on many occasions, thankful and deferential acceptance of such charitable acts may seem less micropolitically costly than being judged ungrateful, testy, and uncivil.

Even when wheelchair users are willing to pay the price of such harsh judgments rather than cooperating in diminishing their interactional place, another consideration often prevents them from doing so. As Goffman (1963[b]:113) observes, the treatment of those who bear a stigma conveys to them that their "real group," the one whose interests they must champion, "is the aggregate of persons who are likely to suffer the same deprivations as [they suffer] because of having the same stigma." Wheelchair users are no exception, and many take this lesson to heart. Therefore they feel a sense of responsibility toward other wheelchair users and worry that their example might influence how other wheelchair users are treated in the future.

> I have people falling all over themselves trying to help me. It used to bother me, but, God, the older you get the less it does. But I know a lot of people it does. I've got one friend that's at the point of being rude. This is bad because it sets a bad example. That person in the future may not be quite so willing to help the next person who really needs it.

As in this woman's case but not her friend's, the contradiction between the wheelchair user's immediate micropolitical interests and the presumably greater interests of his or her "real group" often blocks the wheelchair user's expression of his or her subjective emotional reactions to unsolicited and unwelcome offers and acts of assistance. He or she consequently sacrifices interactional place for the presumably greater good of those who share the stigma of moving through public places in a sitting position.

The Wages of Public Acceptance

As late as the early 1970s, persons with visible disabilities were legally banned from public places in a number of American cities. . . . Today wheelchair users are a common presence in public places, attracting only occasional stares and many minor acts of [assistance]. Yet, the surface acceptance and assistance that others commonly grant them are not without a price. . . .

[W]heelchair users still must endure being treated like children in public places. Sometimes they are treated as open persons who can be addressed at will about their condition and the technical means of their mobility. At other times they are discussed and talked past as if absent. Robert Murphy (1987:201) suggests that people with disabilities are treated like children in part because "overdependency and nonreciprocity are considered childish traits," but wheelchair users seldom exhibit such traits in public. Although wheelchair users often depend on others' friendly assistance when the physical features of public places prove difficult to negotiate, most take pains to avoid exhausting the goodwill and sympathy of those who move through public places in a standing position.

The above discussion demonstrates that wheelchair users more than reciprocate . . . the public acceptance and assistance that others grant them with considerable emotion work and micropolitical sacrifices. That work and those sacrifices profit the walkers who they encounter in public. As Goffman (1963b:121) suggests, wheelchair users' public poise, even temper, and good humor, ensure that walkers "will not have to admit to themselves how limited their tactfulness and tolerance is." On the contrary, wheelchair users' request for and acceptance of public aid provide walkers an opportunity to demonstrate to themselves, if not others, that they are kind and caring people. The wheelchair users' common expressions of gratitude confirm that self-congratulatory moral identity. . . . [Thus], it is an open question whether walkers help wheelchair users as much in public as wheelchair users help them.

Perhaps wheelchair users who frequent public places are still sometimes treated as children because the attention-attracting assistance they sometimes must request, but more often receive, overshadows all the interactional and identificatory assistance they give others. Yet one can easily discern wheelchair users' efforts and sacrifices on others' behalf by looking beyond the glare of physical feats and into the emotional and micropolitical shadows of public encounters. In those shadows wheelchair users stand tall, supporting the emotional weight of public tranquility and their public benefactors' moral identities.

Public Life and Emotion Management

More general lessons await students of social life in the emotional and micropolitical shadows to which wheelchair users' public experiences lead. Strangers in public places may appear to be acting "almost subliminally, demanding nothing of each other" (Strauss 1961: 63–64), but much is demanded of them. . . . Strangers in public places devote considerable energy to preserving their own and one another's privacy, anonymity, and socially valued identities. . . . Wheelchair users' public experiences suggest that [much of that effort is emotional].

Wheelchair users are not the only ones who manage both their own and others' emotions in public places. Walkers who encounter wheelchair users in public undoubtedly sometimes avoid expressing their own private anxieties, aversion, admiration, or sympathetic concern out of concern for the wheelchair users' feelings. It is also doubtful that public encounters between unacquainted walkers and wheelchair users are unusual in this respect. Our public etiquette would seem to proscribe the public expression of emotions that are prescribed by our feeling rules, and public life is often emotionally provocative. Although strangers in public places may take pains to avoid physical contact with one another, nonetheless they touch one another emotionally in a variety of ways. They are touched embarrassingly by one another's presumed judgments as well as by one another's embarrassment. They are caressed reassuringly by others' averted gaze and pinched by fear by others' stares. Others' slights and impositions touch them with anger, and they feel a touch of guilt over their own anger. They touch one another sympathetically when requesting and providing minor acts of public aid, and repay such gifts touchingly in a variety of emotional currencies.

Yet whatever our mode of public mobility, we commonly appear emotionally reserved in public places. We mask our emotions so as not to excite others'. We manage our own expressions and thereby others' feelings. We surface act so as to sustain the tranquil exterior of public life and to avoid being swept away by its emotionally turbulent undercurrents. As suggested by the example of wheelchair users, this is part of the implicit bargain of contemporary public life. It is the price of public acceptance. . . . It is a special characteristic of public anonymity that the very process of producing it socially gives it the appearance of being not only asocial but unemotional as well. Students of social life must look beyond those appearances in order to fully understand public bonds and the bindings of contemporary society. The example of wheelchair users suggests that these bindings include interpersonal processes of emotion management. . . .

References

Cahill, Spencer. 1990. "Childhood and Public Life: Reaffirming Biographical Divisions." *Social Problems* 37:390–402.

Clark, Candace. 1987. "Sympathy Biography and Sympathy Margin." *American Journal of Sociology* 93:290–321.

——. 1990. "Emotions and Micropolitics in Everyday Life: Some Patterns and Paradoxes of Place." Pp. 305–33 in *Research Agendas in the Sociology of Emotions,* edited by Theodore Kemper. Albany: SUNY Press.

Coser, Rose. 1959. "Some Social Functions of Laughter: A Study of Humor in a Hospital Setting." *Human Relations* 12:171–182.

Davis, Fred. 1961. "Deviance Disavowal: The Management of Strained Interaction by the Visibly Handicapped." *Social Problems* 9:121–32.

Emerson, Joan. 1969. "Negotiating the Serious Import of Humor." *Sociometry* 32:169–81.

Goffman, Erving. [1955] 1982. "On Face-Work." Pp. 5–45 in *Interaction Ritual.* New York: Random House.

——. 1963a. *Behavior in Public Places.* New York: Free Press.

——. 1963b. *Stigma.* Englewood Cliffs, NJ: Prentice Hall.

——. 1971. *Relations in Public.* New York: Basic Books.

Gross, Edward and Gregory Stone. 1964. "Embarrassment and the Analysis of Role Requirements." *American Journal of Sociology* 70:1–15.

Hochschild, Arlie. 1979. "Emotion Work, Feeling Rules, and Social Structure." *American Journal of Sociology* 85:551–75.

——. 1990. "Ideology and Emotion Management: A Perspective and Path for Future Research." Pp. 117–42 in *Research Agendas in the Sociology of Emotions,* edited by Theodore Kemper. Albany: SUNY Press.

Murphy, Robert. 1987. *The Body Silent.* New York: Holt.

Simmel, Georg. 1950. *The Sociology of Georg Simmel,* edited by Kurt Wolff. Glencoe, IL: Free Press.

Strauss, Anselm. 1961. *Images of the American City.* New York: Free Press.

19

The Organization of Conversation

Ronald Wardhaugh

Most of us engage in countless conversations daily. Yet we seldom appreciate the intricate and complex organization of even the most casual conversation. We delicately open and carefully close conversations so as not to offend those with whom we talk. We somehow take turns talking without explicitly discussing how we will do so. Although our turns at talk are of varying lengths, we seldom talk at the same time, or at least not for very long, and we rarely fall silent for more than a second or two. We also repeatedly demonstrate our understanding of what has previously been said, correct misunderstandings when they occur, and, in most cases, achieve mutual understanding. Conversationalists may sometimes violently disagree, but they almost always mutually understand that they do disagree.

This selection examines a few of the complex features of conversational interaction. As Wardhaugh notes, we are oriented to a complex set of "rules" or "maxims" of conversation even though we could never articulate them. We may not always follow them but almost always interpret what others do in terms of them. For example, one basic rule of conversation is that a question calls for an answer. There are a variety of acceptable ways to delay answering, but a blatant refusal to answer is an affront to the questioner. It implies that either the question or the questioner was not worth an answer. The reason a blatant refusal to answer a question has such a mutually understood implication is because of our mutual orientation to the rule requiring an answer to a question.

It is because of our mutual orientation to such rules of conversation that even the most casual conversation has a discernable pattern or structure. That structure is not set in advance but built by the conversationalists as they talk and listen to one another. They selectively draw upon a complex set of rules and conversational devices, fitting their talk together into an organized and meaningful conversation.

The study of conversational rules and devices and their uses is central to microsociology. Conversational rules and devices are the materials we use to build mutual understanding and are, hence, the basic building blocks of the social realities that we inhabit. We must understand them in order to understand how we build, sustain, alter, and sometimes damage the social relations that pattern our lives.

Conversation is a social activity, one that always involves two or more people. . . . It is therefore a cooperative endeavour. One very simple and clear illustration of this fact is that, once talk has begun, most conversationalists assume that they have undertaken a definite obligation to keep it going. If they intend to discontinue it, they must do so gracefully. Keeping it going also requires the various parties to "work" so as to seem that all get some satisfaction out of the activity. Endings become a particularly delicate matter. They cannot be arbitrarily imposed by one party on another; they must be negotiated in some way. If for some reason you are forced to end a conversation prematurely, you are required to offer an apology of sorts. If you "break off talks" with others, you make a very strong gesture of non-cooperation, for you deliberately choose to violate the normal assumption that talk will prove to be mutually satisfactory and beneficial to all parties. Cutting talk short is therefore a clear indication of failure or disagreement. . . .

We may also ask ourselves why silence during a conversation creates as much embarrassment to the participants as it sometimes does. It does so because silence signals a failure to keep alive what the participants regard as this essentially cooperative venture. All seem to suffer because the failure is felt to reflect on the participants, both collectively and individually. When a period of silence occurs in a conversation, you can almost sense that everyone involved is searching for a way to fill the hole that has appeared. There is a kind of collective embarrassment and it is not unusual to notice an increase in tension. Sometimes more than one voice will break the silence and the conversation will start up again. When a new topic seems on its way to being established, the hole is filled, and the momentary pause is no more than an embarrassing memory, there is a noticeable reduction in tension, a collective acknowledgement that the day has been saved and that the threat that silence had posed to the group has been successfully removed. . . .

Taking part in a conversation requires your co-operation and participation even when you are not actually talking or intending to talk very much or even at all. You are in a sense always "at risk," even in a group conversation in which you have little or no intention of making a contribution. There is always the risk that one or the other speakers will address you or select you to speak. Being so addressed or selected can result in considerable embarrassment to you if you are not attending to what is going on. So if you want to be involved—without actually desiring to speak—you must still cooperate by listening, on the off chance that you may be called on to say something. You must listen to find out at least two things: whether you might be asked to speak and the topic you might be asked to speak on. Inattentiveness is usually regarded as failure to cooperate. . . .

Conversation is a finely tuned activity. What is particularly remarkable about it is that it does not depend on the subtle manipulation of very few devices. Rather, the devices are quite numerous and their combinations extremely subtle. Confusion and difficulty might seem to be the natural consequences of this diversity, but our common-sense view of most conversations—that they are not very interesting as examples of "creative endeavour"—indicates how easily we manipulate the complexities and navigate ourselves through large areas of potential difficulty. . . .

In one way, any conversation is like a game of chess: it has an opening which is followed by a series of moves, the middle game, and it comes to a conclusion of sorts. However, the rules are by no means as explicit as those of chess, but . . . "rules," "principles," "maxims," "conventions" of some kind do exist to guide the "players." The moves are also not as discrete as those in chess, but they are nevertheless still identifiable as separate moves. The middle game too may often seem to be quite confused. But just as participants in a chess game are required to plan ahead and anticipate some kind of closure, so too must you as a conversationalist constantly take a "prospective," or future-oriented approach to your task. . . .

Most of the moves we make in conversations would not be made if we did not assume that they would be followed by responses whose nature we can predict. We greet others in the expec-

tation that they will return our greetings. We apologize and expect that our apology will be accepted. We make statements which we assume others will believe. We offer someone something in the expectation that our offer will be accepted, unless it is one of those clearly marked, deliberately over-generous offers which we assume will be refused. We also expect that our feelings will be recognized and our beliefs considered by others in framing what they say to us. In these and other ways, we trust that others will take us seriously as we go about our joint conversational endeavour. And we lead others to expect that we will take them just as seriously. It is this trust in the fact that appearance and reality are the same that guides us in dealing with others. It is . . . this same trust that enables us to deceive others and others to deceive us when appearance and reality turn out to be very different.

Many kinds of utterances in conversation appear to require responses of very specific types: a greeting usually calls for a greeting in exchange, a question for an answer, and an invitation for a response. Likewise, challenges, threats, offers, warnings, requests, and complaints call for certain "uptakes" from those to whom they are directed—usually, we would expect, some kind of acknowledgement, acceptance, or refusal. But of course, you can also ignore them by not acknowledging, accepting, or refusing. The consequence is that you have various options when, for example, someone makes a request of you: you can comply, refuse, or simply just ignore what was said to you. And, in complying, refusing, or ignoring, you have a variety of devices available to indicate the "strength" of your response. It is in this way that conversation is at the same time both predictable and unpredictable—certain patterns of behaviour exist, but within these patterns, there is still a vast number of choices available to you.

As we have just indicated, there is a general expectation in conversation that certain kinds of utterances occur in pairs: greetings; questions and answers; requests and either compliances or refusals. Consequently, any response to a greeting, question, or request will be interpreted in relation to this usual paired relationship and will be judged by the initiating speaker to be either an adequate or a deficient second member of the pair. A greeting not returned may cause bewilderment; a question response to a question will leave the original question unanswered—and still to be answered—but the question response itself will be assumed to be relevant to that eventual answering; and a request that is apparently ignored may be treated as a request that has been taken under consideration, and you may expect that, if it is to be refused, some indirect indication of refusal will later be provided.

Silence itself is a potent communicative weapon, and the pairing of utterances in conversation is so strong that you can regard a deliberate breaking of the paired relationship by a failure to supply the second member of the pair as a deliberately uncooperative act. You may proceed to seek an explanation. Consequently, an ignored greeting, a refusal to answer a question, a disregarded request or apology—that is, any situation in which the pairing is not completed—will cause you to wonder what is going on. Since one of the strongest constraints in conversations is being violated—the constraint that an item of type A must be followed by an item of type B—you cannot just completely ignore the resulting silence, that is, the absence of B after A. You must regard this silence as speaking at least as loud as any words that might have been uttered, and you might seek to know the reason for it. . . .

In one sense, the biggest problem you face in conversation is going from silence to speech at the beginning and from speech to silence at the end. Once actual talk is initiated, it follows its own rules, but starting and stopping are not always easy, and, of the two, getting started appears to be the more difficult. After all, you can just stop talking—you can turn away and take the consequences. But getting started requires you to interrupt something—even though that something is only silence—and may also involve a breach of someone else's territory. Clear signaling of your intent becomes necessary very early, so that you can negotiate the opening few moments safely and not close off communication when it has only just begun. . . .

Having managed to begin a conversation, we are faced with the task of keeping it going. A conversation is not just a random series of utterances strung together. Each conversation has its own shape, one "cut" by the participants in the course of conversing. Keeping a conversation going requires, therefore, a set of skills of a different kind from opening that conversation. Failure to exercise the necessary skills will of course bring about

a premature closing. The whole effort will have been abortive.

When we speak, particularly if we want to hold the floor for a while, we must assure ourselves that we indeed do have listeners and continue to have listeners. Moreover, we should try to see to it that our listeners are attending willingly. What we need is some kind of feedback, an assurance that what we are saying is having some effect. When we listen to others, we also feel a need to show we are listening, either to encourage the speaker or merely to be polite. So both speaking and listening require an acknowledgement that the activity of speaking is worthwhile and can be continued. Physical distancing, gestures, facial expressions, nods, and so on are very important indicators of attention. So, too, are certain spoken signals. *Mmms* and *Uh-huhs* serve this function, as do certain words and the various intonations we can employ in uttering them: *Yes, Yeah, Well?, So?, And?, And then?, Exactly, Quite, Correct,* or expressions such as *I see* and *I agree.* To both speaker and listener, these actions, noises, and expressions indicate approval of the act of speaking, but not necessarily, of course, of the content of that speaking. They indicate that one party is willing to give up the floor to the other in the expectation that at some later point the other will be equally as considerate. They are signs of good manners rather than of agreement, although they may sometimes be interpreted as indicators of the latter too—which, of course, they may or may not be according to circumstances. . . .

Most conversations are orderly affairs and not very exciting at all. But there is something remarkable about that orderliness. How is it achieved? For example, speakers must know and subscribe to a set of principles which governs turn-taking in conversation. Who gets to speak and when? Some events proscribe speaking except by certain individuals and often they must speak in fixed formulaic utterances: royal weddings and other important public occasions are good examples. Others have an officially appointed dispenser of opportunities to speak: meetings presided over by a chairperson. . . . Most events, less formally organized than these, use subtle signals either to allow someone to speak or to make it difficult to do so. A look of encouragement may contrast strongly with the pointed ignoring of one or more individuals. . . .

The most general principle governing turn-taking in a conversation is that one and only one person speaks at a time. There may be overlaps and brief interruptions, to be sure, but it is generally quite clear which speaker has the floor at any particular moment. Moreover, that speaker usually gives up the floor voluntarily, that is, he or she willingly hands over the turn to someone else. And just as only one person speaks at a time, so someone speaks at all times. Conversationalists abhor silence; consequently, pauses are usually kept very short and speaker follows speaker in rapid succession. . . .

Having taken a turn in conversation, you can signal that you are coming to the end of what you want to say by using any one of a variety of devices. You can draw out the last syllable or two of what you are saying by pronouncing them extra-slowly and exaggerating the final associated pitch change. Such a signal indicates completion, and someone else can take up the topic. Or you can deliberately pause after you have said something, but without providing any additional change in tempo or pitch. Pauses in conversation tend to get filled. You can attempt to fill the pause yourself—by a *Well!* or some such expression—but others too can use the opportunity that the pause creates either to pick up the topic or to attempt to change it. Some kind of gesture or body movement, for instance, a noticeable relaxation, may also accompany the pause you have created and indicate that you are willing to let another talk. Somewhat more unusually, you can phrase what you are saying grammatically and rhetorically so that it says "I'm finished": however, that kind of technique is a rather formal one and its use is usually restricted to very narrow sets of circumstances.

You can also indicate your desire to take a turn at speaking in a number of ways. Someone who is about to take a turn in conversation tends to increase bodily tension and make certain body movements which draw the attention of others. A noticeable intake of breath is also a clear signal not only that speaking is about to begin but that it is likely to continue for some time. When the speaking actually does begin, it is likely to be a little louder than normal, as an attention-holding device. And, in order to make interruption less likely, a person taking up a turn will very possibly avert his or her gaze from the other participants for a few moments. In this way, the new speaker can resist possible challenges to his or her right to speak by simply not seeing them. . . .

Once you have acquired the turn to speak, you have a strong right to continue speaking until you voluntarily give up the turn. You can give it up either by indicating who you are passing it to or by ending what you are saying and allowing the next speaker to select himself or herself. Once you have been given a turn, there are many ways of keeping it. You can organize what you want to say to prevent interruption. For example, you can indicate that you are making a series of remarks: *First of all* or *To begin with*, followed by *Then, After that, Next, Second*, and so on. Expressions such as *Another thing* and connectors like *So, Because, Moreover, Consequently*, and *However* promote continuity. And, of course, in the same way, it is possible to signal a deliberate coming to an end: *Finally, This shows [means, suggests], All in all, When you think about what I've said* and so on. In other words, you can do much to keep the floor if you are able to control those logical, chronological, and grammatical devices which make a series of utterances a cohesive and coherent account rather than a jumble of thoughts and impressions. But you must always remember that you are participating in a group activity. You cannot have the floor forever, as it were. Consequently, there are severe limits to your use of such devices, and you must be conscious at all times as to how your audience is reacting. Does the feedback they are providing you with show that they are bored and inattentive? If it does, possibly you should hand over the turn very quickly and not seek to get it back too soon. Once again, we can see how co-operation is the essential ingredient in any successful conversation. . . .

Bringing [a conversation] to an end is just as much an art as initiating speech with another person. . . . People do not end conversations arbitrarily. They do not just stop talking and turn away from one another abruptly and without explanation. If they are ever forced to do so—for example, because of an interruption—when the conversation is resumed, one will usually apologize to the other or others for the disruption. A telephone call interrupted through an accidental disconnection will resume either with an outright apology (*Sorry, I cut us off by mistake*) or some other explanation (*Somebody cut us off*). When we seek to close a conversation, we must serve notice that we are rapidly approaching the ultimate cut-off which silence brings, but we often pretend that we are reluctant to cease. We want to leave the other with the impression that there is nothing we would rather do than continue what we are doing; however, some other exterior condition or event stands in the way: *Well, back to work, I must be going, Sorry! [Please excuse me!]* but, *I'd better let you go,* or *I've got to go/run/do X.* Alternatively, we may offer some kind of compliment which acts as a comment on the whole conversation and at the same time marks it as a completed unit: *It's been nice [good] talking to you.* Such a comment indicates that the speaker regards it as time to move on to some new activity because the current one has apparently fulfilled whatever purpose it had—and quite successfully.

You can signal that you intend to bring a conversation to a close in any number of different ways. Diminished eye contact with the speaker can be used to show that you would really prefer to be doing something else. Likewise, a dramatic shift in your posture can signal a new, and different, interest. A glance at a clock or watch is also an effective signal: it indicates that you believe it is time to move on to something else. You can deliberately return to earlier topics that were mentioned and summarize them with words which indicate not only that you are summarizing but also that you are concluding whatever it is you and your listener were doing. Still more deliberate movements and gestures are possible. . . . What is important is that all parties recognize the closing behaviour for what it is and agree to it so that, after perhaps ritualistic exchange of *Goodbyes,* they find that they have negotiated themselves successfully back to silence.

Closing a conversation is a cooperative activity. If one party wants to close and insists on doing so when the other does not, the second party may feel he or she was either shut up or shut out, since the closing was imposed and not negotiated. On certain occasions, it may be appropriate to behave this way: a superior may dismiss or abruptly abandon a subordinate. However, in normal conversation, both parties are required to maneuvre jointly toward a closing. They must agree that they have said all there was to say, that no further topics remain, and that they are willing to disconnect. Expressions such as *Well, OK,* and *So,* hesitations, references to some other activity, or certain movements and gestures can indicate that the parties are about to break off. Once a

sub-routine of this kind is begun, any attempt to bring up an additional topic must be quite clearly signaled: *Oh, I forgot something.* But usually there is no such attempt and the conversation is brought to a conclusion with some form of ritual leave-taking.

Many kinds of expressions are used in preclosing rituals just before the final *Goodbye. I'm sorry I have to go now, I mustn't keep you, Take care, It was nice meeting you, See you,* and *Give my regards to Fred* are just a few randomly chosen examples. If something occurs to you after another person has said one of these to you, you must clearly indicate that you are interrupting the closing routine: *Wait, I've just remembered something, Wow! it's just occurred to me.* A strong expression is called for to acknowledge the break in the parting routine and to indicate that you are aware that you have caused the interruption and that whatever you are going to introduce as new material is important. But, if you have nothing new to introduce, you can be content with an *OK, All right,* a nod of the head, a repositioning of your body, some fixed expression (*Well, I'll be off*), an excuse (*I must go* or *I have to do X*), and so on. These confirm that you agree to the ending. All that is necessary now is for each party to use a *Goodbye* (or some equivalent) and the conversation will be brought to a mutually satisfying end. . . .

Conversations are generally neither structured in advance nor are they entirely "free form." Upon analysis, they do seem to have structures of certain kinds; yet these structures are usually apparent only retrospectively. What structure a conversation has is created by the participants in the very process of their conversing, as they observe the basic principles of conversing. If this is the case, then it follows that the participants in conversation must know what is permissible and what is not: that is, they must be aware that, if the conversation is to succeed, they must do certain kinds of things and not others. Those who study conversational structure attempt to state precisely what these things are. . . .

Any activity that involves conversation is likely to be further illuminated by any understanding we can achieve of the dynamics of conversation. Many such activities are highly specialized, as, for example, radio communication between airline pilots and air traffic controllers. Some may be routine on most occasions but critical on others, as between doctors and patients. And many more may be routine on just about all occasions but cumulatively have profound consequences, as between parents and children and husbands and wives. A large amount of resources of modern societies is devoted to "conversational repair," that is, to activities designed to mitigate and patch up the consequences of failure to communicate. This misunderstanding is unfortunately a fact of life, but fortunately, one located within a much larger context of understanding and cooperation—the very cement of society.

Human beings are uniquely language-using creatures. They are not uniquely social creatures.

Language is important to human beings in creating the kinds of societies in which they have come to live. Human [society] is in large part created and maintained through language use. Ordinary everyday conversation comprises a significant part of that language use, and it is for this reason, if for no other, that it forms such an important area of study. . . .

Part VI

Social Interaction and Relationships

We often speak of social relationships as if they were things that existed apart from social interaction. This is implied, for example, when we say that we *have* a certain kind of relationship with someone. Yet social relationships are not so much something we *have* as something we *do*. Social interaction is the source and sustenance of social relationships. Their only existence apart from interaction is in memory and imagination. And even there, they tend to wither away without the nourishment of social interaction.

Our understanding of different kinds of relationships clearly influences how we interact with one another. For example, most of us do not tell checkout clerks in supermarkets intimate details about our private lives. However, it is because we do *not* do so that our relationship with checkout clerks is fleeting and relatively anonymous. If we did share our intimate secrets with a checkout clerk, and she or he reciprocated, then our relationship would be intimate. Relationships are ways individuals relate to one another, which is just another way of referring to patterns of social interaction.

Social relationships provide the immediate context of our social lives and experience. They support and undermine our sense of self. They emotionally tie us to others in bonds of mutual obligation. Our positions in networks of relationship determine our social standing in the neighborhood, at school, and at work. And, how others relate to us shapes our most personal experiences. The selections in this section examine both the interactional dynamics of relationships and how they, in turn, shape our lives and experience. ✦

20
Uncoupling

Diane Vaughan

In the earlier selection on Codependents Anonymous, Leslie Irvine showed that social relationships provide the anchorage for the self. The stories or narratives of self we tell to others and ourselves are only credible as long as others play their supporting roles in those stories. Close relationships are particularly important in this regard. Closely related individuals frequently and often extensively interact, mutually influencing each other's sense of self and interpretations of experience. In this important sense, they collectively construct their own distinct reality.

Ideally at least, marriage is the archetypal close relationship in our society. As the sociologists Peter Berger and Hansfried Kellner observed some years ago, through continual interaction, marital partners "couple" their previously autonomous identities and build their lives around their relationship. Others come to think of them as a couple, and their identities become publicly coupled in the form of joint checking accounts, credit cards, and home ownership. Berger and Kellner referred to this as the objectivation of the coupled identity. The marital partners' subjectively coupled identity becomes widely recognized, assuming an objective character. In these ways, marital partners come to share a biography and inhabit a distinct subworld that serves as their principal source of self-validation.

That is why Berger and Kellner called marriage a crucial "nomos-building" instrumentality in modern society. A century ago, the sociological thinker Emile Durkheim coined the expression "anomie" (which in Latin literally means lawlessness) to refer to a lack of social norms and regulation. Durkheim argued that, without the guidance of social norms and regulation, individuals would experience life as meaningless. As used by Berger and Kellner, "nomos" is the opposite of anomie, referring to an orderly and predictable social existence that renders life meaningful. Martial partners ideally build just such an existence in the private subworld of their relationship.

However, we know that many marriages are less than ideal and disintegrate long before death parts the couple. In such cases, the couple must part themselves and dismantle their coupled identities, shared biography, and private subworld.

Diane Vaughan describes this process of "uncoupling" in this selection. Based on interviews with recently divorced or soon to be divorced individuals, Vaughan shows that the process of uncoupling has a definite pattern even though it often seems chaotic and disorderly. She also demonstrates that uncoupling is commonly a cooperative endeavor even when there is conflict and bitterness. Although the focus here is on married couples and their uncoupling, much of what is described here and below can also be generalized to other close relationships. It is about how identities and selves are intertwined and subsequently disentangled and about how shared realities are built and subsequently dismantled. This also happens among good friends, lovers, and others who frequently and extensively interact.

Berger and Kellner (1964) describe marriage as a definitional process. Two autonomous individuals come together with separate and distinct biographies and begin to construct for themselves a subworld in which they will live as a couple. A redefinition of self occurs as the autonomous identity of the two individuals involved is reconstructed as a mutual identity. This redefinition is externally anticipated and socially legitimated before it actually occurs in the individual's biography.

Previously, significant conversation for each partner came from nonoverlapping circles, and self-realization came from other sources. Together, they begin to construct a private sphere where all significant conversation centers in their relationship with each other. The coupled identity becomes the main source of their self-realization. Their definitions of reality become correlated, for each partner's actions must be projected in conjunction with the other. As their worlds come to be defined around a relationship with a significant other who becomes the significant other, all other significant relationships have to be reperceived, regrouped. The result is the construction of a joint biography and a mutually coordinated common memory.

Were this construction of a couple identity left only to the two participants, the coupling would be precarious indeed. However, the new reality is reinforced through objectivation, that is, "a process by which subjectively experienced meanings become objective to the individual, and, in interaction with others, become common property, and thereby massively objective" (Berger and Kellner, 1964:6). Hence, through the use of language in conversation with significant others, the reality of the coupling is constantly validated.

Of perhaps greater significance is that this definition of coupledness becomes taken for granted and is validated again and again, not by explicit articulation, but by conversing around the agreed [upon] definition of reality that has been created. In this way a consistent reality is maintained, ordering the individual's world in such a way that it validates his identity. Marriage, according to Berger and Kellner, is a constructed reality which is "nomos-building" (1964:1). That is, it is a social arrangement that contributes order to individual lives, and therefore should be considered as a significant validating relationship for adults in our society.

Social relationships, however, are seldom static. Not only do we move in and out of relationships, but the nature of a particular relationship, though enduring, varies over time. Given that the definitions we create become socially validated and hence constraining, *how do individuals move from a mutual identity, as in marriage, to assume separate, autonomous identities again*? What is the process by which new definitions are created and become validated?

The Berger and Kellner analysis describes a number of interrelated yet distinguishable stages that are involved in the social construction of a mutual identity; for example, the regrouping of all other significant relationships. In much the same way, the *demise* of a relationship should involve distinguishable social processes. Since redefinition of self is basic to both movement into and out of relationships, the social construction of a singular identity also should follow the patterns suggested by Berger and Kellner. This paper is a qualitative examination of this process. Hence, the description that follows bears an implicit test of Berger and Kellner's ideas.

The dimensions of sorrow, anger, personal disorganization, fear, loneliness, and ambiguity that intermingle every separation are well known. Their familiarity does not diminish their importance. Though in real life these cannot be ignored, the researcher has the luxury of selectivity. Here, it is not the pain and disorganization that

are to be explored, but the existence of an underlying orderliness.

Though the focus is on divorce, the process examined appears to apply to *any* heterosexual relationship in which the participants have come to define themselves and be defined by others as a couple. The work is exploratory and, as such, not concerned with generalizability. However, the process may apply to homosexual couples as well. Therefore, the term "uncoupling" will be used because it is a more general concept than divorce. Uncoupling applies to the redefinition of self that occurs as mutual identity unravels into singularity, regardless of marital status or sex of the participants.

The formal basis from which this paper developed was in-depth exploratory interviews. The interviews, ranging from two to six hours, were taped and later analyzed. All of the interviewees were at different stages in the uncoupling process. Most were divorced, though some were still in stages of consideration of divorce. Two of the interviews were based on long-term relationships that never resulted in marriage. All of the relationships were heterosexual. . . . A more informal contribution to the paper comes from personal experiences and the experiences of close friends. Further corroboration has come from autobiographical accounts, newspapers, periodicals, and conversations, which have resulted in a large number of cases illustrating certain points. Additional support has come from individuals who have read or heard the paper with the intent of proving or disproving its contentions by reference to their own cases.

Since the declared purpose here is to abstract the essential features of the process of uncoupling, some simplification is necessary. The separation of a relationship can take several forms. To trace all of them is beyond the scope of this study. Therefore, to narrow the focus, we must first consider the possible variations.

Perhaps the couple identity was not a major mechanism for self-validation from the outset of the union. Or the relationship may have at one time filled that function, but, as time passed, this couple identity was insufficient to meet individual needs. Occasionally this fact has implications for both partners simultaneously, and the uncoupling process is initiated by both. More frequently, however, one partner still finds the marriage a major source of stability and identity, while the other finds it inadequate. In this form, one participant takes the role of initiator of the uncoupling process. However, this role may not consistently be held by one partner, but instead may alternate between them, due to the difficulty of uncoupling in the face of external constraints, social pressure not to be the one responsible for the demise of the marriage, and the variability in the self-validating function of the union over time. For the purpose of this study, the form of uncoupling under consideration is that which results when one partner, no longer finding the coupled identity self-validating, takes the role of initiator in the uncoupling process. The other partner, the significant other, still finds the marriage a major source of stability and identity.

The Initiation of the Process

I was never psychologically married. I always felt strained by attempts that coupled me into a marital unit. I was just never comfortable as "Mrs." I never got used to my last name. I never wanted it. The day after my marriage was probably the most depressed day of my life, because I had lost my singularity. The difference between marriage and a deep relationship, living together, is that you have this ritual, and you achieve a very definite status, and it was that that produced my reactions—because I became in the eyes of the world a man's wife. And I was never comfortable and happy with it. It didn't make any difference who the man was.

An early phase in the uncoupling process occurs as one or the other of the partners begins to question the coupled identity. At first internal, the challenging of the created world remains for a time as a doubt within one of the partners in the coupling. Though there is a definition of coupledness, subjectively the coupledness may be experienced differently by each partner. Frequently, these subjective meanings remain internal and unarticulated. Thus, similarly, the initial recognition of the coupling as problematic may be internal and unarticulated, held as a secret. The subworld that has been constructed, for some reasons, doesn't "fit."

A process of definition negotiation is begun, initiated by the one who finds the mutual identity an inadequate definition of self. Attempts to negotiate the definition of the coupledness are likely to result in the subjective meaning becoming articulated for the first time, thus moving the redefinition process toward objectivation. The secret, held by the initiator, is shared with the significant other. When this occurs, it allows both participants to engage in the definitional process.

Though the issue is made "public" in that private sphere by the two, the initiator frequently finds that a lack of shared definitions of the coupled identity stalemates the negotiations. While the initiator defines the marriage as a problem, the other does not. The renegotiation of the coupled identity cannot proceed unless both agree that the subworld they have constructed needs to be redefined. Perhaps for the significant other, the marriage as it is still provides important self-validation. If so, the initiator must bring the other to the point of sharing a common definition of the marriage as "troubled."

Accompanying Reconstructions

Though this shared definition is being sought, the fact remains that, for the initiator, the coupled identity fails to provide self-validation. In order to meet this need, the initiator engages in other attempts at redefining the nature of the relationship. Called "accompanying reconstructions," these *may* or *may not* be shared with the significant other. They may begin long before the "secret" of the troubled marriage is shared with the other, in an effort to make an uncomfortable situation more comfortable without disrupting the relationship. Or they may occur subsequent to sharing the secret with the significant other, as a reaction to the failure to redefine the coupledness satisfactorily. Time order for their occurrence is not easily imposed—thus, "accompanying reconstructions."

The initiator's accompanying reconstructions may be directed toward the redefinition of (1) the coupledness itself, (2) the identity of the significant other, or (3) the identity of the initiator. A change in definition of either of the three implies a change in at least one of the others. Though they are presented here separately, they are interactive rather than mutually exclusive and are not easily separable in real life.

The first form of accompanying reconstruction to be considered is the initiator's redefinition of the coupledness itself. One way of redefining coupledness is by an unarticulated conversion of the agreed-upon norms of the relationships.

I had reconceptualized what marriage was. I decided sexual fidelity was not essential for marriage. I never told her that. And I didn't even have anyone I was interested in having that intimate a relationship with—I just did a philosophical thing. I just decided it was O.K. for me to have whatever of what quality of other relationship I needed to have. Something like that—of that caliber—was something I could never talk to her about. So I did it all by myself. I read things and decided it. I was at peace with me. I knew that we could stay married, whatever that meant. O.K., I can stay legally tied to you, and I can probably live in this house with you, and I can keep working with you, but you need some resources, because I realize now I'm not going to be all for you. I don't want to be all for you, and I did tell her that. But I couldn't tell her this total head trip I'd been through because she wouldn't understand.

Or, the coupledness may be redefined by acceptance of the relationship with certain limitations. Boundaries can be imposed on the impact the relationship will have on the total life space of the initiator.

I finally came to the point where I realized I was never going to have the kind of marriage I had hope for, the kind of relationship I had hoped for. I didn't want to end it, because of the children, but I wasn't going to let it hurt me any more. I wasn't going to depend on him any more. The children and I were going to be the main unit, and, if he occasionally wanted to participate, fine—and if not, we would go ahead without him. I was no longer willing to let being with him be the determining factor as to whether I was happy or not. I ceased planning our lives around his presence or absence and began looking out for myself.

A second form of accompanying reconstruction occurs when the initiator attempts to redefine the significant other in a way that is more compatible with his own self-validation needs. The initiator may direct efforts toward specific behaviors, such as drinking habits, temper, sexual incompatibilities, or finance management. Or, the redefinition attempt may be of a broader scope.

I was aware of his dependence on the marriage to provide all his happiness, and it wasn't providing it. I wanted him to go to graduate school, but he postponed it, against my wishes. I wanted him to pursue his own life. I

didn't want him to sacrifice for me. I wanted him to become more exciting to me in the process. I was aware that I was trying to persuade him to be a different person.

Redefinition of the significant other may either be directed toward maintaining the coupledness, as above, or moving away from it, as in the case following.

The way I defined being a good wife and the way John defined being a good wife were two different quantities. He wanted the house to look like a hotel and I didn't see it that way. He couldn't see why I couldn't meet his needs.... When he first asked for a divorce and I refused, he suggested I go back to school. I remembered a man who worked with John who had sent his wife back to school so she could support herself, so he could divorce her. I asked John if he was trying to get rid of me. He didn't answer that. He insisted I go, and I finally went.

A third form of accompanying reconstruction may be directed toward redefinition of the initiator. Intermingled with attempts at redefinition of the significant other and redefinition of the coupledness itself is the seeking of self-validation outside the marriage by the initiator. A whole set of other behaviors may evolve that have the ultimate effect of moving the relationship away from the coupledness toward a separation of the joint biography.

What was first internally experienced and recognized as self-minimizing takes a more concrete form and becomes externally expressed in a search for self-maximization. Through investment of self in career, in a cause requiring commitment, in a relationship with a new significant other, in family, in education, or in activities and hobbies, the initiator develops new sources of self-realization. These alternative sources of self-realization confirm not the couple identity but the singularity of the initiator.

Furthermore, in the move toward a distinct biography, the initiator finds ideological support that reinforces the uncoupling process. Berger and Kellner (1964:3) note the existence of a supporting ideology which lends credence to marriage as a significant validating relationship in our society. That is, the nuclear family is seen as the site of love, sexual fulfillment, and self-realization. In the move toward uncoupling, the initiator finds confirmation for a belief in *self* as a first priority.

I now see my break with religion as a part of my developing individuality. At the time I was close friends with priests and nuns, most of who[m] have since left the church. I felt a bitterness toward the church for its definition of marriage that was not best for me.

Whether this ideology first begins within the individual, who then actively seeks sources of self-realization that are ideologically congruent, or whether the initiator's own needs come to be met by a serendipitous "elective affinity" of ideas (Weber 1930), is difficult to say. The interconnections are subtle. The supporting ideology may come from the family of orientation, the women's movement, the peer group, or a new significant other. It may grow directly, as through interaction, or indirectly, as through literature. No matter what the source, the point is that, in turning away from the marriage for self-validation, a separate distinct biography is constructed in interaction with others, and this beginning autonomy is strengthened by a supporting belief system.

The initiator moves toward construction of a separate subworld wherein significant conversation comes from circles which no longer overlap with those of the significant other. And, the significant other is excluded from the separate subworld.

I shared important things with the children that I didn't share with him. It's almost as if I purposefully punished him by not telling him. Some good thing would happen and I'd come home and tell them and wouldn't tell him.

The initiator's autonomy is further reinforced as the secret of the troubled marriage is shared with others in the separate subworld the initiator is constructing. It may be directly expressed as a confidence exchanged with a close friend, family member, or children, or it may be that the sharing is indirect. Rather than being expressed in significant conversation, the definition of the marriage as troubled is created for others by a variety of mechanisms that relay the message that the initiator is not happily married. The definition of the marriage as problematic becomes further objectivated as the secret, once held only by the initiator, then shared with the significant other, moves to a sphere beyond the couple themselves.

Other moves away occur that deeply threaten the coupled identity for the significant other and

at the same time validate the autonomy of the initiator.

I remember going to a party by myself and feeling comfortable. She never forgot that. I never realized the gravity of that to her.

Graduate school became a symbolic issue. I was going to be a separate entity. That's probably the one thing I wanted to do that got the biggest negative emotional response from him.

All that time I was developing more of a sense of being away from her. I didn't depend on her for any emotional feedback, companionship. I went to plays and movies with friends.

The friendship group, rather than focusing on the coupledness, relies on splintered sources that support separate identities. Though this situation can exist in relationships in which the coupled identity is validating for both participants, the distinction is that, in the process of uncoupling, there may not be shared conversation to link the separate subworld of the initiator with that of the significant other.

These movements away by the initiator heighten a sense of exclusion for the significant other. Deep commitment to other than the coupled identity—to a career, to a cause, to education, to a hobby, to another person—reflects a lessened commitment to the marriage. The initiator's search for self-validation outside the marriage even may be demonstrated symbolically to the significant other by the removal of the wedding ring or by the desire, if the initiator is a woman, to revert to her maiden name. If the initiator's lessened commitment to the coupled identity is reflected in a lessened desire for sexual intimacy, the challenge to the identity of the significant other and the coupledness becomes undeniable. As the significant other recognizes the growing autonomy of the initiator, he, too, comes to accept the definition of the marriage as "troubled."

The roles assumed by each participant have implications for the impact of the uncoupling on each. Whereas the initiator has found other sources of self-realization outside the marriage, usually the significant other has not. The marriage still performs the major self-validating function. The significant other is committed to an ideology that supports the coupled identity. The secret of the "troubled" marriage has not been shared with others as it has by the initiator, meaning for the significant other the relationship in its changed construction remains unobjectivated. The challenge to the identity of the significant other and to the coupledness posed by the initiator may result in increased commitment to the coupled identity for the significant other. With the joint biography already separated in these ways, the couple enters into a period of "trying."

Trying

Trying is a stage of intense definition negotiation by the partners. Now both share a definition of the marriage as troubled. However, each partner may seek to construct a new reality that is in opposition to that of the other. The significant other tries to negotiate a shared definition of the marriage as savable, whereas the initiator negotiates toward a shared definition that marks the marriage as unsavable.[1]

For the initiator, the uncoupling process is well under way. At some point the partner who originally perceived the coupled identity to be problematic and sought self-validation outside the coupled identity has experienced "psychological divorce." Sociologically, this can be defined as the point at which the individual's newly constructed separate subworld becomes a major nomos-building mechanism in his life, replacing the nomos-building function of the coupled identity.

The initiator tries subtly to prepare the significant other to live alone. By encouraging the other to make new friends, find a job, get involved in outside activities, or seek additional education, the initiator hopes to decrease the other's commitment to and dependence upon the coupled identity for self-validation and move the other toward autonomy. This stage of preparation is not simply one of cold expediency for the benefit of the initiator, but is based on concern for the significant other and serves to mitigate the pain of the uncoupling process for both the initiator and the other.

For both, there is a hesitancy to sever the ties. In many cases, neither party is fully certain about the termination of the marriage. Mutual uncertainty may be more characteristic of the process. The relationship may weave back and forth between cycles of active trying and passive acceptance of the status quo due to the failure of each

to pull the other to a common definition of the inability of either to make the break.

> I didn't want to hurt him. I didn't want to be responsible for the demise of a marriage I no longer wanted. I could have forced him into being the one to achieve the breach, for I realized it was never going to happen by itself.

> I didn't want to be the villain—the one to push her out into the big, bad world. I wanted to make sure she was at the same point I was.

> I kept hoping some alternative would occur so that he would be willing to break. I kept wishing it would happen.

Frequently, in the trying stage, the partners turn to outside help for formal negotiation of the couple identity. Counseling, though entered into with apparent common purpose, becomes another arena in which the partners attempt to negotiate a shared definition from their separately held definitions of the marriage as savable or unsavable. For the initiator, the counseling may serve as a step in the preparation of the significant other to live alone. Not only does it serve to bring the other to the definition of the marriage as unsavable, but also the counseling provides a resource for the significant other, in the person of the counselor. Often it happens that the other has turned to no one for comfort about the problem marriage. The initiator, sensitive to this need and unable to fill it himself, hopes the counselor will fill this role. The counseling has yet another function. It further objectivates the notion of the coupled identity as problematic.

At some point during this period of trying, the initiator may suggest separation. Yet, separation is not suggested as a formal leave-taking but as a *temporary* separation meant to clarify the relationship for both partners. Again, the concern on the part of the initiator for the significant other appears. Not wanting to hurt, yet recognizing the coupled identity as no longer valid, the temporary separation is encouraged as a further means of bringing the other to accept a definition of the marriage as unsavable, to increase reliance of the other on outside resources of self-realization, and to initiate the physical breach gently.

> Even at that point, at initial separation, I wasn't being honest. I knew fairly certainly that when we separated, it was for good. I let her believe that it was a means for us first finding out what

was happening and then eventually possibly getting back together.

Should the initiator be hesitant to suggest a separation, the significant other may finally tire of the ambiguity of the relationship. No longer finding the coupling as it exists self-validating, the significant other may be the one to suggest a separation. The decision to separate may be the result of discussion and planning, or it may occur spontaneously, in a moment of anger. It may be mutually agreed upon, but more often it is not. However it emerges, the decision to separate is a difficult one for both partners.

Objectivation: Restructuring the Private Sphere

The separation is a transitional state in which everything needs definition, yet very little is capable of being defined. Economic status, friendship networks, personal habits, and sex life are all patterns of the past which need simultaneous reorganization. However, reorganization is hindered by the ambiguity of the relationship. The off-again, on-again wearing of the wedding rings is symbolic of the indecision in this stage. Each of the partners searches for new roles, without yet being free of the old.

For the initiator who has developed outside resources, the impact of this uncertainty is partially mitigated. For the significant other, who has not spent time in preparation for individual existence, the major self-validating function of the marriage is gone and nothing has emerged as a substitute.

> I had lost my identity somewhere along the way. And I kept losing my identity. I kept letting him make all the decisions. I couldn't work. I wasn't able to be myself. I was letting someone else take over. I didn't have any control over it. I didn't know how to stop it. I was unsure if anything really happened I could actually make it on my own or not.

The separation precipitates a redefinition of self for the significant other. Without other resources for self-validation, and with the coupled identity now publicly challenged, the significant other begins a restructuring of the private sphere.

This restructuring occurs not only in the social realm but also entails a form of restructuring that is physical, tangible, and symbolic of the break in the couple identity. For instance, if the initiator

has been the one to leave, at some point the significant other begins reordering the residence they shared to suit the needs of one adult rather than two. Furniture is rearranged or thrown out. Closets and drawers are reorganized. A thorough house-cleaning may be undertaken. As the initiator has moved to a new location that reinforces his singularity, the significant other transforms the home that validated the coupling into one that likewise objectivates the new definition. Changes in the physical appearance of either or both partners may be part of the symbolic restructuring of the private sphere. Weight losses, changes of hair style, or changes in clothing preferences further symbolize the yielding of the mutual identity and the move toward autonomy.

Should the significant other be the one to leave, the move into a new location aids in the redefinition of self as an autonomous individual. For example, the necessity of surviving in a new environment, the eventual emergence of a new set of friends that define and relate to the significant other as a separate being instead of as half of a couple, and the creation of a new residence without the other person are all mechanisms which reinforce autonomy and a definition of singularity.

Though the initiator has long been involved in objectivating a separate reality, frequently for the significant other this stage is just beginning. Seldom does the secret of the troubled marriage become shared with others by this partner until it can no longer be deferred. Although the initiator actively has sought objectivation, the significant other has avoided it. Confronted with actual separation, however, the significant other responds by taking subjectively experienced meanings and moving them to the objective level—by confiding in others, perhaps in writing, in letters or in diaries—any means that helps the other deal with the new reality.

There are some who must be told of the separation—children, parents, best friends. Not only are the two partners reconstructing their own reality, but they now must reconstruct the reality for others. Conversation provides the mechanism for reconstruction, simultaneously creating common definitions and working as a major objectivating apparatus. The longer the conversation goes on, the more massively real do the objectivations become to the partners. The result is a stabilization of the objectivated reality, as the new definition of uncoupledness continues to move outward.

Uncoupling precipitates a reordering of all other significant relationships. As in coupling, where all other relationships are reperceived and regrouped to account for and support the emergence of the significant other, in uncoupling the reordering supports the singularity of each partner. Significant relationships are lost, as former friends of the couple now align with one or the other or refuse to choose between the two. Ties with families of orientation, formerly somewhat attenuated because of the coupling, are frequently renewed. For each of the partners, pressure exists to stabilize characterizations of others and of self so that the world and self are brought toward consistency. Each partner approaches groups that strengthen the new definition each has created, and avoids those that weaken it. The groups with which each partner associates help co-define the new reality.

Objectivations: The Public Sphere

The uncoupling is further objectivated for the participants as the new definition is legitimized in the public sphere. Two separate households demand public identification as separate identities. New telephone listings, changes of mailing address, separate checking accounts, and charge accounts, for example, all are mechanisms by which the new reality becomes publicly reconstructed.

The decision to initiate legal proceedings confirms the uncoupling by the formal negotiation of a heretofore informally negotiated definition. The adversary process supporting separate identities, custody proceedings, the formal separation of the material base, the final removal of the rings all act as means of moving the new definition from the private to the public sphere. The uncoupling now becomes objectivated not only for the participants and their close intimates, but for casual acquaintances and strangers.

Objectivation acts as a constraint upon whatever social identity has been constructed. It can bind a couple together, or hinder their recoupling, once the uncoupling process has begun. Perhaps this can better be understood by considering the tenuous character of the extramarital affair. The very nature of the relationship is private. The coupling remains a secret shared by the two and seldom becomes objectivated in

the public realm. Thus, the responsibility for the maintenance of that coupling usually rests solely with the two participants. When the relationship is no longer self-validating for one of the participants, the uncoupling does not involve reconstruction of reality for others. The constraints imposed by the objectivation of a marital relationship which function to keep a couple in marriage do not exist to the same extent in an affair. The fragility of the coupling is enhanced by its limited objectivation.

Berger and Kellner (1964:6) note that the "degree of objectivation will depend on the number and intensity of the social relationships that are its carriers." As the uncoupling process has moved from a nonshared secret held within the initiator to the realm of public knowledge, the degree of objectivation has increased. The result is a continuing decline in the precariousness of the newly constructed reality over time.

Divorce: A Stage in the Process

Yet a decrease in precariousness is not synonymous with a completion of the uncoupling process. As marriage, or coupling, is a dramatic act of redefinition of self by two strangers as they move from autonomous identities to the construction of a joint biography, so uncoupling involves yet another redefinition of self as the participants move from mutual identity toward autonomy. It is this redefinition of self, for each participant, that completes the uncoupling. Divorce, then, may not be the final stage. In fact, divorce could be viewed as a nonstatus that is at some point on a continuum ranging from marriage (coupling) as an achieved status, to autonomy (uncoupling), likewise an achieved status. In other words, the uncoupling process might be viewed as a status transformation which is complete when the individual defines his salient status as "single" rather than "divorced." When the individual's newly constructed separate subworld becomes nomos-building—when it creates for the individual a sort of order in which he can experience his life as making sense—the uncoupling process is completed.

The completion of uncoupling does not occur at the same moment for each participant. For either or both of the participants, it may not occur until after the other has created a coupled identity with another person. With that step, the tentativeness is gone.

> When I learned of his intention to remarry, I did not realize how devastated I would be. It was just awful. I remember crying and crying. It was really a very bad thing that I did not know or expect. You really aren't divorced while that other person is still free. You still have a lot of your psychological marriage going—in fact, I'm still in that a little bit because I'm still single.

For some, the uncoupling may never be completed. One or both of the participants may never be able to construct a new and separate subworld that becomes self-validating. Witness, for example, the widow who continues to call herself "Mrs. John Doe," who associates with the same circle of friends, who continues to wear her wedding ring and observes wedding anniversaries. For her, the couple identity is still a major mechanism for self-validation, even though her partner is gone.

In fact, death as a form of uncoupling may be easier for the significant other to handle than divorce. There exist ritual techniques for dealing with it, and there is no ambiguity. The relationship is gone. There will be no further interaction between partners. With divorce, or any uncoupling that occurs through the volition of one or both of the partners, the interaction may continue long after the relationship has been formally terminated. For the significant other—the one left behind, without resources for self-validation—the continuing interaction between the partners presents obstacles to autonomy.

> There's a point at which it's over. If your wife dies, you're a lot luckier, I think, because it's over. You either live with it, you kill yourself, or you make your own bed of misery. Unlike losing a wife through death, in divorce, she doesn't die. She keeps resurrecting it. I can't get over it, she won't die. I mean, she won't go away.

Continuities

Continuities are linkages between the partners that exist despite the formal termination of the coupled identity. Most important of these is the existence of shared loved ones—children, in-laws, and so on. Though in-laws may of necessity be excluded from the separately constructed subworlds, children can rarely be and, in their very existence, present continued substantiation of the coupled identity.

In many cases continuities are actively constructed by one or both of the participants after the formal termination of the relationship. These manufactured linkages speak to the difficulty of totally separating that common biography, by providing a continued mechanism for interaction. They may be constructed as a temporary bridge between the separated subworlds, or they may come to be a permanent interaction pattern. Symbolically, they seem to indicate caring on the part of either or both participants.

> The wife moves out. The husband spends his weekend helping her get settled—hanging pictures, moving furniture.

> The husband moves out, leaving his set of tools behind. Several years later, even after his remarriage, the tools are still there, and he comes to borrow them one at a time. The former wife is planning to move within the same city. The tools are boxed up, ready to be taken with her.

> The wife has moved out, but is slow to change her mailing address. Rather than marking her forwarding address on the envelopes and returning them by mail, the husband either delivers them once a week or the wife picks them up.

> The wife moves out. The husband resists dividing property with her that is obviously hers. The conflict necessitates many phone calls and visits.

> The husband moves out. Once a week he comes to the house to visit with the children on an evening when the wife is away. When she gets home, the two of them occasionally go out to dinner.

> A nice part of the marriage was shared shopping trips on Sunday afternoons. After the divorce, they still occasionally go shopping together.

> The holidays during the first year of separation were celebrated as they always had been—with the whole family together.

> During a particularly difficult divorce, the husband noted that he had finally succeeded in finding his wife a decent lawyer.

Continuities present unmeasurable variables in the uncoupling process. In this paper, uncoupling is defined as a reality socially constructed by the participants. The stages that mark the movement from a coupled identity to separate autonomous identities are characterized, using divorce for an ideal-type analysis. Yet, there is no intent to portray uncoupling as a compelling linear process from which there is no turning back. Such conceptualization would deny the human factor inherent in reality construction. Granted, as the original secret is moved from private to public, becoming increasingly objectivated, reconstructing the coupled identity becomes more and more difficult.

Each stage of objectivation acts as a closing of a door. Yet at any stage the process may be interrupted. The initiator may not find mechanisms of self-validation outside the coupling that reinforce his autonomy. Or the self-validation found outside the coupling may be the very stuff that allows the initiator to stay in the relationship. Or continuities may intervene and the reconstruction of the coupled identity may occur, despite the degree of objectivation, as in the following case.

Ellen met Jack in college. They fell in love and married. Jack had been blind since birth. He had pursued a college career in education and was also a musician. Both admired the independence of the other. In the marriage, she subordinated her career to his and helped him pursue a masters degree, as well as his musical interests. Her time was consumed by his needs—for transportation and the taping and transcribing of music for the musicians in his group. He was teaching at a school for the blind by day and performing as a musician at night. They had a son, and her life, instead of turning outward, as his, revolved around family responsibilities. She gained weight. Jack, after twelve years of marriage, left Ellen for his high school sweetheart. Ellen grieved for a while, then began patching up her life. She got a job, established her own credit, went back to college, and lost weight. She saw a lawyer, filed for divorce, joined Parents Without Partners, and began searching out singles groups. She dated. Throughout, Jack and Ellen saw each other occasionally and maintained a sexual relationship. The night before the divorce was final, they reconciled.

The uncoupling never was completed, though all stages of the process occurred, including the public objectivation that results from the initiation of the legal process. Ellen, in constructing an autonomous identity, became again the independent person Jack had first loved. This, together with the continuities that existed between the two, created the basis for a common definition of the coupling as savable.

Conclusions

Berger and Kellner describe the process by which two individuals create a coupled identity for themselves. Here, [I] have started from the point of the coupled identity and examined the process by which people move out of such relationships. Using interview data, [I] have found that, although the renegotiation of separate realities is a complex web of subtle modifications, clear stages emerge which mark the uncoupling process. The emergent stages are like benchmarks which indicate the increasing objectivation of the changing definitions of reality, as these definitions move from the realm of the private to the public. . . .

[A significant finding] is the existence of an underlying order in a phenomenon generally regarded as a chaotic and disorderly process. Undoubtedly the discovery of order was encouraged by the methodology of the study. The information was gained by retrospective analysis on the part of interviewees. Certainly the passage of time allowed events to be reconstructed in an orderly way that made sense. Nonetheless, as was previously noted, the interviewees were all at various stages in the uncoupling process—some at the "secret" stage and some five years hence. Yet, the stages which are discussed here appeared without fail in every case and have been confirmed repeatedly by the other means described earlier.

In addition to this orderliness, the examination of the process of uncoupling discloses two other little-considered aspects of the process that need to be . . . mentioned.

One is the caring. Generally, uncoupling is thought of as a conflict-ridden experience that ends as a bitter battle between two adversaries intent on doing each other in. Frequently, this is the case. Yet, the interviews for this study showed that in all cases, even the most emotion generating, again and again the concern of each of the participants for the other revealed itself. Apparently, the patterns of caring and responsibility that emerge between partners in a coupling are not easily dispelled and in many cases persist throughout the uncoupling process and after, as suggested by the concept of continuities.

A second question that emerges for this examination of uncoupling is related to Berger and Kellner's thesis . . . that, for adults in our society, marriage is a significant validating relationship. . . . Though Berger and Kellner at the outset do delimit the focus of their analysis to marriage as an ideal-type, the question to be answered is, To what degree is this characterization of marriage appropriate today?

Recall, for example, the quote from one interviewee: "I was never psychologically married. I always felt strained by attempts that coupled me into a marital unit. I was just never comfortable as 'Mrs.' " The interviews for this study suggest that the nomos-building quality assumed to derive from marriage to the individual should be taken as problematic rather than as given. . . . A relationship may exist in which the partners are highly interdependent, and the coupled identity does provide the major mechanism for self-validation, as Berger and Kellner suggest. Yet it is equally as likely that the participants are highly independent, or "loosely coupled" (Weick, 1976 . . .), wherein mechanisms for self-validation originate outside the coupling rather than from the coupling itself.

Note

1. This statement must be qualified. There are instances when the partners enter a stage of trying with shared definitions of the marriage as savable. The conditions under which the coupling can be preserved have to be negotiated. If they can arrive at a common definition of the coupling that is agreeable to both, the uncoupling process is terminated. But this analysis is of uncoupling, and there are two alternatives: (1) that they enter with common definitions of the marriage as savable but are not able to negotiate the conditions of the coupling so that the self-validation function is preserved or (2) that they enter the period of trying with opposing definitions, as stated above.

References

Berger, Peter and Hansfried Kellner. 1964. "Marriage and the Construction of Reality," *Diogenes*, 46:1–23.

Weber, Max. 1930. *The Protestant Ethic and the Spirit of Capitalism*, translated by Talcott Parsons. New York: Charles Scribner's Sons.

Weick, Karl E. 1976. "Educational Organizations as Loosely Coupled Systems," *Administrative Science Quarterly*, 21:1–19.

21

Sympathy Biography and Relationships

Candace Clark

The construction and maintenance of relationships clearly involve social exchanges of emotional expressions. Individuals obviously initiate social relationships by exchanging displays of emotion, as in the case of flirting between future romantic partners. Additionally, individuals who already have an ongoing relationship feel that they are owed and owe one another certain emotions. Their failure to meet these often implicit emotional obligations will alter and may even destroy their relationship. That is just one of the ways that individuals may change the form of their relationship through the social exchange of emotions. For example, displays of heartfelt concern can enhance the intimacy of a formally distant relationship while guilt-evoking displays of hurt or anger can alter the distribution of power within a relationship. In these and various other ways, the flow of emotions among individuals ties and reties them into complex relational networks.

This selection focuses on the socially important emotion of sympathy. As Clark notes, we feel that we owe some sympathy to and are owed some sympathy from everyone within our social network. Of course, the amount of and circumstances under which we owe any specific individual sympathy depends on the particular character of our social bond. It also depends on what Clark calls the individual's sympathy biography or past adherence to the implicit feeling rules governing sympathy and its social exchange. Clark identifies the rules of our sympathy etiquette and illustrates how we judge one another's sympathy worthiness in terms of them.

In Clark's words, social relationships provide individuals with sympathy credits that they can draw upon when misfortune strikes. However, they can deplete or lose those credits if they violate rules of sympathy etiquette by falsely claiming, claiming too much, or claiming sympathy too readily. They can also lose sympathy credits if they do not adequately repay displays of sympathy either in kind or with what Clark calls other emotional currencies. If, on the other hand, individuals

never claim sympathy, they may find themselves outside the network of sympathy exchange when they do need and want it.

Clark also explains how the withholding and display of sympathy and its refusal can affect the form of a social relationship. For example, displays of sympathy often enhance the intimacy of a relationship but can also enhance the power of the sympathy donor over its recipient. Hence, an intended recipient of sympathy might well refuse its offer so as to avoid unwanted intimacy or a diminishment of relational power. This is only one example of how emotions and their exchange are implicated in the ongoing negotiation of relationships. Emotions are continually exchanged in what Clark calls the "socioemotional economy," governed by feeling rules and linking members of groups, communities, and societies in networks of reciprocal feeling and interaction. These emotional exchanges create and maintain patterns of social relationship. We are, then, working on more than our own and others' emotions when we manage them.

Sympathy, feeling sorry for or with another person . . . is basic to human society. . . . In the course of everyday encounters, people enter and enact the reciprocal roles-within-roles of sympathy donor and recipient, "sympathizer" and "sympathizee." In my research, I explore the roles of sympathizer and sympathizee in the United States today. . . .

Given the difficulties of observing the interior and often inaccessible aspects of [sympathy] and the need to validate conclusions and search for negative cases, I gathered data eclectically. . . . First, I sought expressions of sympathy in greeting cards, newspaper and television reports, advice columns, etiquette books, song lyrics, and literature. . . . A second source of data is the ethnographic materials produced by generations of sociologists studying victims, the downtrodden, the bereaved, the sick, and other underdogs (Becker 1967) and potential sympathizees. . . . I also involved myself as a participant observer (sometimes more as participant, others more as observer) of sympathy interactions in natural settings (e.g., hospitals, funeral homes, offices, etc.) over a period of two years. . . . A fourth source of data is a survey of northern New Jersey residents (hereafter designated "respondents"). Student interviewers presented vignettes depicting three plights to a cross section of adult nonstudents. The 877 respondents were predominantly Catholics, ranged in age from 18 to 77, and came mostly from the working and middle classes. In one of the vignettes, a hurricane has damaged a family's house; in another, a woman is brutally beaten by a man she "met in passing in a bar"; in the third, a young couple's marriage is jeopardized by one spouse's problems with alcohol. Respondents were asked to read one of these vignettes, to indicate the degree of sympathy they felt for the character(s) (from "extremely sorry" to "somewhat sorry" to "not sorry at all"), and to describe what aspects of the story had affected their responses. . . . Finally, four trained male and female interviewers and I conducted intensive interviews with 12 men and 13 women (hereafter termed "interviewees") between the ages of 25 and 80 living in New Jersey. . . . The interview schedule asked people to describe specific cases in which they had given, not given, received, rejected, expected, feigned, and "worked on" (Hochschild 1983, pp. 35–55) sympathy. . . .

Sympathy Flow

For sympathy to exist, there must be two people—a sympathizee and a sympathizer. (Even if we include self-pity in the category of sympathy, we can say that two selves are involved, one to feel for another.) Rules, meanings, and consequences differ between sympathy donors and recipients.

A set of loose, unwritten rules—an "emotional economy" (Collins 1981)—governs how feelings flow. I am using the term socioemotional economy to mean merely a system, produced and reproduced by interacting group members, for regulating emotional resources in a community. A socioemotional economy is a method for dispersing throughout the group the feeling currency necessary for creating and maintaining connectedness in general—and valued social identities in particular (Franks 1985). It promotes group survival just as a money-based, goods-and-services economy does.

Such capitalist principles as the profit motive usually play little part in the socioemotional economy; to aim for unlimited personal emotional gain at others' expense is, in fact, a violation of the rules. Instead, the people I observed, interviewed, and read about followed a sympathy economy

based on two principles. Sympathizers should adhere to the relatively socialistic tenet of the strong supporting the "deserving" weak. Recipients should reciprocate.

Sympathizers are expected to display sympathy, not indiscriminately, but in a manner appropriate to the person and to the plight. In what may be a split second, a potential sympathizer considers the other's plight, the other's complicity in the plight, and one's own situation relative to the other's. The outcome may or may not be sympathy.

One of the first principles for sympathizers is to determine whether the other person's plight is included in the *grounds* that the society considers sympathy worthy. My data show that in our culture these grounds include loss of a loved one, illness, divorce, loss of one's job, crime victimization, car trouble, and even noisy neighbors or fatigue. . . . Grounds, of course, change over time and vary among [different groups].

My evidence also indicates that sympathizers are influenced by people's social statuses. Children, for instance, often elicit more sympathy than adults with the same problems, and perhaps the middle class elicit more than either the wealthy or the destitute. More sympathy and aid go to disaster victims in friendly nations such as Mexico and Colombia than to those in disliked nations like the [former] Soviet Union. Further, statuses and plights can interact to produce very specific sympathy norms. For my interviewees, women with car trouble warrant more sympathy than men because of men's presumably superior mechanical skills. Widowers with small children often rate more sympathy than widows with children because of women's presumably greater talents in child care. A multitude of norms await further empirical specification.

The giving of sympathy, in addition to being subject to a battery of norms, also has unique meanings for the donor. Giving sympathy sends a dual message: it is a sign of caring or connectedness, and of the superiority or moral worth of the donor. . . . Sympathizing can enhance one's "niceness," but it can also increase one's "softness." Many interviewees tried to strike a balance between seeming hard and seeming sentimental. . . .

As it flows from donor to recipient, sympathy leaves invisible but important ties and debts marking its path. Receiving sympathy can both benefit and obligate the recipient. It benefits, because normal role obligations and standards are re-laxed. In addition, the acceptance, caring, and validation demonstrated by others are rewarding. As Goffman (1952) states, consolation is indeed a prize that can cool out or cool in the victims of life's misfortunes. Beneficial consequences include the tangible as well as the psychological. Receiving sympathy can make the difference between getting fired and not getting fired, between going to prison and going free. . . .

Receiving sympathy obligates, because accepting the role of sympathizee requires one to reciprocate for the gifts of sympathy and acceptance (Simmel 1971, pp. 150–178 . . .). A variety of emotional commodities, such as gratitude, deference, and future sympathy, serve as returns on the original gift.

Many other social variables—such as how intimate a relationship is and how power is configured—affect complex processes of giving and taking sympathy. Space does not permit analysis of them all. The variable to which I turn now is the sympathy margin, or account, set up by the donor for the recipient. Sympathy flow in the socioemotional economy works via sympathy margins. . . .

Sympathy Margin

In life, as in the literature that socializes us, to receive sympathy one must be a "sympathetic character." But what constitutes a sympathetic character? Part of the answer has to do with one's social statuses, and my data suggest that another part is related to relationships built up over time and involving considerable reciprocity. Jacqueline Wiseman (1979), in her analysis of the plight of skid row men and of the agents of social control who deal with them, points to a concept that helps us understand how sympathy and compassion come about. That concept is "social margin," that is, " . . . the amount of leeway a given individual has in making errors on the job, buying on credit, or stepping on the toes of significant others without suffering such serious penalties as being fired, denied credit, or losing friends and family. . . . A person with margin can get help" (1979, p. 223). Wiseman claims that respectability, especially in work and family careers, must be maintained to acquire margin (Wiseman 1979, p. 224).

Wiseman's insights have general utility in explaining interaction in the socioemotional economy of everyday life. One's moral worth and network ties affect how many emotional commodities, including "units" of sympathy and compassion, can be claimed from others and that others feel they owe. Social margin thus includes sympathy margin. Margin (social and otherwise) must be *ascribed by others.* Since we all interact with a variety of others, we may speak of people as having many margins of variable widths—one with each specific other in one's network.

In keeping with Wiseman's terminology, I have drawn a banking analogy with sympathy flow. Each group member has, I maintain, what amounts to an "account" of "sympathy credits" . . . held for him or her by each other group member. A certain number of sympathy credits are automatically on deposit in each of the sympathy accounts of the ordinary group members, available for cashing in when they are needed. They are a right of group membership.

The right to sentiment.—Simply put, group members are expected to feel some sympathy toward each other. How much sympathy (how many credits) each member can claim from each other member varies, but there is some minimum, albeit an unspecifiable and unquantifiable one. In general, people involved in "close" or "deep" relationships have an obligation to create wider sympathy margins for each other than do acquaintances or secondary group members. . . . More sympathy is due per occasion, more *genuine* sympathy is due, and it is due in a wider range of circumstances. We may, for example, feel sympathy for strangers or even enemies in what are considered disastrous or freak circumstances (being pushed under a subway car or being subjected to an earthquake or a terrorist attack), yet our friends and loved ones can call out, and count on, our sympathies for their minor problems as well as for their disasters. Also, credit is more freely given to an intimate than to an acquaintance, even before accounts have been settled.

The right to empathy.—Furthermore, there is an obligation to be empathic and to search for evidence that group members, especially intimates, have problems that merit sympathy. . . . When Goffman (1983, p. 13) discusses the role of "knowership," he recognizes this point, noting that in close relationships, one is supposed to keep the friend's biography in mind, ask questions about how issues in that person's life have been resolved, refer to his or her past illnesses, and the like. Focusing conversation on each other's biographies enhances communication and empathy between "knowers."

The right to display.—Abundant evidence also exists to show that group members are obligated to display sympathy appropriate to the person and the plight. Sometimes words of sympathy are expected, sometimes nonverbal messages and kid glove treatment. Some problems call for "off-the-rack" sentiments available in greeting cards.

Sudnow's (1967) study of hospital staff provides examples of the display norms expected of those dealing face to face with bereaved family members. Physicians giving "bad news" to relatives "cannot, like the telegram deliverer, merely present the news and leave the scene, but must evidence some degree of general concern and responsibility" (p. 129). The relative has the right to cry, moan, scream out, in other words, "to suspend his concern for normally enforceable requirements of . . . composure" (p. 136) on hearing of the death. He or she also has the right to indicate when interaction may proceed after the period of "carrying on" (p. 142). The staff member has the obligation to defer to the other, to present him- or herself solemnly, with appropriate tone of voice, facial expression, and the like.

Among my own interviewees, a 40-year-old professional woman, in reporting her reaction to a friend's illness, said: "I can remember saying to myself, 'Now, this is a shock, and you haven't taken it in yet, but you'd better look serious.'" Another woman, a 36-year-old waitress and college student, in noting violations of display norms, said: "My children were shocked to see [distant relatives] laughing and drinking at *their grandma's* funeral. In fact, so was I!" Interestingly enough, when my interviewees merely began to think, in the interview situation, about their reactions to others' plights, they frequently adopted the facial expressions, postures, and tones of voice appropriate to sympathy display—erasing smiles, knitting eyebrows, sitting up straighter, and speaking in "concerned" tones.

A given sympathy account or margin held by a specific other does not always remain constant. It is continually negotiated and may be increased, decreased, replenished, or used up entirely. Beyond the number of sympathy credits automatically "on account" in one's margins, a group member can earn credits, for example, by investing sympathy, help, and concern in others. The nature of the relationship between the two parties may also change as the sympathy margins of one or both change. Investing in another usually implies (whether as a consequence or a cause) a greater degree of intimacy between the parties.

Sympathy credits can also be cashed in. Claiming or accepting sympathy reduces one's margins, and one should draw against accounts that are solvent. The sick person who does not try to get well, like the skid row man who does not try to reform, may soon find his or her sympathy accounts depleted or even withdrawn (Parsons 1951; Wiseman 1979, p. 223). The number of sympathy credits is limited.

Of course, it is possible to overdraw one's accounts with some people in one's network but not with others. One might, for instance, try to claim equal amounts of sympathy from an acquaintance and from an intimate and find that the former claim is not honored while the latter is. Further, a given sympathy account sometimes depends on the total amount of sympathy a person is receiving. Thus, as several interviewees stated, co-workers may believe that married people will get sympathy from their spouses and, consequently, offer little themselves. My observations show that the members of a network often know each other and discuss among themselves how much sympathy a given member has claimed and how much others have given. The accounts held by some of these people are small because they believe that others are offering "enough." Accounts were drained completely in several cases involving prolonged periods of unemployment, divorce, extended illness, series of mishaps, and claims felt to be exaggerated. The potential sympathizee had to find new networks of significant others—open new accounts—when sympathy was still desired.

To be ascribed sympathy margin by others, one must have dealt properly with sympathy in the past. That is, sympathy margins are affected by one's sympathy biography—previous adherence to the protocols or etiquette for owing, giving, claiming, and accepting sympathy per se. I will now present the rules of sympathy etiquette that my research has uncovered.

Sympathy Etiquette

Rule 1: Do Not Make False Claims to Sympathy

The foremost rule of sympathy etiquette is not to falsely manipulate others' sympathy by pretending to need it, by exaggerating claims, or by courting disaster with the intent of calling out emotions in others. In short, one should not claim another's sympathy needlessly.

Aesop provides an interesting illustrative case, the familiar tale of the boy who cried wolf. The boy's first cries were heeded, but in each case no concrete evidence of the wolf's visit could be found. He was given some margin by others, but eventually his sympathy accounts disappeared. When the wolf actually threatened, the boy was judged to be lying and undeserving of sympathy.

A person who engages in any of the above practices, and who is caught out, erodes bases for trust. All of his or her claims may be called into question. Sympathy accounts may be closed. Others will find themselves not making efforts to empathize, not feeling sympathy sentiments, and/or not feeling obligations to display sympathy in otherwise sympathy worthy situations. A young working-class man explained his reactions to a co-worker's claims: "I can't take the time to sort out which things she claims are real. Now everything she says is suspect to me."

My interviewees were, on the whole, quite concerned about violations of this rule. They reported feeling "taken advantage of," "betrayed," and "conned" when other people played on their sympathies for their own gain. A psychologist in her 50s said of her sister:

> Amy's a disaster area! But . . . she makes her own problems. She calls collect from Hawaii to tell me that her husband is selling the house out from under them. She wants me to say, "Poor Amy!" I have to say to her, "He can't do that unless you sign the papers too." But she won't think or do anything for herself. . . . She makes things bad for herself to get sympathy. . . . I used to feel sorry for her, but now I try to avoid her.

Another interviewee, a 37-year-old real estate agent, spoke heatedly of a man who had got his friend's parents to feel sorry for him because his wife divorced him. The friend's parents were quite sympathetic. They rented him a house cheaply and then sold it to him for half the market value.

The interviewee complained: "He just used the [former landlords], and I could never help him out again knowing what he's like."

What is at issue here is a breach of public trust, a loss of faith that others will play by the rules. Despite the fact that we know to expect cynical and manipulative performances in everyday encounters, it comes as a shock when our expectations are realized and cannot be overlooked or explained away—when the fictions that make interaction easier are shattered. The tags "untrustworthy" and "con artist" are affixed to those who mishandle others' emotions as well as to those who abuse their money or property. One with such a reputation will have little sympathy margin.

Rule 2: Do Not Claim Too Much Sympathy

Even when legitimate grounds exist, do not claim "too much" sympathy "too often" or for "too long." That is, one should not overdraw one's sympathy accounts. The person who does so risks receiving sympathy displays with less sentiment than would be forthcoming otherwise, displays without sentiment, or worse, no displays at all.

Although the point of Aesop's story was that pretenses to sympathy are interpersonally dangerous, I contend that even if there had actually been an unlimited number of wolves, the boy could not have hoped to receive unlimited sympathy. In our terminology here, the boy had cashed in his sympathy credits. After his first few claims were honored, he had already received his sympathy allotment and depleted his sympathy accounts.

There is a variety of ways to ask for too much sympathy. First, one can ask too much for a particular problem. One's own plight may seem dire, but others may have perceived it as low in sympathy-worthiness. For example:

> Every time I see her, I think, "Here we go again!" She's like a broken record. "Sam did this to me; Sam didn't do that for me." I'm sorry, but a lot of us have been through divorces and survived. She's gone completely overboard. [Field notes, teacher in his 30s]

And:

> She looks like she's about 30. I mean, what does she want? Why should I feel sorry for her just because she's having her fortieth birthday? [Field notes, 45-year-old woman]

Second, one can ask for too much for a particular other's present situation. People who have their own problems are, to some extent, exempt from the obligation to feel or display sympathy to others—especially to others in less serious plights. These comments of a survey respondent, a Hispanic custodian in her 50s, show that she applied this "rule for breaking rules" to herself: "Why should I feel sorry for those people in that story [about hurricane damage]? I've got no job, and my husband died."

Third, in specific encounters and relationships, claims to sympathy may be considered excessive, as panhandlers regularly discover. Fourth, one can ask for too much sympathy for a particular setting. For instance, a claim that would be honored at lunch may not be honored in the office. Finally, sympathy may be claimed over too long a period of time—a point that merits further comment.

The estimated duration of a problem is related to the size of one's sympathy accounts in a curvilinear fashion. Problems of either very short or very long duration will engender less, or less consistent, sympathy than intermediate-range problems. Problems that are over quickly, such as a painful medical test lasting only a few moments, elicit minimal sympathy because these situations are not "worth" much. Long-term problems, while they may be worth more sympathy, may call for greater emotional expenditures than others can or will put forth. For instance, those who grieve too long (Wood 1975) or who cannot recover from a divorce or disaster in a timely fashion may find their margins diminished. Chronic illness—arthritis, for example—may thus be awarded less sympathy than an intermediate-range, acute illness, such as pneumonia. . . .

Regardless of one's misfortune, then, claiming and accepting sympathy can seriously diminish others' capacity to sympathize. George Eliot speaks of physical limits on how much sympathy can be felt or displayed:

> If we had a keen vision and feeling for all ordinary human life, it would be like hearing the grass grow and the squirrel's heart beat, and we should die of that roar which lies on the other side in silence. [(1872) 1981, p. 191]

Wiseman concurs:

> Charity and compassion are not available in unlimited supply, the Bible notwithstanding. Like so many other strong emotions, compassion cannot be called forth on every possible occasion without exhausting the giver. [1979, p. 242]

Sympathy recipients are expected to be sensitive to the sacrifices of sympathizers. If they are not, they may diminish others' willingness to sympathize. For both physical and cultural reasons, then, there appears to be a maximum amount of sympathy that an individual may claim from a specific other in a given period.

Those I observed and interviewed recognized these limits on others' sympathy. Several noted that, if they had recently received sympathy, help, time off from work, and the like, they were reluctant even to mention new problems that cropped up soon after. As one man, a carpenter in his 50s, put it,

> That month when I had three deaths in the family and my car broke down and my mother-in-law needed constant care and the kids were sick, well, it was too unbelievable. I was embarrassed to even tell people what was happening. I didn't bring up all the details.

An interviewee in her 30s, who had experienced surgery, a death in the family, and job problems, stated,

> I had to deal with it jokingly. I'd list all the terrible things and laugh. There were just too many things all at once.

She takes care to protect her significant others, thereby protecting her sympathy margins as well.

The other side of this sympathy rule is that, if one does not claim very much sympathy or help very often, one may be, in commonsense terms, "due for" it. Note the case of Mr. F, cited by Locker (1981). He is a stoic who has very rarely claimed sympathy and attention for illness and who is thought by his wife to deserve some:

> . . . . he had very bad flu, it's the first time he's been ill since we've been married, and I couldn't get the doctor to come and see him. OK, so everybody has flu, but he had a high temperature. . . . I felt that if Dr. M. [their former physician] and his old receptionist had been there . . . they would have thought: Mr. F never ever comes near us, he must really not be well, or even if he's not . . . we owe him a visit. [p. 108]

Many of us, like Mr. F, may store up sympathy credits by being competent, functioning group members. (That we can go too far with this practice is the subject of rule 3 below.)

Corollary 2a: Do not accept sympathy too readily.—In addition to not needing too much sympathy, one should not appear to want it too much. One should not expect, take for granted, or demand sympathy but, rather, underplay problems and count blessings.

Giving expressions of strength, independence, and bravery helps one avoid being perceived as self-pitying or as enjoying others' displays of sympathy. The oft-repeated question, "How are you bearing up?" implies that one should be trying to bear up. The appropriate response is, "I'm okay," or "Pretty well." One's tone of voice, energy level, and other nonverbal cues may indicate otherwise. . . . But verbal expressions of bravery are expected. One interviewee pointed out that she often catalogs her misfortunes and problems for others but expressly declines sympathy: "I guess I'm conveying that I could ask for their sympathy, but I'm not. I'm being brave" (young typist).

Underplaying problems is quite common, as Sudnow also found in his (1967) research on dying and the bereaved. "Persons are engaged, so it seems, in the continual de-emphasis of their feelings of loss, out of respect for the difficulties of interaction facing those less intimately involved in the death than themselves" (p. 140). For instance, sympathy phone calls which Sudnow managed to overhear included remarks initiated by the bereaved about the concerns of the sympathizer: "How are your children these days?" (p. 137). Underplaying represents, first, significant emotion work undertaken to align feelings with the norms of various interactional settings and, second, a meaningful gesture to the nonbereaved.

On those occasions when people do not "keep a stiff upper lip," sympathy is, in effect, claimed. And, of course, claims diminish margins. An interviewee, a medical researcher in his 40s, reacted to a sympathy-demanding co-worker as follows: "I always tell people to watch out for Josh. He can be quite a leech if you let him. His problems are endless. You just have to keep your distance." The "greedy" sympathizee is shunned.

The victim of circumstances is also commonly expected to focus on other good luck or blessings that are thought to compensate for the present bad luck. Hurricane victims, interviewed by network newscasters in the fall of 1984, lived up to this expectation. Indeed, none whose interviews were aired failed to strike a positive note. For example: "It could have been worse" (middle-aged woman). "At least we're still alive" (middle-aged man). "We'll just start rebuilding and try to forget all this" (elderly man).

My survey respondents reacting to the vignette about the hurricane victims echoed this theme: "I feel sorry, but at least they've got each other and no one was killed" (housewife in her 50s). "Sometimes a disaster like this draws people together. They're fortunate because they'll probably be closer now" (young secretary).

One typical get well card from Hallmark makes the count-your-blessings norm explicit. It attempts to convince the "unlucky" sufferer that he or she is really "lucky."

> CHEER UP!
> Things could be worse!
> Suppose you had a SNEEZING FIT
> Or you maybe had the GOUT,
> Suppose your ARCHES all FELL IN
> Or all your HAIR FELL OUT—
> . . .
> You're really lucky when you think
> Of what it MIGHT HAVE BEEN—
> But just the same, here's hoping
> You will SOON BE WELL AGAIN!

Other cards, presumably for a male audience, exhort the hospitalized person to pay attention to the nurses rather than to the pain and danger.

To summarize this corollary, one who eagerly and openly accepts sympathy is an embarrassment because she or he is not meeting the role obligations of the sympathizee. Each of us has a right to some sympathy, but interactional strategies that explicitly call for these rights to be honored will diminish sympathy margins rapidly. The resulting sentiment is usually less sincere, and display, if there is any, may be empty.

Rule 3: Claim Some Sympathy

Prescriptions of bravery notwithstanding, to keep sympathy margins viable one should claim and accept some sympathy from others when circumstances are appropriate. This sympathy rule is perhaps less obvious than the others. Taken together with rule 2, it suggests that there is some optimal amount of sympathy to claim. The self-reliant—who remain independent, pay cash, and do not develop credit ratings by borrowing and repaying—may not have sympathy accounts in times of need. Paradoxically, those who have histories of never crying wolf may find no one heeding their legitimate cries. This rule is most clearly applicable in relationships involving intimates or equals, but it operates to some extent for nonintimates, subordinates, and superiors as well.

Just as the act of claiming sympathy has a variety of meanings, so, too, does not claiming or accepting sympathy. In general, one who never claims or accepts sympathy from another over a period of time in a stable relationship may simply come to be defined as an inactive member of the interaction network. (This definition results especially, but not only, when one gives little sympathy to others as well.) Nonaccepters are of the group but not in it. When roles have solidified and become habitual, an out-of-character claim for sympathy may not "compute."

As my interviewees indicated, a number of signals may be sent if one does not, from time to time, claim and accept some sympathy. One may appear too lofty or too self-possessed. In the former case, one is unworthy of sympathy; in the latter, not in need. Or, like a rate-buster's, one's fortune is too good or the ability to cope too expert compared with that of the average person. The following case shows that highly competent people who rarely claim sympathy can easily find themselves defined as not needing sympathy, as not having the problems, worries, or stage fright common among the less able:

> I was so surprised—shocked—at the reaction of my colleagues last week. I had to give a big presentation that lasted two days. I've done shorter ones before, but this was frightening. I found myself getting nervous and tried to talk to my friends about it. They just said, "Oh, you'll do okay. You always do." Not an ounce of sympathy! And these were "near" friends, too, not just people I know.

Although this young editor gives sympathy to others, she rarely finds the need to claim it. The event she describes led her to recognize that she had no sympathy accounts with her co-workers. She reported that she intends to change their perceptions of her by letting them know more about her insecurities—that is, by claiming some sympathy.

My interviewees also attributed such meanings to not accepting sympathy as the unwillingness to incur obligations, the unwillingness to allow others to discharge obligations, and the unwillingness

to admit others into backstage regions where problems and vulnerabilities are apparent. Finally, nonclaimers may give the impression that they feel too "lowly" to expect others' attention and sympathy.

Rule 3 shows that, as a particular sympathy exchange unfolds, group boundaries are created. Insiders and outsiders, intimates and nonintimates are defined. At the same time, group structure—the system of power and status relationship—is affected.

To begin with, A's claim and B's subsequent gift of sympathy create (1) a bond of "knowership" (Goffman 1983, p. 13) or intimacy between them and (2) trust on the part of the sympathizee. Further, the direction of the exchange crystallizes the statuses and roles of those in the relationship along a *superordinate-subordinate* dimension. Mutual exchanges of sympathy commonly symbolize equality, whereas one-way gifts of sympathy usually signify inequality.

If one gives and receives sympathy, one is a friend, intimate, or peer. Former acquaintances who have not been particularly close may find their relationship taking on a more intimate cast, once sympathy has been exchanged.

On the other hand, the person who gives without claiming or accepting sympathy in return does not allow recipients a chance to discharge their obligations. Rather than enhancing equality, these situations engender the "parent-child" relationship between donor and recipient that Mead (1962, p. 367) saw as the essential form of sympathy. And the "parent" may be rightly or wrongly perceived as not requiring or needing sympathy for him- or herself. Furthermore, the state of owing engendered in the "child" (recipient) may be so uncomfortable as to cause resentment against the donor, providing justification for not returning sympathy or actually interfering with feeling it.

To recap, there appears to be an optimal amount of sympathy to claim and/or receive (depending on the relative power and authority of the actor and the desired closeness of the relationship), if one wants to keep accounts open. Claiming too little, as well as claiming too much, may diminish margins.

Rule 4: Reciprocate to Others for the Gift of Sympathy

A final rule for maintaining an adequate supply of sympathy credits is that one must reciprocate. Depending in part on one's position vis-à-vis the donor, one may be expected to repay the gift of sympathy with gratitude, deference, and esteem, or to pay back sympathy. Whether conscious of the fact or not, people usually expect returns when they give sympathy. . . .

As Levi-Strauss (1969, p. 54) points out, returns for social "gifts" do not have to accrue to the original donor to be considered valuable. Returns to family members, friends, and even to charities or the community at large may serve to erase obligations. For instance, if A receives sympathy from B, A can discharge the debt by showing gratitude to B's spouse or by giving sympathy to B's children should they experience problems. But a recipient who never makes a good-faith effort to show appreciation to the group may come to be ignored.

The minimal and most immediate type of return expected for sympathy is gratitude. Paying gratitude for sympathy signifies that one is in, and acknowledges being in, a position of need. She or he is "one-down" or "one-less-up." First, the recipient is in trouble, ailing, or otherwise not able to function in usual social roles, or the sympathy would not be needed. Second, he or she has "burdened" the sympathizer because of these difficulties. Third, the recipient knows that the sympathizer well could have "believed in a just world" and offered blame rather than sympathy. To refuse to pay gratitude can imply, then, a refusal to recognize the state of need, a refusal to accept the sympathy and well-wishes of other group members, or an expectation that sympathy is a right involving no obligations. Any of these signals can create a gap between the sympathizee and the sympathetic other, who may feel (to use my interviewees' words) "used," "taken for granted," or "unappreciated." On the other hand, showing gratitude, even minimally with a nod or a look, can serve to cement ties. In the Outer Hebrides of Scotland and some rural communities in the United States, a gratitude column in which recipients of sympathy visits and flowers publicly give acknowledgments and thanks is a regular feature of weekly newspapers. Some potential sympathizees—students, skid row residents, low-income crime victims—may even be required to display gratitude before they receive sympathy (see Wiseman 1979, p. 243).

The type of gratitude expected in return for sympathy varies with the relative social standings of donor and recipient. Those whom I observed and interviewed rarely mentioned receiving sympathy from a subordinate but noted receiving it from "personages." They remembered and remarked baskets of fruit sent by company presidents at times of bereavement and cards sent to former pet owners by veterinarians (even though such cards were routinely signed and mailed by secretaries). Gifts of sympathy given by superiors (especially when the superior is frugal with such gifts) are imbued with greater value than the same gift from an equal or an inferior. For this reason . . . the returns appropriate for a gift from a superior differ from the returns appropriate for peers. What is owed a superior is gratitude cum deference. Deference is a weightier and dearer commodity than gratitude. Deferential behavior implies that one is inferior to the recipient in a fundamental and perhaps permanent way, grateful for the valuable gift from the superior, and unable to repay the debt with an equally valuable gift. A lack of deference and gratitude is often seen as arrogance, and arrogance can diminish sympathy margin. . . .

Sympathizees must not only show gratitude and deference, they must show them even when the sympathy displays they have received are crude, inept, hurtful, or unwanted. Sudnow's research on bereavement suggests that "offers of sympathy must be accepted without invitation" (1967, p. 156). In some of his cases, an open door policy existed that allowed anyone to enter the house of the bereaved to offer sympathy, whether it was timely or not. Moreover, the awkardness often felt by sympathizers may result in bungled communications, empty phrases ("I just don't know what to say"), jocular attempts to cheer up the victim that actually induce tears of horror, and the like. Another common mode of sympathizing is the recitation of the sympathizer's own problems ("I know just how you feel, because the same thing has happened to me and I . . ."). This sort of communication is intended, one may assume, to refocus the sympathizee's attention and to indicate that one is not alone in misfortune. (A sympathy recipient may feel compelled to listen to or even to elicit such remarks, thereby switching roles with the sympathizer.) The sympathizee must put up with all of the above types of communications, because the mere fact of expressing some sympathy is thought to indicate that the sympathizer means well.

Beyond gratitude, another important type of return is sympathy itself. Paying back past awards replenishes sympathy credits, a fact that I infer from contrary evidence:

> He's having a hard time, but I'm keeping my distance. . . . I gave him a lot of sympathy . . . but he didn't even notice when I needed it. [25-year-old man, teacher]

> I was by her side at her mother's funeral. Where was she when my brothers died? I don't count her as part of the family any more. [Retired secretary, age 70]

Although these people feel that their past investments entitle them to sympathy, there is no FDIC to guarantee emotional returns. The people who failed to repay debts when an occasion arose risked and got closed accounts.

Rules for repaying sympathy with sympathy, like those for paying gratitude, are contingent on power relations. For example, repaying a superior with sympathy (an equal return) may be considered an insult; gratitude is often preferred. The peer or intimate is more likely to receive sympathy for sympathy.

In general, then, sympathizers expect recognition of their gifts of sympathy, and sympathizees acknowledge the fact that they incur debts when they accept such gifts. The rules do not specify commensurate returns in every case, because it is hard to measure how much has been received (and is therefore owed) and because people may want to maintain rather than erode power differences. On the whole, though, most people do not receive much more sympathy than they repay with their gratitude or their own sympathy. Margins not replenished soon become overdrawn. . . .

Conclusions

I have argued that sympathy sentiment and display flow unevenly among group members, usually in patterned . . . ways. People who have acceptable sympathy biographies are ascribed margin by others—they have a right to sympathy in appropriate circumstances. Having an acceptable sympathy biography means following rules of etiquette: not making fraudulent claims, not claiming too much too readily, claiming some sympathy, and reciprocating for sympathy gifts. A

flawed sympathy biography leads to closed accounts, except when rules of niceness or goodness, perhaps combined with duty, motivate people to keep margins open.

[These sympathy rules and processes] are related to the micropolitics of relationships. Because of an awareness of sympathy rules, some people may, consciously or unconsciously, give sympathy to manipulate others into positions of closeness or positions of owing. Indebtedness affects power and status relationships. The debt may not be one that the debtor freely contracts; it can be imposed by the sympathizer. Furthermore, giving sympathy may belittle the recipient because it points up problems and insufficiencies. The following case explicitly illustrates the conscious manipulation of sympathy by a worker to belittle a boss:

> I remember that I once used sympathy on purpose to try to knock someone down a peg. I had a boss who was always doing and saying things to put me down in a semi-nice way. . . . I got tired of it, so I turned it around on him. I was in his office, and I said, "Oh, Mr. Wall, look at all those reports you have to get done. I feel *so* sorry for you. I wouldn't want your job for the world." He changed colors, and I could see he was mad. He just said, "Oh, I can get this done in a snap. Nothing to it!" and edged me out the door. Normally he would have chatted a while. So I really got in a good zinger. [Middle-aged professional woman]

Micropolitics are also affected when, through "deep acting," one manipulates one's own sympathy sentiment to counteract fear, hatred, or anger and maintain a sense of efficacy. Fearing or hating a person may be more unpleasant than feeling sorry for him or her. Flight attendants interviewed by Hochschild admitted working up sympathy when confronted with an unruly or obnoxious passenger they initially detested (Hochschild 1983, p. 55 . . .). Several of my interviewees reported that they had eliminated feelings of dread, annoyance, or "high blood pressure" by "talking themselves into" or "making themselves" feel sorry for children, bosses, co-workers, or spouses toward whom they were inclined to hold more negative emotions. The pitied other seems to threaten or to intrude into one's consciousness less; his or her power to disrupt one's equilibrium is diminished.

Not claiming or accepting sympathy may similarly play a part in power relationships. Refusing to accept sympathy though engaging in one-way sympathy displays can reduce the others' social power and raise or reinforce one's own. In some cases, giving sympathy without receiving it in return becomes "a part of the job" if one is a supervisor, parent, or teacher. A young college professor, normally sympathetic toward students in her course on death and dying, illustrated this link between power and sympathy when a student offered to give her sympathy.

> He wanted me to start telling him all my problems. I thought to myself, "I don't want to get any closer to you. I don't want to tell you any more about myself. And what makes you think *you* can help me?".... I knew what I was doing: trying to preserve my position as professor. [Field notes, Oct. 1985]

Accepting the student's sympathy would have altered the relationship irrevocably, making it closer and jeopardizing her superior standing. Thus, she refused the offered sympathy. The student quickly left, apparently embarrassed by his misstep. The sympathy margin he tried to open for the professor had been purposely rejected.

Finally, people can even pay gratitude in return for sympathy to enhance their prestige in cases where public displays of thanks link the sympathizee with powerful or prestigious others. Gratitude column contributors, for example, show the community that they are worthy of worthy people's sympathy. The ads often thank "friends" anonymously but name superordinate sympathizers.

References

Becker, Howard S. 1967. "Whose Side Are We On?" *Social Problems* 14:239–47.

Collins, Randall. 1981. *Sociology Since Midcentury: Essays in Theory Cumulation.* New York: Academic.

Eliot, George (May Ann Evans Cross). (1872) 1981. *Middlemarch: A Study of Provincial Life.* New York: New American Library.

Franks, David. 1985. "The Sociology of Emotions." Richmond: Virginia Commonwealth University, Department of Sociology.

Goffman, Erving. 1952. "On Cooling the Mark Out: Some Aspects of Adaptation to Failure." *Psychiatry* 15:451–63.

———. 1983. "The Interaction Order." *American Sociological Review* 48:1–17.

Hochschild, Arlie Russell. 1983. *The Managed Heart: Commercialization of Human Feeling.* Berkeley: University of California Press.

Levi-Strauss, Claude. 1969. *The Elementary Structures of Kinship.* Boston: Beacon.

Locker, David. 1981. *Symptoms and Illness: The Cognitive Organization of Disorder.* London: Tavistock.

Mead, George Herbert. (1934) 1962. *Mind, Self, and Society,* edited by Charles Morris. Chicago: University of Chicago Press.

Parsons, Talcott. 1951. *The Social System.* Glencoe, IL: Free Press.

Simmel, Georg. (1908) 1971. *On Individuality and Social Forms,* edited by Donald N. Levine. Chicago: University of Chicago Press.

Sudnow, David. 1967. *Passing On: The Social Organization of Dying.* Englewood Cliffs, NJ: Prentice Hall.

Wiseman, Jacqueline. 1979. *Stations of the Lost: The Treatment of Skid Row Alcholics,* 2nd ed. Chicago: University of Chicago Press.

Wood, Juanita. 1975. "The Structure of Concern: The Ministry in Death-related Situations." *Urban Life* 4:369–84.

22

Popularity and Friendship Among Adolescent Girls

Donna Eder

In most social settings where individuals are in regular contact with one another, relatively stable patterns of relationships tend to develop. These patterns of relationships are often hierarchical or "stratified" with an informal system of social status. Some individuals are well known and liked by many people while others are not. Where more than a few individuals are in regular contact, different relational networks or groups also tend to develop. Members of such groups identify themselves as a distinctive social unit and interact with one another more than they do with those outside the group. These social relational dynamics result in informal social structures that influence subsequent social interaction.

This selection examines social relationships among middle school girls. Over the middle school grades, these girls developed a relatively stable hierarchy of more and less "popular" groups of friends. Cheerleading was the most visible activity for girls in this school and brought instant visibility and popularity. Friendship with an already popular girl was also an important avenue to popularity. Thus, popular girls were not only the center of attention but also much sought after as friends.

By the seventh grade, relatively stable groups or cliques of friends had developed. The more popular girls formed their own groups and avoided interaction with members of less popular groups. The popular girls could not befriend all the girls who wanted to be their friends and apparently worried that associating with less popular girls would threaten their lofty peer status. Less popular girls resented this rejection and came to think of popular girls as "stuck-up" and "snobbish." This resulted in what Eder refers to as "the cycle of popularity" among adolescent girls. Popular girls are first widely admired and liked but then come to be disliked by less popular girls because of their perceived unfriendliness.

This selection illustrates how individuals interactionally create and maintain informal social structures and group boundaries. Once these girls formed more or less popular groups, they tended to interact less with members of other groups and to form stereotypes of them. In turn, these stereotypes discouraged interaction between members of different groups and reinforced group boundaries. These kinds of interactional and relational dynamics are not confined to middle schools. Although the bases of popularity or informal social status and group formation may differ, informal social hierarchies and group boundaries can be found in all variety of social settings. However, the specific character of early adolescent girls' relationships helps explain the consistent finding that they tend to value friendship and popularity over achievement and success in other realms. In the social world of middle school girls, success is measured by peer social status and friendship is central to achieving that status. Their concern with being labeled a "snob" may also discourage them from being more successful than their friends. For them as for us, the patterns of social relationships we interactionally construct then shape our everyday social lives.

One consistent and somewhat troublesome finding in research on adolescent females is that they are more concerned with popularity than with achievement or success. . . . Rosenberg and Simmons (1975) found that girls' concern with being well liked and their lack of interest in success develop during early adolescence. Prior to that, girls and boys are equally concerned with achievement in school and have similar aspirations for success in future jobs. *However between late childhood (ages 8 to 11) and early adolescence (ages 12 to 14), girls' desire to achieve decreases, and their desire to be well liked increases.* During this same period, girls also become more concerned with others' opinions of them and show a marked increase in self-consciousness. In general, during early adolescence, girls' concerns become increasingly differentiated from boys' and become more focused on interpersonal relations than on achievement. . . .

What is most lacking in the literature on adolescents are studies that focus on girls' relationships with other girls. It is often assumed that girls are most concerned with their social success or popularity among boys. But adolescent girls may be equally concerned with their popularity among other girls. Likewise, though it is assumed that girls' avoidance of success stems mainly from a concern with being liked by boys, it may in fact have other motivations as well.

Girls' friendships undergo considerable change with the transition to a middle school setting. First, *students in middle school have a larger population from which to choose friends, which encourages the development of more distinct friendship groups or cliques.* . . . Second, middle school students can participate in more extracurricular activities, which provide new sources of peer status. Specifically, athletic activities provide males with a clear avenue for status, and cheerleading provides an elite group of females with high status. . . .

This article explains why girls become increasingly concerned with interpersonal relationships during the transition to middle school. In particular, it examines how changes in girls' relationships with other girls contribute to an increased concern with popularity and a decreased concern with achievement. It also provides a better understanding of why girls become increasingly other-directed and insecure during early adolescence. . . .

The findings reported [here] are part of a larger study of adolescent peer relations and socialization, which involved in-depth observations of informal and organized peer activities in a middle school. . . . [W]e selected a school that enrolled students from a range of socioeconomic backgrounds, including students from working-class and lower-class families. The school was located in a medium-size midwestern community and enrolled approximately 250 students per grade. Some of the students came from surrounding rural areas. Most of the students were white, but a small number of black students were also enrolled. The school's extracurricular program, which emphasized athletic activities, was typical among middle schools. Vocal and instrumental music programs were also available.

During the first year of the study, two researchers observed extracurricular and informal activities twice a week. . . . We spent much of this time observing interactions during the lunch period, since this was the most opportune time for students to meet informally. In addition, we observed informal interaction before and after school, during special events such as school picnics and dances, and during and between classes.

For two months during the second year, a second research assistant and I made follow-up observations of the same girls and observed some new girls in similar activities. . . .

One advantage of observing during the lunch period was that we could share an activity with students, namely eating lunch, and thus establish rapport fairly quickly. Because of this rapport and because we were in the setting on a regular basis for an extended period of time, we are quite confident that our data represent typical patterns of peer relations at this school. Although we informed students that we were studying adolescent interaction and friendship, we did not take notes openly while observing informal activities. Between lunch periods we wrote brief notes, and immediately after leaving the setting, we recorded detailed notes with a tape recorder. We also tape recorded the interviews and some of the lunch conversations. Our field notes include the seating patterns of the groups we observed and information about the content of their conversations. . . .

Groups were defined according to lunchtime seating arrangements. Any student who sat with a group two or more times was considered a group member. Comments such as "This isn't your group" or "Your group's outside" indicated that these seating patterns reflected meaningful group boundaries. . . .

The Development of Social Stratification

We found considerable differences in peer relations across the three grades. In the sixth grade, there were few stable cliques and no cliques that appeared to have more status than others. In the seventh grade, the cliques were more stable and a hierarchy was beginning to emerge. By eighth grade, there was a clearly defined hierarchical system of stable cliques.

The stratified social system developed from a number of sorting processes. As mentioned, one way students defined group boundaries was through seating arrangements at lunch. During the first year of the study, the three grades had separate lunch periods. Students could sit wherever they wanted during their lunch period, and they expended considerable effort to ensure that they sat with the people they liked. This was accomplished mainly by saving seats for friends. But, this strategy was also used to prevent certain girls from sitting with a group. If one of these girls approached an empty seat at the table, she was often told that the seat was being saved for someone else.

Sixth graders had the most flexible seating patterns during lunch. Few groups sat together regularly throughout the year, and most girls sat with different groups on different days. Because seating arrangements were continually negotiated, we saw open attempts to include and exclude certain girls. In the following example from our field notes, Penny was excluded from a group that she had previously sat with:

> Some visitors were sitting at their table, so they were trying to save the remaining seats for their friends. The main conflict arose when Penny sat in one of those seats and they told her all of them were saved. She looked a little dejected that they weren't going to let her sit with them. Then she looked around and said: "Well, where's Pam's group" and went over and talked to them.
>
> (Field notes, March 10, grade 6)

Seating patterns among seventh graders were more stable; many students sat with the same group for months at a time. Also, a hierarchy of groups, which did not exist among the sixth graders, had developed. The highest status group included seven of the eight cheerleaders and six student council members, including the class president. This was the most stable group in the seventh grade: Twelve of the seventeen girls who sat with this group were permanent members. . . .

Another status division in seating arrangements developed during the seventh grade. All the higher-status groups described above, along with several other groups, sat on one side of the cafeteria. These students often wore name-brand clothes, and many of them appeared to be from middle-class backgrounds. The students on the other side of the cafeteria appeared, from their dress, to be primarily from lower- and working-class backgrounds. It was clear that students were also aware of this difference. One day, a seventh grader asked me if I always sat on this side of the cafeteria. I said "yes" and asked her if she did. She said that she always did, because it was the side where the "good people" sat.

By eighth grade, the seating arrangements were very stable; most students sat with the same group for the entire year. The two top groups merged to form one large mixed-sex group, which included all eight cheerleaders, many of the male athletes, and eleven student council members. The social-class division in seating patterns was also more apparent in eighth grade. Only a few students from middle-class backgrounds sat on the side of the cafeteria with the less popular students.

Changes in group membership during the year provided additional information on the sources of peer-group status among adolescent girls. There were two main avenues for mobility into the elite group—being a cheerleader or being a friend of a cheerleader. For example, during the entire year, only four girls joined the top eighth-grade group. One was a cheerleader and another was her best friend. Both of these girls were welcomed into this very exclusive group. Similarly, one of the cheerleaders who was not already a member of the top seventh-grade group joined it shortly after the year began.

There was no clear top group in sixth grade during most of the year, but after cheerleading tryouts, a large group, which included four of the new cheerleaders, began to sit together quite regularly. Also, after the new cheerleaders did some routines at a pep session in the spring, they made conscious attempts to sit together at lunch. . . .

Near the end of the [second] year, we asked the students in the groups we had been observing if some students in their grade were more popular than others and why. Being a cheerleader and being a friend of a cheerleader, along with having money and being attractive, were considered important avenues for popularity among girls. The following response from two eighth graders was typical:

> R—I wonder how somebody like her gets to be popular in the first place.
>
> D—They hang around with the cheerleaders.
>
> K—Yeah, you hang around popular kids and you usually become popular.
>
> (Interview, May 20, grade 8)

Sixth graders could not participate in cheerleading, but being friends with seventh- and eighth-grade cheerleaders and with popular girls in the sixth grade was important.

> H—She's real popular. She's nice. She's pretty. That's why she's popular.

R—Think so?

H—Then all of her friends are popular and all of their friends are popular.

R—Why are all her friends popular?

H—Because they're all friends I suppose.

(Interview, April 7, grade 6)

Thus, friendships with other girls are important avenues for status, and this has important implications for the meaning of popularity, for peer relations between groups, and for adolescent girls' growing concern with being well liked.

The Meaning of Popularity

From our interviews and informal talks with girls, we found that popularity had a number of different meanings. On the one hand, popular girls were the most *visible* in the school; they were the girls most people knew by name. This was clearly seen as one of the advantages of being popular. According to girls who were not popular, the nice part about being popular is that "everybody knows you." Also, popular girls received the most attention from others. According to one of the popular girls, "the good part [about popularity] is that you get a lot of attention." In contrast, girls who were not popular felt that their achievements were often ignored:

N—Now if I was popular, when I won that contest everybody would have been jumping around and sayin', "Oh! Natalie won! Natalie won!" But it wasn't like that. Since I wasn't popular everybody just kind of thought, like "Big deal!"

(Interview, April 20, grade 8)

Visibility both preceded and followed membership in the elite group. Among sixth-grade girls, one of the main determinants of visibility was attractiveness. Even popular girls admitted that this was an important factor in popularity. The other factor that affected visibility was cheerleading. The cheerleaders were clearly the most visible group of girls in the school. The two athletic events they cheered for—boys' basketball and football—were the main social events in the school.

Becoming a member of the elite group also added to one's visibility, because the entire group was often the focus of the attention of others, particularly those who sat on the same side of the cafeteria. During lunch, the behavior of top-group members was often the topic of conversation among those in other groups, but the top group seldom paid attention to students who were not in their group.

Most of the girls agreed that popular students were more visible, but not all felt that popular students were more well liked. Some girls described popular girls as nice and friendly and considered being well liked another advantage of popularity. But *other girls described popular girls as stuck-up and unfriendly* and clearly stated their dislike for them. Still others expressed some ambivalence on this point. . . .

To the extent that popular girls are well liked, one might ask whether being well liked precedes or follows popularity. Girls who were friendly and outgoing experienced an increase in popularity, but girls who became identified as members of the top group also experienced an initial increase in positive sentiment. This was most obvious among the newly elected cheerleaders. Many of the girls wanted to sit with the cheerleaders at lunch and made special attempts to be friendly toward them. . . .

Cheerleaders and other popular girls experience an increase in positive sentiments because their friendship is an important avenue for social status. When certain girls are first identified as candidates for popularity, many girls want to become their friends. Girls who are outgoing and responsive to others are especially well liked, since their friendship is so highly valued.

However, there is a second stage in this *cycle of popularity*, during which popular girls face increasingly negative sentiment. This stage is also influenced by the importance of social avenues for peer status among adolescent girls and by the nature of social interaction in middle school settings. To better understand this second stage, we will next look at peer relations between groups.

Peer Relations and Social Interaction

One of the important facts about school life is that students have little opportunity to physically separate themselves from other students. Most unstructured activities take place in relatively crowded environments such as the lunch room. Consequently, students develop symbolic ways to distinguish their group from the many students who are always present.

The students we observed used many of the strategies people use to avoid interaction with others in a public setting, such as avoiding body contact and eye contact. . . . For example, students who were in the same class would walk by each other without any acknowledgment. In fact, acknowledgement by someone outside of one's peer group was an important and reportable event.

We also found that students in high-status groups often ignored friendly initiations from students in other groups, giving the impression that they were rude or snobbish. Some of these instances involved members of the same athletic team, as shown in the following notes from gymnastics practice:

> Allison said "Hi" to Patty, who said nothing to her. Allison then made some comment about her being stuck-up. Then she again said "Hi" and again got no response from Patty. She told Marsha, "She's in a bad mood. She's not saying 'Hi' to me." But later she said, "She's stuck-up."
>
> (Field notes, November 6, grade 7)

Allison offered two different explanations for Patty's failure to acknowledge her. First, she explained that Patty was in a bad mood and may not have felt like talking to anyone that day. Then she concluded that Patty was stuck-up. Of these two attributions, the second was more common for this type of behavior. In fact, many of the popular girls in the school were considered snobbish. This was due in part to their failure to engage in interaction with other girls.

> What the sixth graders talked about today was that people try to be nice to a popular girl but that she's very snotty and does not talk to anyone. Apparently, when most people go up to somebody who is snotty and popular, they will not get a response from her and can't even engage in a conversation with her. She just ignores them.
>
> (Field notes, February 10, grade 6)

The concern that popular girls would become stuck-up was so widespread that some girls were warned in advance. For example, in the yearbook of a new cheerleader, someone wrote, "Have fun in high school. Just don't get stuck-up."

Cheerleaders were considered by many to be the most snobbish, but this label was also applied to other girls who sat on the "popular" side of the cafeteria. Many thought that these girls had become less friendly since coming to Woodview Middle School:

> Nancy said how she talked to her at Parkside, and in fact, when they were in seventh grade, they had talked to each other alot, but now this girl never talks to her. It has only been since she came to Woodview that she had turned into such a snob.
>
> (Field notes, February 10, grade 8)

. . . Popular girls were generally considered stuck-up, but some were considered friendly when they were not with other members of their group. This was reported to be true of Susan, who was not in the top group but who did sit on the popular side of the cafeteria:

> She said that Susan was nice if she got her away from Karla. This was another idea that she talked about several times—that some girls would be snotty and not talk to you if they were with one group, but if they were away from one or two of the most popular girls, then they would talk to you.
>
> (Field notes, February 10, grade 6)

Thus, popular girls do not necessarily dislike less popular girls. Rather, they may be concerned about their friends' reactions to their associations with less popular girls. This is probably due to the close relationship between status and friendship among girls. Just as girls become more popular if they have popular friends, they may become less popular if they associate with less popular people. But popular girls may also ignore less popular girls because they simply do not have the time or energy to maintain friendships with all the girls who would like to be their friends.

Popularity and Dislike

These dynamics gave rise to the perception that popular girls were unfriendly and led to an increase in negative sentiment. Some of the students who talked about disliking popular girls were their former close friends. It is not surprising to find that former friends no longer like each other, but the negative feelings toward popular girls were often stronger than those toward other students and frequently took the form of active dislike. As we have seen, friendships with popular girls are an important source of peer status. Consequently, the loss of one of these friendships is salient; the student not only loses a good friend, she loses an opportunity to be more popular. At the same time, the former friend's preference for a new peer group makes the relatively lower status of her old group more salient. This was evident in the reaction to Penny's change in friendships after she made the freshman pom-pom team:

> Bonnie told me that ever since Penny made the pom-pom team she goes over and sits with the popular girls. She told me that she was going to tell Penny something today but that she had chickened out. I asked her what it was and she said, "I was going to tell her if she comes and sits with us, 'Why don't you go over and sit with your new friends if your old friends aren't good enough for you?'"
>
> (Field notes, April 9, grade 8)

Penny's change in group membership was the topic of conversation on several days and led many of her old friends to actively dislike her. Because peer status was so important to these girls, a former friend's transfer to a higher-status group was more painful and led to stronger feelings of resentment than her transfer to another lower-status group.

Popular people were disliked not only by former friends but by many of the students in the school. As discussed earlier, some students felt that members of the top group and other students who sat on the popular side of the cafeteria ignored them. Even though being ignored by other students was extremely common in the school, we mainly heard complaints about being ignored by popular students. Again, it is likely that interaction with popular students was so salient that being ignored by them was also particularly salient. Many students took the snobbery of popular people very seriously, as if it automatically implied they were not as good.

Also, because some students had negative experiences with members of the top group, the whole group was branded with certain labels. We found that some top-group members were less group-oriented than others and initiated interactions with a wider range of girls. Though some girls mentioned these differences, most girls felt that all of the top-group members were stuck-up. They were quick to interpret a lack of response from popular girls as snobbish and tended to apply this interpretation to all group members. This stereotype led many girls to avoid further contact with top-group members, thereby minimizing the possibility of further painful rejection. . . .

Many of the girls formed stereotypes about other girls, but the nature and type of the stereotypes varied depending on their position in the overall social hierarchy. For example, girls who sat on the popular side of the cafeteria but who were not in the top group saw the top-group members as stuck-up but did view themselves that way. They, however, tended to classify all of the students on the other side of the cafeteria as "grits" [a term associated with lower-class people in this region of the country]. The students who sat on the less popular side identified one particular lower-status group as "grits." In general, there was a tendency to apply broader stereotypes to students who were further away in the overall hierarchy and with whom one had less contact. The stereotypes in turn often served to prevent contact and therefore limited the amount of information that students received—information that might have challenged the stereotypes. . . .

Consequences for Group Interaction

One consequence of the negative stereotype of popular girls was a growing tendency to avoid interaction with them. Since the entire popular group was often viewed as snobbish, many girls stopped approaching any of the popular girls for fear of being rejected, even though there were clear difference in the degrees of friendliness among the popular girls.

One of the more popular girls considered this to be one of the main disadvantages of being popular:

> M—Then, a lot of times, people don't talk to the popular kids because they're kind of scared of them and they don't know their real personality. So that's kind of a bummer when you're considered to be popular because you don't usually meet a lot of other people because they just kind of go, "Oh."
>
> (Interview, April 29, grade 8)

As long as interaction between groups was avoided, stereotypes remained unchallenged. Consequently, all the popular girls continued to be viewed by many as stuck-up, despite individual differences in their actual interactional styles.

The negative label was so salient for girls that it also affected interaction within groups. If one group member failed to acknowledge or was not especially friendly to another group member, she was frequently accused of being stuck-up. The considerable anxiety surrounding the use of this label was evident when one girl would tease another and jokingly accuse her of being stuck-up. In most cases, these accusations were taken seriously and denied rather than treated in a light or humorous manner.

Girls who were thought to be better than other group members were accused of being stuck-up, even when they had little control over this perception. For example, in several groups, girls from higher-status families were the least liked members of the group, while in other groups, girls from lower-status families were the least liked. In general, it appears that girls strongly uphold an egalitarian norm and view members who are better or worse than other group members as less desirable friends. Consequently, girls are concerned about being more successful than their friends and about being less successful.

The negative labelling also made it more difficult for shy girls to make friends. Some girls ignored others and failed to respond to friendly initiations because they were shy. In many cases these girls were also perceived as being stuck-up. One girl said that before she got to know and like her friend, she thought her friend was a snob. Several girls told us that it was hard for them to make friends because they were shy and other girls assumed they were stuck-up.

The underlying problem for peer interaction is that ignoring others can be easily misinterpreted. Any behavior can have several potential meanings and can thus be misunderstood, but the act of ignoring someone provides even fewer cues and is therefore even more likely to be misinterpreted. . . .

The Cycle of Popularity

These findings indicate that popularity has a fairly predictable cycle among adolescent girls. First, a few girls become identified through cheer-leading elections as an elite group. Immediately after, many students make offers of affiliation, and these girls experience a marked increase in popularity. In part, this reflects a general tendency for high status people to be liked (Newcomb 1961). This tendency is further strengthened by the fact that friendships with popular girls are important avenues for girls' status.

However, there are limits to the number of friendships that any one person can maintain. Because popular girls get a high number of affiliative offers, they have to reject more offers of friendship than other girls. Also, to maintain their higher status, girls who form the elite group must avoid associations with lower-status girls. For both of these reasons, these girls are likely to ignore the affiliative attempts of many girls, leading to the impression that they are stuck-up. Thus, shortly after these girls reach their peak of popularity, they become increasingly disliked . . .

Discussion

Given the importance of social avenues for status among girls, it is not surprising that they become increasingly concerned with popularity during early adolescence. Furthermore, the salience of being labelled a snob may also contribute to girls' concern with being viewed as friendly and nice. To avoid this label, they are likely to be friendly to people they do not like. Rosenberg and Simmons (1975) found that girls are more likely to act nice to people they dislike and to smile when they are unhappy during middle adolescence than during childhood or early adolescence. This could very well be a response to a greater concern with being viewed as snobbish or stuck-up.

The negative feelings toward high-status girls might also explain why girls become less concerned with achievement during early adolescence. To surpass one's friends appears to have more costs for girls than for boys, because achievement is not a main avenue for peer status for girls and because the avenues that do exist for girls are more arbitrary and therefore less widely accepted. In addition, or perhaps as a consequence, girls appear to value equality more than boys and seek to minimize individual differences.

There is also evidence that this concern with being too successful affects females' academic behavior. Coleman (1966) found that although high school girls tried to get good grades, few sought to be outstanding academically. This avoidance of academic success has previously been attributed to concerns about relationships with boys, but it is possible that it may also be related to concerns about relationships with other girls, specifically to the desire not to be viewed as superior to one's friends. . . .

It is also important to consider the role school activities play in promoting different avenues for peer status for females and males. Many schools now provide equal sports opportunities for females and males, but males' sports still have greater visibility in the school and community. This greater visibility promotes the importance of male athletics and cheerleading as avenues for peer status. . . .

In summary, we found that a system of social stratification developed among students during their middle school years. This system was formed and maintained by a number of interactional processes, including the avoidance of certain individuals and the establishment of group boundaries. . . .

References

Coleman, J. S. 1966. *The Adolescent Society*. New York: Free Press.

Newcomb, T. M. 1961. *The Acquaintance Process*. New York: Holt, Rinehart, and Winston.

Rosenberg, F. R., and R. G. Simmons. 1975. "Sex Differences in the Self-concept in Adolescence." *Sex Roles* 1: 147–159.

23

The Social Contexts of Illness

Arthur W. Frank

We live our lives within webs of more and less intimate and more and less equal social relationships. Those relationships shape our personal experiences and our responses to them. In turn, those relationships change in response to our shifting circumstances and reactions to them. Probably no experience better illustrates this interconnection between social relationships and personal experience than that of critical illness. In this selection, Arthur Frank reflects upon his own experiences with life-threatening illness and others' responses to him when ill. Frank draws general lessons from those reflections about the social shaping of the experience of illness and about the life-affirming importance of sharing and listening to stories of illness.

As Frank notes, when we seek treatment for illness, we become enmeshed in impersonal and subordinating relationships with medical personnel. Physicians and nurses colonize our bodies and reduce us to a disease. They are not interested in what the ill person's experiences mean to her or him but translate those experiences into generalized symptoms of a disease. Medical personnel do not treat the patient as an individual with a rich social life and history but as a carrier of disease. And, according to Frank, the more serious the illness the more distant physicians and others seem to become. In Frank's words, physicians also dominate the drama of illness. The patient must patiently await physicians' verdicts. The patient is continually reminded of how little they know about their own condition. The physician determines what is wrong with the patient and what the patient must do or what must be done to her or him if she or he is to get well. Physicians thereby take control over patients' bodies and, at least temporarily, over their lives.

The particular disease that physicians diagnose also affects both how others respond to the ill person and how the ill person views herself or himself. Frank contrasts his experience of a heart attack with that of cancer. Unlike the heart attack, cancer was stigmatizing both because of the visible signs of its treatment and our collective fear of the disease. The stigma of cancer can lead many friends and family members to deny the illness and the ill person, as did some of Frank's friends and family. However, others, usually those who had also experienced their own or a loved one's critical illness, acknowledged Frank's illness and affirmed their relationship with him. In either case, illnesses such as cancer change how others treat an individual and often how she or he responds to them, changing, undermining, and sometimes strengthening their relationships. It seldom leaves them untouched.

As Frank suggests, the experience of illness is not just bodily but social. How individuals respond to illness depends on how others respond to the illness and the ill person and have responded to him or her in the past. It does not come from inside the ill person but from the web of social relationships in which she or he is and has been embedded. Frank urges the ill to share the experience of illness with others and the rest of us to listen so as to learn to value life for itself. He also implicitly urges us to recognize how profoundly social relationships shape our lives and experience, including the experience of our frail bodies.

I have experienced life-threatening illness twice. I had a heart attack when I was thirty-nine and cancer at age forty. Now that these illnesses are in remission, why go back and write about them? Because illness is an opportunity, though a dangerous one. To seize this opportunity I need to remain with illness a little longer and share what I have learned through it. . . .

I am not an inspiring case, only a writer. By profession I am a university professor, a sociologist with additional training and experience in philosophy, communications, and psychotherapy. These resources helped me put my experiences into words. But I do not write as any kind of expert; I present myself only as a fellow sufferer, trying to make sense of my own illnesses. . . .

Critical illness leaves no aspect of life untouched. The hospitals and other special places we have constructed for critically ill persons have created the illusion that by sealing off the ill person from those who are healthy, we can also seal off the illness in that ill person's life. This illusion is dangerous. Your relationships, your work, your sense of who you are and who you might become, your sense of what life is and ought to be—

these all change, and the change is terrifying. Twice, as I realized how ill I was, I saw these changes coming and was overwhelmed by them. . . .

I have put my body in the hands of physicians off and on since I was born. But until I was critically ill I never felt I was putting my life in their hands. Life-threatening illness gave doctors a new dimension of importance for me. I had never expected so much from them or been so sensitive to their shortcomings. . . .

After [an] ultrasound a physician said, "This will have to be investigated." Hearing this phrase, I was both relieved and offended. The relief was that someone was assuming part of the burden of worrying about what was happening to me. But I was also offended by his language, which made my body into medicine's field of investigation. "I" had become medicine's "this." The physician did not even say, "We'll have to find out what's wrong with you," which would have been a team of real people ("we") speaking to another person ("you").

"This will have to be investigated" was not addressed to me at all. The physician was speaking as if to himself, allowing me, the patient, to overhear.

"This will have to be investigated" assumes that physicians will do the investigation, but they too are left out of the phrase, anonymous. "Will have to be" suggest the investigation happens of its own necessity. Why should a physician speak this way? Because if in the course of this investigation mistakes are made (as the physician who spoke had already mistaken my diagnosis), no individual physician is responsible. The mistakes are just part of a process; they too "have to be." I imagine he spoke out of fear as well as uncertainty. He responded by making himself and other physicians anonymous. And I had to be made anonymous.

I, my body, became the passive object of this necessity, the investigation. I could imagine how native people felt when European explorers arrived on their shores, planted a flag, and claimed their land on behalf of a foreign monarch who would bring civilization to the savages. To get medicine's help, I had to cede the territory of my body to the investigation of doctors who were as yet anonymous. I had to be colonized.

The investigation required me to enter the hospital. Fluids were extracted, specialists' opinions accumulated, machines produced images of the insides of my body, but the diagnosis remained uncertain. One day I returned to my room and a new sign below my name on the door. It said "Lymphoma," a form of cancer I was suspected of having. No one had told me that this diagnosis, which later proved to be wrong, had been confirmed. Finding it written there was like the joke about the guy who learns he has been fired when he finds someone else's name on his office door. In this case, my name had not been changed, it had been defined. "Lymphoma" was a medical flag, planted as a claim on the territory of my body.

This colonization only became worse. During chemotherapy a nurse, speaking to [my wife] Cathie, referred to me as "the seminoma in 53" (my room number). By then the diagnosis was correct, but it had crowded out my name entirely. The hospital had created its own version of my identity. I became the disease, the passive object of investigation and later of treatment. Nameless, how could I be a person who experiences?

The ill person actively tries to make sense of what is happing to her body. She tries to maintain a relationship between what is happening to her body and what is going on in the rest of her life. When a person becomes a patient, physicians take over her body, and their understanding of the body separates it from the rest of her life. Medicine's understanding of pain, for instance, has little to do with the ill person's experience. For the person, pain is about incoherence and the disruption of relations with other people and things; it is about losing one sense of place and finding another. Medicine has no interest in what pain means in a life; it can see pain only as a symptom of a possible disease. Medicine cannot enter into the experience; it seeks only cure or management. It does offer relief to a body that is suffering, but in doing so it colonizes the body. This is the trade-off we make in seeking medical help.

If the treatment works, the passivity is worth it. When I am ill, I want to become a patient. It is dangerous to avoid doctors, but it is equally dangerous to allow them to hog center stage in the drama of illness. The danger of avoiding doctors is immediate and physical, but if we allow them to dominate the drama, they will script it to include only disease. By saying "This will have to be investigated," my physician claimed center stage and scripted the drama to follow; the person within my body was sent out into the audience to watch passively. . . .

Relationships between patients and medical staff, whether physicians or nurses, involve people who are intimate with each other but rarely become intimates of each other. For a truly intimate relationship people need a sharing of time and personal history and a recognition of each other's differences. Medical intimacy categorizes rather than recognizes, and it is one-sided. The patient's life and body are an open book, or chart, to the medical staff. The staff sometimes share their experiences with patients, but in my memory these moments are the exceptions. More important, physicians and nurses can choose what they will tell a patient about themselves, and whether they will say anything at all. There is the real asymmetry, which becomes more complicated during moments that are critical in the patient's life but represent just another day's work for the staff. . . .

I always assumed that if I became seriously ill, physicians, no matter how overworked, would somehow recognize what I was living through. I did not know what form this recognition would take, but I assumed it would happen. What I experienced was the opposite. The more critical my diagnosis became, the more reluctant physicians were to talk to me. I had trouble getting them to make eye contact; most came only to see my disease. This "it" within the body was their field of investigation; "I" seemed to exist beyond the horizon of their interest.

Medical staff often believe they are involved in the patient's personal life. When I was admitted to the hospital, the resident doing my intake physical made a point of saying he was now getting the "social history." Cathie and I were curious to know what the hospital considered important as social history. The resident then asked what my job was. I answered and waited for the next question; he closed the chart. That was it, nothing more. What bothered us was the illusion that he had found out something. The resident took his inquiry into my social history seriously and seemed to have no sense of how little he [had] learned. The irony of there being only one question completely escaped him. He was filling in a category, employment, to give himself the illusion of having recognized me as a "social" being.

The night before I had surgery, I was visited by an anesthesiologist who represented the culmination of my annoyance with this nonrecognition. He refused to look at me, and he even had the facts of the planned operation wrong. When he was leaving I did the worst thing to him I could think of: I made him shake hands. A hand held out to be shaken cannot be refused without direct insult, but to shake a hand is to acknowledge the other as an equal. The anesthesiologist trembled visibly as he brushed his hand over mine, and I allowed myself to enjoy his discomfort. But that was only a token of what I really wanted. I wanted him to recognize that the operation I was having and the disease it was part of were no small thing.

The kind of recognition I wanted changed over the course of my illness. While seeking diagnosis I felt that I was in a struggle just to get physicians to recognize the disease; once I got them onto the stage of my illness, the problem was to keep it my drama, not theirs. The active roles in the drama of illness all go to physicians. Being a patient means, quite literally, being patient. Daily life in the hospital is spent waiting for physicians. Hospitals are organized so that physicians can see a maximum number of patients, which means patients spend maximum time waiting. You have to be patient. Maybe the doctor will come this morning; if not, maybe this afternoon. Decisions about treatment are stalled until the doctor's arrival; nurses and residents don't know what's happening. Hopes, fears, and uncertainty mount.

When the physician does arrive, he commands center stage. I write "he" because this performance is so stereotypically masculine, although women physicians learn to play it well enough. The patient hangs on what brief words are said, what parts of the body are examined or left unattended. When the physician has gone, the patient recounts to visitors everything he did and said, and together they repeatedly consider and interpret his visit. The patient wonders what the physician meant by this joke or that frown. In hospitals, where the patient is constantly reminded of how little he knows, the physician is assumed not only to know all but to know more than he says.

In becoming a patient—being colonized as medical territory and becoming a spectator to your own drama—you lose yourself. First you may find that the lab results rather than your body's responses are determining how you feel. Then, in the rush to treatment, you may lose your capacity to make choices, to decide how you want your body to be used. Finally, in the blandness of the medical setting, in its routines and their discipline, you may forget your tastes and preferences. Life turns to beige. It is difficult to accept the realities of what physicians can do for you without subordinating yourself to their power. The power is real, but it need not be total. . . .

Whenever I told someone I had cancer I felt myself tighten as I said it. Saying the word "cancer," my body began to defend itself. This did not happen when I told people I was having heart problems. A heart attack was simply bad news. But I never stopped thinking that cancer said something about my worth as a person. This difference between heart attack and cancer is stigma. A stigma is, literally, a sign on the surface of the body marking it as dangerous, guilty, and unclean. Stigmas began as judicial punishments in the form of notched ears, brandings, and other visible mutilations of the body. These marks allowed those who came into contact with the stigmatized person to see whom they were dealing with. The stigmatized were expected to go to the margins of society and hide their spoiled bodies. The causes of stigmatization have changed, but the hiding has not.

My heart attack damaged my body but did not stigmatize it. I became short of breath while doing tasks that were normal for a man my age. This was inconvenient and embarrassing but not stigmatizing. The damaged body only fails to perform properly; the stigmatized body contaminates its surroundings. During my heart problems I could no longer participate in certain activities; during cancer I felt I had no right to be among others. As much as I disliked being in the hospital, at least there I felt I belonged. I knew this was foolish. I didn't belong in the hospital; I was hiding there. Ill persons hide in many ways. Some begin to call cancer "c.a.," "the big C," or other euphemisms. I called it cancer, but as I said it I felt that tightness.

Heart attacks are invisible on the body's surface. To myself and to others, I looked no different. One wears cancer. My own visible stigmas were hair loss and my intravenous line. The line created a bulge over my chest, but I could conceal it. Getting dressed each day became an exercise in concealment. I wore shirts that were heavy and loose fitting and equally loose sweaters. A tie under the sweater added some bulk, and a sport coat further obscured the contours of my body. The question, of course, is why I wanted to hide the line from others. The sad answer is that I experienced the visible signs of cancer as defects not just in my appearance, but in myself.

The visible sign most closely associated with cancer is hair loss. Alopecia, or baldness, is caused not by cancer itself but by its treatment. Chemotherapy is not very discriminating. Cancer cells divide rapidly, but so do the cells of hair follicles, the intestinal lining, and gums. The drugs destroy cells in all these areas, creating their particular side effects. Thus there is truth to the folk wisdom that baldness indicates chemotherapy is working. Even knowing this, my enthusiasm for losing my hair was qualified.

My hair fell out several days after my first chemotherapy treatment. First it lost its texture and became thin, then the hair on the sides of my head rubbed off while I was washing it. I was left with a patchy-looking mohawk. It was almost Halloween, but I resisted the temptation to turn my appearance into a punk costume.

Some people try to preserve what hair they have for as long as they can. I thought I looked stranger with some hair than I would with none. Also we got tired of cleaning out the tub and drain every time I took a shower; hot water speeds up the hair loss. So Cathie helped me shave off the rest of my hair, which was truly a labor of love. That shaving marked my full passage into another stage of illness, and it was a sad thing. The loss of hair has to be mourned; it is another break with the younger self you no longer are. . . .

Cancer can do terrible things to the body, but so can other diseases. Cultural historians tell us that for at least a century cancer has been North Americans' most feared disease. This fear is explained only partially by either actual rates of cancer incidence and mortality or by the physical suffering it causes. Society, not the disease itself, makes cancer as dreaded as it is. A culture in which people are unwilling to speak the name of the disease obviously has a special fear. We do not call heart attack "h.a." Cancer alone is mythologized as some savage god, whose very name will invoke its presence. If the name of cancer is unspeakable, what evil does the person with cancer believe can be brought by its presence? Newspaper stories and political speeches use cancer as the metaphor for all the worst that can happen. The ill person then becomes the bearer of these horrors. Just as I tried to hide my intravenous line under my coat, persons with cancer want to hide their disease. Never have I tried so hard to be invisible. . . .

People did not act differently toward me while I had cancer, they only exaggerated how they had always acted. The compassionate ones became more loving, the generous more giving, the ill at ease more defensive. The bullies were peskier than usual, and the ones who were always too busy remained busy. Some people whom I expected to be supportive denied that I was ill at all; medical staff denied that I was anything but the disease. Others affirmed that although I was ill and illness counted, we still had a relationship. These denials and affirmations were not always easy to recognize as they happened. Denials can be subtle; after being with someone I would feel bad and not be sure why.

But illness also exaggerated the ways I acted toward others. I needed other people desperately but, feeling stigmatized, I was cautious of them. One day I would express closeness, the next day distance. My behavior caused others to exaggerate their responses to me, and in my perception of them I exaggerated their actions still further. Even the strongest relationships came under stress. This is how the ill person experiences others during illness: subtle denials, strained affirmations. . . .

The ultimate denial is by friends and loved ones who simply disappear from the ill person's life. In disappearing, they deny that anything special is happening or, alternatively, that the ill person exists at all. Either form of denial can be truly devastating. If I asked these people why they disappeared from Cathie's life and mine during cancer, they would probably say they were busy, they did not want to bother us, and they "knew" we would call if we needed anything. But what we needed was to hear they cared. Such people can't see what their behavior looks like to the ill person and those who are caring for him or her. At Christmas, just after chemotherapy treatment, I was at a small family gathering but was still too weak to get up and circulate among the guests. Someone I had felt close to arrived, a man I had not heard from during my illness. He did not come to the end of the room where I was sitting and did his best not to look in my direction. Per-

haps I was too vulnerable to go to him or just too tired, or perhaps I felt, as I do now, that it was his responsibility to come to me.

A relative tried to excuse the behavior of the people who disappeared from Cathie's and my life during cancer by saying that they "cared silently at a distance." We know cancer is hard for people to confront, but from the perspective of the ill person and caregivers, "caring silently" might as well not be happening. Their distance looks like another denial of the illness. Just as I had expected that physicians would behave differently if I became critically ill, I also expected something more from family and friends. My expectations weren't always met; although the generous became more giving, the busy were still too busy.

Those who best affirmed my experience were often people who had been through critical illness themselves or with someone close. We did not necessarily talk a great deal about specific experiences, but these friends seemed able to look at me clearly and to accept what they saw. They rarely tried to cheer me up, but being with them usually did cheer me. Human suffering becomes bearable when we share it. When we know that someone recognizes our pain, we can let go of it. The power of recognition to reduce suffering cannot be explained, but it seems fundamental to our humanity. . . .

Illness excuses people from their normal responsibilities, but the cost of being excused is greater than it appears at first. An excuse is also an exclusion. When an ill person is told, "All you can do is get well," he is also being told that all he can do is be ill. Telling someone he doesn't have to do anything but get well turns into a message that he has no right to do anything until he can return to his normal tasks. Again, just being ill has no value; on the contrary, the ill person is culpable.

People can't give up the idea that the ill person is responsible for the disease. If the ill person has a responsibility to get well, then presumably he is responsible for having become ill in the first place. The ideal of getting well also excludes and devalues those who will not get well.

If we reject the notion that the ill are responsible for getting well, then what is their responsibility? It is to witness their own suffering and to express this experience so that the rest of us can learn from it. Of course others must be willing to learn; society's reciprocal responsibility is to see and hear what ill people express.

A recent newspaper story suggests how little we understand about the expression of experience as both a right and a responsibility. The story's theme is the need for cancer patients to "talk openly" about their illness. This need is defined as exclusively the patient's; the story does not mention society's need to hear such talk or whether others are willing to listen. The story, a medical-psychological moral fable, contrasts two teenagers with leukemia. One teenager exemplifies openness. When a stranger in a supermarket asks her if she is ill, she raises her wig and says that she is being treated for leukemia. The other teenager withdraws from friends and physicians and refuses further treatment. Without saying so, the article implies that the "open" child will survive and the "withdrawn" child will not.

Stories like this perform a sleight of hand; they make the social context of each child's life disappear. Each teenager has a history of relationships with other people, and it is this history that produces the different behaviors. Their responses to leukemia do not just happen, the way some of us just happen to get leukemia. Whatever causes the disease, the response to it is learned. The teenagers' openness and withdrawal are responses to their experiences with family, friends, schools, and medical staff. The "open" one has been lucky enough to feel valued regardless of being ill. Her sense of stigma at home, at school, and in the hospital has been minimized. She has been allowed to feel that whatever problems her disease creates, illness is not a personal failure. She takes a risk when she shows her bald head to a stranger, but her willingness to do so results from how those around her have already responded to her baldness. The people she has met have acted in ways that allow her to anticipate support from those she now meets; at least she knows she has people to fall back on.

An ill child withdraws when he senses that people do not like what he represents. To his parents he embodies their failure to have a healthy child. He sees them being sad and guilty, and he feels guilty for having made them feel this way. To his siblings he may represent a drain on family time and financial resources. To other children his presence brings a fear of something they understand only enough to worry that it will happen to them. All adolescents experience their bodies changing, and his peers may see in the leukemic their fears of these changes going wrong. To medial staff he represents their failure to cure him. I imagine physicians evaluate their professional self-image in terms of the success of their treatments. They see themselves in a contest with the disease, and when disease persists, they have lost. They cannot think in terms of care that goes beyond treatment.

The child withdraws because he believes others would be happier if they did not have to see him. They may not reject him in any overt way, but he senses from their expressions that he is causing them pain. His withdrawal is no more the result of his "personality" (much less the lack of what some call "fighting spirit") than the other child's openness is. Each child is only looking around, assessing what support is available, and making what seems to be the best deal.

The newspaper story does not talk about the children's circumstances; instead it discusses withdrawal as "psychologically damaging" and openness as being "better adjusted." But the children are not damaged or adjusted; society is. The social group around each child has either helped her adjust or has damaged him, and those groups in turn find support or denial in other groups. The newspaper story makes these groups disappear through its use of the word "psychological," creating the illusion that each child's behavior comes out of that child, the way the leukemia comes from within the child's physiology. Healthy people comfortably accept the social myth that illness behavior is inside the person. We want to enclose the ill person in a psychological language that turns his reality inward, closing off external influence. Then we hand the whole thing to medicine.

The ultimate moral of the story is medical compliance. The open child is the good medical citizen who stays in treatment. The withdrawn child plays his sick role badly. He does not try to get well. As soon as we think of the child's withdrawal as "his" and not a response learned from others, we cannot avoid the implication that he does not deserve to get well. Although the story quotes physicians and passes itself off as "scientific," the science only dresses up the moral fable beneath. The disease is depicted as a fall from grace of a normal childhood. One child redeems herself through the courage of her openness, and the other continues falling. By making disease an issue of the ill person's morality, the story perpetuates a language of stigma.

Where is responsibility in this story? The newspaper account carries a clear implication that the ill person's responsibility is to be a good medical citizen. But the matter is not so simple. I see the children as equally responsible, though only one is happily so. The happy child lifts her wig and proclaims she is a leukemia patient. She performs a significant act of public education, and I have no wish to detract from the honor she deserves. I hope the person she spoke to came away recognizing the ill person's strength as a person, not just a patient. When she perpetuates the openness she has experienced from others, the child widens the circle of public recognition. She has fulfilled her responsibility.

But the withdrawn child is no less responsible, no less a witness to his experience. Like the open child, he reflects the attitudes of those around him. He too acts according to others' cues of what they want of him, which is to disappear. His withdrawal may result in psychological damage, but again the initial damage is not the child's. The damage is caused by those who cannot value the ill.

We may talk about the heroic individual who puts aside society's script for illness, but this is mostly talk. Even the ill person who refuses to let her actions be determined by the way she is treated bases this response on resources developed earlier. Adolescents are more susceptible to the way they are treated at the moment because their personal history is shorter. We who are older are no less creatures of the ways we have been treated; we just have a longer history against which to evaluate our present circumstances.

The responsibility of the ill, then, is not to get well but to express their illness well. And the two have nothing to do with each other. I wish I could believe that those who express their illness well have a greater chance of recovery, but I cannot. Perhaps someday we will understand more of how the mind affects the body. For now I only believe that those who express their illness live their lives fully to the end of the illness. For me this is enough—it has to be enough. If we cannot value life for itself, then we see ill persons only in terms of what they could be doing if they were well, and we see children only as what they will do when they become adults. We fail to value life as a frail bit of good luck in a world based on chance. . . .

Part VII

Structures of Social Life

ocial life is neither random nor constantly changing. It is generally orderly, and its organization more or less enduring. It is, in other words, structured. As the earlier selection on adolescent girls' friendships illustrates, individuals interactionally create social order and structure their social lives. They do so not only in middle schools but where and whenever they engage in social interaction. Yet individuals seldom experience the resulting social structures as their own creation.

The individual is born into a world already populated by different categories of people who engage in particular kinds of activities and participate in established networks of social relationships. For the individual, those social identities, roles, and organizations are simply there. They constitute a massive social structure that seems as inflexible, inescapable, and constraining as the physical environment. For example, contemporary Americans confront a world populated by blacks and whites, children and the elderly, waitresses and customers, rich and poor, and the like. Those social identities and roles largely determine with whom particular individuals interact, how, and under what circumstances. They consequently decide in which networks of social relationships different types of people participate. They structure individuals' experience and shape their lives. Sociologists have long been interested in the interrelationships among social structure, interpersonal interaction, and subjective experience. The selections in this section address various aspects of those complex interrelationships. ✦

24

Social Structure and Experience

Sheldon Stryker

Sheldon Stryker is probably best known for adding the concept of social structure to George Herbert Mead's general ideas about the relationship between the individual and society. Although Mead describes the self as essentially a social structure, he never addresses how the structure of social life structures the self and the individual's inner conversation or subjective experience. That is what Stryker does in this selection.

Stryker conceives of social structure as patterned regularities of interaction between various categories of people. According to Stryker, social positions are symbols for socially recognized categories of people. They are meaningful symbols in that we expect different kinds of behavior from these different categories of people and expect to treat them differently. These different expectations constitute social roles. In turn, social roles imply a whole network of relationships among those in the same and different positions. Thus, social positions and roles are the building blocks of social structure. They structure interactions, relationships, and, consequently, the self and subjective experience.

Stryker notes that individuals define both one another and themselves in terms of social positions. Accordingly, they also subjectively rank their various positional or role identities in terms of their salience or how often the associated roles are played, as well as in terms of the individuals' commitment to the network of relationships that they imply. The self, then, is a structure of social identities ordered into a salience hierarchy and pattern of interpersonal commitments.

Stryker also describes how social structures of positions, roles, and relationships shape individuals' interpersonal and subjective experiences. They determine how social rewards are distributed and, therefore, the resources that different kinds of people bring to their interactions with others. They also influence with whom differently identified individuals will interact, how they will interact, and under what circumstances. If, as Mead argues, meaning is a product of social interaction, then social structures indirectly shape individuals' definitions and interpretations of their experiences. Thus, individuals of different races, ages, classes, and occupations may not only have different experiences, but experience differently as well.

Yet, as Stryker suggests, individuals are not mere social robots. Social positions and roles may constrain us, but we are not under their complete and total control. We periodically escape their confinement and, sometimes, creatively alter them in interaction with others. Social structures are human products and are subject to human modification. We shape social structures at the same time that they shape us.

Humans respond not to the naive world, but to the world as categorized or classified; the physical, biological, and social environment in which they live is a symbolic environment. The symbols that they attach to the environment have meaning, are cues to behavior, and organize behavior. . . . Defining a situation involves naming aspects of the non-human environment; it also involves a process of naming others and naming oneself. A discussion of the former leads directly to the concept of role.

Role theory . . . has used the concept of "status" or "position" to refer to the parts of organized social groups. Symbolic interactionism uses "position" in a more general sense to refer to any socially recognized category of actors. In this usage, positions are symbols for the kinds of persons it is possible to be in society: rich man, poor man, thief, fool, teacher, sergeant, intellectual, rebel, president, and so on and on. Like other symbolic categories, positions serve to cue behavior and so act as predictors or the behavior of persons who are placed into a category. Doing so, they organize behavior with reference to these persons. Attaching a positional label to a person leads to expected behaviors from that person, and to behavior toward that person premised on expectations. The term "role" is used for these expectations which are attached to positions. . . .

Self-definitional activity proceeds largely, though not exclusively, through socially recognized categories and corresponding roles. Since roles necessarily imply relationships to others, so does the self. . . . [And], if social relationships are complex, there must be parallel complexity in the self.

[T]here are [also] empirical issues whose resolution calls for a conception of self as complex and differentiated. . . . Some give higher priority to work than to recreation in exercising choice with respect to activities; others reverse the priority. A man uses his free time to play golf, rather than opting to take his child to the zoo. Under circumstances in which having both marriage and a career is not feasible, one woman chooses to pursue a career rather than to marry, another makes the opposite choice. The analysis of the behaviors represented in these illustrative observations is advanced by a conception of self which is elaborated in ways that go beyond but remain in the spirit of Mead's conceptualization.

This elaboration introduces a new set of concepts: identity (or role identity), identity salience, and commitment. Identities are "parts" of self, internalized positional designations. They exist insofar as the person is a participant in structured role relationships. . . . One may have a long list of identities, limited only by the number of structured role relationships one is involved in. Thus, a woman may have identities as physician, wife, mother, child, tennis player, Democrat, etc., which taken together comprise the self.

"Identity salience" is intended to refer to one possible, theoretically important way in which the self can be organized. Discrete identities may be thought of as ordered into a salience hierarchy, such that the higher the identity in that hierarchy, the more likely that the identity will be invoked in a given situation or in many situations; this probability of invocation is what defines identity salience. . . .

Greater precision in specifying linkages between society and social person is also made possible through the concept of "commitment." . . . To the degree that one's relationship to specified sets of other persons depend on being a particular kind of person, one is committed to being that kind of person. If the maintenance of ties to a set of others is important to the person, and dependent upon being—say—a member of a sorority, that person is committed to being a member of a sorority. Since entering into social relationships is premised on the attribution and acceptance of positions and associated roles, then commitments are premised on identities. . . .

[S]ocial structure . . . refer[s] to the patterned regularities that characterize most human interaction. Whatever may be true of the creative potential of persons in their interactions with one another, as a matter of empirical fact, most of their interactions tend to be with the same or only slowly changing casts of others, and the same sets of persons tend to be bound together or linked in interactional networks, doing essentially the same things on a repetitive basis. Thus, the concepts of group, organization, community, etc., indicate aspects of social life, in which subsets of persons are tied together in patterned interactions and are separated (at least with respect to those interactions) from other persons.

As part of the "patterned regularities" to which it refers, social structure also references the more abstract social boundaries that crosscut all societies, but particularly large, industrialized, contemporary societies. So, for example, any society is likely to have a class structure, a power structure, an age structure, an ethnic structure, and so on.

In any case, the important implication of the generic concept of social structure is that societies are differentiated entities, and that, as a consequence of that differentiation, it is only certain people who interact with one another in certain ways and in certain settings or situations. . . . Thus, if the social person is shaped by interaction, it is social structure that shapes the possibilities for interaction and so, ultimately, the person. Conversely, if the social person creatively alters patterns of interaction, those altered patterns can ultimately change social structure.

Interactions vary in the degree to which they link together persons who are (or are not) in large measure also linked to one another. The concept of "group" can be used to refer to networks of interaction, in which there is a high degree of "closure," in the sense that the persons involved all tend to interact with one another, a recognition of common membership in an organized unit, and a sense of interdependency with respect to common goals. It is important to recognize that groups, so conceived, are structures of interaction . . . [and] units of social structure. . . .

Most interaction takes place within the boundaries of groups or as performances of persons acting as representatives or agents of groups. The relevance of larger social structures lies in the ways they impact on interaction and on the formation, maintenance, or dissolution of groups; and it lies in the ways interaction and group formation, maintenance, or dissolution impact on these larger structures. In general, that relevance is in the form of affecting the probabilities of particular kinds of persons coming into contact in particular kinds of situational settings, and in affecting the probabilities that interaction will take on particular form and content.

Thus, the larger society defines the inventory of the kinds of people it is possible to become; one cannot become a professional athlete in a society which does not provide for athletic competition on a professional basis, and the opportunity to become a soccer player in America today is present in a degree it was not a decade ago. Perhaps more importantly, the evaluational meanings attached to positions that influence the efforts to become one or another kind of person reflect the rewards available in society for attaining these positions. In the same terms, social class alters the probability of becoming—say—a physician by the way it distributes the means, financial and otherwise, for achieving higher education.

The sociological significance of age, class, ethnicity, ecology, or other structural elements in a society lies in part in their impact on just who is brought into contact with whom; that is to say, the interactions that do, in fact, occur, and in their impact on the kinds of interaction that occur. In general, schools bring together persons of roughly the same age and the same class background; thus, the probability of friendship relationships that cross age and class boundaries is less than it might otherwise be. One can only marry someone one meets, and one is much more likely to meet someone living in the same section of a community. Interactions occurring between blacks and whites are more likely to be superficial and conflict laden, if the educational, residential, and occupational structures in a community are essentially segregated. Deviant work schedules or work settings that isolate work crews from the community at large constrain interactions to take place between those who share the deviant schedule or the work setting. . . .

[T]he meanings that persons learn to attach to objects in their world—including themselves—are largely learned through their interactions with others. To the degree, then, that age, class, or other social structures affect group formation and maintenance and resultant interactions, these social structures enter the entire system of meanings of actors.

And . . . structure provides the resources that persons use in their interactions with others. A community organization provides the setting in which the highly educated citizen uses her knowledge of *Roberts Rules of Order* to keep an opposition spokesman from challenging a ruling. The expensive clothes of an upper-class businessman both symbolize and reinforce claims to dominance in an interaction with a skilled worker. The middle-class child learns politeness and courtesy, which can be used to advantage in dealing with secondary others in formal, institutional settings. Institutionalized rules of deference in the relationship of teacher and pupil enable the former to exercise power that might otherwise have little legitimacy.

It should be emphasized that the resources for interactions made available through social structure are important, whether roles are played out in interaction as given or whether they are essentially constructed in the process of interaction. Further, the degree to which roles can be made, rather than simply played, is variable in part as a function of social structure. There is very little room for improvisation in the context of a prison; there is, presumably, a great deal more room for the creative construction of roles in the early stages of a newly formed voluntary association. . . .

The sociological conception of "society" incorporates the idea of patterned, organized interaction. Asking how, or in what terms, society is patterned has led sociology to an image of society in terms of positions and roles. Given that the person is the other side of the society coin, then this view of society leads to an image of the person as a structure of positions and roles which, internalized, is the self. . . . [Yet we must] recognize that not all interactive behavior is captured by the concept of society. . . . That is, only some part of human interaction is describable in terms of a structure of positions and roles; and, since both self and society derive from interaction, only part of the self is describable in these terms. . . .

Reprinted from: Sheldon Stryker, *Symbolic Interactionism*, pp. 56–62, 65–66, 68–71, 79–80. Copyright © 1980 by The Benjamin/Cummings Publishing Company, Inc. Reprinted by permission of Addison-Wesley Longman, Inc. ✦

25

Culture Creation and Diffusion Among Preadolescents

Gary Alan Fine

In this selection, Gary Alan Fine examines the relationship between social structure and the development of distinctive subcultures within a society. He illustrates how culture is created within interacting groups with the example of Little League baseball teams. Members of such groups commonly recombine and revise elements of their previously known and shared culture. They thereby create distinctive systems of knowledge, beliefs, behaviors, and customs, or what Fine calls "idiocultures." He also explains how items from such group cultures spread to other groups through existing channels of communication or social linkages.

However, Fine observes that social-structural divisions are barriers to communication among groups. For example, children tend to interact more freely and openly with older children than with adults, blacks tend to interact more freely and openly with other blacks than with whites, and so on. Novel cultural items consequently spread horizontally or geographically within such social-structural segments of a society more rapidly than they spread vertically between them. A common result is the development of distinctive subcultures within the various segments of a society. Members of those segments of society come to share a distinctive system of knowledge, behavior, customs, and artifacts, and, therefore, a common identity.

Although Fine limits his attention to preadolescent boys, the processes of culture creation and diffusion that he describes are not limited to them. Those same processes are involved in the development of distinctive class, ethnic, and occupational subcultures. They are also processes that perpetuate social-structural divisions. The development of distinctive subcultures among the various segments of a society is yet another barrier to communication across social-structural divisions. Interaction among people who share similar un-derstandings is far less stressful than interaction among people who do not. Therefore, we generally prefer to interact with "our own kind." In other words, social-structural divisions often lead to subcultural divisions that encourage the interactional reproduction of those very social-structural divisions.

For three years, I spent springs and summers observing ten Little League baseball teams in five communities, as they went through their seasons. I observed at practice fields and in dugouts, remaining with the boys after games and arriving early to learn what their activities were like when adults were not present. As I came to know these boys better, I hung out with them outside the baseball setting, when they were "doing nothing." ... By examining Little League baseball teams and preadolescents generally, it should be possible to understand part of the dynamic process by which all cultures are developed by means of small group cultures. ...

While culture may be studied on several analytic levels (the society, subsociety, or small group) I ... begin ... at the most "micro" level—the group. ... Every group has its own lore or culture, which I term its *idioculture*. ... Idioculture consists of a system of knowledge, beliefs, behaviors, and customs shared by members of an interacting group, to which members can refer and that serve as the basis of further interaction. Members recognize that they share experiences, and these experiences can be referred to with the expectation that they will be understood by other members, thus being used to construct a social reality for the participants. This approach stresses the localized nature of culture, implying that it need not be a part of a demographically distinct subgroup but rather can be a particularistic development of any group, such as Little League baseball teams. ...

An idioculture consists of particular examples of behavior or communication that have symbolic meaning and significance for members of a group. Although the list is not exhaustive, phenomena classifiable as idioculture include nicknames, jokes, insults, beliefs, rules of conduct, clothing styles, songs, narratives, gestures, and recurrent fantasies.

The specific content of an idioculture is not created at random. ... Although culture emerges from group interaction, prior knowledge and past experiences affect the form these cultural items take, although not the specific content. Since members know other idiocultures (or latent cultures) through previous or concurrent memberships, the range of potentially known information may be extensive.

In Sanford Heights, a ball hit foul over the backstop is known as a "Polish Home Run." Such a cultural item would have been meaningless had it not been for latent cultural items—what a home run is, and the symbolic opposition of hitting a ball straight over the outfield fence and hitting it over the backstop. In other words, hitting the ball over either *end* of the field is a "home run" (and this was not said of balls that curved outside a foul line). This item also required a knowledge of social stereotypes—that "Polish" is an ethnic slur implying "backward" or "incompetent." Without this cultural knowledge, the identification of such a foul ball as a Polish Home Run could not have become part of the culture of these preadolescents. Likewise, referring to players on the basis of their uniform color as a "green bean" or "chiquita," as was done in Hopewell, suggests that cultural elements are dependent on prior knowledge.

Creativity poses no particular problems since creativity is not *de novo*—rather, it reflects novel combinations of previously familiar elements. . . . These recombinations may be given different meanings from that of their constitutive elements by group members. Players on the Maple Bluff White Sox developed a dress code loosely modeled on observation of major leaguers, although not identical to it. Before one Dodgers' practice in Sanford Heights, several players were hanging on the backstop at the practice field, while one of their teammates shook the fence as hard as possible, an activity he termed the "Chinese pain shake," a phrase apparently created spontaneously. While the term may never have been uttered before, its antecedents exist in the speaker's latent culture—notably the association of Chinese with torture (e.g., the Chinese water torture) and the earthquakes that had affected China during this period, to which this activity was similar. Thus, the creation of this cultural item, although seemingly an idiosyncratic construction, can be interpreted in terms of previous knowledge. The term for that behavior "makes sense" in our culture. . . .

I now focus on cultural transmission in larger social units [and] ask how preadolescent culture can be relatively similar across communities. . . . It is self-evident that contemporary Western societies are not culturally homogeneous. Nations are split by divisions, such as ethnicity, religion, class, occupation, and age. Social-structural divisions correspond to divisions in the knowledge of societal members. The cultural massification in America has not yet wiped out the vitality of specialized cultures. These societal segments have been termed subsocieties, and the knowledge they share is their subculture (Fine and Kleinman 1979). . . .

The subculture construct serves as a gloss for communication within interlocking groups, and for knowledge and behaviors shared by these groups. . . . Information can be shared by individuals on two analytically distinct dimensions I term *horizontal* and *vertical*—metaphors borrowed from the study of social structure. The horizontal dimension corresponds to the geographical region in which [information is shared]. . . . Vertical diffusion represents the extent to which [knowledge] has permeated segments of society, defined structurally rather than geographically. [For example], some vocabulary is known only to a particular group or class within society, while other items are known more widely. Although class distinctions are frequently schematized in terms of their vertical organization, with higher classes being layered on less prestigious ones, the analysis of this vertical dimension uses altitude metaphorically. This vertical dimension includes not only class distinctions, but groupings by occupation, race, religion, and age. . . .

The existence of a cultural element in several groups suggests communication. While the preadolescent community in a local area can be treated as a closed system, the members of this community interact not only with each other; even at this age, these communities are connected with others through a set of *interlocks* or social linkages. These connections take a variety of forms and can be analyzed in terms of either individuals or groups. Individuals, for example, may share membership in several groups simultaneously or sequentially. Groups connect with other groups through mechanisms, such as intergroup communication (i.e., communication from one group to another), multi-group communication (communication from one group or a single individual to a number of groups—as in the mass media), or communication between groups by non-members, who have a role status that requires or encourages such communication. Through these interlocks, cultural information and behavioral options are diffused, resulting in the creation of a shared universe of discourse. I conceive of this social network, rather than the demographic age boundaries of preadolescence, as the referent of the term *subculture*. Not all preadolescents are knowledgeable about "preadolescent culture," while some early adolescents and social scientists are.

Multiple Group Membership

A direct mechanism for the interchange of culture within a population results from the fact that people may belong to several groups simultaneously. Cultural elements that are found in one group can easily be introduced into other groups through overlapping memberships. This is evident in the modern preadolescent's busy schedule—boys may belong to several youth groups in areas outside of their local neighborhood. For example, one boy in Bolton Park attended a gun-safety school which met in another suburb. A boy in Sanford Heights missed a week of the season because of an outing of boys in school patrols. Sports, contests, or summer camps allow the preadolescent to meet peers from all over the region—or the nation (e.g., the Boy Scout Jamboree or the National Spelling Bee). A cultural item can be transmitted readily, if it meets the idiocultural criteria necessary for introduction to the group to which the boy belongs. . . .

When boys return from their adventures, local friends are eager to learn what happened; these personal narratives are a source for the introduction of culture, particularly preadolescent "deviance," such as sexual talk and aggressive pranks. The idea of a *swirly*—sticking a boy's head in a toilet (either clean or unflushed) and flushing—was learned by some Sanford Heights youngsters attending a summer hockey camp in northern Minnesota; one of them almost had that prank pulled on him.

Interchanges among groups in which individuals participate simultaneously are less dramatic, but the new cultural item may be mentioned when relevant. Preadolescents who belong to several groups characterized by few joint members provide a crucial linkage for the spread and alteration of cultural traditions. Memorable cultural products, such as song parodies, spread quickly. These are among the first things individuals perform when they enter another group. Diffusion is motivated by the perceived value of the information. . . .

Weak Ties

No matter how dense or tightly knit their social networks, boys are likely to have acquaintances outside the groups in which they are most active. . . . My data do not allow me to assess the precise extent to which these weak ties are found among children. Because preadolescents do not have easy access to transportation, and because their telephone calls are dialed at the discretion of parents, their acquaintances outside their community are limited compared to those of adults; but they do exist.

The geographically mobile child may maintain friendships over many miles, and it is not uncommon for a boy's former friends to be invited to visit. The childhood pastime of corresponding with pen pals is another example of this same phenomenon. Likewise, the distant (spatially and genetically) cousins who populate American extended families give children others with whom to compare their life situations and cultures. . . . Family visits are common, particularly with preadolescent children who are old enough not to create too much trouble but young enough to be willing to be shown off and to have no choice but to accompany their parents. At these visits, children may meet kin their own age; if these kinfolk live elsewhere, the child may be exposed to novel preadolescent culture. Since children's culture has regional and local variation, kinship ties provide a mechanism by which cultural traditions jump geographical chasms. For example, Barry Rymer, a twelve-year-old Sanford Heights Little Leaguer, was visited by his ten-year-old cousin from a farm near Mason City, Iowa. Although he was teased about being a farmer with "dirty fingernails," he and Barry's friends traded cultural information. For example, instead of calling girls "mutts," the Iowan male subculture calls these creatures "hogs" and uses "moron" rather than calling someone "sick" (field notes, Sanford Heights). Information was traded that may have provided cultural options for Sanford Heights preadolescent boys and for those in Mason City. . . .

Closer to home, a preadolescent boy may know several adolescents or young adults who are willing to tell him about sensitive topics—sex, pranks, insults, etc. A major font of this information is older brothers (though for some topics, older sisters can perform this function). Some older brothers felt a responsibility to their siblings to teach them those cultural traditions helpful for achieving status among the younger boys' peers. Although siblings may not be "close friends" (particularly since they run in different social worlds), these elder siblings are sources for the continuation of cultural tradition. Children without elder siblings learn from those preadolescents who have them. Likewise, a seventh-grade boy may become attached to an older schoolmate who will take him under his wing, and the younger boy will then inform his peers.

Consider the spread of the slang expression *zoid*. *Zoid* was defined by its originator as referring to a boy who is a "loser," or who has a poor reputation and is not a member of any group (as in the sarcastic put-down, "You're a zoid, ya know it?"). The word was created by a twelfth-grade boy in Sanford Heights and spread to his regular baseball friends. The word subsequently was learned by the originator's ninth-grade brother, and the brother used *zoid* with his friends. One of this ninth-grader's friends had a sixth-grade brother playing Little League baseball. This boy added *zoid* to his vocabulary. When the forty-eight twelve-year-olds were interviewed after the season, eleven other boys said they had heard the term.

Structural Roles

A third way in which cultural information spreads within a social system is through individuals who perform particular structural roles in intergroup relations. These are individuals who are not part of these groups but have contacts with them. In terms of preadolescent lore, relatively many individuals have the potential to serve in this capacity. . . . Camp counselors, for example, tell ghost stories and mildly off-color anecdotes for the amusement of their campers. In turn, preadolescents may teach this guardian some of their culture. If the camp counselor is with these campers for two weeks and then a new set of

campers replaces them, the counselor may become a key linkage of diffusion of preadolescent lore. Although he is not a full member of the group, his role allows for diffusion of lore. . . . While the primary role obligation of counselors is not the diffusion of preadolescent cultural traditions, this is an indirect result of their multi-group contacts. These adolescents link groups that lack direct ties. Little League coaches, who work with the same boys over several seasons with 50 percent turnover each year and may coach other sports, also may spread preadolescent lore.

Media Diffusion

The fourth pattern is transmission through the mass media. Television, radio, and films each play a large role in children's lives, and the fact that the media are either national (as in the case of network television and films) or responding to national influences (as in the case of Top 40 Radio or local television programming) implies that the culture displayed by these outlets is relatively uniform. Many groups of preadolescents are simultaneously affected by a single communicator (or communicating group). The effects of a popular television program on children's culture should not be underestimated—as underlined by numerous references to the Fonz or Kojak during this research. One pair of friends named themselves Starsky and Hutch after the television characters. While I was conducting research, the film *The Bad News Bears* was distributed nationally. Boys frequently referred to the film to describe their experiences, and so, a Hopewell boy challenged another boy, invoking the film's memorable line: "Stick it where the sun doesn't shine." Another boy referred to one of Hopewell's teams as the Bad News Bears because of their lack of athletic skill. In the film, the Bears improved to the point that they nearly won the league championship, but the *meaning* of the Bad News Bears in children's interaction is of a team filled with incompetents who curse and belch. . . .

Audiences for media productions are not limited by age alone. These raw cultural elements will generally be viewed by other groups; however, the way in which this culture is used is a function of age and social status. In the case of *The Bad News Bears*, the insults in the film fit the preadolescent culture of aggressive insults, many of which have anal overtones. One might expect that the elements this age group selected from the film are strikingly different from those of their adult guardians. The film ostensibly is about the dangers of over-competition and adult involvement in youth sports. Although accessible to all, media productions are not consumed by a random sample of the population but are selected on the basis of prior interests—interests that reveal the boundaries of the subculture.

These four types of cultural linkages or interlocks illustrate possible transmission mechanisms and together explain how a culture of childhood in American society is possible, even when geographical mobility is restricted and in the absence of child-sponsored media.

Identification

... [T]here are considerable differences among groups of children as to what they know and what they believe is appropriate behavior—one feature that leads to childhood cliques. Even at preadolescence, a boy finds himself with several cultural models available. These models are known by the preadolescents and discussed openly. For example, at one school in Bolton Park, kids are classified as to whether they are daredevils (kids who get into trouble), jocks, or burnies (burn-outs—preadolescents who smoke, drink, and use drugs). Most Little Leaguers consider themselves jocks and, like some older athletes, scorn the burnies (field notes, Bolton Park). Three boys who attended the local Bolton Park parochial school told me that in their school there are three groups of kids: rowdies, in-betweens, and goody-goodies (or Holy Joes)—not surprisingly all considered themselves to be in-betweens. Similar groupings were found in other schools. These distinctions caution against assuming the existence of a homogeneous children's culture and emphasize the importance of understanding the child's identification with his own group. Being part of any subcultural system requires motivation and identification with those who are members. Values, norms, behaviors, and artifacts constitute a subculture, only if individuals see themselves as part of a community whose members give meaning to these "objects." Being classified in a particular age category is not by itself sufficient to predict cultural orientation.

Individuals, even during preadolescence, may identify with specific groups of which they are members or with the large social categories to which they belong (the subsociety). In terms of preadolescent identification, the orientation tends to be directed toward the interacting group or institution (the team or group of friends and even, in some cases, the community). "Class" consciousness has not fully developed by this age, although it does as the child becomes an adolescent and begins to see himself explicitly as a member of that socially defined subgroup. . . .

[The fact] that preadolescents increasingly spend time with their peers has implications for the development of identification of oneself as a peer. . . . The role of peers is indicated by the time-budget study I conducted in Sanford Heights among twelve-year-olds shortly after the season. When I asked about the previous Saturday (after the season ended), the sample claimed to have spent an average of 4.4 hours with friends but only 3.8 hours with parents. While this is not a significant difference, it does suggest that these boys have moved from their parents' orbit. The changing activity patterns of children permit the development of a preadolescent subculture—a subculture that involves identification, as well as shared content. The age segregation found in American society (Conger 1972) is part of this process in that, not only do children spend less time with their parents, but historically they have come to spend less time with all adults who might provide non-peer identification.

The media and adults typically define preadolescence as a social category about which generalizations can be made; members of that age category come to think of themselves in relation to stereotypes offered by older members of the community. This identification with peers, sponsored in part by adults, leads preadolescents to adopt behavior patterns and artifacts defined as particular to their age group.

The Threads of Culture

One of the threads running throughout this analysis . . . is the process by which preadolescent culture—and by implication, all cultures—is created and becomes connected to a group. . . . There is [also] a world beyond the small group. Culture spreads outside of its community of origin, lodging itself in numerous communities and spreading within them. I argue that a subsociety is comprised of numerous interlocking groups in which members identify themselves collectively as a meaningful social segment; a subculture is composed of those cultural traditions that flow through these social networks and that are perceived by members of the subsociety and by outsiders as being particularly characteristic of this social segment. . . .

We are each part of various socially and personally defined societies with their own traditions and values. Although a subculture will be more diffuse than an idioculture of a group that is characterized by face-to-face interaction, it is more definable than a national culture. If we understand culture as disseminated through social relationships, we can then examine these meaningful connections in order to understand the patterns and variations of tradition. . . .

References

Conger, John. 1972. "The World They Never Knew: The Family and Social Change." In *Twelve to Sixteen: Early Adolescence*, ed. by Jerome Kagan and Robert Coles. New York: W. W. Norton.

Fine, Gary Alan and Sherryl Kleinman. 1979. "Rethinking Subculture: An Interactionist Approach." *American Journal of Sociology*, 85:1–20.

26

Everyday Life in Nursing Homes

Timothy Diamond

The source of many challenges we face in our everyday social lives is often far removed from them. Social structures, relatively stable patterns of social relations, link our everyday lives to decisions, actions, and understandings originating elsewhere. For example, decisions made in governmental offices and corporate boardrooms often have far ranging consequences on our lives. Abstract systems of meaning developed elsewhere often organize our lives and clash with our concrete understandings of those lives. We cannot fully understand our everyday social lives without understanding how social relations that stretch far beyond them shape them.

In this selection, Timothy Diamond examines how social policies and the logic of medicine and business shape life in American nursing homes. His focus is patients and nursing assistants who have the most direct contact with patients. Diamond explains how current health care policy leads many nursing home residents down paths of impoverishment. This threat and its realization is often the source of fears and anger that are mistaken for symptoms of residents' fading minds. In addition, the logic of medicine and business that organizes life in nursing homes reduces residents to passive objects of care, to patients, rather than participants in social life. It thereby alienates them from the society outside and, often, from one another. Yet, as Diamond explains, residents are not passive but actively do the work of being patients, no matter how reluctantly.

The working life of nursing assistants or aides are also subject to the logic of business and medicine. Paid little and denied authority, their complex caring work is reduced to units of billable, mostly physical, tasks. Their social relations with patients and the highly skilled work of caring for frail and sometimes dying people disappears in the chart where that work is recorded as discrete units of health care. Those who see only snapshot views of the everyday life of nursing homes or who know it only through the chart or the language of business do not see those relations and that complex caring work. Rather, they see passive and paying patients and unskilled workers performing discrete, menial tasks.

According to Diamond, this is the result of the commodification of care, of making it into something that is bought and sold for a profit. Administrators and supervisory medical staff of nursing homes take this business logic for granted, as just the way things are. Yet, this system of meaning makes little sense on the floor of nursing homes where nursing assistants bathe, feed, talk to and otherwise care for patients who struggle to maintain their sanity in the face of such senselessness. As Diamond suggests, we cannot fully understand life in nursing homes from the perspective of occasional visitors, administrators, or supervisory medical personnel. Much of what occurs in nursing homes cannot be seen from their perspectives. We must start with the perspectives of those who most intimately live that life, residents and nursing aides, and then explore the socially structured relations that shape their everyday lives in nursing homes.

This is a preliminary report on a sociological research project in which I worked as a nursing assistant (or nurses' aide) in a series of nursing homes in the United States. Here, long term care systems are being developed along the organizational model of business and nursing homes are considered an industry. This study focuses on the ongoing creation of that industry. It does so from the standpoint of the everyday life of some of the people inside, especially nursing assistants and patients. . . .

I began the project by attending a vocational school which trains nursing assistants. After completing the training, I worked full time in three nursing homes for a period of just under two years. The primary objective in undertaking the participant observation project was to get to know personally nursing assistants and patients over time, and to experience everyday life in different kinds of homes. This initial analysis describes some aspects of that everyday life and links them to social and political forces beyond them. . . .

The owner of our vocational school stood tall in his three-piece suit on that first night of class as he welcomed the new nursing assistant trainees with a mix of medical and military imagery: "Welcome to the firing line of health care." We were recruits in an area of work that is being formalized as a new profession. While the job of nurses' aide has existed for many years, it is now being organized for nursing homes and home health care. . . . While their work is supervised by the more highly trained registered nurses and licensed practical nurses, nursing assistants are by far the largest group of workers in nursing homes. Although some men do the work, almost all nursing assistants are women.

In the training course, we learned that we were to become members of the health care team, a part of the noblest of professions. We learned elementary biology, and how we were never to do health care without first consulting someone in authority; and we learned not to ask questions but to do as we were told. As one of the students, a black woman from Jamaica, used to joke, "I can't figure out whether they're trying to teach us to be nurses' aides or black women."

Most of the students laughed at the joke; most were black women. The majority of the nursing assistants I met throughout the research were nonwhite. . . . The director of the school turned out to be one of the last white men I was to see in this work, except for administrators and some patients. While men may own and direct nursing homes, it is not a white man's land inside . . . I was not alone as a man, yet as one of the very few white men, my presence was never without suspicion. It was one of the administrators who first expressed the general scepticism of my presence when he asked, "Why would a white guy want to work for these kind of wages?"

It was a shock when I finally began to work and experience the conditions to which he was referring. . . . [M]any nursing assistants with whom I worked . . . complained about not having enough money for essentials—food, rent, utilities, transportation and their children's needs. . . . [T]he newly professionalized health care workers earn less than family subsistence even with a full time job. . . . Solange Ferier [all names in this paper are fictitious] from Jamaica summarized it: "You know, Tim, I done this job for six years in my country. One thing I learn when I come to the States—you can't make it on just one job." Most of the nursing assistants I met work more than one job if they can, and live in hope of overtime. Even a full-time job at slightly over minimum wage is not enough. "Minimum" wage turns out to be an abstraction; it may make sense to policy makers and economists, but it is considerably less than minimum in these people's lives. . . .

Economic Policy and the Path of Poverty

I worked in both private and state-subsidized homes. From the conversations I had with patients in these homes, I conclude that in the United States there is an economic life course involved in being a long-term patient. Meeting people in different homes disrupted my image of nursing home life as a static existence. One does not "end up" in a nursing home; one proceeds on a path that is the consequence of social policy and the embeddedness of nursing homes within the organizational model of business and industry. In the United States, care is based on ability to pay. Long-term patients tell about living through the phases of Medicare, private resources (if any), bankruptcy, and public aid. Given present economic arrangements for long-term care, a patient moves along a path: the more time in long-term care, the poorer one becomes.

There are two types of nursing homes, distinguished by the hours of "skilled" nursing compared with those of "intermediate" care provided. I worked in both types. Medicare, the U.S. federal program, pays only for skilled nursing care (as is the policy of most insurance companies). Medicare enters at the beginning of an acute health crises and pays most of the bill. Yet this is a short-term, rehabilitation-centered program; it has time, sickness, and dollar limits. This is the United States' only federal program for long-term care, but it is actually a very short-term program: one is supported only for a matter of months. It is probably more correct to say that the United States has no federal long-term program, except for Medicaid, which is funded in part by the states. Medicaid, a form of public aid, pays a nursing home for care only after a patient has become indigent. Since long-term care can mean years, indigence is frequently a part of nursing home life.

Many patients told me of their fears as those last weeks of Medicare drew near and, for example, that "damn hip wouldn't heal." Every day Grace DeLong asked me to hand her her checkbook and bank statements. At the time she had about $10,000 in life savings, having worked as a secretary all of her life. She stared at the book for long periods every day, as though to clutch the savings. She had seen it happen to others. Nursing homes are expensive. . . . Medicare lasts only a matter of months, after which patients are on their own, relying on whatever personal resources are available through insurance supplements and savings. . . . [M]ost insurance policies, like Medicare, pay only when one is classified as in need of skilled care. Joyce Horan was nervous that insurance people would visit her; she was afraid they would see she was better enough to be reclassified as only needing "custodial" or intermediate care, be dropped from the rolls, and probably sent to a different ward or home. . . .

Living through long-term care means feeling constant insecurity over having to pay to live in a home, while at the same time realizing the impossibility of doing so for long. It is a journey toward indigence. Grace DeLong, seeing it coming and clenching her checkbook, used to go on and on in her fear; her pleas were quite high pitched and frenzied: "Get me out of here! I can't stay here! I've got to get out of here!" A passer-by or someone who had only a fleeting contact with her might interpret her clamor as senile ranting. But she was afraid of losing that $10,000. She had no one at home to care for her, and felt trapped. . . .

Contrary to the popular image of rest or retirement, nursing home life is not an economically stable situation. This becomes evident in conversations I had with people who linked the experience of private-pay and public aid in their own lives. The women and men I met at the expensive home started out in the posh two lower floors. When their money had run out they were moved to the public aid wings, there to receive noticeably inferior care. There was a certain pressure within the home that many residents complained about. The management had made it clear that they preferred more short-term Medicare patients, since these patients were worth more. One could feel a murmur of fear among the public aid patients that many would be asked to leave or go to another home. No doubt this would happen to some. I know because I met women and men in the poor homes who started as private pay residents in other homes and had been forced to leave them. Meeting them made me understand that there is a distinct economic progression in nursing home life—the longer one stays the more impoverished one becomes, and the more unstable one's environment becomes.

Frequently, nursing homes are approached in our thinking as though they were a series of separate places; the idea is to find a good one, or a good model and eliminate the bad ones. To live in long-term care, however, may well refer to homes in a series rather than a home. One does not live in just "a" home, but moves through a system—a maze of different wards, floors, and homes.

The relationship these people have to the society, then, is precarious even before one begins to consider their physical or psychological conditions. These organizational disruptions (moving from one home or ward to another) are beyond the internal workings of a particular home and something about which anyone inside, including those with authority, can do little. They are a by-product of current social policies related to long-term care. These policies themselves breed a fear that derives directly from living in the society. When Grace was screaming "I've got to get out of here!," she was screaming not just at the nursing home, but also at the society beyond it. I came to change my image of nursing home life as a static enterprise. It is not sitting in a chair "doing nothing." Rather than being passive, it is always a process. The policies that shape this environment inform every moment of nursing home life. Each person is situated somewhere on an overall turbulent path. . . .

The Everyday Making of Patients

Another image of passivity that I carried into the research related to preconceptions I had about patients. Having "ended up" in a nursing home, I thought of them as recipients of someone else's acts, acted upon rather than acting. Patients are formally defined into the organization in a passive way: that is, they are named in terms of diseases, and their basic record of care—the chart—is about what health care goods and services are rendered to them, about what is done to them, not about what they themselves do. It appears as a passive existence to outside observers, visitors who get snapshot views and carry snapshot imagery of people "just sitting." Working in the local reality of everyday relations dissolved that image. From here there is another way of thinking about nursing homes that conceives of patients as actually quite active. The question might be asked, "What kind of work is involved in surviving in a nursing home?" The notion of passive runs close to making patients objects, which, at worst, leads to the ongoing presumption that "they are out of it," and even at best leads to questions like, "What can we do for them?" Yet as one gets to know patients it becomes clear that almost all are thinking, conscious people, however fragile and intermittent that consciousness might be. This point of departure presumes patients to be present, actively aware, conscious, at some level—participants in the setting, not just acted upon, and struggling to be at the helm of their own consciousness, even with all the appearances to the contrary.

I say "struggle" because there can develop within nursing homes an impersonal ethos in which frail, senile patients are assumed to be "out of it." They are inserted into an impersonal mode with pervading notions that their minds are "gone." Yet, getting to know people in their ongoing lives, it becomes evident that being in long term care is not just a passive existence. It is also very active. It takes a lot of effort.

Nursing homes are medical environments. They are not short-term hospitals for these people, yet still they operate on the organizational model of a hospital. When one enters a nursing home, a chart is slid into its slot, there to record the units of health care one receives—all related to the first page of the chart, the diagnosis, or sickness category. One is a patient, treated in an environment that mimics a hospital, with its spotless, sanitized floors, its PA system blaring, its white-uniformed staff, its air of emergency.

In our daily round of work, as in the schooling, the texts and manuals, nursing assistant work was defined in a task-centered, physical way. The first assignment as the day began was usually expressed like this: "Diamond, today you have beds 206 to 230." This did not refer to the beds I had to make, but to the people who occupied them. The first task was to wake the residents, get them up if at all possible, and prepare them for breakfast and medications. This was the hardest part of the day for many nursing assistants, and a source of continual sharing of jokes and complaints. It was hard because it was so hard for the residents, and something they fought against, so the first moments of the day were often spent in conflict. "Work all my life waiting for retirement," Miss Black used to grumble, "and now I can't even sleep in the mornings." I used to try to explain to her that this was a hospital—at least we followed hospital regimens here—but at 7 a.m. that made little sense to her, or to me.

After the patients were awakened, those who were able to leave their beds were transported to the day room for breakfast. Some residents could not perform all the complex tasks of eating, and had to be helped. The rush was on to finish breakfast by 8:30, so there was pressure when one had to help several people eat. The luck of the bad draw was noted in the question, "How many feeders you got today?" "Feeder" referred to a patient who needed help eating. The one who is doing the eating becomes an object in this term, the object of feeding, and under the pressure of time, an object of scorn. Buried underneath this pressured moment, however, was the act of feeding a frail, sick person—a delicate process, requiring much skill. To learn the extremely slow pace of an old person's eating, or how to vary portions and tastes, how to communicate non-verbally while feeding—these are refined skills, but unnamed, indeed, suppressed, by the dictates of the organization.

After breakfast, the "menial" tasks began that would occupy the assistants until lunch: showers or bed baths, toileting or bed pans, changing beds, taking vital signs, continually charting it all. The body was recorded. "Vitals," a word drawn directly from the Latin word for "life," was a continual activity. As the work is lodged in our current vocabulary, it is part of a medical regimen, meaning blood pressure, temperature, pulse, and respiration. Since many people had identical vital signs day in and day out for all their years of residency, this procedure seemed more like a ritual than a requirement of health care, at least to residents, who frequently mocked it. "I guess you got to make sure I'm alive again today, eh?" "Vitals," in the homes, meant physical life, not biography, emotions, or social milieu.

It seems hardest of all for these people to cope when their behavior is called a disease, when that link between this confused present and that known past is severed. Yet even to be placed on certain wards and floors is to be treated as mentally impaired. Meanwhile, a constant life in a total institution is a source of confusion [Goffman 1961] especially for older people. At the very time of their life when they are struggling to maintain their own cognitive abilities and sanity, they become enmeshed in a cultural ethos that says they are "going through their second childhood" or they are "out of their minds." Many residents express anger at this ethos, but a nursing home is not a place where anger is spoken about or permitted. Patienthood is an engulfing identity and, over time, many residents seem to become re-signed in the face of its power.

Yet, sometimes the anger has a clear social and political content. Miss Black had been a math teacher. At 74, when I met her, she was confined to a wheelchair, and had lived through the economic pathway to the public aid phase. She was furious that, as a result, she had lost complete control over her social security check. It was absorbed by the institution as partial payment. She would sit in her wheelchair in the hall and yell, "Where's my social security. Get the administrator! I want my social security checks!" Once or twice the administrators did stop by to explain to her that her check was only part of what it cost to keep her there. That was not an adequate explanation for her. She would get frantic in her fury, trying to move beyond the logic of that answer, trying to reclaim control over the old age support to which she had contributed all her working life. When she yelled too much, the health care staff took over to calm her, sometimes through chemical means. Her anger was then charted in ways congruent with the world of patienthood:

"Miss Black was acting out again today."

Although a nursing home is often a chaotic and angry place, there are within each home and within most patients pockets of creativity, of insightfulness, of competence. Patients are active participants in the setting in complex, humorous, and gracious ways. "And how are you today?" a visiting volunteer or physician or minister would ask Mary Ryan, frequently in a voice too loud. "Oh . . . fine . . . " she would respond, though very slowly. ". . . And you?" Mary was being polite, as she always was to outsiders. She was not fine, she was miserable. She complained about her restraints all day, and after the visitors were gone, she would complain about them once again. The question, "And how are you today?" from a stranger had very little to do with her ongoing life. But in this snapshot visit and irrelevant question, she graciously carried on the conversation, as we all do, with "Fine, thanks. And you?" Meanwhile, the visitors, unaccustomed to her slow, spacey manner (for they lived their lives at a much faster pace than she), and full of presumptions about the institution, walked out the door with a vaguely focused sympathy: "Poor Mary—shame she's so out of it."

While they no doubt mean well, many of the visitors, like the above, will never be more than

strangers, at least emotionally, to the patients. Some patients have friends within the nursing home, but for the most part the home, too, is a gathering of strangers, people alone with others. Some sit next to each other for months and years and do not talk to each other, often do not even know each others' names. One can look out on a room where 40 or 50 people are eating and hear little or no conversation. Residents seem alienated from one another. Ties to the world, even the local world, diminish as the overwhelming passification process of patienthood sweeps over. People curl in socially, as they are continually remade into patients.

"Curl in," however, does not mean passivity. Life inside the home is neither rest nor passive nothingness; it is a repository of effort. It is passive only to outsiders who, with snapshot methods, create a "them" and a "we," and create a passivity. In our creation of images and concepts of passivity, what the patients do while sitting there doing nothing is outside our understanding. Meanwhile patients in long-term care are actively engaged in the work of being a patient. . . .

The Invisibility of Caring Work

In one home it was emphasized repeatedly that the two most important tasks nursing assistants had to accomplish were to make sure patients were available to take their medications and to be sure that everything we did was charted. "If It's Not Charted," read a large sign behind the nurses' station, "It Didn't Happen."

Nursing assistants are trained in and judged in terms of the performance of physical tasks, like taking blood pressures and pulses, giving bed pans, and turning, showering and feeding patients. When these tasks are accomplished, they are coded and recorded in the all-important link between that work and the outside world—the chart. Recording tasks on the chart fits them into the overall organizational scheme of things, called health care. In terms of this participation, what nursing assistants do is considered unskilled.

I found the work that nursing assistants do far more complex than a conception of "unskilled" or "menial" would imply. Much of what they do does not fit into the chart as it is presently constructed. This other, non-physical . . . dimension of what nursing assistants and others might do might be called caring work [Finch and Groves

1983]. . . . [H]olding someone as they grasp for breaths fearing that it might be their last, or cleaning someone, or laughing with them so as to keep them alive, feeding them or brushing their teeth, helping them hold on to memories of the past while they try to maintain sanity in the present—these are constant, essential and difficult parts of the work. They are unskilled and menial practices only if nursing assistants are presumed to be subordinates in a medical world. Yet this caring work is invisible in the language of business and medicine, and is written out of the charts. On the chart it is physical life that is monitored and recorded.

Formally, nursing assistants' tasks have nothing to do with talking to patients. It is, in fact, probably more efficient not to converse. In two homes we were explicitly not allowed to sit with patients. Should the Board of Health appear, or one of the occasional physicians drop in, this would appear as loafing. We were told to keep moving, unless we were charting, for to keep moving is to look busy. Supervisory nurses are under considerable pressure to see that all tasks get charted, and that all patients' units of health care are properly recorded.

Yet there is work beyond this merely physical work that remains invisible and unmentioned. There is a special knowledge and skill involved in caring work. It begins with being in touch with someone else's body, and its need for constant, intimate tending. There is the mental work, much of which is only obvious when it is not done, as when someone turns up poorly dressed, or becomes incontinent when it was the nursing assistant's job to insure against it. There is much more emotional work—holding, cuddling, calming, grieving. There is a great deal of thought work—tending to one patient, thinking of another. What distinguishes this kind of work is that it involves social relations, more than simple tasks. The tasks themselves are only part of wider social relationships, though the only part that gets documented in the formal language and record keeping of the work. In the charting process (but not before), these tasks become the reality of the job, and become separated from social relations.

The lesson that nursing assistants' tasks are performed within the context of social relationships was taught to me best by Mary Gardner, a 14-year veteran of nursing assistant work. It was she who told me, in all seriousness, that "some shit don't stink." I asked her to explain a bit more what she meant. As she was teaching me how to make a bed, she made it perfectly clear: "It depends on if you like 'em and they like you, and if you know 'em pretty well; it's hard to clean somebody new, or somebody you don't like. If you like 'em, it's like your baby." A bit later she made reference to a man with whom she had had to struggle every day: "But now take Floyd, that bastard, that man's shit is foul." Through her explanation it became clear that the work is not a set of menial tasks, but a set of social relations in which the tasks are embedded.

At this point in the development of nursing homes, the social relations of caring work which contextualize these patients' and nurses' aides lives are relegated to an oral tradition. They are not incorporated into the textbooks or charts or reimbursement schemes. They are erased from the formal record. Or perhaps they do not happen at all. For, in this environment, if it's not charted, it didn't happen.

The Commodification of Care

As systems of long-term care develop . . . they increasingly come to be defined in business terms. The nursing home industry is supposed to be a business based on care.

"Care" is the basic stock-in-trade, that which is advertised, bought, and sold. There seems to be a question at this historical moment that is still worth asking, even as nursing homes proceed on what looks like an inexorable course toward corporatization. Can caring be a business? What happens when this web of social relations is placed into the contemporary terms of market discourse? How does day-to-day care for human beings get turned into a commodity?

One day, in a lecture to the workers on our ward, the administrator of one of the homes reprimanded the nursing assistants with a dictum commonly heard in staff meetings: "I hope I don't have to remind you," he said, "that a nursing home is a 24 hour a day, 365 day a year business." He took for granted that he was operating a business, and was chiding us to be more productive in those terms. Business was a taken for granted reality for him. Yet the business model is not a natural fact, but a historically specific mode of organization. The everyday work of human caring and the social relation between carer and patient is molded into the language of business:

costs, beds, profit margins, cost-accountability, turnover, bottom lines. The power of this logic is such that these terms are made to seem reality itself, and dominate everyday life in the homes....

Concrete human relations get changed when they are transformed into the . . . reality of commodities, when care is encoded in reimbursement concepts. The local reality is erased from the view of those whose contact with nursing homes is mediated by these abstract business terms. One of the key notions that facilitates this translation is cost-accountability. To make sense in the language of cost-accountability, units of service have to be coded into dollars and cents, care into units of care. One day during our clinical training we had completed all our assigned tasks and had returned to our instructor to see what our next order might be. After some reflection the R.N. instructor suggested: "Why don't you go do some psycho-social stuff?" Hearing this psuedo-scientific notion for the first time, one of the student trainees (whispering "moron" under her breath) whipped back, "What do you mean, talk to them? What do you think we've been doing all day?" We had continually conversed with our patients while tending to them. Now we were receiving a new, distinct managerial directive and it could be fit into the cost-accountability of the administrative logic, like vitals or showers. Now we could go talk to (or, rather, "do some psycho-social stuff with") the patients and it could be entered into the records as a discrete nursing task, and be separately charted and charged under the heading of hours of nursing care. . . .

In [this example], the reality of the local, everyday life is transformed—annihilated, actually. The administrator's admonition to us that this was a business was certainly correct, more than I imagined when he spoke it. In this language people are market phenomena. It begins in defining people as bodies. The body is conceptualized and treated and recorded in a quantitative way compatible with reimbursement. Terms like beds, costs, turnovers and profit margins are taken for granted as part of nursing home life. These are economic units. The discourse of nursing home life becomes subsumed under that of nursing home management.

Generating a commodity involves transforming a good or service from its everyday meaning as a support for social relationships into an abstract meaning for private profit. Even more than

hospitals, which operate with high technology, nursing homes throughout the western world depend on caring work as a means of profit. In order for commodities to be created, social relations must be redefined. In the process of transforming these social relations into formal tasks, caring work is turned into a commodity. Caring work is turned into discrete and quantifiable tasks; these then become the nuts and bolts that allow nursing homes to run as enterprises for profit. The caring relations are coded into measurable and cost-accountable tasks: talk into "psycho-social stuff," emotional into technical. . . .

One of the dangers of this transformation is that the local reality of patients' lives can become invisible and the caring relations remain implicit and unnamed. . . . [W]hat emerges in their place are separate individuals ("beds") with sicknesses, which demand discrete units of health care, and menial workers to feed, transport, and toilet them—tasks which are all measured in time units required to execute the tasks. The charts record individuals broken down into units of costable measurement; these units can then be built back up as commodities. Life inside the home can then be talked about in terms congruent with any other capitalist organization producing a product for profit. This is the logic of commodities, a logic that informs every moment in the day-to-day production of nursing home life. . . .

Conclusion

Nursing assistants and patients are not classes of people who are essentially silent and passive. They communicate ideas and emotions with specific social and political content—content which is tied directly to the conditions of the organization and, in turn, to the society. Nursing assistants wonder why after 40 [hours of] work they still have to seek overtime just to survive; they wonder why the work they do, even if it is tending to someone during their last days, or even to their deaths, is still dismissed as menial and unskilled. Residents frequently express a desire to reclaim control over their own social security checks, and wonder why after paying into social security all their lives they are now reduced to public aid; they wonder . . . why staff is so convinced that they are crazy. These are questions that permeate life on a ward. They are derived from social conditions. The method of analysis I am suggesting involves seeing these people within the context of these social conditions as political participants in the ongoing productions of everyday life, though at the present time caught in a set of relationships over which they have little or no control. . . .

Current patients and nursing assistants . . . are in a way pioneers. How much of their knowledge gets recorded depends in large part on how effectively researchers bridge the worlds of the everyday and its larger contexts and cultivate the methods for giving them speech. When we get to know patients and nursing assistants as social and political participants, they offer a different perspective on social security, Medicaid, caring work, nursing, and old age. The issues I raise in this study grow out of just a few of the societal relations being lived out in nursing homes, there for us to learn about, or . . . there for the women and men inside to teach.

References

Finch, J. and Groves, D. (Eds). 1983. *A Labour of Love: Women, Work, and Caring.* Boston, MA: Routledge & Kegan Paul.

Goffman, E. 1961. *Asylums.* Garden City, NY: Doubleday.

27

Working and Resisting at Route Restaurant

Greta Foff Paules

The previous selection illustrates how those in social structural positions of power can impose systems of meaning and action on others. Armed with the power of eviction and termination, nursing home administrators impose the logic of medicine and business on the everyday lives of residents and nursing assistants. Similarly, administrators, executives, and managers of other organizations impose systems of meaning and action on their employees, clients, and, often, customers. For example, executives and managers of chain restaurants commonly mandate how tasks will be divided and performed in minute detail, what employees can and cannot wear to work, and how they should interact with customers. Yet, such social structural power has its limits. Those who are subject to it seldom passively accept its dictates and definitions of situations. Rather, they subtly and, sometimes, not so subtly resist the efforts of those in more structurally powerful positions to shape their conduct and thinking. They draw upon local sources of power in those efforts and protect their sense of self from organizational definitions of who and what they should be.

In this selection, Greta Foff Paules illustrates such resistance among waitresses at a chain restaurant that she calls "Kendelport Route." As with most chain restaurants, executives at corporate headquarters attempt to organize and standardize operations at each restaurant. They determine how the restaurants will be designed, equipped, and divided into "stations." They decide what dishes will be offered and how they are prepared. They dictate what employees can and cannot wear at work and how they perform their respective tasks. As Paules notes, they also attempt to promote an image of food service work as servitude. Waitresses are forbidden from eating, drinking, or merely sitting in the presence of customers. They require waitresses to wear plain uniforms that set them apart from customers. They encourage the unilateral use of first names in interactions between customers and waitresses by requiring waitresses to wear name tags or introduce themselves by first name. These and other conventions are symbols of servitude that encourage customers to treat waitresses as mere servants, and as Paules observes, many customers do.

However, waitresses at Route reject this symbolism of service and refuse to think of themselves as servants. Rather, they see themselves as soldiers locked in battle with a rude public. They see themselves as private entrepreneurs earning tips through their own skill and savvy. They feel little loyalty to the company because of the minimal wages they earn. Rather, they believe it is the company's responsibility to provide them with a favorable environment for their business enterprise—earning tips. Most of the waitresses' earnings come from "their" customers rather than the company, limiting its perceived power over them. Waitresses at Kendelport Route also benefit from the severe labor shortage in the area. Managers need experienced, skilled waitresses more than the waitresses need a job at Kedelport Route. They can simply take their business of earning tips elsewhere.

Waitresses draw upon these sources of local power and effectively resist the company's implicit definition of them as servants. Although they often beguile and defer to customers in attempts to earn handsome tips, waitresses are not taken in by their own performances. Rather, they take pride in their ability to "get" tips from customers. They also combat customers' blatant attempts to belittle and intimidate them. They refuse to be treated as submissive servants.

The example of the Route waitresses illustrates both the power of social structure to shape our everyday social lives and its limits. Like the Route waitresses, those in social structural positions of greater power often pressure us to feel, think, and act as they see fit. They often determine the circumstances under which we must act. However, we seldom passively accept their dictates or our circumstances. Rather, we respond to them, sometimes resisting them, sometimes reluctantly bending to them, and often doing a bit of both. Social structural arrangements clearly shape our everyday lives, but they do not determine them because they are, at least in part, of our own making.

This is a study of a small group of women who wait tables in a family-style restaurant in New Jersey. It is a study of women who are neither organized nor upwardly mobile yet actively and effectively strive to protect and enhance their position at work. It is about women who refuse to submit unquestioningly to the dictates of management, to absorb the abuses of a hurried and often hostile public, or to internalize a negative image of self promoted by the symbols of servitude, which pervade their work. It is about women who "don't take no junk."

The restaurant where this study was conducted, referred to here as Route, or Kendelport Route, is located on a busy interstate highway in an area undergoing rapid residential and commercial development. It is surrounded by malls, business parks, research campuses, and housing complexes in various stages of completion. Great expanses of bulldozed forest and billboards announcing forthcoming construction portend continued development in years to come. The entire region, however, suffers from an intense shortage of labor that may temper its growth in the future. Help-wanted signs promising an enjoyable working environment, flexible hours, and good pay and benefits adorn the front windows and doors of many stores and restaurants. Some are never removed. This climate of desperation has far reaching implications for employer-employee relations and for the quality of work life within the restaurant.

Route belongs to a well-known restaurant chain, which developed from a donut stand founded in the early fifties. The chain has more than twelve hundred units or "stores" located throughout the United States and several abroad. The caliber of the chain's food, service, and decor places it in the mid to lower range of the restaurant spectrum. Bon vivant urban professionals do not condescend to dine at Route, which is not greasy enough to be camp. The restaurant does appeal to budget-conscious families, senior citizens on fixed incomes, athletic teams, and church groups. In the predawn hours, Route absorbs the night life that has been dispelled from nearby bars at closing, as well as teenagers who congregate in packs over coffee and fries, and drug dealers who ostentatiously stack fifty- and hundred-dollar bills on booth tables, then stiff their waitresses. Like many roadside restaurants, Route is also the occasional resting place of the homeless, who find refuge on a stool at the counter from the cold, the heat, and the loneliness outside.

Route waitresses include teenagers and women in their sixties; mothers-to-be (three waitresses were pregnant when the research ended),

teen-mothers, grandmothers, and women with no children; full-time workers who have been waiting tables for decades, and women who also hold jobs as telephone operators, cleaning women, cashiers, or companions for the ill. There is a Route waitress who picked cotton and peanuts alongside sharecropper parents when she was six and wore bleached flour sacks for slips, and another whose father is rumored by her co-workers to own "a big, fine mansion . . . with a maid and everything. . . . A girl who was brought up with nannies." In contrast to some restaurants in the area, Route attracts few college students to its waitressing staff. This may be due to the intensely serious work atmosphere or to the stigma attached to Route waitresses. A sense of how the public perceives the restaurant was suggested by a comedian on the "Tonight Show," who hypothesized that Route purposefully hired the ugliest women it could find in order to make the food appear more appetizing.

Approximately thirty waitresses work at Kendelport Route. One to eight waitresses may be on the floor at a given time. The restaurant employs dishwashers or "service assistants," who are often referred to as busboys though they do not bus tables, which is the waitress's job. It employs cooks and prep cooks, and on busy shifts hostesses are scheduled to work the register and seat incoming parties. The managerial staff consists of two managers and a general manager. There are also *PICs* and *SCs* (person-in-charge and service coordinators): employees, usually waitresses, who act as managers for one or two nights a week, allowing managers an occasional night off. Because there are no regular persons-in-charge or service coordinators, *PIC* and *SC* is generally understood as something one does, not is. This is reflected in the language of the restaurant: a waitress is rarely referred to as a *PIC* or *SC*; rather she is said to be *PICing* or *SCing*. . . .

Job categories at Route are segregated along gender lines. During the research period, all managers at Kendelport Route were male, but there were female managers at other units in the district, and women had managed at Kendelport in the past. All but one to two cooks and dishwashers were male. By contrast, virtually all servers were women. Of the few waiters who worked at the restaurant, two were dating waitresses. One, a rugged college student, reported being addressed as "waitress" by inattentive customers: an indication that the public is not accustomed to seeing waiters at Route. Hostesses also tended to be women. . . .

[The Symbolism of Service]

Employees of service industries are encouraged to treat customers with unflinching reverence and solicitude; to regard their concerns and needs as paramount; to look upon them as masters and kings. But to accept this image of the other requires that one adopt a particular image of self. If the customer is king (or queen), the employee by extension is subject, or servant. In the restaurant, a complex system of symbolism encourages customer and worker alike to approach service as an encounter between beings of vastly different social standing, with unequal claims to courtesy, consideration, and respect. Though the customer accepts the imagery of servitude and adopts an interactive posture appropriate to the role of master, the waitress rejects the role of servant in favor of images of self in which she is an active and controlling force in the service encounter. Perhaps because of this, she is able to control the feelings she experiences and expresses toward her customers, and she is neither disoriented nor self-alienated by the emotional demands of her work. . . .

Waitress as Servant

The image of waitress as servant is fostered above all by the conventions that govern interaction between server and served. Much as domestic servants in the nineteenth century did not dine with or in the presence of masters, so today waitresses are forbidden to take breaks, sit, smoke, eat, or drink in the presence of customers. At Route, employees are not allowed to consume so much as a glass of water on the floor, though they are welcome to imbibe unlimited quantities of soda and coffee out of sight of customers. The prohibition against engaging in such physically necessary acts as eating, drinking, and resting in the customer's presence functions to limit contact between server and served and fortify status lines. It is, in addition, a means of concealing the humanness of those whom one would like to deny the courtesies of personhood. When indications of the server's personhood inadvertently obtrude into the service encounter, customers may be forced to modify their interactive stance. One Route waitress commented that when her parents ate at the restaurant her customers treated her with greater respect.

> They look at me like, "Oh my God. They have *parents?*" It's sometimes like we're not human. It's like they become more friendly when my parents are there and I get better tips off them. And I've never gotten stiffed when my parents have been sitting there. . . . They see that outside of this place I am a person and I have relationships with other people. . . .

[T]he waitress is discouraged from adorning herself in a way that might appear cheap. She is also discouraged from dressing above her station. . . . The aggressively plain uniform of the waitress underscores status distinctions between those who render and those who receive service in the same way that the black dress and white cap of the nineteenth-century domestic acted as a "public announcement of subservience" (Rothman 1987: 169; Sutherland 1981: 29–30). . . . In the modern service encounter, the need to underscore the server's inferiority may be especially strong as the status differential between server and served is intrinsically tenuous. The superiority of customer to waitress is limited temporally to the duration of the encounter and spatially to the boundaries of the restaurant. Rigidly defined dress codes, which eliminate all clues of the server's nonwork status, may serve to put the customer at ease in issuing orders to one whose subordination is so narrowly defined. . . .

The linguistic conventions of the restaurant and, in particular, the unilateral use of first names, further emphasize status differences between customer and waitress. . . . [T]he unilateral use of first names signals the subordinate status of the addressee; thus, African Americans, children, and household domestics have traditionally been addressed by first names by those whom they in turn address as *sir, ma'am, Mr.* or *Mrs.*

Restaurants perpetuate this practice by requiring servers to wear name tags which, regardless of the worker's age, bear only her first name, and by requiring servers to introduce themselves by first name to each party they wait on. Waitresses generally have no access to the customer's first or last name (the customer's larger "information preserve" prohibits inquiry) and are constrained to resort to the polite address forms *sir* and *ma'am* when addressing their parties. . . .

[M]odern service organizations must be charged with actively perpetuating the conventions of servitude and, in some cases, inventing new conventions. . . . The restaurant requires the waitress to dress as a maid and introduce herself by first name . . . and the restaurant promotes the degrading term *server*. In preserving the conventions of servitude the company encourages the waitress to internalize an image of self as servant and to adopt an interactive stance consistent with this image. In promoting an image of server as servant to the public, the restaurant encourages customers to treat, or mistreat, the waitress as they would a member of a historically degraded class.

That customers embrace the service-as-servitude metaphor is evidenced by the way they speak to and about service workers. Virtually every rule of etiquette is violated by customers in their interaction with the waitress: the waitress can be interrupted; she can be addressed with the mouth full; she can be ignored and stared at; and she can be subjected to unrestrained anger. Lacking the status of a person she, like the servant, is refused the most basic considerations of polite interaction. . . .

The imagery of servitude is the most insidious and perhaps, therefore, the most dangerous of hazards the waitress encounters. It pervades every aspect of her work, pressuring her to internalize a negative perception of self and assume a corresponding posture of submission; yet, because it is symbolically conveyed and not, for the most part, explicitly advocated, it cannot be directly confronted and may not even be consciously recognized. Nevertheless, the Route waitress successfully resists the symbolism of service, counterpoising company-supported understandings of her role as servant with her own images of self as a soldier confronting enemy forces, or alternatively, as an independent businessperson, working in her own interests, on her own territory.

Waitress as Soldier

If asked, a waitress would certainly agree that waiting tables is much like doing battle, but waitresses do not voluntarily make the comparison explicit. Rather, the perception of waiting tables as waging war and accordingly, the self-perception of waitress as soldier, is expressed implicitly in the waitress's war-oriented terminology:

groups of tables under the control of individual waitresses are referred to as *stations*; the cooks' work area is referred to as the *line*; simultaneously adding several checks to the cooks' wheel is *sandbagging*; to receive many customers at once is to get *hit*; a full station or busy line is *bombed out*; old food and empty restaurants are *dead*; customers who leave no tips, *stiff*; abbreviations used by the waitress to communicate orders to the cook are *codes*; to get angry at someone is to *go off* on or *blow up at her*; to be short an item of food on an order is to *drag* the item; the number of customers served is a *customer count*; the late shift is *graveyard* or *grave*; to provide assistance to a coworker (especially a cook) is to *bail him out*. Waitresses occasionally devise new uses of the war idiom. One waitress commented that when she was pregnant she had her friend *run* the eggs while she went to throw up. Later, when the manager refused to let her go home, the waitress responded by handing him her book and walking out: "I walked off—I abandoned ship," she recalled. Explaining why she objected to a manager having an affair with a waitress, another waitress commented that managers "don't supposed to infiltrate the treaty."

Though much of this is official company terminology, it assumes the connotations of battle only in connection with the waitress's informal, and more blatantly war oriented language. To refer to the nucleus of the kitchen as the *line* does not in itself convey a sense of combat; there are assembly lines and bus lines as well as lines of fire and battle. Only when the cooks' line is regularly said to be *bombed out*, or when stations are repeatedly referred to as *getting hit*, does the battle-oriented meaning of these terms become apparent.

Several of the war idioms used by waitresses are not specific to restaurant work but are used in other occupations, or are common slang. The point here is not that the waitress's view of her work is unique, but that it is a view very different from that promoted by the physical props and interactive conventions of the restaurant. Like many people, and seemingly to a greater degree, the waitress views her work as something of a battle and those with whom her work brings her into contact as the enemy. More important, she views herself, not as a servant who peacefully surrenders to the commands of her master, but as a soldier actively returning fire on hostile forces. The waitress's capacity to sustain this self-image while donning the costume of a maid and complying with the interpersonal conventions of servitude, attests to her strength of will and power of resistance. The same may be said of all subordinate persons who are forced to resist without openly violating the symbolic order (Scott 1985: 33).

Waitress as Private Entrepreneur

During a rush, when the restaurant looks and sounds like a battle zone, the metaphor of service as war and waitress as soldier is most salient. During more peaceful periods, a different image of self assumes prominence: that of waitress as private entrepreneur. While these perceptions of self can be viewed as divergent and even opposed, both convey a sense of power and action.

Evidence that the waitress perceives herself as a private entrepreneur is found in her conceptual isolation of herself from the company and in her possessiveness toward people and things under her jurisdiction. The waitress's self isolation may be expressed relatively directly, as in the following comments of a Route waitress:

> When she [a dissatisfied customer] was getting ready to pay her check, I was ringing it up and she was asking me my name, she was asking my manager's name, she was writing down the regional office's number. So I said, "Look. Do you have a problem? I'm a grown woman. If you have a problem with me, talk to me. If you have problem with Route, call the region. Fine. If you have problem with me, talk to me."

It is also expressed in the waitress's ambivalence toward performing tasks not directly related to the business of making tips. As an independent businessperson, the waitress views her responsibilities to the company as extremely limited. The company pays her a minor retainer, but it is felt to cover few duties beyond those immediately related to waiting tables. Accordingly, *sidework* (stocking supplies and cleaning other than that involved in bussing tables) is performed by the waitress with an air of forbearance as though it were understood that such work was above the call of duty.

The term *sidework* fosters the view that these tasks are peripheral to the waitress's work, but in fact, the thorough completion of sidework duties is critical to the smooth functioning of each shift

and to peaceful relations between shifts. The failure of swing waitresses to stock chocolate fudge spells disaster for grave waitresses faced with twenty orders for sundaes and no supplies. Likewise, the neglect of grave waitresses to fill the syrup dispensers and stock butter creates chaos for the day shift. There is rarely time to stock the necessary items while waiting tables; supplies are often packed in boxes under other boxes on shelves in locked rooms or freezers; they are packaged in jumbo cans and jars, which are heavy and difficult to open; and they sometimes require heating or defrosting before they can be used. Still, stocking and cleaning for the next shift are peripheral to the waitress's work in the sense that they do not directly enhance her tip earnings, and this is the sense that is most significant for the waitress as entrepreneur.

The waitress may, in addition, consider it beyond the call of duty to intervene on the company's behalf to prevent theft of restaurant property.

> I constantly tell Hollinger [a manager] he's a jerk. Constantly. Cause he's an ass. Because, people came in and ripped off place mats on graveyard, and he came in giving me heck. . . . And I said, "Let me tell you something, Hollinger. I don't *care* if they rip off the place mats. If you want somebody to stand by the door, and by the register, then you'd better hire somebody just to do that. Cause that's not my job. I'm here to wait on the people. I take the cash. I can't be babysitting grown adults."

The place mats referred to here were being sold by Route as part of a promotional campaign; waitresses do not use place mats to set tables. The point is significant because . . . waitresses are extremely possessive of, and so likely to protect, restaurant property that they use in their work.

The waitress's tendency to isolate herself from the company, which she perceives as neither liable for her faults nor warranted in requiring her to do more than wait tables, indicates that she does not see herself as an employee in the conventional sense. . . . [H]er sense of independence is fostered by the tipping system, which releases her from financial dependence on the company, and by the circumscription of managerial authority, which indirectly augments the scope of her autonomy. At the same time, the waitress's perception that she is in business for herself may prompt her to assert her independence more strongly.

In keeping with her self-image as entrepreneur, the waitress refers to restaurant property as though it belonged to her. She speaks of *my* salt and peppers, *my* coffee, *my* napkins, *my* silverware, *my* booths, *my* catsups, *my* sugars. Linguistically, people too belong to the waitress who talks of *my* customers, *my* district manager, and *my* manager. The inclusion of managers among the waitress's possessions reflects her view of managers as individuals hired by the company to maintain satisfactory working conditions so she can conduct her business efficiently. . . .

The waitress also exhibits possessiveness in the way she treats her belongings and the belongings of others. Though she is unwilling to discourage customers from stealing company place mats, she may protect items she uses, and so regards as her own. . . . If waitresses are adamantly protective of their own property, they are equally respectful of the property of others. In the restaurant, ownership is determined by location: supplies located in a waitress's station belong to her for the duration of the shift. . . . A waitress who wishes to borrow a cowaitress's catsups, silverware, napkins, or coffee must ask to do so. If she cannot locate the owner and is in desperate and immediate need of an item, she may take it but will apologetically inform the owner as soon as possible that she "stole" the needed article. Borrowing or stealing customers is never acceptable. Apart from those rare occasions when she has obtained her co-worker's consent beforehand, a waitress will not take the order of a party seated in a co-worker's station no matter how frantically the customers wave menus, or how impatiently they glare at passing employees. If, as frequently happens, the "owner" of the party has disappeared, or if there is some confusion concerning the party's ownership, a waitress will search the corners of the restaurant and question every employee in an effort to locate or identify the rightful owner, rather than take the order herself and risk being accused of theft. Indeed, waitresses avoid becoming involved with their co-workers' customers, even in the interest in lending assistance. One waitress recalled that a co-waitress and friend had been caught in the cross fire of a customer food fight and had been doused with orange soda. Asked if she had intervened on behalf of her friend and reprimanded the customers, the waitress responded, "No. I didn't say nothing. Cause that's Mary's people." . . .

Freedom of Emotion

As she resists company efforts to influence her perception of self, so the waitress maintains control over the emotions she experiences and, to some degree, expresses in the service encounter. The waitress may adopt a submissive or energetically friendly manner toward those she serves, but she recognizes this manipulation of self as a means of manipulating the other. The boundary between front and backstage, between manufactured and spontaneous emotion, remains distinct; even in the midst of a performance the waitress does not lose herself in her role or lose sight of her objective.

> This is my motto: "You sit in my station at Route, I'll sell you the world. I'll tell you anything you want to hear." Last night I had this guy, wanted my phone number. He was driving me nuts. And I wasn't interested. . . . He goes, "Well, how come you and your husband broke up?" I said, "Well, he found out about my boyfriend and got mad. I don't know. I don't understand it myself." And he started laughing. And I'm thinking, "*This is my money.* I'll tell you anything." . . . I got five bucks out of him. He didn't get my phone number but *I got my five-dollar tip.* I'll sell you the world if you're in my station. (emphasis added)

The waitress does not sell her customer the world, only a moment of cheerful banter and an illusion of friendship. For this sale she is adequately compensated: "I got my five-dollar tip"—as though she had settled beforehand on a fair price for her illusion.

The success of such an encounter is not measured by monetary rewards alone, however. For the waitress as for all social actors, skillful dissimulation may be an exercise in autonomy, an expression of control. . . . The degree of control the waitress maintains over her inner state is suggested by the ease with which she turns on and off the facade of subservience or conviviality: a smile become a sneer even as she turns away from the table; "yes, ma'am, yes sir" become vehement expletives as soon as she disappears behind the lines.

> I can cuss like a wizard now. Because when they get on your nerves you go in the back and before you know it you saying, "You motherfucker, you God damn bastard, you

blue-eyed faggot" . . . I came out with some names I ain't never thought I knew.

Many servers commented that waitressing had made them tougher and had, in addition, altered their perception of the public.

It's changed me a lot. I have less patience with the public. I found out how rude and cruel people today are . . . I seen two faces of the public, and I don't like it. I don't like their evil side. . . . After you been working with the public for X amount of years, you start seeing the good and the bad in people, and the bad outweighs the good. . . .

As the waitress comes to see the public in an increasingly negative light, she comes to interpret her customers' rudeness and impatience, like their low tips, as evidence of their "evil side," and not a reflection on her waitressing or social skill. In turn, she becomes less willing to tolerate impatience and irritation which she no longer accepts responsibility for provoking. In terms of her own idiom of war, the waitress claims the right to return fire on what she has come to regard as inherently aggressive, hostile forces.

The worst experience I had as far as customer was when I worked graveyard and a family came in . . . two girls and a man and a woman. She obviously was a foreigner, cause she spoke broken English. . . . And she was very rude, very nasty to me. . . . First thing that she did when she sat down was complain. From the time she sat down to the time they ended up walking out, she complained left and right. And she embarrassed me. She tried to embarrass me. She tried everything in the book. She degraded me. But I stood up to her, and I wouldn't let that happen. I stood up to her regardless of whether they were customers, regardless of whether I lost my job. Nobody's going to degrade me like that because I'm a waitress. . . . And then she started getting loud. And boisterous . . . I said, "Look." And then I put my book down. I slammed my book down. I put my pen on the table . . . I said, "Look. If you can do a better job than me, then you write your damn order down yourself and I'll bring it back to the kitchen. When it's ready I'll let you know, and you go back and pick it up." *Then* she called me a foreigner. And that's when the shit hit the fan. I said, "How dare you have the gall to call me a foreigner? *You're* the one that's in America. *You're* the foreigner. The problem with you foreigners, is *you* come in

this country and *you* try to boot Americans out of their *own* jobs, their *own* homes, and you try and take over this country." I said, "Don't you *ever* call me a foreigner, lady. Because I'll take you right by your collar now. I don't care whether I lose my job or not." *Then* she stared cursing at me, and then I cursed right back at her. . . . Then she started arguing with her husband. . . . Called him a MF, bad, bad, vulgar language, right? . . . And he said, "If you call me that one more time . . . I'm going to knock you right in your MFing mouth. And I'll put you on the ground in front of everybody." And she deserved it, and when he said it, I applauded him. I said, "Boy, I'll tell you. If I was married to a bitch like her, I would have knocked her out a long time ago." And he just smiled at me and turned around and walked out.

The waitress slams down her book immediately before releasing her anger on the woman, thereby signaling that she is no longer willing to play the role of compliant servant; she is going to take a stand as a person. In breaking character and expressing her anger she defies company- and customer-supported conceptions of the waitress as one obligated to endure mistreatment at the hands of her supposed social betters. . . .

Another waitress recounted the following episode . . .

I had brought out this lady's chicken fried steak and the middle wasn't cooked enough for her. . . . Instead of her saying, "Ma'am, would you please take this back to the kitchen and have it cooked a little bit more?" she slide that shit over to me and said, "You take this shit back in the kitchen cause it ain't cooked." I turn around to her, I said, "Who the Hell you think you're talking to?" I said, "Do you know who you're talking to?" I said, "Do I look like one of your children? Cause if I do, you better take another look. Now I can understand that you upset cause the middle of your chicken ain't done. . . . But. In the same token, I think you better learn to tone that voice of yours down. Cause you don't talk to me or nobody else like that." "Well" [the woman said], "I don't have to take this. I talk to the mana"—I said, "Damn you, lady, you talk to any damn person you want to talk to." Cause by that time I'd about had it. She [could] kiss my ass far as I was concerned.

[This comment] illustrate[s] the waitress's concern with contesting the belief that a server who is rude to a customer will lose her job. The waitress who related the incident above described the customer's view as follows:

> They figure they say what they want and do what they want; figure you might be afraid to say anything. . . . You know, "She ain't going to say nothing because . . . I go to the boss and tell her boss and she'll lose her job, so she ain't going to say nothing to me.

When assumptions like these surface, in the form of rudeness or threats to contact supervisors, the waitress responds by informing the customer or demonstrating by her actions that she is confident no action will be taken against her.

The following exchange concluded a heated interchange between a waitress and customer regarding the waitress's failure to remember that the customer's boyfriend had not ordered sausage with his breakfast. Note that the waitress volunteers her name to the customer underscoring her lack of concern with being reported. . . .

> She [the customer] said, "Well, I would like to call in the morning and talk to your manager." I said, "Fine. My name is Mae Merrin. You can call him. I been here seven years. I ain't going nowhere. Especially over a couple pieces of meat."

Regardless of whether the waitress directly confronts the issue of her own expendability, her decision to retaliate against an offensive customer challenges the view that she, like a servant, is constrained to submit to abuse as part of her job. The promptness and intensity of her reaction indicate the degree to which this conception diverges from her own perception of self as an independent, but to the company indispensable, businessperson.

Hazards of Personality Control

. . . While interpersonal activity may always and everywhere have demanded maintenance of a facade, individuals are increasingly pressured to experience, rather than merely express appropriate emotions. In *The Managed Heart*, Hochschild (1983) proposes that organizations are no longer content that their workers engage in surface acting, which relies on technical maneuvers to portray feelings, and in which "the body, not the soul, is the main tool of the trade" (1983: 37). Today, workers are encouraged to engage in deep or method acting, in which the worker draws on a reservoir of "emotion memories" to produce an appropriate response (empathy, cheerfulness) for a given role and scene. Toward this end, workers are urged to adopt a view of the service encounter and of the consumer that will evoke a suitable interactive stance. Flight attendants are counseled to look upon the cabin as a living room and passengers as guests, and to regard difficult passengers as children who need attention. The assumption is that flight attendants will feel sincerely sympathetic with passengers they perceive as guests or children and will not be inclined to reciprocate their anger or impatience (Hochschild 1983).

By furnishing the waitress with the script, costume, and backdrop of a servant, the restaurant encourages her to become absorbed in her role or, in Hochschild's terms, to engage in deep acting. In so doing, the company may hope to enhance the authenticity of the performance and reduce the possibility that the server will break character and express emotions incongruous with the role she is expected to play. As one perceives herself as a servant, the waitress should willingly abdicate her claim to the courtesies of interaction between equals; she should absorb abuse with no thought of retaliation; she should fulfill requests however trivial and unreasonable, and accept blame however misdirected, because as a servant it is her job to do so. . . .

More than anything else, the waitress's ability to withstand the symbolic machinery of her work without suffering emotional estrangement testifies to her power of resistance. Though constrained to comply with the interactive conventions of master and servant, while clad in a domestic's uniform, the waitress does not internalize an image of service as servitude and self as servant. In times of stress she sees her work as war and herself as soldier. In times of peace she sees her work as a private enterprise and herself as entrepreneur. Like all social actors, the waitress monitors her projected personality and manipulates her feelings in the course of social interaction, but she does so knowingly and in her own interests. This manipulation of self does not induce self-alienation or emotional disorientation. The waitress distinguishes clearly between emotions expressed in order to please or appease a potential tipper, and emotions that arise spontaneously and are genuine. With experience her ability to separate front and backstage expressions of subservience and conviviality increases and she may silently applaud her powers of deception even as she stands before her audience of customers. To some extent, too, the waitress determines the degree to which she is willing to put up with rudeness in the interests of protecting a potential tip. . . .

Here . . . the intention has not been to deny that waitressing and other direct-service jobs are emotionally taxing and exploitive. Work that regularly provokes outbursts of anger and engenders an embittered view of those with whom one must daily interact, off and on the job, is both injurious and in the strictest sense, coercive. It has also not been the purpose of this discussion to exonerate organizations that perpetuate rituals of deference that threaten the dignity and deny the personhood of those who serve. Though the waitress rejects the symbolic implications of these rituals, her customers do not. The symbolism of service encourages the customer to assume the posture of master to servant, with all accompanying rights of irrationality, condescension, and unrestrained anger. The resulting conflict of perspectives is a constant source of friction between server and served, friction that diminishes the quality of the waitress's work environment and periodically erupts into open fire.

The aim of this discussion has been to explore the ways in which the waitress confronts the emotionally coercive demands of her work. . . . Route waitresses demonstrate that women may respond to the adverse conditions of their work not merely in the passive sense of suffering injuries, but in actively resisting, reformulating, or rejecting the coercive forces they encounter. Like the flight attendant, the waitress is pressured to see and feel about her work in company-endorsed ways; and like the flight attendant, she has little influence over the setting of the stage on which she must act out her work role. And yet the waitress

does not overextend herself into her work, and when she distances herself from her job she does not "feel bad about it." . . .

This investigation has sought to avoid the view that women are resigned to their subjection by examining structure and strategy as interlocking systems, adopting a more comprehensive understanding of action, and reformulating conventional questions about women and work. . . . Rather than ask, *Why are women passive?* we have asked, *How are they active?* In adopting this approach the intent has not been to downplay the difficulties of the waitress's position or deny the need for structural reform that would ensure her greater financial security and eliminate the coercive symbolism of service. Rather, the goal has been to balance pervasive images of female submission and passivity with a glimpse of defiance. . . .

References

Hochschild, Arlie. 1983. *The Managed Heart: Commercialization of Human Feeling.* Berkeley: University of California Press.

Rothman, Robert A. 1987. "Direct-Service Work and Housework." In *Working: Sociological Perspectives.* Englewood, Cliffs, NJ: Prentice Hall.

Scott, James C. 1985. *Weapons of the Weak: Everyday Forms of Peasant Resistance.* New Haven, CT: Yale University Press.

Sutherland, Daniel E. 1981. *Americans and Their Servants: Domestic Service in the United States from 1800 to 1920.* Baton Rouge: Louisiana State University Press.

Part VIII

The Construction of Social Structures

The selections in the previous section examined various ways that social structures profoundly influence individuals' subjective experiences, interactions, relationships, and fates. However, the authors also implied that social structures endure because they are interactionally reproduced. Although social structures often seem self perpetuating, they are perpetuated by individuals who engage in recurrent patterns of interaction. Individuals may experience social structures as an external environment as powerfully constraining as the physical environment, but social structures are quite unlike the physical environment. Their power does not come from nature but from human definition and collective action. They are humanly created and re-created. The selections in this section examine the interactional creation, accomplishment, perpetuation, and redefinition of different types and dimensions of social structure. They remind us that we humans organize and structure our own social lives. Some of us may influence those processes more than others, but we all participate. ✦

28

Society in Action

Herbert Blumer

Herbert Blumer was an important proponent and contributor to the sociological perspective of "symbolic interactionism," a name that he himself gave to it. This approach to the study of social life grew out of George Herbert Mead's ideas about the human self, thought, and interaction. As you may recall, Mead argued that individuals interact with themselves much as they interact with one another. They continually engage in an inner conversation. Rather than blindly responding, they define and interpret their experience. Their action and interaction is symbolic and meaningful.

Blumer argues that the study of social life must start from Mead's basic insights. Human social life is a continual process of individual and collective definition and interpretation. Society, culture, and social structure are not static things but are derived from what people do. And what people do is engage in symbolic interaction, both with one another and with themselves. Through processes of definition and interpretation, humans fit their individual lines of action together and construct joint actions. As Blumer further argues, students of social life cannot afford to ignore the fact that even the action of such human collectivities as societies, nations, and organizations are based on processes of definition, interpretation, and symbolic interaction.

Blumer draws three lessons about the study of social life from this basic insight. First, no matter how stable and orderly, social life is always subject to the "play and fate of meaning." Recurrent patterns of interaction and collective action are based on definitions and interpretations that may change unpredictably. Second, the networks of joint action that are often called "social institutions" are not self-governing and self-sustaining entities, but rather are sustained by human interaction and are governed by human definition and interpretation. Third, the construction of joint action is based on understandings and meanings that emerge from prior interaction. No matter how new they may seem, they have a history. These are the specifications of Blumer's more general lesson: social structures, cultures, institutions, and societies exist only in human action and interac-

tion. Thus, human action and interaction are what students of social life must ultimately study.

Human groups . . . [consist] of human beings who are engaging in action. The action consists of the multitudinous activities that the individuals perform in their lives as they encounter one another and as they deal with the succession of situations confronting them. The individuals may act singly, they may act collectively, and they may act on behalf of, or as representatives of, some organization or group of others. The activities belong to the acting individuals and are carried on by them always with regard to the situations in which they have to act. The import of this simple and essentially redundant characterization is that fundamentally human groups or society *exists in action* and must be seen in terms of action. This picture of human society as action must be the starting point (and the point of return) for any scheme that purports to treat and analyze human society empirically. Conceptual schemes that depict society in some other fashion can only be derivations from the complex of ongoing activity that constitutes group life. This is true of the two dominant conceptions of society in contemporary sociology—that of culture and that of social structure. Culture as a conception, whether defined as custom, tradition, norm, value, rules, or such like, is clearly derived from what people do. Similarly, social structure in any of its aspects, as represented by such terms as social position, status, role, authority, and prestige, refers to relationships derived from how people act toward each other. The life of any human society consists necessarily of an ongoing process of fitting together the activities of its members. It is this complex of ongoing activity that establishes and portrays structure or organization. . . .

The central place and importance of symbolic interaction in human group life and conduct should be apparent. A human society or group consists of people in association. Such association exists necessarily in the form of people acting toward one another and thus engaging in social interaction. Such interaction in human society is characteristically and predominantly on the symbolic level; as individuals acting individually, collectively, or as agents of some organization encounter one another, they are necessarily required to take account of the actions of one another as they form their own action. They do this by a dual process of indicating to others how to act and of interpreting the indications made by others. Human group life is a vast process of such defining to others what to do and of interpreting their definitions; through this process, people come to fit their activities to one another and to form their own individual conduct. Both such joint activity and individual conduct are formed *in* and *through* this ongoing process; they are not mere expressions or products of what people bring to their interaction or of conditions that are antecedent to their interaction. The failure to accommodate to this vital point constitutes the fundamental deficiency of schemes that seek to account for human society in terms of social organization or psychological factors, or of any combination of the two. By virtue of symbolic interaction, human group life is necessarily a formative process and not a mere arena for the expression of pre existing factors.

Human beings must have a makeup that fits the nature of social interaction. The human being is . . . an organism that not only responds to others on the non-symbolic level but as one that makes indications to others and interprets their indications. He can do this, as Mead has shown so emphatically, only by virtue of possessing a "self." Nothing esoteric is meant by this expression. It means merely that a human being can be an object of his own action. Thus, he can recognize himself, for instance, as being a man, young in age, a student, in debt, trying to become a doctor, coming from an undistinguished family, and so forth. In all such instances, he is an object to himself; and he acts toward himself and guides himself in his actions toward others on the basis of the kind of object he is to himself. . . .

[T]he fact that the human being has a self . . . enables him to interact with himself. This interaction is not in the form of interaction between two or more parts of a psychological system, as between needs, or between emotions, or between ideas, or between the id and the ego in the Freudian scheme. Instead, the interaction is social—a form of communication, with the person addressing himself as a person and responding thereto. We can clearly recognize such interaction in ourselves, as each of us notes that he is angry with himself, or that he has to spur himself on in his tasks, or that he reminds himself to do this or that,

or that he is talking to himself in working out some plan of action. As such instances suggest, self-interaction exists fundamentally as a process of making indications to oneself. . . .

The capacity of the human being to make indications to himself gives a distinctive character to human action. It means that the human individual confronts a world that he must interpret in order to act instead of an environment to which he responds because of his organization. He has to cope with the situations in which he is called on to act, ascertaining the meaning of the actions of others and mapping out his own line of action in the light of such interpretation. He has to construct and guide his action instead of merely releasing it in response to factors playing on him or operating through him. He may do a miserable job in constructing his action, but he has to construct it. . . .

This view of human action applies equally well to joint or collective action, in which numbers of individuals are implicated. Joint or collective action constitutes the domain of sociological concern, as exemplified in the behavior of groups, institutions, organizations, and social classes. Such instances of societal behavior, whatever they may be, consist of individuals fitting their lines of action to one another. It is both proper and possible to view and study such behavior in its joint or collective character instead of in its individual components. Such joint behavior does not lose its character of being constructed through an interpretive process in meeting the situations in which the collectivity is called on to act. Whether the collectivity be an army engaged in a campaign, a corporation seeking to expand its operations, or a nation trying to correct an unfavorable balance of trade, it needs to construct its action through an interpretation of what is happening in its area of operation. The interpretive process takes place by participants making indications to one another, not merely each to himself. Joint or collective action is an outcome of such a process of interpretative interaction.

As stated earlier, human group life consists of, and exists in, the fitting of lines of action to each other by the members of the group. Such articulation of lines of action gives rise to and constitutes "joint action"—a societal organization of conduct of different acts of diverse participants. A joint action, while made up of diverse component acts that enter into its formation, is different from any one of them and from their mere aggregation. The joint action has a distinctive character in its own right, a character that lies in the articulation or linkage as apart from what may be articulated or linked. Thus, the joint action may be identified as such and may be spoken of and handled without having to break it down into the separate acts that comprise it. This is what we do when we speak of such things as marriage, a trading transaction, war, a parliamentary discussion, or a church service. Similarly, we can speak of the collectivity that engages in joint action without having to identify the individual members of that collectivity, as we do in speaking of a family, a business corporation, a church, a university, or a nation. . . .

In dealing with collectivities and with joint action, one can easily be trapped in an erroneous position by failing to recognize that the joint action of the collectivity is an interlinkage of the separate acts of the participants. This failure leads one to overlook the fact that a joint action always has to undergo a process of formation; even though it may be a well-established and repetitive form of social action, each instance of it has to be formed anew. Further, this career of formation through which it comes into being necessarily takes place through the dual process of designation and interpretation that was discussed above. The participants still have to guide their respective acts by forming and using meanings.

With these remarks as a background, I wish to make three observations on the implications of the interlinkage that constitutes joint action. I wish to consider first those instances of joint action that are repetitive and stable. The preponderant portion of social action in a human society, particularly in a settled society, exists in the form of recurrent patterns of joint action. In most situations in which people act toward one another, they have in advance a firm understanding of how to act and of how other people will act. They share common and pre-established meanings of what is expected in the action of the participants, and accordingly each participant is able to guide his own behavior by such meanings. Instances of repetitive and pre-established forms of joint action are so frequent and common that it is easy to understand why scholars have viewed them as the essence or natural form of human group life. Such a view is especially apparent in the concepts of "culture" and "social order" that are so dominant in social-science literature. Most sociological schemes rest on the belief that a human society exists in the form of an established order of living, with that order resolvable into adherence to sets of rules, norms, values, and sanctions that specify to people how they are to act in their different situations.

Several comments are in order with regard to this neat scheme. First, it is just not true that the full expanse of life in a human society, any human society, is but an expression of pre-established forms of joint action. New situations are constantly arising within the scope of group life that are problematic and for which existing rules are inadequate. I have never heard of any society that was free of problems nor any society in which members did not have to engage in discussion to work out ways of action. Such areas of unprescribed conduct are just as natural, indigenous, and recurrent in human group life as are those areas covered by pre-established and faithfully followed prescriptions of joint action. Second, we have to recognize that even in the case of pre-established and repetitive joint action, each instance of such joint action has to be formed anew. The participants still have to build up their lines of action and fit them to one another through the dual process of designation and interpretation. They do this in the case of repetitive joint action, of course, by using the same recurrent and constant meanings. If we recognize this, we are forced to realize that the play and fate of meanings are what is important, not the joint action in its established form. Repetitive and stable joint action is just as much a result of an interpretative process as is a new form of joint action that is being developed for the first time. This is not an idle or pedantic point; the meanings that underlie established and recurrent joint action are themselves subject to pressure as well as to reinforcement, to incipient dissatisfaction as well as to indifference; they may be challenged as well as affirmed, allowed to slip along without concern as well as subjected to infusions of new vigor. Behind the facade of the objectively perceived joint action, the set of meanings that sustains that joint action has a life that the social scientists can ill afford to ignore. A gratuitous acceptance of the concepts of norms, values, social rules, and the like should not blind [us] to the fact that any one of them is subtended by a process of social interaction—a process that is necessary not only for their change but equally well for their retention in a fixed form. It is the social process in group life that creates and upholds the rules, not the rules that create and uphold group life.

The second observation on the interlinkage that constitutes joint action refers to the extended connection of actions that make up so much of human group life. We are familiar with these large complex networks of action involving an interlinkage and interdependency of diverse actions of diverse people—as in the division of labor extending from the growing of grain by the farmer to an eventual sale of bread in a store, or in the elaborate chain extending from the arrest of a suspect to his eventual release from a penitentiary. These networks with their regularized participation of diverse people by diverse action at diverse points yields a picture of institutions that have been appropriately a major concern of sociologists. They also give substance to the idea that human group life has the character of a system. In seeing such a large complex of diversified activities, all hanging together in a regularized operation, and in seeing the complementary organization of participants in well-knit interdependent relationships, it is easy to understand why so many scholars view such networks or institutions as self-operating entities, following their own dynamics and not requiring that attention be given to the participants within the network. Most of the sociological analyses of institutions and social organization adhere to this view. Such adherence, in my judgment, is a serious mistake. One should recognize what is true, namely, that the diverse array of participants, occupying different points in the network, engage in their actions at those points on the basis of using given sets of meanings. A network or an institution does not function automatically because of some inner dynamics or system requirements; it functions because people at different points do something, and what they do is a result of how they define the situation in which they are called on to act. A limited appreciation of this point is reflected today in some of the work on decision-making, but on the whole the point is grossly ignored. It is necessary to recognize that the sets of meanings that lead participants to act as they do at their stationed points in the network have their own setting in a localized process of social interaction—and that these meanings are formed, sustained, weakened, strengthened, or transformed, as the case may be, through a socially defining process. Both the functioning and the fate of institutions are set by this process of interpretation as it takes place among the diverse sets of participants.

A third important observation needs to be made, namely, that any instance of joint action, whether newly formed or long established, has necessarily arisen out of a background of previous actions of the participants. A new kind of joint action never comes into existence apart from such a background. The participants involved in the formation of the new joint action always bring to that formation the world of objects, the sets of meanings, and the schemes of interpretation that they already possess. Thus, the new form of joint action always emerges out of and is connected with a context of previous joint action. . . .

[H]uman society [is] people engaged in living. Such living is a process of ongoing activity in which participants are developing lines of action in the multitudinous situations they encounter. They are caught up in a vast process of interaction in which they have to fit their developing actions to one another. This process of interaction consists in making indications to others of what to do and in interpreting the indications as made by others. . . . This general process should be seen, of course, in the differentiated character which it necessarily has by virtue of the fact that people cluster in different groups, belong to different associations, and occupy different positions. They accordingly approach each other differently, live in different worlds, and guide themselves by different sets of meanings. Nevertheless, whether one is dealing with a family, a boy's gang, an industrial corporation, or a political party, one must see the activities of the collectivity as being formed through a process of designation and interpretation.

Reprinted from: Herbert Blumer, *Symbolic Interactionism: Perspective and Method*, pp. 6–7, 10, 12–13, 15, 16–20. Copyright © 1998. Reprinted by permission of Prentice Hall, Inc., Upper Saddle River, NJ. ✦

29

Borderwork Among Girls and Boys

Barrie Thorne

Gender is one of the most fundamental dimensions of the social structure of all known human societies. Yet gender is as much a human creation as any other dimension of social structure. Anatomical sex may be a natural fact of human life, but its meanings are not. It is these meanings, rather than reproductive biology, that constitute gender. Femininity and masculinity are as much products of human definition, interpretation, and interaction as any other human meanings. In this selection, Barrie Thorne examines the construction and reproduction of gender among elementary-school children. She concentrates on a recurrent pattern of interaction that she calls "borderwork."

An earlier selection noted that most children define themselves as either a boy or girl during the preschool-age years. Once they do, they tend to prefer the company of "their own kind." The result is a kind of self-imposed segregation between girls and boys. Boys tend to play with other boys and girls tend to play with other girls. Although girls and boys do continue to interact with one another, much of that interaction serves to erect, rather than break down, the invisible symbolic barrier between them. This kind of interaction is what constitutes the borderwork pattern.

Thorne examines three varieties of borderwork: chasing games, such as "chase-and-kiss"; rituals of pollution, such as "cooties"; and invasions, usually of girls' activities and territories by boys. As she demonstrates, these familiar and memorable forms of interaction create gender divisions and perpetuate prevailing gender stereotypes. When engaged in borderwork, girls and boys treat each other as members of opposing, if not antagonistic, teams. Their gender identities take priority over their personal identities. For example, a boy who is being chased by a girl is much more likely to exclaim, "Help, a girl's chasing me!" than "Help, Susie's chasing me!" They also tend to lump all boys and all girls together. "Boys are mean." "Girls have cooties." They thereby exaggerate gender difference and perpetuate gender stereotypes.

Thorne suggests that interaction between men and women often resembles the borderwork of school-age children, in that adults also enact gender stereotypes and exaggerate gender difference. Like boys and girls, men and women interactionally produce and reproduce their gender and the often rocky relations between the sexes. And what is interactionally produced can be interactionally changed. Gender—the meanings of anatomical sex—is not imposed on us by nature or social structure. To borrow from Blumer, our femininity and masculinity are derived from what we do, not from what we are.

My husband, Peter, and I became parents several years after I had . . . started to teach and do research on gender. . . . Parenting returned me to the sites of childhood—the Lilliputian worlds of sandboxes, neighborhood hideouts, playgrounds, elementary-school lunchrooms. I found that these sites, that the sheer presence of groups of children, evoked memories of my own childhood. . . . Those memories, and my experiences as a parent, whetted my interest in learning, more systematically, about girls' and boys' daily experiences of gender. I decided to hang out in an elementary school, keeping regular notes on my observations, especially of boys' and girls' relationships with one another. . . .

During the 1976-77 school year, I observed for eight months in a public elementary school in a small city on the coast of California. I gained initial access to this school, which I will call Oceanside (all names of places and people have been changed), through the teacher of a combined fourth-fifth-grade class. I regularly observed in Miss Bailey's classroom and accompanied the students into the lunchroom and onto the playground, where I roamed freely and got to know other kids as well.

In 1980, when I was living in Michigan, I did another stint of fieldwork, observing for three months in Ashton School, my pseudonym for a public elementary school on the outskirts of a large city. . . . In addition to observing in an Ashton kindergarten and a second-grade classroom, I roamed around the lunchroom, hallways, and playground. This experience helped me broaden and gain perspective on the more focused and in-depth observations from the California school. . . .

Borderwork

Walking across a school playground from the paved areas where kids play jump rope and hop-scotch to the grassy playing field and games of soccer and baseball, one moves from groups of girls to groups of boys. The spatial separation of boys and girls constitutes a kind of boundary, per-haps felt most strongly by individuals who want to join an activity controlled by the other gender. When girls and boys are together in a relaxed and integrated way, playing a game of handball or eat-ing and talking together at a table in the lunch-room, the sense of gender as boundary often dis-solves. But sometimes girls and boys come together in ways that emphasize their opposition; boundaries may be created through contact as well as avoidance.

The term "borderwork" helps conceptualize interaction across—yet, interaction based on and even strengthening—gender boundaries. This no-tion comes from Fredrik Barth's [1969] analysis of social relations that are maintained across eth-nic boundaries (e.g., between the Saami, or Lapps, and Norwegians) without diminishing the participants' sense of cultural difference and of dichotomized ethnic status. Barth focuses on more macro, ecological arrangements, whereas I emphasize face-to-face behavior. But the insight is similar: *although contact sometimes undermines and reduces an active sense of difference, groups may also interact with one another in ways that strengthen their borders.* One can gain insight into the mainte-nance of ethnic (and gender) groups by examin-ing the boundary that defines them rather than by looking at what Barth calls "the cultural stuff that it encloses" [Barth 1969, p. 15].

When gender boundaries are activated, the loose aggregation "boys and girls" consolidates into "the boys" and "the girls" as separate and rei-fied groups. In the process, categories of identity, that on other occasions have minimal relevance for interaction, become the basis of separate col-lectivities. Other social definitions get squeezed out by heightened awareness of gender as a di-chotomy and of "the girls" and "the boys" as op-posite and even antagonistic sides. Several times I watched this process of transformation, which felt like a heating up of the encounter because of the heightened sense of opposition and conflict.

On a paved area of the Oceanside playground, a game of team handball took shape (team hand-ball resembles doubles tennis, with clenched fists used to serve and return a rubber ball). Kevin ar-rived with the ball, and, seeing potential action, Tony walked over with interest on his face. Rita and Neera already stood on the other side of the yellow painted line that designated the center of a playing court. Neera called out, "Okay, me and Rita against you two," as Kevin and Tony moved into position. The game began in earnest with serves and returns punctuated by game-related talk—challenges between the opposing teams ("You're out!" "No, exactly on the line") and sup-portive comments between team members ("Sorry, Kevin," Tony said, when he missed a shot; "That's okay," Kevin replied). The game pro-ceeded for about five minutes, and then the ball went out of bounds. Neera ran after it, and Tony ran after her, as if to begin a chase. As he ran, Rita shouted with annoyance, "C'mon, let's play." Tony and Neera returned to their positions, and the game continued.

Then Tony slammed the ball, hard, at Rita's feet. She became angry at the shift from the ongo-ing, more cooperative mode of play, and she flashed her middle finger at the other team, call-ing to Sheila to join their side. The game contin-ued in a serious vein until John ran over and joined Kevin and Tony, who cheered; then Bill ar-rived, and there was more cheering. Kevin called out, "C'mon Ben," to draw in another passing boy; then Kevin added up the numbers on each side, looked across the yellow line, and trium-phantly announced, "We got five and you got three." The game continued, more noisy than be-fore, with the boys yelling "wee haw" each time they made a shot. The girls—and that's how they now seemed, since the sides were increasingly de-fined in terms of gender—called out, "Bratty boys! Sissy boys!" When the ball flew out of bounds, the game dissolved, as Tony and Kevin began to chase after Sheila. Annoyed by all these changes, Rita had already stomped off.

In this sequence, an earnest game, with no commentary on the fact that boys and girls hap-pened to be on different sides, gradually trans-formed into a charged sense of girls-against-boys/boys-against-the-girls. Initially, one definition of the situation prevailed: a game of team handball, with each side trying to best the other. Rita, who wanted to play a serious game, objected to the first hint of other possibilities, which emerged when Tony chased Neera. The frame of a team handball game continued but was altered and eventually overwhelmed when the kids began to evoke gender boundaries. These boundaries brought in other possibilities—piling on players to outnumber the other gender, yelling gender-based insults, shifting from handball to cross-gender chasing—which finally broke up the game.

Gender boundaries have a shifting presence, but when evoked, they are accompanied by stylized forms of action, a sense of performance, mixed and ambiguous meanings . . . and by an array of intense emotions—excitement, playful elation, anger, desire, shame, and fear. . . . These stylized moments evoke recurring themes that are deeply rooted in our cultural conceptions of gender, and they suppress awareness of patterns that contradict and qualify them. . . .

Chasing

Cross-gender chasing dramatically affirms boundaries between boys and girls. The basic elements of chase and elude, capture and rescue are found in various kinds of tag with formal rules, as well as in more casual episodes of chasing that punctuate life on playgrounds. These episodes begin with a provocation, such as taunts ("You creep!" "You can't get me!"), bodily pokes, or the grabbing of a hat or other possession. A provocation may be ignored, protested ("Leave me alone!"), or responded to by chasing. Chaser and chased may then alternate roles. Christine Finnan (1982), who also observed schoolyard chasing sequences, notes that chases vary in the ratio of chasers to chased (e.g., one chasing one, or five chasing two), the form of provocation (a taunt or a poke); the outcome (an episode may end when the chased outdistances the chaser, with a brief touch, wrestling to the ground, or the recapturing of a hat or a ball); and in use of space (there may or may not be safety zones). Kids sometimes weave chasing with elaborate shared fantasies, as when a group of Ashton first- and second-grade boys played "jail," with "cops" chasing after "robbers," or when several third-grade girls designated a "kissing dungeon" beneath the playground slide and chased after boys to try to throw them in. When they captured a boy and put him in the dungeon under the slide, two girls would guard

him while other boys pushed through the guards to help the captured boy escape.

Chasing has a gendered structure. Boys frequently chase one another, an activity that often ends in wrestling and mock fights. When girls chase girls, they are usually less physically aggressive; for example, they less often wrestle one another to the ground or try to bodily overpower the person being chased. Unless organized as a formal game like "freeze tag," same-gender chasing goes unnamed and usually undiscussed. But children set apart cross-gender chasing with special names. Students at both Oceanside and Ashton most often talked about "girls-chase-the-boys" and "boys-chase-the-girls"; the names are largely interchangeable, although boys tend to use the former and girls the latter, each claiming a kind of innocence. At Oceanside, I also heard both boys and girls refer to "catch-and-kiss"; and, at Ashton, older boys talked about "kiss-or-kill," younger girls invited one another to "catch boys," and younger girls and boys described the game of "kissin'." In addition to these terms, I have heard reports from other U.S. schools of "the chase," "chasers," "chase-and-kiss," "kiss-chase," and "kissers-and-chasers." The names vary by region and school but always contain both gender and sexual meanings.

Most informal within-gender chasing does not live on in talk unless something unusual happens, like an injury. But cross-gender chasing, especially when it takes the form of extended sequences with more than a few participants, is often surrounded by lively discussion. Several parents have told me about their kindergarten or first-grade children coming home from school to excitedly, or sometimes disgustedly, describe "girls-chase-the-boys" (my children also did this when they entered elementary school). Verbal retellings and assessments take place not only at home but also on the playground. For example, three Ashton fourth-grade girls who claimed time-out from boys-chase-the-girls by running to a declared safety zone, excitedly talked about the ongoing game: "That guy is mean, he hits everybody." "I kicked him in the butt."

In girls-chase-the-boys, girls and boys become, by definition, separate teams. Gender terms blatantly override individual identities, especially in references to the other team ("Help, a girl's chasin' me!" "C'mon Sarah, let's get that boy!" "Tony, help save me from the girls!"). Individuals may call for help from, or offer help to, others of their gender. And in acts of treason, they may grab someone from their team and turn them over to the other side. For example, in an elaborate chasing scene among a group of Ashton third-graders, Ryan grabbed Billy from behind, wrestling him to the ground. "Hey girls, get 'im," Ryan called.

Boys more often mix episodes of cross-gender with same-gender chasing, a pattern strikingly evident in the large chasing scenes or melees that recurred on the segment of the Ashton playground designated for third- and fourth-graders. Of the three age-divided playground areas, this was the most bereft of fixed equipment; it had only a handball court and, as a boy angrily observed to me, "two stinkin' monkey bars." Movable play equipment was also in scarce supply; the balls were often lodged on the school roof, and, for a time, the playground aides refused to hand out jump ropes because they said the kids just wanted to use them to "strangle and give ropeburns." With little to do, many of the students spent recesses and the lunch hour milling and chasing around on the grassy field. Boys ran after, tackled, and wrestled one another on the ground, sometimes so fiercely that injuries occurred. Girls also chased girls, although less frequently and with far less bodily engagement than among boys. Cross-gender chases, in every sort of numeric combination, were also less physically rough than chasing among boys; girls were quick to complain, and the adult aides intervened more quickly when a boy and a girl wrestled on the ground. Cross-gender chasing was full of verbal hostility, from both sides, and it was marked by stalking postures and girls' screams and retreats to spots of safety and talk.

In cross-gender and same-gender chasing, girls often create safety zones, a designated space that they can enter to become exempt from the fray. After a period of respite, often spent discussing what has just happened, they return to the game. The safety zone is sometimes a moving area around an adult; more than once, as I stood watching, my bubble of personal space housed several girls. Or the zone may be more fixed, like the pretend steel house that the first- and second-grade Ashton girls designated next to the school building. In the Oceanside layout, the door to the girls' restroom faced one end of the playground, and girls often ran into it for safety. I could hear

squeals from within as boys tried to open the door and peek in. During one of these scenarios, eight girls emerged from the restroom with dripping clumps of wet paper towels, which they threw at the three boys who had been peeking in, and then another burst of chasing ensued. . . .

'Cooties' and Other Pollution Rituals

Episodes of chasing sometimes entwine with rituals of pollution, as in "cooties" or "cootie tag" where specific individuals or groups are treated as contaminating or carrying "germs." Cooties, of course, are invisible; they make their initial appearance through announcements like "Rochelle has cooties!" Kids have rituals for transferring cooties (usually touching someone else, often after a chase, and shouting "You've got cooties!"), for immunization (writing "CV"—for "cootie vaccination"—on their arms, or shaping their fingers to push out a pretend-immunizing "cootie spray"), and for eliminating cooties (saying "no gives" or using "cootie catchers" made of folded paper) While girls and boys may transfer cooties to one another, and girls may give cooties to girls, boys do not generally give cooties to other boys. Girls, in short, are central to the game.

Either girls or boys may be defined as having cooties, but girls give cooties to boys more often than vice versa. In Michigan, one version of cooties was called "girl stain." . . . And in a further shift from acts to imputing the moral character of actors, individuals may be designated as "cootie queens" or "cootie girls." Cootie queens or cootie girls (I have never heard or read about "cootie kings" or "cootie boys") are female pariahs, the ultimate school untouchables, seen as contaminating not only by virtue of gender, but also through some added stigma such as being overweight or poor. And according to one report, in a racially mixed playground in Fresno, California, "Mexican" (Chicano/Latino) but not Anglo children give cooties; thus, inequalities of race, as well as gender and social class, may be expressed through pollution games. In situations like this, different sources of oppression may compound one another.

I did not learn of any cootie queens at Ashton or Oceanside, but in the daily life of schools, *individual* boys and girls may be stigmatized and treated as contaminating. For example, a third-grade Ashton girl refused to sit by a particular boy, whom other boys routinely pushed away from the thick of all-male seating, because he was "stinky" and "peed in his bed." A teacher in another school told me that her fifth-grade students said to newcomers, "Don't touch Phillip's desk; he picks his nose and makes booger balls." Phillip had problems with motor coordination, which, the teacher thought, contributed to his marginalization.

But there is also a notable gender asymmetry, evident in the skewed patterning of cooties; *girls as a group are treated as an ultimate source of contamination*, while boys *as* boys—although maybe not, as Chicanos or individuals with a physical disability—are exempt. Boys sometimes mark hierarchies among themselves by using "girl" as a label for low-status boys and by pushing subordinated boys next to the contaminating space of girls. In Miss Bailey's fourth-fifth-grade class, other boys routinely forced or maneuvered the lowest-status boys (Miguel and Alejandro, the recent immigrants from Mexico, and Joel, who was overweight and afraid of sports) into sitting "by the girls," a space treated as contaminating. In this context, boys drew on gender meanings to convey racial subordination. In contrast, when there was gender-divided seating in the classroom, lunchroom, music room, or auditorium, which girls sat at the boundary between groups of girls and groups of boys had no apparent relationship to social status.

Boys sometimes treat objects associated with girls as polluting; once again, the reverse does not occur. Bradley, a college student, told me about a classroom incident he remembered from third grade. Some girls gave Valentine's Day cards with pictures of Strawberry Shortcake, a feminine-stereotyped image, to everyone in the class, including boys. Erik dumped all his Strawberry Shortcake valentines into Bradley's box; Bradley one-upped the insult by adding his own Strawberry Shortcake valentines to the pile and sneaking them back into Erik's box.

Recoiling from physical proximity with another person and their belongings because they are perceived as contaminating is a powerful statement of social distance and claimed superiority. Pollution beliefs and practices draw on the emotion-laden feeling of repugnance that accompanies unwanted touch or smell. Kids often act out pollution beliefs in a spirit of playful teasing, but the whimsical frame of "play" slides in and out of the serious, and some games of cooties clearly

cause emotional pain. When pollution rituals appear, even in play, they frequently express and enact larger patterns of inequality, by gender, by social class and race, and by bodily characteristics like weight and motor coordination. When several of these characteristics are found in the same person, the result may be extreme rituals of shaming, as in the case of cootie queens. Aware of the cruelty and pain bound up in games of pollution, teachers and aides often try to intervene, especially when a given individual becomes the repeated target. . . .

Invasions

. . . [I]n chasing, groups of girls and groups of boys confront one another as separate "sides," which makes for a kind of symmetry, as does the alternation of chasing and being chased. But rituals of pollution tip the symmetry, defining girls as more contaminating. Invasions, a final type of borderwork, also take asymmetric form; boys invade girls' groups and activities much more often than the reverse. When asked about what they do on the playground, boys list "teasing the girls" as a named activity, but girls do not talk so routinely about "teasing boys." As in other kinds of borderwork, gendered language ("Let's spy on the girls" "Those boys are messing up our jump-rope game") accompanies invasions, as do stylized interactions that highlight a sense of gender as an antagonistic social division.

On the playgrounds of both schools, I repeatedly saw boys, individually or in groups, deliberately disrupt the activities of groups of girls. Boys ruin ongoing games of jump rope by dashing under the twirling rope and disrupting the flow of the jumpers or by sticking a foot into the rope and stopping its momentum. On the Ashton playground, seven fourth-grade girls engaged in an intense game of four-square; it was a warm October day, and the girls had piled their coats on the cement next to the painted court. Two boys, mischief enlivening their faces, came to the edge of the court. One swung his arm into the game's bouncing space; in annoyed response, one of the female players pushed back at him. He ran off for a few feet, while the other boy circled in to take a swipe, trying to knock the ball out of play. Meanwhile, the first boy kneeled behind the pile of coats and leaned around to watch the girls. One of the girls yelled angrily, "Get out. My glasses are in one of those, and I don't want 'em busted." A playground aide called the boys over and told them to "leave the girls alone," and the boys ran off.

Some boys more or less specialize in invading girls, coming back again and again to disrupt; the majority of boys are not drawn to the activity. Even if only a few boys do most of the invading, disruptions are so frequent that girls develop ritualized responses. Girls verbally protest ("Leave us alone!" "Stop it, Keith!"), and they chase boys away. The disruption of a girls' game may provoke a cross-gender chasing sequence, but if girls are annoyed, they chase in order to drive the boy out of the space, a purpose far removed from playful shifting between the roles of chaser and chased. Girls may guard their play with informal lookouts who try to head off trouble; they are often wary about letting boys into their activities. . . .

Why Is Borderwork So Memorable?

The imagery of "border" may wrongly suggest an unyielding fence that divides social relations into two parts. The image should rather be one of many short fences that are quickly built and as quickly dismantled. . . . [Earlier] I described a team handball game in which gender meanings heated up. Heated events also cool down. After the team handball game transmuted into a brief scene of chasing, the recess bell rang and the participants went back to their shared classroom. Ten minutes later the same girls and boys interacted in reading groups where gender was of minimal significance. . . .

[W]hy [then] are the occasions of gender borderwork so compelling? Why do episodes of girls-chase-the-boys and boys-against-the-girls *seem* like the heart of what "gender" is all about? Why do kids regard those situations as especially newsworthy and turn them into stories that they tell afterward and bring home from school? And why do adults, when invited to muse back upon gender relations in their elementary school years, so often spontaneously recall "girls-chase-the-boys," "teasing girls," and "cooties," but less often mention occasions when boys and girls were together in less gender-marked ways? (The latter kinds of occasions may be recalled under other rubrics, like "when we did classroom projects.")

The occasions of borderwork may carry extraperceptual weight because they are marked by conflict, intense emotions, and the expression of forbidden desires. These group activities may also rivet attention because they are created by kids themselves, and because they are ritualized, not as high ceremony, but by virtue of being stylized, repeated, and enacted with a sense of performance. . . . [For example,] cross-gender chasing has a name ("chase and kiss"), a scripted format (the repertoire of provocations and forms of response), and takes shape through stylized motions and talk. The ritual form focuses attention and evokes dominant beliefs about the "nature" of boys and girls and relationships between them.

Erving Goffman [1977, p. 321] coined the term "genderism" to refer to moments in social life, such as borderwork situations, that evoke stereotypic beliefs. During these ritually foregrounded encounters, men and women "play out the differential human nature claimed for them." Many social environments don't lend themselves to this bifurcated and stylized display, and they may even undermine the stereotypes. But when men engage in horseplay (pushing, shoving) and mock contests like Indian wrestling, they dramatize themes of physical strength and violence that are central to [prevailing] constructions of masculinity. And, in various kinds of cross-gender play, as when a man chases after and pins down a woman, he pretends to throw her off a cliff, or threatens her with a snake, the man again claims physical dominance and encourages the woman to "provide a full-voiced rendition [shrinking back, hiding her eyes, screaming] of the plight to which her sex is presumably prone" [Goffman 1977, p. 323]. In short, men and women—and girls and boys—sometimes become caricatures of themselves, enacting and perpetuating stereotypes.

Games of girls-against-the-boys [and] scenes of cross-gender chasing and invasion . . . evoke stereotyped images of gender relations. Deeply rooted in the dominant culture . . . of our society, these images infuse the ways adults talk about girls and boys and relations between them; the content of movies, television, advertising, and children's books; and even the wisdom of experts. . . . This [prevailing] view of gender—acted out, reinforced, and evoked through the various forms of borderwork—has two key components:

1. ***Emphasis on gender as an oppositional dualism.*** Terms like "the opposite sex" and "the war between the sexes" come readily to

mind when one watches a group of boys invade a jump-rope game and the girls angrily respond, or a group of girls and a group of boys hurling insults at one another across a lunchroom. In all forms of borderwork, boys and girls are defined as rival teams with a socially distant, wary, and even hostile relationship; heterosexual meanings add to the sense of polarization. Hierarchy tilts the theme of opposition, with boys asserting spatial, physical, and evaluative dominance over girls.

2. ***Exaggeration of gender difference and disregard for the presence of crosscutting variation and sources of commonality.*** Social psychologists have identified a continuum that ranges from what Henri Tajfel [1982] calls the "interpersonal extreme," when interaction is largely determined by *individual* characteristics, to the "intergroup extreme," when interaction is largely determined by the *group membership* or social categories of participants. Borderwork lies at the intergroup extreme. When girls and boys are defined as opposite sides caught up in rivalry and competition, group stereotyping and antagonism flourish. Members of "the other side" become "that boy" or "that girl." Individual identities get submerged, and participants hurl gender insults ("sissy boys," "dumb girls"), talk about the other gender as "yuck," and make stereotyped assertions ("girls are cry-babies," "boys are frogs; I don't like boys").

Extensive gender separation and organizing mixed-gender encounters as girls-against-the-boys set off contrastive thinking and feed an assumption of gender as dichotomous and antagonistic difference. These social practices seem to express core truths: that boys and girls are separate and fundamentally different, as individuals and as groups. Other social practices that challenge this portrayal—drawing boys and girls together in relaxed and extended ways, emphasizing individual identities or social categories that cut across gender, acknowledging variation in the activities and interests of girls and boys—carry less perceptual weight. . . .

The frames of "play" and "ritual" set the various forms of borderwork a bit apart from ongoing "ordinary" life. As previously argued, this may en-

hance the perceptual weight of borderwork situations in the eyes of both participants and observers, highlighting a gender-as-antagonistic-dualism portrayal of social relations. But the framing of ritualized play may also give leeway for participants to gain perspective on dominant cultural images. Play and ritual can comment on and challenge, as well as sustain, a given ordering of reality.

. . . I [once] watched and later heard an aide describe a game the Oceanside students played on the school lunchroom floor. The floor was made up of large alternating squares of white and green linoleum, rather like a checkerboard. One day during the chaotic transition from lunch to noontime recess, [a boy named] Don . . . jumped, with much gestural and verbal fanfare, from one green square to another. Pointing to a white square, Don loudly announced, "That's girls' territory. Stay on the green square, or you'll change into a girl. Yuck!"

It occurred to me that Don was playing with gender dualisms, with a basic structure of two oppositely arranged parts whose boundaries are charged with risk. From one vantage point, the square-jumping game, as a kind of magical borderwork, may express and dramatically reaffirm structures basic to . . . the gender relations of the school. In the dichotomous world of either green or white, boy or girl, one misstep could spell transformative disaster. But from another vantage point, Don called up that structure to detached view, playing with, commenting on, and even, perhaps, mocking its assumptions.

References

Barth, Fredrik. 1969. "Introduction." Pp. 9–38 in *Ethnic Groups and Boundaries*, edited by F. Barth. Boston: Little, Brown.

Finnan, Christine. 1982. "The Ethnography of Children's Spontaneous Play." Pp. 358–380 in *Doing the Ethnography of Schooling*, edited by George Spindler. New York: Holt, Rinehart, and Winston.

Goffman, Erving. 1977. "The Arrangement between the Sexes." *Theory and Society* 4:301–336.

Tajfel, Henri. 1982. "Social Psychology of Intergroup Relations." *Annual Review of Psychology*, 33:1–39.

30

The Black Male in Public

Elijah Anderson

This selection by Elijah Anderson illustrates how social structural divisions influence interaction and, in turn, how patterns of interaction perpetuate those divisions. It focuses on interactions, involving young black men on the streets of two adjoining neighborhoods in an American city. Of course, race has long been an important dimension of the American social structure that has profoundly influenced interaction both between and among blacks and whites. Although many of the social structural barriers separating blacks from whites have been lowered in recent years, the influence of racial identification on patterns of interaction is still profound. Anderson suggests that recent increases in poverty and crime in the black ghettos of many American cities have even magnified the influence of the overlapping identities of young, black, male and poor on public interaction in American cities.

According to Anderson, being a young black man from the ghetto is what many sociologists call a "master status." That is, others give that status or identity priority over all other characteristics in defining and deciding what to expect from such an individual. As far as many Americans are concerned, the master status or identity of young black man from the ghetto clearly implies that the individual is potentially dangerous and untrustworthy. Newspapers, television, and often personal experience confirm and perpetuate that stereotype, even among young black men themselves. As Anderson describes it, those who encounter such an individual in public places react accordingly.

On the other hand, Anderson argues, young black men often confirm others' typification of them as potential predators. They often do so inadvertently and sometimes do so quite purposefully. Young black men are hardly immune to the dangers of city streets and protect themselves by assuming a cool and aggressive pose. Yet that very pose may scare not only potential assailants but everyone else they encounter as well. According to Anderson, young black men sometimes also exploit others' fear of them, so as to claim public places as their exclusive turf. They apparently consider this just compensation for others' public treatment of them.

Anderson does suggest that whites may be more indiscriminate in their fear of young black men than other blacks. He observes that blacks, including young black men, often greet one another in an apparent attempt to allay fears and establish mutual trust. Whites who have little contact with blacks are unaware of this custom. They fearfully avoid even glancing at young black men on city streets, treating them all similarly. The result, in Anderson's words, is a vicious circle of suspicion and mistrust that perpetuates long-standing racial divisions in the American social structure. Public interaction between blacks and whites becomes a form of what Thorne calls "borderwork." Rather than breaking down barriers between blacks and whites, it reinforces them. This is only one example of the many subtle ways that individuals interactionally reproduce the very social structures that shape their experience and lives.

From summer 1975 through summer 1989, I did fieldwork in the general area I call the Village-Northton, which encompasses two communities—one black and low income to very poor (with an extremely high infant mortality rate), the other racially mixed but becoming increasingly middle to upper income and white. When my wife Nancy and I moved to the Village in 1975, I had not planned to study the area; but this changed as I encountered the local community and discovered what seemed an ideal urban laboratory. . . .

Particularly during the 1980s, the problems of United States cities grew more and more insistent, if not intractable to many. With rising unemployment, brought on in part by increasing "deindustrialization" and the exodus of major corporations, the local black community suffered. The employment lives of its members are further complicated by continuing racial prejudice and discrimination, which often frustrate efforts to make effective adjustments to these changes and the emerging reality. Many who have difficulty finding work in the regular economy become ever poorer and may join the criminal underground, which promises them huge financial rewards, a certain degree of "coolness," and happiness—that seems never to fully materialize. Yet in hot pursuit, many alienated young people commit themselves to this way of life, adopting its morality and norms and serving as role models for other youths. In this way the drug economy has become elaborated, and drug use has grown widespread among the local poor. As the black community of Northton has undergone social deterioration, the adjacent Village has experienced "spillover" crime and public incivility.

These developments had profound consequences for the more general area I was studying, requiring further refinement of my research plans from a limited ethnographic representation of the gentrifying neighborhood of the Village to a more inclusive study of the relationship between it and the adjacent black ghetto of Northton. I found that I could not truly understand the Village independent of Northton, and vice versa, particularly where the two communities met, and that realization posed insistent sociological . . . questions. How do these diverse peoples get it on? How are their everyday public lives shaped and affected by the workings of local social institutions? What is the culture of the local public spaces? What is the public social order? Is there one? How are the social changes in the two communities affecting the residents of both?

From the mid-1970s through the 1980s, moving to the city and refurbishing inner-city areas seemed to young professionals like a brilliant idea, and a good investment to boot. They could afford an inner-city home that they could treat as a starter house, and the antique bargains held a special allure. Many were alienated from the lifestyles of their suburban parents and sour on what the suburbs represented to them—social and cultural homogeneity—and they saw the city as a place where they might define their own lives in a different manner, close to work and play. This group contributed to the process we know today as gentrification. Yet commitment to such projects had its costs and brought some uncertainty. Crime in the street and wariness about strangers have always been recognized as costs of living in the city, but today many feel such realities have become worse. With looming municipal budget deficits, higher local taxes, a decline in city services, and growing inner-city poverty, drug use, and crime, many gentrifiers have come to see their own fortunes as inextricably inked to those of the nearby ghetto. They realize that changes in the neighboring black community directly and indirectly affect not only their sense of well-being but also their property values. This acknowledge-

ment has slowed down—but not yet reversed—the process of gentrification.

I mean my descriptions and analysis to convey . . . how individuals come to interpret and negotiate the public spaces in the community I have been studying. Much of what I learned came through informal interviews and direct ethnographic observation over an extended period, and it draws on my experiences in the Village-Northton and in nearby communities that share some of the area's more prominent features. . . .

An overwhelming number of young black males in the Village are committed to civility and law-abiding behavior. They often have a hard time convincing others of this, however, because of the stigma attached to their skin color, age, gender, appearance, and general style of self-presentation. Moreover, most residents ascribe criminality, incivility, toughness, and street smartness to the anonymous black male, who must work hard to make others trust his common decency. . . .

Anonymous black males occupy a peculiar position in the social fabric of the Village. The fear and circumspection surrounding people's reactions to their presence constitute one of the hinges that public race relations turn on. Although the black male is a provocative figure to most others he encounters, his role is far from simple. It involves a complex set of relationships to be negotiated and renegotiated with all those sharing the streets. Where the Village meets Northton, black males exercise a peculiar hegemony over the public spaces, particularly at night or when two or more are together. This influence often is checked by the presence of the local police, which in turn has consequences for other public relationships in the Village.

The residents of the area, including black men themselves, are likely to defer to unknown black males, who move convincingly through the area as though they "run it," exuding a sense of ownership. They are easily perceived as symbolically inserting themselves into any available social space, pressing against those who might challenge them. The young black males, the "big winners" of these little competitions, seem to feel very comfortable as they swagger confidently along. Their looks, their easy smiles, and their spontaneous laughter, singing, cursing, and talk about the intimate details of their lives, which can be followed from across the street, all convey the impression of little concern for other pedestrians. The other pedestrians, however, are very concerned about them.

When young black men appear, women (especially white women) sometimes clutch their pocketbooks. They may edge up against their companions or begin to walk stiffly and deliberately. On spotting black males from a distance, other pedestrians often cross the street or give them a wide berth as they pass. When black males deign to pay attention to passersby, they tend to do so directly, giving them a deliberate once-over; their eyes may linger longer than the others consider appropriate to the etiquette of "strangers in the streets." Thus the black males take in all the others and dismiss them as a lion might dismiss a mouse. Fellow pedestrians in turn avert their eyes from the black males, deferring to figures who are seen as unpredictable, menacing, and not to be provoked—predators.

People, black or white, who are more familiar with the black street culture are less troubled by sharing the streets with young black males. Older black men, for instance, frequently adopt a refined set of criteria. In negotiating the streets, they watch out particularly for a certain *kind* of young black male; "jitterbugs" or those who might belong to "wolf packs," small bands of black teenage boys believed to travel about the urban areas accosting and robbing people.

Many members of the Village community, however, both black and white, lack these more sophisticated insights. Incapable of making distinctions between law-abiding black males and others, they rely for protection on broad stereotypes based on color and gender, if not outright racism. They are likely to misread many of the signs displayed by law-abiding black men, thus becoming apprehensive of almost any black male they spot in public. . . .

Two general sociological factors underlie the situation in which the black man in the Village finds himself. The first, the "master status-determining characteristic" of race (Hughes 1945), is at work in the most casual street encounter. . . . In the minds of many Village residents, black and white, the master status of the young black male is determined by his youth, his blackness, his maleness, and what these attributes have come to stand for in the shadow of the ghetto. In the context of racism, he is easily labeled "deviant." . . . In

public, fellow pedestrians are thus uncertain about his purpose and have a strong desire to make sense of him quickly, so that they can get on with their own business. Many simply conclude that he is dangerous and act accordingly. Thus in social encounters in the public spaces of the Village, before he can be taken for anything as an individual . . . he is perceived first and foremost as a young black man from the ghetto. . . . Here the second element comes into play. An assessment like this is really a *social definition*, normally something to be negotiated between labeler and labeled. . . .

In a city one has many encounters with anonymous figures who are initially viewed as strangers, about whom little is known or understood. As Goffman (1959) suggests, there are ways strangers can rapidly become known or seen as less strange. In negotiating public spaces, people receive and display a wide range of behavioral cues and signs that make up the vocabulary of public interaction. Skin color, gender, age, companions, clothing, jewelry, and the objects people carry help identify them, so that assumptions are formed and communication can occur. Movements (quick or slow, false or sincere, comprehensible or incomprehensible) further refine this public communication. Factors like time of day or an activity that "explains" a person's presence can also affect in what way and how quickly the image of "stranger" is neutralized. . . .

If a stranger cannot pass inspection and be assessed as "safe" (either by identity or by purpose), the image of predator may arise, and fellow pedestrians may try to maintain a distance consistent with that image. In the more worrisome situations—for example, encountering a number of strangers on a dark street—the image may persist and trigger some form of defensive action.

In the street environment, it seems, children readily pass inspection, white women and white men do so more slowly, black women, black men, and black male teenagers most slowly of all. The master status assigned to black males undermines their ability to be taken for granted as law-abiding and civil participants in public places: young black males, particularly those who don the urban uniform (sneakers, athletic suits, gold chains, "gangster caps," sunglasses, and large portable radios or "boom boxes"), may be taken as the embodiment of the predator. In this uniform, which suggests to many the "dangerous underclass," these young men are presumed to be troublemakers or criminals. Thus, in the local milieu, the identity of predator is usually "given" to the young black male and made to stick until he demonstrates otherwise, something not easy to do in circumstances that work to cut off communication. . . .

In the Village a third, concrete factor comes into play. The immediate source of much of the distrust the black male faces is the nearness of Northton. White newcomers in particular continue to view the ghetto as a mysterious and unfathomable place that breeds drugs, crime, prostitution, unwed mothers, ignorance, and mental illness. It symbolizes persistent poverty and imminent danger, personified in the young black men who walk the Village streets (see Katz 1988, 195–273). The following narrative of a young black indicates one response of Villagers to the stereotype they fear so much:

A white lady walkin' down the street with a pocketbook. She start walkin' fast. She get so paranoid she break into a little stride. Me and my friends comin' from a party about 12:00. She stops and goes up on the porch of a house, but you could tell she didn't live there. I stop and say, 'Miss, you didn't have to do that. I thought you might think we're some wolf pack. I'm twenty-eight, he's twenty-six, he's twenty-nine. You ain't gonna run from us.' She said, 'Well, I'm sorry.' I said, 'You can come down. I know you don't live there. We just comin' from a party.' We just walked down the street and she came back down, walked across the street where she really wanted to go. So she tried to act as though she lived there. And she didn't. After we said, 'You ain't gotta run from us,' she said, 'No, I was really in a hurry.' My boy said, 'No you wasn't. You thought we was gon' snatch yo' pocketbook.' We pulled money out. 'See this, we work.' I said, 'We grown men, now. You gotta worry about them fifteen-, sixteen-, seventeen-year-old boys. That's what you worry about. But we're grown men.' It told her all this. 'They the ones ain't got no jobs; they're too young to really work. They're the ones you worry about, not us.' She understood that. You could tell she was relieved and she gave a sigh. She came back down the steps, even went across the street. We stopped in the middle of the street. "You all right, now?" And she smiled. We just laughed and went on to a neighborhood bar.

Experiences like this may help modify the way individual white residents view black males in public by establishing conditions under which blacks pass inspection by disavowing the image of the predator, but they do little to change the prevailing public relationship between blacks and whites in the community. Common racist stereotypes persist, and black men who successfully make such disavowals are often seen not as the norm but as the exception—as "different from the rest"—thereby confirming the status of the "rest."

In the interest of security and defense, residents adopt the facile but practical perspective that informs and supports the prevailing view of public community relations: whites are law-abiding and trustworthy; anonymous young black males are crime-prone and dangerous. Ironically, this perceived dangerousness has become important to the public self-identity of many local black men. . . .

[B]oth blacks and whites are cautious with strangers and take special care in dealing with anonymous young blacks. This caution is encouraged by a certain style of self-presentation that is common on the street. Many black youths, law-abiding or otherwise, exude an offensive/defensive aura because they themselves regard the streets as a jungle. A young black man said:

A friend of mine got rolled. He was visiting this girl up near Mercer Street. He come out of this house, and somebody smacked him in the head with a baseball bat. He had all these gold chains on. Had a brand new $200 thick leather jacket, $100 pair of Michael Jordan sneakers, and they were brand new, first time he had them on his feet. He had leather pants on too. And I'm surprised they didn't take his leather pants. I mean, he had a gold chain this thick [shows quarter-inch with his fingers]. I mean pure gold—$800 worth of gold. He came out this girl's house, after visiting his baby. Cats hit him in the head with a baseball bat, and they took everything. Took his sneaks, his coat, everything. When the paramedics got there he had no coat, no sneaks on. They took his belt, took his Gucci belt, the junkies did. I went to visit him in the hospital, and I'm sorry I went in there. I seen him. The boy had stitches . . . they shaved his head, stitches from here to all the way back of his head. Beat him in the head with a baseball bat. They say it was two guys. They was young boys, typical stupid young boys. Now my boy's life is messed up. He home now, but poor guy has seizures and everything. It's a jungle out here, man. But he sold drugs; the cops found cocaine in his underwear. They [the muggers] got what they wanted.

The young black males' pose is generally intended for people they perceive as potentially aggressive toward them. But at the same time it may engender circumspection and anxiety in law-abiding residents, both black and white, whose primary concern is safe passage on the streets.

In this public environment, pedestrians readily defer to young black males, who accept their public position. They walk confidently, heads up and gazes straight. Spontaneous and boisterous, they play their radios as loud as they please, telling everyone within earshot that this is their turf, like it or not. It may be that this is one of the few arenas were they can assert themselves and be taken seriously, and perhaps this is why they are so insistent.

Other pedestrians withdraw, perhaps with a defensive scowl, but nothing more. For the Village is not defended in the way many working-class neighborhoods are. As the black youths walk through late at night with their radios turned up, they meet little or no resistance. This lack of challenge shows how "tame," weak, or undefended the neighborhood is, except in certain areas where white college students predominate and fraternity boys succeed in harassing apparently defenseless blacks such as women with children, lone women, and an occasional single black man. Black youths tend to avoid such areas of the Village unless they are in groups.

The same black youths might hesitate before playing a radio loud in the well-defended territories of Northton, however. There they would likely be met by two or three "interceptors" who would promptly question their business, possibly taking the radio and punching one of the boys, or worse, in the process. No such defending force exists within the Village. . . .

Another aspect of claiming turf rights is public talk—its idiom, duration, intensity, and volume. At times the language of young black males, even those who are completely law-abiding, is harsh and profane. This language is used in many public spaces, but especially at trolley stops and on trolleys and buses. Like the rap music played loudly on boom boxes, it puts others on the defensive. The "others" tend not to say much to the offenders; rather, they complain to one another (though some residents have in fact come to appreciate the young males and enjoy the music).

On public transportation young blacks, including some girls, may display raucous behavior, including cursing and loud talk and play. Because most people encounter the youths as strangers, they understand them through the available stereotypes. Law-abiding black youths often don the special urban uniform and emulate this self-presentation, a practice known as "going for bad" and used to intimidate others. As one young black man said:

> You see the guys sometimes on the bus having this air about them. They know that the grown people on the bus hope that these guys are not problems. The boys play on that. I'm talking about with women old enough to be their mothers. Now, they wouldn't be doing this at home. But they'll do it on that bus. They'll carry on to such an extent. . . . Now, I know, especially the young boys. I know they [older people] be scared. They really wondering, 'cause all they know is the headlines, "Juvenile Crime . . ." "Problems of Youth Kids," or "Chain Snatchers." This is what they know. And these people are much more uncertain than I am, 'cause I know.

In some cases black males capitalize on the fear they know they can evoke. They may "put on a swagger" and intimidate those who must momentarily share a small space on the sidewalk. When passing such a "loud" dark skinned person, whites usually anticipate danger, though they hope for a peaceful pass. Whites and middle-income blacks are often more than ready to cross the street to avoid passing a "strange" black person at close range. Young blacks understand this behavior and sometimes exploit the fear, as illustrated in the following narrative by a young white woman:

> I went out for something at the store at about 9:00, after it was already dark. When I came back, there was no place to park in front of my house anymore. So I had to park around the corner, which I generally don't do because there's a greater chance of getting your car broken into or stolen over there, since a lot of foot traffic goes by at night. So I parked the car, turned out the lights, and got out. I began walking across the street, but I got into a situation I don't like to get into—of having there be some ominous-looking stranger between me and my house. So I have to go around or something. And he was a black fellow between twenty and thirty, on the youngish side. He certainly wasn't anybody I knew. So I

decided not really to run, just sort of double-time, so I wouldn't meet him at close distance at the corner. I kind of ran diagonally, keeping the maximum distance between him and me. And it must have been obvious to him that I was running out of fear, being alone at night out in the street. He started chuckling, not trying to hide it. He just laughed at what I was doing. He could tell what he meant to me, the two of us being the only people out there.

At times even civil and law-abiding youths enjoy this confusion. They have an interest in going for bad, for it is a way to keep other youths at bay. The right look, moves, and general behavior ensure safe passage. However, this image is also a source of subtle but enduring racial and class distinctions, if not overt hostility, within the community.

Some black youths confront others with behavior they refer to as "gritting," "looking mean," "looking hard," and "bumping." Youths have a saying, "His jaws got tight." Such actions could easily be compared to threatening animal behavior, particularly dogs warning other dogs away from their territory or food. Gritting is a way of warning peers against "messing with me." To grit is to be ready to defend one's interests, in this case one's physical self. It conveys alertness to the prospect of harmful intent, communicating and defining personal boundaries. As one black man said concerning strategies for negotiating the Northton streets near the Village:

> When I walk the streets, I put this expression on my face that tells the next person I'm not to be messed with. That 'You messing with the wrong fellow. You just try it.' And I know when cats are behind me. I be just lookin' in the air, letting them know I'm checkin' them out. Then I'll put my hand in my pocket, even if I ain't got no gun. Nobody wants to get shot, that shit burns, man. That shit hurt. Some guys go to singing. They try to let people know they crazy. 'Cause if you crazy [capable of anything], they'll leave you alone. And I have looked in they face [muggers] and said, 'Yo, I'm not the one.' Give 'em that crazy look, then walk away. 'Cause I know what they into. They catch your drift quick. . . .

The youth is caught up here in a cultural catch-22: to appear harmless to others might make him seem weak or square to those he feels a need to impress. If he does not dress the part of a young black man on the streets, it is difficult for him to "act right." If he is unable to "act right," then he may be victimized by strangers in his general peer group. The uniform—radio, sneakers, gold chain, athletic suit—and the selective use of the "grit," the quasi-military swagger to the beat of "rap" songs in public places, are all part of the young man's pose.

Law-abiding and crime-prone youths alike adopt such poses in effect camouflaging themselves and making it difficult for more conventional people to know how to behave around them, since those for whom they may not be performing directly may see them as threatening. By connecting culturally with the ghetto, a young black may avoid compromising his public presentation of self, but at the cost of further alienating law-abiding whites and blacks.

In general, the black male is assumed to be streetwise. He also comes to think of himself as such, and this helps him negotiate public spaces. In this sense others collectively assist him in being who he is. With a simple move one way or the other, he can be taken as a "dangerous dude." He is then left alone, whereas whites may have more trouble.

Civility and law-abidingness are stereotypically ascribed to the white male, particularly in the public context of so many "dangerous" and "predatory" young blacks. (In fact, white men must campaign to achieve the status of being seen as dangerous in public places.) The white male is not taken seriously on the streets, particularly by black men, who resist seeing him as a significant threat. They think that most white men view conflict in terms of "limited warfare," amounting to little more than scowls and harsh words. It is generally understood that blacks from Northton do not assume this but are open to unlimited warfare, including the use of sticks, stones, knives, and guns, perhaps even a fight to the death.

Most conventional people learn to fear black youths from reading about crimes in the local papers and seeing reports of violence on television, but also by living so near and having the chance to observe them. Every time there is a violent crime, this image of young blacks gains credibility. Such public relations attribute to blacks control over the means and use of violence in public encounters, thus contributing to dominant stereotypes and fear. As is clear from the following interview, black men pick up on that fear:

They [white men] look at you strange, they be paranoid. Especially if you walkin' behind 'em. They slow down and let you walk in front or they walk on the other side. You know they got their eye on you. I walk past one one time. My mother live on Fortieth and Calvary and I did that. I said, 'You ain't gotta slow down, brother. I ain't gonna do nothin' to you, I ain't like that.' He looked at me and laughed. He knew what I meant, and I knew what he was thinkin'. He had a little smile. It was late at night, about 1:00 A.M. He let me get in front of him. He was comin' from a bar, and he had a six-pack. I'm a fast walker anyway; you can hear my shoes clickin'. I see him slowing down. I said, 'I ain't gonna do nothin' to you, I ain't like that.' He just laughed; I kept on walking and I laughed. That's the way it went.

Whereas street interactions between black strangers tend to be highly refined, greetings of whites toward blacks are usually ambiguous or have limited effectiveness. This general communication gap between blacks and whites is exacerbated by the influx of white newcomers. In contrast to the longtime residents, the newcomers are unaccustomed to and frequently intolerant of neighboring blacks and have not learned a visible street etiquette. The run-ins such new people have with blacks contribute to a general black view of "the whites" of the Village as prejudiced, thus undermining the positive race relations promoted over many years by egalitarian-minded residents.

The result is that the white and black communities become collapsed into social monoliths. For instance, although blacks tend to relate cautiously to unknown black youths, they are inclined to look at them longer, inspecting them and noting their business to see whether they deserve to be trusted. Whites, on the other hand, look at blacks, see their skin color, and dismiss them quickly as potential acquaintances; then they furtively avert their gaze, hoping not to send the wrong message, for they desire distance and very limited involvement. Any follow-up by black youths is considered highly suspect unless there are strong mitigating factors, such as an emergency where help is needed.

A common testimonial from young blacks reflects the way whites encounter them. They speak about the defensiveness of whites in general. White women are said to plant broad grins on their faces in hopes of not being accosted. The

smile may appear to be a sign of trust, but it is more likely to show a deference, especially when the woman looks back as soon as she is at a safe distance. When the black stranger and the perceived danger have passed, the putative social ties suggested by the smile are no longer binding and the woman may attempt to keep the "dangerous" person in view, for a sudden move could signal an "attempted robbery" or "rape." . . .

A young black man who often walks through the Village reports this reaction from white women:

> They give the eye. You can see 'em lookin' right at you. They look at you and turn back this way, and keep on walkin'. Like you don't exist, but they be paranoid as hell. Won't say hello. But some of 'em do. Some of 'em say hi. Some of 'em smile. But they always scared.

One young white woman confirmed this: "I must admit, I look at a black [male] on the street just for a few seconds. Just long enough to let him know I know of his presence, then I look away." . . .

Out of a sense of frustration, many young blacks mock or otherwise insult the whites they see in public spaces, trying to "get even" with them for being part of the "monolithic" group of whites. When they encounter whites who display fear, they may laugh at them or harass them. They think, "What do I have to lose?" and may purposely create discomfort in those they see as "ignorant" enough to be afraid of them. Of course the whites of the Village are anything but a monolithic group. But it is convenient for certain blacks to see things this way, placing all whites, whom they see as the source of their troubles, into an easily manageable bag. In this way blacks as well as whites become victims of simplistic thinking.

Black men's resentment, coupled with peer-group pressure to act tough, may cause them to shift unpredictably from being courteous to whites to "fulfilling the prophecy" of those who are afraid and uncomfortable around blacks. When confronting a white woman on the streets some youths may make lewd or suggestive comments, reminding her that she is vulnerable and under surveillance. The following account describes such an encounter:

> On a Wednesday afternoon in June at about 2:00, Sandra Norris pushed her nine-month-old daughter down Cherry Street. The gray stone facades of the Victorian buildings spar-

kled in the sun. The streets seemed deserted, as the Village usually is at this time. Suddenly three black youths appeared. They looked in their late teens. As they approached her, one of the young men yelled to the others, 'Let's get her! Get her!' Making sexual gestures, two of the youths reached for her menacingly. She cringed and pulled the stroller toward her. At that the boys laughed loudly. They were playing with her, but the feigned attack was no fun for Mrs. Norris. It left her shaking.

As indicated above, an aggressive presentation—though certainly not usually so extreme—is often accepted as necessary for black youths to maintain regard with their peers. They must "act right" by the toughest ghetto standards or risk being ridiculed or even victimized by their own peers. Feeling a certain power in numbers, some groups will readily engage in such games, noisily swooping down on their supposed "prey" or fanning out in a menacing formation. Children, white and black, sometimes are intimidated and form fearful and negative feelings about teenage "black boys."

Such demeanor may be a way of identifying with the ghetto streets, but it is also a way of exhibiting "toughness" toward figures who represent the "overclass," which many view as deeply implicated in the misfortunes of their communities. Such conduct is easily confused with and incorporated into ordinary male adolescent behavior, but the result is complicated by race and gender and the generalized powerlessness of the black community. Understandably, middle-class residents, black and white, become even more likely to place social distance between themselves and such youths, conceptually lumping anonymous black males together for self-defense.

Of course not everyone is victimized by crime, but many people take incivility as an indication of what could happen if they did not keep up their guard. When representatives of Northton walking through the Village intimidate residents either verbally or physically, many middle-class people—whites in particular—become afraid of black males in general. They may have second thoughts about "open" and to some degree friendly displays they may previously have made toward blacks in public. Blacks and whites thus become increasingly estranged. In fact there is a vicious circle of suspicion and distrust between the two groups and an overwhelming tendency for public

relations between them to remain superficial and guarded.

It is not surprising that the law-abiding black man often feels at a disadvantage in his interactions with whites. Most whites, except possibly those who are streetwise . . . and empathic about the plight of inner-city blacks, are conditioned to consider all black male strangers potential muggers. The average black, because of his own socialization on the streets and his understanding of the psychology of whites, understands this position very well and knows what whites are thinking.

Many blacks and whites seem alarmed when a black youth approaches them for any reason, even to ask the time. Such overtures may simply be the youth's attempt to disavow criminal intent or to neutralize the social distance generally displayed on the streets. But these attempts are easily interpreted as a setup for a mugging, causing the other person to flee or to cut off the interaction. The public stigma is so powerful that black strangers are seldom allowed to be civil or even helpful without some suspicion of their motives. . . .

Even law-abiding black men who befriend whites and belong to biracial primary groups face "outsider" status. For example, when a black visits a white friend's house, knocks on the door or rings the bell and waits, he risks being taken by the neighbors as someone whose business on the stoop is questionable. Some people will keep an eye on him, watching every move until their neighbor comes to the door. It may not matter how well the visitor is dressed. His skin color indicates his "stranger" status, which persists until he passes inspection when the white person answers the door. The white man with the same self-presentation would pass much sooner.

Although they do not usually articulate the problem in just this manner, many black middle-income Villagers feel somewhat bitter about the prejudice of their white neighbors, who are caught up in a kind of symbolic racism. Dark skin has a special meaning, which Village residents have come to associate with crime. Though white Villagers may not have contempt for blacks in general, they do experience anxiety over the prospect of being victimized. So, since blacks are believed to make up a large proportion of the criminals, pedestrians tend to be defensive and short with strange black males. The same people may have intimate black friends and may pride themselves on their racial tolerance. Yet, concerned with safety, they regard blacks as an anonymous mass through which they must negotiate their way to their destination. They may pass right by black "friends" and simply fail to see them because they are concentrating not on the friend but on the social context. Such reactions frustrate many black-white friendships before they have a chance to begin. Blacks generally complain more than whites about such shortcomings of friendly relations. But as blacks make their way around the streets, they too may miss a "friend" of the other color. Such events may have more to do with the ambiguous nature of public race relations than with racial feeling itself. But whatever the cause, these problems are an impediment to spontaneous and biracial interactions. . . .

References

Goffman, Erving. 1959. *The Presentation of Self in Everyday Life*. Garden City, NY: Doubleday.

Hughes, Everett. 1945. "Dilemmas and Contradictions of Status." *American Journal of Sociology*, 50: 353–359.

Katz, Jack. 1988. *Seductions of Crime: Moral and Sensual Attraction in Doing Evil*. New York: Basic Books.

31

Managing Emotions in an Animal Shelter

Arnold Arluke

Social structures endure because one generation transmits to the next the symbols, classification systems, meanings, and rules that structure action, interaction, and social life. Each subsequent generation consequently engages in recurrent patterns of action and interaction that reproduce those social structures. They seldom perfectly replicate social structures, but alter them in various ways that sometimes lead to profound restructuring over time. Even such imperfect replication of social structures is not guaranteed but subject to what Herbert Blumer called "the play and fate of meaning." Yet, social structures are more or less enduring thanks to processes of socialization.

For example, the medical students discussed by Smith and Kleinman in an earlier selection eventually reproduced the affectively neutral culture and social structure of modern medicine. Their teachers and training at medical school subtly but effectively transmitted feeling rules and emotion management strategies that encouraged them to do so. They learned how to control their emotions and, thereby, how to control and distance themselves from their patients. That is, they learned how to reproduce physicians' authority over patients and the conventional structure of the physician-patient relationship.

This selection examines another instance of how emotional socialization promotes the reproduction of social structure, in this case a specific social institution. It concerns a Humane Society shelter where euthanasia of animals was and is routine. As Arluke observes, people in Western societies have inconsistent and often conflicting attitudes toward animals. On the one hand, we believe that at least some sentient creatures deserve affection and care. On the other hand, we regard others, even of the same species, as utilitarian objects to be used as we see fit. Arluke shows how such conflicting meanings caused new workers at the shelter emotional difficulties. Kinds of animals that they had previously learned to love, care for, and protect were being rou-

tinely killed, often with their involvement. Yet, similar to medical students, they learned emotion management and interpretive strategies that relieved their emotional discomfort and convinced them of the nobility of their gruesome tasks. This socialization process produced a new generation of workers who would reproduce the social institution of the animal "kill shelter."

We may be more similar to these kill shelter workers than we might first recognize. Our work often requires us to do things that we find morally troubling and emotionally disturbing. However, we usually learn ways of excusing what we do that calm our emotions. Like the "kill shelter" workers, we learn how to live with all the little murders that we commit as part of our jobs, convincing ourselves that they are necessary and perhaps even noble. The reproduction of social structures requires sacrifices, and most of us learn to make them with hardly a thought and only a twinge of emotion.

From the sociologist's perspective, what is most interesting in the study of conflicts in the contemporary treatment of animals is not to point out that such conflicts exist or to debate the assumptions that underlie them—a task more ably served by philosophers—but to better understand what it is about modern society that makes it possible to shower animals with affection as sentient creatures while simultaneously maltreating or killing them as utilitarian objects. How is it that a conflict that should require a very difficult balancing of significant values has become something that many people live with comfortably? Indeed, they may not even be aware that others may perceive their actions as inconsistent. How is it that instead of questioning the propriety of their conflicts, many don ethical blindfolds?

As with any cultural contradiction, these attitudes are built into the normative order, itself perpetuated by institutions that provide ways out of contradictions by supplying myths to bridge them and techniques to assuage troubled feelings. . . .

Humane and scientific institutions, for example, must teach newcomers in shelters and laboratories to suspend their prior, ordinary or commonsense thinking about the use and meaning of animals and adopt a different set of assumptions that may be inconsistent with these prior views. The assumptions are not themselves proved but rather structure and form the field upon which the activity plays out its life. Typically, these assumptions are transmitted to nascent practitioners of a discipline, along with relevant empirical facts and skills, as indisputable truths, not as debatable assumptions. They must come to accept the premise of the institution—often that it is necessary to kill animals—and get on with the business of the institution. But exactly how do they get on with this business?

In addition to learning to think differently about the proper fate of animals in institutions, workers must also learn to feel differently about them in that situation. Uncomfortable feelings may be experienced by newcomers even if the premise of the institution is accepted at an intellectual level. Although institutions will, no doubt, equip newcomers with rules and resources for managing unwanted emotions, researchers have not examined how such emotion management strategies actually work and the extent to which they eliminate uncomfortable feelings. In the absence of such research, it is generally assumed that newcomers learn ways to distance themselves from their acts and lessen their guilt. These devices are thought to prevent any attachment to and empathy for animals (Schleifer 1985) and to make killing "a reflex, virtually devoid of emotional content" (Serpell 1986:152).

To examine these assumptions, I conducted ethnographic research over a seven-month period in a "kill-shelter" serving a major metropolitan area. Such a case study seemed warranted, given the sensitivity of the topic under study. I became immersed in this site, spending approximately 75 hours in direct observation of all facets of shelter work and life, including euthanasia of animals and the training of workers to do it. Also, interviews were conducted with the entire staff of sixteen people, many formally and at length on tape, about euthanasia and related aspects of shelter work. . . .

The Newcomer's Problem

Euthanasia posed a substantial emotional challenge to most novice shelter workers. People seeking work at the shelter typically regarded themselves as "animal people" or "animal lovers" and recounted lifelong histories of keeping pets, collecting animals, nursing strays, and working in zoos, pet stores, veterinarian practices, and even animal research laboratories. They came wanting to "work with animals" and expecting to spend much of their time having hands-on contact with animals in a setting where others shared the same high priority they placed on human-animal interaction. The prospect of having to kill animals seemed incompatible with this self-conception.

When first applying for their jobs, some shelter workers did not even know that euthanasia was carried out at the shelter. To address this possible misconception, applicants were asked how they would feel when it was their turn to euthanize. Most reported that they did not really think through this question at this time, simply replying that they thought it was "Okay" in order to get the job. One worker, for instance, said she "just put this thought out of [her] mind," while another worker said that she had hope to "sleaze out" of (or avoid) doing it. Many said that having to do euthanasia did not fully sink in until they "looked the animal in its eyes." Clearly, newcomers were emotionally unprepared to actually kill animals.

Once on the job, newcomers quickly formed strong attachments to particular animals. In fact, it was customary to caution newcomers against adopting animals right away. Several factors encouraged these attachments. At first, workers found themselves relating to shelter animals as though they were their own pets because many of the animals were healthy and appealing to workers, and since most of the animals had been pets, they sometimes initiated interaction with the workers. Newcomers also saw more senior people interacting with animals in a pet-like fashion. Shelter animals, for example, were all named, and everyone used these names when referring to the animals. While newcomers followed suit, they did not realize that more experienced workers could interact in this way with animals and not become attached to them. Moreover, newcomers found that their work required them to know the individual personalities of shelter animals in order to make the best decisions regarding euthanasia and adoption, but this knowledge easily fostered attachments. Not surprisingly, the prospect of having to kill animals with whom they had become attached was a major concern for newcomers. This anticipated relationship with shelter animals made newcomers agonize when they imagined selecting animals for euthanasia and seeing "trusting looks" in the faces of those killed. They also worried about having to cope with the "losses" they expected to feel from killing these animals.

Further aggravating the novices' trepidation was the fact that they had to kill animals for no higher purpose. Many felt grieved and frustrated by what they saw as the "senseless" killing of healthy animals. Several newcomers flinched at the shelter's willingness to kill animals if suitable homes were not found instead of "fostering out" the animals. In their opinion, putting animals in less than "ideal" homes for a few years was better than death.

The clash between the feelings of newcomers for shelter animals and the institution's practice of euthanasia led newcomers to experience a caring-killing "paradox." On the one hand, they tried to understand and embrace the institutional rationale for euthanasia, but on the other hand, they wanted to nurture and tend to shelter animals. Doing both seemed impossible to many newcomers. Acceptance of the need to euthanize did not remove the apprehension that workers felt about having to kill animals themselves or to be part of this process. Their everyday selves were still paramount and made them feel for shelter animals as they might toward their own pets—the thought of killing them was troubling. They even feared getting to the point where they would no longer be upset killing animals, commonly asking those more senior, "Do you still care?" or "Doesn't it still bother you?" Experienced shelter workers acknowledged the "paradox" of newcomers, telling and reassuring them that:

> There is a terrible paradox in what you will have to do—you want to care for animals, but will have to kill some of them. It is a painful process of killing animals when you don't want to. It seems so bad, but we'll make it good in your head. You will find yourself in a complex emotional state. Euthanizing is not just technical skills. You have to believe it is right to make it matter of fact.

Emotion Management Strategies

How did shelter workers manage their uncomfortable feelings? Workers learned different emotion management strategies to distance themselves enough to kill, but not so much as to abandon a sense of themselves as animal people. These strategies enabled workers at least to hold in abeyance their prior, everyday sensibilities regarding animals and to apply a different emotional perspective while in the shelter.

Transforming Shelter Animals Into Virtual Pets

New workers often had trouble distinguishing between shelter animals and their own pets. Failure to make this dinstinction could result in emotionally jarring situations, especially when animals were euthanized. However, they soon came to see shelter animals as virtual pets—liminal animals lying somewhere between the two categories of pet and object. In such a liminal status workers could maintain a safe distance from animals while not entirely detaching themselves from them.

One way they accomplished this transformation was to lessen the intensity of their emotional attachments to individual animals. Almost as a rite of passage, newcomers were emotionally scarred by the euthanasia of a favorite animal, leaving them distraught over the loss. They also heard cautionary tales about workers who were very upset by the loss of animals with whom they had grown "too close" as well as workers whose "excessive" or "crazy" attachments resulted in harm to animals—such as the person who was fired after she released all the dogs from the shelter because she could no longer stand to see them caged or put to death. Newcomers soon began consciously to restrict the depth of their attachments. As one worker observed: "I don't let myself get that attached to them."

On the other hand, certain mottoes or ideals were part of the shelter culture, and these underscored the importance of not becoming detached from their charges or becoming desensitized to euthanasia. One worker, for instance, told me that you "learn to turn your feelings off when you do this work, but you can't completely. They say if you can, you shouldn't be on the job." Another worker noted: "If you get to the point where killing doesn't bother you, then you shouldn't be working here."

While they stopped themselves from "loving" individual shelter animals, because of their likely fate, workers learned that they could become more safely attached by maintaining a generalized caring feeling for shelter animals as a group. As workers became more seasoned, individual bonding became less frequent, interest in adopting subsided and a sense emerged of corporate attachment to shelter animals as a population of refugees rather than as individual pets.

Workers also came to see shelter animals differently from everyday pets by assuming professional roles with their charges. One role was that of "caretaker" rather than pet owner. As a worker noted: "You don't set yourself up by seeing them as pets. You'd kill yourself; I'd cut my wrists. I'm a caretaker, so I make them feel better while they are here. They won't be forgotten so quickly. I feel I get to know them. I'm their last hope." Comparing her own pet to shelter animals, another worker noted: "No bell goes off in your head with your own pet as it would with a shelter animal, where the bell says you can't love this animal because you have to euthanize it." If not caretakers, they could become social workers trying to place these animals in homes of other people.

New workers came to view their charges as having a type of market value within the larger population of shelter animals. Their value was not to be personal and individual from the worker's perspective. Rather, they were to be assessed in the light of their competitive attractiveness to potential adopters. This view was nowhere more apparent than in the selection of healthy and well behaved animals to be euthanized in order to make room for incoming animals. An experienced shelter worker described these "tough choices" and the difficulty newcomers had in viewing animals this way:

> When you go through and pull [i.e., remove an animal for euthanasia]—that's when you have to make some real tough choices. If they've all been here an equal amount of time, then if you've got eighteen cages and six are filled with black cats, and you have a variety in here waiting for cages, you're going to pull the black ones so you can have more of a variety. It's hard for a new employee to understand that I'm going to pull a black cat to make room for a white one. After they've been here through a cat season, they know exactly what I'm doing, and you don't have to say anything when you have old staff around you.

In addition, newcomers learned to think differently when spending money for the medical care of shelter animals than they would when spending on their own pets. Although an occasional animal might receive some medical attention, many animals were killed because it was not considered economically feasible to treat them even though they had reversible problems and the cost might be insubstantial. For example, while two newcomers observed the euthanizing of several kittens, an experienced worker pointed to a viral infection in their mouths as the reason behind their deaths. One newcomer asked why the kittens could not be treated medically so they could be put up for adoption. The reply was that the virus could be treated, but "given the volume, it is not economical to treat them."

Keeping shelter mascots further helped workers separate everyday pets from their charges, with mascots serving as surrogate pets in contrast to the rest of the shelter's animals. Cats and dogs were occasionally singled out to become the group mascots, the former because workers took a special interest in them, the latter because workers hoped to increase their adoptability. Unlike other shelter animals, mascots were permitted to run free in areas reserved for workers, such as their private office and front desk, where they were played with and talked about by workers. Importantly, they were never euthanized, either remaining indefinitely in the shelter or going home as someone's pet. Although most shelter workers interacted with the mascots as though they were pets, one shelter worker, akin to an owner, often took a special interest in the animal and let it be known that she would eventually adopt the animal if a good home could not be found. Some of their actions toward these mascots were in clear contrast to the way they would have acted toward regular shelter animals. In one case, for example, a cat mascot was found to have a stomach ailment requiring expensive surgery. In normal circumstances this animal would have been killed, but one of the workers used her own money to pay for the operation.

Using the Animal

By taking the feelings of animals into account, workers distracted themselves from their own discomfort when euthanizing. Workers tried to make this experience as "good" as possible for the animals and, in so doing, felt better themselves. Some workers, in fact, openly admitted that "it makes me feel better making it [euthanasia] better for the animal." Even more seasoned workers were more at ease with euthanasia if they focused on making animals feel secure and calm as they were killed. A worker with twenty years' experience remarked that "it still bothers you after you're here for a long time, but not as much. Compassion and tenderness are there when I euthanize, so it doesn't eat away at me."

One way workers did this was to empathize with animals in order to figure out how to reduce each animal's stress during euthanasia. By seeing things from the animals' perspective, workers sought to make the process of dying "peaceful and easy." As a worker pointed out: "You make the animal comfortable and happy and secure, so when the time to euthanize comes, it will not be under stress and scared—the dog will lick your face, the cats will purr." In the words of another worker: "They get more love in the last few seconds than they ever did." Workers were encouraged to "think of all the little things that might stress the animal—if you sense that some are afraid of men, then keep men away." For example, one worker said that she decided not to have cats and dogs in the euthanasia room at the same time. Observation of euthanasia confirmed that workers considered animals' states of mind. In one instance, where a cat and her kittens had to be euthanized, the mother was killed first because the worker thought she would become very upset if she sensed her kittens were dying. And in another case a worker refused to be interviewed during euthanasia because she felt that our talking made the animals more anxious.

Another way that taking animals into consideration helped workers distract themselves from their own concerns was to concentrate on the methodology of killing and to become technically proficient at it. By focusing on the technique of killing—and not on why it needed to be done or how they felt about doing it—workers could reassure themselves that they were making death quick and painless for animals. Workers, called "shooters," who injected the euthanasia drug were told to "focus not on the euthanasia, but on the needle. Concentrate on technical skills if you are the shooter." Even those people, known as "holders," who merely held animals steady during the injection, were taught to view their participation as a technical act as opposed to a demonstration of affection. In the words of a worker:

> The holder is the one who controls the dog. You have your arm around her. You're the one who has got a hold of that vein. When they get the blood in the syringe, you let go. But you have to hold that dog and try and keep him steady and not let him pull away. That's my job.

Bad killing technique, whether shooting or holding, was bemoaned by senior workers. As one

noted: "I get really pissed off if someone blows a vein if it is due to an improper hold."

Since euthanasia was regarded more as technical than as a moral or emotional issue, it was not surprising that workers could acquire reputations within the shelter for being "good shots," and animals came to be seen as either easy or hard "putdowns"—a division reflecting technical difficulty and increased physical discomfort for animals. If the animal was a "hard putdown," workers became all the more absorbed in the mechanics of euthanasia, knowing that the sharpness of their technical skills would affect the extent of an animal's distress. . . .

Workers could also take animals into consideration, rather than focus on their own feelings, by seeing their death as the alleviation of suffering. This was easy to do with animals who were very sick and old—known as "automatic kills"—but it was much harder to see suffering in "healthy and happy" animals that were killed. They too had to be seen as having lives not worth living. Workers were aware that the breadth of their definition of suffering made euthanasia easier for them. One worker acknowledged that: "Sometimes you want to find any reason, like it has a runny nose." Newcomers often flinched at what was deemed sufficient medical or psychological reason to euthanize an animal, as did veterinary technicians working in the adjoining animal hospital who sometimes sarcastically said to shelter workers and their animals: "If you cough, they will kill you. If you sneeze, they will kill you."

Workers learned to see euthanasia as a way to prevent suffering. For example, it was thought that it was better to euthanize healthy strays than to let them "suffer" on the streets. One senior worker told newcomers:

> I'd rather kill than see suffering. I've seen dogs hung in alleys, cats with firecrackers in their mouths or caught in fan belts. This helps me to cope with euthanizing—to prevent this suffering through euthanasia. Am I sick if I can do this for fifteen years? No. I still cry when I see a sick pigeon on the streets, but I believe in what I am doing.

Once in a shelter, healthy strays, along with abandoned and surrendered animals, were also thought better dead than "fostered out." A worker noted: "I'd rather kill it now than let it live three years and die a horrible death. No life is better than a temporary life." Even having a potential adopter was not enough; the animal's future home, if deemed "inappropriate," would only cause the animal more "suffering." One worker elaborated:

> Finding an appropriate home for the animal is the only way the animal is going to get out of here alive. The inappropriate home prolongs the suffering, prolongs the agony, prolongs the neglect, prolongs the abuse of an animal. The animal was abused or neglected in the first place or it wouldn't be here.

This thinking was a problem for newcomers who believed that almost any home, even if temporary, was better than killing animals. Particularly troubling were those people denied an animal for adoption even though their resources and attitudes seemed acceptable to workers. Some potential adopters were rejected because it was thought that they were not home often enough, even though by all other standards they seemed likely to become good owners. In one case, a veterinary hospital technician wanted to adopt a four-month-old puppy, but was rejected because she had full-time employment. Although she retorted that she had a roommate who was at home most of the time, her request was still denied.

But newcomers soon learned to scrutinize potential adopters carefully by screening them for certain warning flags, such as not wanting to spay or neuter, not wanting to fence in or leash animals, not being home enough with animals, and so on, in addition to such basics as not having a landlord's approval or adopting the pet as a gift for someone else. Most workers came to see certain groups of people as risky adopters requiring even greater scrutiny before approval. For some workers, this meant welfare recipients because they were unwilling to spay or neuter, or policemen because they might be too rough with animals.

Although workers accepted the applications of most potential owners, they did reject some. But even in their acceptances, they reaffirmed their concern for suffering and their desire to find perfect homes; they certainly did so with their rejections, admonishing those turned down for whatever their presumed problems were toward animals. Occasionally, rejected applicants became irate and made angry comments such as "You'd rather kill it than give it to me!" These moments were uncomfortable for newcomers to watch since, to some extent, they shared the rejected applicant's sentiment—any home was better than death. More experienced workers would try to cool down the applicant but also remind newcomers that some homes were worse than death. In one such case, the shelter manager said to the rejected applicant, but for all to hear, "It is my intention to find a good home where the animal's needs can be met."

Resisting and Avoiding Euthanasia

New workers, in particular, sometimes managed their discomfort with euthanasia by trying to prevent or delay the death of animals. Although there were generally understood euthanasia guidelines, they were rather vague, and workers could exert mild pressure to make exceptions to the rules. Certainly, not all animals scheduled or "pink-slipped" to be killed were "automatic kills." As a worker noted. "If a 12 year-old stray with hip dysplasia comes in, yes, you know as soon as it walks in the door that at the end of the stray holding period it's going to be euthanized, but not all of them are like this." A worker described such an instance:

> Four weeks is really young. Five weeks, you're really pushing it. Six weeks, we can take it, but it depends on its overall health and condition. But sometimes we'll keep one or two younger ones, depending on the animal itself. We just had an animal last week—it was a dachshund. She is a really nice and friendly dog. In this case, we just decided to keep her.

Sometimes a worker took a special liking to a particular animal, but it was to be euthanized because the cage was needed for new animals, or it was too young, too old, somewhat sick, or had a behavior problem. The worker might let it be known among colleagues that they were very attached to the animal, or they might go directly to the person making the euthanasia selection with a plea for the animal's date of death to be delayed in the hopes of adoption. One worker had a favorite cat that was to be euthanized, but succeeded in blocking its euthanasia, at least for a while, by personally taking financial responsibility for its shelter costs.

However, opposing euthanasia had to be done in a way that did not make such decisions too difficult for those making them. Workers could not object repeatedly to euthanasia or oppose it too aggressively without making the selector feel uncomfortable. One worker felt "guilty" when this happened to her:

> There was one technician—Marie—who used to make me feel guilty. I have to make room for new animals because we have so few cages. I must decide which old ones to kill to make room for new ones. Marie would get upset when I would choose certain cats to be killed. She would come to me with her runny, snotty nose, complaining that certain cats were picked to be killed. This made me feel guilty.

If opposing euthanasia failed, workers were able to avoid the discomfort of doing it. One worker said that he would not "be around" if his favorite cat was killed, and noted:

> There's not an animal I'm not attached to here, but there's a cat here now that I like a lot. There's a good chance that she'll be euthanized. She's got a heart murmur. I guess. It's a mild one, but . . . any type of heart murmur with a cat is bad. She's also got a lump right here. They've already tested her for leukemia and it's negative, so they are testing her for something else. But she's just got an adorable face and everything else with her is fine. I like her personality. But I have two cats at home. I can't have a third. I won't be around when they euthanize her. I'll let somebody else do it. I would rather it be done when I'm not here.

Although workers could be exempted from killing animals with whom they had closely bonded, there was a strong feeling that such persons should be there for the animal's sake. Yet if present, they could indicate to others that they did not want to be the "shooter" and instead be the "holder," allowing them to feel more removed from the actual killing. A worker said:

> Especially if it's one I like a lot, I would rather be the one holding instead of injecting. If you don't want to inject, you just back up and somebody else does it. Everybody here does that. I just look at it, I don't want to be the one to do it. Even though people say that holding is the harder of the two, I would look at it as, well, I am the one who is doing this. And sometimes, I don't want to be the one to do it.

Customizing the division of labor of euthanasia to fit their own emotional limits, other workers preferred not to do the holding. One worker observed:

> One of the ways that I detach myself from euthanasia is that I do the shooting rather than the holding so that I don't feel the animal dying. I'm concentrating on the technical skill behind the actual injection. And with a dog, you literally feel the animal's life go out of it in your arms, instead of giving the injection and letting it drop.

Using the Owner

Shelter workers could also displace some of their own discomfort with euthanasia into anger and frustration with pet owners. Rather than questioning the morality of their own acts and feeling guilty about euthanasia, workers came to regard owners, and not themselves, as behaving wrongly toward animals. As workers transferred the blame for killing animals to the public, they concentrated their energies on educating and changing public attitudes to pets and making successful adoptions through the shelter.

The public was seen as treating animals as "property to be thrown away like trash" rather than as something having intrinsic value. One worker bemoaned:

> A lot of people who want to leave their pets have bullshit reasons for this—like they just bought new furniture for their living room and their cat shed all over it.

This lack of commitment resulted in many of the surrendered animals being euthanized because they were not adoptable and/or space was needed. Speaking about these owners, one worker candidly acknowledged:

> I would love to be rude once to some of these people who come in. I'd like to say to these people, "Cut this bullshit out!"

Another worker concluded: "You do want to strangle these people."

Even if pet owners did not surrender their animals to the shelter, they became tainted as a group in the eyes of workers, who saw many of them as negligent or irresponsible. A common charge against owners was that their pets were allowed to run free and be hurt, lost or stolen. One senior worker admitted: "A bias does get built in. We're called if a cat gets caught in a fan belt. We're the ones that have to scrape cats off the streets." Owners were also seen as selfish and misguided when it came to their pets, thoughtlessly allowing them to breed, instead of spaying or neutering them. Workers often repeated the shelter's pithy wish: "Parents will let their pets have puppies or kittens so they can show their children the miracle of birth—well, maybe they should come in here to see the miracle of death!" Workers could be heard among themselves admonishing the public's "irresponsibility" toward breeding and the deaths that such an attitude caused. A worker explained: "The only reason why it has been killed is that no one took the time to be a responsible pet owner. They felt the cat deserved to run free or they didn't want to pay the money to have it spayed or neutered, or that she should have one litter. Well great, what are you to do with her six offspring?" Even owners who declared great love and affection for their pets sometimes came across in the shelter environment as cruel to their animals. These were owners who let their animals suffer because they could not bear to kill them. A worker noted:

I'll get a 22-year-old cat. And the owner is crying out there. I tell her, "You know, twenty-two years is great. You have nothing to be ashamed of. Nothing." But you get some others that come in and they [the animals] look absolutely like shit. You feel like taking hold of them and saying "What in the hell are you doing? He should have been put to sleep two years ago."

According to shelter workers, owners should have to suffer pangs of conscience about their treatment of animals, but did not. Some owners seemed not to want their pets, and this shocked workers, as one noted: "You'd be surprised at how many people come right out and say they don't want it any more. They are usually the ones who call us to pick it up, otherwise they'll dump it on the street. And of course, we're going to come and get it. I feel like saying 'It's your conscience, not mine, go ahead, do it.' Of course, I don't do that." Many surrenderers, in the eyes of shelter workers, just did not care whether their animals lived or died. At the same time that surrenderers were seen as lacking a conscience, shelter workers were afforded the opportunity to reaffirm their own dedication to and feelings for animals. A worker commented:

Some surrenderers take them back after we tell them we can't guarantee placement. Most

say, "Well that's fine." Like the owner of this cat, he called this morning and said, "I've got to get rid of it, I'm allergic to it." Of course, he didn't seem at all bothered. He goes, "That's fine." Or somebody is going to surrender a pet because they're moving, well, if it was me, and I'm sure quite a few other people here feel the same way, I'd look for a place where pets were allowed. People are just looking out for themselves and not anything else.

In the opinion of the workers, it was important for newcomers to learn not to bear the "guilt" that owners should have felt. To do this, they had to see owners as the real killers of shelter animals. As one worker put it, "People think we are murderers, but they are the ones that have put us in this position. We are morally offended by the fact that we have to carry out an execution that we didn't necessarily order." A senior shelter worker recounted how she came to terms with guilt:

Every night I had a recurring dream that I had died, and I was standing in line to go to heaven. And St. Peter says to me, "I know you, you're the one that killed all those little animals." And I'd sit up in the bed in a cold sweat. Finally, I realized it wasn't my fault, my dreams changed. After St. Peter said, "I know you, you're the one that killed all those little animals," I turned to the 999,000 people behind me and said, "I know you, you made me kill all these animals." You grow into the fact that you are the executioner, but you weren't the judge and jury.

Shelter workers redirected their emotions and resources into changing public attitudes about pets in order to curtail the never-ending flow of animals—often called a "flood"—that always far exceeded what was possible to adopt out. Overwhelmed by this problem, workers wanted to do something about it other than killing animals. By putting effort into adoption or public education, they felt they were making a dent in the overpopulation problem instead of feeling hopeless about it. For many, combating pet overpopulation became addictive and missionary. Rather than chew over the morality of their own participation in euthanasia, they felt part of a serious campaign—often described as a "battle"—against the formidable foe of the pet owner and in defense of helpless animals.

Owners were used in ways other than as objects of blame. Successful adoptions helped to accentuate the positive in a setting where there were few opportunities to feel good about what workers were doing. Finding homes for animals came close to the original motivation that brought many workers to the shelter seeking employment. One worker commented: "For every one euthanized, you have to think about the one placed, or the one case where you placed in a perfect family." Another worker said that "you get a good feeling when you see an empty cage." She explained that she did not think that it was empty because an animal had just been killed, but because an animal had just been adopted. Indeed, out of self-protection, when the cage of someone's "favorite" was empty, workers did not ask what happened to the animals so they could assume that it was adopted rather than killed. They talked about how all of their animals were "either PWP or PWG—placed with people or placed with God." Shelter workers felt particularly satisfied when they heard from people who had satisfactorily adopted animals. Sometimes these owners came into the shelter and talked informally with workers; at other times, they wrote letters of thanks for their animals. Besides taping this mail on the walls for all to see, workers mounted snapshots of adopters and their animals in the shelter's lobby.

Dealing With Others

For workers to manage their emotions successfully, they had to learn to suspend asking hard ethical questions. While this was easy to do within the confines of the shelter, it was more difficult outside. Many reported feeling badly when outsiders learned they killed animals and challenged them about the morality of euthanasia. Workers dealt with these unwanted feelings in two ways.

Outside work, they could try to avoid the kinds of contact that give rise to unwanted emotions and difficult questions. Workers claimed that roommates, spouses, family members, and strangers sometimes made them feel "guilty" because they were seen as "villains" or "murderers." As one worker said, "You expect your spouse, your parents, your sister, your brother, or your significant other to understand. And they don't. And your friends don't. People make stupid remarks like, 'Gee, I would never do your job because I love animals too much.'" Workers claimed that they had become "paranoid" about being asked if they killed animals, waiting for questions

such as, "How can you kill them if you care about animals so much?" Sometimes people would simply tell workers: "I love animals, I couldn't do that." One worker claimed that these questions and comments "make me feel like I've done something wrong." Another said, "So what does it mean—I don't love animals?" If workers were not explicitly criticized or misunderstood, they still encountered people who made them feel reluctant to talk about their work. One worker noted that "I'm proud that I'm a 90 per cent shot, and that I'm not putting the animals through stress, but people don't want to hear this."

In anticipation of these negative reactions, many workers hesitated to divulge what they did. One worker said that she had learned to tell people that she "drives an animal ambulance." If workers revealed that they carried out euthanasia, they often presented arguments to support their caring for animals and the need for euthanasia. As one worker noted, "I throw numbers at them, like the fact that we get 12,000 animals a year but can only place 2,000." While concealing their work and educating others about it were by far the most common strategies used with outsiders, some workers would occasionally take a blunter approach and use sarcasm or black humor. The following worker talked about all these approaches:

> People give me a lot of grief. You know, you tell them where you work, and you tell them it's an animal shelter. And they say, "Well, you don't put them to sleep, do you?" And I always love to say, "Well actually I give classes on how to do that," just for the shock value of it. Or it's the old, "I could never do what you do, I love animals too much." "Oh, I don't love them at all. That's why I work here. I kill them. I enjoy it." But sometimes you don't even mention where you work because you don't want to deal with that. It depends on the social situation I am in as to whether I want to go in to it or not, and it also depends on how I feel at a given time. Some people are interested, and then I talk about spaying and neutering their pets.

Another way workers dealt with outsiders was to neutralize their criticism of euthanasia. The only credible opinions about euthanasia were seen as coming from those people who actually did such killing as part of the shelter community. Humor was one device that helped workers feel part of this community. It gave them a special language to talk about death and their concerns about it. As with gallows humor in other settings, it was not particularly funny out of context, and workers knew this, but learning to use it and find it humorous became a rite of passage. For instance, people telephoning the shelter might be greeted with the salutation, "Heaven." Referring to the euthanasia room and the euthanasia drug also took on a light, funny side with the room being called "downtown" or the "lavender lounge" (its walls were this color) and the drug being called "sleepaway" or "go-go juice" (its brand name was "Fatal Plus").

But no ritual practice gave more of a sense of "we-ness" then actually killing animals. No single act admitted them more into the shelter institution or more clearly demarcated the transition of shelter workers out of the novice role. As they gained increasing experience with euthanasia, workers developed a firmer sense of being in the same boat with peers who also did what they did. They shared an unarticulated belief that others could not understand what it was like to kill unless they had also done so. Even within the shelter, kennel workers often felt misunderstood by the front-desk people. As one worker reflected, "It does feel like you can't understand what I do if you can't understand that I don't like to kill, but that I have to kill. You'd have to see what I see. Maybe then." Since outsiders did not share this experience, workers tended to give them little credibility and to discount their opinions. By curtailing the possibility of understanding what they did and communicating with others about it, workers furthered their solidarity and created boundaries between themselves and outsiders that served to shield them from external criticism and diminish any uncomfortable feelings easily raised by the "uninformed" or "naive."

The Imperfection of Emotion Management

Certainly, the killing of animals by shelter workers was facilitated by the kinds of emotion management strategies that have been discussed. Yet it would be wrong to characterize these people, including those with many years' experience, as completely detached. These strategies were far from perfect. It would be more accurate to say that their institutional socialization was incomplete. All workers, including those with many

years of experience, felt uneasy about euthanasia at certain times.

For the few who continued to experience sharp and disturbing feelings, quitting became a way to manage emotions. For example, one worker felt "plagued" by a conflict between her own feelings for the animals which made killing hard to accept and the shelter's euthanasia policy with which she intellectually agreed. She said it was "like having two people in my head, one good and the other evil, that argue about me destroying these animals." This conflict left her feeling "guilty" about deaths she found "hard to justify." After nine months on the job, she quit.

For most workers this conflict was neither intense nor constant, but instead manifested itself as episodic uneasiness. From time to time euthanasia provoked modest but clearly discernible levels of emotional distress. There was no consensus, however, on what kind of euthanasia would rattle people and make them feel uncomfortable, but everyone had at least one type that roused their feelings.

The most obvious discomfort with euthanasia occurred when workers had to kill animals to which they were attached or that they could easily see as pets. While newcomers were more likely to have formed these attachments, seasoned workers could still be troubled by euthanasia when animals reminded them of other attachments. As one veteran worker reflected:

> I haven't been emotionally attached to a dog, except for one, for quite a while. I know my limit. But there are times when I'll look at a dog when I'm euthanizing it and go, "You've got Rex's eyes." Or it's an Irish setter—I have a natural attachment to Irish setters. Or black cats—I hate to euthanize black cats. It's real hard for me to euthanize a black cat.

Even without attachments, many workers found it "heartbreaking" to euthanize young, healthy and well-behaved animals merely for space because they could have become pets. Without a medical or psychological reason, euthanasia seemed a "waste."

For many, euthanasia became unsettling if it appeared that animals suffered physically or psychologically. This happened, for example, when injections of the euthanasia drug caused animals to "scream," "cry," or become very disoriented and move about frantically. But it also happened when animals seemed to "know" they were about to be killed or sensed that "death was in the air." "Cats aren't dumb. They know what's going on. Whenever you take them to the room, they always get this stance where their head goes up, and they know," observed one worker. Another said that many animals could "smell" death. These workers became uneasy because they assumed that the animals were "scared." "What is hard for me," said one worker, "is when they are crying and they are very, very scared." Another said that she could "feel their tension and anxiety" in the euthanasia room. "They seem to know what's happening—that something is going to happen," she added to explain her discomfort.

Ironically, for some workers the opposite situation left them feeling unsettled. They found it eerie when animals were not scared and instead behaved "as though they were co-operating." According to one worker, certain breeds were likely to act this way as they were being killed: "Greyhounds and dobermans will either give you their paw or willingly give you their leg, and look right past you. It's as though they are co-operating. The other dogs will look right at you."

Killing large numbers of animals in a single day was disconcerting for nearly everyone. This happened to one worker when the number of animals killed was so great she could not conceptualize the quantity until she picked up a thick pile of "yellow slips" (surrender forms), or when she looked at the drug log and saw how many animals had been given euthanasia injections. The flow of animals into the shelter was seasonal, and workers grew to loathe those months when many animals were brought in and euthanized. The summer was a particularly bad time, because so many cats came in and were killed. As one worker said, "They are constantly coming in. On a bad day, you might have to do it [euthanasia] fifty times. There are straight months of killing." Another observed, "After three hours of killing, you come out a mess. It drains me completely. I'll turn around and see all these dead animals on the floor around me—and it's "What have I done?" And yet another worker noted:

It's very difficult when we are inundated from spring until fall. Every single person who walks through the door has either a pillow case, a box, a laundry basket or whatever—one more litter of kittens. And you only have X number of cages in your facility and they are already full. So the animal may come in the front door and go out the back door in a barrel. It's very difficult if that animal never had a chance at life, or has had a very short life.

Even seasoned workers said that it did "not feel right" to spend so much time killing, particularly when so many of the animals they killed were young and never had a chance to become a pet.

All workers, then, experienced at least some uneasiness when facing certain types of euthanasia, despite their socialization into the shelter's culture. The emotions generated by these situations overruled attempts by the shelter to help them manage their emotions and objectify their charges. When emotion management and objectification failed, workers felt some degree of connection and identification with the animals which in turn elicited feelings of sadness, worry, and even remorse.

Conclusion

The initial conflict faced by newcomers to an animal shelter was extreme—because of their prior, everyday perspective toward animals, killing them generated emotions that caused workers to balk at carrying out euthanasia. However, on closer inspection, this tension was replaced by a more moderate and manageable version of the same conflict. The conflict was repackaged and softened, but it was there, nonetheless. Shelter workers could more easily live with this version, and their emotion management strategies got them to this point. These strategies embodied an underlying inconsistency or dilemma between the simultaneous pulls toward objectifying the animals and seeing the animals in pet-related terms—a conflict between rational necessity and sentimentality, between head and heart, between everyday perspective and that of the institution. . . .

A final look at these strategies reveals this underlying tension. By transforming shelter animals into virtual pets, the workers could objectify the animals to some degree, while also categorizing them as something like, yet different from, everyday pets. When it came to actually killing them, workers could play the role of highly skilled technicians efficiently dispatching animal lives seen as not worth living, simultaneously trying to take the emotional and physical feelings of animals into account. Being able to avoid or postpone killing was itself viewed as a struggle between emotion and rationality; importantly, this was allowed, thereby acknowledging some degree of emotion but within limits that reaffirmed a more rational approach. When it came to their view of owners (perhaps a collective projection of a sort), it was the public, and not themselves, that objectified animals; whatever they did, including the killing, paled by comparison and was done out of sentiment and caring. Indeed, outsiders came to be suspected, one-dimensionally, as a distant and alien group, while workers increasingly cultivated a strong sense of we-ness among themselves—humans, too, seem to have two fundamentally different kinds of relations with each other. . . .

It is . . . not surprising that these strategies were sometimes imperfect, failing to prevent penetration of the everyday perspective toward animals into the shelter. Even the most effective programs of organizational socialization are likely to be fallible when workers face situations that trigger their prior feelings and concerns. Many shelter workers may have felt uneasy because at certain times their personal, everyday thinking and feeling about animals in general may have taken precedence over the institutional "rules" for thinking and feeling about animals. . . .

Yet, in the end, by relying on these strategies workers reproduced the institution (e.g., Smith and Kleinman 1989), thereby creating a new generation of workers who would support the humane society model and the kind of human-animal relationship in which people could believe they were killing with a conscience. Far from being a unique situation, the shelter worker's relationship with animals is but our general culture's response to animals writ small. It is not likely that we ourselves are altogether exempt from this inconsistency, as our individual ways of managing our thought and feelings may similarly dull the conflict just enough for it to become a familiar uneasiness. For shelter workers, the conflict is merely heightened and their struggle to make peace with their acts is more deliberate and collective.

References

Schleifer, H. (1985) "Images of death and life: food animal production and the vegetarian option," in P. Singer (ed.) *In Defense of Animals*, New York: Harper & Row, pp. 63–74.

Serpell, J. (1986) *In the Company of Animals*, Oxford: Basil Blackwell.

Smith, A., and Kleinman, S. (1989) "Managing emotions in medical school: students' contacts with the living and the dead." *Social Psychology Quarterly* 52:56–68.

Part IX

The Politics of Social Reality

One of the central themes of this volume is that humans inhabit socially constructed realities. Through interaction with one another, we endow the world of brute physical facts with meaning and create symbolic universes that transcend that world. We interpret and structure our subjective experience in terms of social symbols and meanings. Thus, our reality is socially constructed and decided.

However, individuals' definitions of their subjective experience, themselves, one another, social situations, relationships, their society, and the surrounding environment do not always coincide. When such definitional contests occur, power usually decides whose definition will prevail. In our society, for example, the medical profession's authoritative definitions of illness commonly prevail over the Christian Scientists' definitions; psychiatrists' definitions of subjective experience prevail over their patients'; social service providers' definitions take precedence over clients' definitions of their own problems; and so on. The politics of reality decide who will participate in the social construction of reality and how much they will contribute.

The more familiar form of politics also involves contested definitions of reality. The social problems that policymakers are urged to address are particular constructions of reality. People and groups make different claims about what social conditions are problems, what kind of problems they are, and how they should be addressed. The politics of reality decide what conditions get defined as social problems, how they get defined, and what actions are taken to address them. These politics of reality are the most fundamental politics of human social life that decide what reality everyone in a given social circle will inhabit, and, in some cases, whether they will live at all. The selections in this section examine various aspects of the politics of social reality and their consequences. ✦

32

The Moral Career of the Mental Patient

Erving Goffman

The politics of reality are perhaps most obvious in mental hospitals. Yet students of social life paid little attention to the political struggles of reality construction in mental hospitals before the publication of Goffman's widely read study Asylums. They simply assumed the perspective of mental health professionals and did not take seriously their patients' often clashing views of reality. Goffman took a different tack. He attempted to learn about the social life of a mental hospital from the perspective of its patients. This selection, taken from Asylums, reveals the politics of reality at that hospital and how they shaped patients' moral careers.

What is at stake in the politics of reality that brings individuals to a mental hospital and keeps them there is their very definition of self. In this selection, Goffman reports that family members, friends, and mental health professionals commonly form a political coalition against patients even before they get to the mental hospital. Once there, the patients' past lives and current circumstances are interpreted so as to justify admittance. From that point forward, patients' definitions of self are hostages to the definitional power of the institution and its staff.

Like those outside the walls of the mental hospital, patients attempt to maintain "face" or effective claims to positive social value. Yet their very presence in the institution indicates that they have fallen from social grace. As Goffman observes, the mental hospital is a mirror that continually reflects unflattering self-images to patients. Although patients attempt to counter these mortifying definitions of self with what Goffman calls "sad tales," they are challenged by everything around them and by everyone in the hospital. Their misdeeds are recorded in case records, reported at staff meetings, and discussed informally. Patients' own presentations of self cannot counter the weight of information that the hospital's staff possesses about them. They consequently have little influence over how others define and treat

them. In the politics of reality of the mental institution, patients are virtually powerless.

The goal of the mental institution and its staff is to convince patients to internalize the psychiatric view of reality and themselves. Yet, as Goffman observes, the constant assaults upon patients' definitions of self may have a quite different effect, at least temporarily. Unable to claim or maintain face, patients may conclude that they have nothing to lose by acting shamelessly and do so. Thus, the very institution that is supposed to entice deviant individuals back to the official social reality may sometimes drive them further away. Therein lies a more general sociological lesson. Those who have no power to wield over the politics of reality may simply choose not to participate.

In 1955-56, I did a year's field work at St. Elizabeths Hospital, Washington, D.C., a federal institution of somewhat over 7000 inmates that draws three quarters of its patients from the District of Columbia. . . . My immediate object in doing field work at St. Elizabeths was to try to learn about the social world of the hospital inmate, as this world is subjectively experienced by him. . . .

It was then and still is my belief that any group of persons—prisoners, primitives, pilots, or patients—develop a life of their own that becomes meaningful, reasonable, and normal once you get close to it, and that a good way to learn about any of these worlds is to submit oneself in the company of the members to the daily round of petty contingencies to which they are subject. . . .

The world view of a group functions to sustain its members and expectedly provides them with a self-justifying definition of their own situation and a prejudiced view of nonmembers, in this case, doctors, nurses, attendants, and relatives. To describe the patient's situation faithfully is necessarily to present a partisan view. (For this last bias, I partly excuse myself by arguing that the imbalance is at least on the right side of the scale, since almost all professional literature on mental patients is written from the point of view of the psychiatrist, and he, socially speaking, is on the other side). . . .

Traditionally the term *career* has been reserved for those who expect to enjoy the rises laid out within a respectable profession. The term is coming to be used, however, in a broadened sense to refer to any social strand of any person's course through life. The perspective of natural history is taken: unique outcomes are neglected in favor of such changes over time as are basic and common to the members of a social category, although occurring independently to each of them. Such a career is not a thing that can be brilliant or disappointing; it can no more be a success than a failure. In this light, I want to consider the mental patient. . . .

The category "mental patient" itself will be understood in one strictly sociological sense. In this perspective, the psychiatric view of a person becomes significant only in so far as this view itself alters his social fate—an alteration which seems to become fundamental in our society when, and only when, the person is put through the process of hospitalization. I, therefore, exclude certain neighboring categories: the undiscovered candidates who would be judged "sick" by psychiatric standards but who never come to be viewed as such by themselves or others, although they may cause everyone a great deal of trouble; the office patient whom a psychiatrist feels he can handle with drugs or shock on the outside; the mental client who engages in psychotherapeutic relationships. And I include anyone, however robust in temperament, who somehow gets caught up in the heavy machinery of mental-hospital servicing. In this way, the effects of being treated as a mental patient can be kept quite distant from the effects upon a person's life of traits a clinician would view as psychopathological. . . .

The career of the mental patient falls popularly and naturalistically into three main phases: the period prior to entering the hospital, which I shall call the prepatient phase; the period in the hospital, the inpatient phase; the period after discharge from the hospital, should this occur, namely, the ex-patient phase. This paper will deal only with the first two phases. . . .

The Prepatient Phase

The prepatient's career may be seen in terms of an extrusory model; he starts out with relationships and rights, and ends up, at the beginning of his hospital stay, with hardly any of either. The moral aspects of this career, then, typically begin with the experience of abandonment, disloyalty, and embitterment. This is the case even though to others it may be obvious that he was in need of treatment, and even though in the hospital he may soon come to agree. . . .

In the prepatient's progress from home to the hospital, he may participate as a third person in what he may come to experience as a kind of alienative coalition. His next-of-relation presses him into coming to "talk things over" with a medical practitioner, an office psychiatrist, or some other counselor. Disinclination on his part may be met by threatening him with desertion, disownment, or other legal action, or by stressing the joint and exploratory nature of the interview. But typically the next-of-relation will have set the interview up, in the sense of selecting the professional, arranging for time, telling the professional something about the case, and so on. This move effectively tends to establish the next-of-relation as the responsible person to whom pertinent findings can be divulged, while effectively establishing the other as the patient. The prepatient often goes to the interview with the understanding that he is going as an equal of someone who is so bound together with him that a third person could not come between them in fundamental matters; this, after all, is one way in which close relationships are defined in our society. Upon arrival at the office, the prepatient suddenly finds that he and his next-of-relation have not been accorded the same roles, and apparently that a prior understanding between the professional and the next-of-relation has been put in operation against him. In the extreme but common case, the professional first sees the prepatient alone, in the role of examiner and diagnostician, and then sees the next-of-relation alone, in the role of adviser, while carefully avoiding talking things over seriously with them both together. And even in those non-consultative cases where public officials must forcibly extract a person from a family that wants to tolerate him, the next-of-relation is likely to be induced to "go along" with the official action, so that even here the prepatient may feel that an alienative coalition has been formed against him. . . .

The final point I want to consider about the prepatient's moral career is its peculiarly retroactive character. Until a person actually arrives at the hospital, there usually seems no way of knowing for sure that he is destined to do so, given the determinative role of career contingencies. And, until the point of hospitalization is reached, he or others may not conceive of him as a person who is becoming a mental patient. However, since he will be held against his will in the hospital, his next-of-relation and the hospital staff will be in great need of a rationale for the hardships they are sponsoring. The medical elements of the staff will also need evidence that they are still in the trade they were trained for. These problems are eased, no doubt unintentionally, by the case-history construction that is placed on the patient's past life, this having the effect of demonstrating that all along he had been becoming sick, that he finally became very sick, and that if he had not been hospitalized much worse things would have happened to him—all of which, of course, may be true. Incidentally, if the patient wants to make sense out of his stay in the hospital, and, as already suggested, keep alive the possibility of once again conceiving of his next-of-relation as a decent, well-meaning person, then he, too, will have reason to believe some of this psychiatric work-up of his past. . . .

The Inpatient Phase

The last step in the prepatient's career can involve his realization—justified or not—that he has been deserted by society and turned out of relationships by those closest to him. Interestingly enough, the patient, especially a first admission, may manage to keep himself from coming to the end of this trail, even though, in fact, he is now in a locked mental-hospital ward. On entering the hospital, he may very strongly feel the desire not to be known to anyone as a person who could possibly be reduced to these present circumstances, or as a person who conducted himself in the way he did prior to commitment. Consequently, he may avoid talking to anyone, may stay by himself when possible, and may even be "out of contact" or "manic" so as to avoid ratifying any interaction that presses a politely reciprocal role upon him and opens him up to what he has become in the eyes of others. When the next-of-relation makes an effort to visit, he may be rejected by mutism, or by the patient's refusal to enter the visiting room, these strategies sometimes suggesting that the patient still clings to a remnant of relatedness to those who made up his past, and is protecting this remnant from the final destructiveness of dealing with the new people that they have become. . . .

Once the prepatient begins to settle down, the main outlines of his fate tend to follow those of a whole class of segregated establishments—jails, concentration camps, monasteries, work camps, and so on—in which the inmate spends the whole round of life on the grounds, and marches through his regimented day in the immediate company of a group of persons of his own institutional status.

Like the neophyte in many of these total institutions, the new inpatient finds himself cleanly stripped of many of his accustomed affirmations, satisfactions, and defenses, and is subjected to a rather full set of mortifying experiences: restriction of free movement, communal living, diffuse authority of a whole echelon of people, and so on. Here one begins to learn about the limited extent to which a conception of oneself can be sustained when the usual setting of supports for it are suddenly removed. . . .

Once lodged on a given ward, the patient is firmly instructed that the restrictions and deprivations he encounters are not due to such blind forces as tradition or economy—and hence dissociable from self—but are intentional parts of his treatment, part of his need at the time, and, therefore, an expression of the state that his self has fallen to. Having every reason to initiate requests for better conditions, he is told that when the staff feel he is "able to manage" or will be "comfortable with" a higher ward level, then appropriate action will be taken. In short, assignment to a given ward is presented not as a reward or punishment, but as an expression of his general level of social functioning, his status as a person. Given the fact that the worst ward levels provide a round of life that inpatients with organic brain damage can easily manage, and that these quite limited human beings are present to prove it, one can appreciate some of the mirroring effects of the hospital.

The ward system, then, is an extreme instance of how the physical facts of an establishment can be explicitly employed to frame the conception a person takes of himself. In addition, the official psychiatric mandate of mental hospitals gives rise to even more direct, even more blatant, attacks upon the inmate's view of himself. The more "medical" and the more progressive a mental hospital is—the more it attempts to be therapeutic and not merely custodial—the more he may be confronted by high-ranking staff arguing that his past has been a failure, that the cause of this has been within himself, that his attitude to life is wrong, and that if he wants to be a person he will have to change his way of dealing with people and his conceptions of himself. Often the moral value of these verbal assaults will be brought home to him by requiring him to practice taking this psychiatric view of himself in arranged confessional periods, whether in private sessions or group psychotherapy.

Now a general point may be made about the moral career of inpatients which has bearing on many moral careers. Given the stage that any person has reached in a career, one typically finds that he constructs an image of his life course—past, present, and future—which selects, abstracts, and distorts in such a way as to provide him with a view of himself that he can usefully expound in current situations. Quite generally, the person's line concerning self defensively brings him into appropriate alignment with the basic values of his society, and so may be called an apologia. If the person can manage to present a view of his current situation which shows the operation of favorable personal qualities in the past and a favorable destiny awaiting him, it may be called a success story. If the facts of a person's past and present are extremely dismal, then about the best he can do is to show that he is not responsible for what has become of him, and the term "sad tale" is appropriate. Interestingly enough, the more the person's past forces him out of apparent alignment with central moral values, the more often he seems compelled to tell his sad tale in any company in which he finds himself. Perhaps the party responds to the need he feels in others of not having their sense of proper life courses affronted. In any case, it is among convicts, "winos," and prostitutes that one seems to obtain sad tales the most readily. It is the vicissitudes of the mental patient's sad tale that I want to consider now.

In the mental hospital, the setting and the house rules press home to the patient that he is, after all, a mental case who has suffered some kind of social collapse on the outside, having failed in some over-all way, and that here he is of little social weight, being hardly capable of acting like a full-fledged person at all. These humiliations are likely to be most keenly felt by middle-class patients, since their previous condition of life little immunizes them against such affronts, but all patients feel some downgrading. Just as any normal

member of his outside subculture would do, the patient often responds to this situation by attempting to assert a sad tale proving that he is not "sick," that the "little trouble" he did get into was really somebody else's fault, that his past life course had some honor and rectitude, and that the hospital is, therefore, unjust in forcing the status of mental patient upon him. This self-respecting tendency is heavily institutionalized within the patient society where opening social contacts typically involve the participants' volunteering information about their current ward location and length of stay so far, but not the reasons for their stay—such interaction being conducted in the manner of small talk on the outside. With greater familiarity, each patient usually volunteers relatively acceptable reasons for his hospitalization, at the same time accepting without open, immediate question the lines offered by other patients. Such stories as the following are given and overtly accepted:

> I was going to night school to get a M A degree, and holding down a job in addition, and the load got too much for me.

> The others here are sick mentally, but I'm suffering from a bad nervous system and that is what is giving me these phobias.

> I got here by mistake because of a diabetes diagnosis, and I'll leave in a couple of days. [The patient had been in seven weeks.]

> I failed as a child, and later with my wife I reached out for dependency.

> My trouble is that I can't work. That's what I'm in for. I had two jobs with a good home and all the money I wanted.

The patient sometimes reinforces these stories by an optimistic definition of his occupational status. A man who managed to obtain an audition as a radio announcer styles himself a radio announcer; another who worked for some months as a copy boy and was then given a job as a reporter on a large trade journal, but fired after three weeks, defines himself as a reporter. A whole social role in the patient community may be constructed on the basis of these reciprocally sustained fictions. For these face-to-face niceties tend to be qualified by behind-the-back gossip that comes only a degree closer to the "objective" facts. Here, of course, one can see a classic social function of informal networks of equals:

they serve as one another's audience for self-supporting tales—tales that are somewhat more solid than pure fantasy and somewhat thinner than the facts.

But the patient's apologia is called forth in a unique setting, for few settings could be so destructive of self-stories except, of course, those stories already constructed along psychiatric lines. And this destructiveness rests on more than the official sheet of paper which attests that the patient is of unsound mind, a danger to himself and others—an attestation, incidentally, which seems to cut deeply into the patient's pride, and into the possibility of his having any.

Certainly, the degrading conditions of the hospital setting belie many of the self-stories that are presented by patients, and the very fact of being in the mental hospital is evidence against these tales. And, of course, there is not always sufficient patient solidarity to prevent patient discrediting patient, just as there is not always a sufficient number of "professionalized" attendants to prevent attendant discrediting patient. As one patient informant repeatedly suggested to a fellow patient:

> If you're so smart, how come you got your ass in here?

The mental-hospital setting, however, is more treacherous still. Staff have much to gain through discreditings of the patient's story—whatever the felt reason for such discreditings. If the custodial faction in the hospital is to succeed in managing his daily round without complaint or trouble from him, then it will prove useful to be able to point out to him that the claims about himself upon which he rationalizes his demands are false, that he is not what he is claiming to be, and that in fact he is a failure as a person. If the psychiatric faction is to impress upon him its views about his personal make-up, then they must be able to show in detail how their version of his past and their version of his character hold up much better than his own. If both the custodial and psychiatric factions are to get him to co-operate in the various psychiatric treatments, then it will prove useful to disabuse him of his view of their purposes, and cause him to appreciate that they know what they are doing, and are doing what is best for him. In brief, the difficulties caused by a patient are closely tied to his version of what has been happening to him, and if co-operation is to be secured, it helps if this version is discredited. The patient must "insightfully" come to take, or affect to take, the hospital's view of himself.

The staff also have ideal means—in addition to the mirroring effect of the setting—for denying the inmate's rationalizations. Current psychiatric doctrine defines mental disorder as something that can have its roots in the patient's earliest years, show its signs throughout the course of his life, and invade almost every sector of his current activity. No segment of his past or present need be defined, then, as beyond the jurisdiction and mandate of psychiatric assessment. Mental hospitals bureaucratically institutionalize this extremely wide mandate by formally basing their treatment of the patient upon his diagnosis and hence upon the psychiatric view of his past.

The case record is an important expression of this mandate. This dossier is apparently not regularly used, however, to record occasions when the patient showed capacity to cope honorably and effectively with difficult life situations. Nor is the case record typically used to provide a rough average or sampling of his past conduct. One of its purposes is to show the ways in which the patient is "sick" and the reasons why it was right to commit him and is right currently to keep him committed; and this is done by extracting from his whole life course a list of those incidents that have or might have had "symptomatic" significance. The misadventures of his parents or siblings that might suggest a "taint" may be cited. Early acts in which the patient appeared to have shown bad judgment or emotional disturbance will be recorded. Occasions when he acted in a way which the layman would consider immoral, sexually perverted, weak-willed, childish, ill-considered, impulsive, and crazy may be described. Misbehaviors which someone saw as the last straw, as cause for immediate action, are likely to be reported in detail. In addition, the record will describe his state on arrival at the hospital—and this is not likely to be a time of tranquility and ease for him. The record may also report the false line taken by the patient in answering embarrassing questions, showing him as someone who makes claims that are obviously contrary to the facts:

> Claims she lives with oldest daughter or with sisters only when sick and in need of care; otherwise with husband, he himself says not for twelve years.

Contrary to the reports from the personnel, he says he no longer bangs on the floor or cries in the morning.

. . . conceals fact that she had her organs removed, claims she is still menstruating.

At first, she denied having had premarital sexual experience; but when asked about Jim, she said she had forgotten about it 'cause it had been unpleasant.

Where contrary facts are not known by the recorder, their presence is often left scrupulously an open question:

The patient denied any heterosexual experiences, nor could one trick her into admitting that she had ever been pregnant or into any kind of sexual indulgence, denying masturbation as well.

Even with considerable pressure, she was unwilling to engage in any projection of paranoid mechanisms.

No psychotic content could be elicited at this time.

And, if in no more factual way, discrediting statements often appear in descriptions given of the patient's general social manner in the hospital:

When interviewed, he was bland, apparently self-assured, and sprinkles high-sounding generalizations freely throughout his verbal productions.

Armed with a rather neat appearance and natty little Hitlerian mustache, this 45-year-old man, who has spent the last five or more years of his life in the hospital, is making a very successful adjustment living within the role of a rather gay liver and jim-dandy type of fellow who is not only quite superior to his fellow patients in intellectual respects, but who is also quite a man with women. His speech is sprayed with many multi-syllabled words which he generally uses in good context, but if he talks long enough on any subject it soon becomes apparent that he is so completely lost in this verbal diarrhea as to make what he says almost completely worthless.

The events recorded in the case history are, then, just the sort that a layman would consider scandalous, defamatory, and discrediting. I think it is fair to say that all levels of mental-hospital staff fail, in general, to deal with this material with the moral neutrality claimed for medical statements and psychiatric diagnosis, but instead participate, by intonation and gesture, if by no other means, in the lay reaction to these acts. This will occur in staff-patient encounters as well as in staff encounters at which no patient is present.

In some mental hospitals, access to the case record is technically restricted to medical and higher nursing levels, but even here, informal access or relayed information is often available to lower-staff levels. In addition, ward personnel are felt to have a right to know those aspects of the patient's past conduct which, embedded in the reputation he develops, purportedly make it possible to manage him with greater benefit to himself and less risk to others. Further, all staff levels typically have access to the nursing notes kept on the ward, which chart the daily course of each patient's disease, and hence his conduct, providing for the near present the sort of information the case record supplies for his past. . . .

The formal and informal patterns of communication linking staff members tend to amplify the disclosive work done by the case record. A discreditable act that the patient performs during one part of the day's routine in one part of the hospital community is likely to be reported back to those who supervise other areas of his life where he implicitly takes that stand that he is not the sort of person who could act that way.

Of significance here, as in some other social establishments, is the increasingly common practice of all-level staff conferences, where staff air their views of patients and develop collective agreement concerning the line that the patient is trying to take and the line that should be taken to him. A patient who develops a "personal" relation with an attendant, or manages to make an attendant anxious by eloquent and persistent accusations of malpractice, can be put back into his place by means of the staff meeting, where the attendant is given warning or assurance that the patient is "sick." Since the differential image of himself that a person usually meets from those of various levels around him comes here to be unified behind the scenes into a common approach, the patient may find himself faced with a kind of collusion against him—albeit one sincerely thought to be for his own ultimate welfare.

In addition, the formal transfer of the patient from one ward or service to another is likely to be accompanied by an informal description of his characteristics, this being felt to facilitate the work of the employee who is newly responsible for him.

Finally, at the most informal of levels, the lunch-time and coffee-break small talk of staff often turns upon the latest doings of the patient, the gossip level of any social establishment being here intensified by the assumption that everything about him is in some way the proper business of the hospital employee. Theoretically, there seems to be no reason why such gossip should not build up the subject instead of tear him down, unless one claims that talk about those not present will always tend to be critical in order to maintain the integrity and prestige of the circle in which the talking occurs. And so, even when the impulse of the speakers seems kindly and generous, the implication of their talk is typically that the patient is not a complete person. For example, a conscientious group therapist, sympathetic with patients, once admitted to his coffee companions:

> I've had about three group disrupters, one man in particular—a lawyer [*sotto voce*] James Wilson—very bright—who just made things miserable for me, but I would always tell him to get on the stage and do something. Well, I was getting desperate and then I bumped into his therapist, who said that right now behind the man's bluff and front he needed the group very much and that it probably meant more to him than anything else he was getting out of the hospital—he just needed the support. Well, that made me feel altogether different about him. He's out now.

In general, then, mental hospitals systematically provide for circulation about each patient the kind of information that the patient is likely to try to hide. And, in various degrees of detail, this information is used daily to puncture his claims. At the admission and diagnostic conferences, he will be asked questions to which he must give wrong answers in order to maintain his self-respect, and then the true answer may be shot back at him. An attendant whom he tells a version of his past and his reason for being in the hospital may smile disbelievingly, or say, "That's not the way I heard it," in line with the practical psychiatry of bringing the patient down to reality. When he accosts a physician or nurse on the ward and presents his claims for more privileges or for discharge, this may be countered by a question which he cannot answer truthfully, without calling up a time in his past when he acted disgracefully. When he gives his view of his situation during group psychotherapy, the therapist, taking the role of interrogator, may attempt to disabuse him of his face-saving interpretations and encourage an interpretation suggesting that it is he himself who is to blame and who must change. When he claims to staff or fellow patients that he is well and has never been really sick, someone may give him graphic details of how, only one month ago, he was prancing around like a girl, or claiming that he was God, or declining to talk or eat, or putting gum in his hair.

Each time the staff deflates that patient's claims, his sense of what a person ought to be and the rules of peer-group social intercourse press him to reconstruct his stories; and each time he does this, the custodial and psychiatric interests of the staff may lead them to discredit these tales again. . . .

Learning to live under conditions of imminent exposure and wide fluctuation in regard, with little control over the granting or withholding of this regard, is an important step in the socialization of the patient, a step that tells something important about what it is like to be an inmate in a mental hospital. Having one's past mistakes and present progress under constant moral review seems to make for a special adaptation consisting of a less than moral attitude to ego ideals. One's shortcomings and successes become too central and fluctuating an issue in life to allow the usual commitment of concern for other persons' views of them. It is not very practicable to try to sustain solid claims about oneself. The inmate tends to learn that degradations and reconstructions of the self need not be given too much weight, at the same time learning that staff and inmates are ready to view an inflation or deflation of a self with some indifference. He learns that a defensible picture of self can be seen as something outside oneself that can be constructed, lost, and rebuilt, all with great speed and some equanimity. He learns about the viability of taking up a standpoint—and hence a self—that is outside the one which the hospital can give and take away from him.

The setting, then, seems to engender a kind of cosmopolitan sophistication, a kind of civic apathy. In this unserious yet oddly exaggerated moral context, building up a self or having it destroyed becomes something of a shameless game, and learning to view this process as a game seems to make for some demoralization, the game being such a fundamental one. In the hospital, then, the inmate can learn that the self is not a fortress, but rather a small open city; he can become weary of having to show pleasure when held by troops of his own, and weary of having to show displeasure when held by the enemy. Once he learns what it is like to be defined by society as not having a viable self, this threatening definition—the threat that helps attach people to the self society accords them—is weakened. . . .

In the usual cycle of adult socialization, one expects to find alienation and mortification followed by a new set of beliefs about the world and a new way of conceiving of selves. In the case of the mental-hospital patient, this rebirth does

sometimes occur, taking the form of a strong belief in the psychiatric perspective, or, briefly at least, a devotion to the social cause of better treatment for mental patients. The moral career of the mental patient has unique interest, however; it can illustrate the possibility that, in casting off the raiments of the old self—or in having this cover torn away—the person need not seek a new robe and a new audience before which to cower. Instead he can learn, at least for a time, to practice before all groups the amoral arts of shamelessness.

Reprinted from: Erving Goffman, *Asylums*. Copyright © 1961 by Erving Goffman. Reprinted by permission of Doubleday, a division of Random House, Inc. ✦

33

Taking Anti-Depressant Drugs

David A. Karp

Even before the publication of Goffman's Asylums, there was a growing trend away from the hospitalization of those deemed mentally ill, a so-called deinstitutionalization movement that has continued to the present. Today, individuals who are diagnosed as mentally ill are more likely to be treated with psychotropic drugs on an outpatient basis than hospitalized. This may save them from the kind of assaults upon the self that Goffman describes in the preceding selection, but taking psychotropic drugs also profoundly affects individuals' definitions of themselves, as David Karp illustrates in this selection.

Karp focuses on people who have been diagnosed as clinically depressed and on their experiences with anti-depressant medications. The individuals whom Karp interviewed initially resisted doctors' and psychiatrists' advice to start taking anti-depressant drugs because it implied a redefinition of self. The prescription of anti-depressant drugs is based on the medical definition of depression as a biochemical illness. Thus, it implies that the depressed individual is not simply troubled but the victim of a biochemical disease. The biochemical explanation of depression may absolve depressed individuals of responsibility for their past and present troubles, but at the expense of portraying them as victims of biochemical forces beyond their control. For depressed individuals, taking anti-depressant medications involves sacrificing their sense of personal efficacy, and many resist that redefinition of themselves.

However, their suffering eventually drives them to agree to take prescribed anti-depressants for a limited time, on a trial basis. A few may experience immediate relief, but most remain emotionally troubled and troubled by noxious side effects while doctors and psychiatrists experiment with different drugs and dosages. If and when relief does come, the depressed individual experiences it as a miraculous spiritual redemption. Karp likens this to a religious conversion. The individual is converted to a new view of self and reality. He or she embraces the biomedical model and redefines himself or herself as ill rather than troubled.

Yet, for many, the success of this therapy and their conversion to biomedical reality is short-lived. They experience relapses while taking the miraculous drug that had supposedly cured them. Not only the drug but their new reality fails them. They consequently start once again to question the biomedical model and their doctors' advice and authority. Many start altering prescribed dosages of their anti-depressants, and some stop taking them altogether. They thereby reclaim their lost sense of personal efficacy and their prior definition of self.

This is a clear example of the politics of reality. The depressed individual initially battles doctors and psychiatrists for definitional authority over their personal troubles and themselves. The doctors' and psychiatrists' power and legitimacy eventually win out, and the depressed individual internalizes the biomedical model of reality and defines herself or himself in terms of it for a time. However, when the promises of that construction of reality prove hollow, the individual again battles its powerful advocates by ignoring their instructions and reasserting definitional control over his or her self, life, and reality. As Karp concludes, this example is an argument for a more democratic politics of reality between doctor and patient in the treatment of emotional problems.

The purpose of this paper is to explore the symbolic meanings attached to taking anti-depressant medications. The decision to embark on a course of drug taking is not a simple matter of unthinkingly following a doctor's orders. In fact, a patient's willingness to begin a drug regimen and stick with it involves an extensive interpretive process that includes consideration of such issues as the connection between drug use and illness self definitions, the meanings of drug side effects, attitudes towards physicians, evaluations of professional expertise, and ambiguity about the causes of one's problem. As Conrad (1985) points out, available studies rarely deal with such issues and so explain noncompliance only from a doctor-centered perspective. This view improperly slights the range of responses patients make to drug use.

The perspective taken in this study fits with a general literature in social psychology arguing that the subjective experience of taking drugs is deeply connected with individual and collective interpretations about the drug taken. . . .

The case of anti-depressant medications is especially valuable for analysis because these drugs are linked with the meaning of emotional experience. They are designed to alter "abnormal" moods and emotions. If there is a question in patients' minds about the value of taking medications for such clearly physiological problems as epilepsy and diabetes, decisions about taking drugs for "emotional illness" are still more problematic. Despite the psychiatric professions' clear adoption in recent years of a biochemical paradigm for understanding emotional problems, it is, we shall see, far from clear to patients whether their emotional problems warrant designation as an illness requiring biochemical intervention. . . .

Although prior research [has] clarified how patients understood and legitimated their use of psychotropic drugs in a global way (for example, as a resource for helping them to fulfill family and work roles), this research did not explore how the meanings attached to psychotropic drugs change over the period of their use. An important promise of symbolic interaction theory is that the meanings of objects, events, and situations are constantly being renegotiated and reinterpreted (Blumer, 1969). Correspondingly, this paper argues that the use of anti-depressant medications articulates with a more general depression "career" path characterized by ongoing redefinitions of self, illness, and, here, the meaning of medication itself.

In an earlier paper (Karp 1992) I identified clear stages in the evolution of an illness consciousness among depressed persons. Certain events in the course of an illness become critical identity markers that reflect a profound shift in how persons see themselves. . . . At such junctures persons are transformed in a way that requires a redefinition of who they were, are, and might be. The data to follow illustrate that the eventual decision to take medications was a major benchmark in the way my respondents came to see themselves, the nature of their problem, and their images of the future. The consequent decisions to continue and then eventually to stop a drug regimen are complicated and sometimes the product of years of confusion, evaluation, and experimentation.

Although it would do violence to the complexity of persons' responses to drug treatment to say that everyone moved through absolutely determined stages of interpretation, the stories I heard suggest clear regularities. These "moments" in the way respondents simultaneously tried to make sense out of drugs and their illness include an initial *resistance* stage during which they were unwilling to take anti-depressant medications. However, despite their ideological and psychological opposition, those interviewed eventually became desperate enough to try medication and thus capitulated to the advice of medical experts. During a second period of *trial commitment*, individuals express a willingness to experiment with drugs for a short period of time only. Having made the decision to try medications, they begin to accept biochemical definitions of depression's etiology. Such a redefinition is critical in becoming committed to a medical treatment model. For several, taking the drugs has a marginal or even negative impact on their problem. However, by now even these individuals have become *converted* to a belief in biochemical explanations of depression and begin a search to find the "right" drug. Finally, even those who experienced a "miracle" and felt "saved" by medication eventually have other episodes of depression and become *disenchanted* with drugs. They feel a need to get off the drugs "to see what happens," to see whether they can "go it alone." . . .

Method

Between August, 1991 and May, 1992, I conducted the 20 in-depth interviews which constitute the basis for this paper. A number of avenues were used to solicit interviewees. Initial interviews were done with personal acquaintances whom I knew had long histories with depression (10 cases). In addition, advertisements were placed in local newspapers and this strategy yielded a number of responses (6 cases). Finally, after each interview respondents were asked to describe my study to friends whom they knew had histories of depression and to refer names of willing participants (4 cases). In all instances, only those who had been officially diagnosed and treated by mental health professionals were included in the study. . . .

Although it is impossible to know what information persons might have withheld, I found it remarkable how candidly most of those interviewed appeared to speak about their experiences, including such difficult topics as child abuse, drug addiction, work failures, broken relationships, and suicide attempts. Several times interviews were punctuated by tears as persons recounted especially painful incidents. In every case, I reserved time at the end of the interview for respondents to "process" our conversation and to communicate how they felt about the experience. Nearly everyone expressed gratitude for the chance to tell their story, often saying that doing the interview gave them new perspectives on their life. . . .

Interpreting the Drug Experience

There is considerable variability in the time persons take to move through their individual depression careers. In large measure these variations related to how early in life trouble with depression begins and then whether bouts with depression are chronic or intermittent. Several of the persons interviewed realized, in retrospect, that they were deeply troubled from ages as young as four or five, and others did not experience "serious" depression until early adulthood. Consequently, some of those interviewed move into the therapeutic worlds of counselors, therapists, psychiatrists, and drugs by their teenage years, or even earlier. Others go for years before their trouble is diagnosed as depression and only then embark upon a course of therapy. However long it took the respondents to recognize and label their difficulty as depression, their eventual treatment by physicians involved use of prescribed medications. As indicated earlier, an individual's response to medication can be described as a process of unfolding consciousness and identity change consisting of four broad stages: resistance, trial commitment, conversion, and disenchantment.

Resistance

On rare occasions persons with whom I spoke sought out physicians explicitly to obtain anti-depressant medications. Perhaps this will increasingly be the case as both psychiatry and pharmaceutical companies "educate" the public about the nature of depression and as drugs like Prozac are touted in the media as revolutionary cures for depressive "illness." Normally, however, the idea to take medications is first raised by a therapist or doctor, a suggestion that is met with considerable

resistance. Typically, respondents offered a number of reasons for initially resisting drugs. Some described themselves nearly identically by saying "I'm the kind of person who doesn't even believe in taking aspirin for a headache." Others were appropriately concerned about the unknown and possibly long-term effects of powerful medication. It is interesting that even respondents who had earlier in their lives experimented with all kinds of drugs (for example, marihuana, cocaine, and LSD) were opposed to taking these drugs. Without denying their stated reasons, there appears to be a central underlying dynamic to their resistance. Taking anti-depressant medication would require a dramatic redefinition of self. Taking the drug would be a clear affirmation that they were a person with a stigmatized emotional disorder. In this respect, a willingness to begin a regimen of psychiatric medications is far from a simple medical decision. It is a decisive juncture in one's self redefinition as an emotionally ill rather than merely a troubled person.

> I didn't want to be told that I had something that was going to affect the rest of my life, and that could only be solved by taking pills. It was sort of definitive. I had a label and it was a label that I thought was pejorative. I didn't want to be this quietly depressed person, that there was something wrong with me. And it was sort of a rebellion in that [I said] "No it isn't, I'm not like that. I don't need you and your pills."

> My internist said, "You're depressed. You need an anti-depressant." I mean, I didn't understand the word exactly. She sent me to (names a psychiatrist) for anti-depressants. I went to (names psychiatrist) and said "I don't need anti-depressants, but I do need somebody to talk to." Drugs, I was against drugs. I didn't understand them either. But if he would talk to me, maybe we could work our way out of it. . . .

For several respondents the first clear communication that they needed medications followed a crisis that pushed them into a psychiatrist's office or, sometimes, into a hospital. New patients often perceived doctors as unwilling to pay significant attention to their feelings and were, as they saw it, altogether too eager to prescribe medications. Especially in hospitals, respondents sometimes acutely experienced the paradox that psychiatrists didn't want to spend much time hearing about their feelings despite the fact it was their bad feelings that forced them into the hospital. As individuals often saw it, their problems were situational and their souls were wounded. Such a perspective on the causes of their misery did not seem to square with the assessment that they had a disease in the form of unbalanced brain chemicals and should be treated with medication.

While persons suffering from depression often express anger towards those whom they view as implicated in the creation of their problem, I was surprised throughout these interviews by the virulence of the animosity expressed toward psychiatrists. Eventually, many of the persons interviewed found psychiatrists whom they trusted and from whom they benefitted. However, early in their treatment, individuals saw psychiatrists as oppressively evangelistic "true believers" in biochemical causes of depression, a view that they did not then hold. Their initial negative evaluation of psychiatry and psychiatrists I caught in the frequency and regularity with which respondents angrily labeled their doctors as "pill pushers."

> This particular doctor was such an asshole. He sounded like a used car salesman for antidepressants. He was just like so gung-ho. "Oh yuh, you're the typical depressed [person], here's the drug that will cure you. Let me know if you go home and just want to kill yourself or something. We'll try something different for you." And I hated him. I just really hated him. . . .

> Everything can be cured with a drug. Everything. They've got a drug for everything. Most [psychiatrists], they like to tinker with the body through these drugs, rather than trying to, you know, have people express what they're feeling. They just took one look at me, and pronounced me depressed, and wanted to put me on a battery of anti-depressants.

> [I feel] a real disenchantment with the traditional psychiatrists like the one that I had, and the ones who resort very quickly to pills. And I certainly have doubts about the degree to which the doctors are hooked up with the drug companies.

By the time patients arrive for treatment in doctors' offices or hospitals they have already moved through a number of changes in self definition. When asked about the unfolding of the recognition that they were depressed, individuals ordinarily describe an early time of inchoate feelings of distress, followed by feeling that "something is really wrong with me," and then to some variant of "I can't continue to live like this." Even after a crisis severe enough to precipitate hospitalization, individuals are, as we have seen, still resistant to taking medications. Resisting medication is a way of resisting categorization as a mentally ill person. However, the depth and persistence of their misery proves great enough that, under the proddings of physicians and sometimes other patients and family members, individuals begin to waver in their resolve not to take medication. Several persons described themselves as eventually "coming around" to the decision to take drugs because they became willing to try anything to diminish their suffering. Over and again respondents described their capitulation to medications as a consequence of the desperation they felt.

> But I also didn't want to do it [take drugs] because I felt such shame. I felt like, "Well I'm not depressed, someone else is depressed." Like I couldn't believe it was me. It was like some wonder drug or something. And I was thinking, "No way, I don't want to jump on this bandwagon." I was so scared of it. I felt like five years from now they'd find out that it gave me cancer or something. I just didn't want to take medication at all. But then at the same time I wanted so desperately for something to fix me. So I was just willing to try anything. He just said, "Give it a week, think about it."

> I was very leery of it [taking medications]. I mean I was concerned about what the effects might be and I didn't like the idea of putting myself on some sort of medication, but at a certain point it just seemed to me that I had to try it and the problem was so great that I really wanted to do anything that would alleviate it. . . .

> I couldn't drag myself around any more. I couldn't sleep. I didn't eat. . . . I just felt physically like there was something wrong with me, and that I had to stop and I think there is a physical component, because now that I've been on medication long enough I think it has helped.

In an especially evocative comment a respondent equated taking the medication with "swallowing" her will.

> I have a hard time taking medication . . . I don't like taking pills. I didn't like taking aspirin. I mean, I've generally been very conservative at

that, so I kind of swallowed, you know, my will and that's when I took Prozac.

The moment individuals decide to try medications is decisive in beginning a reorientation in their thinking about the nature of their difficulty and of their "selves." Putting the first pill into one's mouth begins both a revision of one's biochemistry and one's self. Social psychologists have long understood that embarking upon a new life direction, especially one that departs from earlier held views of reality, requires the construction of a new "vocabulary of motives" (Mills, 1972) and new "accounts" (Lyman and Scott, 1968) for behavior. . . . Rather than understanding behaviors as always being propelled by clear motives, we know that behavioral changes often precede motive productions. Taking the medication is the beginning of a process of commitment to biochemical explanations of affective disorders.

Trial Commitment

In his well-known paper entitled "Notes on the Concept of Commitment," Howard Becker (1960) illuminates the idea that commitments to new ways of life do not happen suddenly, all at once. Commitments are built up slowly, gradually, and often imperceptibly through a series of "side bets" or personal decisions, each of which seems of little consequence. Persons, for example, may become committed to work organizations through a series of side bets such as paying into a pension plan, accepting a promotion and new responsibilities, buying a home based on current income, and so on. As Becker explains, each of these apparently independent decisions is like putting individual bricks into a wall until one day it suddenly becomes clear that the wall has grown to such a height that one cannot climb over it—a commitment has been made that is not easily reversed.

The decision to take a medication is sometimes preceded by a *negotiation* with doctors about how long one is willing to try it. . . . Negotiations reflect patients' ambivalence that they have not yet accepted doctors' definitions of them as having a biochemically based illness.

And so then I started taking this Prozac. And the only reason I would take it is that he promised I would only be on it for three months. I ended up being on it for nine months, probably longer, nine or ten months. If I had known that, I don't think I'd ever gone on it because I just didn't want to put any kind of substance in my body.

The psychiatrist . . . said, "Look, I just think you should stay on it through the end of this year, you know, and then you can go off it." So I decided . . . I wasn't thinking of it quite so blatantly, but I was sort of thinking, "All right, I'll just take this eight months and see what happens."

Negotiations aside, taking medications coincides with a growing acceptance of official medical versions about the causes of depression. Everyone who suffers from depression feels obliged to construct theories of causation in order to impose some coherence onto an especially hazy, ambiguous life circumstance and to evaluate the extent to which they are responsible for their condition. Although it is impossible ever to fully resolve whether nature or nurture, or some combination, is responsible for depression, every person I interviewed eventually accepted in greater or lesser degree a biochemical explanation of depression.

Adoption of the view that one is victimized by a biochemically sick self constitutes a comfortable "account" for a history of difficulties and failures and absolves one of responsibility. On the negative side, however, acceptance of a victim role, while diminishing a sense of personal responsibility, is also enfeebling. To be a victim of biochemical forces beyond one's control gives force to others' definition of oneself as a helpless, passive object of injury. Holstein and Miller (1990:120) comment that "victimization . . . provides an interpretive framework and a discourse that relieves victims of responsibility for their fates, but at a cost. The cost involves the myriad ways that the victim image debilitates those to whom it is applied." The interpretative dilemma was to navigate between rhetorics of biochemical determinism and a sense of personal efficacy. However, everyone with whom I talked eventually adopted some version of biological causation of depression, as the following representative comments illustrate.

WELL, DO YOU FEEL LIKE A VICTIM?

I would say that uh in me, [it is] my brain chemistry that is prone to depression and that, given like the amount of trauma in [my life], it really added up and had no way to pass or flow and really built up. And like the drug helps it to flow or something. And then the way that I understand I'm no longer on it [medications] is that it's [the brain chemistry] kind of working OK on its own right now.

YOU SEEM TO DOUBT THE PSYCHIATRIC MODEL OF ILLNESS.

I don't doubt it. I don't know. You know, I'm not a psychopharmacologist and I'm not going to say "It's a problem with serotonin uptake in my brain," and I'm not a psychoanalyst and I'm not going to say, "It's you know, the Oedipal whatever." But I feel that it's an illness because it's something you don't have any control over. . . .

There was a sense of relief to a certain extent when I started finding out that the medication was helpful, because then I could say that this certainly partly is a chemical problem, and that I'm not a looney tunes, and I'm not, you know, it's not a mental illness, which really sounds bad to me. I think I'm much less negative about it than I was, even in 1982. But at that time the fact that there might be a chemical imbalance that was being rectified by medication was of great comfort to me.

Well, you know, as a result of that more recent one, more recent depression, I've kind of come around more to the biochemical explanation. . . .

Conversion: Muddle or Miracle

Once patients have accepted and internalized a rhetoric of biochemical causation, they become committed to a process of finding the "right" medication. Such a discovery often proves elusive as persons enter upon a protracted process of trial and error with multiple drugs. This process is often extremely confusing as persons deal with a variety of side effects ranging from such relatively benign problems as dry mouth, constipation, and weight gain to more dramatic experiences like fainting in public places. In several interviews drug "horror stories" were a prominent theme, as in the case of a hospitalized woman whose therapy, along with drugs, consisted of physical exercise.

I was on every drug under the sun. Just everything (said with exasperation). It was like a cocktail. I mean I was really out of control . . . I'll never forget this little vignette where they would drug me and say, "Well, you've got to get out there and be more active . . . I'll never

forget—tennis . . . I was so drugged up I could barely see my fingers and this therapist took us out to the tennis courts. He was hitting balls and I couldn't even see the ball. This asshole, I couldn't even see and he's worried about my backhand. It's stupid. You know, at the time I don't think I thought it was too funny. I thought, "What's wrong with me." So things went from bad to worse.

Sometimes individuals stayed on a medication for months that had no discernible positive effect or which they perceived only modestly influenced their condition. The search for the "right" drug seems analogous to a process of serial monogamy in which individuals move through a series of unsatisfying, bad, or even destructive relationships, always with the hope that the right person will eventually be found. Just as individuals internalize the notion of romantic love with its attendant ideology that one's perfect mate is somewhere in the world, respondents maintained their faith, in spite of a series of disappointments, that they would find the right medication.

Anyway I think I continued on the imipramine, but they gave me other drugs. Out of all the drugs that I had I can't say that any one really made me feel better. You know and I can only say that when you find the right drug you really know. "Oh, this is what it means to be better." But I do remember it wasn't imipramine.

It's [names drug] been effective and I haven't felt the need for anything else. But I also have the feeling, "I wonder if there is something better that I could take a lower dose of that would be effective." Or, "Isn't there something else now that might be better." I always feel that way (laughs).

I'm feeling very hopeless [right now]. I'm still taking the Trazadone. I'm also taking an anti-anxiety drug once in a while and I feel like I'm treading water. I'm waking up at five o'clock in the morning even with the Trazadone. I wake up in horror that, you know, I'll be a bag lady, that I'm not going to be able to get through my work day today. Every once in a while I wonder "Have I tried enough stuff. Is there something that would work better?"

Many of those interviewed never find a drug that dramatically influences things for the better. These people continue to take the medications, but remain only partial believers in biochemical explanations. However, equal numbers among the respondents interviewed describe the "miracle" of medication. It is among these persons that the metaphor to religious conversion is most apparent. For them, the drug truly provides a "revelation" because it makes them feel "normal," often for the first time in their lives. In these instances, any trace of uncertainty about the biochemical basis for their problem disappears. Finding the right medication is, in fact, described as a spiritual awakening, as an ecstatic experience.

> All I can tell you is, "Oh my God, you know when you're on the right medication." It was the most incredible thing. And I would say that I had a spiritual experience.

> So I started taking this Trazadone. It may have been a week or two. I had never experienced such a magical effect in my whole life. It was just magical. Thoughts that I had been having . . . I had been having these horrible, tortured depressed thoughts and the only thing I can say is that they just stopped being in my head and it was like they had run around in my blood and I just didn't think that way any more. And I started thinking better thoughts, happier thoughts. It was very clear to me that it wasn't the same as being high. Astonishing. It was wonderful. . . . After two weeks. I mean, it was just magical. My life began to change profoundly at that point.

> And then I start seeing this therapist last September twice a week and he recommends going to see a psychiatrist. I go to him and he recommends Doxepin and I start taking that. And then at the end of November it just kind of kicked in. It was a miracle. It really was. Quite extraordinary.

> Well, I'd had a headache for four months and they treated that with Amitriptyline. And then I changed doctors. I went to the (names a university) health plan. Anyway, I saw a psychiatrist and had been seeing her for a while and I guess probably giving all the classic symptoms that I didn't know existed. And finally she said, "Well, you know, I think one of the problems here is that you're depressed and I'm putting you on Imipramine and see if that's going to work." And when it started working it was like a miracle. It was just like "wow." I know specifically of other times I was very depressed and then when I got out of it I would describe to people "I feel like I've come out of a tunnel."

While there is a danger in relying too heavily on one biography, it seems worthwhile to present in some detail the dialogue I had with a respondent whose words express particularly well the complexity of depression, the powerful effects of a medication in providing new and plausible realities, and even the uncertainty about "giving up" depression. Although it is not within the province of this paper to offer a full discussion of the "positive" features of depression, several respondents claim that the agony of depression has been instrumental in their spiritual growth. One unanticipated aspect of depression revealed in the interviews is the connection between depression and spiritual life. Several persons in my sample have seriously experimented with Buddhist teachings which they claim, more satisfactorily than Western religions, understands the place of human pain and suffering. Others connect their depression with creativity and insight. The following woman, quoted at length, is a writer. Her comments illuminate the breathtaking impact of feeling normal after years of non-stop pain, the religious-like dimensions of the drug conversion experience, and the uncertainty attached to giving up any long held identity, even one that has been deeply troublesome. Our conversation went like this:

HOW WOULD YOU DESCRIBE THE EXPERIENCE OF PROZAC?

> I went on Prozac. I was like, cracking up, a couple of years ago, and sort of got back to the mental hospital—time number five. And I think the psychiatrist I was seeing, she didn't know what to do with me, so she sent me to this . . . psychopharmacologist, and he prescribed Prozac for me, and within five days, it was very, very strange. . . . I mean, it was hard to explain, but, I was just incredibly fearful and anxious, and I really at that point was going to kill myself, because I just was like, "Forget it." You know, "I've worked too hard and tried to conquer this thing too much, and I can't do it." And there was a tremendous amount of anger. But within five days of going on the Prozac it was like the obsessions reduced, and it was a very weird feeling. What was strange about it was that it took away the feeling of depression that I've had in my stomach for years, ever since I was a little girl. It was gone. And I remember not wanting to tell anybody about it, because I thought, this is really strange.

NOT WANTING TO TELL ANYBODY BECAUSE?

Like, "I think this is working." I was kind of like, "Jesus Christ, what's going on here." Because I'd been on medications that never had done anything for me, and this was so dramatic. . . . It was very dramatic because I was on the brink of really cracking up, and then within five days I wasn't anywhere near cracking up. And actually it's interesting, because I loved it, but I also wanted to go off of it, because I was sure it was going to take away my creativity.

SO, ITS BACK TO THE PAIN/ CREATIVITY LINK.

Oh, because I couldn't write. I was used to being in an anxious state all of the time, and suddenly I didn't care as much about my writing any more. That was what the weird thing was. It [writing] didn't mean as much to me. Nothing meant as much to me. In a way that was incredibly freeing. And at the same time, I built my whole identity around being a person who was, you know, driven, intense, and I tried sort of whipping myself up into an intense state, you know, and it didn't work.

YOU MEAN, SOMETHING THAT YOU HAD NO TROUBLE WITH BEFORE. . . .

It [the intensity] wasn't there and as much as I hated it before. I also felt like it was who I was, and the Prozac took it away, and I remember thinking, "This is very nice. I should take this when I go on vacation, you know, and [otherwise] get me off of this stuff, because this is going to make a moron out of me."

SO WHAT'S THE END OF THE STORY? STILL TAKING IT?

Well I remained on it, but the course is kind of rocky because then I was a convert to Prozac, and I was like, "This stuff is incredible." I was thinking, "This stuff is just the greatest stuff I've ever taken in the world." I mean, "this is a miracle." And I would think, "This is a miracle." And it was a miracle, it really was a miracle to me. For that one year, I was so happy. . . . And at this point the Prozac has become so intertwined with the millions of meanings that I've given it. Even a God [meaning] for a while.

. . . Persons' commitment and conversion to drugs is completed when those drugs become a routine part of their daily life. The process of adopting the medical version of depression's proper treatment is accomplished when the respondent's initial resistance to drugs completely vanishes. What normally started out as a tentative and ambivalent experiment with medications typically becomes a taken-for-granted way of life. In effect, the persons interviewed have undergone a socialization process that has transformed the meanings to them of medication. The negotiated experiment begun with trepidation has become institutionalized, habitualized, and ritualized. To use the vocabulary offered by Peter Berger and Thomas Luckmann (1967), a once alternative and alien "symbolic universe" has become an accepted and seemingly immutable reality. That is, taking medications now appears as an absolutely unquestioned feature of daily reality. Consider the casualness with which those initially opposed to drugs sometimes come to regard them.

What's interesting to me about the drug now, or at least my attitude toward it, is that I regard it almost as a food supplement. It's just something I eat that's going to have a certain effect. So I don't quite see it as unnatural the way I used to.

And then I decided, "Hey, this stuff's pretty good, you know? I can be happy or be less anxious and do productive work." So I thought, "OK, I'll stay on it forever." So it was a total turnaround.

[Now] taking medication is pretty much just a reflex.

I'm convinced maybe I have to take it for the rest of my life. I'd certainly rather feel like this than like that, and if it's two little pills I've got in my mouth every day that makes me stay this way, then so be it.

Disenchantment and Deconversion

Those who study conversions must include in their analysis the factors that sometimes account for the disenchantment, defection, and deconversion of large numbers of persons from their respective groups or belief systems. Some persons, of course, retain their commitments to alternative realities over the long term. Equally, though, are those who come to question the utility and correctness of the explanatory schemas with which they had experimented and then fully embraced. Of course, even converts stand at different places on a continuum of commitment. Some are never fully convinced of the value of new behaviors and beliefs, are easily disenchanted with new problem-solving perspectives, and return relatively quickly to old perspectives and identities. A few among those studied stayed on drugs for only a short time, deciding that they were not sufficiently effective to put up with noxious side effects. After experimenting with medications, these persons were easily able to return to the view that their problems were environmentally based and that drugs would not be their salvation. The failure of a belief system is much more devastating, of course, when persons had embraced it unreservedly. This was certainly the case for those who had experienced a drug miracle, but who subsequently suffered a relapse. The young woman writer quoted earlier described her response to the eventual failure of the drug after her ecstatic revelatory experience.

> Then I decided I was going to go away to Kentucky and live in Appalachia for two months and do an internship in interviewing women down there. And then again I thought, this is the kind of thing I can do, because now I'm on Prozac and I won't freak out, whereas before that kind of change would have freaked me out. And I went, and I freaked out, and that's when I completely like, relapsed. . . . Now I have a somewhat more balanced view of the Prozac in that I can become obsessive, anxious, depressed on it, even very obsessive and anxious and depressed. It's not a miracle drug. It hasn't saved me. And it's been a long time coming to terms with that. It helps somewhat, sometimes, and that's where it's at. And, I did for a while think, I am going to be cured. . . . It was the ultimate disappointment. You know, it was connected with an intense sense of loss and a sense of redemption, and I do not overstate [things]. It really was that.

The complexity of stopping medications is evident in the fact that even when they do not appear to fundamentally alter depressive feelings, respondents sometimes become psychologically dependent upon them. Once having experimented with the drugs and having accepted biochemical definitions of their condition, persons feel uncertain about stopping. Whatever their current problems, several individuals were afraid that things might deteriorate if they stopped taking the medications.

> I'm afraid to not take it, but it really hasn't done much of anything.

> I mean, it's almost to the point now where I take it sometimes but like I really don't feel like

I have the need for it. But I'm sort of afraid not to take it . . . I'm on such a low dosage [now]. He's (doctor) got me on one pill a night. And it's taken, you know, ten years [to get to that point].

> If I had listened to myself I would have just said "Screw the medications." But also I think I was probably afraid, afraid that if I went off them completely that I would get worse, and I guess there is some evidence for that. . . .

And sometimes persons are afraid to stop the medication because they believe their systems have become physiologically dependent on them.

> I'm on anti-depressant medicine right now, have been since '83, around there, and I wanted to go off them and I can't. There's no way I can go off them. There is just no way. I would have to spend six months to a year pretty much in a very controlled environment, as my body, my nervous system reacted to not having the stuff.

Ultimately, the respondents in this study, like the epilepsy patients interviewed by Conrad (1985), become, at the least, ambivalent about the role of medications in dealing with their difficulty. They may feel dependent on the drugs and worry about the consequences of stopping, but they also begin to question the wisdom of staying on the medications. Just as Conrad's epilepsy patients eventually discover that the medications are not the "ticket to normality," it eventually becomes apparent to sufferers of depression that a medical "cure" is not forthcoming. In both instances, patients become disenchanted with the side effects of the drugs, begin to question their efficacy, experiment with dosage levels and sometimes decide even to stop taking them. Conrad describes a number of non-compliance responses of epilepsy patients which reflect efforts to regain control over their illness. He notes (1985:36) that "[self] regulating medication represents an attempt to assert some degree of control over a condition that appears at times to be completely out of control." His findings certainly seem generalizable to the case of depression, as the following comments illustrate.

> I guess I myself was curious to see what would happen if I were to stop taking it. Partly my wife didn't like the idea that I was on a drug.

She's concerned about long range effects and I guess I was a little concerned about that too.

I wanted to go off it all along and it started giving me headaches. I wanted to get off it already.

I had gained a lot of weight on the pills. I was always a very thin person and here I was carrying forty more pounds. My sense of physical identity was damaged and I wanted out.

In other cases individuals finally rebel against taking medications as a way of reclaiming selves that they believe have been lost because of their involvement with anti-depressant medications. These persons who vow never to go on the drugs again have plainly had a deconversion experience.

Now in between the new and the old [medications] there would be a period when they would take me off the thing. And my friends during that stretch without fail would say, "You seem like yourself again." And if I had listened closely I would have said, "Gee, the implication of this is that these pills are fucking me up." [Finally] I would go in and say, "Can I get off it? Can I get off it?" And he would say, "Try it longer." Finally I thought, "I'm not going to ask this son of a bitch any longer. I'm just going to take myself off it." And I did and he either forgot about it or didn't raise it. I just took myself off. . . . [And] I will never take another fucking pill in my life. And I'm not generalizing to other people. . . . But for me, I had gotten so fucked up with this stuff that I will never do it again.

I mean, I put my foot down about the Trazadone. I was at the point where I could say, "I'm just going to stop."

Discussion

Although the persons quoted in this paper may stand at different points in their drug taking careers, most commonly move through a socialization process which involves overcoming initial resistance to drug taking, negotiating the terms of their treatment, adopting new rhetorics about the cause of depression, experiencing a conversion to medical realities, and eventually becoming disenchanted with the value of medications for solving their problems. This process bears a strong similarity to descriptions of religious conversion and deconversion. That is, one's willingness to begin,

sustain, and sometimes stop a doctor-prescribed regimen of anti-depressant medications must be understood in the broader context of adopting a new, identity-altering view of reality; namely, that one suffers from a biochemically based emotional illness. For this reason, the experience of taking antidepressant medication involves a complex and emotionally charged interpretive process in which nothing less than one's view of self is at stake.

The process described in this paper helps in thinking about some of the social psychological dynamics that are part of the "medicalization" (Conrad and Schneider, 1980) of society more broadly. . . . The medical model begins with the easily accepted assertion that normalcy is preferable to abnormalcy. However, normalcy then becomes a synonym for health and abnormalcy a synonym for pathology. Health and pathology, in turn, are defined in terms of the presumed scientific, objective, unbiased standards originating from experimentation and laboratory research. Because it is better to be healthy than to be sick, the medical model supports physicians' decisions, whether requested or not, to provide health for the patient. By defining certain characteristics of the human condition as "illness," and therefore in need of cure, physicians also provide themselves the right to explore every part of the human anatomy, to prescribe a myriad of curative agents, and frequently, to compel treatment.

The medical model is used to support the political reality created by a coalition of physicians, teachers, judges, and other health professionals. Peter Berger and Thomas Luckmann (1967) refer to this coalition as "universe maintenance specialists." These specialists from different disciplines set the norms defining proper and improper behavior, deviant and conforming behavior, normal and pathological behavior, sick and healthy behavior. Thus, therapy "entails the application of conceptual machinery to ensure that actual or potential deviants stay within the institutionalized definitions of reality. . . . This requires a body of knowledge that includes a theory of deviance, a diagnostic apparatus and a conceptual system for the 'cure of souls'" (1967:112).

Nowhere, of course, is the struggle over definitions of illness reality and, literally, the mind of the patient more apparent than in psychiatry. The materials presented earlier illustrate that acceptance of medical versions of reality is not an automatic thing. Psychiatric patients are initially resistant to illness definitions of their problem and "come around" to prescribed medical treatments only with great difficulty. Although everyone described in this paper eventually capitulates to medical versions of reality, their conversion is incomplete as they lose faith in the efficacy of drug treatment and sometimes rebel against it altogether. It seems reasonable to speculate that as part of a general and increasing "democratization" of professional/client relationships, resistance to medical authority will become more intense. Moreover, the terrain of this struggle over reality is most likely to be in the psychiatric arena where the legitimacy of a purely medical model is most suspect. . . .

The persons interviewed eventually realize that doctors, despite their best efforts, will not clear away their confusions about depression. The socialization process described in this paper involves hope that medication will provide the solution to their problem. In most cases, however, this optimistic attitude was replaced with disillusionment and sometimes anger. The failure of medical treatments for depression provides fertile soil for the emergence of self help groups which offer the view of affective disorders as troubles that must ultimately be remedied by the individuals who suffer from them (Karp, 1992). Such a definition suggests an anti-psychiatry ideology that demands, at the very least, a greater democ-racy between doctor and patient in efforts to treat the problem. . . .

References

Becker, H. (1960). "Notes on the concept of commitment." *American Journal of Sociology* 66:32–40.

Berger, P. and Luckmann, T. (1967). *The Social Construction of Reality.* Garden City, NY: Doubleday.

Blumer, H. (1969). *Symbolic Interaction: Perspective and Method.* Englewood Cliffs, NJ: Prentice Hall.

Conrad, P. (1985). "The meaning of medications: Another look at compliance." *Social Science and Medicine* 20:29–37.

Conrad, P., and Schneider, J. (1980). *Deviance and Medicalization.* St. Louis, MO: Mosby.

Holstein, J., and Miller, G. (1990). "Rethinking victimization: An interactional approach to victimology." *Symbolic Interaction* 13:103–122.

Karp, D. (1992). "Illness ambiguity and the search for meaning." *Journal of Contemporary Ethnography* 21:139–170.

Lyman, S., and Scott, M. (1968). "Accounts." *American Sociological Review* 33 (December):46–62.

Mills, C. W. (1972). "Situated actions and vocabularies of motive." In *Symbolic Interaction*, ed. by J. Manis and B. Meltzer. Boston: Allyn & Bacon.

34

The Rise and Fall of the Freeway Shootings Problem

Joel Best

Social problems are as much a matter of definition as other aspects of human reality. Many social conditions have negative consequences for someone. Some are simply not recognized by most people; others are considered personal rather than social problems; and still others are considered an unfortunate but inevitable fact of human life. Such social conditions only become social problems when they gain the attention of the public and policymakers as a particular kind of problem that can and must be addressed. In most cases, activists, such as Mothers Against Drunk Driving, or professionals, such as doctors and social workers, make claims that a certain social condition, such as alcohol-related traffic accidents or some forms of adults' treatment of children, are serious problems requiring public concern and intervention. These "primary claimsmakers" also define the characteristics of the problem or just what kind of problem it is, such as "drunk driving" or "child abuse." In some cases, the media then publicize those claims with print and broadcast stories about the problem. The media then become "secondary claimsmakers," promoting public concern about the problem and increasing pressure on policymakers to address it. In other cases, the media identify and define the problem and are the primary claimsmakers. Sometimes there are competing claims about the nature of the problem and, by implication, how it should best be addressed. For example, are the recent incidents of school shootings a problem of inadequate parenting, media violence, or the ready availability of guns? There is also competition among claimsmakers for different social problems for public attention and that of policymakers. Those conditions we consider social problems are products of such politics of reality. The study of social problems construction helps us better understand the political processes that shape the social realities we inhabit.

In this selection, Joel Best examines the rise and decline of the social problem of freeway shootings in 1987. In this case, the media were the primary claimsmakers. Newspapers, television news broadcasts, and news magazines defined violent incidents on freeways as instances of a new and growing social problem. Best shows how news reports about freeway shootings followed the standard template for social problems stories. They described the problem and offered explanations and various interpretations of it. In doing so, they drew upon existing cultural resources such as imagery from popular films and stereotypes of Southern California, humor, and the general fear of random violence in contemporary America.

Best also identifies some factors that contributed to the emergence of the social problem of freeway shootings and to its sudden demise. The problem was first identified by the influential Los Angeles Times, the incidents occurred in Southern California where national trends are often set, and those incidents occurred during the summer when there is often a shortage of news stories. However, the ambivalent and often humorous descriptions of the problem, the lack of sufficient incidents across the country, and the failure of primary claimsmakers to adopt the problem as their own led to the disappearance of the problem as the media turned its attention elsewhere. Incidents of freeway violence probably continued to occur but were no longer reported as instances of a serious social problem. More recent claims about the social problem of road rage have arguably revived this social problem but with an expanded "domain" of possible instances. The road rage problem involves not just traffic-related shootings and other violence but all kinds of expressions of anger on roadways including shouted insults and vulgar displays of middle fingers.

The freeway shooting problem was short-lived, but it illustrates how social conditions and events are constructed into social problems. Incidents are treated as instances of a trend and a growing problem that does or might directly or indirectly affect many people. Explanations and interpretations are provided that define the particular characteristics and causes of the problem. Policies are then proposed to address the problem. Claims that receive media exposure and resonate with wide-spread cultural understandings tend to be successful and become part of the socially taken-for-granted reality. For example, few Americans would question whether drunk driving, child abuse, and, perhaps, road rage are social problems. Yet, these social problems are of relatively recent construction. They are not mere reflections of harmful social behaviors, but products of ef-

fective claimsmaking, media exposure, public perceptions, and public policies. The effective construction of these and other social problems, and unsuccessful claims regarding others, can reveal much about the politics involved in the social construction of reality.

Theories of social problems construction argue that the concerns policymakers and the public have about particular social problems are not simply a reflection of objective facts about social conditions. . . . Rather, social problems emerge—become a focus for concern—through a process of claimsmaking. This process determines, not only which phenomena come to be designated social problems but the characteristics ascribed to those problems. Problems can always be depicted in more than one way: rape as a sex crime or a crime of violence; marijuana as a cause of psychosis, a precursor to hard drugs, or a threat to economic productivity; and so on. Explaining how and why particular images of problems emerge has become a central task for constructionist analysts (Best 1989).

Typically, constructionist explanations examine the organization of the claimsmaking process, assuming that claims originate with activists, professionals, or others with vested interests in bringing attention to an issue and/or promoting a particular image of the problem. The news media then transforms the primary claims of these individuals and relay the resulting secondary claims to the public. . . . According to this two-stage model, the resulting images of problems depend, in part, on the primary claimsmakers' interests and ideology, the constraints imposed by the media's routines, and the rhetoric adopted in making both primary and secondary claims (Best 1990).

Although others' primary claims usually shape news coverage of social issues, the media's role need not be reactive; the press can act as primary claimsmaker, discovering and constructing social problems on its own. In such cases there might seem to be few constraints on how the media characterize the problem. Yet in practice, the press usually presents these problems within familiar frameworks and describes them in familiar terms. Shootings on Los Angeles freeways offer an example: during the summer of 1987, the press discovered, promoted, and then dropped this problem. Examination of this coverage re-

veals conventional elements, common to discussions of many other social problems. The conventional nature of this coverage is this paper's topic. Unconstrained by independent primary claimsmakers, the press might have characterized freeway violence in many different ways. In fact, the media's treatment of freeway violence resembles most other social problems coverage. What accounts for this standardized, taken-for-granted treatment?

Sociological studies of the news media suggest that the answer lies in the nature of news work: reporters and editors work within constraints (e.g., broadcast time-limits) for which they develop routines (e.g., television news favors stories which can be illustrated with videotape). . . . No doubt such routines helped shape the media's treatment of freeway violence, but they alone cannot account for the particular way the problem was described.

The press's coverage also drew upon a fund of cultural resources. In constructing freeway violence as a social problem, the media adopted a familiar template of elements routinely used in social problems coverage, borrowed familiar cultural images, and otherwise located the problem within a taken-for-granted cultural framework. Examining the use of cultural resources in claimsmaking about freeway shootings reveals the role of cultural concerns in the larger process of social problems construction.

Methods

This paper analyzes the imagery used to construct the 1987 freeway violence problem in three major news media: newspapers, . . . magazines, . . . and national television broadcasts. . . . While not a systematic sample of press coverage, the sources examined include many of the most significant treatments—both local and national—of the freeway violence problem.

This analysis does not try to contrast the media's construction with the "reality" of freeway shootings, if only because it is impossible to convincingly draw such a contrast. Media coverage is virtually the only source of information about freeway violence; the short-lived problem produced no official records, victimization surveys, or public opinion polls, and only a single social scientific study of the phenomenon. In 1987, for instance, no agency kept official statistics on the incidence of freeway shootings, nor was there any way to determine whether the rate of incidents had changed from the preceding years. Reporters covering the story compiled their own lists of violent incidents and argued that these incidents reflected a new social trend. The issue is not whether this was a "real" trend—a largely unanswerable question—but how journalists used "trend" and other language to characterize freeway shootings.

Evaluation of the freeway violence problem begins by examining the template—the standard elements of description, explanation, and interpretation—used in stories about social problems. [I] consider three sorts of imagery—popular culture, humor, and random violence—used as cultural resources in constructing freeway violence as a social problem and [suggest] some circumstances which affect claimsmakers' choices of images. Finally, an explanation is offered for the emergence and disappearance of freeway shootings as a social problem.

Freeway Shootings and the Template for Social Problems Stories

The 1987 freeway shootings problem seems to have been discovered in a June 26 *Los Angeles Times* column, "No Shelter From Freeway Violence," which suggested "there is a malevolence loose on those roads . . ."(Sauter 1987a). A month later, freeway violence received nationwide notice: all three television networks broadcast stories on their evening news programs; all three major newsweeklies ran stories; and feature articles, columns and editorial cartoons appeared in newspapers throughout the country. . . . After about three weeks, the national news media turned to new topics, although freeway shootings occasionally resurfaced. . . .

While short-lived, the media's treatment of freeway violence resembled coverage of other, better-established social problems. The press described freeway shootings as a social phenomenon, offered explanations for the violence, and located the problem within familiar interpretive schemes. These elements—description, explanation, and interpretation—form a template for social problems coverage. Although most contemporary news stories about social problems fit this template, the emphasis on description, explana-

tion, and interpretation is socially constructed. Different news templates occur in other times and places, such as framing news stories in moralistic or ideological terms. . . .

Describing the Problem

On June 24, the *Los Angeles Times* ran a brief story, "2nd Freeway Shooting Incident Is Investigated," noting that there had been two apparently unrelated shootings during the previous weekend (Stewart 1987). This story seems to have performed a central task in social problems construction: it established a new category (freeway shooting), thereby redefining the two *incidents* as *instances* of a new problem. In Fishman's (1978, p. 534) language, freeway violence became a "news theme," which "presents a specific news event, or a number of such events, in terms of some broader concept." The new category inspired the June 26 column which claimed there had been "four unrelated freeway shootings over the past 10 months" (Sauter 1987a). Sauter later explained that this column reflected "a desire to seize on a trendoid—the journalistic category reflecting something new, potentially interesting and possibly—just possibly—indicative of a trend" (1987b). *Times* reporters recall that they were now "watching for a trend." An editor assigned reporter Lonn Johnston to write a feature article on the topic. Completed after a few days, the story "was held [i.e., not published] for a couple weeks" (Bill Billiter and Lonn Johnston, telephone interview 1989).

Journalists have a rule of thumb: once a third thing happens, you have a trend. The July 20 *Times* news story—"Traffic Dispute Results in Third Freeway Shooting"—revived the concept (Billiter 1987). The next day, Johnson's feature article (amended with a "new top" referring to the newest incident) appeared, shifting the focus from news reports about particular incidents to a general analysis of the freeway violence problem ("a new kind of urban warfare") (Johnston 1987). The same day, the *Los Angeles Herald Examiner's* (1987) editorial cartoon showed a motorist shopping for "the ultimate freeway defense vehicle"—a tank.

The category was now familiar. A July 26 story began: "While police searched for suspects in the latest highway shooting . . . " (Kendall 1987); it was the first of four front-page *Times* pieces over five days. (The *Herald Examiner* ran front-page freeway violence stories on twelve of the four-teen days from July 21 to August 3.) As the story received more attention, the freeway shooting category began showing elasticity: not all re-ported incidents occurred on freeways, and not all involved shooting. Some reporters began using broader terms to refer to the problem [such as] "traffic-related shootings" or "roadway violence," and a variety of incidents were presented as in-stances of the category, including rocks thrown at windshields (ABC "Nightline", July 30) and:

> . . . one copycat moved from the freeways to the busy Southern California skyways. The pilot of a Cesna says he was threatened by the pilot of another plane, who flew close—along-side—and pointed a handgun. (CBS, August 5)

Press reports described freeway shootings as a series of incidents—a "sudden evolution," "trend," "wave," "spate," "spree," "upsurge," "fad," "rash"—an "epidemic," "plaguing Southern California," "reaching alarming proportions." However, some reporters acknowledged that is was impossible to document increasing freeway violence. The cate-gory had no official standing; no law enforcement agency kept records of freeway shootings as such, and the press had no way to measure shifts in inci-dence. Instead, reporters quoted officials to the effect that violence seemed more common and referred to a running total of incidents, usually beginning with shots fired at a motorcyclist on June 18 (a case not mentioned in any of the early *Times* stories). By August, the list included over forty incidents.

Descriptions of the shooting emphasized that they had begun with mundane traffic disputes, [and] that they seemed random, without clear motive, irrational. CBS anchorperson Dan Rather noted, "authorities are dealing with, literally, mur-derous rage" (CBS, July 24) but other stories spoke of copycats and "triggermen out for a cruel joke" (NBC, July 29). The result, reporters sug-gested, was freeways becoming "shooting galler-ies," "scenes of combat," "war zones," or a "terror zone."

If freeway shootings were random and sense-less, then their context was irrelevant. For in-stance, the first network news story about free-way violence featured a typifying example:

REPORTER JERRY BOWEN: Nineteen-year-old Jiang Nan was shot by another motorist last month during a race for a freeway exit.

[video: shots of Jan in hospital bed] (CBS, July 24)

Three nights later, Nan reappeared in a story on another network:

REPORTER KEN KASHUIHARA: Jiang Nan was shot in the arm because, he says, he honked his horn at another driver. [video: Nan walking bandaged]

NAN: You can't go around people, shooting people because people just honk your horn. You know. That's not right. [video: close-up of Nan speaking, sitting in car's driver seat, labeled "Jian Nan-Victim"] (ABC, July 27)

CBS and ABC used Jiang Nan's experience to ex-emplify the randomness of freeway violence. In contrast, the *Los Angeles Times* story about the same incident offered more information about its context:

> Alhambra Police Detective Jim Varga said Sunday's shooting occurred after two cars approached the New Avenue freeway on-ramp in Alhambra at about the same time, and the drivers 'began jockeying for position to see who would get on first.'
>
> Once on the freeway, occupants of both cars threw paper cups and other items at each other, and the other driver tried to prevent Nan from changing lanes, Varga said. When Nan headed for the Atlantic Boulevard exit, the gunmen opened fire, striking Jan in the arm. (Stewart 1987)

This description makes the shooting seem less ran-dom, less an irrational response ("shooting people because people just honk your horn"), and more like the escalating "character contests" which of-ten precede interpersonal violence (Luckenbill 1984). While the press did not offer detailed ac-counts of every incident, other reports showed vi-olence emerging from a context of conflict. For instance, the aerial gun-waving incident men-tioned above involved rival planes engaged in fish-spotting (Trippert 1987). Some reporters seemed to restrict the concept of freeway shootings to ran-dom incidents: "investigators believe that as many as four of the recent shootings involved gang activ-ity or narcotics and may not have been examples of random roadway violence" (Kendall and Jones 1987, p. 20). In other words not all shootings on freeways were "freeway shootings." (In 1987, the media attributed five deaths to freeway violence, but [Centers for Disease Control, or CDC] researchers, after eliminating cases involving prior disputes, found only two [one on a freeway]. [Onwuachi-Saunders, Chukwudi, Lambert, Marchbanks, O'Carroll, and Mercy 1989].

If freeway shootings were random and on the rise, then all motorists were potential victims. The media reported that fear was widespread, that some motorists were buying bulletproof windshields or arming themselves to fight back, and that there had been a "courtesy surge by drivers fearful of reprisals" (Dean 1987; Gest 1987).

In short, the media described freeway shootings as a growing problem, characterized by random violence and widespread fear. Without official statistics or public opinion polls bearing on the topic, reporters relied on interviews with their sources to support these claims. Thus, the eleven network news stories used thirty-eight clips from interviews: eleven with law enforcement officials promising to take action or advising caution; thirteen victims describing their experiences; ten person-in-the-street interviews revealing public concern; and four experts offering explanations.

Explaining the Problem

Having discovered and described freeway violence, the press sought to explain the new social problem. These explanations came from interviews with experts, mostly psychiatrists and social scientists who offered some version of frustration-aggression theory. . . .

> Maybe you have a short fuse. Maybe you have a gun in the car. You're wrapped in steel armor, plenty of power under your foot, but constantly boxed in by traffic. A feeling of impotence and anger, and then someone cuts you off. That, authorities say, is how the shootings began. Then perhaps some people began firing for fun. (NBC, August 3)

In this view, driving in congested "creep-hour traffic" produced stress and frustration which, in turn, led to anger and escalated into shootings and other violent acts (Lobue 1987). Almost all press reports offered some version of this explanation; some added secondary accounts. Several stories suggested that a car's anonymity made aggression less risky ("It's the private bubble that brings out Mr. Hyde" [Johston 1987, p. 3]); others implied that media coverage encouraged copycat crimes. Still others alluded to the effects of summer heat. . . .

Interpreting the Problem

If freeway violence was a social problem, what sort of problem was it? There were several answers to this question, examples of what Gamson and Modigliani (1989, p. 3) call interpretive packages:

> A package has an internal structure. At its core is a central organizing idea, or *frame*, for making sense of relevant events, suggesting what is at issue. . . . Finally, a package offers a number of different condensing symbols that suggests the core frame and positions in shorthand, making it possible to display the package as a whole with a deft metaphor, catchphrase, or other symbolic device. (emphasis in original)

These interpretations offered different orientations to understanding freeway violence and had different implications for social policy.

Perhaps the most straightforward interpretation treated freeway shootings as a *crime problem*. Government and law enforcement officials emphasized this theme. One Highway Patrol officer declared: "These are difficult crimes to try to stop for law enforcement. They are ty—, these are crimes of passion which are akin to the types of crime that occur, uh, between family members" (NBC, August 3). If freeway violence was a crime problem, then its solution lay in increased patrols, better investigations, and more effective prosecution. All three freeway-violence bills which became law fit this model: [Assembly Bill] 2416 added officers to the Highway Patrol; [Assembly Bill] 2142 forbade probation for convicted offenders; and [Senate Bill] 117 created an additional five-year penalty for persons convicted in freeway shootings (Gillam 1987).

Other analysts portrayed freeway violence as a *traffic problem*, a product of congested highways. While Los Angeles Police Chief Daryl Gates (1987) warned of a "breakdown in self-discipline," his Op-Ed piece concentrated on ways to improve traffic flow, such as closing rush-hour freeways to single-occupant cars. Interpreting freeway violence as a traffic problem implied a need for new freeways, mass transportation, or other means of reducing congestion, although such long-term solutions rarely received detailed discussion.

Still others treated freeway violence as a *gun problem*, one more consequence of the ready availability of firearms. Newspaper editorial pages favored this interpretation; the *Times* (1987a; 1987c) and *San Francisco Chronicle* (1987b) editorials on freeway shootings advocated gun control, and the *Washington Post* (1987) ran a Herblock cartoon, showing a roadside gun stand with signs reading "Last Chance to Reload Before Freeway" and "NRA Freeway Special."

Several commentators spoke of a *courtesy problem*; they viewed the violence as a product of aggressive, hurried, self-centered driving habits. One "recovering Type A" urged people to change their habits: "It takes self-confidence to be a freeway wimp" (Brenner 1987). The CDC researchers offered a *medical* interpretation: "the full public health impact of roadway violence has never been investigated. Roadway assaults could have an enormous emotional impact on drivers in Los Angeles County as well as throughout the United States" (Onwuachi-Saunders et al. 1989, p. 2264). Finally, there were suggestions that freeway shootings were really a *media problem*, "a combination of coincidence and media hype" (Royko 1987a). But even these critics seemed to agree that more than one hype was at work; after describing the "media circus," *Newsweek* went on to discuss traffic congestion—"the real cause of L.A.'s sudden evolution from 'Have a Nice Day' to 'Make My Day'" (Kaus 1987).

The Template for Social Problems Coverage

In covering freeway violence, then, the press concentrated on description, explanation, and interpretation. These are, of course, standard elements for stories about social problems; they form a template for social problems coverage. Because the press places a premium on the novel and the exotic, description is central to the construction of new social problems. Explanation and interpretation offer accounts for these problems. . . .

The only unusual feature of the press coverage was the diversity of interpretive schemes presented. Stallings (1990, p. 90) argues that the media prefer monocausal explanations; while early press coverage may offer competing interpretations, "later accounts tend to converge on a single factor." This failed to happen in the case of freeway violence, probably because the media continued to play the role of primary claimsmaker. Most social problems coverage follows the lead of the independent primary claimsmakers who promote a particular interpretation. Because the press discovered freeway violence, there was no single authoritative interpretation, and commentators adapted several familiar interpretive packages. . . .

Culture and Claims

Constructionist analysts suggest that it is easier to promote claims which "fit closely with broad cultural concerns" (Hilgartner and Bosk 1988, p. 64), which "resonate with larger cultural themes" (Gamson and Modigliani 1989, p. 5). The media's treatment of freeway shootings was noteworthy for the ease with which it incorporated imagery from other sources. Often, claimsmakers who presented different interpretations of freeway violence drew upon similar images.

Popular Culture

Discussions of freeway violence frequently borrowed images from violent films. Reporters invoked references to crime thrillers ("Make My Day"), action pictures set in post-Vietnam ("Freeway Rambos") or post-apocalyptic society ("Road Warriors," "a Mad Max mentality"), and Westerns ("hairtrigger impulses reminiscent of the frontier West" [Cummings 1987]). These images fit nicely with interpretations of freeway shootings as a crime or gun problem.

The importance of the film industry to Los Angeles no doubt encouraged these allusions to contemporary movies, and the frequent use of violent automotive chase scenes in action pictures must have helped forge the link between freeway shootings and movie imagery. But references to popular culture are not uncommon in constructions of social problems; most obviously, "Star Wars" has become a standard referent in defense policy debates.

Popular culture is a readily available cultural resource, offering a vast array of familiar images which are easily adapted to claimsmaking. There are advantages to using these images: they suggest that the claimsmaker is clever or up-to-date and they make claims more accessible or more interesting to a wider audience. But those advantages come at a cost. When popular cultural images typify a problem, they shape perceptions of it.

Thus, suggestions that freeway shootings somehow resembled the extraordinary violence in formula films implied an ambivalence toward violence, since popular culture simultaneously celebrates and deplores violence. And, since U.S. popular culture tends to locate good and evil within individual hero[e]s and villains, the movie imagery may have helped define freeway shootings in terms of deviant individuals. Finally, likening brief incidents of freeway violence to the prolonged, dramatic violence found in films implied a level of violence far greater than that found in press reports of particular freeway shootings. Although the references to Mad Max and Rambo were playful, they exaggerated the problem's seriousness.

Humor

Reports of freeway violence also inspired cartoonists and humor columnists. Most often, their work used exaggeration to make the problem seem ridiculous. Instead of depicting freeways as scenes of criminal violence, cartoonists militarized the problem (e.g., depicting a middle-class couple in a car, with the middle-aged female passenger wearing a Rambo-style headband and aiming a rocket launcher [*Los Angeles Times* 1987b], or showing a traffic reporter's helicopter under fire [*San Francisco Chronicle* 1987a]). Playing on reporters' references to war zones and Rambo, these cartoons extended the problem to a ridiculous extreme, showing ordinary people taking extraordinary violence for granted. Other cartoons contrasted freeway violence with earthquakes and drunk driving (*Los Angeles Times* 1987d; 1987e), suggesting that shootings were just one added problem faced by long-suffering urbanites. The humor lay in the implication that freeway shootings were mundane, not at all extraordinary, that random danger is simply another hazard of urban life. . . .

Other humor depended on freeway shootings having emerged in Los Angeles, notorious for its heavy, fast-moving freeway traffic. Thus, a CBS (July 24) story began: "It's always been crazy on the Southern California freeways—a real zoo—but these days the animals are armed and dangerous," while columnist Lewis Grizzard (1987) noted, " . . . there are more crazy people in Los Angeles than anywhere else in the country." Here, stereotypes of Southern California provided a cultural resource for the humorists. Other humorists warned that the roots of freeway violence were mundane, that aggressive driving was widespread, and that it was only a small step from

everyday hostility to extraordinary violence (cf. Royko 1987b). Thus, all parties—and the larger culture—were to blame when incidents escalated to violence. As these examples suggest, claimsmakers incorporated humor into almost all of the competing interpretations of freeway violence.

Random Violence

The humorists' treatments of freeway shootings, like the reporters' references to Rambo, suggest a failure to take the problem completely seriously. However, most of the humor was not pointed; it made fun of the phenomenon, rather than the people involved. At the same time, press reports emphasized the random, senseless qualities of freeway violence, warning that ordinary drivers, going about their everyday business, were potential victims. This drew upon a more general, contemporary concern with irrational, capricious villains. The 1980s saw the construction of other villains said to strike at random, including serial murderers, strangers abducting children, and product-tampering copycats. . . .

In the 1960s and 1970s, asserting randomness became a standard tactic for claimsmakers seeking to raise social concern; defining all children as potential child-abuse victims or all women as potential rape victims gave the widest possible audience an interest in confronting these problems. But it is easy to move from saying "X happens to all sorts of people," to "X can happen to anyone," to "X occurs randomly." And defining events as random encourages people to ignore or deny patterns in social life. Thus, claims that freeway shootings were random linked this problem to those involving other menacing deviants, while discouraging critical analysis of the problem's nature.

Incorporating Cultural Images

Because there were no independent primary claimsmakers guiding the interpretation of freeway shootings, the media had a relatively free hand in constructing the problem. However, rather than treating freeway violence as a unique phenomenon, the press located the problem within a set of existing—and not necessarily consistent—cultural concerns. Freeway shootings were said to resemble violent elements in popular culture, to have humorous features, and to reflect the random impulses of violent criminals. Confronted with a "new" problem, the media borrowed established cultural images to discuss it, with advocates of very different interpretations adopting similar imagery.

The problem's Southern California setting explains the frequent references to the film industry, the Los Angeles freeways, and the character of Californians. Not surprisingly, a different imagery characterized media coverage of an earlier "outbreak" of freeway violence in Houston, Texas in 1982 (King 1982; Ivey 1983). In particular, there were references to the frontier West ("gunfighter," "posse"), while the most prominent explanation held that Houston's economic boom had attracted "Texas newcomers," producing a "clash of cultures on the highway." A 1987 *Houston Post* article ("Freeway free-for-all: Why Los Angeles' highways and not Houston's?") argued that, while Houston led the nation in traffic congestion, the city's recent economic slowdown had reduced the influx of newcomers and slowed the "frantic pace of life," causing a decline in freeway shootings (Flood 1987).

The contrasting treatments of freeway violence in Los Angeles and Houston suggest that primary claimsmaking by the media will usually draw from a pool of available imagery. This resembles Swidler's (1986, p. 273) model of culture "as a 'tool kit' of symbols, stories, rituals, and worldviews, which people may use in varying configurations to solve different kinds of problems." In this view, "individuals select the meanings they need . . . from the limited but nonetheless varied cultural menu a given society provides" (Schudson 1989, p. 155). Thus, reporters covering the 1987 freeway shootings incorporated familiar images—references to recent films, expertise from psychiatrists and social scientists, humorous stereotypes about Californians and their freeways, and warnings about random violence. If nothing else, the time constraints of news work make this sort of borrowing likely.

The problem with the tool-kit model is that it does not help us predict which images will be used to construct which problems (Schudson 1989). But claims do not emerge in vacuum; they have an organizational context which affects the choice of imagery in at least three stages of the claimsmaking process. First, primary claimsmakers have ideologies, professional training, perceived interests, and other concerns which shape their construction of social problems. Claims-

makers' identities affect their characterization of problems; where moralists see sin, medical authorities detect disease.

Second, primary claimsmakers find themselves competing with one another for media attention. Not all claims receive coverage, and the press favors those which are dramatic, sponsored by powerful groups, and "relate to deep mythic themes" (Hilgartner and Bosk 1988, p. 64). Thus, bigots, political radicals, religious fundamentalists, and others outside the political and cultural mainstream have trouble getting the press to listen to their claims and often complain that the coverage they do receive distorts what they have to say. The media's role as a filter is less obvious when (as in the case of freeway violence) they act as primary claimsmakers. Here, reporters have insiders' knowledge of what makes a good story; they understand the template for social problems stories and shape their reports to fit.

In turn, media coverage shapes the reactions of policymakers and the public. Gamson and Modigliani (1989) discuss this third stage, arguing that the impact of claims depends upon the rhetoric and activities of primary and secondary claimsmakers and upon whether the claims have "cultural resonance." Claims presented in terms which are unfamiliar or ill-matched to the larger culture's concerns have little impact.

In short, while primary claimsmakers may seem to have a great deal of freedom in composing claims, they are in practice constrained by their own perceptions of the problem, the expectations of the press, and the concerns of policymakers and the public. Even so, the language and imagery used by independent primary claimsmakers are likely to be more diverse than the rhetoric adopted when the press serves as primary claimsmaker. When not prompted by outside claimsmakers, reporters and editors construct social problems within the familiar limits of news-work conventions. These constraints help explain why, in the case of freeway violence, the media adapted familiar explanations, interpretations, and images in their presentation of the problem. Still, the impact of those claims depended on a set of contingencies which shaped the rise—and fall—of the freeway shootings problem.

The Natural History of a Short-Lived Problem

Three contingencies accounted for the emergence of freeway violence as a social problem. First, the "freeway violence" category had to be discovered; someone had to define separate incidents as part of a larger pattern. The resulting category had its own appeal: it offered both drama (as a violent crime) and immediacy (i.e., most people were part of freeway traffic and therefore at risk). Yet freeway violence was not controversial; the media's construction of the problem did not threaten any powerful interests. And television had little difficulty illustrating the problem with videotape of dense traffic, bulletholes in cars, and interviews with victims. Once discovered, freeway violence fit several of the media's requirements for a good social problems story.

Still these features alone cannot explain freeway violence becoming a focus for national attention. Most crime waves attract only local news coverage (Fishman 1978). Other outbreaks of freeway shootings—in California in 1977 (*Los Angeles Times* 1987a), Detroit in 1989 (*New York Times* 1989), and Houston in 1982—failed to attract as much national attention as the 1987 Los Angeles incidents.

This suggests the importance of a second contingency: the *Los Angeles Times* discovered freeway shootings. As the most authoritative newspaper in its state and region, it sets the agenda for Southern California print and electronic news coverage; a story treated seriously by the *Times* is likely to be picked up by radio and television stations, as well as other newspapers (Best 1986). . . . Moreover, as a major metropolitan region and the center for the entertainment industry, Los Angeles has more than its share of reporters. Major newsmagazines and newspapers station correspondents there. All three [major] television networks own and operate affiliates in Los Angeles, and the network news programs favor reports from owned and operated stations. . . . Moreover, the widespread perception that Southern California often sets styles for the rest of the country makes it more likely that a Los Angeles "trend" will receive coverage in the national press.

Third, timing may have been important. There seem to have been relatively few stories competing for media attention. Journalistic folklore speaks of summer "dog days" and the "silly season" when news is slow, reporters must look harder for stories, and marginal stories are more likely to receive coverage. It may well be easier to gain coverage for social-problems claimsmaking during the summer. Consider the "crack epidemic" of 1986, freeway shootings of 1987, and the interest in polluted beaches in 1988. Claimsmakers must compete for media attention but, to the degree that this competition is seasonal, there may be periods when relatively weak claims can rise to visibility.

Taken together, these contingencies—the discovery of the category, by the *Los Angeles Times*, during a slow news season—help account for the rise of freeway violence to national prominence. Because freeway shootings emanated from Southern California—often a source for new trends—the media anticipated that violence would spread. On CBS (August 5), Dan Rather asked: "Is it a local phenomenon, or does it indicate something in the country as a whole, something in society at large?" Broadcasting from Chicago, ABC's (August 6) Peter Jennings noted, "There haven't been any incidents here in the Midwest . . . " But the *Wall Street Journal* argued that the violence was nationwide: "the nation's freeways now resemble something out of the Wild West" (Gonzales 1987). In its August 17 issue, *Time* noted: "Highway officials in Arizona, Washington, Utah, and Northern California reported armed confrontations last week" (Trippert 1987); three months later, a short item reported freeway violence "appears to have faded on the West Coast but is all the rage in southern Illinois and is spreading to eastern Missouri" (*Time* 1987). However, these isolated reports were apparently insufficient to maintain interest in freeway violence as a spreading problem.

The failure to document a dramatic spread in freeway shootings helps account for their disappearance as a social problem. Freeway violence both emerged and disappeared quickly. Why? The news media constructed the problem, but the story did not develop in any of the ways which might have let it remain visible. The lighthearted tone of some coverage discouraged people from taking the problem seriously. The press did not find sufficient cases to portray freeway violence as spreading throughout the country, nor did reporters find a growing number of incidents in Los Angeles; there was no dramatic new news to keep the story alive. Moreover, there were no independent primary claimsmakers interested in pursuing and promoting the story. The media brought freeway violence to public attention without prompting from outside claimsmakers. Once the problem achieved visibility, it might have been adopted by claimsmakers outside the press, but this did not happen, probably because the principal interpretations of the problem called for solutions which seemed unworkable. Whatever the arguments for expanded freeways, mass transportation, or other long-term solutions to Los Angeles traffic problems, few advocates expected progress, let along solutions, in the near future. And defining freeway shootings as a gun problem offered little advantage; the tiny number of freeway homicides could not affect the entrenched debate over gun control. In other words, no constituency emerged to adopt the newly-constructed freeway shooting problem, to nurture it and help it develop into a well-established social problem.

Conclusion

Freeway violence offers an example of a short-lived social problem in which the media acted as primary claimsmakers. The problem was discovered and constructed by enterprising reporters and press commentators. In 1987, theirs were the only voices to be heard on the subject. Because they had a free hand in constructing this problem, we can view the result as a prototype of social-problems construction as practiced by the media. Most striking are the similarities between the construction of freeway shootings and the media's treatment of other social problems. The press framed its coverage within a standard structure, using a template of elements—descriptions, explanations, and interpretation—usually found in contemporary social-problems stories. Moreover, the media adapted a variety of cultural resources, such as references to popular culture and random violence, to depict freeway shootings. The particular construction which emerged—a frightening yet funny spectacle of Los Angelinos, pushed beyond endurance by the frustrations of freeway driving, turning to random shootings and somehow incorporating this violence into their everyday lives—was engaging enough (and the immediate competition for media attention weak enough) to catapult freeway violence into national visibility. However, there was little to sus-

tain the media's interest, and the attention soon faded.

By mid-August, 1987, freeway violence had disappeared from national news coverage. Still, the problem retains some familiarity and remains the subject of occasional asides. . . . Freeway shootings, then, have become a cultural resource in their own right, available for use in the construction of other social problems.

References

Best, Joel. 1986. "Famous for Fifteen Minutes." *Qualitative Sociology* 9: 372–382.

———. 1989. *Images of Issues*, edited by Joel Best. New York: Aldine de Gruyter.

———. 1990. *Threatened Children*. Chicago: University of Chicago Press.

Billiter, Bill. 1971. "Traffic Dispute Results in Third Freeway Shooting." *Los Angeles Times* (July 20): I3.

Brenner, Martin. 1987. "Power to the Freeway Wimps." *Los Angeles Times* (August 5): II7.

Cummings, Judith. 1987. "On Congested Highways, California Motorists Turn to Violence." *New York Times* (July 28): I10.

Dean, Paul. 1987. "Defensive Driving." *Los Angeles Times* (August 5): V1.

Fishman, Mark. 1978. "Crime Waves as Ideology." *Social Problems* 25: 531–543.

Flood, Mary. 1987. "Freeway Free-for-All." *Houston Post* (August 9): 1A, 20A.

Gamson, William and Andre Modigliani. 1989. "Media Discourse and Public Opinion on Nuclear Power." *American Journal of Sociology* 95: 1–37.

Gates, Daryl F. 1987. "Highway Hostility Must be Stopped." *Los Angeles Times* (August 23): V5.

Gest, Ted. 1987. "Rambo's Brothers Cruise Clogged Expressways." *U.S. News and World Report* 103 (August 10): 6.

Gillam, Jerry. 1987. "Bills Signed to Combat Violence on Freeways." *Los Angeles Times* (September 27): I21.

Gonzales, Monica. 1987. "Motorist Mayhem." *Wall Street Journal* (August 3): 1, 14.

Grizzard, Lewis. 1987. "How to Avoid Getting Shot." *Atlanta Constitution* (August 2): B1.

Hilgartner, Stephen, and Charles L. Bosk. 1988. "The Rise and Fall of Social Problems." *American Journal of Sociology* 94: 53–78.

Ivey, Mark. 1983. "Where the Commuter Is a Gunfighter." *Business Week* (May 1): 20A, B.

Johnston, Lonn. 1987. "Stress on Freeways Sparks 'War Out There.'" *Los Angeles Times* (July 21): I3.

Kaus, Mickey. 1987. "Gunplay on the Freeway." *Newsweek* 110 (August 10): 18.

Kendall, John. 1987. "Death Raises Level of Fears on Highways." *Los Angeles Times* (July 26): I1.

Kendall, John, and Jack Jones. 1987. "4 Men, Woman Held in Highway Shooting Death." *Los Angeles Times* (July 29): 11, 20.

King, Wayne. 1982. "'Unfriendly Driving' Explodes into Violence on Texas Freeways." *New York Times* (December 17): A16.

Lobue, Ange. 1987. "Mayhem on the Freeways." *U.S. News and World Report* 103 (September 28): 9.

Los Angeles Herald Examiner. 1987. Editorial cartoon. (July 21): A14.

Los Angeles Times. 1987a. "Guns and Tire Irons" (editorial). (August 6): II10.

——. 1987b. Editorial cartoon. (August 8): II2.

——. 1987c. "Guns in Cars" (editorial). (August 23): II4.

——. 1987d. Editorial cartoon. (August 23): V5.

——. 1987e. Editorial cartoon. (October 10): II9.

Luckenbill, David. 1984. "Character Coercion, Instrumental Coercion, and Gun Control." *Journal of Applied Behavioral Science* 20: 181–192.

New York Times. 1989. "Outbreak of Road Shootings Plagues Detroit." (February 12): 27.

Onwuachi-Saunders, F. Chukwudi, Beborah A. Lambert, Polly A. Marchbanks, Patrick W. O'Carroll, and James A. Mercy. 1989. "Firearm-Related Assaults on Los Angeles Roadways." *Journal of the American Medical Association* 262: 2262–2264.

Royko, Mike. 1987a. "California 'Trend' Strictly a Misfire." *Chicago Tribune* (August 4): 3.

——. 1987b. "Were They Cruising for a Shooting." *Chicago Tribune* (August 10): 3.

San Francisco Chronicle. 1987a. Editorial cartoon. (August 10): 54.

——. 1987b. "Limiting Guns in Motor Vehicles" (editorial). (August 21): 72.

Sauter, Van Gordon. 1987a. "No Shelter from Freeway Violence." *Los Angeles Times* (June 26): V1.

——. 1987b. "Too Much Ado About Freeway Shootings?" *Los Angeles Times* (August 3): II5.

Schudson, Michael. 1989. "How Culture Works." *Theory and Society* 18: 153–180.

Stallings, Robert A. 1990. "Media Discourse and the Social Construction of Risk." *Social Problems* 37: 80–95.

Stewart, Jill. 1987. "2nd Freeway Shooting Incident Is Investigated." *Los Angeles Times* (June 24): II1.

Swidler, Ann. 1986. "Culture in Action." *American Sociological Review* 51: 273–286.

Time. 1987. "Homicide on the Highway." 130 (November 23): 31.

Trippett, Frank. 1987. "Highway to Homicide." *Time* 130 (August 17): 18.

Washington Post. 1987. Editorial cartoon. (August 3): A14.

35

Nazi Doctors at Auschwitz

Robert Jay Lifton

Although humans socially construct reality, they seldom experience it as their construction. We usually take the socially constructed reality that we inhabit for granted as the reality rather than a reality. We dismiss alternative constructions of reality as symptoms of demonic possession or mental illness or as products of ignorance or depravity. Humans' faith in the inevitability of their particular reality provides security and meaning in a sometimes senseless world. However, it has also led to such horrors as war and oppression throughout human history.

There is probably no better example of the power and potential horrors of socially constructed reality than Nazi Germany. The Nazis constructed a reality in which Jews and other so-called "undesirables" were the cause of all Germany's problems, and National Socialism was its savior. Those who embraced this construction of reality or were merely caught up in it either participated in or ignored all manner of human atrocities. This selection examines how Nazi ideology or interpretations of reality and the reality of the infamous Auschwitz concentration camp led physicians to participate in mass murder. Robert Jay Lifton describes these Nazi doctors' socialization to killing and to the horrific reality of Auschwitz based on interviews with surviving doctors and camp prisoners. He focuses on the doctors' participation in "selections" of Jewish prisoners for immediate execution in Auschwitz's infamous gas chamber or for, usually temporary, survival as camp workers. Although many doctors were initially reluctant to participate in such "selections," their reluctance was overpowered by the reality of Auschwitz and their own Nazi ideology. They came to view the largely hidden and efficient extermination of Jews as less disturbing than the living horrors of Auschwitz. Over time, most came to accept the mass murder of Jews and their participation in it as inevitable, necessary, and routine. They even considered the killing necessary to protect the health of inmates who were spared that fate. Although not all doctors approved of the mass execution of Jews by gassing, all were convinced that the "Jewish problem" needed to be solved and that this "Final Solution" would finally solve it.

Lifton argues that these doctors' acceptance of the horrific reality of Auschwitz involved the psychological process he calls "doubling." Faced with that horrific reality, Nazi doctors developed an Auschwitz self alongside their existing "normal" self. The Auschwitz self was the dutiful and efficient medical supervisor of mass killing. Their other, humane self was nurtured by occasional acts of kindness and medical concern toward still living inmates and regular visits with family and friends away from the camp. However, the doctors kept their lives at the camp and away from it quite separate, supporting the psychological schism between their two selves. According to Lifton, it is this psychological doubling that allowed doctors to participate in killings without thinking of themselves as murderers. Rather, they could think of themselves as normal people who had to do a dirty but necessary job.

Lifton suggests that Auschwitz illustrates the power of a social situation to command the psychological doubling that enables individuals to commit atrocities. It was the reality of Auschwitz and Nazi ideology that led doctors who had taken the Hippocratic oath to participate in the routine taking of human life and not some psychological disposition toward cruelty. That is a sobering lesson. It suggests that under certain social conditions, just about anyone can become a killer or tormentor in the cause of some construction of reality. The example of Nazi Doctors at Auschwitz alerts us to the kind of social situations and realities that can transform us into such monsters.

I gained an important perspective on Auschwitz from an Israeli dentist who had spent three years in the camp. We were completing a long interview, during which he had told me about many things, including details of SS dentists' supervision of prisoners' removal of gold fillings from the teeth of fellow Jews killed in the gas chambers. He looked about the comfortable room in his house with its beautiful view of Haifa, sighed deeply, and said, "This world is not this world." What I think he meant was that, after Auschwitz, the ordinary rhythms and appearances of life, however innocuous or pleasant, were far from the truth of human existence. Underneath those rhythms and appearances lay darkness and menace.

The comment also raises questions of our capacity to approach Auschwitz. From the beginning there has been enormous resistance on the part of virtually everyone to knowledge of what the Nazis were doing and have done there. That resistance has hardly abated, whatever the current interest in what we call "the Holocaust." Nor have more recent episodes of mass slaughter done much to overcome it. For to permit one's imagination to enter into the Nazi killing machine—to begin to experience that killing machine—is to alter one's relationship to the entire human project. One does not want to learn about such things.

Psychologically speaking, nothing is darker or more menacing, or harder to accept, than the participation of physicians in mass murder. However technicized or commercial the modern physician may have become, he or she is still a healer—and one responsible to a tradition of healing, which all cultures revere and depend upon. Knowledge that the doctor has joined the killers adds a grotesque dimension to the perception that "this world is not this world." During my work I gained the impression that, among Germans and many others, this involvement of physicians was viewed as the most shameful behavior.

When we think of the crimes of Nazi doctors, what come to mind are their cruel and sometimes fatal human experiments. Those experiments in their precise and absolute violation of the Hippocratic oath, mock and subvert the very idea of the ethical physician, of the physician dedicated to the well-being of patients. . . .

Yet when we turn to the Nazi doctor's role in Auschwitz, it was not the experiments that were most significant. Rather it was his participation in the killing process—indeed his supervision of Auschwitz mass murder from the beginning to end. This aspect of Nazi medical behavior has escaped full recognition—even though we are familiar with photographs of Nazi doctors standing at the ramp and performing their notorious "selections" of arriving Jews, determining which were to go directly to the gas chamber and which were to live, at least temporarily, and work in the camp. . . .

My assumption from the beginning, in keeping with my twenty-five years of research, was that the best way to learn about Nazi doctors was to talk to them; interviews became the pragmatic core of the study. But I knew that, even more than in earlier work, I would have to supplement the interviews with extensive reading in and probing of all related issues—having to do not only with observations by others on Nazi medical behavior but with the Nazi era in general, as well as with German culture and history and with overall patterns of victimization in general and anti-Jewishness in particular. . . .

I interviewed three groups of people. The central group consisted of twenty-nine men who had been significantly involved at high levels with Nazi medicine, twenty-eight of them physicians and one pharmacist. . . . I interviewed a second group of twelve former Nazi nonmedical professionals of some prominence: as lawyers, judges, economists, teachers, architects, administrators, and Party officials. . . . Very different was the third group I interviewed: eighty former Auschwitz prisoners who had worked on medical blocks, more than half of them doctors. . . .

While Auschwitz genocide came to encompass Gypsies, Poles, and Russians, only Jews underwent systematic selections. For the primary function of Auschwitz . . . was the murder of every single Jew the Nazis could (in Himmler's words) lay their hands on anywhere.

The SS doctor did no direct medical work. His primary function was to carry out Auschwitz's institutional program of medicalized genocide. Consider the SS doctor's activities in Auschwitz. He performed initial large-scale selections of arriving Jewish prisoners at the Birkenau camp. . . . These selections were usually conducted according to formula: old and debilitated people, children, and women with children all selected for gas chamber; while relatively young adults were permitted to survive, at least temporarily. . . .

After the selection, the presiding doctor was driven in an SS vehicle usually marked with a red cross, together with a medical technician (one of a special group of "disinfectors" . . .) and the gas pellets, to a gas chamber adjoining one of the crematoria. As *Führer*, or "leader," of the team, the doctor had supervisory responsibility for the correct carrying out of the killing process, though the medical technician actually inserted the gas pellets, and the entire sequence became so routine that little intervention was required. The doctor also had the task of declaring those inside the gas chamber dead and sometimes looked through a peephole to observe them. This, too, became routine, a matter of permitting twenty minutes or so to pass before the doors of the gas chamber could be opened and the bodies removed.

SS doctors also carried out two additional forms of selections . . . Jewish inmates were lined up on very short notice at various places in the camp and their ranks thinned in order to allow room for presumably healthier replacements from new transports. The other type of selections took place directly in the medical blocks in a caricature of triage. Rather than simply permitting those closest to death to die—in order to use limited medical resources to treat those who might be saved—as in traditional medical triage (the meaning given the term as originally used by the French military), the Nazis combined triage with murder by sending to the gas chamber those judged to be significantly ill or debilitated, or who required more than two or three weeks for recovery. . . .

Socialization to Killing

Virtually all Nazi doctors in Auschwitz complied in conducting selections, although they varied in how they did so and in their attitudes toward what they were doing. . . . [A]ll SS doctors were greatly influenced by . . . practical . . . issues: their shared relationship to an institution and to its selections demands, as regulated by higher medical and command authorities. And as greater numbers of transports arrived, selections were going on much of the time: as Dr. B. put it, "There was no way of avoiding [viewing] them if one had work to do in camp."

Under increasing pressure to select, most SS doctors underwent what he viewed as an extraordinary individual-psychological shift from revulsion to acceptance: *"In the beginning it was almost impossible. Afterward it became routine. That's the only way to put it."*

This shift involved a *socialization* to Auschwitz, including the important transition from outsider to insider.

Alcohol was crucial to this transition. Drinking together, often quite heavily, evenings in the officers' club, doctors "spoke very freely" and "expressed the most intimate objections." Some would "condemn the whole thing" and insist that "this is a filthy business . . . !" Dr. B. described these outbursts as so insistent as to be "like a mania . . . a sickness . . . over Auschwitz and . . . the gassings."

Such inebriated protest brought about no repercussions—indeed, may even have been encouraged—and was unrelated to commitment or action. Consequently, "whether one condemned it or not was not really so much the issue." The issue, as Ernst B. defined it, was that "Auschwitz was an existing fact. One couldn't . . . really be against it, you see, one had to go along with it whether it was good or bad." That is, mass killing was the unyielding *fact of life* to which everyone was expected to adapt.

Whenever an SS doctor arrived at Auschwitz, the process was repeated as questions raised by the newcomer were answered by his more experienced drinking companions:

> He would ask, 'How can these things be done there?' Then there was something like a general answer . . . which clarified everything. What is better for him [the prisoner]—whether he croaks . . . in shit or goes to heaven in [a cloud of] gas? And that settled the whole matter for the initiates. . . .

This ostensibly humane argument, Dr. B. was saying, was itself an assertion of Auschwitz reality as the baseline for all else. His language of initiation is appropriate in that selections were the specific "ordeal" the initiate had to undergo in order to emerge as a functioning Auschwitz "adult." And by exposing and combating doubts, the drinking sessions helped suppress moral aspects of the prior self in favor of a new Auschwitz self. . . .

At the same time there was constant pressure from above toward maximum involvement in selections, particularly from the spring of 1944 when dentists and pharmacists were also ordered to take their turns on the ramp. One of those dentists later testified that his plea to [Eduard] Wirths that he did not feel capable of performing selections, and wished to leave the camp, was met with a cool declaration that "according to a 'Führer order,' service in a concentration camp was considered front-line duty, and that any refusal was considered a desertion." . . .

Pressure and mentorship could combine, as in the case of Franz Lucas who, known to have a certain reluctance to select, was taken to the ramp by Wirths and [Joseph] Mengele and more or less shown how to go about things. Lucas apparently tried several ploys, including feigned illness, to avoid selecting; and even after complying, his kindness and medical help to prisoners led to a dressing down and an eventual transfer. . . .

The socialization of SS doctors to Auschwitz killing was enhanced by the camp's isolation from the world outside. The connecting medical figure with outside authority was Enno Lolling, who came frequently to the camp from his Berlin office and was essentially incompetent and a heavy drinker. Ernst B. had the impression that Lolling's superiors preferred not to know too many details about the camps, and that there was a general policy of "screening them off" from regular SS units. Camp doctors perpetuated this isolation by their reluctance, in Dr. B's phrase, to let others "see their cards." The result was, as he put it with only partial exaggeration, that "a concentration camp [became] a totally self-contained entity, absolutely isolated from everything—especially Auschwitz."

Doctors assigned there, then, had limited contact with anything but Auschwitz reality. They became preoccupied with adapting themselves to that reality, and moral revulsion could be converted into feelings of discomfort, unhappiness, anxiety, and despair. Subjective struggles could replace moral questions. They became concerned not with the evil of the environment but with how to come to some terms with the place.

They then became creatures of what Dr. B. described as the all-important Auschwitz milieu or atmosphere: "In that atmosphere everything is seen differently from the way it would be viewed now." On the basis of all the pressures and adaptive inclinations I have described, "after a few weeks in that milieu, one thinks: 'Yes.'" . . . Participation in selections was also enhanced by a sense that they did not come first in the hierarchy of horrors. Dr. B., for instance, stressed that "other things were much worse"—such as scenes of starving children in the Gypsy camp, where 80 percent of the inmates in general were starving to death while a few could be "living very well." He stressed the difficulty of "having this in front of you every day, continuously," and how "it took a long time to be able to live with that."

There, as in other situations, what mattered was what one could see, what confronted one's senses: "The killing was mostly excluded [from conversation], . . . [since] it was not what was directly visible. But very visible were the so-called *Muselmanner* [or living corpses]. [Also] visible

were the ones who were starving . . . to death. . . . That was a bigger problem. . . . One was more oppressed by that."

By not quite seeing it, doctors could distance themselves from the very killing they were actively supervising. The same purpose was served by drawing upon their having witnessed what they claimed were worse horrors—in camps for Russian prisoners of war and in other concentration camps—which enabled them to conclude that "they've got it a lot better here." . . .

Doctors were further enabled to do selections by the shared sense that Auschwitz was morally separate from the rest of the world, that it was, as Dr. B. put it, "extraterritorial." He referred not to Auschwitz's geographical isolation, but to its existence as a special enclave of bizarre evil, which rendered it exempt from ordinary rules of behavior. . . .

[L]egitimaters . . . of medicalized Auschwitz killing were aided in their function by their sense that all Jews were already condemned. What Dr. Magda V. said of Mengele applies more generally to SS doctors. "It didn't matter to him [whether he selected someone or not] because he thought that sooner or later they're going [to the gas chamber]. . . . For him I think we . . . were just dead anyhow." Another survivor similarly called the whole process "only a play": that is a staged drama in which "we were all there to be killed. The question was only who was to be first."

For the SS doctor, efficiency in selections became equated with quarantine arrangements and the improvement of actual medical units, all in the service of keeping enough inmates able to work and the camp free of epidemics. Within that context, the SS doctor inevitably came to perceive his professional function to be in neither the killing nor the healing alone, but in achieving the necessary balance. That *healing-killing balance*, according to the SS doctor Ernst B., was "the problem" for Auschwitz doctors. From that standpoint, as he further explained, the principle of "clearing out" a block when there was extensive diarrhea—sending everyone on it to the gas chambers—could be viewed as "pseudo ethical" and "pseudo idealistic." Dr. B. meant that such a policy in that environment could be perceived by the doctors themselves as ethical and idealistic in that they carried out their task to perfection on behalf of the higher goal of camp balance. . . .

Ideology and the 'Jewish Problem'

Crucial to the capacity to perform selections was a doctor's relationship to Nazi ideology. Important here was the basic early attraction on the part of most of these doctors to the Nazi promise of German resurgence—a tie that could sustain them through reservations and discomfort: "We looked at it [Auschwitz] as a totally messed-up thing. [But] you could not change it, you see. That's like in a democracy, where you may find many things wanting, but you cannot change it. Or rather, you stick with it nonetheless. Because [you] think democracy is better." The strong implication is that Nazism *even with Auschwitz* was the best of all possible worlds.

However ironic, these medical participants in mass murder were held to the regime behind the murder by the principles of what Dr. B. called "coherent community" . . . and "common effort" . . . in discussing his and others' sense of the Nazi movement's commitment to overcoming staggering national problems. Hence he could speak of "a faith" . . . and, more than that, of a "practiced faith" joined to a community; in all this, "the bridge . . . is the ideology." And that "bridge" could connect the Nazi doctors to an immediate sense of community and communal purpose in their Auschwitz work.

Anti-Jewishness was an active ingredient in that ideology. While there was individual variation, Dr. B. claimed that "all physicians were absolutely convinced that the Jews were our misfortune. . . . When I mentioned the phrase "gangrenous appendix" an SS doctor had applied to Jews, . . . Dr. B. quickly answered that the Nazi doctors' overall feeling was: "Whether you want to call it an appendix or [not], it must be extirpated. . . ." He went so far as to say that even the policy of killing all Jews was readily justified by this "theoretical and ideological" stance, so that "of course they supported it." . . .

Doctors could call forth an absolutized Nazi version of good and evil as both justification for what they were seeing and doing and further avoidance of its psychological actuality (as Ernst B. explained):

> Precisely because they were convinced of the justness . . . or of the . . . National Socialist "world blessing" . . . and that the Jews were the root evil . . . of the world—precisely because they were so convinced of it did they believe, or were strengthened—[in that belief], that the Jews, even existentially, had to be absolutely exterminated. . . .

And although "not everybody approved of the gassing" and "many theories were discussed," one had to admit that gassing was an improvement over the inefficiency of previous methods:

> The main argument for the gassing was that when one tried to create ghettos . . . they never lasted longer than one or two generations. And then the ghetto—let us say—would become porous. . . . That was the main argument for the gassing. Against the gassing there were a number of different kinds of the most nonsensical speculations . . . forced sterilization and so on. . . . Lots of theorizing went on.

Now there was a more successful approach to the "Jewish problem" and, as Dr. B. added, "a means of confirmation" of the success.

In talking about these matters, he never directly answered one question I repeatedly asked him: whether doctors disagreed with one another about the necessity to kill Jews, or agreed about that and disagreed only about the means. I believe that the ambiguity has psychological significance beyond his evasion. From what Dr. B. and other observers have conveyed, it is probably accurate to say that most Nazi doctors in Auschwitz believed that something they perceived as "Jewishness" had to be eliminated, whether that meant sending Jews to Madagascar, forcing Jews to leave Germany while permitting a small well-established minority to remain and undergo complete assimilation, or murdering every last one of them. By clinging to this ambiguity, Nazi doctors had an additional means of avoiding the psychological reality of the decision for mass murder and its implementation. And by viewing the whole matter as a problem that needed to be "solved," by whatever means, that pragmatic goal could become the only focus. The very term . . . "Final Solution" served both psychological purposes: it stood for mass murder without sounding or feeling like it; and it kept the focus primarily on problem solving. So given a minimum agreement on the necessity of solving the "Jewish problem," doctors and other Nazis could come to accept, even to prefer, the mass-murder project, because it alone promised a *genuine* solution, a clearing up of the matter once and for all, and a *final* solution. . . .

The Schizophrenic Situation: Doubling

The SS doctor was deeply involved in the stark contradictions of the "schizophrenic situation" that Ernst B. considered to be the key to understanding Auschwitz; I see it as a further expression of "extraterritoriality"—of the sense that what happened there did not count. The heart of that schizophrenia for doctors lay in the idea of doing constructive medical work within a "slaughterhouse." A related dimension of the schizophrenia, as B. explained, was the "split situation" between the idealism of a world-bettering great German state along with the specific Nazi "world blessing" and what he called (still reluctant to speak directly of mass murder) "the other situation, the one working with those . . . methods there." . . .

[One] way Nazi doctors coped with Auschwitz was to lead a double life that both reflected and enhanced their psychological doubling. Thus, they spent most of their time in the camp (except for occasional professional or pleasure trips to nearby areas) but went on leave for a few days every other month or so to spend time, usually in Germany, with their wives and children. They remained extremely aware of the separateness of the two worlds. One's wife, children, and parents came to stand for purity, as opposed to an inner sense of Auschwitz filth. Ernst B., for instance, managed to get home every two or three months for about a week's time but spoke strongly against the idea of his wife ever visiting him at Auschwitz: "I could never have subjected my wife to a closer look at things. . . . I can't even express myself properly, [but] the thought of her coming there would have caused [me] great [inner] resistance. One simply gave it no consideration whatsoever."

Dr. B. observed that each SS doctor could call forth two radically different psychological constellations within the self: one based on "values generally accepted" and the education and background of a "normal person"; the other based on "this [Nazi-Auschwitz] ideology with values quite different from those generally accepted." The first tendency might be present one day, the second on the next, and it was hard to know which to expect on a given occasion or whether there would be a mixture of both.

Only a form of schism or doubling can explain the polarities of cruelty and decency in the same SS doctor. Klein is perhaps the best illustration here. This cruel and fanatical racist was seen by Dr. Magda V. as profoundly hypocritical and simply a "bad man," and by another prisoner physician, Olga Lengyel, as "one of the fervent zealots" who ran the Nazi annihilation project. Yet this latter doctor also spoke of him as a person capable of kindness, as when he brought her medicine for her patients and protected her from cruel SS personnel . . . ; he was, Lengyel said, "the only German in Auschwitz who never shouted."

Another prisoner also had a surprisingly positive experience with Klein: when walking in the camp, this man took the highly unusual and dangerous step of approaching the SS doctor directly in order to ask him to have his (the prisoner's) wife, a nurse, transferred from an attic working place, where a great deal of sawdust caused her to cough incessantly, back to a medical block where she had worked in the past. Instead of saying, "Away with this fellow!" as everyone thought he would, Klein complied. This survivor commented, "These things are so intermingled—murdering and extermination on the one hand, and the very small details where something could work out quite the other way." He further reflected:

> When I tell this . . . after thirty-five years, I think, How could it be possible? . . . That one could influence this god and make a man who . . . exterminated thousands of people . . . to have interest in one prisoner girl, and save her. . . . There are things that happen in human nature . . . that an experienced analyst even cannot understand. . . . This split, . . . it can be very delicate. . . . Maybe with these small [positive] things—with Klein, there [was] something of . . . medical tradition in them. But, in general, I believe they were no longer doctors. They were SS officers. In these things, the group spirit is one thousand times mightier than the individual spirit.

This survivor was saying that Klein functioned primarily in relation to the collective SS ethos, or what I call the "Auschwitz self"; but that he had available a humane dimension of self that could emerge at certain times.

The existence of that humane element of self may, in fact, have contributed to Klein's and other Nazi doctors' cruelties. For instance, when SS doctors asked pregnant women to step forward so that they could receive a double food ration—only to send those who did to the gas chamber the following day—it is possible that a brief sense of potential "medical activity" (improving the diet of pregnant women) contributed to the doctors' psychological capacity to carry out this hideous hoax.

In my interviews with Dr. Lottie M., she raised several questions she asked me to explore with Nazi doctors: How far did they look upon all of Auschwitz as "an experiment [on] how much a person can stand"? How much were they able to recognize "the irrationalism of . . . the racial theory"? At what point had "they started to be afraid of the end"? But what she was most curious about was "this question of split loyalty"—of conflicting oaths, contradictions between murderous cruelty and momentary kindness which SS doctors seemed to manifest continuously during their time at Auschwitz.

For the schism tended not to be resolved. Its persistence was part of the overall psychological equilibrium that enabled the SS doctor to do his deadly work. He became integrated into a large, brutal, highly functional system. Thus Dr. Henri Q. could wisely urge me to concentrate upon Nazi doctors' relation to this system rather than upon a single, infamous individual such as Mengele: "What impressed us was the fact that Auschwitz was a collective effort. It was not just a single person, but many. And the disturbing thing was that it was not something passionate [irrational]. It was something calm—there was nothing emotional about Auschwitz." . . .

The key to understanding how Nazi doctors came to do the work of Auschwitz is the psychological principle I call "doubling." . . . Doubling is an active psychological process, a means of *adaptation to extremity*. That is why I use the verb form, as opposed to the more usual noun form, "the double." The adaptation requires a dissolving of "psychological glue" as an alternative to a radical breakdown of the self. In Auschwitz, [the Nazi doctor] needed a functional Auschwitz self . . . [a]nd that Auschwitz self had to assume hegemony on an everyday basis, reducing expressions of the prior self to odd moments and to contacts with family and friends outside of camp. Nor did most Nazi doctors resist that usurpation as long as they remained in the camp. Rather they welcomed it as the only means of psychological function. If an environment is sufficiently extreme, and one chooses to remain in it, one may be able to do so *only* by means of doubling. . . .

Indeed, Auschwitz as an *institution*—as an atrocity-producing situation—ran on doubling. An atrocity-producing situation is one so structured externally (in this case, institutionally) that the average person entering it (in this case, as part of the German authority) will commit or become associated with atrocities. Always important to an atrocity-producing situation is its capacity to motivate individuals psychologically toward engaging in atrocity.

In an institution as powerful as Auschwitz, the external environment could set the tone for much of an individual doctor's "inner environment." The demand for doubling was part of the environmental message immediately perceived by Nazi doctors, the implicit command to bring forth a self that could adapt to killing without one's feeling oneself a murderer. Doubling became not just an individual enterprise but a shared psychological process, the group norm, part of the Auschwitz "weather." And that group process was intensified by the general awareness that, whatever went on in other camps, Auschwitz was the great technical center of the Final Solution. One had to double in order that one's life and work there not be interfered with either by the corpses one helped to produce or by those "living dead" (the *Muselmänner*) all around one. . . .

No individual self is inherently evil, murderous, genocidal. Yet under certain circumstances virtually any self is capable of becoming all of these. A self is not a thing or a person but an inclusive representation or symbolization of an individual organism—as experienced by a particular person and . . . by other people. To emphasize activity, shift, and change, we may speak of "self-process." . . .

The self's capacity for [mass killing] is always influenced by ideological currents in the environment. . . . [I]n terms of self-process, the sequence from ordinary doctor to Nazi doctor to ordinary doctor suggests the extraordinary power of an environment to issue a "call" to genocide. Everything said here about the self's response to that call depends importantly upon idea structures of a collective nature, upon shared mentality rather than any isolated self. . . .

Nazi doctors doubled in murderous ways; so can others. Doubling provides a connecting principle between the murderous behavior of Nazi doctors and the universal potential for just such behavior. The same is true of the capacity to murder endlessly in the name of national-racial cure. Under certain conditions, just about anyone can join a collective call to eliminate every last one of the alleged group of carriers of the "germ of death."

Yet my conclusion is by no means that "we are all Nazis." We are *not* all Nazis. That accusation eliminates precisely the kind of moral distinction we need to make. One of these distinctions concerns how, with our universal potential for murder and genocide, we for the most part hold back from evil. A sensitive healer aghast at discovering her own impulses to slap a patient who had become unruly wrote to me of this "problem of our daily humanity." But we learn from the Nazis not only the crucial distinction between impulse and act, but the critical importance of larger ideological currents in connecting the two in ways that result in mass evil. . . .

Reprinted from: Robert Jay Lifton, *The Nazi Doctors: Medical Killing and the Psychology of Genocide,* pp. 1, 2, 6, 7, 147–148, 193, 195–200, 202–206, 210–213, 419, 422, 425, 498, 503. Copyright © 1986 by Robert Jay Lifton. Reprinted by permission of Basic Books, a member of Perseus Books, L.L.C. ✦

Part X

Postmodern Social Reality

Some students of contemporary social life maintain that we have entered a new epoch of human history. Current modes of transportation and electronic means of communication have profoundly altered social life. We may now watch television programs on Kenya in the morning, telephone someone in Japan that afternoon, send a computer message to someone in Israel later, and fly to the Bahamas for the weekend that evening. Such travel and communication expands and multiplies networks of social interaction and relationships. It exposes us to numerous and often clashing versions of reality. Moreover, the diverse array of goods and services sold in the marketplace enable us to create collages of such diverse realities. We may dress like a New England woodsman, courtesy of L.L. Bean, in our Chicago apartment with Southwestern decor, while listening to rap music and feasting on Thai food. We see a kaleidoscope of realities on television, on city streets, and during our travels. Under these conditions, it is difficult to believe that any human reality is inevitable. Even supposedly authoritative experts are suspect. They often disagree and quickly change their minds. Nothing seems certain. This is what many students of social life call the postmodern condition. Some welcome it while others condemn it, but they all agree that human social life and experience is profoundly changing right before our eyes. They also agree that students of social life who ignore those changes will be left behind. The following selection is one attempt to understand postmodern social experience. ✦

36

The Dissolution of the Self

Kenneth J. Gergen

Many of the selections in this volume explain and illustrate how the self is formed and shaped by social experience. This most basic principle of sociological psychology clearly implies that the character of the self would change as the character of social life historically changes. That, in turn, suggests that our inner lives and selves are quite different from those of all but our most immediate ancestors. There seems to be little doubt that the character of social life in most human communities has undergone profound changes during the twentieth century. Kenneth Gergen examines some of the psychological consequences of these changes in this selection.

In an earlier selection, George Herbert Mead observed that the individual's adoption of the attitude of an organized community, or generalized other, unifies her or his self. Today, however, such a unification of self is more difficult. Contemporary modes of travel and communication expose us to the often inconsistent attitudes of countless people and communities. They allow us to maintain relationships, despite physical separation, and to participate in communities spread over great distances. Television and movies, not to mention newspapers, magazines, and books, bring us into contact with numerous other actual and fictional people and communities. This is what Gergen calls social saturation, and it leads to an increasingly dense population of the self. The voices of countless significant and generalized others fill our heads, and those voices are seldom in unison or even in harmony.

Our adoption of the attitudes of such countless and contentious significant and generalized others does not unify our selves but pulls them apart. Gergen calls this new pattern of self-consciousness "multiphrenia," which literally means many minds. We are many different things to many different people and to ourselves. We interpret our experiences and define ourselves in many different and often incompatible ways and evaluate ourselves according to many different and incom-patible standards. According to Gergen, that is why we often feel overwhelmed, inadequate, and uncertain. Neither our hearts nor our minds speak with a single voice or for a unified self. Consequently, Gergen argues, the belief that we possess a single true or real self begins to erode. We become increasingly aware that it is our connections to others that make us what we are. We no longer ask ourselves "Who am I?" We ask others "Who can I be with you?" This is what Gergen calls postmodern being—a new kind of human being living a new kind of social life.

... Cultural life in the twentieth century has been dominated by two major vocabularies of the self. Largely from the nineteenth century, we have inherited a *romanticist* view of the self, one that attributes to each person characteristics of personal depth: passion, soul, creativity, and moral fiber. This vocabulary is essential to the formation of deeply committed relations, dedicated friendships, and life purposes. But since the rise of the *modernist* world-view beginning in the early twentieth century, the romantic vocabulary has been threatened. For modernists, the chief characteristics of the self reside not in the domain of depth, but rather in our ability to reason—in our beliefs, opinions, and conscious intentions. In the modernist idiom, normal persons are predictable, honest, and sincere. Modernists believe in educational systems, a stable family life, moral training, and rational choice of marriage partners.

Yet, as I shall argue, both the romantic and the modern beliefs about the self are falling into disuse, and the social arrangements that they support are eroding. This is largely a result of the forces of social saturation. Emerging technologies saturate us with the voices of humankind—both harmonious and alien. As we absorb their varied rhymes and reasons, they become part of us and we of them. Social saturation furnishes us with a multiplicity of incoherent and unrelated languages of the self. For everything we "know to be true" about ourselves, other voices within respond with doubt and even derision. This fragmentation of self-conceptions corresponds to a multiplicity of incoherent and disconnected relationships. These relationships pull us in myriad directions, inviting us to play such a variety of roles that the very concept of an "authentic self" with knowable characteristics recedes from view. The fully saturated self becomes no self at all. ....

I . . . equate the saturating of self with the condition of postmodernism. As we enter the postmodern era, all previous beliefs about the self are placed in jeopardy, and with them the patterns of action they sustain. Postmodernism does not bring with it a new vocabulary for understanding ourselves, new traits or characteristics to be discovered or explored. Its impact is more apocalyptic than that: the very concept of personal essences is thrown into doubt. Selves as possessors of real and identifiable characteristics—such as rationality, emotion, inspiration, and will—are dismantled. . . .

The Process of Social Saturation

A century ago, social relationships were largely confined to the distance of an easy walk. Most were conducted in person, within small communities: family, neighbors, townspeople. Yes, the horse and carriage made longer trips possible, but even a trip of thirty miles could take all day. The railroad could speed one away, but cost and availability limited such travel. If one moved from the community, relationships were likely to end. From birth to death, one could depend on relatively even-textured social surroundings. Words, faces, gestures, and possibilities were relatively consistent, coherent, and slow to change.

For much of the world's population, especially the industrialized West, the small, face-to-face community is vanishing into the pages of history. We go to country inns for weekend outings, we decorate condominium interiors with clapboards and brass beds, and we dream of old age in a rural cottage. But as a result of the technological developments just described, contemporary life is a swirling sea of social relations. Words thunder in by radio, television, newspaper, mail, radio, telephone, fax, wire service, electronic mail, billboards, Federal Express, and more. Waves of new faces are everywhere—in town for a day, visiting for the weekend, at the Rotary lunch, at the church social—and incessantly and incandescently on television. Long weeks in a single community are unusual; a full day within a single neighborhood is becoming rare. We travel casually across town, into the countryside, to neighboring towns, cities, states; one might go thirty miles for coffee and conversation.

Through the technologies of the century, the number and variety of relationships in which we are engaged, potential frequency of contact, expressed intensity of relationship, and endurance through time all are steadily increasing. As this increase becomes extreme, we reach a state of social saturation.

In the face-to-face community, the cast of others remained relatively stable. There were changes by virtue of births and deaths, but moving from one town—much less state or country—to another was difficult. The number of relationships commonly maintained in today's world stands in stark contrast. Counting one's family, the morning television news, the car radio, colleagues on the train, and the local newspaper, the typical commuter may confront as many different persons (in terms of views or images) in the first two hours of a day as the community-based predecessor did in a month. The morning calls in a business office may connect one to a dozen different locales in a given city, often across the continent, and very possibly across national boundaries. A single hour of prime-time melodrama immerses one in the lives of a score of individuals. In an evening of television, hundreds of engaging faces insinuate themselves into our lives. It is not only the immediate community that occupies our thoughts and feelings, but a constantly changing cast of characters spread across the globe. . . .

Populating the Self

Consider the moments:

- Over lunch with friends, you discuss Northern Ireland. Although you have never spoken a word on the subject, you find yourself heatedly defending British policies.

- You work as an executive in the investments department of a bank. In the evenings, you smoke marijuana and listen to the Grateful Dead.

- You sit in a cafe and wonder what it would be like to have an intimate relationship with various strangers walking past.

- You are a lawyer in a prestigious midtown firm. On the weekends, you work on a novel about romance with a terrorist.

- You go to a Moroccan restaurant and afterward take in the latest show at a country-and-western bar.

In each case, individuals harbor a sense of coherent identity or self-sameness, only to find themselves suddenly propelled by alternative impulses. They seem securely to be one sort of person, but yet another comes bursting to the surface—in a suddenly voiced opinion, a fantasy, a turn of interests, or a private activity. Such experiences with variation and self-contradiction may be viewed as preliminary effects of social saturation. They may signal a *populating of the self,* the acquisition of multiple and disparate potentials for being. It is this process of self-population that begins to undermine the traditional commitments to both romanticist and modernist forms of being. It is of pivotal importance in setting the stage for the postmodern turn. Let us explore.

The technologies of social saturation expose us to an enormous range of persons, new forms of relationship, unique circumstances and opportunities, and special intensities of feeling. One can scarcely remain unaffected by such exposure. As child-development specialists now agree, the process of socialization is lifelong. We continue to incorporate information from the environment throughout our lives. When exposed to other persons, we change in two major ways. We increase our capacities for *knowing that* and for *knowing how.* In the first case, through exposure to others, we learn myriad details about their words, actions, dress, mannerisms, and so on. We ingest enormous amounts of information about patterns of interchange. Thus, for example, from an hour on a city street, we are informed of the clothing styles of blacks, whites, upper class, lower class, and more. We may learn the ways of Japanese businessmen, bag ladies, Sikhs, Hare Krishnas, or flute players from Chile. We see how relationships are carried out between mothers and daughters, business executives, teenage friends, and construction workers. An hour in a business office may expose us to the political views of a Texas oilman, a Chicago lawyer, and a gay activist from San Francisco. Radio commentators espouse views on boxing, pollution, and child abuse; pop music may advocate machoism, racial bigotry, and suicide. Paperback books cause hearts to race over the unjustly treated, those who strive against impossible odds, those who are brave or brilliant. And this is to say nothing of television input. Via television, myriad figures are allowed into the home who would never otherwise trespass. Millions watch as talk-show guests—murderers, rapists, women prisoners, child abusers, members of the KKK, mental patients, and others often discredited—attempt to make their lives intelligible. There are few six-year-olds who cannot furnish at least a rudimentary account of life in an African village, the concerns of divorcing parents, or drug-pushing in the ghetto. Hourly, our storehouse of social knowledge expands in range and sophistication.

This massive increase in knowledge of the social world lays the ground work for a second kind of learning, a *knowing how.* We learn how to place such knowledge into action, to shape it for social consumption, to act so that social life can proceed effectively. And the possibilities for placing this supply of information into effective action are constantly expanding. The Japanese businessman glimpsed on the street today, and on the television tomorrow, may well be confronted in one's office the following week. On these occasions, the rudiments of appropriate behavior are already in place. If a mate announces that he or she is thinking about divorce, the other's reaction is not likely to be dumb dismay. The drama has so often been played out on television and movie screens that one is already prepared with multiple options. If one wins a wonderful prize, suffers a humiliating loss, faces temptation to cheat, or learns of a sudden death in the family, the reactions are hardly random. One more or less knows how it goes, is more or less ready for action. Having seen it all before, one approaches a state of ennui.

In an important sense, as social saturation proceeds we become pastiches, imitative assemblages of each other. In memory, we carry others' patterns of being with us. If the conditions are favorable, we can place these patterns into action. Each of us becomes the other, a representative, or a replacement. To put it more broadly, as the century has progressed, selves become increasingly populated with the character of others. . . .

Multiphrenia

It is sunny Saturday morning, and he finishes breakfast in high spirits. It is a rare day in which he is free to do as he pleases. With relish, he contemplates his options. The back door needs fixing, which calls for a trip to the hardware store. This would allow a much-needed haircut; and, while in town, he could get a birthday card for his brother, leave off his shoes for repair, and pick up shirts at the cleaners. But, he ponders, he really should get some exercise; is there time for jogging in the afternoon? That reminds him of a championship game he wanted to see at the same time. To be taken more seriously was his ex-wife's repeated request for a luncheon talk. And shouldn't he also settle his vacation plans before all the best locations are taken? Slowly, his optimism gives way to a sense of defeat. The free day has become a chaos of competing opportunities and necessities.

If such a scene is vaguely familiar, it attests only further to the pervasive effects of social saturation and the populating of the self. More important, one detects amid the hurly-burly of contemporary life a new constellation of feelings or sensibilities, a new pattern of self-consciousness. This syndrome may be termed *multiphrenia*, generally referring to the splitting of the individual into a multiplicity of self-investments. This condition is partly an outcome of self-population, but partly a result of the populated self's efforts to exploit the potentials of the technologies of relationship. In this sense, there is a cyclical spiraling toward a state of multiphrenia. As one's potentials are expanded by the technologies, so one increasingly employs the technologies for self-expression; yet, as the technologies are further utilized, so do they add to the repertoire of potentials. It would be a mistake to view this multiphrenic condition as a form of illness, for it is often suffused with a sense of expansiveness and adventure. Someday, there may indeed be nothing to distinguish multiphrenia from simply "normal living."

However, before we pass into this oceanic state, let us pause to consider some prominent features of the condition. Three of these are especially noteworthy.

Vertigo of the Valued

With the technology of social saturation, two of the major factors traditionally impeding relationships—namely time and space—are both removed. The past can be continuously renewed—via voice, video, and visits, for example—and distance poses no substantial barriers to ongoing interchange. Yet this same freedom ironically leads to a form of enslavement. For each person, passion, or potential incorporated into oneself exacts a penalty—a penalty both of *being* and of *being*

with. In the former case, as others are incorporated into the self, their tastes, goals, and values also insinuate themselves into one's being. Through continued interchange, one acquires, for example, a yen for Thai cooking, the desire for retirement security, or an investment in wildlife preservation. Through others, one comes to value whole-grain breads, novels from Chile, or community politics. Yet as Buddhists have long been aware, to desire is simultaneously to become a slave of the desirable. To "want" reduces one's choice to "want not." Thus, as others are incorporated into the self, and their desires become one's own, there is an expansion of goals—of "musts," wants, and needs. Attention is necessitated, effort is exerted, frustrations are encountered. Each new desire places its demands and reduces one's liberties.

There is also the penalty of being with. As relationships develop, their participants acquire local definitions—friend, lover, teacher, supporter, and so on. To sustain the relationship requires an honoring of the definitions—both of self and other. If two persons become close friends, for example, each acquires certain rights, duties, and privileges. Most relationships of any significance carry with them a range of obligations—for communication, joint activities, preparing for the other's pleasure, rendering appropriate congratulations, and so on. Thus, as relations accumulate and expand over time, there is a steadily increasing range of phone calls to make and answer, greeting cards to address, visits or activities to arrange, meals to prepare, preparations to be made, clothes to buy, makeup to apply. . . . And with each new opportunity—for skiing together in the Alps, touring Australia, camping in the Adirondacks, or snorkling in the Bahamas—there are "opportunity costs." One must unearth information, buy equipment, reserve hotels, arrange travel, work long hours to clear one's desk, locate babysitters, dogsitters, homesitters. . . . Liberation becomes a swirling vertigo of demands.

In the professional world, this expansion of "musts" is strikingly evident. In the university of the 1950s, for example, one's departmental colleagues were often vital to one's work. One could walk but a short distance for advice, information, support, and so on. Departments were often close-knit and highly interdependent; travels to other departments or professional meetings were notable events. Today, however, the energetic academic will be linked by post, long-distance phone, fax, and electronic mail to like-minded scholars around the globe. The number of interactions possible in a day is limited only by the constraints of time. The technologies have also stimulated the development of hundreds of new organizations, international conferences, and professional meetings. A colleague recently informed me that if funds were available, he could spend his entire sabbatical traveling from one professional gathering to another. A similar condition pervades the business world. One's scope of business opportunities is no longer so limited by geography; the technologies of the age enable projects to be pursued around the world. (Colgate Tartar Control toothpaste is now sold in over forty countries.) In effect, the potential for new connection and new opportunities is practically unlimited. Daily life has become a sea of drowning demands, and there is no shore in sight.

The Expansion of Inadequacy

It is not simply the expansion of self through relationships that hounds one with the continued sense of "ought." There is also the seeping of self-doubt into everyday consciousness, a subtle feeling of inadequacy that smothers one's activities with an uneasy sense of impending emptiness. In important respects, this sense of inadequacy is a by-product of the populating of self and the presence of social ghosts. For as we incorporate others into ourselves, so does the range of proprieties expand—that is, the range of what we feel a "good," "proper," or "exemplary" person should be. Many of us carry with us the "ghost of a father," reminding us of the values of honesty and hard work, or a mother challenging us to be nurturing and understanding. We may also absorb from a friend the values of maintaining a healthy body, from a lover the goal of self-sacrifice, from a teacher the ideal of worldly knowledge, and so on. Normal development leaves most people with a rich sense of personal well-being by fulfilling these goals.

But now consider the effects of social saturation. The range of one's friends and associates expands exponentially; one's past life continues to be vivid; and the mass media expose one to an enormous array of new criteria for self-evaluation. A friend from California reminds one to relax and enjoy life; in Ohio, an associate is getting ahead by working eleven hours a day. A relative from Boston stresses the importance of cultural sophistication, while a Washington colleague belittles one's lack of political savvy. A relative's return from Paris reminds one to pay more attention to personal appearance, while a ruddy companion from Colorado suggests that one grows soft.

Meanwhile, newspapers, magazines, and television provide a barrage of new criteria of self-evaluation. Is one sufficiently adventurous, clean, well traveled, well read, low in cholesterol, slim, skilled in cooking, friendly, odor free, coiffed, frugal, burglar proof, family oriented? The list is unending. More than once, I have heard the lament of a subscriber to the Sunday *New York Times*. Each page of this weighty tome will be read by millions. Thus, each page remaining undevoured by day's end will leave one precariously disadvantaged—a potential idiot in a thousand unpredictable circumstances.

Yet the threat of inadequacy is hardly limited to the immediate confrontation with mates and media. Because many of these criteria for self-evaluation are incorporated into the self—existing within the cadre of social ghosts—they are free to speak at any moment. The problem with values is that they are sufficient unto themselves. To value justice, for example, is to say nothing of the value of love; investing in duty will blind one to the value of spontaneity. No one value in itself recognizes the importance of any alternative value. And so it is with the chorus of social ghosts. Each voice of value stands to discredit all that does not meet its standard. All the voices at odds with one's current conduct thus stand as internal critics, scolding, ridiculing, and robbing action of its potential for fulfillment. One settles in front of the television for enjoyment, and the chorus begins: "twelve-year-old," "couch potato," "lazy," "irresponsible." . . . One sits down with a good book, and again: "sedentary," "antisocial," "inefficient," "fantasist." . . . Join friends for a game of tennis, and "skin cancer," "shirker of household duties," "underexercised," "overly competitive" come up. Work late and it is "workaholic," "heart attack-prone," "overly ambitious," "irresponsible family member." Each moment is enveloped in the guilt born of all that was possible but now foreclosed.

Rationality in Recession

A third dimension of multiphrenia is closely related to the others. The focus here is on the rationality of everyday decision-making instances in which one tries to be a "reasonable person." Why, one asks, is it important for one's children to attend college? The rational reply is that a college education increases one's job opportunities, earnings, and likely sense of personal fulfillment. Why should I stop smoking? one asks, and the answer is clear that smoking causes cancer, so to smoke is simply to invite a short life. Yet these "obvious" lines of reasoning are obvious only so long as one's identity remains fixed within a particular group.

The rationality of these replies depends altogether on the sharing of opinions—of each incorporating the views of others. To achieve identity in other cultural enclaves turns these "good reasons" into "rationalizations," "false consciousness," or "ignorance." Within some subcultures, a college education is a one-way ticket to bourgeois conventionality—a white-collar job, picket fence in the suburbs, and chronic boredom. For many, smoking is an integral part of a risky lifestyle; it furnishes a sense of intensity, offbeatness, rugged individualism. In the same way, saving money for old age is "sensible" in one family, and "oblivious to the erosions of inflation" in another. For most Westerners, marrying for love is the only reasonable (if not conceivable) thing to do. But many Japanese will point to statistics demonstrating greater longevity and happiness in arranged marriages. Rationality is a vital by-product of social participation.

Yet as the range of our relationships is expanded, the validity of each localized rationality is threatened. What is rational in one relationship is questionable or absurd from the standpoint of another. The "obvious choice" while talking with a colleague lapses into absurdity when speaking with a spouse, and into irrelevance when an old friend calls that evening. Further, because each relationship increases one's capacities for discernment, one carries with oneself a multiplicity of competing expectations, values, and beliefs about "the obvious solution." Thus, if the options are carefully evaluated, every decision becomes a leap into gray vapors. Hamlet's bifurcated decision becomes all too simple, for it is no longer

being or non-being that is in question, but to which of multifarious beings one can be committed.

Conclusion

So we find a profound sea change taking place in the character of social life during the twentieth century. Through an array of newly emerging technologies, the world of relationships becomes increasingly saturated. We engage in greater numbers of relationships, in a greater variety of forms, and with greater intensities than ever before. With the multiplication of relationships also comes a transformation in the social capacities of the individual—both in knowing how and knowing that. The relatively coherent and unified sense of self inherent in a traditional culture gives way to manifold and competing potentials. A multiphrenic condition emerges in which one swims in ever-shifting, concatenating, and contentious currents of being. One bears the burden of an increasing array of oughts, of self-doubts and irrationalities. The possibility for committed romanticism or strong and single-minded modernism recedes, and the way is opened for the postmodern being. . . .

As belief in essential selves erodes, awareness expands of the ways in which personal identity can be created and re-created. . . . This consciousness of construction does not strike as a thunderbolt; rather, it eats slowly and irregularly away at the edge of consciousness. And as it increasingly colors our understanding of self and relationships, the character of this consciousness undergoes a qualitative change. . . . [P]ostmodern consciousness [brings] the erasure of the category of self. No longer can one securely determine what it is to be a specific kind of person . . . or even a person at all. As the category of the individual person fades from view, consciousness of construction becomes focal. We realize increasingly that who and what we are is not so much the result of our "person essence" (real feelings, deep beliefs, and the like), but of how we are constructed in various social groups. . . . [T]he concept of the individual self ceases to be intelligible. . . .

Reprinted from: Kenneth J. Gergen, *The Saturated Self*, pp. 6–7, 61–62, 68–71, 73–80, 146, 170. Copyright © 1991 by Basic Books, Inc. Reprinted by permission of Basic Books, a member of Perseus Books, L.L.C. ✦